Volume II

Stories of Eastern
Montana's Pioneers

As told to:
    Mrs. Morris (Gladys Mullet) Kauffman

Gladys Kauffman

Sweetgrass Books

Cover Logo
The logo used in the original "As I Remember" series
in the Glendive Ranger-Review

Rear Cover Photo
Kauffman Family Photo
Wing's Studio, Glendive, Montana

-Contact Information-
www.As-I-Remember.com
gmk311@hotmail.com

Project Manager, Kent Kauffman

Printed in the United States of America

ISBN 10: 1-59152-037-1
ISBN 13: 978-1-59152-037-5

Sweetgrass Books
A Division of Farcountry Press
Helena, Montana

Table of Contents

Introduction
Forward
Loaned Photo Acknowledgements

Photo Section
Unpublished Stories

Glossary
Complete List of Interviews

Introduction

In 1964, during Montana's territorial centennial year, Mrs. Morris (Gladys Mullet) Kauffman of Glendive, Montana noticed the dwindling number of pioneers who had settled Eastern Montana. Too many of them were taking their stories to the grave. Surely someone should record those stories! Of course, there was no 'someone' so Mrs. Kauffman, despite having nine children at home, undertook the task.

During the next twelve years she interviewed over 160 of the early Eastern Montana pioneers and published their stories in Glendive's newspaper, the Ranger-Review, naming the column "As I Remember."

Mrs. Kauffman, herself the daughter of early settlers, reflects her love of history and her affection for Eastern Montana in her writing. She vividly brings to life the colorful pioneer era as she retells the heartaches, joys, laughter, and hardships of those hardy settlers.

As Mrs. Kauffman interviewed the old timers they related their experiences as they recalled them. Thus the name "As I Remember." The reader may notice variations in the different recollections, but we do not attempt to reconcile discrepancies. These stories are 'their' memories.

As I Remember, Volume I was released in June 2006. It included the first twenty-nine interviews, published in the Ranger-Review in 1964, as well as fifty other stories. Volume II contains most of the remaining interviews.

Although most of the stories were written by Mrs. Kauffman, a few were submitted in writing by others for the original series. In the book we have not changed the original submissions to conform to our format. The same applies to other sources, such as newspapers. These entries appear in italics.

In 1974 Mrs. Kauffman began taking classes at Dawson Community College in Glendive, which limited time for her "As I Remember" column. Consequently several of the original interviews were never published. These interviews, as well as several stories compiled from later submissions from other people, are included in a section at the end of this volume.

And now a note about language: The reader should keep in mind that these stories were recorded between 1964 and 1975 and reflect life experiences in the late 19th and early 20th century. These interviews are in the language of the time and no attempt has been made to 'update' the stories to conform to today's standards.

In the back of the book, a glossary explains some terms and locations that may be unfamiliar to the reader. These terms are marked by an asterisk* in the book to indicate their inclusion in the glossary.

Also in the back of the book is a complete list of all the interviews Mrs. Kauffman recorded between 1964 and 1975. They are listed alphabetically, with volume and page number reference.

Let "As I Remember" take you back to another era and also help you appreciate the times in which you live!

Kent Kauffman, Project Manager

Foreword

Ever since the "As I Remember" series began in 1964, people have encouraged me to compile the stories into a book. Over thirty years have passed since the last article was printed. Prospects for a book looked bleak, but I am blessed to have a supportive family.

At considerable sacrifice of time and money, my son Kent undertook the resurrection of "As I Remember" stories that had been published in the Ranger-Review. From 1964 to 1975 I had interviewed pioneers who, mostly between 1880 and 1910, had settled Eastern Montana. Kent undertook the role of project manager, searching out a publisher, handling the endless details of preparing a manuscript, making necessary contacts, traveling with me to collect photos and retrieve from the Ranger-Review office sections of stories missing from my collection, and to get further information for Volume I. All this was in addition to typing the manuscript and distributing it to proofreaders.

He took considerable time off work to concentrate on this endeavor and his diligence in preparing Volume I laid the groundwork for Volume II. In short, without his determined persistence, there would have been no Volume I, much less Volume II of As I Remember.

The rest of the family has been no less supportive. Considerable assistance with typing came from my daughter Twila. My son Vance was a big help with the website we created for the project (www.As-I-Remember.com) and with invaluable technical assistance. Daughter Vaughn is supportive with phone calls and brainstorming and is diligent in promoting the project. Gaylene and Valerie, here in Bozeman, help with packaging, mailing, and distribution. Other family members contributed time as well.

We could not have succeeded without the help of many others. Cindy Mullet, reporter for the Ranger-Review, was an immense help in tracking down and copying articles we were missing. The staff at the Ranger-Review in general have been most cooperative. Our friend Doris Gnagey in California and my daughter-in-law Sharon in Wyoming spent hours proofreading stories for us.

We are grateful to the many people who loaned us photos (see the Loaned Photo Acknowledgements section) and to Matt Yovich who provided technical assistance with the photos.

We have enjoyed working with Kathy Springmeyer and Farcountry Press and have appreciated Kathy's help in the many aspects of the project.

A myriad of 'people connections' facilitated various aspects of the project and it was gratifying to see everything come together. We hope the book promotes both an appreciation of our past and a gratitude for our present. Enjoy!

Thank you to all!

Gladys Kauffman

Loaned Photo Acknowledgements

First Impressions

When the early settlers arrived in Eastern Montana, their first impressions were not always flattering. Nevertheless, many of those pioneers grew to love the rolling hills and badlands and remained to raise their families. What drew them here? What kept them here? The <u>As I Remember</u> stories provide glimpses into both the land and the people that settled the land. Here are a few samples of first impressions.

"A man must really have a grudge against himself to live in this kind of country." That was Andrew Larson's reaction to Eastern Montana as he traveled through on a train in 1885, headed for California. Little did he guess that seven years later he would return and spend the next sixty-seven years in Glendive.
Mrs. Andrew Larson, Volume I, Page 46

"When I came, I thought this was the most desolate place in the world!" exclaimed Mrs. Peter Quilling as she recalled her introduction to the Treasure State in 1907. Then she hastened to add, "But I'm all for Montana now!"
Mrs. Peter Quilling, Volume I, Page 235

Miss Dougherty, coming from the mild Emerald Isle (Ireland) where snow never fell, was greeted in Glendive by a foot of it. When she stepped off the train and saw what lay before her she exclaimed, "If this is Glendive, God help me!"
Joe Kelly, Volume I, Page 50

What a sight that little shack was to greet a mother with her three young girls, fresh from the 'civilization' of the city! She was expecting the worst, but hardly this bad! In spite of the bleak introduction, the days on the homestead* were happy ones.
Mrs. Frank Hasty, Volume II, Page 104

Mr. Stangeland's first impression of Glendive was dismal indeed. He arrived March 1, with a cold wind blowing, dust flying. Viewing the uninspiring scene was enough to start a fellow talking to himself, and the question he was asking was, "Why did I ever come here?" The only reply he could give himself was, "I wish I could get out!" He probably could have, some time or another in the next sixty-six years, but he's still here.
Jacob Stangeland, Volume II, Page 90

Mrs. Frank Fritsch

December 1965

Rattlesnakes and windstorms! Mrs. Frank Fritsch, a native of Illinois, with her husband joined the homesteaders Montana-bound in 1910. She immediately took a liking to her adopted state, but the snakes and the windstorms she would have gladly omitted.

Even before her first encounter with a rattler, she had a dread of the creatures, especially that she would sometime meet one and not recognize its warning rattle until it was too late. Her husband assured her, "If you hear that rattle you'll know what it is," but she just didn't see how she could be sure. When she'd hear the buzz of a grasshopper (and there were many grasshoppers in Montana that first year she was here) she'd flee to the house, fearing the worst. Mr. Fritsch tried to give her a better idea of what to expect by shaking a handful of flax seed as about the closest imitation but still she worried. And then one day she heard it – and she recognized it.

She had started out on horseback for her brother's place about four or five miles from her home and had to dismount to open a gate. As she started for the gate a sudden rattle stopped her in her tracks. It was no grasshopper and no flax seed and she didn't need her husband to tell her so. A quick look in the direction of that menacing buzz revealed a rattler coiled just a few feet from her. She was terrified at the sound and sight, yet she felt she must try to kill the snake. She was wearing an apron with a full skirt so she hurried to the plowed field nearby, filled her apron with clods of dirt, then came back and began firing them at the snake. Maybe her aim would have been more accurate if she hadn't been so scared but, as it was, she "didn't come within a mile of it," to quote Mrs. Fritsch.

A series of futile attempts to put a clod where the snake was convinced her she would do better to go on to her brother's place and get some help. By that time she was so weak and shaky she found she couldn't get on her horse (no doubt some more of you would testify to a 'shaky feeling' after an encounter with a rattler!) so she walked and led her horse the rest of the way. The hired man came along back with her and they found the snake in the same spot. He thought she ought to try to kill it with the long stick he had brought but that idea was not at all to her liking. At his urging she finally took the stick, howbeit with great reluctance, and took a mighty whack at the snake. Had she connected, it surely would have been the death of him because she hit so hard she broke the stick in two, but she missed the snake entirely. That left only a short piece of stick for the hired man to use but with it he quickly put an end to the rattler. Mrs. Fritsch was astonished to see that such a light blow would stun the snake.

Not until many years later did she see another rattlesnake. They were living in West Glendive by then and she had gone to the garden to get an armful of Swiss chard for their rabbits when, again, she heard that unmistakable warning.

2

She dropped her Swiss chard, grabbed the hoe and finished off that snake without any assistance this time. Then she draped the dead remains over the garden fence to prove to her family that she actually had done the deed.

As for windstorms, she had reason for prejudice. The second summer they were in Montana, the wind gave them a frightening experience. They had a well on their place but the water was alkaline and not fit for drinking – nor for much else either. They had to haul their drinking water the five miles from her brother's home. One hot summer afternoon as they were going home with the water they noticed big, black, threatening clouds rolling up from the west. They hurried on home and Mr. Fritsch quickly stabled the horses while the others of the party (Mrs. Fritsch's parents were with them) dashed to the house. Mr. Fritsch himself just had time to get inside the door when the storm broke in all its fury. As the wind tore at the little one-and-a-half story house the occupants suddenly felt a shift and the house was no longer on its foundation. After a time (it seemed a long time!) the storm subsided and the Fritsches were much relieved that their house was still intact if not where it was supposed to be. Later Mr. Fritsch obtained some big telephone poles and pushed it back onto the foundation. But from then on Mrs. Fritsch had a dread of storms. Soon after that they dug a root cellar and she 'waited out the storms' down there.

Before coming to Montana Mr. and Mrs. Fritsch had lived a little more than fifty miles from Chicago. When news of Montana's homestead offer reached them, both her father and his father decided to come to the Treasure State* and look over the situation. They were favorably impressed with what they saw and returned to urge the young people to trust their future to the new country. That is how it happened that Mr. and Mrs. Fritsch, as well as two of his brothers and two of her brothers, pioneered in Montana. The entire group located between Glendive and Wibaux.

Mr. Fritsch came out to Montana in March, moving livestock and furniture in immigrant cars* to get a house ready for his wife and two-and-a-half year old son. The cars were unloaded at Wibaux where he stored the household goods until they had a place to put them. Mrs. Fritsch had canned a good supply of fruit to help stock the larder in their new home, but when she came in May and they took inventory of goods moved into their house, they found that someone had stolen all those jars of fruit. This was most distressing because commercially canned foods were not available in the stores of that day.

Mrs. Fritsch was impressed, as were many others of the new settlers, with the friendliness of the Westerners. There was much visiting back and forth between neighbors and they had wonderful times together but hospitality wasn't limited to your neighbors. Anyone who stopped in near mealtime was invited to eat with them as a matter of course.

One pair of neighbors, an old ranch couple to the north, raised wonderful gardens – such rhubarb they had! Those gardens inspired the Fritsches to try a garden too, and they determined to raise, among other things, watermelon. The melons grew nicely and when they should have been getting ripe, Mr. Fritsch started 'tapping' them to test them but they just didn't have the right sound.

Finally Mr. Fritsch decided it was time to try one, regardless of sound but when he attempted to cut it, the knife wouldn't cut. By that time, he was not to be easily diverted from his purpose so he took the axe and chopped that melon open only to find that instead of watermelon they had citron melon*! Mrs. Fritsch made lots of citron preserves that fall.

To help overcome the alkali water problem, they dug a big cistern. Throughout the winter months when there was plenty of clean snow, Mr. Fritsch would go with team and wagon to the draws where the drifts were deepest, load the wagon with the snow and haul it to the cistern. It was surprising how well that cistern water held out through the summer months. Water from the cistern was fine for general household use and for washing clothes (Mrs. Fritsch was fortunate to have a washing machine – one of those with a wooden tub and a handle on the side which was pushed back and forth to agitate the clothes) but they hauled water for drinking and cooking all the time they lived on the farm.

The cistern was useful for more than one purpose; it also served as an efficient cooler. They'd tie ropes on tall cans of milk and suspend them in the water to keep them cool. Mrs. Fritsch made butter to sell in Glendive, and many an afternoon she sat in the shade of the house and turned the handle of the old churn. They sold eggs in town as well. Their chickens blew away in the same storm that moved their house off its foundation, but they got more chickens and sold more eggs.

Lack of schools presented a problem here just as in many another pioneer community. When their first child, Glen, was ready to start, there was no school for him but there happened to be a schoolteacher nearby. Mary Ashworth, one of the Wibaux schoolteachers, had homesteaded in their neighborhood so for his first school, Glen rode horseback to her claim throughout the summer months and she taught him.

The next year Mrs. Fritsch moved into Allard with him during the school term. Here again, water was a problem, perhaps even more so than at home. There they could at least use a team and wagon to haul the water but in Allard, she and little Glen had to walk about a half-mile and carry the water back in a bucket. The teacher at Allard that year, Nora Carroll (now Mrs. Hurd) roomed with them in their little 'Town' house.

The school situation wasn't getting any better in the community where they lived so the next year they moved into Glendive for the school year and spent the summers on the farm. During that winter while they were in town, their farmhouse burned to the ground – probably because of an overheated stove.

After another year or so the family moved into town and Mr. Fritsch employed himself hauling coal from the Clyde Clapp mine to Glendive residents, using a team and wagon. Later on they bought land and built up a place in West Glendive. There they lived until Mr. Fritsch passed away in 1959. After his death Mrs. Fritsch moved to an apartment in Glendive so she would be within walking distance of stores and businesses but she still likes the wide, open spaces.

4

W.A. Brubaker (as told by Albert Brubaker)

March 1966

"Say, I bet the deputy'll be President some day!" Hearing the prediction, the cowboys hooted, but Joe Ferris, who became W.A. Brubaker's father-in-law, had the last laugh.

W.A. Brubaker, back in 1905, was watching a poker game in Medora, North Dakota, when one of the old ranchers sitting in asked him, "Why don't you start a bank in Terry? They need one out there." So Brubaker started a bank out there. He was not a banker by occupation or background or training, but he was equal to the challenge.

Brubaker had come to the West at the close of the Spanish-American War in 1902. Originally from New Carlisle, Ohio, he enlisted in the United States Army at the outbreak of hostilities with Spain and was sent to the Philippines. While in the service he was in the communications division and improved upon the telegraphic skills which he had picked up as a youngster while hanging around the depot in his hometown. He became a skilled operator so when he was discharged (his sons still have his discharge papers) with an excellent record and $804.02 mustering out pay (he was justly proud of having saved that much in three years at a time when a soldier's pay was hardly more than $20 a month), he sought employment as a telegrapher.

He landed a job with the Northern Pacific Railroad and was sent to Big Horn, Montana. From Big Horn he was transferred to Tusler, then to Terry, then Medora. And that's how he happened to be on hand to receive the suggestion that he start a bank in Terry. Brubaker went to work immediately to organize the bank, which opened for business January 1906. The bank's subscription records show the names of many old Medora ranchers.

That same year, 1906, Brubaker married Carrie Ferris, daughter of Joe Ferris of Medora. Joe, along with his brother Sylvane and A.W. Merrifield, had immigrated to North Dakota from New Brunswick, Canada. The three young adventurers went as far as the railroad could take them (the Northern Pacific had not crossed the Little Missouri at that time), and there they settled.

A few years later a young Easterner, interested in hunting buffalo, showed up in the badlands country. The great buffalo herds by that year, 1883, had been pretty well wiped out so a guide was a necessity, but the stranger, before he ever attempted to find a guide, had two counts against him: not only was he a New Yorker (which was bad enough); he even wore glasses! Glasses may have attained some degree of respectability in the East by that time, but on the Frontier anyone wearing them was definitely suspect. As a result, the other guides would have nothing to do with the would-be hunter. It was with no little reluctance and with considerable misgiving that Joe Ferris finally agreed to perform that service for Theodore Roosevelt on his first buffalo hunt.

Joe, according to his grandson, was of – shall we say sedentary? – inclinations, so while Roosevelt rode horseback, Ferris took it easy with a horse and buggy on the hunt. Roosevelt got his buffalo, and before the hunt was over Ferris had changed his mind about the 'tenderfoot'. That hunt marked the beginning of a life-long friendship.

Roosevelt became interested in cattle ranching in the badlands, and before he returned to New York he purchased the Chimney Butte or Maltese Cross Ranch and made an agreement with Joe's brother Sylvane and their friend Merrifield to look after the cattle for him. Joe wasn't interested in running cattle so he wasn't involved with Roosevelt's ranching, but in his Medora home one room was 'Roosevelt's room'. This room was reserved solely for Roosevelt's use on his trips to North Dakota. Roosevelt's health was rather delicate when he first came west so every evening Mrs. Ferris placed a large pitcher of milk on the table of his room. Roosevelt liked to go to bed and read, and every evening he would drink the entire two quarts of milk before going to sleep. A certain pitcher, with its two matching glasses, was always kept in 'his' room for his special use. That same pitcher, the two glasses, and a small bowl belonging to the set, are still in the Brubaker family's possession, a treasured heirloom.

Another heirloom much prized by the family is the doll buggy given to the Brubaker boys' mother, Carrie Ferris, by Theodore Roosevelt when she was a little girl. The Brubakers' only daughter died when she was just three years old, so the buggy was handed down to the first granddaughter. Now the great grandchildren of Carrie Ferris Brubaker occasionally play with the buggy that was a gift from the president-to-be.

Joe Ferris made probably the first prediction that Teddy Roosevelt would some day be president. A feature appearing in the <u>Minneapolis Sunday Tribune</u> in 1943 describes how he happened to make that prediction:

A yellow dust pall hovered over the flag-draped streets of the little cow-town of Dickinson, Dakota Territory. It was late in the afternoon of July 4, 1884, and the tiny frontier hamlet was concluding its first Independence Day celebration. All day long the thinly-scattered prairie settlers had poured into the town, filling its streets and bars to overflowing: homesteaders with their sunbonneted wives and innumerable children crowded into crude buckboards*; tanned cattlemen and cowhands mounted on agile ponies; stolid, blanket-wrapped Redskins, openly curious at the palefaces' strange ceremonies. It had been a day of rude and simple sports — wrestling, foot racing, roping. But to these pioneer men in the terrible isolation of lonely homesteads, it had been a blessed respite from monotony.

Not for years were the great sister states of North and South Dakota to be carved from the territory and made a portion of the Union. Not yet could they feel themselves a part of the nation they were helping to build with their toil, tears and sweat. Perhaps that was why even the bars were empty when the final event on the day's program was reached — the first Fourth of July address in the history of the lonely frontier outpost.

It was not an impressive scene. Rough planks, laid over upended beer kegs, provided seats for the feminine portion of the audience. Most of the men slouched against nearby buildings or squatted cowboy-fashion on the dry earth. In the background, the lines of tethered ponies pawed and fidgeted at the hitching posts. On the rude, bunting-draped rostrum, the orator of the day fidgeted as nervously as any pony. He was a stranger to most of the crowd, a short, slight young fellow in his twenties, who had come from somewhere in the East a year or two before. He was a deputy sheriff now in the nearby cattle town of Medora. And — most of the audience thought with sinking hearts — he didn't look like much of a talker.

But with the youthful orator's opening phrases the crowd fell silent. In the eager, intense features and the shrill, penetrating voice there was something that commanded attention and respect. As they listened, even tipsy cowhands filled to their neckerchiefs with 'red likker' were caught in the spell of the young man's bold and vigorous speech. To the gnarled homesteaders and their drab, toil-worn wives who huddled on the rude benches, he drew with quick, vigorous strokes a portrait of an America such as they had never dared dream of. With the magic of his speech he peopled the barren plains with towns and cities, and foretold the future of the prairies as the breadbasket of a continent.

In his puckered, intense countenance was the calm certainty of a clear vision and a sure faith, as he sketched for them the pattern of a nation's future — a nation whose broad acres and teeming peoples stretched from sea to sea, a beacon-light of liberty and progress for the oppressed of all the earth.

In the thunder-crash of applause that followed the youthful orator's peroration, young Joe Ferris leaned over and spoke to the man sitting next to him. "Say," he said excitedly, "I bet the deputy'll be president some day!" In the crowded bar room that night, the cowhand was telling about it. "And would you believe it?" he chuckled, "that fool Joe Ferris says the deputy's going to be president when he grows up!" The bartender flicked his towel at an imaginary fly and eyed the grinning cowhands sourly. "Maybe Joe ain't such a fool as you think," he said. "If the deputy DON'T ever get to be president, it won't be because he's afraid of the job. Did I ever tell you what I saw him do over in the saloon in Medora?"

"No, tell us," chorused a half-dozen eager voices. "Well, it was one night last fall. A few of the boys were in the place having a sociable card game. The deputy was there, too. But he wasn't playing. Just sitting quiet behind the stove. And then in comes this tough guy." The bartender paused and grimaced disgustedly at the recollection. "He WAS tough, too," he continued. "and full up to the ears with red likker. Nothin' else would do but that all the boys in the house should have a drink with him."

"And to prove he meant it, he laid his hardware plumb on the bar, where anybody otherwise inclined could see it. Well, the boys all moved up pretty fast to name their poison, and they were busy drinkin' it when this tough hombre spots the deputy sitting behind the stove. 'Hey, you,' he yells, 'Why aren't you drinking? Don't you like my company?' And he picks up his gun and starts for the deputy. Well, I didn't see what happened very clear; but the next thing I knew the tough hombre was sitting on

7

the floor holding his chin, and his gun was lying on the floor across the room. 'No,' the deputy says, casual like, 'I don't like your company.' And that's all there was to it." The bartender paused and eyed the cowhands for a moment. "Except," he added, "that he hasn't had any trouble with tough cowpunchers since."

The punchers grinned. "All right, Old Timer," one of them chuckled, "we'll even let him be president, like Joe Ferris says, if you want us to." "I think Joe always was a little optimistic," said a clear voice behind them. The cowhands turned, grinning sheepishly, to face the smiling young deputy sheriff who had walked in unseen. The deputy tossed a bill on the bar. "Go ahead, fellows," he said, "If I'm going to be president I ought to buy a drink. It's too bad, though, that my sponsor, Joe, isn't here to get in on it."

It was a long time before young Joe Ferris ceased to hear the last of his frontier presidential candidate. The great blizzards of 1887 wiped out the stock of most of the smaller Dakota ranchers – and among them was the herd of the fearless young deputy. He gave up his ranching activities and drifted away to other adventures.

The slow wheel of the years turned on, and Joe Ferris heard now and then of his former friend, sometimes by letter, sometimes word of mouth. He was reported in Texas, the Philippines, in New York. Next, he had received a high governmental post in the nation's capital, where he was rapidly becoming a prominent national official.

And seventeen years after that memorable Fourth of July in the little cow-town, Joe Ferris had his revenge on the friends and neighbors who had twitted him about his youthful and impulsive remark. It was a letter, signed by the deputy sheriff himself:

"THE WHITE HOUSE, WASHINGTON, D.C.
My Dear Joe:
    No telegram that I received pleased me more than yours, and I thank you for it. Give my warm regards to Mrs. Joe, Sylvane and all my friends,
Sincerely yours,
Theodore Roosevelt, The Medora President."

The original of that closing letter, dated November 10, 1904, and sent by the President of the United States to Joe Ferris (actually, the letter is addressed to both Joe and Sylvane) on that memorable occasion is carefully preserved in the safe of the State Bank of Terry.

When Joe Ferris died in California, the following observations and poem appeared in the Los Angeles Free Press:

"Editor's Note: The Free Press printed last Wednesday a story of the death of Joseph A. Ferris, 80-year-old plainsman, at the home of his daughter, Mrs. R.E. Richardson, on East Telegraph Road. The story gave an account of his early acquaintance with the late Theodore Roosevelt on the plains of North Dakota when the two men, then young, hunted together with Ferris as guide to the New Yorker who

8

was 'out west' seeking the health that later carried him through years of strenuous work as rough rider, statesman and president. The friendship between the two men appealed to James W. Foley, well-known California writer. In Monday's issue of the Pasadena Star News, to which he is a daily contributor, appeared the following poem by Mr. Foley in his editorial page column, 'The Top of the Evening:'"

THEODORE AND JOE

On saddle ponies tough and strong
They jogged the prairie trails along,
The youngsters Theodore and Joe,
That nearly sixty years ago,
To camp beneath the sparkling stars,
Where were no fences, gates or bars.
The grass was soft to trotting feet,
The prairie air was cool and sweet,
When they pledged friendship long ago,
The youngsters Theodore and Joe.

And there was friendship true as steel
Forged by an old chuck-wagon wheel,
When saddle leather creaked and cried
As they rode with it, side by side
The lush-grassed prairie lands among,
And both were ardent, keen and young,
With courage high and spirits hale
They rode upon the Friendship Trail.
That nearly sixty years ago,
The youngsters Theodore and Joe.

And oft in prairie's summer glow,
In winter's blizzard and the snow,
In springtime roundup and the fall
They rode the trail and heard the call
Of the great spaces far and wide
Where noble dreamings come to ride.
One kept along the old, old trail,
But both kept faith with long ago,
The youngsters Theodore and Joe.

There may be Happy Hunting Grounds
Where scouts and hunters make their rounds,

And roundups in far spaces wide,
Where old time cowboys meet and ride.
There may be campfires of the stars
Where are no fences, gates or bars,
In all life's lure and mystery
Who is to say what things may be
And two may meet and cry Hello
The youngsters Theodore and Joe.
James W. Foley

After W.A. Brubaker and Carrie Ferris were married they set up housekeeping in Terry and spent the rest of their lives there. The home they built in Terry is one of the oldest dwellings in the town and is now occupied by one of their sons, Harold.

Mrs. Brubaker passed away in 1918, victim of the influenza epidemic, leaving her husband and three young boys. Her parents, Mr. and Mrs. Joe Ferris, came and lived with their widowed son-in-law about a year and a half to help him adjust to the task of caring for his children, but from then on the banker carried on alone.

W.A. Brubaker wasn't a very tall man, but anything he might have lacked in stature (according to his army discharge papers he was 5' 5 1/2" tall) he made up in spirit. Nobody could 'buffalo' him! He was a stalwart member of the community and through the years made many civic contributions. He passed away in Terry in 1956, just after the bank's fiftieth anniversary.

A few weeks before his death he turned the presidency of the bank over to his oldest son, Albert, the present president. All three of his sons, Albert, Jack, and Harold, make their homes in Terry, active in the bank their father started in 1906.

Doll carriage given to Carrie Ferris by Theodore Roosevelt

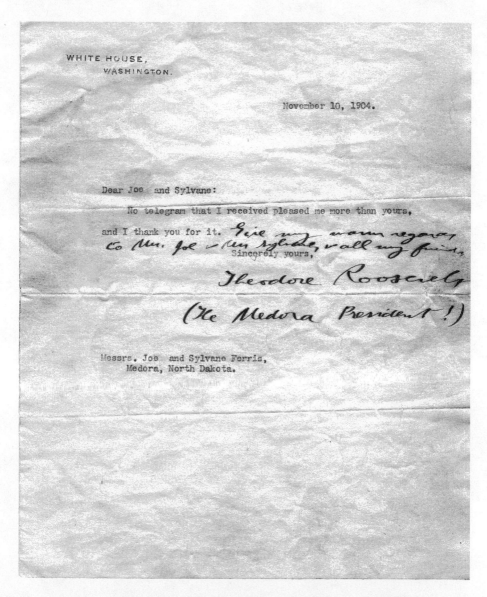

WHITE HOUSE,
WASHINGTON.

November 10, 1904.

Dear Joe and Sylvane:

No telegram that I received pleased me more than yours,

and I thank you for it. *Give my warm regards*
to Mr. Joe - Mr. Sylvane, & all my friends,

Sincerely yours,

Theodore Roosevelt

(He Medora President!)

Messrs. Joe and Sylvane Ferris,
Medora, North Dakota.

Thank you letter from President Theodore Roosevelt to Joe Ferris

Back: William Merrifield, Sylvane
Ferris, Joe Ferris, George Meyers
Seated: Teddy Roosevelt
Bull Moose Convention 1912

Stith Outhouse, built 1905
Only steam-heated outhouse west
of the Mississippi River
Terry, Montana

Theodore Roosevelt National Park, Medora, North Dakota

Mrs. R. J. (Kathryn Ehlen) Kennedy

February 1965

Mrs. R.J. Kennedy has been no stranger to heartache and hardship since she came to Montana, but she says she would be glad to turn back the pages of time and relive those days she shared with her husband and their growing children.

Montana's incomparable Indian summer greeted her when she arrived with her sister and brother-in-law on October 17, 1907. They had made the trip from Wisconsin to Mondak on the Great Northern Railroad, but at that point public transportation facilities abruptly ended. Her brother-in-law, William Fink, had spent the summer with a partner mining coal near Tokna for some of the camps along the Lower Yellowstone Irrigation ditch then being built. That fall he went back to Wisconsin to get his family, and Kathryn (Ehlen) came with them, her brother following with an immigrant car*.

They reached Mondak on a Sunday morning, and Fink, too impatient to wait until Monday for the stage, wanted to leave the rest of the party at Mondak while he started walking to Tokna. His wife was considerably less than enthusiastic about the plan but insisted that if he started walking, she would walk, too.

They made a picturesque procession as they started toward the river — Kathryn, Mr. and Mrs. Fink with their year-old baby, five grips, and a phonograph. The phonograph was not a little record player, but one with a big brass horn that used to accompany those audio marvels. Little wonder observers laughed to see the procession coming, joking that they carried their music with them.

They reached the river just as a freighter's outfit was being loaded onto the ferry so they crossed together, and the freighter gave them a ride to Tokna. The wagon had no box, just a couple loose planks the length of the frame. Mrs. Kennedy remarked that she's often wondered how they managed to stay aboard. They had had no breakfast so the stop at Fairview for dinner was a welcome one. After dinner they continued on and were beyond Sidney by dusk. They camped for the night in a schoolhouse, sleeping on the floor and again starting on in the morning without benefit of breakfast. By the time they reached Tokna, about eleven o'clock that forenoon, they were more than ready to eat.

Their household goods, her brother accompanying them, were coming by immigrant car and didn't arrive until a week or so later. In the meantime they camped in a little tent. Quarters proved to be rather close, however, so they rigged a 'lean-to', or at least a wind break, out of some of the many gunny sacks that had been tossed aside by the freighters who stopped there.

Since the autumn weather was mild they found their improvised lodgings tolerably comfortable, but when a freighter finally delivered their household goods, they quickly unpacked the little kerosene heater and set it up in the 'lean-to' to warm the atmosphere a bit more. The atmosphere wasn't all that was warmed. About the middle of the night the gunnysacks caught fire and provided more than a little excitement before the blaze was extinguished. Fortunately most of their possessions were still on the wagon – the stove was about all they had taken time to unload – so they didn't lose much in the conflagration.

They were hardly settled when Fred Baker, a nearby rancher, had to accompany a carload of cattle to Iowa so he arranged for Kathryn to stay with his wife during his absence. Soon after his return Tom Neece made a similar trip so she spent some time at the Neece's. It was while she was working there that she first met a young cowboy, Bob Kennedy. Bob was riding for L.D. 'Ren' Matthews, manager on one of Senator McCone's ranches. Bob's proficiency must not have been limited to riding horses and punching cows because the following summer he claimed Kathryn for his bride. They were married June 24, 1908.

Bob came to Montana in 1903, but then suffered an attack of homesickness and went back to Michigan for a spell. Before long he was ready to return to the West, and in the West he stayed the rest of his life. He did some freighting when he first came out, then started working for Matthews. He liked action and lively horses and found both on the ranch, especially at roundup time, where rough breaks and hard knocks were commonplace.

One of those hard knocks left him 'laid up' for quite some time. He, with 'Ren' and Henry Matthews and Mr. Cole (Mrs. Minnie Danskin's father), was trying to cut a bunch of cattle when one of the cows dashed back to the herd. Bob dashed, too, and didn't see a couple steers fighting at the edge of the main herd. When he tangled with them it was too late for seeing.

One minute he was riding hard to turn that cow; the next thing of which he was aware he was sitting on the ground, his hat beside him and his horse grazing a short distance away. About then he noticed the boss coming toward him. Still befuddled, he mentally puzzled that he couldn't remember falling asleep! The boss soon enlightened him as to what had happened and asked him if he was able to ride to the ranch. Bob assured him that he was and started, but the farther he rode the sicker he got. It was many a day before he chased another cow.

About the time the Kennedys were married, Mr. Mason, a rancher on Burns Creek, had to leave on account of his health so he wrote to them about taking over the ranch. They agreed and lived on the ranch about two years before deciding to take a homestead.

In 1910 they filed on a quarter* twelve and one half miles straight east of Bloomfield on the western edge of Murphy's Table. Making a living on the homestead was by no means a life of ease – nor yet the now much-publicized 'security'. The 1914 crop finally held promise of real returns and neighbors predicted they'd get fifty bushels of wheat to the acre. Then the weather turned hot – scorchingly hot. The fifty-bushel prospect shriveled and withered until he harvested eighteen bushels to the acre of number four wheat. Bob was so discouraged he declared he was going to rent to the first fellow who came along.

His wife didn't think he really meant it, but before the fall was over he had rented to Dan Nissley.

The Nissleys moved onto the homestead between Christmas and New Year that winter, and the Kennedys, with three children by this time, moved to the Tommy Allen place. Mrs. Kennedy decided to keep account of all their expenses so from January 1, 1915 to January 1, 1916 she wrote down everything they spent. At the end of the year the total spent for groceries was $250. Of course, she added, she had had a nice garden; they raised chickens, and milked a cow, all of which helped to keep the grocery bill to a minimum, but even so.... They were poor but, Mrs. Kennedy emphasized, they were happy.

After they left the homestead Kennedy worked at various jobs, including quite a bit of work for the county. The last farming they did was on the Lieper place in 1920-22. It was while they were living there that real tragedy struck their little family. Mrs. Kennedy was washing clothes (she had no washer of any kind to lighten that chore), and thinking to bleach the clothes a little whiter, she set the tub on the stove to bring the water to boiling.

Little Louis liked to help her carry the water for the washing, and by the time she was ready to remove the tub from the stove, he had awakened from his nap. As she set the tub on the floor where she could more vigorously 'stomp' the clothes with a stomper, she warned the little fellow to stay away from the hot water. He assured her that he knew the water was hot and that he wouldn't fall in. He was playing with his kitty, pretending it was a baby, walking it on its hind legs. She explained to him that she just wanted to make sure he knew so he'd stay away, and he again affirmed his intention of keeping a safe distance.

The room was about twenty-four feet long, and while she was at the opposite end of the room he called to her, "Mama, see my baby walk!" followed almost immediately by his screams. She whirled to see him sit himself part way out of the scalding water, but his hands slipped and he fell back the second time before she could reach him. Their little Louis died the next night.

From Lieper's place they moved to Glendive for a couple years, then to a ranch northwest of Glendive, now owned by Johnny Horst. The depression came, and they weren't making much out on the ranch so after the World War II started and the boys had gone to the Service, leaving Mr. and Mrs. Kennedy alone, they moved to Glendive again.

They had spent fifty-five happy years together before Mr. Kennedy passed away in 1963. Of their eight children who grew to maturity, all are still living, all but two in the Glendive vicinity.

Mrs. Kennedy commented that she'd like to go back to Fairview sometime and see how it looks now. In the more than fifty-seven years that she's been here, she's never been back to Fairview or Mondak, the site of their illustrious introduction to the West.

Ed Haskell

April 1966

Ed Haskell is no newcomer needing an introduction to Ranger-Review readers but no series on old timers would be complete without Ed's story so meet him again. When a R-R reporter, calling Ed recently on the occasion of his ninety-second birthday, asked him when he came to Glendive, he informed her that he had come with the original surveying crew that laid out the channel for the Yellowstone River. However, Billy Wood tells us that the day after his arrival in the Gate City* he crossed the Yellowstone in a rowboat, and he maintains that he came before Ed did, so somebody has his story mixed. And Billy insists that it isn't he.

Back in Melrose, Massachusetts, where Ed originated, 100 miles was a long trip. In fact, although he was a traveling salesman for a wholesale grocery company, he had never been 100 miles from his hometown when he started on the 2,600 mile trip that brought him to Montana.

The train trip was quite an experience for the Haskells – Ed, his wife and two children. They stopped over in St. Paul to visit some friends, a former steam laundry operator in Melrose. Sunday forenoon these friends called the hotel where Haskells were staying and invited them to go for a drive with them.

The drive to Minnehaha Falls, in the four-passenger carriage behind a spirited team, was an enjoyable one. They were almost back to the hotel when suddenly all Ed's enjoyment drained away: He remembered that when he went to bed the night before he had put his billfold, containing all his money, under his pillow and when he left the hotel for the ride, the billfold had stayed under the pillow!

He went through some bad moments before he got back to that room. Then he found that the maid who had made the bed had carefully replaced the billfold, contents intact, under the pillow. Mr. Haskell observed that he hasn't put his billfold under his pillow since.

They arrived in Glendive on the heels of a May blizzard. Instead of the brother he had expected to meet them, he was amazed to see on the depot platform a plumber who had disappeared from Melrose two years before. Nobody there knew where he had gone so it's little wonder that Haskell was surprised to meet him 2,600 miles from home.

The ex-plumber (he told Ed he was plumbing in Glendive too, but Ed was rather dubious about that; he couldn't see that much plumbing had been done in Glendive in 1899) explained that Brother George would be in the next day to welcome the newcomers and take them to the ranch.

They had come into town about five o'clock in the evening so, after getting the family settled in the hotel, the Melrose friend offered to show Ed the town. Wouldn't take long, he explained, because there wasn't much of it. One place the friend pointed out was the Gilmore house, a show place in Glendive in those early days.

16

As Ed recalls, there were about three trees in Glendive when he made that first sight-seeing tour; two in front of the Yellowstone Hotel (these were pre-Jordan days), and one beside Esther O'Neil's (then the Cavanaugh) home.

The friend was right; it didn't take long to see the town. Next day on the way to the ranch, eighteen miles southwest of Glendive on Clear Creek, they didn't see much either because the snow was piled high, the white expanse stretched to the skyline. Already they were beginning to have their suspicions that this was going to be quite a change from Massachusetts. And it was.

The change from a seventeen-room mansion to a rough log cabin was an adjustment that Ed Haskell found he could take in stride better than his wife could. The new environment was completely foreign to Easterners accustomed to a beautiful home with the most modern conveniences and even luxuries – central heating, gas lights, lovely furniture, fine china, silver, linen. Now they were housed in a crude log cabin with an oilcloth-covered table, apple box cupboards, straw filled ticking for mattresses – and bed bugs.

Mrs. Haskell 'stuck it out' until September but then tired of fighting bed bugs, announced to her husband, "I'm going back home." "Don't you like it out here?" Ed asked her. "I've been trying," she told him, "but I haven't reached that stage yet. If you'll build a house in town so Helen (their five-year-old daughter) can go to school I'll come back."

What had brought two brothers from far away Massachusetts to such an unlikely place as a Montana sheep ranch? Ed's brother, George, was working for the General Electric Company in St. Paul and had met several stockmen from Montana. He had become interested in the possibilities in the stock business, so he wrote back to Massachusetts and suggested that his brother there interview Mr. Gilmore, also a resident of Melrose.

Boston was the principal wool-buying center for the United States and through that contact Massachusetts-born Mr. Gilmore became interested in raising sheep. He is supposed to have been the first man to bring sheep into eastern Montana. Certain it is that he started a number of Dawson County's 'big' sheep men in the business. The first sheep were driven overland from Mexico.

While Mr. Gilmore was enthusiastic about Montana as sheep-raising country, he took a dim view of fellows accustomed to 'civilization' trying to adjust to the primitive conditions on the frontier, warning them it was 'rough and woolly with no conveniences'. It would be a tough proposition, but if George really wanted to come, he'd be glad to give him a job. George 'really wanted to come' and did so in May of 1898. He worked on the Cole ranch out on Burns Creek at first.

If there is anything designed to discourage someone contemplating going into the sheep business, it would be going through lambing* season – the season George arrived – rain, snow, working all hours of the day and night. But George liked it and when he heard about a ranch for sale over on Clear Creek, he immediately investigated.

Mr. McClain (uncle of Billy Wood) had a ranch in a nice location, but his two sons who had been ranching with him had decided to quit the sheep business and join the gold rush to Alaska so Mr. McClain wanted to sell. Since the ranch was only eighteen miles from Glendive he could get into town readily so he bought it.

George's wife, unlike Ed's wife, fell in love with this country and was entirely willing to settle down here. She had an advantage, though, in that they came into town frequently and had a better chance to get acquainted. Since she was a talented musician, both vocally and instrumentally, and George also was very musical, they participated in a home talent show, "Little Tycoon" which helped them get acquainted.

Even out on the ranch, every Sunday folks would drive out –one or two or a dozen – from Glendive, bringing their instruments along, and they would have a great time.

Ed, in keeping with his bargain with his wife, built a house in town. In fact, he built two little houses, almost alike, across from Quanrad, Brink & Riebold*. Gene Blaze was his contractor and built the two houses for a cost of $1,340.

Even though the house in town had become a reality, Aphia could not seem to bring herself to risk coming back to the wild and woolly west. Ed loved his wife and children but the vision of helping develop a new land gripped him and it seemed he had to stay. He made four different trips to Melrose to try to get her to change her mind, but she was as determined to stay in the East as he was to stay in the West so they finally separated.

Ed's sister, back in Boston, shared Aphia's lack of enthusiasm for 'roughing it'. She came out one fall for a visit, planning to stay until spring. He told her, when she was making her plans, that if she stayed through the winter she should stay for the spring too, because that was the nicest time of the year.

She stayed two weeks. Then she told Ed, "I think you and George are just crazy leaving the kind of home you had back there to come out here!" And she went back to Massachusetts.

Mr. Haskell can't recall that he ever saw a live sheep until he got to the ranch, but he saw plenty then. By 1903, with the homesteaders coming in, he felt that the sheep were getting too numerous for the range so he and his brother divided the sheep and Ed put his out on shares near Watford City, North Dakota. In 1905 he sold his sheep and went to work for the Exchange State Bank in Glendive. Two years later he married Miss Mable Batchelor of Glendive.

A few years later Haskell saw possibilities opening up for a brand new business. Dr. Hathaway was driving a new car around town – the first Mr. Haskell remembers seeing in Glendive. In 1908 Ed ordered a train carload of automobiles to sell – a one-cylinder runabout, a two-cylinder roadster, a two-cylinder touring car, and a one cylinder one-ton truck.

When he started in the car business, he was still with the bank, but in 1910 he quit the bank and went into the auto business full time (the first full time auto dealer in the state, he believes). He made a trip to the Reo* Factory to see the new four cylinder cars they were putting on the market.

He was favorably impressed with what he saw and made a deal for forty cars to be delivered as he wanted them. His former business associates told him bluntly and in none-too-complimentary terms what they thought about his new venture. "You sure are plumb crazy, Ed, to quit a good job at the bank and try something like this. You'll never sell forty cars around here!" But he sold them and a good many more in the years that followed. Those first years, he declares, were the best years in the automobile business. Everybody paid cash and there were no trade-ins.

During his years in the auto business he sold about every kind made, but his biggest deal was with Buick. His contract covered all the territory from the North Dakota line to Columbus and included quite a bit of northern Wyoming. During this time he had sub-dealers in all the different towns in the area.

Twice while he had the garage he had a car auction to 'clean up' the used cars on his lot. One year he had a Spokane auctioneer who specialized in car auctions. The auctioneer was here a week before the sale date directing preparations. The auction was held inside the garage where a platform of double car length had been built. Each car sold had to be able to climb the steep grade to the platform and then stop in a very short distance.

The day of the sale the auctioneer took his place but when he began to speak he could hardly be heard. He hoarsely explained that he had a cold and his right lung seemed affected. Then he continued, his voice rising a little more with each word, "But my left lung is ALL RIGHT!" and began to cry the auction with full volume.

In 1923 Haskell was thrilled to have John Phillip Sousa and his 100-piece band visit Glendive. He had heard the band several times in the East and felt strongly that Glendive just couldn't pass up this opportunity for such a wonderful musical treat so when others said it couldn't be done, that Glendive just couldn't guarantee the thousand dollar booking for the band, Mr. Haskell personally campaigned until he had the assurance of the minimum, then presented the matter again to the Kiwanis Club and arrangements were completed.

The opera house wasn't large enough to accommodate the expected crowd so a garage, which Haskell used for a repair shop and showroom, was converted into an auditorium for the occasion. An overflow crowd proved that Haskell's faith in Glendivians' musical appreciation was not misplaced. He treasures yet the autographed photograph presented to him by the famed 'March King'.

He sold his garage to Bert Hilger in 1936 and retired, but he didn't stay retired long. When a fellow is only sixty-two years young he needs something to do so he started selling insurance. He continued with that business for almost twenty years, but after the death of his wife in 1955, he sold it to his daughter Leone and her husband, Cecil Dyer, and retired the second time. He reasoned that he was old enough to die any time so why keep plugging away?

Perhaps one factor contributing to Mr. Haskell's long and vigorous life is his abstinence from tobacco, although that was hardly his motive in abstaining. He remembers that when he was a little fellow he didn't get to see too much of his father, who hurried to catch the 8:10 train for Boston in the morning and was gone until the 6:00 train brought him home in the evening.

After dinner in the evening his father would retire behind his newspaper as he relaxed in his favorite chair, and smoke his cigar. Little four-year-old Ed was fascinated by the smoke rings that drifted ceiling-ward from behind that newspaper and one day he decided he would try making some himself.

Stealing one of those big cigars, he hid behind the old barn, but though he puffed away valiantly, he could not make smoke rings; he just made himself desperately sick. Presently his mother saw him sitting on the big wooden curbing around the well. Perhaps noticing a greenish hue to his countenance, she asked him what was the matter and he admitted that he didn't feel well.

She smelled the smoke and asked him if he had been smoking, but he told her he hadn't. Mother knew otherwise and warned him that if he didn't tell her he might die. He didn't want to die right then so he confessed. He hasn't been able to smoke since. He could chew tobacco, however, but he lost his appetite for that too, soon after he came to Montana. He hadn't been at the ranch long when his brother suggested one morning that he go on up to the lambing camp and they would tell him there what to do.

It was a dreary, rainy morning and the slicker he was wearing didn't make him any more dexterous as he straddled a western saddle for the first time. He had been told to say, 'giddup, giddup', whatever that meant, and kick the horse in the ribs so he did, and that 'gentle horse' promptly bucked him off. He had a 'chew' of tobacco in his mouth when he mounted that horse, and he swallowed the whole thing when he so unceremoniously dismounted. Sick! He was so sick he wanted George to send him back home, but George assured him, "Oh, you'll get over it." After several days, he realized he was going to recover, and he did, but since that he hasn't chewed either.

Cottontail rabbits were plentiful those first years Ed was in Montana, especially around a big butte not far from the ranch buildings, and occasionally he made a rabbit pie. One of the sheepherders used to come up to the ranch house for dinner sometimes, and one day he came just after Ed had made a rabbit pie.

"You like chicken pie, Mose?" Ed asked him. "Sure do." "Well, we have chicken pie for dinner." Mose ate three servings. Then Ed remarked, "Once in awhile we make jack rabbit pie around here." Mose emphatically made it known that, though he could eat cottontails, he could not eat jack rabbits so it wasn't long until Ed made a point of having a jack rabbit pie when Mose came just so he could chuckle as he watched the unsuspecting sheepherder partake with gusto.

One day as he and Billy Wood discussed hunting cottontails, Billy asked him, "Do you shoot them?" "How else would I get them?" Ed wanted to know. "I sure can't catch them on foot." "No, no," Billy explained, "You don't try to outrun them. Rabbits are curious, just like antelope, so you set out a lantern at night, and they will sit and watch that lantern until it makes their eyes water. As the water drops to the ground it will start to freeze until finally it builds up right to their eyes and the rabbits are frozen fast. All you have to do is go out in the morning and pick them off the icicles!"

When Mr. Haskell came to Montana, there were only about 1,800 people in the entire county (the county then reached to the Canadian line), and fewer than a 1,000 in Glendive so he has had ample opportunity to watch the town grow. Not long ago someone asked him, "How does it seem to grow old?" (Perhaps it was Billy Wood who asked.) Haskell replied, "You will have to ask someone older; I don't know yet."

In 1956 Mr. Haskell married Miss Effie Ekberg, a former teacher at Dawson County High School. According to Mr. Haskell, he and Effie have been married ten years, and she says it doesn't seem like more than twenty.

Even with all his other interests, Mr. Haskell has still found time for community and church activities. He was a charter member and was present at the laying of the cornerstone when the first Congregational Church* was built in 1937 and had the honor of laying the cornerstone for the new structure built fifty-eight years later.

He has been president of the Kiwanis club, member of the City Council, and of the Chamber of Commerce, is the oldest living past master of Glendive Masonic Lodge 31 AF & AM and a fifty-seven year member of Al Bedoo Masonic Lodge of Billings.

Mr. Haskell remarked that as you grow older you love to reminisce. There's only one citizen remaining in Glendive with whom he can do this – Billy Wood. One of the stories that came to his mind as he thought of that reminiscing was the time during spring break-up when a flood threatened Glendive. Everyone who had a car was ready to flee to higher ground, and Mr. Haskell parked his car in front of the house to be ready at a moment's notice. The crisis passed without incident. The next morning he went out to drive to work, drove the car around the corner of the block, and ran out of gas!

Then there was the time in one of the parades when he hauled a ton of sacked flour on one of his trucks to show how powerful it was.

When the Dawson Country Club was 'going strong', members were to dress formally for the big parties. On one of his trips to Chicago, Mr. Haskell stopped over long enough to have a full dress suit made – this was about 1915. He still has that suit and at one of his recent birthday parties – he loves parties and hasn't missed having a birthday party since he came to Glendive – he wore that suit. (He admits it's a little tight, but he can wear it.) One of the guests, when greeted at the door, asked him, "Are you the butler or the host?"

Over the years, the easterner from 'civilized' Massachusetts has made a noteworthy contribution in bringing 'civilization' to Montana, too.

Mrs. Isaac (Elsie Guss) Jones

December 1965

"We didn't come until 1910 so we really weren't early enough to be classed as pioneers," Mrs. Elsie Jones was careful to explain as she began describing her introduction to Montana.

Although many parts of the county had scarcely been touched at that time, Thirteen Mile Valley was pretty well settled, and all the homestead land had been taken. Mr. and Mrs. Ike Jones considered themselves fortunate indeed to be able to buy a homestead that was already proved up* right in the location they wanted, between Bloomfield and Red Top.

Many of the settlers in the area around Bloomfield had come from Bloomfield, Nebraska. Among those coming was Theodore Jones, brother to Ike. Letters going back to Nebraska from the homesteaders persuaded Ike that a farm in Montana would be a good investment as well as an inviting place to live so here it was that he brought his bride of less than a month.

Elsie Guss had been a schoolteacher in Nebraska before her marriage to Ike Jones. The news that they planned to move 'Out West' after their marriage was received with horror by her family, particularly her sisters. "What will you do out there in that wild country?" was their chief theme as they tried to dissuade her. Actually, she wasn't too sure herself what she was going to do 'out there', but she was game to find out.

Before moving to their new home in the 'Wild West' the newlyweds took a long look at civilization. Their wedding trip took them first to Sioux City, then to Chicago, Niagara Falls, New York City, Washington D.C., and Norfolk, Virginia. They concluded their train trip at Glendive, ready for what the West might offer.

In Glendive Mrs. Jones received the surprise of her life. While teaching in Nebraska she would usually spend the weekend in her parents' home, but on Sunday evening she had to go to the nearby town of Wassau, spend the night in the hotel, then take the train next morning to get to her school. It seems that most of the little towns around there had one thing in common: dinky, dirty, 'nasty' hotels with only primitive accommodations. With such hotels in Nebraska, what could one expect in a small Montana town? Mrs. Jones was expecting the worst, and that's where she got her surprise. They spent their first night in the Treasure State* in the Jordan Hotel, and Mrs. Jones declared that it was as nice as any of the hotels they had stayed in on their trip through the east. The room, the food, the service – everything was just fine. And here she was expecting a little old Wild West hotel! Then she added that, of course, fifty-five years ago it couldn't compare with the present Jordan Hotel.

When they reached Glendive they were still more than thirty miles from their new home so they rode out to Bloomfield with the mail carrier, Mr. Coleman, in his spring wagon. It was an all-day trip, and Mrs. Jones recalled how, at noon, Mr. Coleman stopped to eat his lunch and build a little fire to heat his coffee.

At their farm a new house was waiting for them. Brother Theodore had built the house before their arrival so it was all ready for them to move into. Thede and his family, living in the new house while they finished it, stayed to greet the newcomers and had a hot supper ready for them. Even though they came in September the ride out from Glendive had been a cold one so the travelers were happy for the warm welcome. Thede had homesteaded on Burns Creek so they moved back over to their own home as soon as the owners of the new house arrived to occupy it.

Mr. and Mrs. Jones had bought their farm from Miles Borntrager. Borntrager and his wife had each filed on a claim but hers was several miles east of Red Top so he was glad for the opportunity to sell his homestead and buy land closer to where they were living.

Folks back home in Nebraska, apprehensive of the new venture from the start, now besieged them with questions, wanting to know what it was like 'out there'. As soon as she had opportunity to familiarize herself a bit with the country, Mrs. Jones began sending reports. One of the most persistent questions was, "How big a town is Bloomfield?" By way of reply she told them Bloomfield was really a big town; the post office was a mile from the middle of town and the blacksmith shop was a mile-and-a-half the other way. What she didn't bother to mention until some time later was that Mrs. Nettie Gibbs had the post office in her shack on her homestead west of Bloomfield (it was a mile from the middle of town!) and Frank Stone's blacksmith shop was on his homestead south of town.

Mrs. Jones mentioned that when she and her husband came to Montana, two farmers in the area still farmed with oxen. One of them was Jens Scarpholt (still farming in the Thirteen Mile Valley though not now with oxen) and the other was Louie Swanson. She said that after a time Swanson bought a team but they ran away while he had them hitched to a binder and he was killed.

The summer of 1915 was one of the coldest summers Mrs. Jones remembers. Her mother came out to visit them and declared she was cold the whole time she was here – except for one day. They did have one warm day so they went on a picnic down at Intake and that was the one day Mrs. Guss was able to get really warm.

Pioneering wasn't new to the Guss family. Mr. and Mrs. Guss had moved from Pennsylvania to Nebraska when daughter Elsie (Mrs. Jones) was only two years old. Nebraska, at that time, was more of a frontier than Montana was in 1910. They settled on the edge of the Indian reservation at a time when trouble with the Indians was still common. Mrs. Jones pointed out that her mother believed in being fair to the Indians and always made a practice of giving them something to eat any time they stopped. The Indians were always friendly to them, even helping them on occasion – perhaps replenishing the woodpile or some other such act of kindness. "Be good to an Indian and he'll be good to you," was Mrs. Guss's philosophy. Their experience seemed to bear that out.

Less than thirty miles from their home the white settlers of an entire village were massacred by the Indians on the warpath but no harm ever came to the Guss family.

They lived in a dugout the first year they were in Nebraska, then moved to a two-story house. They were ahead of schools, just as the first Thirteen Mile settlers had been, and the first school was held in the second story of their new house. Although little Elsie was only four years old when the school was opened, she too, had to go to school. This was not much to her liking so one day, instead of going to school, she slipped down to the creek and climbed up into a tree. Her vacation was brief indeed. Presently she saw her mother coming with a big stick. Mother climbed the tree and brought Elsie down, then applied 'the board of education to the seat of learning'. That was the first, last, and only time Elsie ever played 'hookie'.

Mrs. Jones laughingly recalled that when she was a little girl, her mother always talked about Pennsylvania, then when she moved to Montana and became a mother herself, she talked about Nebraska. After their son graduated from high school the family went to Nebraska for a visit but Son just wasn't much impressed. "You mean," he asked, "this is the country you've been talking about all these years? Just all up and down, no valleys, no tables, just hills!" Since then she says she's had to be pretty careful what she says about Nebraska.

Seriously though, Mrs. Jones observed that she liked Montana from the start and never was interested in moving back to Nebraska. Perhaps what impressed her most about the new country was the friendliness of all the people – not just your friends but of everyone. This was a sharp contrast to what she had observed when she traveled east and even 'back home' in Nebraska.

In 1943 Mr. and Mrs. Jones moved into Glendive. Mr. Jones was reluctant to leave the old farm that he loved but the winter in town was easier for him. The next spring he passed away. Mrs. Jones still considers Montana's people the friendliest and feels Montana is the best place to live. She just looks back with pleasure on all the good times she's had in Montana.

As she spoke of the good times she remembered how they used to get together for Sunday dinner – thirty or forty of them in one place. Once, when they were at Uncle Thede's they were going to make ice cream but they ran out of milk. They solved that simply, not by running to the store (Bloomfield was thirteen miles away) but by going to the pasture and milking the cow. They had their ice cream!

Angelo Tomalino

August 1965

Poverty dominated much of Italy in 1900. What peasant would dare dream that he might some day retire in California? A wild dream – but dreams do sometimes come true. Carlo Tomalino heard that across the thousands of miles of land and sea the United States was giving away land in Montana – 160 acres to a man, just for the taking. He wasn't thinking California then, but surely a man with 160 acres could soon accumulate a fortune, come back to Italy, and "have it made." So Carlo Tomalino left his wife and two small sons in Italy and came to Montana to get a home ready for them.

He chose a quarter section* on Murphy Table, about six miles northwest of Intake, for his homesite and began to make improvements on it. Homestead requirements were liberal, and he didn't have to stay on the homestead all the time so he was able to work out a good deal. George McCone and Jack Martin were his main employers.

He soon learned that 160 acres of dry land in Montana were not to be reckoned as 160 acres in Italy. But who could hope for 160 acres in Italy? The homestead held more promise than the Old Country, and after about four years he was able to send for his family. And after about fifty years he moved to California.

Angelo was rather small to remember much about his arrival in this country, but he does recall that his father came in a wagon to meet them at the train. The bottom of the wagon was covered with straw so they snuggled down into the straw and slept a good part of that last stage of their journey. Night fell before they reached Murphy Table, and the bright shining of the stars made a deep impression on him.

Aboard ship two things made an impression on him – the propeller and the food. There was a hole in the floor of the ship where you could look down and see the big propeller churning the water. The hole had a fence around it to prevent accidents, but fences don't mean too much to a five-year-old boy. He had slipped away from his mother and when she found him, he was lying on his stomach under that fence, gazing down at the fascinating sight below. His mother, however, was not fascinated and jerked him out in a hurry.

And the food. They had not been eating very well in Italy, and to him the food was wonderful. Some of the other passengers evidently didn't enjoy it quite so much because quite a number of them were sick during the voyage. He remembers, too, standing at the rail watching for whales, but the whales kept out of sight.

Angelo's formal education began in the Burns Creek School. He and his brother were fortunate to have a horse and buggy to go to school. Angelo recalls that one time he got a little too cocky and instead of sitting on the buggy seat, he perched on top of the back rest. His cockiness was unceremoniously dashed when the driver whipped up the horse, the buggy lurched, and he tipped backwards. He landed in the back of the buggy, but he had such a good rolling start that he kept right on rolling until he hit the ground.

School then differed considerably from its present-day counterpart. The big boys were BIG and many of them uncouth. They illustrated their idea of 'fun' by roping Angelo's brother and dragging him around the yard until Slim Graves discovered them and came to the rescue.

During recess they liked to slip away from the school and go wading in the creek. There would be water snakes and frogs and other creatures to make their 'field trip' even more interesting, and sometimes they'd get so interested they'd forget to think of the time. Then they'd have to hustle like good fellows to get shoes and socks on and get back to the school when the bell rang.

If there were still wolves in the country (and that was the report), Angelo never actually saw one, but he imagined he saw plenty of them. The older boys thought it a good joke to yell "Wolves!" The Burns Creek area was liberally supplied with rocks and boulders, and each rock and boulder, especially when late afternoon gave way to dusk, could pass for a wolf.

In the spring they would watch for the Indians to return from their winter quarters. They always found the visits interesting, yet they were about half scared to have them come. The Indians carried a generous supply of beads. One or two would come to the door and knock, then trade beads for loaves of homemade bread. They couldn't understand each other's language, but the Indians managed to make their wants known, and Mrs. Tomalino, a bit apprehensive about having them around when her husband was out working, would quickly accommodate them. The last year the Indians came through they were driving a Model T Ford. The radiator was steaming and they were having a hard time keeping it going, but they were traveling in style.

As Angelo looks back to his boyhood encounters with cowboys and Indians he says he just can't see much resemblance to the cowboys and Indians portrayed in present-day shows.

According to Angelo he never was too much of a horseman. His brother Joe could handle the horses, but his own interests were directed more to machinery. His dad used to say that if anybody could have a run-a-way, Angelo could. There were no tractors and certainly no 'power takeoffs' to furnish power for a feed mill so they ground feed with a mill powered by horses going 'round and 'round to turn the mill. One day as they were grinding feed one of the lines to the horse's bridle broke so they started going straight instead of following their circle. That meant the feed mill started following them. The first thump of the mill coming off its pedestal was enough to scare the horses, and each succeeding bounce scared them a little more. They were a couple miles away before they were stopped.

Prairie fires were a very real hazard in those early days of tall grass and few plowed fields. Each farmer made a practice of plowing a few furrows around his buildings as a measure of protection. Some of the fires came close enough to their home to cause their mother real concern (the boys were generally more excited than alarmed), but none of them actually reached their buildings. A prairie fire was everybody's business, and everyone within sight of the smoke would come hurrying to fight fire, beating at the flames with wet gunnysacks.

Angelo reflected that the doctor situation was quite different in those days. When a doctor was needed someone would go for the doctor, then the doctor would hire a chauffeur and car from one of the garages and hurry to the scene of need. They could usually count on getting stuck about a half-dozen times either in mud or snow, depending on the season. And they charged ten dollars.

About the time Angelo started to high school the family left the homestead (although they kept possession and continued to farm it) and moved to a place down along the river. During his four years of high school Angelo would stay in town for the school term, boarding with a local family – thirty dollars a month for room and board. He confesses that he looked upon school as more or less of a picnic, a vacation from hoeing corn or potatoes or similar work. They had no cultivator except the hoe, and he got so he hated to see a lot of corn planted because he knew it was going to mean a lot of hoeing. Compared with that, school certainly was no drudgery. Perhaps there would be fewer school dropouts if the alternative were more in the nature of hoeing corn in the hot sun!

After high school Angelo started working for the county surveyor and worked under several different surveyors. The Roosevelt 'landslide' of 1932 swept his boss out of office so Angelo was out of a job. He had been interested in radio for some time and had taken a radio course by mail so now he took to radio repair full time. His 'office' was wherever he could rent a little space – a corner of Dick Statham's garage, a spot in E.G. Ufer's Standard Mercantile hardware store, a little space in the G.D. Hollecker Store. For the latter he paid five dollars a month. Finally he decided it would be more satisfactory to move into quarters of his own, and he opened a shop on North Merrill.

In the early days of radio when not many homes boasted a set, Angelo made a practice of setting up a radio on the sidewalk to let the public listen. One of his early ads in THE DAWSON COUNTY REVIEW invited: "Listen to the Louis-Schmeling Fight via RCA radio in front of the Standard Mercantile Co. Wednesday, June 22."

He reports that a regular mob would gather around to listen to such a special feature. You could draw a bigger crowd with a little radio set than with color TV now. People marveled that the words and the music could come from that little box, but now it's an old story and they take the picture for granted, too.

The senior Tomalinos now live in Glendale, California. Three of their four children are still living: Joe on the farm near Intake, Angelo in Glendive, and Elsie (Mrs. Bob Adams) in California. Carlo Jr., remembered by many for his singing, passed away in California about eight years ago.

Mrs. Joe (Fanny Hostetler) Stoll

August 1967

"Papa's coming! Papa's coming!" Even though 'Papa' was still several miles away, in the still of the evening Jake Hostetler's children could hear and recognize the rumble of his wagon. It had steel wheels as well as steel tires so as it rattled down 'Gravel Hill' (the descent from Morgan Table to Thirteen Mile Valley) the noise from his wheels was distinct from other wagons with wooden wheels. The trip to Glendive took two days, and his children always listened eagerly for the signal that Papa would soon be home from town.

The trips to town were made fairly regularly for a pioneer settlement – perhaps once a month – because they sold butter and eggs in the little town on the Yellowstone. They hauled for the neighbors, too, and sometimes took in as much as fifty pounds of butter and thirty dozen eggs. Their main customer was Mrs. Morse, proprietor of the Morse Rooming House on Bell Street, just on the east end of the bridge.

The Hostetlers came to Dawson County in the spring of 1905. In those days any time someone from the small settlement made the trip to Glendive, the county seat and almost the only shopping center between the Missouri River and Miles City, all the other neighbors would send with them for supplies that were running short. Not only did the town-goer bring supplies; he also brought the mail. No one considered once a month too often to get the mail! With the establishment of the Adams post office, five miles away instead of thirty, mail service was much improved.

Mrs. Hostetler's parents, the Johnny Millers, had moved to Thirteen Mile in the fall of 1904. They had bought a section* and a half of railroad land and had built a real house, not just a shack as many dwellings were at the start. It had a full basement under it, and Dave Chupp, Sr. had 'rocked up' the sides of it.

The efficient equipment in the basement for handling cream made a distinct impression on the little granddaughter, Fannie. Along one wall of the basement was a long, drop-leaf table, and on this table were placed the crocks for the milk skimming. Grandma waited until the milk was slightly sour before she skimmed it so she could get all the cream. About 1910 or '12 they bought one of the first cream separators on the market. To insure prompt cooling of the cream and milk they sank a tub, with a hole in the bottom of it, into the dirt floor. Then they would carry cold water from the well at carefully spaced intervals to keep the tub filled and their products cold. People did live without refrigerators!

Jake Hostetler had come from Kansas to North Dakota as a young man, and there he had married Lydia Miller. His parents didn't want him to stay in the north and probably were convinced it was even worse when he left North Dakota for the sparsely settled plains of Montana. He moved his stock and furniture by immigrant car* while his wife and three children – Fannie, Ed, and Amos – followed by passenger train. Emma, also a daughter of the Johnny Millers, accompanied her sister and the children on the train.

28

It was well she did. Otherwise who, a few years later, would have taught the first school in the Valley? And where would bachelor John Kauffman, one of the very first homesteaders to come to the Valley (in the spring of 1903) have found his wife? Unattached women were scarce in pioneer country, and John didn't overlook the opportunity provided when Miss Emma joined the settlement. Their wedding was the first in the new community.

Before the wedding, though – the school. With more settlers constantly coming, including about fifteen children of school age, there was soon a demand for a school. To prove a need they had to first hold a three-month term before the county would establish a district.

The shanty that Dave Chupp, Sr. had built (about a mile south of Red Top Church) when he first came to Montana in the fall of 1904 was converted into a school. Desks were shelves built along the walls, and the pupils sat on backless benches with their backs to each other and facing the shelves. It was hardly the modern architect's idea of a school, but it served the purpose and proved that if a district were established there would be pupils to attend.

Miss Emma, who had homesteaded immediately south of the site later chosen for the school, was reluctant to tackle the job of teaching, but no other teacher was available so she was prevailed upon. As the scholars sat on their backless benches they studied their lessons diligently. The teacher could easily tell which ones were studying diligently because they all studied out loud.

Later when the district was established and the new schoolhouse was built, someone suggested to her, "We'll name the school after you," but Emma's reply to that was, "Oh, no, you don't!" Instead it was called the Adams School, but the name was later changed to Red Top when the roof was painted red. Roy Reed was the first teacher in the new school, followed by Lester Brown and then Mabel Reed. When the schoolhouse was built, it became the center for community activities. Sunday School was held there on Sundays. A little later, often on Friday evenings, it was the scene of spell-downs or ciphering matches.

Fannie recalls that one evening they had a debate on the pros and cons of drinking intoxicating beverages. Harvey Boston, a homesteader (not famous for his temperance) who lived a couple miles from the school, somehow turned up arguing with the cons. She remembers vividly his concluding statement: "As for me, I never took a drink in my life," (pronounced pause to appreciate the gasp with which his audience greeted such bare-faced mishandling of the truth), then finished, "unless I was with somebody or by myself!"

When the Jake Hostetler family moved to the Thirteen Mile Valley in 1905, they built on the northeast corner of 'Grandpa's' (Johnny Miller) land. There was a ready market for hay in those early years so Mr. Hostetler put up a lot of prairie hay, which he would then sell to the livery barns in Glendive. Fannie remembers riding to town on one of those loads of hay. She observed that if she got to town once a year in the summer during those childhood years she thought that was wonderful. And why not? One fellow who had come when just small told of going to Glendive just three times before he was twenty-one.

The pasture in which they ran their cattle was a mile long so their little yellow dog was much appreciated. Even when the cattle were at the far end of the pasture, they could tell him, "Sic, 'em; bring the cows," and he would bring them, yet he never ran them. The faithful dog had been with the family even in the days when they lived in North Dakota before coming to Montana. One afternoon little Fannie had disappeared, and no trace could be found of the dog, either. As Mrs. Hostetler searched she noticed a certain path where the tall wheat was waving in the field so she pursued the 'waves' and caught up with a little girl and a pup just before they reached the main road.

In 1910 the family left the Bloomfield area and moved to Wisconsin where Jake's brother lived. They sold their livestock and left the yellow dog with Grandma. After their departure the dog refused to eat. They had sold their black and white team to Eli Borntrager, and one day he came driving that team east past Grandpa's. The little dog eagerly ran down to the road, only to droop disappointedly when he realized the team was not transporting those he sought.

The family stayed in Wisconsin only two years before they returned to the Treasure State. Upon their return they lived first on 'the Bendon place' (originally the Dave Chupp home, south of the Red Top School), then on Uncle John Kauffman's place. His three-room granary substituted for a house quite acceptably. During this time Jake worked for various farmers in the community.

While they lived at Uncle John's he undertook the remodeling of his garage and chicken house. One of the children, carrying little Matilda (the ten-month-old baby) dropped her and her head struck a scrap of lumber. The injury did not seem to be severe, but her condition grew worse, and a week later she died. This fall took place just a week before they moved to the C.A. Buller place. Bullers had gone to Michigan so Hostetlers farmed his place during his absence.

When Bullers returned after one year in Michigan, Hostetlers bought a quarter of a section from Monie Schrock, one mile east of Glen Borntrager's home, and lived there until the fall of 1919 when they had a sale and moved to Oregon. They bought a place near Hubbard, and during the ten years they lived there tragedy struck the family twice. First the mother passed away, then a few years later one of the boys, Oscar, was struck by a car and killed.

That same year, 1929, the father of the family with one son, Ed, and Ed's wife returned to Montana. By this time most of the children had married and established homes of their own. Fannie, instead of returning to Montana at that time, had gone first to Canada, then to Hesston, Kansas, where she attended school. Later she did come to Montana and made her home here for a number of years. Ed, his wife and family have remained in Montana until the present, but after a few years Jake Hostetler moved back to Oregon again and has lived there since. Now, at ninety-one-and-a-half years, he lives in the Home for the Aged in McMinnville.

Two others of the family members live in Oregon, as they have since 1919: Amos lives in Salem, and Celesta in Sheridan. Fred is near Tofield, Alberta, and Fannie's home is near Detroit Lakes, Minnesota.

Bill Blue

July 1966

Bill Blue took the long way 'round to get to Montana, but even so he reached the Richey area well ahead of the crowd. He was there in time to get the full benefit of the hostility of the ranchers toward the 'Honyockers' (the disparaging term ranchers applied to the homesteaders).

Natives of the Hoosier State, the Blues happened to be in Washington when they heard about the homestead opportunities in Dawson County. Mrs. Blue's cousin was married to the head of the mathematics department at Bozeman, Mr. Tallman. Mr. Tallman was also a surveyor, and it was he who had surveyed the Richey area, making way for the homesteaders. Mrs. Tallman wrote to her cousin, urging them to look into homestead possibilities, so in September 1909, Mr. Blue came to investigate.

If transportation in 1909 had been what it is in 1966, Blue would likely have located in the Lindsay area rather than Richey. He had contacted the land office, and by the time he reached Glendive, one of the real estate agents locating the homesteaders had picked out a site for him near Lindsay. Blue tried to hire someone to take him out to look at the place, but he wasn't able to get a ride for a few days, and in the meantime someone else filed on it.

Blue was obliged to look elsewhere so when he heard there was plenty of land to the northwest of Glendive, he began looking for a ride out there. An early settler from that region, a man by the name of Bancroft, happened to be in Glendive so Bill asked what he would charge to haul him out. Bancroft's hearty reply was, "I want neighbors; it won't cost you a cent!"

Bancroft was as good as his word. He not only gave Mr. Blue a ride out to his own home, fifty miles from Glendive; he hauled him around for almost a week and refused pay even for that. The only compensation Bancroft ever did accept was when, in the years that followed, he peddled groceries around the country. Then, if he was in Blue's neighborhood, he would stay overnight with them. The Blues would have extended that hospitality to anyone needing a bed for the night so they could never feel that that was in any sense 'pay' for what Mr. Bancroft had done for them.

Back in his home state of Indiana Bill Blue had been a schoolteacher. At forty or fifty dollars a month he didn't feel there was much future in teaching school so he began to look for greener pastures. He had a farm in Indiana, too, but as the population there increased, the farms were becoming smaller and smaller so he felt that farming prospects left much to be desired, too.

In 1905 Bill Blue married Blanche Hott, a girl he had known since childhood. In the first few years of their marriage they did a good bit of traveling – until they found that 'right spot'. They started their travels with a honeymoon trip to Denver where they attended the International Epworth League Sunday School convention. Six months later they headed south again, this time to Oklahoma City.

31

An uncle of Bill's who was a land agent for a railroad company wrote and asked Bill to come help him sell some land in Texas. Mr. and Mrs. Blue made plans to go – even had their tickets bought – when uncle wired that he'd disposed of all the Texas holdings but come to Oklahoma City anyway. They spent Christmas with him in Oklahoma and still smile at their own surprise to find people celebrating Christmas with fireworks. Since they had their tickets to Texas they used them and went on over into Mexico, too.

That trip proved to be the start of a long chain events – a chain that ended in Montana. As they returned homeward they stopped to visit relatives in Kansas. Some of those Kansas farmers had gone to Alberta to raise wheat, so Blue caught the Canadian wheat fever and decided he'd go North. He went in the fall of 1907, but when he reached Calgary, he found them trying to harvest wheat that was lying flat on the ground. It was so flat on the ground they couldn't cut around the fields; the binder could cut only one direction. Two feet of wet snow had depressed the wheat, and it depressed him as well. He abruptly recovered from his wheat fever and decided this was no place to homestead. Now he concludes he would have been lucky to go ahead and homestead: the location he was considering is in the middle of the oil country. From Calgary he went to British Columbia and looked at the big fruit ranches. The fruit grew prolifically, but lack of transportation made marketing too costly for profit so they kept on going.

At Loomis, Washington, they rented a squaw man's* estate. The place had eighty acres of alfalfa along with ample space for truck gardening and seemed the ideal place, but then the panic of 1908 struck. Money tightened, mines and lumber industries in the surrounding area shut down, and everybody left so there went his market. He couldn't sell his produce so he traded it for horses and two covered wagons and headed for Wenatchee. It's been close to sixty years since they made that trip, but the recollection of that road is still vivid. The road was cut out of solid rock with a sheer drop of a thousand feet to the Columbia River in some places. All the horses were required to have bells on them, and when you approached a curve, you stopped to listen so you would know if another team was coming. If you heard bells – wait.

He hauled lumber that year and made good money because those roads were dangerous, too, and teamsters weren't eager to haul over them. His horses proved to be a good investment, and he used them for land leveling as well as hauling so when he decided to homestead in Montana, he had a little 'laid by' to start him out. Good thing he did. He put in his first Montana crop in 1910, one of the driest years in the memory of the old timers.

Bill Blue filed on his homestead in September of 1909, but he didn't take up residence until the spring of 1910. When he moved from Washington, he shipped two immigrant cars of livestock and other belongings for equipment in his new venture. One of the first jobs he had in Montana was hauling big timbers to the Ditch* under construction as part of the new Intake Dam project. Again he put those horses to good use.

32

He broke up eighty acres of sod on his claim that spring and declares that the summer was so dry that what he planted didn't come up until August (they had a rain in August) and froze in September. He built a little shack that spring, too. He really intended it for a hen house, but when he saw what kind of crop the summer was producing, he moved it over the basement he had dug and they used it for a house. He wasn't at all sure he was going to be around to build a real house!

While he was digging the basement he dug out a badger. He decided that badger didn't have such a bad idea, living underground, so he rocked up the walls (those walls are two feet thick), plastered them, and lived below ground level, too. They still use that original part of the house for a kitchen and have always found it warm in winter and cool in summer. At one end of the kitchen is the storeroom on the same level. There they store fruits and vegetables and canned goods. In all these years nothing has ever frozen in the storeroom.

By 1914 the Blues were convinced that crops could be raised in Dawson County after all and had decided to make this their permanent home. They built their house, joining it to the original shack. Unlike many homesteaders, Blue hired a carpenter, Isaiah Kauffman, to build their house instead of just doing it himself with the help of some neighbors. Kauffman built a number of houses throughout the area, including Glen Borntrager's, Walter Seekins', and Menno Mullet's.

An interesting feature of the Blue home is the cistern, eight feet deep, built under the porch on the south side of the kitchen. Mr. Blue explained that it was hard to find good water in that area because there was so much alkali, but with the cistern to catch the rain water and melting snow they had a good supply of soft water for washing, cleaning, anything but drinking. As for drinking, they used more milk than they did water. In addition to the two immigrant cars from Washington, Mr. Blue shipped two more from Indiana when he went back to get his wife and family where they had gone while he got a place ready for them to live. Included in the load in those cars were some Devonshire cows, excellent milk stock. Here he crossed the Devonshires with Herefords and built up a herd with which he was very well pleased.

While Mr. Bancroft was pleased at the prospect of neighbors, others in the area were not. Cattlemen, horsemen, and sheepmen fought among themselves, and all of them fought against the homesteaders. Some of them were frankly determined to run Bill Blue out of the country – and he was determined to stay. Among other things, someone killed Blue's bull and hauled it into Lambert. This wasn't the first such incident, and an aroused community banded together to do something about it.

This wasn't just a local concern; widespread rustling had been going on throughout Dawson, Richland, and McCone counties so the sheriffs of those counties, along with a posse of 100 citizens, set out to round up the gang responsible for the rustling. They found the hideout near a big clay butte. Besides apprehending five men and two women, they found a hundred bushels of hides that the thieves had hidden in the surrounding brush.

The wily law-evaders cut steps into the butte and used it for a lookout. From the top of the butte, anyone approaching could be seen from a considerable distance, and the fugitives would have time to escape, but with such a concentrated search under way a lookout wasn't enough. They were captured.

Another time one of Bill's neighbors happened along just in time to witness the unauthorized butchering of one of his cattle so he allowed the butcher the privilege of walking clear to Glendive to the sheriff's office. Just to make sure the privilege wasn't forfeited, he followed along close by on his horse.

Blue had several sections of land to supplement his homestead, and one of these sections he fenced for pasture. He'd send the children over to check on the cattle and make sure everything was all right, but he was puzzled when sometimes they would bring back a report of stray horses in that section – as many as a hundred. Finally he discovered that horse thieves were using his pasture for a stopping place as they moved them from the north down toward the river. Yes, things were interesting in those early years, sometimes more so than was desirable.

By the spring of 1910 many homesteaders had flocked into the community where Bill Blue located. Along with the homesteaders came their children, and Blue, with children of his own, felt that schools were imperative. The ranchers didn't share his views. Ranchers felt that schools would be one more anchor to hold the farmers, and they didn't want the farmers anchored. Schools would mean a rise in taxes, too, and the ranchers were bitterly opposed to paying more taxes to provide schools for the 'honyockers' kids'. That would be heaping insult upon injury! Anyway, most of the ranchers were bachelors so why bother about schools?

In 1912 when Blue bought a kerosene-powered Rumley* tractor, he had to go to Glendive twice weekly to get fuel for it. This proved to be a good opportunity to work with the county superintendent toward getting a school started so now he could work from both ends. Back at the Richey end, Blue was one of the board members, Clyde Richey, postmaster, another member, and Eldon Walker, mail carrier from Bloomfield to Richey, the other member. When Walker brought the mail from Bloomfield, Blue would ride over to Richey's home (where the post office was located and for whom the town was named), and they'd have a school board meeting.

There were problems a plenty to be faced, not the least of which was lack of money. How could a decent schoolhouse be built with so little money? Getting the lumber hauled out was another problem. It had to be brought from Stipek or Glendive, a four-day trip from Blues, and no one seemed interested in hauling lumber. Blue hauled most of it himself, but a neighbor brought out one load. He made the occasion memorable by driving clear through to Glendive, with liquor at the end of the drive, in one day. On the return trip he didn't make such fast time.

Eventually they did get enough lumber hauled to build a school and enough money to hire someone to build it. Bill's brother, Frank Blue, built that first school. Now as he views Richey's fine school system Mr. Blue feels that it was well worth the struggle to get it started.

A motorist today cruising comfortably along on the oiled highways in the Richey area in a late model car – any model car – may have difficulty visualizing problems facing the pioneers even fifty years ago. The motorist might, that is, unless he happens to be one of those pioneers, such as Bill Blue.

When Blue homesteaded fifty miles northwest of Glendive, it wasn't just oiled roads that were lacking; roads of any kind were non-existent. Why would there be roads where no one had ever traveled or even had occasion to travel? Those first years there were no roads, no railroads, no markets, no elevators, and some years – no crops. Blue did his first breaking sod in Dawson County in 1910 and a less-determined character might well have decided that would be his last, but Blue tried again. No crop in '10, half a crop in '11, then in '12 – ah, in 1912! That was the year! That was the year of his first bumper crop. In spite of dismal returns those first two years, Blue believed Montana could produce, and he broke up several thousand acres of sod with his big Rumley. Not only did he break for himself and his father and brothers, but for many other homesteaders as well.

Even though 1912 yielded a wonderful crop his problems weren't all solved. Rather, some of them were intensified – his marketing problem, for example. He didn't get all of the year's crop shipped until the railroad reached Richey! At first he had to haul to Glendive, a four-day trip. He used seven horses and a wagon with a trailer to make those trips, four horses on the lead wagon, three on the trailer. When he came to the steep hills he'd hitch all seven horses to the wagon, then when he got it to the top, he'd take the seven back to the trailer and pull it up the hill.

In 1913 the Northern Pacific Railroad reached Savage, then in 1914 the Great Northern was completed to Lambert, just twenty-two miles from Blue's farm. Toward Glendive by that time there was at least a wagon trail, but toward Lambert there was nothing. You just had to wander around through the hills and figure out for yourself where you could cross the coulees.

With the railroad headed their way, farmers in Blue's area formed a corporation and tried to sell stock to be ready to build an elevator when the railroad arrived, but most of the farmers didn't have any money to buy shares. And certainly the stockmen weren't interested in putting money into an elevator! For Blue it meant digging into his own resources, even selling his life insurance policy and his Indiana farm before the elevator was established.

When the rails reached Richey, they were organized and ready to bring lumber to start building, but getting it built was not the end of their problems. It went broke two or three times after it began operating (with opposition from stockmen no small part of the reason), but persistence was rewarded with success, and Richey farmers had a market.

Blue is a strong believer in land conservation, and even before he came to Montana he had cooperated in experiments. Back in Indiana in 1902 he associated with Purdue University as a field man to increase yield and quality.

He had a twenty-acre field where, instead of buying commercial fertilizer, he plowed under English clover and planted it to corn. At a time when the average corn yield there was twenty-eight bushels per acre, his field yielded 100 bushels to the acre.

In Montana he continued to apply known principles of conservation and to experiment with others. He built a system of dams to hold the spring runoff and rains, built ditches for drainage and practiced contour farming, working in cooperation with the county extension agent. One year he made more on ten acres of potatoes than on a section of wheat! However, he has had good success with grains, also. His highest yield of wheat was sixty bushels to the acre, his highest yield of flax thirty-five bushels to the acre.

Blue is now in his eighty-sixth year, but he carries those years lightly. He explained that as boys both he and his brother hoped to become professional ball players so they started a program of training toward that goal. They thought it would be great to be in the circus, too, but their uncle, Ben Wallace, a circus man, discouraged that. Bill changed his mind about a career (his brother did play with St. Louis fifty-six years ago), but he kept up a physical fitness program and accredits his agility today to exercise.

Mr. and Mrs. Blue still live in their home on the old homestead. Interesting relics of another era grace their living room. Mrs. Blue's diploma, certifying the graduation of Blanche Hott on May 17, 1905, from Amboy Academy in Indiana, hangs in its frame on the wall. An old-fashioned reed organ, given to her by her parents as a Christmas gift when she was ten years old, stands in one corner. And of course, the clock. The clock would surely catch the eye of anyone interested in antiques or in the unique.

The clock, which belonged to Mrs. Blue's parents and was in their home as far back as she can remember, has two separate dials. The upper dial has Roman numerals for indicating the time. The lower dial has numbers to thirty-one with a hand to indicate the day of the month, the other to show the day of the week. Although the clock is not now in running order, all those features are quiet reminders that time marches on.

Mrs. Perry (Annie Johnson) Walker

May 1966

When Mrs. Perry Walker first came to Glendive back in 1907 (she was Miss Annie Johnson then), she spent her first two nights in the comfortable Jordan Hotel, but after that her accommodations were somewhat less sophisticated; her living quarters were in a tent.

She was one of the many immigrants from Bloomfield, Nebraska, who settled near Bloomfield, Montana, giving that village its name. Joseph Walker and his son Perry were among the land seekers who had come to Dawson County in the fall of 1906 and filed on homesteads. They then returned to their Nebraska home for the winter and made preparations to move the next spring.

Late in March they made the permanent move to their new home, loading livestock, machinery (not the array a farmer might move now), and household necessities into the westbound immigrant car*. Included in the assortment was a large tent which was to provide their shelter from the elements in the months to come.

Three weeks later Mr. Walker's wife, in company with Mrs. Jinks Linder, Miss Lizzie Ruth (later Mrs. Oberhofer), and Miss Annie Johnson, followed her husband. Perry came to Glendive to get them, bringing two outfits. He drove a team hitched to a buggy and trailed another team and wagon. That way he could take out a load of lumber on the wagon while the ladies rode in the buggy. Trips to Glendive were long, drawn-out affairs so there was nothing like making the most of each one.

Mr. Walker was crippled, so much of the physical labor depended upon son Perry, their only child. In the three weeks that the two Walker men had been in Montana they had been busy getting the wind-swept prairie, never before inhabited, ready for a home.

They had set up the big tent which was to serve, not only as a summer dwelling for the family, but also as a shelter for the cow and the horses which had been brought from Nebraska. Perry had partitioned off one end of the tent, stacking bales of hay for a divider.

For a time Annie Johnson lived with the Walkers. No well had been dug as yet so she and Perry's mother would carry water for washing clothes and dishes and for other cleaning chores from a low place nearby where the melting snow formed a pond of water. Drinking water was secured by melting the snow.

The winter had been a very severe one, and there was still much snow in coulees and low places. Some of the Nebraska folks had come earlier, planning to spend the winter on their homesteads. They had arrived just after Christmas, but a heavy snowstorm had arrived just ahead of them. Responsible people in Glendive wouldn't let them venture out into the country, certain they could not survive such an attempt.

Some of those who remember have likened that winter to our recent 1964-65 siege. One blizzard followed another and the snow piled deeper and deeper so the Nebraska 'early birds' just had to settle down in Glendive and wait for the winter to relent and allow them to go on to their destinations.

Surely before those winter months had passed, the home seekers must have been wondering if every winter followed that pattern and if so, questioned the wisdom of their move. But spring reluctantly came at long last, and the snowbound reached their homesteads just a short time before Mr. Walker and son who had waited out the winter in Nebraska.

There were no telephones to spread news then, but soon word got around that a single girl was in the country (the feminine population was even slimmer numerically than the male population in 1907 and there weren't many males) so it wasn't long until Mr. and Mrs. Ira Bendon came driving by. They needed someone to help Mrs. Bendon so almost before she had time to realize she was on a Montana homestead, the Nebraska girl found herself on a Montana ranch.

At that time the Bendons lived on the Bar M Ranch on Burns Creek. Mr. Bendon usually had three or four men working for him so there was plenty of cooking to be done. In addition to cattle and horses, he had quite a big bunch of sheep so during lambing* season there were extra men and they were extra busy. Annie was the 'hired girl', as domestic help was called on the frontier. Men might come in at any hour of the night for something to eat and it was up to her to get up, build a wood fire in the kitchen range, and fix them something.

Homesteaders at that time were allowed only 160 acres so Mr. Walker and Perry filed on adjoining quarters*, two miles straight north of Bloomfield (or what later became Bloomfield). In the fall they put up a small house on the parents' quarter and later a little shack on Perry's. The buildings on both homesteads were as close to the dividing line as possible so residence requirements for both places could be satisfied, yet Perry could be close enough to help his crippled father.

By the time Perry had proved up on his claim, Annie Johnson was old enough to file so she took another quarter in the same section as the Walkers (Robert Linder had the fourth quarter). Perry no longer needed his shack particularly so they moved it over onto her quarter and she lived in it as necessary to meet the homestead regulations but still 'worked out' a good deal.

In 1911 Annie and Perry were married. A few years later 'the old folks' built a new house so the young couple lived in the original homestead house. When, almost forty years later, the 'young couple' retired and moved closer to town, it was that first little house that they moved to their new location and fixed up, building onto it, for their retirement home. Mrs. Walker is still living in the home they made thus.

When Annie and Perry were first married, all farming, of course, was still done with horses. She helped outside a good deal, and one of her regular tasks was to harness and hitch up the team used by the crippled senior Walker. Once the horses were hitched to an implement, he could drive them, but he could not manage getting them ready or putting them away when he was through.

Usually he got along all right, but one time when he had three horses hitched to a binder, they decided the pace he directed was too slow so they speeded it up. When he saw that he wasn't going to be able to persuade them differently, he tumbled himself off the outfit and let them go. As a rule, however, the horses behaved themselves quite respectably. They were 'home grown', as Mrs. Perry Walker put it, not the bronco type that some of the homesteaders bought after they had come to Montana.

As she reflected over the years in the Treasure State, Mrs. Walker observed that some years they had a crop, some years they didn't. Sometimes there wasn't much money, but in spite of the hardships, they were happy and healthy.

They had six children so she didn't get around much when the children were small. She recalled that there was one period of three years when she didn't even get to Glendive. But didn't she get lonesome? She was busy!

They had none of the 'modern conveniences' to lighten their work. Perry mined their coal for heating and cooking in the badlands a few miles to the west. Although they did in later years have a gasoline lantern, kerosene lamps supplied most of their artificial light. It was a chore to keep those lamps clean and filled. Not until 1948, just two years before they left the homestead, did they get electricity.

She got her first power washing machine (gasoline powered) soon after her youngest son was born. For sixteen years she had scrubbed the clothes clean on a washboard. She always had a big garden to help meet the family's food need, and even now, when she's all alone, she still puts in a garden each summer.

Mrs. Walker had to smile as she thought of some early experiences. Rattlesnakes were plentiful in those early days, and once when she and Perry's mother were helping him load hay, she picked up a forkful of hay and a rattler dropped out. But that didn't shake her as much as a very recent encounter did.

Just last summer she noticed a snake lying across the road near her lane. The snake looked so dirty and dried up that she figured a truck had run over it and killed it. With no question in her mind that it was dead, she walked up to it and pushed at its tail with her toe. To her consternation that 'dead' snake reared straight up! She beat a hasty retreat while she hunted for a big rock and resolved that next time she'd use a stick if she was going to poke a rattler.

Mr. and Mrs. Walker had been in Montana almost forty-five years before they returned to Nebraska for their first visit. One of their Montana neighbors, Mrs. Ike Jones, (Elsie Guss), had been Mrs. Walker's closest neighbor in Nebraska and was also one of her school teachers.

Mr. Walker passed away in 1959. Mrs. Walker continues to live in their home on Dry Creek. Her children had some questions about her staying there, but she feels that as long as she is able, she'd rather stay 'home'.

"My children," she testifies, "are all very good to me and also good for me. I don't feel that they owe me anything. I had my reward during the years they were growing up. And what wonderful years they were! Now all I ask is patience and understanding. I have a wonderful daughter and son-in-law, and I love them all and my sixteen grandchildren. I feel that with God's help I've come this far, and I know He won't desert me now!"

Fritz Massar

December 1965 – January 1966

"There's a long, long trail awinding" between Glendive and Circle, even though the present-day motorist, skimming over the broad new oiled highway, might not realize it. But the old timers who traveled that route on a rough dirt trail, winding around the peaks and through the canyons of the Redwater-Yellowstone Divide* in mud and in snow, in wind and cold, know things about that trail that most of this later generation have never experienced.

It was when Fritz was freighting for Pete Rorvik, who ran a general store in old Circle, that he became most familiar with trails and storms and the Divide. One of those trips that he isn't likely to forget was in the dead of winter. He had started out from Glendive with team and wagon and had gone as far as Greens the first day where he stayed overnight, as was the custom of freighters going long distances. The next morning there was wind and snow in the air and the mercury was registering thirty-five degrees below zero.

Mr. Green urged Fritz not to start out, but Fritz was young and of a restless nature so he started out anyway. Later in the day as he battled the storm he realized he should have heeded that advice. He was not going to be able to make Circle before nightfall in that weather. Homes were few and far between along that route so when he came to one he stopped and asked permission to stay overnight.

Old-time western hospitality has been widely extolled, but here was one instance that was a disgrace to the country. Who, even in our day, would turn a man from their door in weather like that? But in answer to his request for lodging, they flatly refused him.

Fritz told them he would sleep in the barn – any place – if only they would let him unhitch and feed his horses and give him shelter for the night, but still they would not permit him to stay. Crossing Mt. Antelope, darkness was coming on. He was becoming chilled through and through and had to face the fact that he just couldn't make it to Circle that night. He knew that somewhere along the way, distant from the trail, were two ranch houses, but he didn't know how to find his way to them. Then he found fresh wagon tracks in the snow so he followed them where they turned off the trail until, to his immeasurable relief, he saw a dim light ahead. This was what was later the Henry Hildebrand ranch house. They welcomed him in and he spent the night there. His feet were frozen and his body completely chilled, but the next day he made it to Circle with his team and wagonload of freight. Dr. Koehler, Circle's young practicing physician, treated his feet and saved them from ill effects, but he suffered for years from chilblains as a result of that experience.

Early in spring Fritz purchased a wagonload of oats from a farmer over Bloomfield way, part of it for Pete Rorvik and part for himself to seed on his homestead. The ground was frozen as he crossed the Divide (near Mink) with his team and wagon to go to Bloomfield, but by the time he returned the

40

ground had thawed just enough to make that gumbo* greasy. It was so slick the horses could not pull the wagon up the Divide so Fritz unloaded those sacks of oats, drove the horses and wagon to the top of the hill, then carried the sacks, one by one, up to the wagon and reloaded them so he could continue on his way to Circle. "Where there's a will, there's a way."

Fritz Massar, twenty years old, had arrived in Montana September 12, 1910 with $25 in his pocket after bumming his way on a freight train from Arlington, South Dakota. He borrowed money to buy a saddle horse and worked out to finance his homestead. As an example, while he was working for Pete Rorvik, he received the handsome wage of one dollar per day. And this was no eight-hour day, nor yet a five-day week. He worked from five in the morning until nine, ten, or eleven in the evening, seven days a week. In this way he was able to pay for a house on his homestead, fifty miles southwest of Circle, and to make other improvements.

Aside from his homestead, his first business venture was an ice cream parlor in old Circle. (Old Circle was farther south right along Redwater.) He didn't have electric freezers to make his ice cream but he did have ice which he had put up during the winter, storing it in a dugout which he had made in the side of a hill. He'd make the ice cream early in the morning, then go off to work leaving the door to his establishment open. As ranchers came in during the day, they'd help themselves to ice cream. In the absence of the parlor's proprietor, they might leave the chairs and tables stacked up or turned upside down, but they always left a paper bill far exceeding the cost of the ice cream they ate. He made more that way than if he had stayed and tended shop!

While Fritz's business was in Circle, his homestead was just three miles from Brockway. On the other hand, O.A. Moxness, cashier of the First State Bank, moved to Brockway to start a bank there and his homestead was near Circle. They decided it would be to their mutual advantage to trade homesteads so they exchanged, just as they might have swapped jack knives as boys in days gone by.

One cold winter while he was at his homestead, a neighboring homesteader became seriously ill with pneumonia. Fritz rode for help, fifteen miles in forty below zero weather, to the homestead of Miss Inga Ryerson, a trained nurse. He led another saddled horse as he went and the courageous Nurse Ryerson quickly prepared to ride back with him in the bitter weather. No sulfa drugs made her task easier but she nursed young Burdette back to health.

In 1914 Fritz purchased a new Model T Ford so it became his mission to drive the young doctor, newly located in Circle, to the homes of the ill, near and far, in summer and in winter, in mud or in snow, in all that vast area when the roads were just two wagon tracks winding over the prairies.

When Circle was moved to its present site in 1913, Fritz and rancher Albert Klaus established a meat market, the first to be located in what is now McCone County. They bought cattle and butchered them in the open prairie to supply meat for their shop. Ice from the dugout kept the meat cold. Later Fritz bought out Klaus, continuing to operate a grocery store in conjunction with it until 1943.

For a time in those early days of the meat market, Fritz shared a room in the rear of the First State Bank with O.A. Moxness, bank cashier, and O.J. Thompson, Circle attorney. The meat market business called for early rising while bankers and attorneys had no duties until nine – if then. So it was that while his companions slept, Fritz was up and about early while it was still dark. As the other two fellows told it, Fritz got up early and chased about with a lantern trying to find daylight.

Those were the days before modern inventions furnished effortless entertainment. There were no radios, no movies, and of course, no television. Folks provided their own amusement, and these young men did well at that, usually with jokes on Fritz because of his emphatic reaction. They delighted in such tricks as tracking dead mice on his very clean white meat counter in a moment when he was not watching. Or perhaps when he had a date, while Fritz quickly changed from his working clothes, these usually slow-moving, leisurely pals would radically change their pace and get a wheel jacked up on Fritz's new Model T Ford or figure out some other trick to harass him.

The numerous bachelors who helped make up Circle's early-day population found suitable accommodations scarce. During that period the Christiansons were Home Mission missionaries in Circle for the Congregational Church. Mrs. Christianson, an ambitious little body, saw the need for a boarding and rooming house, but their salary was meager and they had no funds for such an undertaking. However, Mr. Krug, of Glendive, saw the possibilities for such an establishment so he financed the project and in 1914, the Home of the Hungry Hounds – 3-H for short – was opened.

The 3-H was a two-story building with five sleeping rooms on the second floor while on the first floor the Christianson family had their living quarters, the kitchen, a quite spacious dining room and a room for a helper.

Now the three young men, Massar, Moxness, and Thompson who had been sharing the little room in the rear of the First State Bank, sleeping on cots, each had a private room and slept on real beds. Other single men of the town also promptly occupied the other two rooms. Mrs. Christianson served meals family style in the dining room and it was open for the public.

The 3-H building is still in use in Circle, now as an apartment house under the ownership of Mr. and Mrs. Fred Becker. After the Christiansons moved from Circle it was used in a variety of ways before Mr. and Mrs. F.S. Kalberg purchased the property and converted it into apartments.

During the era of the Hungry Hounds House (1915), a young schoolteacher, Jeanette Ward, from Indiana made her entrance on the scene. Her aunt and uncle, Mr. and Mrs. Ben Bean, had homesteaded north of Circle in 1912. Just prior to that they had completed a five-year term of missionary service in China and because of a persistent cough which Uncle Ben had contracted there, they had decided to homestead on the Montana prairie with its pure, exhilarating air.

Now their home school needed a teacher so Aunt Maggie wrote back to Indiana, "Of all my nieces and nephews who are school teachers, could not one come and teach our school, stay in our home and be company for me?" Jeanette's brother responded to her plea, but when his father met death by drowning it was necessary for this only son to return home and take over the farm. So it was that Jeanette journeyed to Montana in his place. Thus began an era which she had never, in her wildest dreams, anticipated. Uncle Ben met her in Glendive in his model T Ford which he had named Andrew because, he explained, its mission was to go out and win souls.

In this country eligible bachelors considerably outnumbered marriageable young ladies, and few were the single school marms who stayed single for long. Jeanette Ward was not one of the exceptions. Before long Fritz Massar became acquainted with her and began courting. In 1916 they were married with Uncle Ben the officiating minister.

They spent their four-day honeymoon on Fritz's homestead fixing fence. Then his business had to have attention so they returned to Circle and he took his bride to the 3-H for a two-week stay until their own little three-room house in north Circle was ready for occupancy. The little house later gave way to a spacious eight-room home, but the Massars have lived their forty-nine years of married life on this same spot. Here they reared their children, all of whom are now married and have families of their own.

Mrs. Massar, too, had occasion to find the trail between Circle and Glendive a long one even though she was not engaged in any freighting enterprise. Before the birth of their first child Mr. Massar planned to bring her to Glendive because there was no hospital in Circle. That winter was the kind of winter old timers talk about, with cold and snow. What trail there was had been buried under drifts of snow long before the end of February when they started for Glendive so they didn't even attempt to follow a road. They kept to the ridges whenever possible and hoped they could somehow get across the coulees.

They started out about eleven o'clock in the morning in their little Model T behind the mailman in his Nash, hoping that this way they could get through. The United Brethren minister also went along to help with the pushing and shoveling that were sure to be needed. The coulees, of course, were blown full of snow as they had known would be the case. In general, their policy was to 'hit 'em hard' and hope they'd get through. When they broke a spring on the Ford, they borrowed a rail from a fence to fix it up so they could go on. After more pushing and more shoveling they finally had to leave the Ford and all went on in the mailman's car. Mrs. Massar remembered to have her suitcase transferred to the other car but later realized that in the commotion and excitement, the suitcase containing the baby clothes had been left behind.

By five o'clock they had managed to get as far as Union, thirty miles. Mrs. Olson quickly set out a lunch for them, which was much appreciated, and then they headed on toward Glendive. They found the road a little better from there on so they were able to complete their journey that day, reaching their destination about nine o'clock that evening. Three days later the Massars became the parents of a new baby girl. But that wasn't the end of the stress and strain, not for Mr. Massar, anyway.

He went back out to Circle with the mailman but a few days later managed to get back in to see her; though he seemed quiet. He said nothing about not feeling well. However, as he started home again with the mailman, he became deathly sick about eleven miles from Glendive and had to be brought back to the hospital, a victim of the flu. Nothing was said to Mrs. Massar about his being in the hospital, and even when he was released and came to see her again, she didn't know why he looked so pale and drawn.

After that visit, Mr. Massar went on out to their home in Circle. A few days later he contracted small pox. Back in Glendive, Mrs. Massar could have gone home but the river ice had 'gone out' and all of what is now West Glendive was under water with big chunks floating around. No vehicles could traverse the submerged road. To get the mail to Circle (only first class mail was sent) a man carried it across the railroad bridge and handed it to the mailman, at the same time receiving the incoming mail. The news of Mr. Massar's illness reached Glendive but it did not reach his wife. He had absolutely forbidden them to tell her anything of his battle for life.

While she waited for the floodwaters to subside so she could go home, Mrs. Massar and the baby were staying in a rooming house. One of her friends there received a letter with the ominous report, and as she read she kept glancing oddly at Mrs. Massar, but not a word did she say about the part that concerned Mr. Massar. Not until he was out of danger did Mrs. Massar learn that her husband had been at death's door. But he by-passed that door then and has now reached the age of eighty years.

Mr. Massar has served for many years as County Administrator and still fills that office. In addition he performs many services which have no title such as assisting at funerals with ushering, guest books, flowers, general arrangements or whatever he can do in his sympathetic way.

Joe S. Beres

May 1966

Few old timers are still around who were in Glendive early enough to move away in 1904, but Joe Beres did. The Beres family came to Glendive the winter of 1900-1901 from their homestead southeast of Dickinson. Joe's father had preceded the family to Glendive to get a job and find a home for the family.

Before coming to Glendive Mr. Beres had been acquainted with several Glendive men, among them John Grundhauser, and it was through them that he found a job in a barbershop. They moved into a little house on the south side of town, far from neighbors – far that is for being in town. About all Taylor Avenue and beyond could boast was sagebrush, but there were a few houses scattered through the sagebrush.

Joe started to school in the Lincoln School in the fall of 1903. The Lincoln at that time was a one-room frame building standing in the same block occupied by the present brick structure. Miss Ruth Hunter was the teacher. Miss Hunter had come to Montana from Watertown, South Dakota to teach a three-month term of school at Tokna (near the site of the present town of Savage) in the spring of 1901. She was well satisfied with her wages of $35 per month.

Her sister, Mrs. August Frederickson, was living at Tokna, and had written with suggestions for things they might do after school was out. Miss Hunter wrote back to make no plans because she would be returning to Watertown at the end of the term. However, while she was at Tokna, Glendive school officials contacted her, and Miss Hunter contracted to teach the next term in Glendive so she spent the summer with the Fredericksons after all. That fall she began teaching at the Lincoln School. After several years she married a Glendive lawyer, Theodore Lentz, and they later moved to Missoula.

The first bridge across the Yellowstone River had washed out before the Beres family came to Glendive, but the new bridge was dedicated while they were here. If there were speeches given at the ceremonies, they didn't make much of an impression upon a small boy. What did impress him was the professional diver who dived off the new bridge into the Yellowstone and was then picked up in a boat.

Mr. Beres remembers that, as a boy, he and his chums used to enjoy standing on the river bank and watching as cattle swam across the river. Large numbers of cattle trying to cross on the new bridge shook it too much so rather than trying to divide a big bunch into units small enough to be allowed on the bridge, cowboys often chose to swim them across.

Another event from those early days that clings to his memory was the sight of a crowd of men in the courthouse yard early one morning. He and his father had gone fishing early, and as they cut across the block next to the courthouse, they saw the crowd still milling about the yard, which had gathered to watch the hanging of the deputy sheriff for the murder of the sheriff.

45

Joe and his cousin, two years older, were an enterprising pair and early started in business. They would collect agates, wash them, then take them down to the depot at train time and sell them to the passengers. They were doing a pretty good business, selling the agates for a nickel or a dime apiece, until too many others tried the same thing, and the depot agent put a stop to it.

In 1904, the family moved back to Dickinson, and that's how it happened that Mr. Beres was rooting for the opposing side when Dickinson and Glendive played that notorious grudge baseball game a few years later, about 1908. The Dickinson team and fans made up a caravan of cars and traveled to Glendive, no mean accomplishment in the first decade of the 20th century. There was no road through the badlands so they helped each other up the hills and across or around the canyons, probably the first cars ever to negotiate that terrain, and arrived in Glendive the second day in plenty of time for the game, a couple hours to spare.

Some of the old timers who were living in Glendive when that controversial game was played perhaps remember the story a little differently so we may get some calls on this, but according to the Dickinson version Glendive had hired a suspended major league pitcher for the game. Dickinson got wind of the bit of trickery so they got in 'cahoots' with the pitcher and bought him off. He agreed to 'throw the game' for $1,000, and the guarantee that Dickinson men would get him out of town as soon as Glendive pulled him from the game.

Glendive, with their professional pitcher, had the game 'in the bag' so betting was heavy and the odds long. If that pitcher hadn't made arrangements to get out of town promptly, he never would have made it alive. When the game was lost, Glendive's gamblers were out for blood. He escaped, though, and the Dickinson cohort made enough on their bets so they could well afford to ship their cars and likewise themselves back to Dickinson by train. Certainly, economy could hardly have been the motive prompting them to travel that tortuous route by car to come to Glendive. One Dickinson fan who had come to Glendive by train for the game didn't even get to see it. He was a railroad man, and when he hit the Gate City*, some of his railroad buddies got hold of him and started making the rounds. After a time he passed out so his faithful pals put him on a flatcar on an eastbound train. When he woke up, he found himself on a siding at Curry, four or five miles from town – a long way when you have to walk it.

Joe Beres's father was among those who made the automobile trip to Glendive for the game, but Joe himself didn't get back to Glendive again until 1915 when he came through on a motorcycle. He and a friend decided to take a trip to Yellowstone National Park, and the two started out in high spirits. Two miles from Belfield they overtook a bunch of young fellows leisurely bouncing along in a touring car. They ate dust for awhile but then decided to pass so Joe's pal, a Swede, started around. He made it all right, but when the driver of the car saw what was happening, he speeded up so Joe didn't get around so easily. Forced to the edge of the road (which was only a trail), Joe hit a hole that sent him and his motorcycle somersaulting through the air. Luckily he escaped without serious injury, but his cycle didn't fare so well; the frame broke.

He pushed the broken vehicle back to Belfield where he found a blacksmith who could put a clamp on it and told him he could probably get it welded at Beach. The clamp must have been a strong one because it held through all the stress and strain of the badlands. At Beach he succeeded in getting the frame welded, but he just got across the railroad track at the edge of town, and it broke again. He had had the forethought to carry the clamp with him, so he put the clamp back on and went back to the blacksmith.

Now the blacksmith told him he couldn't weld it satisfactorily, but maybe he could get it fixed in Glendive. At Glendive his luck was no better, but at Miles City he found a place where they sold Indian Motorcycles. They agreed to sell him a frame if he'd strip it, so strip it he did, then mounted his motor and accessories on it. Fortunately 'the Swede' was a good mechanic so that operation wasn't the problem it might have been. Mr. Beres pointed out that you just about had to have a mechanic along in those days!

After Miles City, they sailed along smoothly until they reached the Huntley irrigation project. Wherever the road crossed an irrigation ditch there was a hump in the road, and it was fun going over those humps about forty miles an hour. It was fun, that is, until they crossed one with a sharp turn just on the other side. The Swede made the turn, but Joe, right behind him, landed in the irrigation ditch, motorcycle and all. Swede was surely disgusted with him, but Joe was glad he had a traveling companion who knew how to clean carburetors.

When they reached Gardiner, they found that motor vehicles were not allowed inside the park because they might scare the horses. They weren't about to go in without their cycles so they went to Hunter's Hot Springs instead, and spent a week there.

On the westward trip it seemed that everything happened to Joe, but on the return trip trouble at last caught up to the Swede, too. They were about thirty or thirty-five miles from Dickinson when the Swede's motorcycle had a flat tire. It was getting toward evening and Joe's headlight had broken in the Belfield mishap so Swede told him to go on into town before dark, and he'd follow when he had the tire fixed. That sounded reasonable so Joe headed on into Dickinson and reached home about eight o'clock. About eleven o'clock a thoroughly disgruntled Swede pulled into Dickinson, too. They didn't carry spare tires with them, but instead had repair kits for patching tires. Swede patched his tire, then realized that the tire pump had gone along into Dickinson with Joe. He'd had to push his motorcycle about five miles to Fryburg before he could get air for the tire.

The following year Joe Beres again found himself in Glendive, this time as chauffeur and best man for a wedding party. Joe had now graduated from a motorcycle to a car, a little more accommodating for passengers. Automobile travelers met with frequent obstacles in those early days of motorized transportation when roads were chiefly wagon trails. As the wedding party proceeded from Dickinson to Glendive, one of their first obstacles was the

Little Missouri River. Later that year a bridge was built across the Little Missouri at Medora, but that didn't help on this trip so Joe tried fording the river.

He covered the radiator with his raincoat, hoping thus to keep the distributor and wires from getting wet, then lined up with the tracks on the opposite bank and eased into the river nice and slow. They were going along just fine, but then all of a sudden the front end dropped into a hole. Now what! They looked around, then noticed a fellow sitting beside the livery barn on the river's bank so they motioned him to come over. He leisurely mounted one of his team horses and rode over to them bringing along a chain. Upon reaching them he tossed the end of the chain to Joe and let him get down into the water and hook the chain to the car, then pulled them out. On dry ground once more, the dripping best man asked what the charge would be and winced at the $5 blandly named. The explanation that if he had been called in the first place the charge would have been just two dollars offered small consolation, especially since it was Joe who had to get wet.

The wedding took place at Wibaux. Joe's sister had come along to be bridesmaid, and after the wedding they came on to Glendive. Next day they started back to Dickinson. This time when they reached the Little Missouri, Joe determined to cross on the railroad bridge rather than risk a duplicate performance of their first crossing. The grade approaching the bridge was about a block-and-a-half long, so that and the bridge made a long drive on railroad ties, but they made it across. They got into trouble with the depot agent though.

It was getting late in the evening and a heavy rain had made the roads impassable so they had to spend the night in Medora, but funds were running low (that $5). To relieve a critical situation, Joe hunted up a fellow he knew and borrowed enough money to pay for hotel rooms, meals and train fare next morning to Dickinson, all for the party of four. He told Nels about the $5 river crossing, then Nels told him it was no accident that they had dropped into that hole. He explained that the livery stable attendant took a fresno* and deliberately made a ditch across the place where the trail lined up with the tracks on the opposite bank. Natives were familiar with the trick and knew they had to go around the hole, but unsuspecting strangers would head straight across, drop into the hole, and pay $5 to get pulled out.

The first job Joe Beres held (aside from odd jobs such as selling agates) was that of shoeshine boy in his father's Dickinson barber shop. In 1912 he started as a bellhop in the St. Charles Hotel, then advanced to clerk. In 1917 he decided to try to get on with the Northern Pacific Railroad and came to Glendive in January of that year to apply and get his physical. He still has the canceled check, dated January 19, 1917, that paid his expenses, including his stay at the Jordan Hotel, while he was in Glendive.

He accepted and started working out of Mandan, making his first trip February 13, 1917. He made his last trip February 28, 1966. In the intervening years he worked out of Mandan, Forsyth, Dickinson, and Glendive. In 1949 he was moved to Glendive and has been here since.

When World War I broke out, he was working in Forsyth so he registered there. He was in the service fourteen months, part of that time in France. After his discharge he went back to the railroad with no loss of seniority for his time in the army. In 1927 he married Appolonia 'Appie' Grasl from near Dickinson. They have three children, two of whom are married and living in Glendive – Jack, manager of the Federated Store, and Mrs. Tom Hughes. One single son is in the Service in New York. Seven grandchildren help them keep young.

He hasn't lost his interest in agates. He didn't mention selling any at the depot lately, but he enjoys cutting and polishing them and spends considerable time with his hobby since his retirement from the railroad.

Joe Beres on his Harley Davidson

Isabelle Kierzek / Mr. and Mrs. John Zabrocki

August 1974

When Isabelle Kierzek's parents came to America from Poland in 1884, they brought along three children, the youngest only six weeks old. They first settled in Winona, Minnesota where other Polish people lived. Her father was a carpenter, but fourteen years after their arrival in America, he filed on a homestead near Greenbush, Minnesota, in Roseau County.

In 1908 two of the boys traveled to Montana and filed on homesteads in Wibaux County. Later their father moved the rest of the family to the Treasure State to help the boys. Everything was brought to Montana in a railroad boxcar, including the cattle and horses. Several families came to this virgin country the same way at this time. Mr. Zabrocki liked the Montana country so well that he bought a farm, built a home, and farmed until he retired in 1919.

The community where the Zabrocki family settled was made up mostly of Polish people. About 1911 they began to build a Catholic Church and a parish house for the priest. The name St. Phillip was picked because one of the parishioners, Phillip Wicka, donated a large sum of money to build the church and also purchased the statue of St. Phillip that was put into the church. The land was donated by Henry Schuster. All the building supplies for the church were hauled in by horse and wagon.

Before long a general store and post office were put up across the street from the church. This land was owned by Mrs. Kierzek's brother, Felix. Then a home was built next to the store for one of the partners of the store. The partners were John and Frank Losinski, also from Winona. A school had already been built, some years before, about three miles from St. Phillip. This school was called the 'Red Cap School', and Isabelle attended this school for a few years. Later a larger school was needed and a new one was built in St. Phillip. It was then called the St. Phillip's School. The Red Cap School was given its name because it was near a scoria* hill – a hill with a 'red cap'.

The St. Phillip village continued to grow. John Floreck started up a blacksmith shop, and later another general store was built with an attached dance hall. This was run by Nick Peplinski. As time went on Mr. Zabrocki and other farmers wanted to retire from farming. Wishing to be near the church, they built in St. Phillip. Soon about half-a-dozen houses were added to the cluster of businesses and dwellings. Church services were held in Polish. A priest from Poland, Father Chezleviech, came and served the community church. People traveled as far as twenty miles with horse and buggy to attend services.

When the Zabrockis first came to Wibaux County, they found the country was not only new but rather wild as well. One day, as one of the boys was cutting hay, a couple wolves started following him around the field. He yelled at Isabelle to get his rifle so she took it to him. That same evening he walked to visit a friend nearby and took the rifle with him. Coming home in the dark he met the two wolves. He shot at the shining eyes, and even though in the darkness he missed, the shot scared the wolves away.

Andrew Floreck also had a memorable encounter with wolves. There was a coal mine near the community and everyone mined their own coal. Andrew had taken his drill, a tool about six feet long, to be sharpened, and on the way home, with about a mile left to go, he was threatened by a wolf. He kept swinging the drill around him and was able to get on home.

Today the original St. Phillip's church is no longer there: it burned down in the 1950's. A new brick church is there in its place. There are no other buildings left in St. Phillips except the Parish House and a community hall. And there is a large cemetery. The St. Phillip's School has been moved to the Wibaux County Fairgrounds and is used as a museum.

Mrs. Kierzek reflects that her memories are of good and bad times, both. She lived there most of her life, married there, and raised her family there until her husband died in 1944. She now lives in Miles City.

Early immigrant family — Wheelwright working on wheel

Old sheep wagon – a sheepherder's solitary home for months at a time

Shearing sheep and sacking the wool

Branding at the + S Ranch

Haying early 1900's

Early Glendive Roundup

Mrs. Harry C. (Claire Berard) Anderson

April 1964

In 1904 Mr. Peter Berard, father of Mrs. Harry Anderson of Glendive, arrived from Missoula with an immigrant car bearing a team, a wagon, a walking plow, and some household goods. His oldest son was with him and they were headed for Four Mile Creek, eleven miles northwest of what is now Fairview, and homestead land. There was no Northern Pacific branch line to Sidney at that early date so the immigrant car had to be unloaded in Glendive and the remainder of the journey made with the team and wagon, a two day trip.

Mrs. Anderson's grandparents, both maternal and paternal, were born in France. Each had emigrated to Canada near Montreal with their respective families at an early age. Life was not easy for the newcomers, and the family of Mrs. Berard moved to Rhode Island when she was eight.

There she went to work in a J & P Coates factory operating a loom when she was only nine years old. No child labor laws protected children of that day, and she would sometimes get so tired she would lay her head on the loom and go to sleep. Then a man would come around carrying a long stick with a rabbit's foot tied to its end and waken her. Later the family moved back to St. Hyacinth in Canada, and it was there she met and married Peter Berard.

They were both young when they married. Three months after their marriage in 1886 they moved to Missoula. There Berard worked in the lumber mills at Frenchtown, a small French settlement near Missoula, for eighteen years. About the turn of the century two of their friends from Frenchtown moved to eastern Montana and homesteaded, both on the site of the present town of Fairview. As a result of their reports the Berards thought it would be nice if they could own some land too, so they decided to homestead.

Father and eldest son came first and made preparations for the family to join them. A place to live held top priority so they cut and hauled logs from the Missouri River to build a one-room log house, and in April, 1905, the family joined them. Claire (now Mrs. Anderson), her older sister, little brother, and mother came on the Great Northern to Mondak, then crossed the Missouri River on the ferry. They rode with the mailman in his spring wagon* to the home of their friends on Fairview's site where they stayed overnight; then Mr. Berard came the next day to take them to the homestead.

A new era began for the Berards. Until this time both had always lived in French-speaking communities, and Mrs. Berard could speak no English when they came to Dawson County. (It was Dawson then; now it is Richland.) She learned, though. She made many other adjustments, too. She very much missed the trees when they came to these wide open spaces. Neighbors were few and far between, and she was lonely in this great empty country, but in time she became accustomed to the distances and the scattered population.

Perhaps the hardest adjustment for her to make was the difficulty of getting proper food for her children. Mrs. Anderson mentioned that she remembers her mother crying when she had no milk for the little two-year old boy. In an effort to substitute she would mix some cornstarch and water with a little sweetening, cook it and give to him. They had a wonderful neighbor, Ben Doyle, a bachelor who lived about two-and-one-half miles from the Berards. He was a rough and rugged individual, but he had a heart of gold. He knew his new neighbors weren't able to get enough of the right kind of food that first year on the homestead so he would often come, always walking, bringing milk or eggs, or sometimes even a quarter of beef. How Mrs. Berard did rejoice when she had milk to give to her family!

He was such a kindly man that the Berards soon learned to love him dearly. When the Berards' oldest boy did some work for him, he gave them a lovely heifer calf as payment so the next year there was milk for the little ones. Later Mr. Doyle married a fine girl who came out from Chicago and took up a homestead in the community.

That first summer they were on the homestead Claire's oldest brother learned to use the shotgun and would hunt the wild ducks that landed on the alkali ponds of Four Mile Creek. That was their chief supply of meat those first months.

The little log house provided good protection against the winter cold, but the summer rains (when they came) would saturate the dirt roof and soak through the nice board ceiling. Mrs. Berard soon learned to have bowls and pans handy for setting in strategic spots to 'catch the drip'. The first winter after the family came – that notorious winter of 1905-06 – Mr. Berard cut and hauled more logs from the Missouri bottom lands to build an addition to the house. They added two more rooms on the main floor and an upstairs, divided into two rooms, over the entire first floor. The original house now became the kitchen. The logs made a substantial house (it's still standing), and the thick walls provided space for nice window seats. Later they plastered the interior and put siding on the exterior of the house.

Hauling logs that winter demanded much endurance and perseverance. There was no road to follow, just a trail, and as the horses and sleigh made repeated trips, the snow packed harder. The snow kept falling, much as it did that winter sixty years later. The trail kept building up on that hard pack. The horses tried to follow the trail, and as long as they could stay on it, team and sleigh stayed on top, but to the sides the snow was softer. Just missing the edge of the trail by a few inches meant an upset sled. And an upset sled meant a log slide. Any logs that did stay on the sled had to be unloaded before the vehicle could be righted, then loaded again.

Finally Berard hit upon a plan for marking the trail. He equipped himself with a bunch of branches, then lying on his stomach on top of the logs, he leaned over the edge of the load and drove stakes into the hard-packed trail as he drove along. From then on he was able to stay on the trail. He also hauled logs that winter to build a barn.

An ample supply of good water on the homestead was supplied by the well, forty feet deep, which Berard dug with a shovel. As he dug deeper into the well, he loaded the dirt into a bucket and other members of the family hoisted it to the surface with a windlass*. From the depths of the well Berard made the surprising announcement that he could see stars in broad daylight. His family thought he must be fooling them, but then Claire was lowered into the well in the bucket to observe, and she confirmed his report; from the darkness of the shaft, the stars were clearly visible.

The Berards did most of their trading in those early days at Mondak. Mondak was also the shipping point for their grain. Usually they waited to haul their grain until the Missouri River froze over. Then they could haul across on the ice and save the ferry fare. Their freighting, of course, was done with a wagon, pulled by a four-horse team.

Early homesteaders found tall grass almost everywhere. Sometimes a buffalo skull that had been hidden by the verdant growth would be discovered. The abundant grass was a blessing when they wanted to make hay, but it was a bane if a fire started in it. Mrs. Anderson recalls waking one night and seeing a big red glow against the sky. Her mother was in the kitchen preparing lunch for some of the fire fighters. Every settler in the area, be he rancher or homesteader, would drop what he was doing and hurry to fight a fire as soon as he noticed it. Some homesteaders would go with their teams and plows to make a fire guard while others would fight with wet sacks. The cowboys had a method all their own. They would kill a steer, split it in two, tie it behind a horse with a lariat and drag it along the fire line.

Mrs. Anderson remembers her father putting up the native grass for feed. One day as her mother was helping him load hay he pitched up a forkful, and a rattlesnake dropped onto the rack. Mrs. Berard had left the two youngest children in the shade of a hay cock, and her first thought at the sight of the rattler was for her children. With a scream she jumped from the wagon and, almost hysterical, rushed to the hay cock where they were playing. They were safe, however, and no snake was in their vicinity. In fact, the rattlesnake that landed on the hay rack was the one and only snake of its kind they saw in that vicinity in all their years on the homestead!

Mrs. Anderson did make the acquaintance of rattlesnakes during her girlhood days in other communities. There were no schools on Four Mile so when her older sister married and located in the vicinity of a school, Claire stayed with her one year to go to school. Their teacher rode horseback to school, and each day Claire and one of her school mates, a part-Indian girl, would take the teacher's horse to a neighbor's place for water. One day as they took the horse they found a rattlesnake coiled on top of a post close to the watering place. They killed that one, and another time she killed a rattler as she walked to school. She had been warned that there were many snakes in the Hardscrabble area so she always carried a long stick when she went to school. She was glad for the stick when she met the snake.

The next year a school was established two miles from her parents' home so she and her brother both were able to go to school now. Because of the difficulty in getting to school during the severest winter months, school was suspended, then continued late into the summer and resumed in August to make it easier for the children to attend. Mrs. Anderson recalls only once ever getting a ride to or from school. That day her parents had gone to town, and as they came home it was raining very hard, so since it was about time for school to be dismissed, they picked up the children and took them along home. Other than that, the children always walked the two miles in the morning and again in the evening.

Since Claire was necessarily late in starting her schooling her older brother helped her learn to read and do simple arithmetic. She soon found great enjoyment in reading so by the time she started to school she was reading on a sixth grade level but was far behind in other subjects. Her teacher encouraged her to proceed as rapidly as she could with her other subject matter so she was soon able to bring her other studies up to her reading level.

When Claire was ready for high school, her parents sent her to Willow City near Rugby, North Dakota, to a school operated by French sisters. Their Mother House was located on the Island of Jersey off the coast of France, and all but two of the fifteen sisters were from France. After her graduation from high school she began teaching in a rural school back in Montana, getting her training by attending summer school. During her first term she gave a basket social, and a young homesteader from the Sioux Pass country, Harry Anderson, bought her basket. This was her introduction to him and the beginning of a friendship which culminated in their marriage four years later.

Harry had come from Iowa with an older brother a few years before. His mother had died when Harry was very young, leaving his father with nine children. When his older brother came to Montana to homestead, Harry came with him, even though he was not yet old enough to file. As soon as he was eligible he selected the site for his home, locating about fifteen miles from the Berard homestead. This was the home to which he took his bride, and they lived there until 1939 when they moved to Glendive.

One daughter, Mary Claire was born to the Andersons. She is now married to Al Pontrelli and living in Missoula. After Mr. Anderson's death in 1953, Mrs. Anderson went back to her school teaching and taught another eleven years but is now retired, living in her Glendive home.

In 1954 she was privileged to visit for the first time the homeland of her forefathers. She participated in a guided tour of Europe and experienced a great thrill as she realized, when she caught her first glimpse of Mt. Blanc, that this was the land where her grandparents first saw life. In 1960 she made a second trip to Europe. She plans this summer to visit her parents' early homes near Montreal.

Charles W. Grandey

April - May 1971

Charles W. Grandey came to Terry in August 1907, from Gurnee, Illinois, a little town twenty-five miles north of Chicago. In Illinois he had charge of the high schools for Northwestern University, directing the high schools for a number of towns and districts around there as well as in Gurnee.

Because he contracted a touch of tuberculosis, his doctor recommended that he change climate and suggested Montana. Grandey, with a wife and child, didn't have the money to go out to the 'Great American Desert' but the doctor's sister was teaching in Miles City and she put him in contact with the Terry school board. The Milwaukee Railroad was coming through the next year and Terry wanted to get a high school started, especially with the population growth expected. Grandey arranged with his school board to release him for one year, and Terry hired him to start a high school.

He came out with a Life Certificate from the University of Illinois so he was not required to take state examinations. That Life Certificate was the key that opened the door for him to the state superintendent, the governor – everything. The original plan was for him to come for one year but in January the Terry school board told him, "If you will stay we'll build you a good school." At that time he was holding school in a four-room house. He stayed and they built the two-story Grandey building still in use in Terry, now as a grade school. There was not a single vote against the building.

Grandey wrote to his Illinois board that he wasn't coming back. His health was good and everything else was good too. He stayed forty years with the school system and still lives in Terry fifty-four years later.

When he came to Terry they had fifty-five pupils in the grade school. That first year he organized a high school, and he taught grades five through nine. There was no need that first year for grades beyond ninth because there were no eligible pupils. However, grades ten through twelve were added in successive years. While Grandey was holding classes in the four-room house, the primary grades were conducted in the then-existing school building. That school was on the grounds where the present high school is located. Mrs. Hale, whose husband had a dray* in Terry, taught the primary grades. Mrs. Hale now lives in South Dakota. In the next six or seven years while Grandey was superintendent of the Terry schools, seven rural schools were built in District 5, the Terry district. The district was large, reaching to Southerland on the Powder River.

Grandey's first home in Terry was in a house built by a Civil War veteran. It was a nice house on the corner by the Grandey building. Grandey, with his wife and son, lived in this two-room house until larger quarters were found.

Editor J.A. McKinley came to Terry the same year Grandey did and started the Tribune that year. He suggested starting a commercial club, and it was organized in September that same year. Mr. W.A. Brubaker was president and Mr. Grandey secretary.

58

Also that year (1907 was an eventful year!) Mr. McKinley and Mr. Grandey each took up a homestead on a bench seven miles southeast of Terry. This 160 acres was the beginning of Grandey's ranch which now includes 2,240 acres. Later he bought railroad land to increase his holdings. He named his homestead Broadview.

In 1908 Grandey raised the first wheat in Terry country and marked the beginning of farming in the area. (Prior to this some ranchers had raised feed grain but had not 'farmed'.) That fall he entered some of his wheat in the Custer County fair and took first prize.

There was no minister in Terry when Mr. Grandey came, and he was often called upon to conduct funerals. He well remembers the first funeral he held. The poor fellow, an alcoholic, was found in the ash heap behind the saloon. They found a letter from his daughter in his pocket saying she was glad he had a job and that she and Mother would be coming out.

Another funeral Mr. Grandey well remembers conducting was that of an old Indian fighter, Red McDonald. Red was one of the first individuals, aside from his school board, that Mr. Grandey met after arriving in Terry, and that first meeting was hardly prophetic of a friendship developing.

The morning after he arrived in Terry, Mr. Grandey was to meet with the school board. Since one of the board members ran a saloon, the meeting was to be held there. On the way to the meeting they met Red and one of the board genially invited, "Come on, Red; have a drink on the new school man."

Mr. Grandey spoke up, "Gentlemen, I don't drink but I'll go into the saloon with you where we're having our meeting." Red was a sarcastic old man. Looking the 'new school man' up and down he caustically commented, "We didn't expect a school marm to have a man's drink." In spite of this introduction, Mr. Grandey and Red became good friends and when the latter died in Butte several years later, a telegram came to Terry that Mr. Grandey was to have the funeral. The funeral in Terry was attended by many old timers – real old timers: hunters, trappers, ranchers. One came wearing a coonskin cap. Red, who had a horse ranch, had been around for many years and was known for miles around. Theodore Roosevelt had become acquainted with him while he was ranching in the badlands of North Dakota, and when he came through Terry after his rise to national fame, Red was in the crowd at the depot to greet him and Roosevelt spoke to him from the platform.

Mr. Grandey recalls that after the funeral the owner of a lumberyard there in Terry asked him for the sermon but his answer was, "No, that sermon is buried with him." Another time when he had the funeral for an old fellow, all six of the pallbearers, one of them a Catholic, asked him to have their funerals in Brockway and Circle.

During the time Terry had no minister, Mr. Grandey filled the pulpit from February to September one year. He also preached in three different churches in Miles City (Presbyterian, Methodist, and Baptist) and in both the Presbyterian and Methodist churches in Kalispell.

Although he came as an educator, Mr. Grandey was pressed into a variety of services in the community. Two of the big mercantile establishments had him keep their books. A hardware store had him make out their invoices.

The grade for the coming Milwaukee Railroad was in when he came but the track was not, and he helped the surveyor line up the track. Mr. Grandey served for a time as secretary of Terry's Chamber of Commerce and during this period they started working for a bridge across the Yellowstone between Miles City and Glendive. At the time it was a long way around for folks midway between those two points, as they had to go to one of those towns to cross on a bridge.

He went clear to Ekalaka to get votes for the bridge. When he came to Terry in 1907 there was a Woodmen Lodge of about 100 men. He had been an officer in this lodge back in Illinois and was soon elected Council (head of the Woodmen) in Terry. He went to Ekalaka to install officers there and that's how he happened to get acquainted at Ekalaka and so to get votes for the bridge.

This issue did not pass unanimously as did the bond issue for his school building, but it passed by a good margin and Terry got a bridge. It was built in 1910 for a cost of $50,000. This bridge later washed away one spring when the Yellowstone River ice broke up and flooded. A replacement bridge was built in 1960. Mr. Grandey "had his fingers in the pie" when the 1960 bridge was built too. At that time he was in the state legislature and was able to get the $750,000 needed for the new bridge.

In 1917, Mr. Grandey conducted his first summer training school for teachers. This school was held in Glendive, but it was a cooperative venture of several counties and was supervised by the state superintendent of schools. Cooperating counties were Richland, Fallon, Prairie, Custer, and Dawson. Teacher's tuition for attending summer school was paid by the county from which she came rather than by the individual teacher.

Mr. Grandey had not been in Montana long when he had realized the need for such an effort. When he attended his first teachers' convention in Miles City in November of 1907, (his first year in Montana) he was secretary of the convention. As such he called the roll and only one of the teachers responding was from Montana! This one teacher was the county superintendent from Glendive and was one of the superintendents who later helped start the summer school. It was this lack of native teachers that pointed up the need for a training school in Eastern Montana.

In 1919 the school was held in Terry with 121 teachers enrolled. Miss Lucille Hennigar was the primary teacher training supervisor while Mr. Grandey supervised the upper grades. The summer school girls organized a baseball team and Miss Hennigar played first base. They had a great time, but the girls complained that they couldn't find first base because she stood on it!

Unquestionably, many of Miss Hennigar's former pupils will concur with Mr. Grandey that she was a wonderful teacher. She was, he adds, a firm disciplinarian and had the respect of her pupils. He recalled an incident related to him by one of her fellow teachers – a man teacher, it happened – illustrating her firm discipline. The man teacher had walked past the room where Miss

Hennigar was teaching and found a boy sitting in the hall. The boy was supposed to be inside playing the trumpet so the teacher asked him why he was out in the hall. Rather sheepishly the youth explained, "I came late so I'm out here." Not only did she have the respect of her pupils but of the parents as well. They were back of her, Mr. Grandey asserts, and the kids knew it!

The chancellor of Montana appointed Mr. Grandey director of teacher training schools for Custer County, and he served in this capacity from 1921 until 1935 when the Eastern Montana Normal School* was started in Billings. These schools were conducted as an extension of the normal school at Dillon.

The enrollment in Miles City was as high as 289. Years later he gave an Armistice address in Kalispell, and afterwards he was approached by a tall gray-haired lady who greeted him with "You don't remember me, of course." But Grandey replied, "Oh yes I do; you went to normal school in Miles City. That was in the days when girls didn't eat breakfast and you fainted away in my classroom!" Mr. Grandey mentioned incidentally, that the Glendive school board passed a rule that teachers were not to go out on school nights, just weekends. Suppose the rule is still on the books?

In the earlier days, examinations for teachers were held in Miles City and Terry and the state superintendent appointed him to the State Teachers' Examination Board. One year he graded 800 papers in Helena.

In 1910, the governor of Montana appointed him to reorganize school laws with regard to enrollment. The legislature later passed an enrollment law requiring that the names of both the father and the mother, as well as the first and middle name of the child, appear on the enrollment form. Opposition to the law was expressed by an old sheepman who declared, "Too many kids around here don't know who their father is."

In 1918, Mr. Grandey took a team of basketball players from Terry to the state tournament in Livingston. The state tournament then involved all schools regardless of size competing in one tournament rather than divisions according to size. The tournament heretofore had always been held in Bozeman but this year the location had been changed to Livingston. In Terry's first game they faced Butte – and won. (Quite a triumph for one of the smallest schools in the state against one of the largest!) In their second game they played the team that had defeated Helena in the first round and they won that game too. The tide turned then and they wound up sixth in the state. Even though they didn't place in the tournament, Mr. Grandey was well pleased with their performance and felt they made a good showing for a small school. Neighboring Miles City took second place in the tournament and Bozeman won first.

In 1918 Mr. Grandey was chosen to serve on the board of control of the State Athletic Association, and in 1922 he was elected vice president of the association. That particular period was a tumultuous one in the history of athletics in Montana. Prior to this time schools hadn't been too particular about the age of their players, but the board had decided it was time to clamp down. Consequently, they disqualified Billings for playing an ineligible man. Because of the resulting furor the president and three board members resigned. Thus Vice President Grandey found himself head of the association.

The tumult was by no means settled. Other schools, too, were using ineligible players and paying the resulting penalties. Missoula, for example, was found to have an over-age player on their team when they were due to meet the Havre Blue Ponies for the state championship. Mr. Grandey wired Mr. Ketchum, principal of the Missoula high school to drop the ineligible player before the game. They played him in spite of the warning (Havre won the championship anyway), so Missoula, too, was disqualified for a year.

A little later the high school athletic association was reorganized and when the reorganization was completed, they had elected all new officers. The superintendent of schools from Havre presided. When he called for election of president, Missoula's Mr. Ketchum stood and announced, "I came to this meeting for one purpose only; to see that Mr. Grandey is elected President. He has straightened out this high school association and deserves it."

Mr. Grandey was elected and served as president of the Montana Athletic Association for twenty-five years. This year they had a banquet in Helena for fellows who had been fifty years with the high schools of Montana and invited him as a special guest but he didn't quite feel equal to going. Mr. Grandey is ninety-two years old and, though alert, he has had to cut down on his activities.

He has a life pass from the Montana High School Association "to all Interscholastic Games, Events, and Activities" which directs, "Admit Free and without Challenge."

After Mr. Grandey's retirement from the school system he served in the Montana Senate. They had a bill before the legislature that would require all who installed indoor plumbing to have it examined by a licensed plumber. The bill would have applied to all, even farm dwellings miles from anyone (including a plumber). Grandey himself had a farm and he knew what it would be like to try to comply with such a law. In opposing the bill he pointed out that, in his case (and there would be many other such cases) there was only one plumber within eighty miles and he wouldn't come out to the farm.

The bill was defeated in the senate by six votes. Afterwards the sponsor of the bill (the secretary of the plumber's union from Butte) met him in the hall and demanded, "Why did you kill my bill? We could hear you up in the gallery and we could hear you say, 'Vote no!'" In view of the arguments he had presented on the floor, it was hardly necessary to answer that. One of those who had voted against the bill was a plumber. Asked why he voted as he did he replied, "Anything good enough for Grandey is good enough for me." He had been one of Grandey's pupils at Terry.

Three days later the sponsor of the defeated plumbing bill came around to talk with him again. He opened the conversation with, "You're a pretty tough hombre." This was a rather surprising approach and Grandey, of course, asked him why he said that. The fellow went on to explain, "When you were president of the Montana Athletic Association you told Great Falls to play Havre or forfeit, and they played." (Great Falls claimed Havre would not play them.

Actually, Great Falls had asked to play on a date that was taken.) Grandey mildly pointed out, "There were other men on the board who agreed with me."

When the oil drilling came into Montana, the state shared a good deal of the leasing, putting $2,000,000 into the state treasury. Grandey contended that the money should be put into the school fund where it would draw interest and the interest should be paid to the schools of the state. However, the Butte delegation wanted the money immediately distributed to the schools. Finally the question was put before the Montana State Supreme Court – a court which, just then, had three members from Butte. It came as no surprise when the court ruled that the money could be distributed immediately to the schools.

An old senator approached Grandey. "You recite poetry," he began, "and I like to hear you speak. Won't you say something against the Supreme Court action?" Grandey agreed to do so. He asked the lieutenant governor to be off the record and out of order and permission was granted. So he said, "The Supreme Court has seen fit to distribute this money to the schools but the children of the future won't get it. I'll have to recite a little ditty:

A woman got a divorce from her old man.
She says, "There ain't no justice in this land.
But I have to laugh at the court's decision.
They gave him the kids, and they aren't his'n!"

He didn't get censored for his poetry.

On one occasion while Mr. Grandey was in the Senate the House asked him to come and open their session with prayer. He did and that was the only time he knows that the House asked a senator to serve in this capacity.

Mr. Grandey has done a lot of traveling since his retirement from teaching in 1947. Following his retirement he was employed as a state representative for the MacMillan Book Company until he was elected to the State Senate in 1952.

In 1950, he was elected State Rotary Governor and as state governor he addressed Rotary Clubs in Mississippi, Virginia, and California as well as in twenty-eight Montana cities.

When he spoke before the commercial Club and Rotary of Whittier, California, his oldest son, Don, introduced him. Don, a past president in Whittier, announced, "It has been my honor to introduce many celebrities, including your beloved Dick (Nixon) to this club, but it is my honor today to introduce the greatest man I've ever known – my father who is Rotary Governor of Montana. Thank you."

Later one of the club members told him, "I'd be glad to pay the $10 fine to have my son introduce me like that!" (The club had a rule that anyone putting in a personal 'plug' for business or family had to pay a fine.)

While he was serving in the school system he gave commencement addresses in twenty schools in Montana including the normal schools at Dillon and Billings as well as a number of high schools – Fariview, Sidney, and Glendive among them.

Mrs. Grandey passed away in 1937, the result of a heart condition. The couple's three sons are a source of great comfort – yes, and pride too – to their father. And well he may be proud of them. Although their education began in a small town school, they have certainly demonstrated that this was no handicap.

While Mr. Grandey's sons, from their small town schools, have gone on to positions of prominence, they are not the only Terry boys to do so. As far as Mr. Grandey in concerned, "his boys" include far more than his own three sons. Many of his Terry graduates have achieved nationally strategic positions and he is just as proud of them as of his own sons.

One such 'boy' is Lyle Woods who retired this year from Boeing Aircraft after forty-five years with the company. Lyle was in charge of the Minute Man program and he spoke to the Billings Rotary Club on this subject while Mr. Grandey was Rotary Governor of Montana.

Mr. Grandey, of course, was there to hear him and Lyle, in his opening remarks, told his audience, "I am just a small town boy and went all the way with the professor here that you fellows call governor. He was a stickler for attendance and discipline and the boys who came out of his office were so impressed. One boy who had played hooky and had been called to the office was not eating his supper that evening and his mother noticed. She pointed out to him that his supper was getting cold and the burdened lad explained, 'Well Mother, I am bad in school and Mr. Grandey is liable to throw me in the furnace.' His mother went to Mr. Grandey to find out what he'd said. Mr. Grandey had told the boy that if he didn't improve his attendance he was going to drop him from the register!"

Mr. Grandey never tires of telling about the various students. Perhaps it's because he took a personal interest in each one that he seems to be able to remember them all.

Terry High School graduated its first senior in 1912 – just one. This first graduate was Beryl Stith. Beryl went on to graduate from Dillon and from Chicago University and then taught in Terry six years. (It was her father, J. W. Stith, who wrote to Grandey in the first place about his coming to Terry to start a high school and sent him a contract.)

In 1913 and again in 1914, there was one graduate. Then in 1915, the class increased to four. One of the graduates that year was Harry Ross who later became superintendent at Saco, then principal in Billings. Another 1915 graduate taught school in Spokane. Percentage wise, Mr. Grandey was turning out a lot of teachers from his high school. Four more students graduated in 1916. Then in 1917 there was a class of seven. With the enrollment increasing, a third teacher was added in 1917. From 1908 until 1917, Mr. Grandey and Mr. A.O. Gullidge had handled the entire teaching load.

Mr. Gullidge had graduated from Gurnee, Mr. Grandey's former school, and had been superintendent of schools at Grays Lake, Illinois. He had joined Mr. Grandey in Terry in 1908. Even though Terry High School had only two teachers, it was an accredited high school, approved by the State Department of Education. Mr. Gullidge taught in Terry until 1934, then, upon Mr. Grandey's recommendation, became superintendent of schools at Baker – for twenty-one years. He ended up on the State Board of Education as the High School

Inspector for the state. The third teacher for Terry High was Cora Harmon, graduate of Stanford and daughter of the State Superintendent of Schools.

Mr. Grandey introduced in Terry the second school transportation system in the state. Other schools at this time were building dormitories to house out-of-town students but Mr. Grandey was opposed to this. He believed high schoolers should be home with their parents at night so he started 'bussing' children to and from school each day – with a team and spring wagon.

He hired a driver who started from the Tusler Ranch each morning at six o'clock, went up over Broadview Bench and on into Terry picking up students. After school the driver made the return trip then stayed overnight at Tusler's to start the route again next morning. Three of his basketball players came in on the 'bus'.

While Mr. Grandey has been active and influential in Montana's educational circles, on the state as well as the local level, his activities and influence have by no means been limited to educational circles. Positions already mentioned in this series of articles would make a lengthy list but there have been many others as well both in and out of educational circles.

In 1912 when Terry was organized as a town, Mr. Grandey was appointed town clerk. About that same time he served as secretary and treasurer of the Broadview Telephone Line. Almost from the time of his arrival in Montana, he has been a 'pillar' in the Terry Community Church, an elder and chairman of the board of trustees as well as filling in as preacher many times.

He was part owner of the Terry Drug Store and managed it three summers. In 1913, he became secretary and treasurer of the Masons Building Association and in 1914, Master of the Lodge. In 1917, he became a member of the Glendive Knights Templay, in 1924 the Al Bedoo Shrine. Also, the National Board of the DeMolay in New York honored him.

In World War I, he was chairman of the Four Minute Men and received a citation from President Woodrow Wilson. During this same period, Mr. Brubaker was chairman of the committee that sold bonds and Mr. Grandey was a member of that body. Mr. Brubaker and Mr. Grandey worked together in many efforts, one of which was getting the organization of Prairie County adopted. They both, Mr. Grandey asserts, wore out their cars in their campaigning to get Prairie carved out of Custer County.

He served on the committee with the University of Montana and Montana State College to revise the Course of Study for Montana schools in about 1926. He was appointed by the governor of Montana to the State Water Board in the interest of the Tongue River Project and Musselshell.

Mr. Grandey is a lifetime member of the National Education Association and past president of the Montana Teachers' Association. Just last month, on April 5, 1971, he was given a lifetime membership in the Terry Commercial Club. He is also a lifetime member of the Masonic Lodge.

Although to ninety-two year old Mr. Grandey his sons are still 'boys', each of them would also qualify as an old timer. His oldest son, Don was born in Illinois so he came to Montana the same year his dad did – in 1907.

Don attended elementary and high school in Terry then went to Bozeman for college. He graduated Cum Laude from Bozeman in 1928 with a degree in Industrial Engineering and went to work for California Edison as clerk and bookkeeper in Santa Barbara. From this beginning forty-three years ago he worked his way up to his present position of manager of three districts, which include six cities. In 1938, he was transferred to Inglewood. Mr. Grandey relates with pardonable fatherly pride that while he was visiting his son in Inglewood, the mayor told him he'd asked the company (California Edison) not to move Don from there. But, they transferred him anyway.

During World War II, Don was assigned the task of camouflaging war plants. From a plane, Mr. Grandey tells us, the plants looked like a garden. Also during the war General Electric awarded the Bomber Award for increasing production in war plants by 200,000 man-hours.

While he was manager at Montebello, the manager at Whittier died so for a time he managed both places. Then his assistant took over at Montebello and Don was transferred to Whittier, his present location. He was in charge of putting in the White Way – a brilliantly lighted stretch on Whittier Boulevard.

Two years ago Don was voted Man of the Year by the Quaker College in Whittier. He was also on the committee planning the college's seventy-fifth anniversary. He has served as president of the Whittier Commercial Club. While he was president of the Rotary Club, he and his wife were sent to Honolulu for the Rotary Convention. He and his wife, Eve, have two children, a boy and a girl, both now married. Their daughter lives in Alhambra and their son is a Whittier policeman. Don will be retiring this summer.

Son number two, Charles E. Grandey, was born in Terry. Charles graduated from the State University of Montana with an LLB in Law in 1931 and was immediately admitted to practice law in the Treasure State. He practiced two years in Terry and served two years as county attorney of McCone County. From McCone County he went to Washington, D.C. where he was an assistant to the Director of Litigation of the National Rifle Association from January of 1935, to November that same year. In November he was transferred to the Federal Trade Commission and remained there until he retired in 1969.

Charles served in numerous positions with the Commission, the most important of which were director, Bureau of Consultation (1954 – 1959) and assistant general counsel for Voluntary Compliance (1959 – 1969).

Coincident with his transfer to the Assistant General Counsel position, The Commission gave him a Distinguished Service Award "For outstanding contribution to law enforcement in the field of voluntary compliance since 1954 and particularly for his efforts in promoting the Guides Program of the Federal Trade Commission. His advocacy of the Guides program which set forth criteria for cigarette advertising, tire advertising and pricing, has enabled the Commission to pinpoint particular areas of consideration for the guidance of all concerned as to what the law requires to protect the public and competition in the public interest. He has, with outstanding success, promulgated these guides on a nationwide basis and his efforts stand as a monument of personal achievement in the new program of the Federal Trade Commission."

Son Charles' biography was published in the 1951-52 'Distinguished Leaders in the Nation's Capitol', published by the American Press and Publishing Corporation. In 1954, "Advertising Age" named him as one of the ten men in the nation who made advertising news that year. Its citation reads in part, "He unhesitatingly pushed out a cigarette advertising Code and the cigarette companies fell into line... He opened FTC's door for advertisers."

In 1961 he was admitted to practice before the Supreme Court of the United States. The 1961 edition of Marquis' "Who's Who in the South and Southwest" included his biography. Prior to his retirement he was a member of the American Bar Association and had served successively as a member of five committees of the Association.

He has been an active member of the Church of Christ since 1937 as a worker and leader in personal work, a substitute preacher, and the author of four religious pamphlets, one of which has been translated into a number of foreign languages and has been internationally distributed.

He is married to the former Elizabeth Allsup of Macon, Mississippi and they have two daughters, both of whom are married and each has two children. Charles and Elizabeth are living in Arlington, Virginia.

The youngest of Mr. Grandey's sons, Arthur, graduated from Montana State College in 1931, a straight A student, after which he moved to Santa Barbara, California and went to work for Southern California Edison Company. He was with this company ten years during which he married Margaret Chenourth of Great Falls.

In 1938 he started working for the Aluminum Company of America (Alcoa) and spent twenty-seven years with them. While he was superintendent of the Magnesium Plant he designed and produced the largest cast wing section ever made for an experimental guided missile for Northrup Aircraft Company.

His dad explains that they couldn't cast an entire wing because the oxygen would ignite the magnesium so when he cast this section thirty feet in width, he sat up all night to watch it and make sure it didn't ignite. The original is now in the Smithsonian Institute in Washington D. C.

In 1965, Arthur retired from Alcoa and moved to Indio, California where he purchased the Towne Mobile Home Park and ran it until 1970. Now he and his wife, Margaret, are having a good time touring the United States in a trailer.

Their two children are both grown and married. Jim, an engineer with Lockheed, lives in San Jose, California with his wife and two girls. Their daughter, JoAnne, and her husband live in El Paso, Texas where he is a regional executive for Goodyear Tire and Rubber Company. They have a boy and a girl.

If space would only permit, Professor Grandey would be happy to relate the accomplishments of all his Terry students. He will also tell you about them if you stop in to visit him in the retirement wing of the Terry hospital.

Art Schrumpf

April 1966

When Art Schrumpf started his banking career back in 1919, the bank where he worked boasted just two mechanical adding machines in the entire establishment. All the rest of the computation was done by brain and recorded by hand. As he remembers, outside of one or two long-term real estate mortgages, they didn't have any mortgages whatsoever. Their outstanding loans, perhaps 99% of them, were to local cattlemen and to business houses on unsecured notes. Yet he doesn't recall that they ever had any trouble collecting.

Another conspicuous difference between 'then' and 'now': all transactions were in gold and silver. The State National Bank of Miles City, where Schrumpf got his first banking experience, was a Federal depository, and they handled post office funds, Indian funds, and the payroll for nearby Fort Keogh. The paper currency was either gold or silver certificates in the same denominations as the present Federal Reserve Notes. The gold certificates had a gold backing and the backings of the silver certificates were silvery, more of a 'whitish' hue than the Federal Reserve Notes.

Art Schrumpf was born in Chicago. His father was a dentist (he graduated from the Chicago College of Dentistry in the same class with Glendive's Dr. Moe) and ran a barbershop, too. He even played a zither. One evening in 1902, the Renn brothers from Cabin Creek southeast of Glendive, who had accompanied a shipment of cattle to Chicago, were walking past his barbershop and heard him playing the zither. They went in, got acquainted, and wound up convincing the elder Mr. Schrumpf he ought to move to Miles City.

Miles City's only dentist was retiring so Mr. Schrumpf bought him out, and then he was the only dentist in that metropolis – and for many miles around. Sometimes he'd pack his tools into a case, take his collapsible dental chair and board the train for Fallon or Terry where he'd set up an 'office' for a few days in a hotel room to give residents of those areas opportunity to take care of their teeth. In 1910 they bought their first car – a Buick.

During World War I Art spent eighteen months in France. After his discharge he returned to Miles City and went to work at 'Pierre Wibaux's bank', the State National. He had experience in several other Miles City banks before coming to Glendive in 1937 to work for Mr. Watson in the Merchant's National.

When the First National bought out the Merchant's Bank in 1946, Schrumpf moved to the First as cashier, the same position he had held in the Merchant's. He continued with the First National until his retirement at the end of 1960.

As he looks back over the years and compares, Mr. Schrumpf sees a great change in banking procedures. Among other things, it is becoming increasingly mechanized, the volume of business has multiplied, and a greater variety of services is offered.

Mrs. Jens (Birgette Nielsen) Mortensen

January 1967

The winter of 1908-09 was a mild one in eastern Montana, and for that the Jens Mortensens were thankful. They hadn't had much time to 'get ready for winter' so the milder the better.

Birgette Nielsen, a native of Denmark, decided in 1907 to join her brother who had migrated to South Dakota. Cupid works fast in South Dakota and before the year was out, Birgette became the bride of Jens Mortensen, her sister-in-law's cousin. Jens had also come from Denmark, but they had never met until they reached South Dakota.

Homestead lands in that area were taken by this time, but in many areas of eastern Montana they were just opening up so the Mortensens decided to investigate. Jens made the investigative trip in October of 1908 and filed on a quarter section* northeast of Lindsay, two-and-one-half miles west of where the Twin Buttes School was later located. He returned home and immediately made preparations for a grant car with livestock, equipment, and household necessities to make the move to the Treasure State.

By this time they had a small baby so Mrs. Mortensen and the baby camped with a neighbor while their house was built. Neighbors were a scarce commodity in those parts but they were fortunate to have located within a quarter mile of another family. Much less time went into the building of the usual homestead shack than is considered necessary to build a house these days. Of course, there was quite a contrast in the finished product too!

Mrs. Mortensen and baby Hannah arrived on November 12 and on the 15th they moved into their own home. It was just a little one-room structure and by the time they had the kitchen range, the heating stove, table, bed, and a few other essentials in it, they hardly had any space to walk but they managed.

For fuel that winter they mostly burned wood, using coal only to hold the fire at night. Mr. Mortensen and three neighbors worked together cutting and loading wood for the four families. Mortensen was the only one who had a team and wagon so he supplied all the transportation as they hauled to each family.

In South Dakota they had burned mostly corn cobs and flax straw so they didn't know much about burning coal – particularly the lignite available here. Any coal they had burned previously was the hard coal, but with plenty of wood to burn they managed to keep warm in their little shack, its 2x4 studs covered with boards, then tarpaper, and over that a thick red paper. Little wonder then that they were glad for a mild winter.

Besides their horses, the Mortensens had brought with them three cows and a dozen chickens so another item on the agenda that first fall was building a barn. By digging back into a bank they had a maximum of shelter for a minimum of cost and time.

With so much to do in those first months they didn't attempt to dig a well but hauled their water from a neighbor's well over in 'Stinking Coulee'. (That illustrious appellation resulted from the distinctive odor given off by some dead animals in the coulee about the time the first family settled in that vicinity.) One horse could pull the stoneboat* they used to transport the barrel of water from the neighbor's well. So they managed through the winter but the next spring they dug a well of their own. Even then, of course, the water had to be carried from the well to the house. Water from a faucet was a luxury far into the future.

When spring came, Mr. Mortensen began turning the virgin sod with his breaking plow*, plowing where no furrows had ever been turned before. About all they planted that year was some oats and a garden. That fall the oats provided feed for the livestock and the garden produced potatoes, carrots, pumpkins, and cucumbers, supplying a welcome addition to the family diet.

By the spring of 1909 more homesteaders were flocking to the Lindsay area and that summer the ladies of the community decided there were enough of them to form a Ladies Aid so they did just that. The six members who formed the first Ladies Aid group were Mrs. Ed Lervold, Mrs. Ole Lervold, Mrs. Sam Mathison, Mrs. Andrew Minde, Mindes' daughter Clara, and Mrs. Mortensen. Their group was small and they didn't have much money but they had a good time getting together and making aprons, pillowslips, and other small articles. Every meeting they each gave ten cents to buy materials. Mrs. Ole Lervold made a dress for each one and they gave the money to the aid instead of to her.

At Christmas that winter – Mortensens' second Christmas in Montana – all the neighbors gathered in the home of Andrew Mindes and had a tree. No school had been started yet in the community so they had a program that same evening. The parents had taught their children some verses to recite for the occasion and they all sang together. They had such a good time that some of them stayed all night. A few of the men went home to do chores and build up the fires, but they came back for breakfast. The early settlers didn't go very far very often but they knew how to have good times with their neighbors.

During the summers they enjoyed getting together for picnics. The Paquettes, homesteaders in the same section as the Mortensens, had an icehouse so they would supply ice to make ice cream. What a treat that homemade ice cream was on a hot summer day!

The Mortensens' second winter in Montana taught them a few things about the capriciousness of the weather in their chosen state. One February morning – Valentine's Day, to be exact – Jens told his wife he was going over to Wolds (they had the post office then) to get the mail and have his team shod. It was a beautiful morning; so warm that water from melting snow was standing in every little depression. She suggested that before he left he should bring in some more coal but he assured her he would be back by noon and, warm as it was, there was plenty of coal in to last until he returned. The forenoon wasn't very old before the temperature began to drop and a chill wind rose to drive the snow that was beginning to fall. Before noon a full scale blizzard had developed.

They were accustomed to feeding the cattle about midday so at noon she started for the barn to do the feeding. As she floundered through the snow, trying to find her way to the barn, she became utterly confused. Quite by accident she stumbled against the fence that Jens had built between the house and barn to keep their oldest girl from exploring the barnyard, so she was able to follow the fence to the barn and also back to the house. Coal that was supposed to last until Jens came home didn't. She tried to get some from the pile outside but she couldn't pry it loose. She didn't know what she was going to do because she had to have more coal to keep from freezing. Then a neighbor came. Ole Lervold knew that Jens had gone to Wolds that morning and also knew that he hadn't returned yet because he would have brought the Lervold mail too, and he hadn't stopped in with it. Knowing that Mrs. Mortensen was home alone with two little ones, he decided he'd better check to see if they were all right. What a blessing! He carried in plenty of coal to last through the storm and made sure everything else was all right before he went back home. Everything was all right, that is, except that Jens still hadn't returned. Through the long afternoon she couldn't quell the nagging fear that perhaps he wouldn't.

Meanwhile, over at the Wolds', it was dinner time before the horse shoeing was completed so Jens ate dinner, then started home about one o'clock. All signs of the trail had been obliterated, and there was no fence to follow so he was soon lost in the swirling snow. All afternoon he wandered, his sense of direction completely gone. As the temperature continued to drop he walked a good deal to keep himself from freezing. When he had left home that morning, he had not foreseen any need for his warmest clothing. Now the struggle for survival was on. When hope seemed almost gone, he came to a fence. Fences were scarce in those parts so he felt sure that he must be near Paquettes.

Hopefully, he followed the fence and soon saw a glimmer of light from a window. Never was a light more welcome! He stumbled into Paquettes yard and soon found himself in the warm kitchen. It was seven o'clock, six hours since he had left the Wolds' five or six miles away. Mrs. Paquette quickly prepared some supper for him to eat before he started out again. As he headed across the section for the last lap of his journey he had no further difficulty. By this time the storm had subsided somewhat and a dim moon was shining, helping to guide him home where he arrived safely about eight o'clock.

Mortensens hadn't harvested much of a crop in 1909 because they hadn't had time to break much ground for planting but in 1910, though they had more ground broken, they harvested even less. Old timers look back upon that summer as one of the driest they ever experienced. As a result, that winter of 1910-11 wasn't the kind to inspire nostalgic memories. It's better to just forget but some things aren't easy to forget. There was no anti-poverty program then and no welfare agency to help the needy. You just made out the best you could.

They lived mostly on white beans that winter. Jens had been able to cut some prairie hay so he sold some and they were able to get a little flour. Their cows were dry so they were deprived of even the dairy products which would have made such a difference in their diet. Today's food authorities can stress the importance of balanced meals; their problem was just to find something for a meal. Somehow they did survive.

No church houses stood on the prairies waiting for the first settlers to use them but they could worship without the benefit of special buildings. Andrew Minde, one of the neighbors whom Mrs. Mortensen describes as a very religious man, went to Glendive to get a preacher and took him out to their community to hold a worship service. The neighbors gathered in Minde's home for their first service. At that time even Glendive had no resident Lutheran minister so they could not have regular services, but sometimes a missionary would come through and the little group would meet.

At the first service, held in the Minde home, two of Mortensen's children, Hannah and Dora, and Ed Lervold's boy were baptized. In 1914, the East Deer Creek Church was built and then services were held fairly regularly. One neighbor would go to Glendive to get the minister, then another would take him back. Nile Mortensen was the first person baptized in the new church.

The Mortensens hadn't been in Montana many years before his health began to decline. In 1918 he spent three months in the hospital, then in 1921 he passed away leaving his widow with nine children ranging in ages from five months to thirteen years old. They had known hard times before, and more hard times followed as she struggled to provide for her family of four boys and five girls. They moved around a good deal during the next two decades. One boy and one girl died before maturity. In 1942, her oldest boy, Lyle, entered the service and returned in 1945. The following year he and Nile, the next oldest son, bought a little home in West Glendive where they lived with their mother. The others were all away from home by this time.

Lyle had a job hauling tar for the highway crews and one hot July day in 1947 a tank exploded, burning him so severely he lived only a few days. That left just Nile and Mrs. Mortensen in their West Glendive home. Mrs. Mortensen will be eighty years old this spring, but she is still active and has managed to keep her sense of humor all these years.

Team of horses and modified stoneboat

Erling Fosfjeld

October 1965

Some young fellows today may figure they're starting out on a shoestring (perhaps a borrowed one), but it's doubtful that any of them would know what it means in the sense that Erling Fosfjeld experienced. They may think they have to go into debt to buy the latest machinery or equipment, but when he started out he 'made do' with what he had until he could afford more.

Erling had come from Norway to Glendive in 1909 with a party of eleven friends. His brother had been in Montana, and he came back to Norway with such glowing reports of how good it was that they decided to try it, too. Pretty hard times in Norway then, Mr. Fosfjeld explained. As with many another of the early settlers, he figured he would come over and make a little money, then go back to Norway. But again as many another, he came – made a little money (in time) – and stayed.

The group arrived in April and planned to go lambing*, but the first thing Erling did was get sick. It was a week before he was able to work, and then he started for the Northern Pacific Railroad. He kept that job for about a year, but quit to go lambing for Joe Holtz when the next spring rolled around.

Holtz had a sheep ranch just across the Yellowstone/Redwood divide* when Erling started working for him, but his lambing band was down on Sioux Creek so Erling lambed on the exact location that was later to become his ranch. After herding sheep for Holtz the rest of the summer, he spent two-and-a-half years in the Terry area, still with sheep. He first worked for 'Powder River Louie', then for John Derham.

About that time he began getting other ideas - matrimonial ideas - and after another short period with the N.P. he married Sina Idland. Perhaps the ideas weren't very new. He had known Sina in Norway before coming to the New World. Now he managed to get over to see her fairly regularly even though it meant quite a walk. Her father had also come to this country in 1909 (he had been in Montana before, near Big Timber, but had gone back to Norway) and homesteaded on Redwater. In 1910 Sina joined her father. Her mother had died when she was just a young girl so she and a married sister were all the immediate family Mr. Idland had.

The first couple of years here she worked in town – she's the only lady still living in Circle who worked in 'Old Circle'. Old Circle was a little south of the town's present location and boasted little more than a store, post office, hotel, and a dwelling house or two when Sina worked there in Erling Njaa's hotel. Later a dance hall was built, but little other building was done – a few houses – before the town was moved to its present site. The hotel was sold and used for a sheep shed.

The homestead fever that swept the country finally affected Sina, too, but by the time she became interested she found there was only one homestead left – a half section on Sioux Creek. She and her friends joked about "the one left just for Sina" and she filed on it. Proving up on her homestead meant living about ten miles from town, alone, with no means of transportation except that provided by her own two feet. While she was fulfilling residence requirements she worked part of the time for neighbors, Mr. and Mrs. Sam Undem.

Non-citizens were allowed to file on a homestead but couldn't get their final papers until they had become citizens. Her citizenship requirement was solved simply by her marriage to Erling Fosfjeld. The law at that time provided that when a man received his naturalization papers, his wife automatically became a citizen, too, so they both became citizens in 1915.

Erling and Sina were married in Glendive in 1913, and their ride to her homestead in a lumber wagon was their honeymoon. She had a little one-room shack, but that was her only building. With no livestock she had no need for a barn, but now that a saddle horse had come along with the husband, a barn was needed.

Erling's only tools were an axe and a spade, but that barn was needed so he went ahead with what had to be done. First he made a dugout, then cut posts in the coulee and snagged them home with his saddle horse. He used the posts for the sides of the barn, then cut poles for rafters. But what about a covering for the roof? Bare rafters weren't going to keep out much cold or precipitation. One of his neighbors had raised flax that summer and told him he could have the straw, but that presented another problem. How was he to get that straw home? When he doesn't have the equipment he needs, a resourceful fellow figures out a substitute – and Erling Fosfjeld was resourceful! He filled his bed tarp with straw, tied it onto his saddle horse, hauled it home, and piled it on the poles for a roof.

Later he bought some cows, some horses, a little machinery, and continued to make improvements, including adding a lean-to*. He did a little farming but was more interested in livestock.

One of his nephews and Martin Undem helped him when he was ready to dig his well. They dug it by hand, using a bucket and windless to haul the dirt to the surface. Martin, down in the well filling the bucket, was digging so enthusiastically that when the nephew thought it was time to quit, he couldn't get Martin out of that well. Martin just kept piling the dirt in the bucket so the nephew kept pulling it up. It's hard telling when Martin would have called it a day, but gas down in the well began to bother him so he climbed onto the rope and gave the signal to be hoisted to the surface. But now the nephew had the upper hand, literally and figuratively. When he had Martin part way up, he asked, "Can you still smell the gas?" Martin answered in the negative and Nephew gave a few more turns to the windless. Again he asked, "Can you smell it now?" Martin shouted back, "No, I'm above it now," so Nephew decreed, "Then you have to go back," and down into the well he went again until the nephew figured his score was settled and cranked him to the surface.

In 1916 the First Lutheran Church of Circle was organized with Mr. and Mrs. Fosfjeld among the charter members, of whom only seven are still living. Plans are already underway for the church's fiftieth anniversary celebration next

74

year. Prior to 1916 there was no Lutheran minister in the Circle area, but a Congregational minister had homesteaded in that vicinity so the residents of the community asked him to preach for them, holding services in a schoolhouse. He was not too well acquainted with the language and sometimes ran into a little difficulty, but he could communicate the Gospel so they were glad for his messages. Mr. Fosfjeld facetiously commented that if the Lutherans hadn't sent out a minister they probably would all have turned out to be Congregationalists.

In 1919 the Fosfjelds sold their livestock and went back to Norway. By doing so they missed that hard winter of 1919-1920 that wiped out many a homesteader and even some of the ranchers, but they didn't gain much either. When they came back to the homestead a year later, he had just $20 in his pocket. He had money coming from different individuals, but how can you collect money from someone who is broke? About all he ever realized from those accounts was a few cows and horses and some old machinery.

It was when he started over again after their return from Norway that he started concentrating on sheep. But raising sheep didn't automatically make everything rosy from then on. There were still plenty of hard times to weather. They haven't forgotten the year they had to sell 400 yearlings and two-year-old ewes for $3.50 each in order to pay the bank. That left them with only old sheep – about 800 of them – but in time they were able to build up their flock again.

One winter he ran out of feed during bitterly cold weather and had to go to Circle with the team and bobsled to get a load of pellets. That morning, when he started back for the ranch with his load, the mercury registered fifty-five degrees below zero! He thought he was dressed warmly, but by the time he reached home his legs were frozen, and he had just about 'had it'. Even the horses, which normally could have pulled the ton of pellets over the snow without too much difficulty, were 'played out' by the extreme cold.

Another time he almost ran out of hay near the spring of the year. When a fellow told him, "You'd better get hold of some more hay," Mr. Fosfjeld replied (more optimistically than he felt), "When the hay is gone spring will be here." He didn't add that he couldn't buy more hay because he didn't have the money. But as it turned out, spring did come in time to save the day for him.

Two years ago the Fosfjelds celebrated their fiftieth wedding anniversary. An account of the celebration was carried in the CIRCLE BANNER:

A hundred and thirty people gathered at First Lutheran Church Sunday afternoon to extend congratulations to Mr. and Mrs. Erling Fosfjeld on their 50th wedding anniversary.

During the noon hour a turkey and ham dinner was served to sixty-eight people, mostly relatives of the honored couple and a few local friends.

Rev. and Mrs. James Schoeld were among the invited guests and following the dinner the Reverend spoke briefly on the meaning of marriage and of the work of this esteemed couple in the church. Both are charter members of First Lutheran.

Rev. Schoeld also read an interesting poem entitled 'This Earthly House' which had been sent to the Fosfjelds by Mr. and Mrs. Njadl Siqveland of Marysville, Washington. Mr. Siqveland was a former Circle resident.

An interesting feature of the program was a story in Norwegian on the life of Erling and Sina while residents of Norway and later in America when they took up life on the Sioux Creek homestead. This was followed by a Norwegian song composed by Sig Fosfjeld, here on visit from Norway, and Mrs. Jennie Idland of Circle.

Erling Fosfjeld and Sina Idland were married at Glendive Lutheran Church by the Rev. Grafton on Nov. 6, 1913. Witnesses to the ceremony were Tom Ueland, formerly of Glendive and Marie Idland of Circle, a sister of the bride.

The happy young people immediately took up residence on Mrs. Fosfjeld's homestead on which she had filed in 1912. They continued to reside there until 1953 when they retired from the farm and took up residence in Circle.

They still have the six silver coffee spoons sent to them back in 1913 as a wedding present from Mrs. Fosfjeld's sister in Norway. They observed, wryly, that they had to pay such a heavy duty on the spoons that it was almost as though they had to buy their wedding present.

The Fosfjelds have now made seven trips to visit their friends and relatives in Norway, making their seventh trip this last summer. They traveled by jet plane for the first time. Instead of spending eight to twelve days crossing the ocean, this time they left Norway at eight o'clock Monday morning and were back in Circle by ten o'clock the next morning.

It was because of Mrs. Fosfjeld's poor health that they decided it was best to leave the ranch and move into Circle, but her health is much better now. When Mr. Fosfjeld was asked to explain how he managed to keep such thick hair, he answered that he had told one of his herders that if you want to keep your hair you shouldn't wash it more than four times a year – it needs a little fertilizer. Whatever his explanation, baldness certainly doesn't appear to be any threat to him. Neither, for that matter, does age. In the words of the poem, "These few short years can't make me old; I feel I'm in my youth. Eternity lies just ahead, full life and joy and truth."

On the following page is the poem Mr. and Mrs. Siqveland sent to the Fosfjelds for the celebration of their fiftieth wedding anniversary.

This Earthly House
"For we know that if our earthly house of this tabernacle were dissolved we have a building of God, a house not made with hands, eternal in the heavens." II Cor 5:1

You tell me I am getting old, but that's not really so;
The house I live in may be worn, and that of course I know.
It's been in use a good long while and weathered many a gale,
I'm therefore not surprised to find it's getting somewhat frail.

You tell me I am getting old, you mix my house with me;
You're looking at the outside, that's all that most folk see.
The dweller in the little house is young and bright and gay,
Just starting on a life that lasts through long, eternal day.

The color changing of the roof, the windows looking dim;
The walls a bit transparent and getting rather thin.
The foundation's not so steady as once it used to be,
And that is all that YOU observe, but it's not really me.

I patch the old house up a bit to make it last the night;
But soon I shall be going to my house of endless light.
I'm going to live forever there, my life goes on, it's grand,
How can you say I'm getting old? You do not understand.

These few short years can't make me old, I feel I'm in my youth;
Eternity lies just ahead, full of life and joy and truth.
We will not fret to see this house grow shabby day by day,
But look ahead to our new home which never will decay.

I want to be made fit to dwell in that blest house above;
Cleansed in the precious blood of Christ, and growing still in love.
The beauty of that glorious home no words can ever say,
'Tis hidden from these mortal eyes, but kept for us some day.

My house is getting ready in the land beyond the sky;
Its Architect and Builder is my Saviour now on high.
But I rather think He's leaving the furnishing to me.
So it's 'treasures up in heaven' I must store each day, you see.

Mr. and Mrs. Njadl Siqveland

Don Gibson

November – December 1970

When Grant Gibson and an older brother left Flint, Michigan in 1891, they were headed west, but they hadn't decided just how far they would go. At Glendive they had just seventeen cents left so that was the deciding factor. If he'd had another dollar or so, his son Don reflects, he might have gone to Billings.

As it was, he went to work in the Glendive area. He herded sheep first for some man on Morgan Creek, then worked some time for Harpsters and also on the Parson ranch. But sooner or later he got a job with Elmer Herrick out in the Divide* Country at the head of Clear Creek – south of where the highway now is that connects Glendive and Circle. No highway then of course, they were lucky if they found a trail in the early 1890's!

So, that's how it happened that Grant Gibson from Michigan was working at Elmer Herrick's in 1900 when Inez Broughton from Minnesota came to visit Mrs. Herrick. Inez and Mrs. Herrick had been school chums in Waseca, Minnesota, and their friendship had continued through the years. Grant evidently was not a man to waste time because in January of 1901 he arranged so that Mrs. Herrick's friend could visit her more often: he married the girl.

Inez had never been in the west before so during her first visit Grant and one of the other cowboys thought they would put on a show for her. She, however, wasn't much impressed; about the time the horses got to bucking good she turned around and went back into the house. The bucking may not have impressed her but one of the riders must have.

The change from Minneapolis to ranch life in Dawson County in 1901 must have been something of a cultural shock for a city girl, but the new Mrs. Gibson adapted admirably. They were forty miles from Glendive and there were no other towns any closer (Circle, Lindsey, Union, weren't there yet). They made probably two trips to town in the fall of the year and that was about it, hauling in grain and bringing groceries back, a four-horse wagonload each time.

They had a storehouse attached to the bunkhouse and it was stocked just like a grocery store – like a grocery store of the early 1900's, you understand, not like a super market today! Most of the products lining the shelves of the modern supermarket had never been dreamed up when the Gibsons set up housekeeping.

The pioneer cook had to depend much more upon her own resourcefulness and ingenuity to serve varied meals. Some, of course, were satisfied with meat and potatoes and navy beans, but others weren't. Young Mrs. Gibson was neither resourceful nor ingenious when she married, but her new husband taught her how to cook – did a great job.

Canned fruit as we know it now was not to be bought – nor vegetables either, with the exception of tomatoes. They did have dried fruit – chiefly apples, prunes, peaches, and apricots. Flour, sugar, salt, macaroni, rice, and other staples occupied considerable space in the storehouse.

The ranch housewife better have her list complete when shopping time came. Don recalls hearing his mother tell that one year she failed to get the quantity of baking powder she should have so she just had to do without. You didn't run to town in the middle of the year for baking powder! But then they ran out of salt for the stock – and a trip to town was made without delay.

Another canned product available was pumpkin but one of their sheepherders didn't take to it very enthusiastically. Eddie Garfield was camp tender at the hay camp down on Hay Creek, and one day while he was gone to the home ranch on some errand the herder opened the can of pumpkin. He didn't know what it was supposed to be (he couldn't read), and tried to eat it, just as it came from the can. Ever taste unsweetened pumpkin? When Eddie got back to camp, the herder informed that the stuff in that can was spoiled. He couldn't eat it, and anything he couldn't eat must be spoiled.

The house in which they set up housekeeping had only three rooms – big enough for just two. However, as their family grew to three boys and a girl they needed more space, and in 1915 they built a new house, a big one.

When the Gibsons made one of their infrequent trips to town, they came in across Poverty Flat. Hastys had a roadhouse so when the trip was made in cold weather, they came as far as Hastys' the first day, on to Glendive to load and back to Hastys' the second day, home the third. In warm weather, instead of staying at the roadhouse, they camped at Eleven Mile Spring.

When the Grant Gibsons' first child was due, Mrs. Gibson went back to Minneapolis so Howard was born in Minnesota. Their other three children, however, were born in Glendive. Don, the second son, was born at the Burt Maternity Home. There was a Dr. Burt and Don says he was always under the impression Dr. Burt was a medical doctor, but a few years ago a fellow in the courthouse declared he was a veterinarian! Regardless of Dr. Burt's profession, there was no question, Mr. Gibson insists, about what kind of maternity home his wife maintained.

'Neighbors', when the Grant Gibsons started raising their family, were few and far between – far enough away that they'd hardly be considered neighbors by most people now. And children, it seemed to the Gibson small fry, were even fewer. Heides, just over the Divide (about twelve miles horseback; three or four miles farther if you went by buggy) had children and Earl Simes did. Simeses were about fifteen miles northwest, where Cottonwood Creek joins Redwater. Then in about 1908 the Billy Rust family moved to a location about four miles from Gibsons and they had youngsters Don's age.

Mention of Billy Rust reminded Don of how his dad and Billy used to hunt wolves together. Billy was small of stature so he could crawl into a hole after a wolf, hook a hind leg and pull it out. Once the wolf was out of the hole it would snap at anything within reach and the teeth marks on Grant's gun barrel bore mute testimony to the many times it had been bitten.

Other neighbors included Billy Wood (he had arrived in Montana about the same time Grant Gibson did and they soon became fast friends), twenty miles southeast, and Libbys, fifteen miles to the northeast. Any wonder that when neighbors went visiting (and old timers say it was more often than now) they took the children along and stayed two or three days? Joe Storm also lived in the area, at the head of Sioux Creek. Joe had a bunch of hounds he used to hunt coyotes.

Miss Josephine Gathwright, who had a homestead near Albert Skillestad's – same section in fact – was a seamstress. She traveled about the neighborhood sewing in the various homes, making clothes and mending as was needed. She would make her home with the family until she had their sewing done, then go on to another home until she had her rounds made. Between times she lived on her homestead. Miss Gathwright was a good friend of Camelia Osborne, an early county superintendent of schools, and they shared many activities. Mrs. Gibson learned to develop pictures so she took many and her family now has a number of pictures of the early pioneers, including one of the few of Miss Osborne.

Grant Gibson mostly raised cattle and horses but during two different periods he did run sheep. Sam Undem, a confirmed cattle man, used to jibe that Grant would raise cattle until he went broke, then turn to sheep to get him back on his feet. Sheep, though, weren't always such a good bet either. One year – this was after Don was old enough to remember it – 500 sheep went over a bank, "follow the leader" style, on the Divide and were killed. They spent most of that winter, he recalls, skinning sheep to save the pelts – nothing else to save.

Grant never did farm much so his boys did more riding than plowing. Every day Don and Howard, his older brother, would have to check on the cattle down on Sioux Creek. They'd ride down around them and turn them back so they didn't stray too far away. Usually there was other riding to be done as well, including a ride about once a week up to Mt. Antelope to get the mail.

In the early years of his parents' marriage they had to go clear to Glendive to get mail, but by the time Don was big enough to be riding, mail was being taken to Circle and some routes were established along the way.

Don and his brothers and sister learned to ride an old brown horse they had. Sometimes all four of the children would be on him at the same time. The patient old horse would plod 'round and 'round the house with his cargo and if a rider fell off he'd stop and wait for him to get back on again.

The Indian pony they had was of a different nature. He chose to carry one at a time and if they tried to double up on him, he'd unload them. Mr. Gibson had traded a lump-jaw steer for the pony when some Indians went through one time.

Prairie fires can strike dread to the heart any time, but before the coming of the farmer with his plowed fields, range fires were even more of a threat. When a fire started on a rampage, any rancher within sight of it turned out to fight it. As homesteaders began coming in they, too, joined the battle when there was a fire to be fought.

80

Don remembers one fire, especially, that came very close to their home. The Gibson children were attending High Point School at the time and as the fire threatened at closer range, the teacher dismissed them and sent them home from school.

Their father, of course, was out fighting fire but their mother was home and immediately put them to carrying water. The spring, which supplied them with water, was about 200 feet downhill from the house. Mr. Gibson had cut steps into the hillside to facilitate descent and climbing. Now the children carried water up the hill and filled tubs – pails – everything available so if the fire came close to the house they would be ready to fight it. The fire did come within a half-mile of the house but no closer so they didn't have to use their water.

Before her marriage, Mrs. Gibson had worked for an architect so when they built their new house they got the plans from the firm of her former employers. Having the house-building crew around supplied an interesting diversion for the boys. In one case, at least, the boys supplied diversion for the crew.

Mr. Gibson had gone to Glendive for a load of shingles and while there, picked up an extra man for the crew. On the way home they camped out for the night as usual, and Mr. Gibson learned that the new man was afraid of snakes – so afraid that he would not sleep on the ground but spent the night on the load of shingles. That isn't the kind of information that keeps very well, and the boys decided this provided too good an opportunity to pass up. Mr. Gibson prefaced the telling of this incident with, "You don't have to print this," but he didn't forbid it so . . . Bullsnakes had a den in a pile of rocks not far from the house so the boys captured and killed three of the snakes and took them to the bunkhouse. They put one in the new carpenter's bed; one they stretched out on the floor; and the third, which was still wriggling, they tied to a chair. The new carpenter terminated his services abruptly.

Having the crew around provided diversion for Mr. Gibson too. Each night they'd play horseshoes, the loser milking the cow. Sometimes they played so late they'd – no, they didn't turn on the yard light – tie a candle to the stakes to see them.

Our rural residents still have school problems, but the problems were even more so when the Grant Gibsons were raising their family. They had one boy older than Don (Howard) and twins; a boy and a girl (Ray and Faye) younger. When Don was five there was no school around so Grant built a little one-room cabin in their yard, hired a teacher at his own expense, and sent his children to school.

Their first teacher was Miss Laura Powers, later Mrs. Claude Gunnett. The Gibson children went to their own private school for two years; then the High Point School, about three miles from the Gibson home – as the crow flies – was started so they began attending there. Most of the time they rode horseback but one year Jeanne Libby stayed with them to go to school and that year they used a buggy most of the time.

Don remembers yet the time they were discriminated against – he figured – in favor of their buggy horse. His folks had been to a dance the night before and didn't get home until morning. Hard telling how far away the dance had been but the snow was deep and Dad figured the horse was too tired to make another three miles to school so the children walked and the horse stood in the barn all day.

When Howard, the oldest boy, graduated from the eighth grade, private school was resumed in the Gibson yard with Miss Isabella Peterson – Mrs. Fred Rilla – teaching the three younger children in the elementary grades and Howard his first year of high school. (We didn't ask him but it might be interesting to know how Don voted on the high school bond election last summer!)

By the time Howard was ready for his second year of high school, Mr. Gibson decided it was time to make other arrangements. Mrs. Gibson's mother and stepfather had retired from their Iowa farm and were living in town so in the fall of 1916, the Gibsons moved to Iowa, and took over management of the farm while the children pursued their high school education

It was during their Iowa sojourn that Grant Gibson bought his first car, in 1917. It was a Model T. First time he drove it into the garage he hit the door. He hollered, "Whoa, Dick!" but Dick didn't stop. He never did learn to drive a car very well – drove horses too long perhaps – and left most of the driving to his boys.

As for his wife, she never would try to drive a car. After Don was married, he kept telling his wife, Peggy, that sometime he would have to teach her but – always some other day. She had learned to ride horseback, this city girl turned ranch wife, and could drive horses – had her own buggy team – but a car, no.

One of Don's early cars is still running and is frequently seen on the streets of Glendive. Delton Peuse drives a Model A that Don bought years ago for his hired man to use.

Don and Peggy were married in 1926. They met while the Gibsons were in Iowa for educational pursuits. Peggy lived in Des Moines and went to high school with Don's younger sister, Faye. She laughingly recalled that the first time she saw Don he was just getting over "a big old case of the measles." She and her family had driven out to the farm where the Gibsons were living to see Faye.

Grant brought his family back to Montana in February, 1926. Don, also, had bought a car while they were in Iowa, but he didn't bring it when the family moved. In June he went back to get his Model T but that wasn't all. While he was there he and Peggy were married so he brought back his new wife, too.

Peggy's June arrival as a bride was quite different from that of her mother-in-law. One of the experiences Don's mother always remembered, and to which she occasionally referred, was her own January arrival in Glendive and the trip to the ranch.

At that time there was no bridge across the Yellowstone – the first one had been washed out, the second one had not yet been built. There was a ferry for crossing the river but when the river was frozen the ferry couldn't run and they had to cross on the ice. Crossing on the ice wouldn't have been so bad but on this particular occasion the ice had water on it. That didn't inspire much confidence. They made the crossing without mishap, however, and the trip on out to the ranch was uneventful – if a forty-mile trip with team and buggy in the middle of winter could be deemed uneventful.

Along with his ranching, Don carried mail in the Union area for sixteen years. Helped make ends meet during the '30's, he explained. He started out with a Model T Ford and when he couldn't go with the Ford he went with the team and sled or horseback or however he could get through. In those days you carried the mail, regardless. His route called for delivery three times a week and if you didn't get through one day you started out again the next morning and kept trying until you did get through. They used to quip that it was a tri-weekly route – if you didn't make it through one week you tried again the next.

Don Gibson has served two terms as county commissioner and was just reelected to a third. This is the first time, as far as they could determine, that anyone has been elected to three terms as county commissioner. Anyone remember otherwise?

The Gibson's only son, Danny, lives in Bellingham, Washington, and if you give him a chance, Don will be glad to show you a picture of their new grandson, almost five months old.

Don's father died in 1947, his mother in 1952. In the thirties Grant had had a tractor accident; he fell off a big Rumley* and the plow ran over him. Then the tractor circled back and he had to roll to one side or the Rumley would have gone over him too. After that he always had a stiff leg. He was not one to complain, but he was never very well after the accident.

Don is the only one of his family still living in eastern Montana. His oldest brother, Howard, passed away in 1937 while he was serving as county agent in Torrington, Wyoming. The twins both live east of the Mississippi: Ray in Detroit, Michigan and Faye in Fremont, Ohio.

Don and his wife, Peggy, live on the ranch but they have rented an apartment in town for the winter. Since he will be working full time as commissioner he wants to be in where he can get to work more easily. Even a county commissioner can't guarantee that his roads won't be blocked! At best, from the ranch to Glendive and back again each day gets to be a lot of driving.

The beginning of retirement, maybe you'd say.

Mrs. Fred (Ullman) Grulke

July 1965

If whipping, ear-twisting, tail-twisting and kicking him won't start a balky horse, what can you do? Mrs. Fred Grulke saw first hand how one stage driver handled it.

When her brother Robert Ullman returned to Fairview with his new bride after they were married in Glendive, the Grulkes accompanied them in their buggy for a visit in that area. In the Grulkes' home state of Wisconsin there might have been a train or streetcar to take them back to Glendive, but in primitive Montana they had to make the trip by horse-drawn stagecoach. The stage made a daily trip between Mondak and Glendive, starting about seven in the morning and arriving about ten o'clock in the evening. They'd change horses about twenty miles along the way to assure maximum speed, but on this particular trip at one of the changes the 'speed' was slow getting started when one of the horses chose to balk. With passengers, luggage, mail all loaded, ready to go, the other horses dancing, eager to be off, that equine refused to budge. The driver tried all the tricks in his bag to change its mind. Talk about mules being stubborn – that horse could 'out mule' a mule. As a last resort, after trying all of the above, they piled an armload of straw under the unwilling quadruped and lit a fire. That horse took off then and didn't slow down until they were almost to the next station.

Mrs. Grulke had come to the Treasure State from Wisconsin's 'civilization', where she had grown up on a farm along with nine brothers and sisters. During the winter months they went to an English school which was only a quarter of a mile away, but during the summer they attended a German school, walking three miles in the morning and again in the afternoon.

She remembers how they made their own soap using tallow or fat or drippings, mixed with lye which they made from wood ashes. Maple syrup – real maple syrup – on the table three times a day was routine. And with fresh bread to soak up the syrup – what more could anyone ask? They had their own maple trees, and 'tapping season', when they went out in the big sleigh to gather the sap from the trees, was a highlight every year. On a warm day they sometimes gathered as much as eight quarts from a single tree.

The big sheet-metal trough (8'x3') in which they cooked the sap after it was gathered was located in an open lean-to*, and it was great fun to sit in the evening and watch the sap simmering while the big logs glowed underneath. Sometimes they would cook the sap all night so it may not have been so much fun for the man who had to stay up to watch it and stir it. As the sap cooked down, fresh sap would be added and the cooking continued. Mrs. Grulke recalled that one time it wasn't watched carefully enough so it boiled dry. Then a bird got stuck in the gluey concoction and couldn't get loose. What a scrubbing followed to get the trough usable again!

When the syrup was ready for the table their father would put it into jugs – half-gallon, gallon, or even two-gallon jugs – and peddle it in the residential district of a nearby town for a dollar a gallon. The children delighted in the rare occasions when they'd get to make maple sugar. Their dad didn't allow it often, but sometimes when he was gone, they'd get their coveted sugar.

Mr. and Mrs. Grulke had been married about three years when they decided to try the West. Four of her brothers and one of her sisters had already found their way to Eastern Montana. Mr. Grulke had been a cheesemaker back in Wisconsin, but when they heard about the homestead land out West, they decided to look into the possibilities offered. Once in Montana, however, he walked into a job plastering and building and never did get around to looking at the homesteads.

Mrs. Grulke's sister, Helen, and her husband, Henry Larson, were living in Glendive so the Grulkes moved into the upstairs of their house when they first came. It was Mr. Larson for whom Fred worked. During this period Mr. Larson contracted to build the original Zion Lutheran Church* in the Gate City* (the building now owned by the Latter Day Saints) so Mr. Grulke had his hand in the building of it, too.

The Grulkes soon built a home of their own on Towne Street. Since they, like most other Glendive residents at that time, didn't have water in the house they had water barrels that were filled daily from the wagon that delivered water about town. They had to keep the barrels covered so the cows wouldn't drink the water. The drinking water was hauled from a well instead of the river and was, of course, kept separate. When they did get a water system installed in the house, they had to have a filter on the faucet.

Many of the town's residents had a cow or two (or more) so each morning some boys would gather the 'city herd' and take them to pasture – over in the direction of the Meisner Addition – and bring them back each evening. So it was that any uncovered water barrel could substitute as a drinking trough for thirsty or curious cattle.

Automatic gas or electric heating units were far in the future when they built their first house. They used lignite coal or cedar wood for fuel, and there was no taking your heat for granted when you had to get up in the middle of a bitterly cold night to add more fuel to the fire. Mrs. Grulke knows all about that because after her husband started driving the fire truck he often worked nights. Then it was her responsibility to 'keep the home fires burning'.

Riverview Park dwellers who think of their section of the city as rather recently developed may be surprised to learn that this part of town was platted and development promoted over fifty-five years ago. Mrs. Grulke has some of the material put out by the Glendive Land Company, the aim of which was to inform the reader of 'one of the best investments which can be made in the most promising state in the Great North West'. The literature includes a map of Glendive labeled "Bird's-eye view of Glendive, Montana, Showing the Advantages of Riverview Park Addition." The map, copyrighted 1910, was definitely visionary, and we still haven't reached the potential pictured there. No sign of Caine's Coulee is evident on the map, and it pictures houses instead of Whipkey Field and the South Side Park just to the north of the Riverview

Addition. Perhaps most Glendivians couldn't tell you where to find Alsip Ave. and Baer Ave., but a glance at the map shows that they are the next two streets beyond Patt Ave.

The map bears a quotation from Theodore Roosevelt: "Every person who invests in well selected real estate in a growing section of a prosperous community adopts the surest and safest method of becoming rich."

The accompanying booklet is informative and features on its first two pages pictures of the company's officers: J.W. Patt, president; C.E. Wharton, E.E. Devaul, H.P. Burt, and E.G. DeVaul. Next we find an essay describing the city and prophesying the progress to come. The prophecy may not have been entirely accurate, but it's interesting:

There is good reason for Glendive being credited as one of the best towns in Montana today. Being an important division point on one of the great transcontinental railway lines, holding the key to a hundred thousand acres of fertile lands in the Lower Yellowstone, and being the commercial, financial and social center of a great undeveloped empire larger than many eastern states, Glendive has a right to feel proud of its natural resources and can afford to anticipate its future with confidence.

So rapidly have come the changes that mark the evolution of a primitive frontier town into a modern progressive city, that even few of those who have had an active part in the industrial growth of Glendive realize that the town is really on the verge of a tremendous development and that the next few years will witness still further transformations that are going to make this one of the most important towns within that portion of the state that lies east of the continental divide. But the town's future may best be gauged by a review of the present conditions which have given it such a flattering reputation. Glendive is located in Dawson County, Montana, near the eastern border of the state and is on the south and east bank of the Yellowstone River at the point where it curves from east to the north and mingles its waters with the Missouri. It lies on a level bench between the river and a spur of high hills – the first glimpse of the foothills of the Rockies that the westbound traveler obtains. The principal business street, paralleling the N.P. railway, is solidly built up with splendid business blocks of brick and stone and all of the business institutions of the town display an air of prosperity, neatness and newness that is a revelation to the eastern visitor. The residence district is also compact, well laid out and the town is notable for the architectural beauty of many of its homes.

The town has today a population of about 4500 and is growing at the rate of 500 to 1000 a year. Although Glendive is a livestock and wool center, the fact that it is a division point has given it, in addition, a large and permanent pay roll which is distributed monthly among its hundreds of railway employees. The Northern Pacific Railway has always taken an active and commendable interest in the welfare of the community and besides paying out its $65,000 in wages monthly at this point, has furnished free hydraulic water to the city for fire protection and likewise supplies it to the employees of the company. The company has also borne the cost of extensive development of the agricultural resources in the vicinity of Glendive and these experiments have done much to convince the world of the splendid possibilities of dry land farming on many thousands of acres of benchlands in Dawson County.

Glendive today has four strong banks that take an active part in the development of the town, a newly organized commercial club that has just started an effective campaign for the upbuilding of a Greater Glendive, has many stores with large and complete stocks, a fine modern hotel, two hospitals, five flourishing churches, three schools, a new county High School erected at a cost of $40,000, a full complement of secret societies, a county social club with over one hundred members, a local electric light company and telephone company, three stage lines, three newspapers, and, in fact, all of the needful institutions of a live and progressive community.

The fact that Glendive last year shipped over 1,500,000 pounds of wool is an index to its importance as a shipping and marketing point and its record of from one to two thousand horses a month during the horse sales is an index to its growing importance as a market for range horses.

During the past year, Glendive felt the direct benefit of being the center of construction of two great projects that are still under way and which will be completed within the present year. The first is the government irrigation project that will result in the reclamation of over a hundred thousand acres in the Lower Yellowstone Valley, land that is to be sold or homesteaded under federal supervision and is already partially taken up. This work, involving the construction of a huge canal and a great dam across the Yellowstone near Glendive has given employment to thousands of laborers. The other project is the extension of the Northern Pacific Railway from Glendive to Sidney, a town about fifty miles north of Glendive on the Yellowstone. This work is still under way and is being pushed forward so vigorously that the company expects to run trains before snow flies again. The grading has practically been finished and steel will soon be in place. This road will, when the plans are carried out, be extended to connect with the Great Northern Railway at the Missouri River and Glendive will then occupy a more strategic location as a railway point. This branch will open up all of the irrigated land under the Yellowstone project and thus add materially to Glendive's trade territory.

And now one word about Glendive's future expansion and its effect on real estate. The town is at present hemmed in by the river on one side; a deep ravine to the east effectually stops its expansion in that direction so that whatever growth it will make must naturally be south and west of the Northern Pacific Railway tracks. Our addition lying in a compact body, smooth as a floor and every foot suitable for a home site, is within two and a half blocks of Main Street. It is generally conceded and is entirely probable that the business center will shift westward bringing it opposite the proposed location of the Northern Pacific's new depot which will make our new *addition the most accessible residence district in Glendive. It is also near here that the Sidney branch leaves the main line on its way down the valley.*

These are all facts, briefly stated, that by the logic of history, indicate Glendive's coming era of prosperity. In the Dakotas there are today, within a few hour's ride of Glendive, many prosperous cities that with fewer natural advantages and much smaller tributary territories, have within a few years, grown at an amazing rate merely because the farmer replaced the cattleman and the old time range has been cut up into farms. The immigration to the Northwest is now on, and the settlement of the millions of acres of plow land in Glendive's tributary territory will all rebound to the upbuilding of this, the Gateway to Montana.

The booklet then goes on to explain more specifically the Glendive Land Company's plans for Riverview Park with:

How Riverview Park Is Platted

Riverview Park consists of about 600 lots or propositions; lots varying in size; none of them being smaller than 40 x 142 feet and the largest about three acres. All streets are 60 feet in width and alleys 16 feet in width. Water mains, concrete walks, shade trees and electric light service. Five corner lots 50 x 142 feet, in which are five beautiful houses built; worth from $1,500.00 to $4,000.00 each.

Description and photographs of same will be found in this book. There are also 135 corner lots, size 50 x 142 feet which are more valuable than inside lots. The price for each and every lot without regard to size the $4,000.00 house and lot and the other four houses and lots is the same, $120.00, $10.00 down and $10.00 each month until you pay $120.00. No interest on deferred payments. No city or county tax for one year. Eight per cent discount if you prefer paying cash.

IF YOU WANT

> *Large profits - Quick returns*
> *Easy money - invest at least part*
> *of your money in Riverview Park.*

MONEY TALKS -

> *But usually says*

GOOD-BYE

> *Pretty Homes,   Large Tracts, Corner Lots*
> *Inside Lots, with Improvements, All for $120.00*
> *$10.00 down and $10.00 a month.*

The first house pictured is the one now owned by Matt Duffner. Its original owner purchased it for $120.00, according to the development plan. Each purchaser 'Drew' for his lot but was assured

IT IS NO LOTTERY OR NO GAMBLE

You are sure of receiving your full money's worth; because the least you can get is a lot 40 x 142 feet. If you are lucky you may be one of the five who find a house on their lot or you may get a tract which is larger than the average lot, or one of the corner lots which are more valuable than the inside lots.

DON'T DELAY - ACT TODAY

Mrs. Grulke's brother, Robert Ullman, was one of the purchasers of a Riverview Park lot. He had homesteaded near Fairview where he had broken the sod with a team of oxen. However, as he anticipated the need for schools for his children, he decided it would be wise to move to Glendive so he accepted the Glendive Land Company's offer. He didn't get one of the lots with a house on it, but he built and lived there until his death in 1956.

Mr. Grulke took an early interest in cars and was one of the first in town to get one in about 1910. Those first cars, of course, had to be cranked by hand so when their little daughter, about five years old, saw a grain binder on her uncle's farm she asked him, "Do you have to crank it?"

Mrs. Grulke well remembers their first trip by automobile to Yellowstone Park. Their party, in three cars (two Fords and Grulke's Chandler), left Glendive at five in the morning and reached Billings about dusk. All the trouble on the way seemed to concentrate on the one Ford. First they had a flat tire; then a broken spring (they weren't traveling on an oiled highway, you know); next they were caught in a rainstorm and this same Ford hit a farmer's cow and broke the radiator hose. The hose was still long enough so they could hook it up and limp on into Billings, but progress was slow. After one of these unplanned stops, when they had traveled some miles down the road, Mrs. Grulke missed her handbag. They stopped the caravan to start an anxious search and were relieved to find it still hanging on the unlucky Ford. Slipping from the fender where she had laid it, it had caught on a nut and was still hanging there.

The Grulkes have three children. Daughter Edna is in Dickinson, Clarence is in Portland teaching school, and Ray (Jeff) works in the post office in Glendive.

Through the years Mrs. Grulke has been active in various clubs, including the Eastern Star, the Women's Benefit Association, and the Women's Club, as well as in the Congregational Church*.

Mr. and Mrs. Grulke celebrated their golden wedding anniversary in 1955. Since Mr. Grulke's passing in 1957, Mrs. Grulke has continued to live in the home on Barry Street they occupied together. With her eightieth birthday a couple years behind her, she still keeps up her yard, with the help of her brother, and does her own housework.

Jacob Stangeland

November 1971

Jacob Stangeland was born in Norway in 1875 (do you realize that was almost 100 years ago?) and came to the United States in 1892 for one simple reason – to make money. He explains (tongue in cheek) that he had heard that money grew on trees and bushes here so he was going to pick some, then go back to the old country. That was seventy-nine years ago. Jacob is still here.

He and his brother made the long ocean voyage together, then continued across a good part of the North American continent to South Dakota where they knew some fellows that had come from Norway earlier. Jacob could speak no English, but there were quite a few Norwegians there so he managed.

His first job in this country was on a farm where he was paid $8 a month, plus room and board. His workday started at 4 a.m. and lasted until 10 or 11 p.m., but he was pleased that he was making good wages. Now he says of those days, "I didn't know any better. Strong back and weak mind!" But it was better than he could make in 'the old country'. After a number of years in South Dakota he began hearing about the good wages paid in Montana so in 1905 he decided to find out for himself and boarded a train for Glendive.

Mr. Stangeland's first impression of Glendive was dismal indeed. He arrived March 1, with a cold wind blowing, dust flying. Viewing the uninspiring scene was enough to start a fellow talking to himself, and the question he was asking was, "Why did I ever come here?" The only reply he could give himself was, "I wish I could get out!" He probably could have, some time or another in the next sixty-six years, but he's still here.

He soon learned that rumors about the wages were true. He began working for Neil Stewart who had a roadhouse near Intake where freighters would stop for the night. His wages were a handsome $40 a month with room and board. His next job was with Pete Evans on Crackerbox. Evans was an early rancher in the Glendive area, running sheep and horses. Later he sold his sheep and went to farming. He bought a big steam engine, and in addition to his own farming he did a lot of breaking sod for others, charging $4 an acre. During spring work Evans had a crew of twenty men working for him. That steamer created a lot of employment! He mined his own coal to fuel the steamer so he needed men to mine it and men to haul it. They piled the coal like a haystack.

The engine was kept going day and night. One man had to steer, one man shoveled coal, and another set the plows. Still another man was needed to haul water for the boiler. Stangeland was the water man. He had a big tank with a pump on the wagon and a long hose to fill the boiler. Sometimes he had only a short distance to haul the water, other times as much as two miles, and the steamer would have to wait for the water to come. Some of the country was rough and hilly, and four horses were needed to pull the wagon.

Then Evans gave him two mules to use on the water wagon. Mr. Stangeland well remembers the first time he approached 'the rig' with those mules. They had never been used in this capacity before and weren't eager to be initiated. When they heard the boiler letting off steam – and that besides the noise of the engine – they quit the country in a hurry, taking the water wagon and Jacob with them. But he managed to bring them under control before they broke anything. Those mules could really pull, and once they became accustomed to the constant 'sshhsshh' of the boiler they got along fine.

Jacob also worked for Pete's brother, Martin, before he went to work on the Lower Yellowstone Irrigation Project. He started working on 'the ditch' in the fall of the year and the ground was already frozen. They used a big, heavy plow to break the sod to start the ditch. Rocks from the big hills nearby were loaded onto wagons by hand and hauled to the dam site for fill. He operated a Fresno*, sometimes driving two horses, other times four.

His next job was working on the railroad tracks being laid between Glendive and Sidney. Again his wages were $40 a month and room and board. But $40 went a long way then. A few dollars bought good work shoes and fifty cents a full meal at the Chinaman's restaurant in Glendive.

In 1909 Stangeland decided to homestead and chose a half section about twenty-six miles southwest of Glendive on Crackerbox Creek. He explained that because he was more than five miles from the railroad he could take a half section*, even in 1909. Practically every homestead section had two families on it; Herigstad filed on the other half of Jacob's section.

Two men signed a note for him so he could borrow $60 from the Exchange State Bank to build a shack on his claim. And $60 bought enough lumber – good lumber – to build a shack. Then he borrowed a team and wagon from Pete Evans, who lived about ten miles from him, to haul the lumber from Glendive. Later he hauled logs from the creek to build a barn, but there was no hurry about that because at first he didn't have anything to put in the barn.

His home site was about ten miles from where Highway 10 is now, but then there was no road. There were no fences, either, so you went where you wanted and made your own road. Handy sometimes, other times not so convenient.

At first he carried his water, a bucket in each hand, from a spring two miles away. Then he hand-dug a well, seventy-five feet deep. He boarded it up with planks so it wouldn't cave in, and drew the water up with a windlass* and bucket. Later he had a well drilled, 105 feet deep, at a dollar per foot. He put a pump and a windmill over this well, making it easier to get water.

His furnishings were sparse when he 'set up housekeeping'. He had a few stools, a rocking chair, and a camp stove from a sheep wagon. He used the camp stove both for cooking and for heating, even during his first winter in the shack. It did a passable job of supplying heat for the cooking, and he got by with it for heating, but he explains that you stood against it and warmed one side, then turned and warmed the other side. Winters around here aren't what they used to be? Maybe our houses and heating systems influence our thinking! He burned cottonwood for fuel. His diet consisted mainly of biscuits and beans, ham and bacon. He couldn't keep potatoes during the winter because they would freeze in his little shack. Later he dug a root cellar, but he found that he didn't dig it deep enough to prevent freezing in the coldest weather so he still couldn't keep potatoes during the winter.

The first spring he was on the homestead Jacob Stangeland had Pete Evans break up twenty-five acres of sod for him, the minimum for proving up* on his claim. He planted flax and laconically observes that he harvested "almost enough to live on." At first he had no team – in fact, not even one horse – so when he went some place he walked. Sometimes he would catch a ride to Glendive with a neighbor. He bought his first team from Oftedal for $300.

His experiences with crops were much the same as that of other pioneers, battling drought, grasshoppers, and hail. One year he was hailed out in the middle of June, but he had insurance and was able to collect a thousand dollars. Then, to his surprise, the wheat grew up again, and he harvested eight bushels to the acres. Another year, however, he was not so fortunate. That year some of the neighbors were working together, and they were scheduled to pull into his field the next morning when a hailstorm struck. The stones were as big as hen's eggs so the once-promising crop was pounded to nothing. There was no time for it to grow up again, and he had no insurance that year.

Prairie fires were always a threat in those early years, what with the tall grass on miles of unplowed prairie. One fire, started by a spark from a steam engine, came too close to his home for comfort. When he saw it coming, he took his sulky plow* and plowed a fire guard around his buildings before he joined the fire fighters, but they were able to put it out before it reached his place.

Fire in summer, snow in winter. One snowstorm was so wild that he couldn't get to his barn to feed the cows for a couple days. The wind drifted the snow faster than he could shovel it so he just had to wait until it calmed down. When he was able to get to the barn, he found snow had drifted inside, too. It doesn't take much of a crack for snow to blow in with that kind of wind driving it. He even had three or four inches of snow on his bed where it blew in through the keyhole in the door to his shack! He had no chimney – just a stovepipe through the roof so that same storm blew snow down the pipe and kept it sizzling in the stove. Snow blew under the shingles too, so when it melted, the plaster ceiling got wet, and the whole ceiling came down.

During one particularly severe summer windstorm in 1928 he took his dog and cat with him and sought refuge in the root cellar. When he emerged, his house was all right, but the wind had folded his windmill wheel.

The first time his cat had kittens a tomcat killed them so the next time she went two miles to a neighbor's place to have them. Then when the kittens were about three weeks old, she carried them home – four of them – making the round trip of four miles for each kitten!

When Mr. Stangeland was seventy-eight years old, he decided it was time to retire and he moved to Glendive. Now, at ninety-six, he lives in the nursing wing of the Glendive Community Hospital. He's still alert, still able to get around. When a fellow gets that close to 100 he should be entitled to a little relaxation, and he appreciates the care he receives at the home.

Andrew E. Anderson

March 1965

When Andrew E. Anderson came to America, sixty-one years ago this Easter (1904), he thought he'd work a year or two (he was fifteen years old when he came) and have so much money he could go back to Norway and buy a sailing ship. It didn't work out that way. Instead of being a master of navigation, he turned out to be master of a dry land ranch. Instead of going back a year or two later, he went back fifty-six years later and then for just three months.

Andy's father had come to the New World earlier, bringing the family to Chicago. With more than twenty-five years experience as sailor and cook before leaving his native land, he soon hired on as first cook with a Great Lakes ship. Andy's first job was second cook on the ship. The Great Lakes were navigable only nine months of the year so when that job closed for the winter, Andy went to work for the Western Electric Company. He was getting along all right, but after a few years one of his cousins, on his way back to Norway for a visit, told about the good wages in Montana. When the cousin returned, Andy left the rest of the family and came to Montana with him.

After reaching Glendive he lay around town for about a month until his money was gone before he found a job. Most of the folks in Glendive at that time kept a cow or horse so one of his 'odd jobs' during that time was unloading a load of hay. His pay? Twenty-five cents. As Mr. Anderson related this incident, he couldn't resist adding, "Imagine a young fellow now unloading a load of hay for twenty-five cents!" But his pay was enough to buy a meal.

He found out what the good wages were when he started working for the railroad on a section gang, laying track fifteen miles west of Glendive. He worked ten hours a day, and after his room and board were deducted he had ninety-six cents a day left. Nine months of that was enough. He quit the railroad and went to the country to work.

For the next couple years he herded sheep for Eivend Kalberg on Morgan Creek, then two years for Adolphus Kent on Seven Mile, and finally, before he moved onto his own homestead, he herded two years for Rollef Undem on Clear Creek. He had homesteaded in 1910 but had continued to work out. While he worked for Kent he herded the sheep on his own land, just a few miles down Seven Mile Creek from the Kent ranch. In this way he could make improvements and build up his homestead while working out.

During the time he worked for Undem he became acquainted with Mrs. Undem's sister who had come from Norway in 1909 to visit. She had stayed, doing housework in Glendive, but after five years in this country she took on a permanent housekeeping job which to date has lasted almost fifty-one years. She married Andrew E. Anderson in the fall of 1914. Last November fifth they celebrated their golden wedding anniversary. An open house in their honor at the Zion Lutheran Church was attended by more than two hundred people.

They even received a telegram of congratulations from Norway where Mrs. Anderson's sister still lives.

When Mr. Anderson filed on his homestead, some of the homesteaders farther north warned him he wouldn't last two years there, but he outlasted most of his 'warners'. His homestead included the spot where the early settlers farther from town, as they made their slow trips to Glendive, would stop to feed and water their horses. The hills were dry, but the creek had water in it the year round, something unusual in that part of the country. One of his brothers, who also came to Montana and filed on the half section north of Andrew's, contracted the dread flu of 1918 and died before he had proved up*. Their father, then, was entitled to prove it, but he was down in Florida and didn't want the land so Andrew was permitted to prove up that half section also.

Many of the homesteaders, especially at first, went in for farming, but Mr. Anderson majored in stock – sheep and cattle. Perhaps that was the secret of his success when others failed. Most of their years on the homestead were without the convenience of electricity or telephone. Their well, eighteen feet deep with seven feet of water was, according to Mr. Anderson, their 'deep freeze, refrigerator, and all'. They lowered things into the well in a bucket by means of a windlass and found that the water did a good job keeping things cold. In later years they built an ice house and put up ice to use during the warm months. When the first Rural Electrification Association line came through the area, it stopped several miles up the creek from Andersons so they made several trips to Circle, R.E.A. headquarters, to get the line extended to serve them and two other families. They were finally successful in getting the electricity. The telephone was also added to the list of their conveniences several years before they sold the ranch.

Naturalization laws, at the time the Andersons came, permitted the minor who entered the United States to automatically become a citizen at age twenty-one. Thus Mr. Anderson became a citizen and because Mrs. Anderson married a citizen, she too, was accredited with citizenship without the process of naturalization.

In retrospect Mr. Anderson reflected that their years on the ranch included good ones and bad ones. The Andersons, along with many 'old timers', recalled that day in 1910 when smoke from forest fires completely obscured the light of day. That next winter brought extreme cold, with the temperature dropping to sixty-three degrees below zero.

His area was generously populated with rattlesnakes when he took up his abode there. One summer as they were putting up hay, he threw a forkful of hay onto the hayrack, and a rattler dropped out of it, falling back onto his shoulder and sliding to the ground. Evidently the snake also found the experience disconcerting and didn't have time to collect his wits – or his striking powers – because Mr. Anderson escaped unharmed. There was a den of the rattlers on his ranch, but each spring and fall when the snakes were bunched up around their den, Mr. Anderson would kill as many as he could so they are getting scarce. Coyotes gave him more trouble than the rattlesnakes did. Someone had to be with the sheep all the time because if they were left alone for even an hour, one or two would be missing.

The dust storms of the thirties were like nothing he had ever before experienced. Mr. Anderson recalled that when the first big storm hit, it was toward evening, and he was trying to get his sheep into the corral which he had near Joe Hajek's place. Before he could get them into the shelter, the dust rolled down upon them like a huge wave. He threw himself flat on the ground and held onto the sagebrush, but the wind was so strong that lambs rolled past him like tumbleweeds until they hit the coulee.

Mr. and Mrs. Anderson visited Norway in 1960 and again in 1964, staying three months each time. In the fifty-six years of his absence it seemed to him things had changed one hundred percent. Most of his relatives were gone – they were able to find only one niece of his family – but Mrs. Anderson has many relatives still living there.

In June of 1963 the Andersons sold the ranch and moved into Glendive. Mr. Anderson says it's too easy for him, but Mrs. Anderson says they like it just fine.

Mrs. Henry (Mary Barber) Wienke

July 1969

Mrs. Mary Wienke, then Mary Barber, came to Montana as a girl of seventeen with her mother and younger sister. Thinking back, she had to do a little figuring to decide just what year she came to the Treasure State, then came up with the conclusion it had to be in 1907. She's five-and-one-half years older than her sister Viola, and Viola was twelve – that she remembered for sure. They came in June and Viola had had her twelfth birthday on May 1.

Then, as now, children under twelve were allowed to travel for half-fare on the railroad. If they had only come about six weeks sooner.... They hadn't, but it was so close that Mrs. Barber bought a half-fare ticket for Viola anyway, and no questions were asked – none, that is, until they were halfway to Montana. Then a different conductor took over.

As he came through their car checking tickets he sized up Viola, then asked Mrs. Barber how old the girl was. That six weeks.... The mother truthfully acknowledged that the twelfth birthday had been passed, just the month before. Seemed as though six weeks shouldn't have made that much difference, but the conductor made her 'dig up' the other half fare.

The Barbers came to Montana from Bloomfield, Nebraska. Charlie Barber, one of the older sons, had come earlier and homesteaded. He kept writing to the 'folks back home' telling them how good it was until finally the widowed mother decided to come, too.

Homesteading was nothing new to Mrs. Barber. She and her husband, in their young days, had moved from New York to Nebraska where he had filed on a homestead. They had helped build up that Midwest state, along with the other pioneers who had moved 'West'. Now Nebraska was well settled and the frontier had been pushed many miles farther west.

She had no idea of pioneering all over again, even when Charlie was seized with homestead fever and moved west. She just didn't think she wanted to go through all that again; at twenty it was all right, but at fifty-eight it was a different story. But in spite of her age, Charlie's urging finally prevailed. She decided, with her youngest son, Levi, and her two youngest daughters (out of twelve children) to try it once more.

They loaded their belongings into an immigrant car*, and Levi went with it. Destination: a new home in Montana. The women folk followed by passenger train. Mrs. Barber and the girls stopped off for awhile in Sioux, Iowa to visit with one of the older sons so they arrived a couple weeks after Levi and the immigrant car.

When their train pulled into Glendive that June afternoon, three very hot, very tired, very dusty passengers descended from it. They expected to stay overnight in town, but Charlie was there to meet them and persuaded them they should go on out right away. It would be so hot in Glendive, he pointed out to them, that it would be better to head right on out to the homestead.

His homestead was located about four miles west of where Bloomfield is now. Not much of a drive, is it? Thirty miles of oiled highway, four of gravel – for today's cars, there's nothing to it. But for the Barbers in 1907 it was a different story.

There was a good wagon trail – by 'good' we mean clearly discernible through the tall grass – to follow, but traveling with the team and buggy took a good part of the night to cover the intervening miles. It was true that the night in town would have been hot. It was also true that driving out under the burning sun next day would have been hot. But to the bone-weary travelers, jolting along in the buggy, the night ride seemed endless. Day was just beginning to break as they pulled up to the little shack out in the middle of nowhere.

Charlie's home on the homestead was a tiny little shack – probably not more than 10'x12'. Mrs. Wienke doesn't remember the measurements exactly but she remembers that, even with the meager furnishings it contained, there wasn't much room in it for five people. Next day – or rather, that day – she and her sister Vi wanted to take a nap so they lay down outside the shack to rest up. They slept soundly and woke up with a grand case of sunburn.

Those first two or three weeks in Montana, Mary was dreadfully homesick and wondered how she would ever stand it here. Soon, however, they began getting acquainted and started going places, and the homesickness wore off.

Mrs. Mary Wienke's brother, Levi, and her mother, Mrs. Barber, each filed on a homestead when they came to Montana in 1907. (Mary was too young to file.) The homesteaders filed on adjoining quarters* close to the top of the Yellowstone-Redwater Divide.

Since there were two claims there had to be two houses so they built just across the line from each other. They had stayed with Charlie when they first came, then pitched a tent and moved onto their claim. They had a time keeping the tent from blowing away but lived in it until they had time to make kind of a dugout in the bank, where they lived most of the summer. Before winter they had a house built farther on up the hill.

Until they could get around to digging a 'proper' well they substituted with a hole in the coulee. They found that if they'd dig a hole with the posthole digger and wait awhile water would run in. Mrs. Wienke remarked that she doesn't know where the water came from – just seepage, maybe, but it tasted good and nobody got sick from it.

Mrs. Wienke was born Mary Barber in an old log house eighteen miles north of Bloomfield, Nebraska, in a community known as the Devil's Nest. Where the community got its name isn't clear, but since it was along the Missouri River perhaps rough breaks gave it its name. There might have been other reasons, but we'll give it the benefit of the doubt until somebody tells us otherwise.

From a hill on the Barber farm they could see, not only the river, but across it the state of South Dakota. The house in which Mrs. Wienke was born was built from trees that her parents themselves had cut when they migrated to Nebraska from New York.

The family moved into Bloomfield, Nebraska (from which Bloomfield, Montana got its name) when Mary was eleven years old. Her father passed away when she was just a girl. In the years that followed most of the older children had married and set up homes of their own so only the three youngest of her twelve children were living with Mrs. Barber when she made the momentous decision to join another son Charlie in his homesteading venture.

When Richey earned for itself a place on the map it was twelve miles north and a little west of where the Barbers homesteaded. For fuel in those early days on the homestead, Levi (Mary's brother) cut wood in the divide and mined their coal from one of the many veins that lay close to the surface in eastern Montana.

Mrs. Wienke, when she was still Mary Barber, worked one summer at the Chet Murphy Ranch. The Murphy Ranch was one of the larger horse ranches in Dawson County – and Dawson County in 1910 was quite an extensive piece of territory. The Missouri River was its northern boundary and the North Dakota line was its eastern border.

Although she was ranch house cook, she cooked for the cowboys, too; they all ate in the ranch house. But she didn't cook frog legs. Frog legs may be considered a delicacy by some people, but that isn't the way they're listed in Mrs. Mary Wienke's book. She laughed to recall the time a bunch of the cowboys tried to persuade her to join them in a 'banquet' of frog legs. She had seen them in the afternoon, after a heavy rain, catching the frogs and making their preparations. When the feast was ready, a delegation came to the house to invite her to eat with them, but the menu just didn't appeal to her. She was game for a lot of new things, but not frog legs. She firmly declined the honor and continued with her supper preparations in the house.

She worked on the ranch during roundup time and never knew how many would show up at the table, particularly in the evening. At noon probably only Mr. and Mrs. Murphy and a few men who weren't riding would be at the table, but in the evening all the Murphy cowboys and a bunch more might show up.

The ranch house had a large kitchen and a big dining hall next to it with a long table. Everyone, from Mr. and Mrs. Murphy to the last cow hand, ate at this table. They had a large bunkhouse where the men slept. Mary had her own private bunkhouse, a guest house a short distance from the ranch house.

To the girl from Nebraska the Murphy Ranch, with its big corrals and big barns, was an impressive place. She enjoyed working at the ranch – the Murphys were really nice people – but toward the end of the summer her mother became ill so her brother came to get her so she could help at home.

About three miles north of the Barber homesteads another young Nebraskan homesteaded. Henry Wienke had come with his parents when a 'whole slug' had come from Bloomfield, Nebraska. Mary had known him casually in their native state, but she got to know him much better when they became neighbors in Montana. They were married in 1911.

Those early settlers were accustomed to going miles on horseback or with a team and buggy for picnics, parties, dances or any kind of get-together. Mrs. Wienke recalled one time when she and Henry were going together, they had gone to a picnic over on Deer Creek. They had started home in their topless buggy when they noticed "the awfulest clouds coming up" – black clouds with shades of green and white, rolling and churning in the sky. From the looks of the clouds the young couple expected hail with the storm, and there they were, miles from everywhere with no shelter in sight.

As Henry put the team to a gallop to try to get some place (they weren't quite sure where) before the storm broke, he told her, "If you see any place to get into we'll dash for it." The storm was almost upon them when they did see a place. No one was living there, but there was an open shed or barn and a little shack. They drove 'pell mell' to the shed and right on into it with the team and buggy, then made a dash for the shack as the storm broke. The wind blew so hard they thought the shack would blow over, but it remained intact while they sat and waited for the rain to stop. When the storm finally blew itself out there was mud and water everywhere, but at least it was under them and not soaking them.

Even though the pioneers went long distances horseback or with team and buggy when they did decide to go to some gathering, they didn't run around much. They mainly amused themselves at home, and that without benefit of radio or television. They always seemed to find something to do, Mrs. Wienke reflected.

Of course, with kerosene lights there wasn't much temptation to stay up later than necessary in the evening. On the homestead they depended upon kerosene lights entirely. Not until after Mary and Henry had been married several years and had moved into Richey did they have a gas lantern. The gas lantern gave a wonderful light compared to the regular kerosene lamp, and they used that until electricity came to Richey, bringing electric lights.

Mary and Henry were married in Glendive in October 1911. They didn't think about it until afterwards, but they picked Halloween for their wedding day. Her sister, Viola, and his brother, Art, were their attendants.

They traveled to Glendive by team and buggy, of course, and as they started away from Henry's folks that morning it was 'snowing to beat the band', but the weather was not cold. As they started to drive away, Henry's mother came running out with an umbrella for Vi and Art (how about the bride and groom!) so they all had a lot of fun over the snow and umbrella.

When they reached Glendive they had quite a time finding a minister to marry them. Mary had attended the Congregational Church* so they expected to have the Congregational minister marry them, but he was out of town. They hardly knew what to do then, but after some hunting around they finally found the Scandinavian Lutheran minister who performed the ceremony for them.

Henry, who had been living in an 8'x16' shack on his homestead, intended to build a new house for his bride. He got the lumber hauled out all right, but then the weather turned cold so they couldn't start. With that cold spell winter was there for the season so building had to wait until spring. When spring came, the crop had to have priority so they didn't get their new house built until well into the summer.

They started out as farmers, but the next five or six years they dried out so much that they decided to move into Richey, which by that time had grown into quite a little town. It even boasted a railroad (they had made a point of being in town for rail day, the day the railroad reached Richey), and Henry went to work for the Great Northern.

He started out on the section gang, then was promoted to machinist. In 1949 he was transferred to Glasgow, then to Helena. He was stationed in Havre when he retired. After his retirement they moved to the Flathead country where they lived for three-and-a-half years before he passed away in 1960.

Mrs. Wienke came back to Richey for awhile, then moved to California where two of her sons live. The Wienkes had six children, five boys and one girl, but the oldest died in infancy. Besides the two sons in California, she has a son in Wolf Point and another in the home town of Richey. Her only daughter, Mrs. Robert Eggebrecht, also lives in Richey.

Although her home is now in California, just out of Los Angeles, she generally spends her summers in Montana. This year she came a little earlier than usual so she could be here in time for the wedding of one of her granddaughters. This year, also, four new great grandchildren (including the twins born to Mr. and Mrs. Dick Raisl last Christmas) awaited her first inspection.

Mrs. Wienke's arrival in 1907 as a seventeen-year-old might seem to 'date' her but don't expect to meet an old woman. She modestly suggested in response to a comment that if she doesn't look her seventy-eight years, perhaps it's because she has never had a serious illness, but it could be that her wonderful sense of humor and her generally cheerful outlook on life have helped to keep her young.

Frank Hasty

May 1968

Either side you start from, Frank Hasty's forebears acquainted themselves with Glendive when there wasn't much of Glendive with which to get acquainted. His mother came in 1881, his father seventeen years later – still in the nineteenth century.

His mother was only eight years old when she arrived here. Her father, Sherman M. Rigby, had reached eastern Montana (then still a territory) the same year the Northern Pacific Railroad did, with the railroad just enough earlier so that he could use its facilities to get here.

When Grandfather Rigby arrived, there were no houses to rent or buy for the simple reason there were almost no houses. A carpenter by trade, he promptly set about remedying that situation and soon had a house ready for his family. This house at 411 Hughes is now the Roy McDonough home.

Hughes Street was 'way out' when Rigby built there, and there were no other houses nearby. Much of Glendive was still up on the airport flat (current site of the fairgrounds) where the town had been started. When the Northern Pacific Depot was built the town moved down to the depot.

Eight-year-old Edith (Frank's mother) was afraid to sleep in her little lean-to bedroom at the back of the house because she could hear too clearly the howling of the coyotes. Grandfather Rigby described to his grandchildren the buffalo slaughter on the plains. Even when he came there were remains of many buffalo on Sawyers Island. They had been killed for their hides and the carcasses left to decay.

Frank's father, also named Frank Hasty, came to Montana in 1898 from Minneapolis, although he was originally from Maine. He and his brother Fred were headed for Alaska and the gold rush, but they only made it to Glendive. Frank and Fred were the only members of the family with sights set on Alaska, but their entire family moved to Montana. In Minneapolis they had become acquainted with an Englishman who had started a sheep and cattle ranch on Cabin Creek and he prevailed upon them to come out and work on this ranch.

Later on the rest of the family moved to Baker and Frank (Sr.) came to Glendive. The Hastys were among the very first settlers in Baker. Fred and Frank ran a freight line between Baker and Terry before the Milwaukee brought rail service to the former.

When Frank, Sr. settled in Glendive he, too, did carpenter work. He always had a team of horses, and when carpenter work was slack, he'd haul gravel – coal – anything that needed hauling. He came to Glendive early in 1898, and in the fall of that same year he married Edith Rigby. When they were first married, they lived on the ranch on Cabin Creek. Three years later they moved to Glendive and occupied the house her father had built at 411 Hughes Street. That is where they were living when their two boys were born, and that is where they were living when the boys, Frank and Jack, started to school.

They kept Frank out of school until Jack was ready to start, then sent them both together. They went to the Lincoln School the first three grades. When they started to school the first grade was held in a frame building beside the present school, while classes for grades two through six were held in the old part of the present Lincoln School building.

About the time the boys completed the third grade, Hastys homesteaded out on 'Poverty Flats', the site currently planned for the new airport. At first there was no school at all on Poverty Flats, then a three-month term was held in a little shack. They used the little shack for two years before there was money enough in the district to build a schoolhouse. Although there were probably a dozen families on the flat by then, only one other family had school children. Three Larimer girls and the two Hasty boys made up the school census.

Before the influx of homesteaders the flat had been sheep territory, and shearing pens were located on the south side of Hasty's claim. With the homesteaders taking over the grazing lands, the sheep had to be moved elsewhere, and the shearing pens were abandoned. The pens were last used the spring that Hasty filed on his claim. He freighted the wool from the pens to Glendive, and in return for his labor he was given the pens. Hasty used the lumber from which they were constructed to build their new house on the homestead.

The house which Frank Hasty's father built out of sheep shearing pens on their Poverty Flats homestead has a varied history. After serving as home for the Hasty family and as a roadhouse for freighters on the homestead, it was sold and moved to West Glendive where Fred Voorhies lived in it.

Later Jake Holzworth moved it to another location in West Glendive, back of the Derrick Cafe. While the Ralph Kalloch family lived in it they had a fire which damaged but did not destroy the house. At that time they found in the wall some newspapers bearing the name of Frank Hasty so there is no question about where the house came from. Still standing back of the Derrick Cafe, the house now provides a home for the manager of the cafe.

Since the Hasty homestead was conveniently located on the Paxton-Glendive road, they decided to offer roadhouse facilities where freight haulers could sleep and get their meals. They were just far enough from town that freighters stopping for the night could easily get into Glendive the next day, take care of their business, and get back to Hasty's for the next night, putting them well on their homeward way.

They equipped the big bunkhouse (the first building constructed on the homestead and used by the family until the house was ready) with double bunks and it could accommodate as many as twelve men. The big barn, built into the bank below the house, offered plenty of room for the teams, and Mrs. Hasty was a proficient cook so the Hasty Roadhouse was a busy place during freighting season. Freight haulers at times would make reservations to assure accommodations at the roadhouse just as motorists do now for motels.

They lived on the homestead until 1926. Mr. Hasty recalls that in their early years on Poverty Flats rattlesnakes contested their rights to the land. The boys didn't carve notches on their guns, but in the spring they would start tucking snake rattles into their hat bands each time they killed a rattler and see how many they could collect by fall. They were careful, especially those first years on the flat, to use a fork when shocking grain rather than handling the bundles by hand because each bundle was a potential hideout for a rattlesnake.

Mr. Hasty well remembers when automobiles began coming into popular use. He especially remembers the time Amos Beatty drove his new car out to the Hasty farm to help with the threshing. He got along fine driving out, but when he reached the separator (threshing machine), he couldn't remember how to stop his new machine so he drove 'round and 'round the rig, hollering for someone to stop him.

Electrical storms are nothing new in this country, and during a severe one while the Hastys lived on the homestead lightning struck the chimney of their house. It followed the nails in the rafters and showered everything with splinters. Mr. Hasty especially remembers how the freshly sliced tomatoes on the table looked. Everyone was knocked down, and Grandmother Hasty (the grandparents were living with them at the time) was knocked unconscious, causing them some concern before she revived. She and Grandfather were both near the chimney, and after the excitement calmed down Grandfather (a tall man) philosophically observed, "Good thing I wasn't standing up; would have scorched my hair!"

Frank's father was an early truck owner and hauled coal many years for Glendive residents, doing other kinds of freight work as well. After they moved to Glendive in 1926 he continued his freight work and also took care of the Glendive Golf Course. He passed away in 1940 at the age of sixty-nine. Frank's mother, Edith Rigby Hasty, lived another seventeen years to the age of eighty-seven. Frank settled down in Glendive, where he worked for Montana-Dakota Utilities Company, while Jack, his younger brother, went into the filling station business in Livingston.

Frank's first wife passed away, and in 1948 he married Hazel Winkler Keenast, whose first husband had been killed in an airplane accident. December 1, 1967 he retired after forty years of service with MDU*, but he and his wife continue to live in Glendive.

Mr. Hasty has seen a lot of changes come to Glendive, but perhaps the change that impressed him the most was when the cinder paths and wooden sidewalks were taken out and replaced with cement walks. The period of growth that has seemed most outstanding to him has been that since World War II. Working as he was, in the power plant for MDU, he was in a unique position to notice the expansion as power demands increased.

Mrs. Frank (Hazel Winkler) Hasty

May – June 1968

Back in the Twin Cities the Winklers heard all about the wild cowboys in Montana so when they homesteaded near Circle they knew just what to expect. The first time a bunch of cowboys rode up to their house (it would be when the man of the house was gone) Mrs. Winkler and her three girls were just scared to death (almost).

In 1909 Frank J. Winkler closed up his Singer Sewing Machine business (he sold Edison phonographs, too) in St. Paul and headed for Montana. He had heard about the free land available in the eastern part of the state so he, along with a number of others from the cities who also had heard about the free land, hurried West to make his fortune.

He came in the fall and made preparations for his family to join him in the spring, building a little shack, digging a well (why were wells always located down hill from the house so you carried the empty bucket down and the full bucket up the hill?), and getting things in general arranged to accommodate a family.

When the family arrived in Glendive in the spring, Mr. Winkler had made arrangements with Fred Golding, the land promoter who had located him on his claim, to bring them to the homestead in his big touring car. (Not too many cars were available in 1910 to haul people around.)

What a sight that little shack was to greet a mother with her three young girls, fresh from the 'civilization' of the city, when Mr. Golding deposited them at the doorstep! She was expecting the worst, but hardly this bad!

As they huddled beside the unprepossessing little shack, Mrs. Winkler wailed, "What will we do if we get sick, way out here, sixty miles from a doctor?" (It probably seemed more like a hundred miles to her just then.) In St. Paul the girls had always caught everything that went around, but as it turned out, they didn't get sick all the time they were on the homestead.

In spite of the bleak introduction, the days on the homestead were happy ones. They hadn't been there long when they had their first encounter with cowboys, an encounter that reeducated them. They (the cowboys) had been rounding up horses and were holding them with a rope corral on the flat near the Winkler shack. When Mrs. Winkler saw several of them approaching the house, she was terrified and quickly herded her girls behind her. She had no idea what they wanted, but from what she had heard back in the cities they would probably shoot her and her girls down in cold blood.

It was a great relief to find that she couldn't have been more wrong. They turned out to be the nicest fellows you could want to meet, and their intentions were no more violent than to explain that they would like to camp for the night on the flat where they were holding the horses. In succeeding roundups Hazel was even permitted to ride with them as they searched for the horses.

There was a good watering place on the Winkler land so not only the cattlemen and horsemen liked to camp there but the sheepmen, as well. When they camped there, they would often invite the homestead family down for meals, and many a 'late' lamb was given to the girls to raise.

Since the Winklers' house was so small, they built a 'summer' house as a supplement. Actually the summer house was just a platform with a tent over it; the platform helped to discourage snakes, and the tent helped to discourage the rain soaking them. They halfway lived in the platform house during the summer.

There was always plenty of work on the homestead, including chores for the girls, but Hazel enjoyed the outside work. Usually, that is. But there were times.... like the time the cow ran away with her. They had staked a cow with a newborn calf near the house, and at milking time Hazel would lead her down to the barn.

She remembers that her father had strictly warned her not to tie the rope around her waist (so she figures she must have tried it before), but on this particular evening she untied the rope from the stake – and tied it around her waist.

Just about the time she got the rope fastened, the dog started to bark, and away went the cow. Desperately she tried to get the rope untied, then, failing that, she tried to slip it down over her feet, but she couldn't manage that either so all she could do was bounce along through the cactus behind the runaway cow. And she wasn't bouncing on her feet, either. For a month after that she had to use a pillow every time she rode horseback.

They farmed only half-a-section, but that was enough to provide Hazel opportunity to help with the field work. They farmed with live horse power (four work horses and one saddle horse), and Mrs. Hasty especially remembers riding a two-wheeled cart behind the harrow up and down the field.

At threshing time all the neighbors came and helped, then when the threshing was completed at one farm, they'd all move on to the next, following the threshing rig. There were plenty of errands to run and chores to do when 'Mom' was cooking for threshers!

Battling a prairie fire that swept across the northwest corner of their section was the most frightening experience of their homestead tenure. They figured it must have started from the sun shining on a tin can because they couldn't account for it in any other way. When they saw the fire, Mr. Winkler tried to get far enough ahead of it to plow a furrow while others attacked the flames directly with wet sacks. All the neighbors within sight of the fire ('all' wasn't very many) came to help, and, although the fire burned across their stubble field, they were able to control it before it reached any buildings.

The fire was the most frightening experience, but rattlesnakes always managed to scare her plenty, too. Scared though she was of snakes, she always killed them if she had a chance. Whenever she killed one, she would hang the remains over the edge of the hayrack so she could show her dad (who knew she was deathly afraid of them) that she had killed one.

But she doesn't remember whether she got to the hayrack with the one they killed in the kitchen. Someone had left the door open, and the next thing they knew, there was a rattler in the culinary department. Mother grabbed the broom and Hazel ran for the rake to get it out to where they could kill it. Another time a snake crawled down its hole before they could stop it so Hazel went after it with a shotgun, but she almost shot off her mother's toe before they got the snake. No excitement on the farm?

During the four years they lived on the homestead the girls attended a little country school – the Winkler School, seven miles northwest of Circle. They used a stoneboat* for transportation, setting off each morning with lunch buckets for the girls and a bale of hay for their horse.

There wasn't much going for recreation on the farm, but then there wasn't much time for recreation. Yet Mrs. Hasty looks back on those days as some of the happiest of her life.

The one saddle horse on the Winkler homestead was a great 'pal' as well as a great help. Hazel loved those outdoor days with the horse as her companion. That was much better than riding a broomstick horse!

They had a pet steer that they played with a good deal, and sometimes they rode even him – around the barnyard, that is; they couldn't ride him for any practical purposes. They had a lot of fun with him, though.

Coyote hunting might seem to be strange recreation for a girl. There were plenty of coyotes to hunt in those days when their natural habitat had not yet been invaded to any great extent by man. While the ranchers and farmers did hunt the coyotes with rifles on occasion, their main thrust was to locate the dens and dig them out.

Mrs. Hasty recalls the great thrill they all felt when her father came driving home in their first car. They had, of course, ridden in cars before, but to have a new one all their own was something entirely different. Probably there are few owners of '68 models whose pride and elation could match Mr. Winkler's in his new Cadillac touring car. He even had a new cap duster, and gauntlet gloves, and topcoat to do justice to the occasion.

Hazel soon learned to drive the new car, too, and was sometimes sent on errands with it. Although their community was rather remote, a minister from Circle held Gospel meetings in the schoolhouse from time to time. Since Winklers had a car they were glad to go to Circle to pick him up, and since Hazel could drive, she was glad to be the one to go.

One Sunday when she had brought him out he was invited to their house for dinner so after the service Hazel started for home with the minister. Even the roads were only trails so instead of bothering with the trail, she just cut across the pasture, wasting no time. She was accustomed to the bouncing over the rough places, but the minister wasn't and as they careened across the prairie he clung for dear life to the sides of the car and finally begged, "Hazel, Hazel, slow up!" Mrs. Hasty would probably view a similar ride now much as the minister did then.

The new car did not eliminate the long trips to Glendive which had to be made with team and wagon. The car was fine for hauling groceries and smaller supplies, but freighting still required two days to go to town and two days to return. Mr. Winkler found the Hasty Road House on Poverty Flats a convenient place to stay overnight when he had to make those long trips. He became acquainted with Frank Hasty long before his daughter did!

One of the homesteaders, Jim Bowers, had a huge house, and the people of the neighborhood sometimes gathered there for dances. They didn't get baby sitters then to stay with the children while the parents went to the dance. Instead they fixed a lunch, loaded up the whole family, and then spent the whole night dancing. Children played with other children until they were tired, then found a place to curl up and go to sleep.

Mrs. Winkler's brother had also moved to the Circle country, and one evening when there was nothing going on at Bowers he decided to go to a dance about twelve miles away. He persuaded his sister to go along with him, and Hazel, too, was permitted to go. They started out with horse and sleigh, but about three-quarters of the way there the horse took sick so they had to get out and walk and lead the horse. It was midnight before they got to the party.

In 1914 Frank J. Winkler started a garage in Circle so they moved into town. Mrs. Hasty's earliest recollections of Circle include a rooming house, livery stable, Joe Rorvik's store, a drug store, and a mercantile store – and Ben Larson right along in there some place. By the time they moved in, a movie house had been added and other businesses and dwellings besides.

Winkler's town house was a pleasant contrast to the little shack they had lived in on the homestead. It was a two-bedroom structure and one of the first homes in Circle to have Delco lights* – a real luxury.

Mr. Winkler had the agency for Ford so, of course, it was only fitting that he drive a Ford himself. Mrs. Hasty recalls that she was sure they could never all fit in the Ford (Mr. and Mrs. Winkler and the three girls) after the Cadillac touring car to which they had become accustomed, but she found that they could.

She remembers, too, a pickup that her father had in the garage which he refused to let her drive. One day when he was gone and Joe McCan was in charge of the shop, she coaxed him to let her drive it until he jestingly told her, "If you can crawl through that hole," (the little half moon in the glass of the cashier's window) "I'll let you take the pickup."

He thought he was playing it safe, but he underestimated (over-estimated) Hazel. Somehow she wriggled through the hole so he felt he had to keep his word. She exultingly drove the pickup and got back to the garage just fine, but then as she attempted to drive in she hit the garage door!

About a year after he started the Circle garage Frank Winkler extended his operations to Glendive but retained his Circle interests and continued to live in Circle at first. However, when the girls were ready to start high school, about a year later, they moved into Glendive for the school term (they lived in the old Aiken house on Douglas Street), then the next fall moved in on a permanent basis.

When Winkler started his Ford garage in Glendive his quarters were across the street from the city hall in the building now occupied by the Greyhound bus depot*. A few years later a contractor by the name of C.S. Johnson built new quarters for him on the corner of Towne and Kendrick – the building which now houses the Farm and Home Furniture store. His grand opening there was really grand with the nationally famous Sousa's band performing.

Ed Garfield worked for Winkler in the garage, and one day in an idle moment sat down on a crate of batteries that had just come in. He then went on about his work until noon when he put on his coat and started home. It was winter and cold outside, and he was no more than out the door when he turned to hurry back inside, wondering what had happened to him. He wasn't long in finding out that the whole seat of his trousers had dropped qut, eaten away by the battery acid.

A young fellow by the name of Frank Hasty palled around with some of the mechanics that worked at the garage, and occasionally they'd go hunting together for ducks or chickens. Winkler himself sometimes went along with them, and they used to kid him about his nose.

He was left-handed, but all the guns were for right-handers so when the shell ejected, he had to dodge or it would have come back at his nose. So they'd tell him, "If you didn't have such a big nose you'd get more game." Little did Frank realize then that he would some day marry Winkler's daughter.

When Mr. Winkler was ready to retire he sold the garage to a Smith, but Smith only had it about six months when he became ill. Jack Reid, Winkler's son-in-law, then bought it. While Reid had the garage he moved it to the corner of Towne and Merrill where Kampschror's Radio and TV is now. Later Reid sold the garage to Urbanec who moved it to its present West Glendive location.

After he sold the garage Jack and Myrtle (Mrs. Hasty's sister) moved to Big Fork, Montana where they still live. The youngest Winkler girl, Frances, was killed in a car accident in Oregon in 1937. Mr. Winkler had passed away in 1934, but Mrs. Winkler lived until 1960.

In 1921 Hazel married Clarence Keenast and they moved to St. Paul, but they had moved back to Miles City when he was killed in an airplane accident in 1945. In 1948 she married Frank Hasty. They are now retired, the girl from the homestead and the boy from the roadhouse, and live in Glendive.

Walton Baker

May 1965

TV programs may give the impression that about all cowboys had to do was endlessly gallop their horses and shoot Indians or each other, but Walton Baker knows that the life of a cowboy often involved long hours and hard work, especially during roundup times. Since 1922, Baker has lived in Glendive and worked for the Northern Pacific Railroad in the car department, but previous to that date railroads were a foreign element in his life, and horses were his specialty.

He was born in Canada to parents recently immigrated from England. The Baker family in England had had considerable means but both parents died while Walton's father was still a minor so the estate was left in the care of guardians. By the time he reached the legal age when he could assume control of his property, he found that there wasn't much of it left. Consequently, a few years after he married, he and his wife with their two children decided to emigrate to Canada. They settled near Winnipeg, Manitoba, but found it hard to make a living midst the unfriendly elements. The growing season was so short that the wheat varieties then used would often freeze before harvest. Winters were long and the snow deep so the Bakers decided to move again, this time to Montana.

Mr. Baker came ahead of the family and settled on the Tongue River south of Miles City in 1890. There he engaged in ranching and prepared for his family to join him. During this time, for some ready cash, he also cooked for a big horse ranch, Brown and Scott.

Mr. and Mrs. Baker both were college-educated. It's a little beyond Walton yet to figure out why they would choose to settle in primitive ranch country rather than some place where they could use that education to greater advantage. But they chose the ranch country, and that's why Walton Baker grew up in the saddle, so to speak.

Walton's mother was an accomplished pianist, as was his father. His father also played the violin and was much in demand for providing the music at the community dances. He used to tuck his violin under his arm and ride twenty miles horseback to play for a hoedown. When the dances were closer to home, he'd pile some straw into the wagon and take the whole family. The youngsters would play until they were tired, then curl up in a corner and go to sleep. Mr. Baker pointed out that in those days you didn't see fellows drinking at a dance. No respectable woman would dance with them if they did. When the boys were older, Walton with a violin and one of his brothers with a banjo took over the music making. He still has his own violin as well as his father's, the latter over a hundred years old.

About the only holiday celebrated in the Baker home was Christmas. Christmas wasn't commercialized then as it is now, and their simple festivities were a far cry from today's lavish and extravagant displays. Their father would go up into the hills and cut a pine for their Christmas tree, then the sisters would pop corn and string it to drape over the branches to decorate it. The girls also made candy while their mother would make pastry – the old-style flake pastry. She'd make little individual mince pies and a big mince pie ahead of time and then, if desired, warm them up at serving time. A little hard candy and perhaps an apple comprised the gifts, yet Mr. Baker feels that they enjoyed their celebration as much – perhaps more than – families do now. A number of bachelors lived in the neighborhood ('neighborhood' included a radius of probably at least ten miles) and his mother would invite them to share their Christmas dinner.

There were nine children in the Baker family, but there was quite an age span between the oldest and the youngest so they were seldom all home at once. Still it seemed there was always a gang around the Baker home. Because of their location on the frontier Walton had very little opportunity to get schooling of any kind. His father tried to get a school started, but law required there be at least nine pupils, and there just weren't nine pupils in the area. His parents boarded children in their home to get the required number, and in this way they were able to have three-month terms several different years, but it's rather hard to get an education at that rate.

When Walton was a little older he had a chance to go to a school over on Pumpkin Creek ten miles south of Miles City for a nine-month term. He worked for his room and board on a road ranch five miles from school. Ranchers going into Miles City would stop at the ranch for the night, go on into town the next day, load and return to the ranch another night, then on to their own ranch the next day. That meant that there would usually be five or six extra teams to care for morning and evening besides fourteen cows to milk. Weekends there would be stables to clean, coal to haul, and the numerous other chores associated with a ranch. The temperature that winter dropped to sixty degrees below zero one night, but Walton rode his horse the five miles to school next morning despite the biting cold. No one else showed up, not even the teacher, so he rode the five miles back to the ranch again.

He didn't give up the idea of getting more education, and after he was grown he tried again but feels now that he went about it in the wrong way. In retrospect he concludes that he'd have made more progress if he had taken some night courses in Miles City, but instead he enrolled at the St. Thomas College in St. Paul.

He soon realized he'd undertaken to fill a big order, and then he was informed that someone was contesting his rights to the homestead on which he had previously filed back in Montana. He and his brothers were in the cattle business together, and his claim was being worked, but he decided he'd best get home and take care of the matter. He quit school and kept the homestead, but now he figures it would have been a good thing for him if the other fellow had got it. Later when he enlisted in the army during World War I he sold it and accepted a note for it, but the note was worthless, and he never did get anything out of it.

110

He had learned to ride horseback almost as soon as he'd learned to walk, and when he was still in his teens he went to work punching cattle. There were some big spreads in the country then, and Walton rode from the Powder River to Rosebud Creek, with the Tongue River and Pumpkin Creek between, and as far north as the Yellowstone. He put in considerable time with the George Hawkins outfit, a cattle ranch where they branded from 800 to 1,000 calves a year. They had three or four bands of sheep, too (2,000-3,000 sheep to a band), but not many horses – only what they needed for the ranch. Everything on the ranch was done with horses. Mr. Baker reflected that when horses were used for transportation and working, it wasn't often that a man was hurt or killed by them. Some of the horses were mean, all right, but the man who knew how to handle them could usually take care of himself.

Spring roundup, starting about the first of June, generally lasted about a month. They didn't like to start earlier because brands were too hard to read before the cattle had shed their shaggy winter hair. The roundup wagon, with up to forty men to a wagon, would move every day, sometimes twice a day, while the riders searched every draw, gully, and canyon for cattle. The surrounding ranches would each send a man, a rep*, to ride with the different wagons to watch for any of their stock that had strayed onto other ranges. Often the rep was just called by the brand of his particular outfit so, although they rode and ate together for weeks, they might not even know the fellow's name.

When roundup time came, nobody bothered changing clocks for daylight savings time because they were already using all the daylight hours. Up at break of day (and day breaks in the wee hours in June) they rode long hours and covered long miles. No eight-hour day, forty-hour week for them!

There was always plenty of excitement as men and horses prepared for the day's work. At least half-a-dozen horses would be concentrating on dislodging their riders, and it wasn't unusual for some of them to succeed. These horses weren't barnyard stock; many of them had never been handled – perhaps had never seen a man except when they were branded – until they were five or six years old. By that time they were pretty well set in their ways. They were tough and hard to handle, but the cowboys were tough, too.

Horses would be brought in from the range earlier in the spring, and the boys would start getting their horses ready for the season; clip manes and tails, trim hoofs if necessary, take care of any details pertinent to a well-groomed horse. Not that that made any difference in the way the horse pitched when the cowboy was ready to ride him!

Sometimes a man would choose to break a horse in the corral, but others would ride them out in the open. Perhaps they would blindfold the horse until they were firmly in the saddle, then they'd jerk the blindfold off and the fireworks would start. No admission was charged for watching those rough-riding contests.

Another technique was to tie the horse down until his rider was in the saddle, then a helper would turn him loose and both horse and rider would display their skills. Mr. Baker cheerfully acknowledged that he didn't always stay in the saddle when he intended to, but he had plenty of company. There were some of those bronc riders, though, that a horse, as long as he stayed on his feet, just didn't throw. Many of the cowboys who never participated in a rodeo were just as skillful as those who did. By the time the roundup started, the horses were 'broke' to a degree, but most of them could by no stretch of the imagination be called gentle.

Each cowboy would have seven or eight horses in his 'string' and ride perhaps five different horses in one day, depending upon the amount of riding to be done. As they rounded up the cattle, they branded the calves that belonged on the range, probably 200 a day, and turned them loose. Strays (cattle that belonged on a different range) were thrown into the 'herd' until the roundup was completed and they were taken back to their home range. The herd had to be guarded night and day to keep them together, so already short hours for sleep were cut even shorter when a cowboy had to take his turn at night guard.

The night guard started at eight and changed every two hours, and the fellows who drew the midnight to 2 a.m. shift didn't expect much sleep after they were relieved. The frequency with which they had to stand guard depended upon the number of men with the wagon. Each man usually had a special horse that he used for night herding. Any little noise out of the ordinary might 'spook' the herd, especially at night, so the night watchmen had to be extra careful. It didn't take much to start a stampede but once started it was mighty hard to stop.

Ranchers then didn't sell their steers until they were five or six years old, and that much beef on the run was nothing to trifle with. Mr. Baker remarked that he never happened to be around when they had a really bad stampede, but he didn't evidence much regret at being deprived of the experience.

The saddle bunch, too, had to have a night watchman, who was called the 'night hawk'. When a severe electrical storm appeared to be in the offing, the wagon boss would ask another man to keep his horse up so he could go to the aid of the night hawk when the storm hit. With 200 or more high-strung horses to watch, the night hawk was liable to need help. Horses seem to draw lightning, and Mr. Baker explained that you could often see light dancing around the horses until it looked as though you could reach out and grab balls of fire from above their ears. Actually, the horses weren't as hard to hold during the storm as afterward when the cold rain had chilled them, making them want to run.

Spring roundup was likely to mean working in heat and dust while the fall roundup frequently spelled cold and mud or snow. Sleeping on the ground wasn't bad in the spring, but in the fall it could be plenty disagreeable. Some of the fellows had small tents, but many of them just spread their bedrolls on the freezing ground out in the open.

One night when they were camped on Rosebud Creek, Walt was sleeping in the cook tent, and the wind blew the tent down around him. As he disentangled himself, he was obliged to crawl out into four inches of snow. A fellow wasn't likely to feel especially picturesque or glamorous getting out of bed into a snow bank, but such was the life of a cowboy at times. Of course the weather wasn't always bad. There were pleasant days, too, and they took the bad with the good.

On the roundup the prairie was their dining hall and the big sky was their ceiling. The menu was generally rather limited, but nobody expected much variety on the roundup; they just expected the food to be substantial and plenty of it. Meat and potatoes were their mainstay and hot baking powder biscuits often livened up the fare. Once in awhile you'd find a cook who would take time to bake pies, but usually they were too busy.

He recalls that one fellow they had was a real good cook and even made pies fairly often, but he was so cranky you hardly dared stick your head inside the tent. He was a drinker, too, but he was so clever that for a long time no one knew where he kept his liquor hidden. Finally someone discovered that he kept his rolling pin (a long beer bottle) filled with whiskey!

In good weather the cook usually prepared the meals out in the open, but in inclement weather a tent served for his kitchen. When the meal was ready the cook's yell "Ch-u-ck!" brought everyone to the mess wagon on the double. Details such as tables and tablecloths had no part in a roundup. Each cowboy grabbed his tin plate and utensils, filled them from the kettle or pan, then sat on the ground or wherever suited him. When he finished the meal, he brought his equipment back to the wagon.

At the back of the wagon was a large box with shelves built above it. This was the 'mess box', and here the dishes, cookware, and food supplies, smaller items, were stored. Since at least once a day and sometimes twice a day the wagon had to be ready to bounce and joggle over the unmarked prairie to the next roundup site, its contents weren't of the fragile sort.

On the roundup anything could happen and frequently did. One day after dinner as they made ready to move, the cowboys had their horses saddled, the teams hooked to the wagons, and were almost ready to start. One of the fellows was an outstanding rider, even in a company of good riders, and it seemed he was always breaking a horse for someone or taming a horse that was too mean for anyone else. With that kind of horse under his saddle it wasn't surprising to anyone that while Elmer was helping with the bed wagon, his horse found an excuse for alarm and abruptly left camp – unattended. Walt was mounted so he gave chase, racing along the creek, dodging the big red boulders strewn over the ground in that region.

The bronc wasn't planning to surrender his freedom without giving Walton a run for his money, and as the horses skimmed over the ground (about the closest thing to flying before Wright Brothers) the bronc's bridle reins streamed in the wind. The distance between them was narrowing, and Walton saw the lines almost within his grasp. He leaned to grab them but his shifting weight threw his straining horse off balance, and the horse turned a complete somersault. He flipped high enough in the air that as Walton whirled underneath him he completely cleared the ground and was able to free himself, unscathed, from the saddle before the horse fell. Mr. Baker accounted for his escape simply with, "The Lord had his arms around me." His horse was somewhat stunned but quickly recovered, and Walton used him the rest of the afternoon for riding circle.

Another time while they were on the roundup they came across a big gray wolf with five young ones. There happened to be about fifteen or twenty fellows together when they spotted them, and they quickly decided to try their luck roping wolves. They had to get within roping distance first so cowboys and wolves were soon flying in every direction. The lay of the land was hardly conducive to racing – some of the roughest country along Graveyard Creek up from Hathaway – so the wolves certainly had the advantage. Mr. Baker remarked that he doesn't know how he happened to be that lucky, but he was riding a good horse, and he managed to get close enough to rope one of those half-grown wolves. He's tried to rope bobcats and coyotes, too, he says but was never as lucky as with that wolf.

There were still quite a few of those gray wolves in the country then, and they were bad medicine for livestock. While coyotes had to content themselves with sheep, a wolf could pull down a grown steer. Coyotes were so numerous and so bold that while a herder was on one side of a band of sheep, a coyote might be on the other side of the band, pulling one down.

A couple years before the United States' entry into World War I Walton had a bout with pneumonia that almost cost him his life. He was halter-breaking some horses early in October when a man came who wanted to trade some bulls. The bulls were out on the range so Walton rode with the trader to get them. When they got in late that evening Walton was feeling rather rough, and he wasn't any better the next morning. He lay around home for a few days, but his condition continued to worsen so his brother went to Miles City for a doctor. (No telephone then.) Dr. Garberson came right out, diagnosed his illness as pneumonia, and immediately took him to the hospital. The next days were days of fever and delirium. A special nurse was assigned to him, and Mr. Baker still can't figure out when the man ever slept; whenever he roused enough to know what was going on, the nurse was always alert.

When the schoolteacher to whom he was engaged received word of his critical condition (she was back at her home in Wadena, Minnesota, just then) she hurried to Montana. The crisis passed, he recovered, and as soon as he was out of the hospital they were married.

When the United States entered World War I Walton was given a deferred classification because of his cattle and farming interests. After a time, though, it seemed that everyone else had gone, and he began to feel that perhaps he should go, too, so he volunteered.

He and his wife decided it would be best if she went back to Minnesota near her folks while he was gone so he went back with her before it was time for him to go. His call had come by the time their first child was born, but then the doctor told him that his wife had a little poisoning so it would be better if he didn't go right away. The doctor wrote to his Miles City draft board and arranged for him to wait and go with the next bunch. But before the next bunch left the armistice was signed so he didn't go at all.

When they came back to Montana after the war he worked around at different jobs. The year of 1920 was a hard one that just about cleaned out a lot of farmers and stockmen, and jobs weren't plentiful. He worked for the highway for awhile, then came to Glendive to see what he could find. The railroad was a little short of men just then because of a strike or something so they took him on. He started to work at noon one day in 1922, not knowing how permanent the job would be, and worked steadily until his retirement in 1959.

Mrs. Baker passed away in October, 1962, but four of their five children are still living. One daughter is in Mandan, two are in Seattle, and his only son, Jack, lives in Glendive.

When Mr. Baker was asked if he had any old pictures to go along with his story, he expostulated, "It's bad enough to print that stuff for them to read without asking them to look at a picture, too!" We're sorry that he didn't happen to have any handy, but as he relates incidents of his younger days, his word pictures vividly portray the West as it was when the cowboy was King.

Mrs. Alfred (Edna Miller) Doane

August 1965

Since Edna Miller Doane was only six years old when she made the covered wagon trip from northeastern North Dakota to the Thirteen Mile Valley in Dawson County the details that stand out in her memory are naturally the ones that impressed a child, not necessarily what an adult might remember.

One of their North Dakota neighbors, Jacob B. Mullet, had come to Montana in 1903 in search of a tract of land suitable for settlement by a number of families. He felt that he had found such a tract along the Thirteen Mile Creek, thirty miles northwest of Glendive, and brought back a favorable report to his neighbors. His oldest son, Joe Mullet and family, and the Amos Miller family moved to Montana yet that year, Mr. Mullet and his family the next summer, and now two more families were ready to move. Eli Chupp had also come over earlier, and on October 1 his family and the Dan Miller family started for the new home sites. Their caravan, as it started down the trail, consisted of a covered wagon, a hayrack, (each pulled by a two-horse team), a herd of cattle, Mrs. Eli Chupp with her four children, Mr. and Mrs. Dan Miller with five children, and eighteen-year-old Jacob J. Mullet, who had returned to North Dakota to assist in moving preparations and to act as guide on the way.

They had bunks along each side of the wagon, and at night a bed was fixed on the floor between the back wheels for her parents. As they jogged along over the prairie the children, except the 'cowboys', had to stay pretty much in the wagon so when camping time came in the evening, they were ready for some exercise. One evening as they gave vent to their pent-up energies one little tow-headed fellow, about three years old, fell into the creek, but his older brother quickly pulled him out, none the worse for the impromptu bath.

The oldest boy of each family, nine-year-old Ammon Chupp and eight-year-old Mose Miller, were the 'cowboys' who drove the cattle. They made the entire trip horseback. Ammon's younger brother complains that when they passed through a town he had to help with the cattle, too, only he had to do it without benefit of a steed.

One day as the party was stopped for dinner an Indian wagon came to their camp so the boys on horseback quickly skedaddled into the brush; they had heard enough tales about Indians that they were taking no chances on losing their saddle horses! However the visit passed with no untoward incident.

Their food along the way, as Mrs. Doane recalls, consisted largely of crackers, half-moon pies (apple, baked before they started on their journey), and milk. Since they were bringing the cows with them, they had plenty of milk along the way. Mrs. Doane especially remembers the crackers since it was her responsibility at each meal to bring them. To get into the wagon she always climbed up over the wagon tongue and one time as she was getting down with them, stepping down backwards, her crackers spilled to the ground. She didn't want to get scolded and so, not knowing any better, she carefully put her crackers back into the bowl and served them anyway. When they had started on their trip, they didn't stock up with a bunch of little two-pound cartons. Their crackers were packed in big wooden boxes, more like apple boxes now.

They were blessed with beautiful Indian summer weather during most of their trip. One night, however, the wind blew so hard they feared the wagon might tip over so they parked it between a fence and the hayrack, but the anticipated trouble didn't materialize.

When they arrived in the valley Dan Millers stayed with the Amos Miller family (Amos and Dan were brothers) until they could get their house built. This house still serves as part of the Jens Scarpholt residence, a few miles east of Bloomfield. Only Bloomfield wasn't there when the house was built.

The Valley boasted no school when the Millers came because there had been no need for one. And there was no school for a few years thereafter. Edna started school on her ninth birthday, March 6, 1907. This first school was held in a sod house in the Dave Chupp yard (across from the present home of Elmer Borntrager). They had a three-month term with Emma Miller (Edna's aunt) as teacher. Mrs. Doane stated, "She wasn't a teacher, but she taught." Educational requirements for teachers in the Dawson County of 1907 weren't very strict.

Mrs. Doane remembers that on the closing day of school that first term they had a program and each of the children gave a 'speech' or recitation. The three speeches that she can recall give us a sample of what we might have enjoyed had we been able to attend that event. Her own was:

Little deeds of kindness, Little words of love,
Make the mighty ocean, And the heaven above.

The other speeches she can remember didn't offer quite such lofty sentiments. The one proclaimed: "Here I stand so big and stout. I like 'Speck' and sauerkraut!" (Speck is German for bacon.) And the other: "I had a little dog, and his name was Rover. And when he died, he died all over." The next year the Red Top schoolhouse was built five miles east of Bloomfield and Roy Reed was their teacher.

All mail, groceries, and other supplies had to be brought from Glendive. Such is largely the case now, too; the difference is that in the early 1900's the trip required two days. No fences interfered with their traveling so their trails followed the easiest routes. Neighbors took turns going to town, each bringing the mail and supplies that might be needed for the rest of the community. After a few years Jacob B. Mullet applied for a post office at his home, one-half mile south of Gregg Jones' home and named it Adams. Mrs. Doane still has some post cards bearing the Adams address. One, addressed to her late husband, Alfred Doane, was dated January 24, 1909. The sender wrote, "Got a raise the first of the year and now get $65 a month, but I may quit for I think I can get better wages in the gas business. I will be nineteen next Saturday."

In 1928 Mr. Miller became ill and finally decided he'd have to see a doctor so he got one of the neighbors, Lester Brown, to take him to Glendive. He told his family he would get a check-up and come right home, but they never saw him alive again. He was kept in the hospital and within a few days he passed away. In less than a year his wife became ill and died also.

In 1935 Edna married Alfred Doane. Alfred had come to Montana in 1906 from Bloomfield, Nebraska, and had homesteaded a few miles from the Miller homestead. In 1941 they moved to a farm on Morgan Creek. Mr. Doane passed away in March of 1962. He had reached Montana on St. Patrick's Day and his death came the day after St. Patrick's Day, fifty-six years later. Mrs. Doane continues to live on their Morgan Creek farm, and her two sons do the farming.

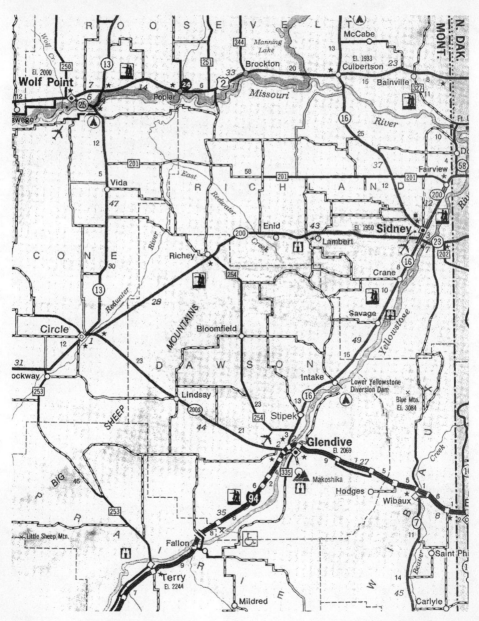

Preceding Page:
Map of Dawson County, Montana and Surrounding Areas
Map courtesy of Montana Department of Transportation

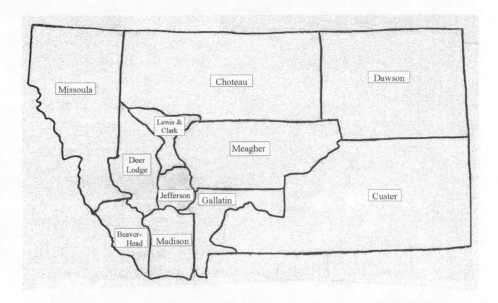

Montana Counties 1879

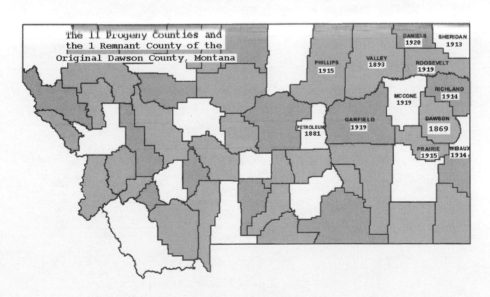

The counties carved out of the original Dawson County
including date of each county's creation
Map and information couretsy of Norman Hyatt

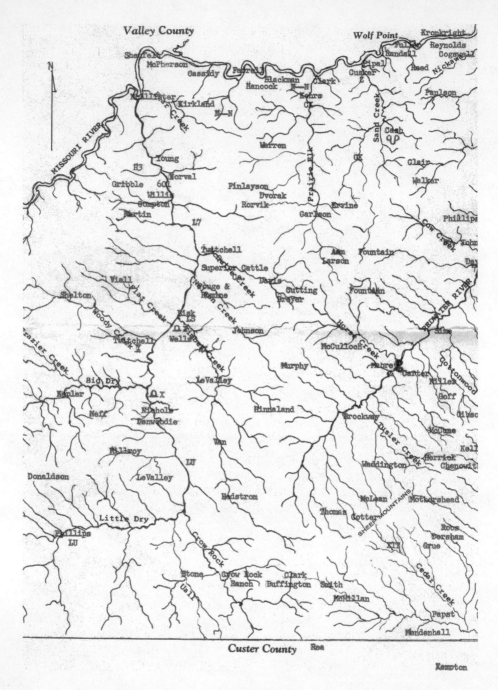

Map of the eastern two-thirds of Dawson County, circa 1900
when the county stretched from North Dakota to the Musselshell River

Early Montana ranches added to map by Marie MacDonald 1967

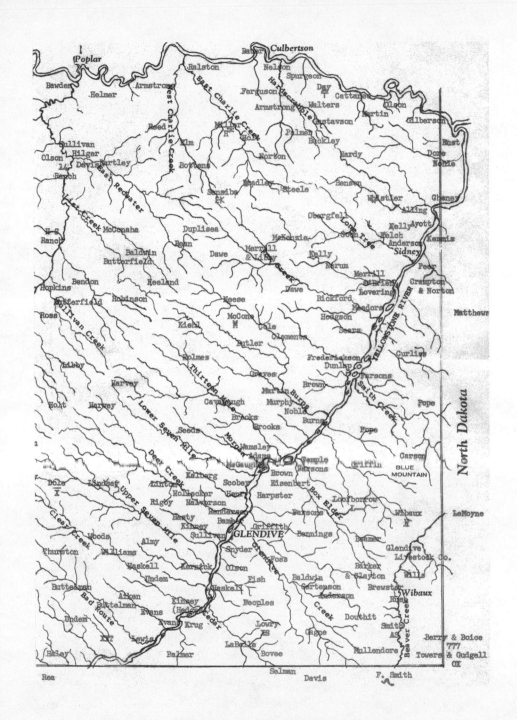

Map copyrighted 1967 by Marie MacDonald
used by permission of the Marie MacDonald family

Carl Colbrese

September 1965

Thirteen year old Carl Colbrese met with a cold reception when he arrived in Glendive from sunny Italy. Back in his old home region in Italy the climate was much like that of California, and the temperatures seldom dropped to the freezing mark. Not so in Montana, he found, and especially not that winter of 1908. Much of the time that winter the mercury hovered around thirty-five to forty degrees below zero, and that was what greeted him when he landed in the Gate City the fifteenth of January that year. And snow! There was more than he had seen in all his life before, and it just kept coming. It seemed to him there was more snow than anything else in Glendive.

Carl's brother Lawrence had come to Glendive in 1905, lured here by a cousin who had come still earlier, and it was the two of them who 'pulled' young Carl to the New World. One of his uncles came with him so Carl didn't make the long voyage alone. Lawrence was working for the Northern Pacific Railroad, and it wasn't long until Carl, too, was able to get a job with the N.P., carrying water from the cisterns. That marked the beginning of his railroad career, and he stayed with it until his retirement in 1957.

The three young fellows, Carl, Lawrence, and their cousin, lived together in a boxcar along the railroad, doing their own cooking and housekeeping. Carl didn't mind the cooking – in fact, he rather enjoyed that – but he didn't like the dishwashing.

Rabbits were plentiful in those days, but no one seemed to think of eating them until the Colbrese boys introduced them on their own private bill of fare. Then rabbit meat became so popular among their friends that one Thanksgiving some of their bachelor cronies asked Carl to cook them a rabbit dinner to celebrate the holiday.

Carl couldn't resist playing a practical joke when the opportunity presented itself, and opportunity came begging this time when a bobcat got in front of his gunsights. He cut up the cat and made 'Hungarian goulash', adding his own special combination of seasonings, and served it up in style, the nature of the meat completely concealed. His guests partook heartily of his Thanksgiving dinner, and when the stew was gone, he asked them how they liked it. They were enthusiastic in their response, assuring him, "It was good!" "Not enough of it!" "Bring on more!" Instead of bringing on more stew, he slipped outside to where the head of the bobcat lay and brought it in, whiskers and all, and set it on the table. What an uproar was triggered by the sight of that head! And the diners, without exception, had had enough.

But not all of his stews produced such a turbulent climax. Several years after he joined his brother and cousin in the boxcar three young ladies set up housekeeping in a little shack next door. The girls, whose parents had emigrated from Poland and homesteaded near Circle, could speak only Polish, and Carl's speech was still something of a mixture of Italian and English so conversation

122

was a problem. But food has a universal language and the girls couldn't resist the smell of Carl's stews. They wondered how they might get an invitation to dinner, and once Carl got a hint of their interest in his culinary accomplishments it was simple; he invited them.

After this their acquaintance grew, and in time Carl developed a special interest in one of the young ladies, Agnes Molenda. The interest was mutual and this they managed to communicate to each other even though they didn't speak the same language. Carl was able to propose marriage, and she accepted.

Now they were faced with the problem of getting permission from her folks. Since the family lived beyond Circle and this was in the dead of winter, transportation was even more of a problem than communication had been.

After considerable counseling with his bride-to-be and her two sisters and her brother-in-law, they decided the safest and most comfortable solution was for them (the bride-to-be, sisters, and brother-in-law) to go in a sheep wagon while Carl went ahead on a saddle horse. There wasn't much of a trail between Glendive and Circle then and what trail there was was pretty well covered with snow. Carl decided to see if he could find a better route. The blowing snow was confusing and in the unfamiliar territory, Carl lost his way completely. He couldn't even find his way back to the trail he had left.

Darkness overtook him, and after what seemed an interminable interlude he saw a light. It was his only hope, and he headed for it. His knock on the door was answered by a rough-looking character who apparently had never shaved. Carl wondered if it had been a mistake to come here for help, but there was no turning back now so he mustered his courage to explain to the fellow that he was lost and would like to be directed to Circle, hastening to add that he would be glad to pay for the help.

He was soon made to realize that his fears were groundless. The man not only showed him which way to go, but he saddled his own horse and rode with him about ten miles until they were back to the trail (the same trail that Carl had left in search of a better) and refused the offered pay. Carl finally caught up with the rest of his party in the sheepwagon and they continued on their way.

Mr. and Mrs. Molenda granted permission for the marriage, but then the party had to come back to Glendive before the young couple could get married. There was no church and not much of anything else in Circle in 1915 so the wedding took place in Glendive in the Catholic Church which was then located on the south side of town in the building later known as C.Y.A. Hall*. The hall was demolished several years ago.

A couple weeks after Carl's marriage Lawrence also decided to get married, and since he was marrying Agnes's cousin, he too, had to go to the Circle area to get permission. He decided he'd try going with a car he had bought from Hildebrand so Carl went along with him to help him with the snow shoveling that was sure to be encountered.

Thanks to the snow it was dark by the time they reached Circle. The trail on out to the homestead was so vague and unfamiliar it was hard enough to follow in daylight so they decided to stay in Circle for the night. They found a room in the only hotel, but plaster kept falling from the ceiling until they decided they'd better get out of there. They spent the remainder of the night in a café, waiting for dawn so they could continue their journey. Once they reached their destination the desired permission was granted, they came back to Glendive, and Lawrence, too, made the trip to the altar.

The newlyweds didn't set up housekeeping in a 'newly decorated' or 'completely furnished' apartment, nor did they start monthly payments on a new house. They had the new house, all right, but there were no monthly payments involved. Carl and Lawrence each built small one-room houses out of 'boxcar lumber' – rough lumber that had been discarded by the railroad company. They supplied their own labor so the cost was nominal. Their furnishings were simple, but they managed very well – even without a TV set.

While this generation takes for granted such conveniences as automatic electric or gas ovens, they didn't even have ovens! Before he was married Carl and his brother made their own oven. They piled up dirt to make a bank out of the gumbo*, then dug back into it (that gumbo was so solid they had to pick or chisel some of the dirt loose) to make a hole perhaps three-and-one-half feet square and three feet deep, with a hole or 'chimney' in the top so their fire would draw. On baking day they filled the hole with wood and started a fire.

They had a special trough for mixing the bread and made their own bread pans out of sheet metal they got from the railroad company. They made big pans and big loaves, each loaf weighing three pounds or more, and baked six or seven loaves at a time.

After the wood was all burned, they carefully raked out all the coals and ashes, covered the chimney, then tossed in a piece of paper to test the temperature. If the paper burned up, the oven was too hot, but if the paper started to brown, it was time to put in the bread. During the baking process they'd look in occasionally to see if the bread was baking too fast. If it was starting to burn they'd uncover the 'chimney' for a little while to lower the temperature a bit. The baking process took about an hour or hour and a half. When the bread was done, they'd set the pans of bread on a board, and it would take two men to carry the load into the house. And it was good bread, too!

When Carl started with the railroad upon his arrival in the Treasure State, he worked for a dollar a day, carrying water. From that beginning he worked his way up through the various jobs the roundhouse offered until he reached the position of machinist, the job he held when he retired in 1957. Mr. Colbrese reflected that in the railroad's early days in Glendive they offered many concessions to their workers, including free rent in the company's houses, to keep them in this frontier town. The engines then were small and pulled two coaches at a time. The trip to Miles City would take five or six hours. He mentioned that he bought a horse and buggy because he figured he could go faster that way than on the railroad.

Marriage in no way diminished his enjoyment of a practical joke. One day as his wife was walking home from town (their shack was on what would now be Sargent Avenue) he saw her coming, and thinking to give her a little scare, he lay down in the road and started rolling around, groaning and hollering, making a great ado. Seeing the strange figure and hearing the weird noises, she didn't come close enough to see that it was her husband but turned instead and started to run back toward town. At that turn of events Carl stopped his acting and jumped to his feet, calling to her to come back, but she wouldn't even look back to assess the developments. She just kept running until she reached the safety of the populated main street. That was more scare than he had bargained for, but her brother proved he could out perform even that performance.

Carl happened to hear his wife ask her brother to go to the cellar to get some potatoes so, unknown to either of them, Carl slipped down through the trapdoor into the cellar before Joe got there. When Joe lifted the door and started to swing down into the cellar, Carl grabbed his legs. With a terrified shriek Joe jerked away, jumped back from that hole and took off, almost hysterical. That was far beyond the reaction Carl had anticipated, and he never tried a trick like that again.

Not long after they were married, Carl and his new wife arranged to visit her parents. They could go as far as Circle with a team and wagon, but from there on out to the homestead the snow was so deep only a sleigh could go. His wife's cousin met them in Circle with a sled to take them on out to Molendas. It was dark by the time they reached Circle and darker, if possible, when they started on in the sled. Blowing snow obscured the trail, and in the darkness the hills all looked alike so before long they were completely confused. All night they wandered around in the cold – and it was bitter cold! – trying to find their way to the homestead.

Wolves were still numerous in that region, and their howling didn't make that long, miserable night any more pleasant. The wanderers, of course, had no guns with them because they had started out for a visit, not for a hunt, and they were acutely aware that they had no means of protecting themselves should those wolves get too close. Not until five o'clock the next morning did they, very nearly frozen, locate the Molenda home with its offer of warmth and food.

As Mr. Colbrese reminisced about wolves he described their cunning in pulling down cattle. He explained that the wolves would fill up with water at the water hole, then unload it on a slope where the cattle trailed to water. Ice formed on the slope so as the cattle started down they'd slide and as soon as they were down the wolves would be upon them to kill.

Carl liked to hunt, especially coyotes. The bounty then was $2.50 per coyote so that sport could be a profitable pastime. Some of his hunting experiences stand out vividly in his memory yet. One time he and his work partner went to Hodges on the train, then started off across country to hunt. They thought they were going to take a short cut back to town, but instead of that they got lost and after hunting all day, wandered around all that night and most of the next day. Finally they spotted the smoke from the N.P. smokestack and followed it into town. They had killed a rabbit to get a little something to eat, but that was sadly inadequate and they were two hungry, cold fellows when they got home. They had been expected at work that morning, but how are you going to report for work when you're miles out in the hills and no way to get back to town? No one knew where they were so there was no way to get them to work that day.

Another time three of them were hunting together, and of the three, Carl was the only one wearing boots. They came to a creek so Carl successfully carried one of his companions across, then went back for the second. This time they didn't fare so well. He stepped into a hole and they both went down, almost drowning besides soaking themselves to the skin so that by the time they got home they were both on the verge of pneumonia. Not only that, they lost a good gun in the bargain. Not too profitable, that trip.

Carl bought his first car, a Dort, soon after he was married. That car was a far cry from his present Pontiac. Cars then had little power, little speed (it took about all day to go to Circle) and the radiator seemed to be always steaming. Later on, after they had moved out onto a farm (the one where Jim Brown lives now) he got a Dodge. That was quite an improvement over the Dort, but still left much to be desired, measured by later models. For one thing it had no brakes and for another it always backfired. Once as they were going home from town, it started backfiring going down the hill toward the creek and caught fire. Mrs. Colbrese was sitting in the back seat holding the baby so Carl called to her not to jump out until he could get the car slowed down more. He coasted on through the creek and managed to bring it to a stop as he started up the hill on the other side, then turned to tell his wife it would be all right to get out now. But she wasn't there. She had jumped out before they crossed the creek.

Mr. and Mrs. Colbrese raised a family of five girls and three boys, all of whom are still living. Since Mrs. Colbrese passed away in 1962, Mr. Colbrese has lived alone in the house they bought in 1956. At present he is living in the basement and renting out the main floor. Besides doing all his own yard work he raises a garden. He likes to visit, and in addition to his friends and children he enjoys his thirty-six grandchildren.

126

Mrs. Ed (Kathryn Cruikshank) Rigby

June 1967

With America on the move road maps are much in demand today. Before Calvin Cruikshank started from Iowa to Montana fifty-four years ago, he procured a map, too, but he wasn't interested in filling stations; his map of Iowa showed every windmill along the route he expected to take. The map also showed every schoolhouse with an adjacent cyclone cellar where one could find shelter from the terrific wind and electric storms so common to that region.

In January of 1913 Calvin Cruikshank had suffered a serious attack of pneumonia which left one of his lungs severely damaged, and the attending physician recommended a move to a higher altitude. The family felt they had no alternative. If a higher altitude and dryer climate would help restore the father's health, such a location must be sought, but where?

Just when they were trying to decide they received a letter from a relative who had homesteaded in the Lindsay area of Dawson County. He wrote glowing accounts of the advantages this new country had to offer, and finally the family pinpointed Glendive, the nearest town of any size, as their destination.

The decision to move had not been an easy one to make. It meant pulling up stakes, selling their home, and starting out as strangers in a strange land. Doleful predictions of relatives and friends that the trip would be too much for an invalid did not ease the situation.

There were questions to consider: What if Mrs. Cruikshank found herself a widow before they reached their destination? Far from relatives, how would she care for the children (four daughters) in such an event? With the father's health at stake, they decided they'd cross that bridge if they came to it and hope their course didn't lead that way.

It was August before Calvin felt that he was physically able to start the journey. Careful preparations were made. The trip was to be made in a covered wagon pulled by a team of spirited black horses. Neighbors made predictions about those horses, too. They were much too light for such a long trip and would surely play out before they reached their destination. However Calvin felt he knew his horses and he did not intend to force them. They would take their time along the way, their only concern that they reach their destination before cold weather set in.

Much planning went into the packing for the trip. Articles not often used but which would be needed occasionally or at least at the end of the journey were packed first. A feather bed, ticks and other bedding were placed over this part of the load. Here the family could rest in comfort at the end of the day. As they traveled the girls could take turns resting on the beds, riding up in front with their parents or, tiring of both, they would walk beside the wagon and explore the countryside.

Fastened to the back of the wagon was a three-burner kerosene stove and hanging from the sides were lantern, buckets and a shovel. Someone with a sense of humor tacked on an automobile license plate, which stayed in place during the entire trip. A tent for camping, an important piece of equipment, was included. And then of course there was Jack. Jack was the family dog and must not be left behind. He could walk beside the wagon or ride up front as he saw fit. For the most part he saw fit to walk.

Mr. Cruikshank felt that it would be dangerous to carry much money with them along the way (no traveler's checks then) so he entrusted a sum of money to a brother-in-law with instructions to send it to various banks along the way and the date on which it should be at each place. He also arranged for mail to be sent to certain designated post offices.

At last all was packed and they were ready to go. The covered wagon with the two blacks, Kit and Flash, in the traces creaked out of the yard and onto the road. It was with mixed feelings that Mr. and Mrs. Cruikshank and their four daughters, Lela, Katherine, Jessica, and Mable, left their country home, five acres near Des Moines, Iowa and began their long trek westward.

The Cruikshank family found the Iowa segment of their journey not too eventful. They reveled in the beauty of the lush green countryside, the many lakes, the lovely trees. Their stop at Spirit Lake was perhaps their most memorable during that part of their trip. They drew water from the lake to wash clothes, and the girls had great fun making mud pies, using the foam from the lake for frosting. They had a wonderful time wading in the lake, too.

And the friendly people! One late afternoon they were driving hard to reach some kind of shelter before the electric storm which they could see was brewing should strike. As they approached a farm with a large barn they saw the farmer come out, and he waved them in through his gate. He didn't stop with waving them into his yard but threw open the huge barn doors and told them to drive in, wagon and all. That night the children were invited to sleep in the house because it was raining too hard to set up a tent.

They weren't quite so fortunate in another of the storms they encountered. Caught in the open, Mr. Cruikshank drove to the side of the road and unhitched the horses, then he and his wife worked desperately to save the top from blowing off the wagon as it swayed in high winds. A big farmhouse was visible not far away so they sent the children there to seek shelter. When they reached the house, they found no one there except a tramp standing on the porch knocking for admittance.

As they stood there in the wind the storm suddenly broke, with cloudburst proportions. Four young girls, two of them crying, getting drenched to the skin, and a tramp — and the tramp makes a sudden dash for a nearby shed. The little girls darted after him, but he slammed the door shut and held it tightly so they couldn't get in. Perhaps he was afraid of them? They felt forlorn and forsaken, but then Lela noticed another shed and led her younger sisters to that one.

When the storm subsided they rejoined their parents who had undergone some anxious moments. The storm-battered travelers then drove about half-a-mile farther down the road and spent the night in the entrance hall of a schoolhouse because everything on the wagon was too wet to try to make a comfortable camp. While they were at the schoolhouse a man came by and questioned them about their use of the building but seemed satisfied to let them remain when they explained their presence.

Although they had an automobile license plate tacked onto their covered wagon, they still didn't have much in common with automobiles, and the plate didn't give the horses any more appreciation for those noisy carriages they would occasionally meet. Fortunately, those occasions were rare.

When an auto was sighted (or heard) approaching, Mr. Cruikshank would drive to the side of the road, get down from the wagon, and stand at the horses' heads, firmly holding their bridles. He would send the dog under the wagon and warn everyone in the wagon to hold on tight, then speak soothingly to the horses until the clamorous (and we didn't say glamorous) monstrosity had passed.

As the days of travel progressed the lushness of Iowa was left behind. The country gradually became more sparsely settled, the towns much farther apart, and the roads considerably less traveled. There came a time when the Cruikshanks found themselves off course, lost, in what seemed to them a vast wilderness. They had passed only two houses since breaking camp that morning, and at each of those only the women folk were at home. They were of Russian descent and unable to speak the English language so were of no help in aiding the travelers in finding their bearings.

This was not the day Calvin would have chosen to become ill, but then – he wasn't choosing. His mounting temperature added to the anxiety of being lost. When toward the middle of the afternoon, farm buildings were sighted, he announced to the family that they would set up camp until he felt better and could get definite information regarding their whereabouts.

He hoped too, to be able to buy hay for the horses, but the dear little grandmother he encountered when he knocked on the farm house door dashed his hopes. She spoke no English, but through her young grandson she made clear that she thought they were gypsies.

She assured them they could get better accommodations farther on but was rather vague as to how much farther on. She was not at all vague, however, about her refusal to let them camp or to let them buy feed for their horses. Calvin knew he could not risk going farther so he drove on a short distance from the buildings and unhitched the horses. With suspicious eye the Russian lady watched every move.

However, when she saw Mrs. Cruikshank alight from the covered wagon, then four girls tumble out, her grandmotherly heart melted within her. Coming on over to the wagon she pointed to the smallest child and with gestures asked, "Mein babee? Mein babee?"

From then on she lavished kindness upon the travelers. At her insistence the horses were stabled in her barn with all the hay they could eat. After the tent was pitched her grandson was dispatched with a huge crock of fresh milk and she herself followed with one of those typical Russian loaves of home-baked bread – round, large and delicious.

Her hospitality did not diminish when the days passed with Mr. Cruikshank too ill to leave his bed and move on. Each afternoon it was her delight to visit an hour or so with the campers while her grandson acted as interpreter. And the regular crock of milk was presented each day as her token of friendship.

When Mr. Cruikshank was again able to travel they somehow found their way back to the road (or trail) they were supposed to follow, but the country was still desolate. The sight of vacant houses, many of them sod, became commonplace. One of the abandoned houses they passed was a two-story structure. The ground around it was white with alkali, the water unfit to drink. The day was windy and chilly, but they had fun exploring the empty house. And they picked up buffalo chips to use as fuel for their fire.

The family approached Redfield, South Dakota, with special interest. Not only was it a 'mail stop', it was also one of the towns where money was to be waiting for them at the bank. They collected their mail but were dismayed to find their money had not yet arrived.

They camped outside the town for several days waiting for the money, now critically needed, to arrive. After several inquiries the banker, evidently sensing Mr. Cruikshank's concern, ventured to ask if he would consider accepting a small personal loan from the banker himself until the funds arrived. Wonderful days when man could trust man even though complete strangers!

Their next camping site as they traveled on turned out to be near a gypsy camp. Calvin was afraid to leave camp lest the gypsies should make off with the team or some other of their possessions, so they didn't linger long at that site. In fairness to the gypsies it should be added that they in no way bothered their fellow travelers.

Another time they camped near a farmhouse and Katherine went to the well for a pail of water. As she was walking back to camp a passing car stopped, and two men got out. Their car radiator was boiling so they were going to relieve her of her pail of water, but Mr. Cruikshank saw them and came to her rescue.

As they came closer to Montana they saw 'tons' of buffalo berries, but they didn't know what they were and were afraid to eat them for fear they were poisonous. What a joy, then, to find them again in Montana and to discover that, far from being poisonous, they made delicious jelly.

It was a day of triumph when Kit and Flash (who, according to the folks back home, were supposed to have dropped by the wayside from sheer exhaustion) first set foot over the North Dakota line and onto Montana soil.

They looked forward to reaching Wibaux because that had been designated as a mail stop for them. They thought they must be getting close so when they met an old timer, they asked him about the road conditions to "Y-box." Imagine their disappointment when he told them there was no such place! After a bit of consideration he explained to them, "You no doubt are referring to W-i-b-a-u-x, pronounced Wee-bow." What a relief to find that the town with their mail hadn't disappeared after all.

They camped once more after leaving Wibaux before they reached their destination, Glendive. The next day excitement ran high as they broke over the hill by the Northern Pacific Hospital and saw the town of Glendive spread out before them.

A passer-by on the main street of Glendive may or may not have taken notice of the trim covered wagon or the black team tied up at the hitching post opposite the Northern Pacific Railway depot, but to the occupants of that wagon it was a great moment. It marked the end of the 900-mile long journey begun nine weeks before.

They learned that there was a camping ground at the far end of the bridge that spanned the Yellowstone river so when those wagon wheels began creaking again, it was down the main street where a right turn onto Bell Street led directly to the bridge and the camping ground.

At this camping ground the Cruikshanks found an opportunity to meet many of the farmers of the area. It was the month of October, and the year's grain harvest was being delivered to the grain elevators of Glendive. Many farmers had hauls of from thirty to sixty miles so they would camp there overnight before starting the trip home. Other farmers would arrive throughout the night hours, and they found this a convenient place to wait over for business to open up the next morning.

The Cruikshanks spent two days in this camp. While visiting in the city hall where he was inquiring about possible homestead sites, Mr. Cruikshank became acquainted with the Dawson County surveyor, Mr. Reginald Hurdle. Mr. Hurdle had a nice home on the country side of the bridge near the campground. Close by his home was a small cabin owned but seldom used by a homesteader named Orion Steinman,

At Mr. Hurdle's suggestion the Cruikshanks made arrangements to rent this cabin, and they settled down for a pleasant winter. They became close friends with a second nearby neighbor, the Milo Rigbys, whose curly-headed son Edwin was happy to have the Cruikshank girls join him each weekday as they crossed the bridge to attend the city schools.

Mr. Cruikshank secured winter employment from J.A. Morse as night clerk in his hotel, which was located at the very end of the bridge on the city side. During one of his nights on duty here his family, in the cabin at the other end of the bridge, was rudely awakened by loud, angry voices.

Terror struck their hearts as two shots pierced the night. Within yards of the cabin there was the sharp clatter of galloping hoofs and the racing of buggy wheels, then from the bridge a series of distressed calls for help. The voice was loud and clear at the beginning, but each successive cry of 'Help' grew fainter and fainter until at last all was still – still except for the hushed voices of those who had responded to the calls.

Mr. Cruikshank, at his end of the long bridge, had also heard the shots. He had hurried with the sheriff in the direction of the calls and reached the side of the murdered man just before his final call died away. So this was the Wild West.

The spring of 1914 found Mr. Cruikshank again raising the cover over his wagon. This time they were preparing to move to the homestead on which he had filed the preceding fall. In the meantime he had purchased two Holstein cows and a young heifer so they were tied to the back of the wagon as once again Kit and Flash started down the trail.

Cruikshank had filed on 320 acres ten miles south of the Union Post Office. (By 1913 he didn't have much choice.) Miles before reaching the homestead he could point across the prairie and say, "There is our new home."

Rising diagonally across the property was a chain of buttes known as the Diamond G Buttes which served as a landmark to the surrounding area. It was near the base of these buttes that the covered wagon made its final stop. Here the family tent was pitched for the spring and summer months, with a temporary cook shack erected alongside.

All attention was given then to turning the sod in preparation for planting a crop of grain and a large garden. Some fencing also had to be done so it was well into the summer months before work could begin on building a house.

The house was built on the order of most of the homestead dwellings, with a fairly flat bowed roof but without the tar-papered exterior. Instead regular siding was used and finished off with white paint, making a neat and attractive homestead 'shack'.

It was completed and ready for occupancy by the time the chill of the fall months set in, as was also the dugout barn and chicken house with their rocked-up fronts and flax straw roofs. Beside the barn stood a stack of straw and also one long stack of hay made from cutting the buffalo grass of the rangeland. It had been a very busy summer for the whole family.

Busy though it was, somehow there had been time for making the acquaintance of all the closer neighbors. Bordering their property was the Henry Roth homestead. He was a bachelor and took a big interest in helping this newly arrived family get started developing their homestead.

Then there were the Steinmans in whose Glendive cabin the Cruikshanks had wintered; the Bill Ruckman family; Mrs. Anna Mildred; and Lou Heltemes, another bachelor – bachelor, that is, until he and Mrs. Chamberland decided to unite interests, and he became a family man.

Still further to the south lay the Nick Buttleman cattle ranch with its many sections and well known '52' brand. The Cruikshanks found these neighbors all wonderful folk to know, and enjoyed many happy occasions with them throughout the years that followed.

When it was time for school to start the four Cruikshank girls had to walk a distance of three miles directly north to what was known as the Pierce School. Miss Effie Bryan, daughter of one of the farmers of that district, was teacher of this country school, teaching all grades from one through seven.

Things went well during those years the Cruikshanks were proving up on their homestead. Calvin's health improved, thanks to Montana's invigorating climate. The crops were good, and he was building up a fair-sized herd of cattle. Then came the drought years.

Crops withered away for lack of moisture. If precipitation came it was liable to be in the form of hail, which wiped out everything that had managed to survive. Mr. Cruikshank decided to seek employment with the Northern Pacific Railroad in Glendive to support his family while Mrs. Cruikshank and the girls bravely tried to keep the homestead going. With the family thus separated they eventually decided to give the homestead "back to the Indians," though they later sold it for grazing land. It still holds a warm spot in the hearts of the surviving family members.

In 1919 they had opportunity to lease some property four miles from Glendive so they moved in closer and turned their cattle into better pastures. Mr. Cruikshank continued his work with the railroad, however. Soon after the move from the homestead one of the daughters was injured in an automobile accident and left paralyzed for life. This led to the decision to move the family to California in 1920.

Lela, the oldest daughter, remained in Montana and later married G.W. Hall, Northern Pacific depot agent in Wibaux. Katherine, the second daughter, later returned to Montana. She and Ed Rigby, the curly-haired boy with whom she had walked to school that first winter in Montana, had kept up a correspondence. Ed had made three trips to California. On the third trip he brought Katherine back to Glendive with him as his bride. There they made their home for the next forty years.

In the fall of 1966 Ed Rigby retired as an engineer on the Northern Pacific Railroad, and now he and Katherine reside in Walla Walla, Washington, where two of their three daughters live.

They drove overland to Washington but not in a covered wagon. While the trip was made in a few days and without the discomforts and worries that accompanied the Cruikshank's trip to Montana, it was safe to say that they saw less of the surrounding country, had less contact with the inhabitants, and had fewer memorable experiences than the Cruikshank family had on that trip from Iowa fifty-three years before.

Mrs. Hall still lives in Wibaux, and the other two sisters live in California where the Cruikshank family located when they left Montana. Mrs. Cruikshank passed away in 1951 in Pomona. As for the invalid Calvin Cruikshank who was ordered to a higher, dryer climate to survive – he lived to be ninety years old and then died an accidental death!

E. H. Rigby

April 1965

Sherman M. Rigby and the Northern Pacific Railroad reached Glendive the same year – 1881. The railroad was just far enough ahead so that Mr. Rigby could use it to get here. Coming from Wisconsin, he probably chose this newly opened land, then still a territory, chiefly for the sake of adventure. A man who would move his family eleven times in one year, as Mr. Rigby did, must surely have been of an adventuresome nature!

There wasn't just a shortage of houses in the Gate City when Mr. Rigby arrived; there was a dearth. Glendive consisted mainly of some tents and shacks up on the airport flat when he came. (At the time, the airport was beyond the north end of Merrill Avenue near the fairgrounds) He wanted his family to join him as soon as possible so, a carpenter by trade, he promptly set himself to the task of building a house. He must have built well, for the house, with a few changes, is still serving as a dwelling today with the Roy McDonough family living in it.

The house is located at 411 E. Hughes Street and at that time was the only one in the area. There was nothing between it and Hungry Joe*, and at night the howling of the coyotes could be plainly heard. So plainly that Edith, the family's eight-year-old daughter, was afraid to sleep in her little lean-to bedroom at the back of the house because she'd hear those coyotes in the night.

Mr. Rigby (Edwin) recalls his grandfather's description of the buffalo slaughter on the plains. Even when he came, there were remains of many buffalo on Sawyer's Island. They had been killed for their hides, then the carcass left to decay.

After a time Grandfather Rigby decided to homestead and chose a site on the flat above the present Crisafulli place. He didn't have his full acreage there so later he took his other forty acres along the river, between the river and where Hager's Trailer Court is now. It was on this place that his son Milo lived when he came back to Montana after a lengthy sojourn in Oregon.

Grandfather Rigby was a great one to sing hymns and it didn't matter much where he happened to be. One day as he was shingling a house in the red light district he started to sing and a woman popped out of a house with orders for him to quit, complaining that people would think it was a church. He kept on singing so presently she was back out with a repeat command. He still didn't heed so finally she told him she'd throw a rock at him if he didn't stop. By way of reply he reminded her that he had a hammer – and kept on singing hymns.

In his later years he was confined for a time in the Grace Hospital, and he still sang hymns. Often he would waken in the night and, unable to go back to sleep, start singing. However, that interfered with the sleep of other patients so they had to move him to a private home. At different times he lived in the homes of his various children, and sang there, too. He was eighty-four years old when he died in 1916.

134

Sherman Rigby had three children: William, Milo, and Edith. William married a widow, Mrs. Fish, with four sons. The Fish boys were well known in the Glendive area. They ranched with William on Pine Unit for years, then William homesteaded on Poverty Flat. He lived there almost until his death in 1948.

Edith married Frank Hasty and lived here in Glendive. Their son Frank continues as a Glendive resident, working for MDU*, while son Jack has a filling station in Livingston. Edith passed away in 1958.

Milo went to Oregon and embarked upon a teaching career. For a time he was superintendent of schools and rode a bicycle when he went to visit schools. (No cars, of course) In November of 1891 he founded a business college in Medford, Oregon. His son, Glendive's E.H. Rigby, has a copy of the school's 1894-95 catalogue. At that time they had seven different departments, including normal training for teachers. We don't want these excerpts from the catalogue to lure any students from Glendive, but in 1894, Rigby's Business College was asking tuition of, "Only $6.00 per month for the three month term – Furnished room with light, fuel, and board, can be obtained for $3.00 per week." Regarding the shorthand department: "Anyone becoming proficient in shorthand need never be out of employment. The salaries paid shorthand writers are larger than those generally commanded by other clerical position ranging from $600 to $2,000 per annum."

The catalogue also gives us a glimpse of Mr. Rigby's life as pictured by Rev. J.B. Ives, D.D.L.L.D., of Dallas, Oregon.

Having known Prof. Milo E. Rigby for more than twelve years, and believing him to be a true, earnest gentleman, deserving success and worthy of the highest honors, I wish from my own good will and unknown to the professor, to give the following brief sketch:

Milo, we will call him, for such he was called when a boy, was born in Green County, Wisconsin, December 16, 1861, and spent the greater part of his first twenty years on a farm, and like many poor, earnest boys, had few advantages. He attended a country school in the winter, and would help his father on the farm in the summer. We will not follow Milo in his various journeys from county to county and state to state, nor will we try to itemize the difficulties with which he has had to contend, space forbids us that privilege, but we will say that they have been many and of the most discouraging character, and would have baffled a less determined spirit.

Professor Rigby from early childhood has manifested a spirit of firm, unyielding determination, and obstacles that would have blockaded the path of thousands, have been quietly moved aside by his firm, unyielding, yet gentle manners. Professor Rigby as a schoolboy was a gentleman and boasts of having never been punished while attending school. He studied hard, and made rapid progress. As a teacher he has proven himself to be a gentleman in his dealings with his pupils, and as an instructor he has few equals. He is a graduate in thirty-five branches, and carries a life diploma,

135

privileging him to teach in any public school or university without examination. Professor Rigby is a natural artist, and as a penman as well as an instructor in penmanship has few equals.

While in California he received from the State Methodist College of California the degree of Master of Mathematics. And as an expert accountant he has no superiors.

The Rigbys also have the letter, which was written November 7, 1891 in reply to an inquiry regarding the school from Miss Lizzie Hillis. The letter says in part: *The cost of tuition, board and books for three months will be about seventy dollars. Our tuition for three months will be $25.00. We can secure you board here in private families for $3.00 or $3.50 per week. Books and paper for a term of three months will cost about $3.50.*

We hope to see you with us soon and will say, should you join our college, every effort will be put forth by the teachers to advance you in your course, procure you a position when you have finished, and see that you are well cared for while under our tuition.

Hoping to hear from you at your earliest convenience, and also to see you with us at an early date.

We are, Y'rs Respectfully,
Rigby and Part.

The letter is significant because Miss Hillis did come to the school, and a few years later the principal and proprietor procured for her a unique position – wife of the principal and proprietor.

In 1907 M.E. Rigby, with his wife and son, Edwin, and their two other children, returned to Glendive. His own health was failing somewhat, and he also wanted to help look after his folks. They lived on Grandfather Rigby's homestead along the river and found it an excellent garden spot. Glendive itself had no public water system at that time and not many residents had gardens so there was good demand for fresh produce. Mr. Rigby recalls that they had two produce wagons in town from which they sold vegetables.

Later Mr. Rigby (M.E.) homesteaded on Goose Island, the first island upriver. For several years they lived on Goose Island during the summer and on Grandfather Rigby's homestead during the winter. During the winter they would cross to Goose Island on the ice to cut and haul out timber. One day as they were bringing home a load of timber a big grey wolf followed them. Mr. Rigby had the shotgun in the wagon, but the wolf was careful to stay beyond range of the gun. When Mr. Rigby got off the wagon and hid along the edge of the timber, hoping to get closer, the wolf got wind of him and swung into the timber on the opposite side of the island.

One year Edwin walked to school in Glendive from the island until winter closed in and they moved to the nearer place. He had to leave home about seven in the morning, and would get home just about dark.

The Rigbys spent the years 1914-16 in Georgia. After they came back Ed went to work in the roundhouse. In 1918 he started as a fireman and has been

136

on the road since. He is a passenger engineer now but is thinking in terms of retiring before too much longer. What will he do with his time then? He's a rock hound and rocks can take a lot of time.

The year before the Rigbys moved to Georgia marked the arrival of another pioneer family. The Cruikshanks, with their four daughters, immigrated from Iowa in a covered wagon that fall. They began their leisurely trip in August and reached the Gate City in October. Mr. Cruikshank had had pneumonia and the doctor ordered him to a higher, drier climate. This might have been a little drier than he bargained for, while he was trying to farm, anyway, but the therapy must have been effective. He lived to be ninety years old.

The first winter after their arrival, the Cruikshanks camped on the site of the present Buttrey Store*. It was here that Ed Rigby first met Katherine Cruikshank. After the Cruikshanks moved to California Ed and Katherine kept up a correspondence. Ed made three trips to California and the third trip in 1926 he brought Katherine back with him as his bride. They have made their home in Glendive since.

The Rigbys have three daughters – two nurses and a secretary. All three of the girls are married now with families of their own, presenting Mr. and Mrs. Rigby with ten grandchildren. The occasional visits from children and grandchildren make things lively and are much enjoyed at the North Nowlan home.

Mrs. George (Helen Accart) Beeler

October 1968

Mrs. Helen Beeler is an American today because her father and mother happened to have the skills Pierre Wibaux was looking for in servants when he left France for the United States some eighty-odd years ago.

Wibaux was a wealthy young Frenchman with dreams of a cattle empire in the lush grasslands of the Montana Territory. When he first came he was a single man, and it was not until he returned to France where he married and prepared for another trip across the Atlantic that he looked about for servants. He advertised for domestic help, and those interested in applying wrote their names and qualifications – their particular skills – on a piece of paper. All these applications were placed in a box 'like when you vote'.

Although the applications were placed in a box, the process of selection was not merely a matter of 'drawing a name out of a hat'. Mr. Wibaux examined each application carefully. There were plenty to examine, for America was the dream of many Europeans of that day. He chose Jules Accart as gardener and caretaker, and his wife, Victorine (Mrs. Beeler's mother) as chambermaid.

Mrs. Beeler, until fire destroyed her home this summer, had a sizable collection of her father's papers, but the papers were all in Belgian (French). Those papers could have interesting information if they were still available.

Mrs. Beeler recalls stories her mother told her about their immigration to America. 'The menfolk', Mr. Wibaux and Mr. Accart, came over first, then when they had made preparations for the arrival of 'the womenfolk', Mrs. Wibaux and Mrs. Accart came. When the women got off the train at the depot in Wibaux (actually at Keith, one mile east), they found themselves surrounded by Indians – most disconcerting, to say the least – but Mr. Wibaux and a bunch of his cowboys met them and escorted them to the ranch.

One son, Elmer, was born to the Accarts in France, but he was left with his grandmother at the time of this first crossing. Three years later Mrs. Wibaux and Mrs. Accart both returned to France briefly, and when they came back to the United States they brought young Elmer with them. A 'hired girl' was engaged to help Mrs. Accart with the boy on the return trip. Mrs. Accart was strictly personal maid to Mrs. Wibaux, attending her constantly, and was not expected to assist in any way with the cooking or any other household duties. Other servants took care of those responsibilities.

If you take for granted your luxury living in this generation, consider that even French nobility could not boast indoor plumbing and bathrooms in the 1880's. Mrs. Beeler remembers hearing her mother describe one of their 'Indian scares' while they were outside. They saw an Indian coming across the creek toward the house so the two women hid in the tall weeds. The Indian went into the house, helped himself to what he wanted, and left. Another time they were in the house when one of them saw an Indian go past the window. There was no time to flee so they each ran for a closet and hid among the clothes while the

Indian went through the house. They were relieved when he departed without discovering them.

The women's fear at their first encounters with the Indians was not without basis. In the mid 1880's, just a few years after the battle of Custer with the Indians at the Little Big Horn, there was still considerable bad feeling between the red men and white. However, Mrs. Beeler points out that her father (Jules Accart) got along very well with the Indians (no doubt Wibaux, his employer, also did) and received from them the same consideration which he accorded them.

The Wibaux ranch headquarters was located about 12 miles north of the town of Wibaux – or perhaps we should say Mingusville, the name by which the settlement was called prior to 1893. Wibaux built up another ranch about 50 miles north of headquarters, and it was at this northerly ranch that the cowboys stayed. The Wibauxs and the Accarts lived at the former, but Pierre shared his time with the lower ranch as was necessary.

Descendants of Frank W. Kinney shared with us in a former AS I REMEMBER column a letter written by Kinney to his mother in Minnesota about 1885. The exact year is uncertain for, while they have the original copy of the letter, there was no date on it. The entire letter is printed in the Kinney story, Volume I of "As I Remember."

In this letter Kinney tells about finding some horses that had strayed from Wibaux and describes his own efforts to return them. Because the letter gives an 'eyewitness' description of the Wibaux Ranch as well as of their manner of living, a portion of the letter is reprinted here:

Will have to tell you of the long ride I had the first of March. There was five head of western horses that were shipped in here last fall and had strayed from the Wibaux ranch and were taken down on the Little Missouri about fifty miles from the RR track, got away and strayed back this way and I found them (or rather F.G.) and as there was $25 reward offered for them, thought I would undertake to deliver them. But I supposed I had to take them only about 25 miles from here. So I caught the best horse in the lot I have to ride.

Frank was with me the first half day and he left me after we had got about half way and pulled for home and I kept on across the country keeping my direction the best I could but as the day was kind of hazy and there being no road I soon lost sight of the Camels Hump (or the Blue Mountain) and had to go by guess and my horses were wild and I had to drive them on the run most of the time to get them where I wanted them.

About 5 o'clock I struck the creek where the home ranch was but about 10 miles too high up so I headed them down the creek on a good round trot and hardly let them stop until I came up to the ranch where I expected to get rid of my horses.

But on going in I found no one home but the man's wife and servants. As he is quite wealthy he lives in a fine house and she keeps one girl to cook and one to look after family affairs but they have only one child, and that is less than one year old and an old Frenchman to look after the wood and a few chores around the barn.

The men folks stay down at the lower ranch some 50 miles from there. Mr. Wibaux, the owner of the stock, was down below to spend a couple of weeks and as they had so little hay the woman (Note: This would have been Mrs. Wibaux) did not want to take the horses and so I was in a fine pickle. But after hard thinking, concluded to start below in the morning. So went out to corral the horses and after running them for half an hour succeeded in getting them in.

After taking care of my horse with the help of the old Frenchman we went to the house and was taken into the kitchen and allowed the same fare as the servants. As it was after supper hour I was given an abundance of fried potatoes and venison, bread and coffee.

It was served on a rude table without table cloth, and a bench to sit on. And the most interesting part of it was neither the old man or the cook could understand a word of English. But the serving maid could talk a little but she was in but little. When supper was over the old man beckoned for me to follow and we went up stairs.

He began to strip his linen for bed and so I followed suit. As I was tired from my long ride I was soon fast asleep and was awakened by the crowing of a rooster about ten feet from our bed. The old Frenchman had taken in some frozen-toed chickens and one of them was reminding us of morn.

As I was in somewhat of a hurry I was the first one out and as soon as I got breakfast was off. The servant had a big time trying to find out if I wanted a lunch and some oats to take for my saddle horse. Two of them could not understand white man's talk and the other but little and I guess if it had not been for Mrs. Wibaux we would have been jabbering back and forth now. That was the first private house that I ever stayed that the work folks had to eat in the kitchen and I was with the W.F. But as anything goes I did not complain.

Mr. Kinney continues to describe his efforts to return the stray horses to Pierre Wibaux. He lost his way the second day and at nightfall found himself at a ranch on the Little Missouri River so it was about 2 o'clock the third afternoon before he caught up with Mr. Wibaux at the north ranch.

When he was ready to start back, *Mr. Wibaux,* (we quote from Mr. Kinney again) *said if I would wait for him to get ready he would go up with me. I was only too glad to wait and about seven o'clock we pulled out for his home ranch, by the ridge road over fifty miles and not a ranch on it.*

He had two horses, led one and rode the other and changed every 12 or 15 miles. I expected to get left on the trail, but my horse being one of the best of its kind that I ever saw, stayed with the Frenchman to the end which we found about four o'clock making the ride in about 8 hours for we stopped and let our horses graze at noon.

After caring for our horses we went to the house and a supper was soon served. But in quite a different style. Instead of benches and cook table and servants it was filled with easy chairs, nice tables, china dishes, and everything to compare. But I must say the change was so great that I felt a little awkward.

Of course my former reception was all right. I could not expect one in her situation" (Note: Mrs. Wibaux's) *"to do anything different, I being a perfect stranger and making no other pretensions than a cowboy.*

One could see on entering that the house was furnished to a different taste than a 'simon pure' American. One of the oddities was a fire place but as this is out of line will not bother you with more." (We could wish he would have gone on and 'bothered' with a good deal more).

When bedtime came I was shown to a well furnished room where I had the best night's rest I had had since starting from home. That was some difference from the stubby little Frenchman's that slept with his cap on and bed about a foot too short and a hencoop to perfume the room.

As soon as breakfast was over Mr. Wibaux settled with me and thanking him for his kindness I saddled up and directed my horse 'which started off as nimble as ever' through the hills for home some 30 miles due west. And so ends our brief visit at the Wibaux ranch.

The Accarts' second child, daughter Julma, was born on the W Bar Ranch the same day, same house as Cyril, Wibaux's son and only child. According to an article in "The Wibaux Pioneer Gazette" at the time Wibaux's nephew visited the town in 1975, Cyril was born September 25, 1885.

When Pierre Wibaux's nephew J. Sylvain Wibaux visited Wibaux in 1957, the town went all out to welcome him. A full day of activities was planned, climaxed by a Lion's Club banquet in the evening. This banquet was for Lion members only with their invited guests, and Mrs. Beeler, because of family associations, was one of the few invited.

At the time of the nephew's visit the Wibaux Pioneer Gazette featured an article by Mrs. Nora C. Hurd about Pierre Wibaux. In this article mention is made of the beautiful flowers on the Wibaux premises and of the gardener Wibaux brought with him from France. Because the interests of Jules Accart were so closely tied to those of the cattle baron, we quote, with permission, the article here:

One of the most colorful figures in the history of eastern Montana was Pierre Wibaux for whom our town and county were named. Pierre Wibaux and 'Gus' Crissy, former French army officer, came to what is now Wibaux county in 1883 and engaged in ranching. This first venture did not prove profitable and at the end of three years the men found themselves at the end of their resources and in the fall of 1886 both men returned to France.

(Per Don Welsh in <u>The Trail Guide</u>, by March 1885 Pierre Wibaux and Gus Grisy – the correct spelling – had separated completely as business partners. Wibaux adopted as his brand the <u>W</u> and operated successfully on a small scale until the winter of 1886-1887.)

The call of the cow country proved too strong for Pierre Wibaux to withstand and in the spring of 1887, with his young bride, he came back to Montana; came back to find that the winter just passed was one of the most severe in the history of the country, and that approximately 85% of the cattle on the range had perished.

Undisturbed by this tragedy, he bought the remnants of some of the large herds that had survived the winter, and later purchased more cattle from herds trailed into the state. This time he seems to have had an unlimited supply of capital. It is estimated that at one time his herd numbered sixty thousand head.

Mr. Wibaux enlarged the original W Bar ranch, which was located 12 miles north of Wibaux. Here he built a large dwelling house, a house for the ranch foreman, bunkhouses for the 20 cowboys he employed, and a dwelling for the servants whom he brought with him from France.

In addition to this he built up another ranch 60 miles north of Wibaux, and had several line cabins 40 miles apart along the Yellowstone River. He also had a camp at which he stationed a wolfer with about 100 dogs. The dogs were kept in enclosures or stockades and packs of them run on alternate days. The line cabins were always stocked with provisions and line riders* were stationed in them.

The W Bar cattle ranged from the Little Missouri River west to the Yellowstone, and from the Northern Pacific railroad north to the Big Missouri. The spring round-up lasted three months and as many as ten thousand calves were branded in one season.

The office of the W Bar stood on what is now the main street of Wibaux. Some of the trees that once shaded the lawn about this building are still standing, and around town there are to be found fountains and statuary that once graced the grounds and garden around the office.

Pierre Wibaux was a lover of flowers and brought his gardener with him from France. Early residents still speak of the beds of California poppies, portulacas and flaming zinnias that bloomed in this yard, and men who rode for the W Bar tell of Mr. Wibaux inviting them to this spot for rest and refreshment after the cattle to be shipped had reached the end of their long trail and were loaded into the cars.

Mr. Wibaux did not establish a residence in town but lived at the ranch 12 miles north of Wibaux, and it was here that his son, Cyril, was born.

Mr. Wibaux is described as being about 30 years of age at the time of his arrival in Montana. He was above the average in height and weighed nearly 200 pounds. He had the erect carriage of a man who had spent years in military training.

He had a spirited team of black horses which he drove to a cart, tandem. When riding for pleasure he rode a large, carefully groomed saddle horse, and his favorite saddle and bridle were silver mounted, the saddle having a silver horn, six inches in diameter. These saddles with the large horns were designed originally for the Spanish dons, and were made so in order that the tally books might rest on the horn while the cattle were being tallied.

142

The first rodeo in this part of the country was put on by the cowboys of the W Bar for the entertainment of members of the French nobility visiting the Wibaux ranch. One of the features was a roping contest, Mr. Wibaux offering a prize for the man who would first rope, throw and tie a steer. The contest was staged on the plains, without the aid of enclosures now used for such sport.

For all his love of display Pierre Wibaux was no tenderfoot. He was an excellent horseman, he was fond of boxing and few men in the country were his equal in this sport. He often rode on the round-up, taking his place with the men, enduring the mud and the cold rains, and taking orders from his own foreman the same as any other cowboy.

Mr. Wibaux was known as a good man to work for, fair to his men, kind and thoughtful to his proven friends, but overbearing and haughty with those who tried to use his friendship to further their own designs.

Mr. Wibaux continued to run cattle here until 1900 when settlers began to come in such numbers that ranching on a large scale was no longer feasible. After disposing of his interests in Wibaux he was engaged in the banking business in Miles City and invested in mining property in the Black Hills.

Much of his time during the last years of his life was spent in travel. Before his death, which occurred in 1913, he requested that his remains be brought back to Wibaux for interment. His likeness, cast in bronze, and over nine feet in height, surmounts a high granite slab above his tomb. He is represented as wearing a buckskin jacket and trousers, and the familiar Stetson and chaps of the western cowboy. His lariat lies coiled at his feet and one hand rests on a rifle at his side, the other holds a pair of field glasses through which he seems to be gazing out over the country.

Another article with a byline In the same issue of the Wibaux Pioneer Gazette informs us: Mr. Wibaux's biggest cattle operations in Wibaux county and surrounding territory were from 1881 to 1895. He operated the famous W Bar ranch, located approximately 15 miles north of the town of Wibaux located on Beaver Creek.

The W Bar ranch was operated from 1885 to 1895. The stone barn still stands today, but the Wibaux residence proper has been destroyed. Some parts of other buildings (now known as the Schieffer ranch) still remain.

In 1900 Pierre Wibaux moved to Miles City, Montana, where he engaged in the banking business. The years 1907-1908 were his last years in the cattle business near Miles City. A building on main street, formerly a bank, bears his name over the main entry and a city park in Miles City is named after Pierre Wibaux.

Late in 1912 Pierre Wibaux was hospitalized in Chicago, and he died March 21, 1913, in St. Luke's Hospital, Chicago, at the age of 58 years. Death was attributed to liver cancer.

Mrs. Ralph Jones of Glendive owns a matching dresser and commode which formerly belonged to Pierre Wibaux. Her father bought it at auction when the Wibaux estate was settled. Under the dresser's heavy marble top the shipping instructions, 'Glendive Livestock Co., Mingusville', is still clearly legible. The dresser and commode, with their handles of grape clusters and leaves, were shipped from France to Mingusville by Pierre Wibaux as part of the furnishings for his ranch home on the Montana prairies. If furniture could only talk, what a story those two pieces could give us!

Mrs. Beeler doesn't know what year her parents bought a place in Wibaux, one-half-mile south of the cemetery, but even after they did, Mr. Accart continued for some time to work for Wibaux. Each day he rode to the ranch and back horseback. The white horse that he rode was a gift from the Indians. He often gave cream and eggs to the Indians, she explained, and in return, they gave him the horse. One winter during a severe snow storm the gift horse smothered. He had gone into the barn, which was dug into a hill, and the snow drifted over it so tightly that the horse died.

The Accarts were fortunate to escape a similar fate. The house, too, was covered by the snow, but the stovepipe stuck out above the drifts. Mr. Chappell with some others from the town came looking for them, and all that could be seen was the stovepipe. The search party shouted down the pipe, and Mrs. Accart, down in her kitchen, wondered what was the matter with her stove. With windows and door plastered with snow, the interior of the house was completely dark. And now the stove begins emitting weird noises! Not knowing quite what to expect, she lifted the stove lid and was relieved to find that the noises had a human origin. The prisoners and the rescuers could hear each other with ease through the stove and pipe, and Mr. Chappel assured them of a prompt release. With the aid of some other men from the town, he soon had them shoveled out.

Helen Beeler is the youngest of the nine Accart children. She can remember the last time her father made the trip to France with Pierre Wibaux. He made several trips, and she remembers that he brought back souvenirs for the family. Hers was a bracelet. She no longer has the bracelet, but she does have her mother's gold watch. She and her brother Happy are the only remaining members of their family.

When Helen was thirteen years old, she was sent to the convent in Miles City. That was a homesick time. During her stay there she received only one card from home – from Happy – and the sisters in the convent couldn't read that. She was overjoyed when her oldest sister, Julma, living in Wolf Point, came for her. Helen lived with Julma in Wolf Point until her own marriage to George Beeler, brother to Julma's husband.

The Beelers have spent most of their married life in or near Wibaux. Last summer their home on the edge of Wibaux was struck by lightning and destroyed by the ensuing fire so they have moved into one of the older homes in Wibaux. Their nine children are all married and scattered, but Mrs. Beeler's brother Happy still makes his home with them.

Wedding Picture of Mr. & Mrs. Pierre Wibaux, son Cyril in lower left

Art Kitchen

February 1965

Art Kitchen arrived in Montana in March of 1907, too late to get the benefit of most of that record-breaking 1906-07 winter, but he's had plenty of opportunities to see cold and snow other winters.

One winter afternoon, a few years after his Montana debut, Adolph Boje, a close neighbor, stopped in and told Art that he needed a little help. He had to haul some straw, but the rack was off his wagon so he wanted Art to go along home with him and sleep there that night (both were bachelors), then in the morning help him lift the rack onto the wagon frame.

Neighbors were neighbors in those days, and Art went along with him. Next morning as soon as they had eaten breakfast, they went out to assemble the hay rack. The weather was cold, but they didn't give the matter much thought; they had had cold weather before. The rack on the wagon, Boje went to get his load of straw, and Art walked back home – about a mile.

It was bitter cold in the shack when he got there, and his fingers were so numb he had difficulty holding a match to light a fire, but he soon had a roaring fire going and could forget that the weather was cold outside. Not so with Adolph.

After he had his load of straw he went on over to Bloomfield to pick up a few things at the store, then on the way home stopped at another neighbor's, Barry Chaney, who had a government thermometer and kept the weather record. There he was informed that the temperature had dropped to fifty-four degrees below zero! That was too much for Adolph.

He went as far as Kitchen's, put his team in the barn and announced, "It's too cold to go any farther; I'm staying here tonight!" And stay he did. "If he just hadn't found out what that thermometer said," Art chuckled, "he probably would have made it home all right."

Kitchen was one of a number of Thirteen Mile settlers who came from Bloomfield, Nebraska, conferring upon the post office of their new settlement the name of their old home town. Bert Crockett, one of the valley's earlier settlers, had come from the same community in Nebraska and it was as a result of his reports that the migration from the east to the west took place. Art was single and came with the Lou Cole family, selling his saddle horse to get the money for his train fare.

As soon as they reached Glendive, he went out to look over the available land, chose his quarter section, then filed on it. Art spent that summer in Glendive, working for the Goodrich Kaul Lumber Company. The job proved to have more than one advantage; when time came that fall to build his shack out on the homestead, the boss allowed him all the lumber he needed at cost.

He built his shack 12'x14' feet, then later was sorry he hadn't made it 14'x16'. There was no school in the community as yet, even though there were a number of children of school age. Since he was getting his material at cost, he felt that he could just as well have made his abode a bit larger and let the community hold school there until a schoolhouse could be built.

When Art first came there were still some of the 'old' old timers around – ranchers who considered anyone within twenty-five miles (and few enough they were) as their neighbor, and their riders who just about lived in their saddles thought of a fifty or sixty mile ride as part of the day's routine.

There was sort of an unwritten law that a man was invited to eat if he stopped in at mealtime. Mr. Kitchen told about one fellow who had somehow missed the place where he had expected to eat dinner and didn't get anything to eat until he reached the home ranch that evening, after riding since early morning. Asked if he was hungry (superfluous question!), he retorted that he was "hungry enough to eat a horse and chase the rider a mile."

The country was all open range with horses and cattle of every color and description when the homesteaders started coming. The new settlers found they had to fence their holdings to keep out the range stock, and those fences strangled the last of the 'big outfits'.

To get started with his farming operations he bought a team from Edward O'Neil and a breaking plow* and wagon from Pat Dawson. He broke about twenty acres with this walking plow, but later he hired Art Youngquist to break another fifty acres for him. Youngquist used one of those big steam engines that pulled twelve plows, but when he came around with it, it scared Kitchen's team, and they took off on the run with the disc bouncing behind them. When he got them stopped, the disc needed some mending, but he was accustomed to doing his own repair work so he soon had it ready to go again. The sod needed plenty of disking behind the breaker plow.

The first few years he farmed he got a pretty good crop, but then came the dry summers of 1910 and 1911, and they didn't get anything. He joked that when they did get a crop, they worked all summer to raise it, then worked all winter to haul it away. He usually hauled his grain to Intake, using a team and wagon, of course. He could make three trips a week, one day to go down and one day to come back. The wheat price usually wasn't much – perhaps fifty cents a bushel – but at least they didn't have thousands of dollars tied up in equipment as a farmer has now.

Art has been a bachelor all his life, so while he was on his homestead, Mrs. Frank Coryell did his baking and washing, and after the Milt Hills came, he bought butter from Mrs. Hill. There were times when being a bachelor had its drawbacks, though, especially at threshing time. Mose and Joe Mullet owned a threshing rig, and each fall they threshed for the entire neighborhood, moving from one place to the next with the different neighbors making up the crew. A man could hardly be in the kitchen cooking when the threshing crew was at his place, but there were about half-a-dozen bachelors in the 'ring', so they hired Ora Chaney to cook for them at their various places.

Art had started drinking when he was only eighteen, smoking too, and by the time he was thirty-nine he was drinking heavily. One afternoon Clyde Chaney stopped by and asked him to go along to the meeting at the schoolhouse that night. The Methodist circuit preacher, Arch Plummer, was to be there. Plummer, Kitchen says, was highly regarded among the settlers, and he agreed to go along.

The meeting turned out to be a temperance meeting so at its close, Art signed the pledge. He quit, all right, but that signing didn't take away his appetite for intemperance so after about two years of struggling against it, he decided the craving was as bad as the doing so he started in again. Before long he was such a slave to his pipe that when he got up in the morning he would start his pipe going before he dressed, and the only time he laid it down was to eat. Came a time when he was shucking corn for Ike Jones and ran out of tobacco. He recalls that he tried to get Ike to go to Bloomfield and get him some, but Ike wouldn't do it so he went himself and got a dollar's worth.

A couple days later, they had a big rain and he couldn't shuck corn so he just worked around the shed. During the course of the morning he had stopped to refill his pipe and still held the sack in one hand, the match in the other, when suddenly he seemed to hear, "Art, quit it!" And he quit. He emptied his pipe, and at noon when he got to his room, he cleaned out all the sacks and cans of tobacco from his drawer, took them to the creek (running high with the rains), and sent them on their way to the Yellowstone. He became a Christian and had no more trouble with the tobacco habit.

In 1916 he sold his homestead and went to work for Andy Dahl. Dahl had a big Rumley steam engine, and did a lot of breaking for the homesteaders and farmers throughout the area. From that job Kitchen went to Hysham and worked for a big sheep ranch. After lambing* season he was assigned to the job of 'camp tender' – getting supplies from town, hauling and chopping wood, seeing that the different herders had what they needed, and so forth.

When World War I broke out, he was too old for the draft so he went to Billings and enlisted. Four of the men who enlisted with him there were with him throughout the duration of their service, including overseas (they were in the signal corps), and all came back together to part in Billings after the war.

After the war Kitchen returned to the Bloomfield country, bought his father's homestead, and farmed until about 1924. As the mechanization of farming became more necessary he felt he'd rather get into some other kind of work so he sold his place to Rick Johnson and went to Hamilton. In 1938 he came back to Glendive and has made his home here since.

Mr. Kitchen will be eighty-three next May, but he still lives alone in his little shack on Nowlan. Some have suggested to him he should make other arrangements, but as long as he is able to take care of himself, he prefers his independence.

Mr. James Bidwell & Mrs. George (Margaret Bidwell) Pierce

May 1965

The Iowa auctioneer-farmer-stockman found his health continuing to decline despite heavy medication and careful adherence to doctor's recommendations. Perhaps a change of scenery and release from the strain of auctioneering could do what doctors and medicines couldn't, so in 1908 Oscar Bidwell and his wife made a visit to his brother, Everett Bidwell, and nephew, Frank Eaton, near Union, Montana. They were favorably impressed with what they saw so in 1909 Mr. Bidwell returned to Dawson County. After filing on a homestead he returned to his home and made preparations to leave his lovely Iowa farm and move to the dryland homestead on the Montana prairies. He succeeded in leaving his farm behind, but not his auctioneering.

In April of 1909 he took up residence in the Treasure State. Relatives here had built a barn on his claim in anticipation of his arrival so Mr. Bidwell and the nephew who had accompanied him lived in that while they built a house and broke up and seeded ten acres of sod, using horse power for field work, of course. The summer of 1910 was dry, even by Montana standards, and the ten acres yielded nothing, but the house they built that summer still serves as a dwelling today. Further loss that fall resulted from the disappearance of seven mares and a stallion that were evidently stolen from the range. Mr. Bidwell and Frank Eaton rode for two weeks trying to find them but found no trace.

That fall Mr. Bidwell went back to Iowa to get his family. They loaded machinery, livestock, and household goods into immigrant cars*, the family into passenger cars, and were Montana bound. The family arrived in a couple of days, but the journey took the immigrant car a couple weeks. Everett Bidwell, with team and wagon, met the family at the train, and after spending the night in Glendive, they embarked on the last stage of their journey – the journey that marked the beginning of a new era in their lives. Mrs. Pierce recalls that on the way out, jogging along in the lumber wagon, they opened a tin can of tomatoes and found that the cold tomatoes really tasted good. They were accustomed to Mother's home canning, but the tin cans were something of a novelty.

Once at the homestead it was four years before the two girls, seven-year-old Margaret and five-year-old Alice, ever saw town again. Little wonder that 'going to town' was an occasion much anticipated and long remembered. They allowed what they considered to be a reasonable time (about a week) for the immigrant car to get here, then the men folk and ten-year-old Jim came back to town to unload it while Mrs. Bidwell and the other three children stayed at the homestead. The car wasn't in yet, but they thought it would surely arrive any day so they waited for it. They waited a week. The Goodrich Lumber Company had built sheds for just such contingencies so they could sleep there, but there wasn't much to do during the day – especially for a ten-year-old boy. The men could go into the barrooms to warm themselves, but where was the boy to go?

The October weather, though pleasant, was nevertheless chilly. Morning rising was always accompanied by considerable hand-clapping, thigh-slapping, and foot-stomping to warm them a little. They weren't at all sorry when the car finally arrived so they could load their wagons and start for the homestead.

They had come in with three outfits, and there was another team and wagon in the immigrant car. Their four wagons were loaded and ready to leave town by sundown. Young Jim was driving one of the wagons, piled high with furniture. Don't picture the four wagons and the herd of cattle following Highway 20 to Lindsay. There was no road and you had to use your imagination a little to see the wagon trail. Dusk overtook them by the time they had reached the sandhills west of Glendive, and it was difficult to see the chuckholes along the way. More frequently than Jim, walking along side the wagon much of the time, could appreciate, the wheels on one side of the wagon would drop into one of those sand pockets and the wagon with its high load would lurch threateningly. The men were amused at the youthful alacrity with which Jim would jump aside at each lurch, but he was taking no chances with that load.

They camped that first evening at Seven Mile Spring, about seven miles west of Glendive in the vicinity of Dr. Strowd's former summer home near where Joe Morasko now lives. Trailing the cattle was slow business so they had to take their time. They expected to reach the homestead by the second evening, but darkness overtook them and they lost the trail so there was no choice but to camp. With the coming daylight they were able to relocate their trail and soon found that they had camped two miles from their new home.

Neighbors were few and far between in the homestead country when the Bidwells first arrived, and company was always welcome. Whenever someone stopped at one of the scattered dwellings, morning, noon or night, he was invited in. If it was near mealtime, there was an automatic invitation to stay and eat. You might not have much, but you shared what you had. If it was at close of day, he was expected to stay overnight. Doors were left unlocked, and even if no one was home the traveler was free to go in and prepare himself a meal, providing he washed up the dishes and put things away after he was through.

Wood was scarce and every little piece was cherished for kindling. Settlers would go up into the Divide* with teams and wagons to haul out the dead cedar for their firewood, and none was wasted. You used it for starting your fire, but you'd better keep your fire going with coal because that was your allotment of wood for that time.

The first year fresh vegetables were even scarcer than wood. A few potatoes had struggled through the summer's drought, but that was the extent of their produce. They had plenty to eat, but their diet wasn't the kind now considered necessary for good health. The children enjoyed eating the potatoes raw when they were occasionally permitted to do so.

The new land in which they found themselves afforded them freedom of living in the open country, but it did not hand them entertainment on a platter – or on a TV set either, for that matter. They created their own entertainment and had a happy time doing it. During the winter the children coasted down hills, made snow houses, and dug tunnels through the drifts. In the summer they had picnics, waded in the creek, and rode horseback. They always had a variety of pets, which contributed to a full life. Ray, especially (the son just younger than Jim), was a great one to make pets. One year he made pets out of two weaner pigs, which he named Jennie and Jane. Those pigs became a great nuisance, and they didn't improve with age. Nevertheless, when time came for their demise, the family realized they couldn't eat those pigs so they shipped them instead.

Visits from the grandparents were always a highlight of the summer, and the entire family looked forward to them eagerly, as well as visits from the uncles, aunts, and cousins. They didn't have much room, but they made beds on the floor for sleeping accommodations and everyone had a wonderful time with the relatives. The parents of both Mr. and Mrs. Bidwell lived in Iowa, and both families had earlier moved from Wisconsin, although from different parts of the state. Mr. Bidwell's father (Frank Bidwell) was originally from New York State. He was a Civil War veteran and had participated in Sherman's march to the sea.

He had made the trip from New York to Wisconsin in a covered wagon pulled by oxen. The James Bidwells still have the shoes with which his grandfather's oxen were shod, a unique antique. Grandfather Bidwell also fought in some Indian skirmishes in Minnesota after he moved to Wisconsin. In 1881 he moved to Iowa where he very successfully engaged in stock raising. When one of the immigrant cars destined for the Bidwells at Glendive left Iowa, he sent along a little plot of blue grass for his daughter-in-law out Union way. She planted it along one side of the yard and always had a special regard for that little patch of blue grass.

Both Mr. and Mrs. Bidwell were high school graduates, unusual for their generation and Mr. Bidwell had also attended business college. The duties and responsibilities of a pioneer wife left little time for leisure, but Mrs. Bidwell managed to find time for sewing, crocheting, and embroidering, as well as some photography. Not only did she enjoy taking pictures, she also did the developing and printing. She loved good music and had sung in the church choir before leaving Iowa. When they moved to Montana the organ came with them, and the children regarded it as a real treat when Mother played the organ for them. In 1917 they bought an Edison phonograph and some good records so many happy hours were spent listening to the music.

During World War I Mrs. Bidwell was chairman of the Clear Creek Red Cross with their sewing, knitting, and making bandages. During this time Mr. Bidwell was also busy with the war effort, working to sell war bonds. For this he received recognition from President Wilson. After the Clear Creek Home Demonstration Club was organized Mrs. Bidwell also found time for active participation in it, serving as club president for seven or eight years. Busy though she was, on special occasions she always took time to make the table especially attractive with lovely linen and fine china, even in the midst of their primitive surroundings.

One evening at almost dusk the cry went through the neighborhood that a child was lost. Search parties were quickly formed and all through the night they combed the prairies. Mrs. Bidwell stayed up all night, frying doughnuts and making fresh coffee for the searchers. During the night a cold rain fell, causing increased concern for the child's welfare. Each little group had a gun so that when the child was found, shots could be fired to notify the others.

It was daybreak when the welcome signal reverberated through the hills. The child, just a little past two years old, had wandered farther than they had thought possible and was found sleeping in the shelter of an overhanging rock more than two and one-half miles from home. She seemed none the worse for her experience and didn't even catch a cold.

There were no schools in that area when the Bidwells arrived, for the simple reason that there were no children – not enough for school anyway. Even with their arrival there weren't enough to meet the minimum pupil requirements for a school. It was two more years before there were enough children in the neighborhood so they could demand a teacher. Miss Emma Carson was the teacher for that first term of school in the summer of 1912.

School was held in a homesteader's shack, which Mr. Bidwell had previously bought and used for a granary. He moved it to the northeast corner of his homestead, and school began. By the end of that term there were enough children to warrant a schoolhouse so the county supplied the materials, but it was built entirely with volunteer labor by the men of the district. By the fall of 1913 it was ready and school was officially established.

One winter morning the weather was deceptively balmy, and the children didn't wrap very warmly when they left for school. During the day one of our sudden blizzards struck, and temperatures began to drop. Mr. Bidwell and the hired man made ready to go get the children from school, piling plenty of warm blankets in the wagon. By that time the blizzard had reduced visibility to almost zero, but they hitched the team to the wagon and by following the fence they were able to find the schoolhouse. Only then did they realize that in the blowing and whirling snow they had put the blankets into one wagon and hitched the team to the wagon that stood next to it! The Bidwell children were the only ones to get home that night. All the others stayed at the schoolhouse.

During another blizzard when Mr. Bidwell came for them in the bobsled, he was wearing a curly black fur coat. They had to follow the fence that time, too, to find their way so progress was slow, and by the time they reached home, his overcoat pockets were tightly packed with snow that had blown into them.

The first year they were here their address was Two-EE, Montana. The post office, in the home of Cora and Mattie Aulbe, was near the Billy Wood Ranch and borrowed its name from his brand. Next a post office was established in the home of Albert Skillestad and named Union. Later it was transferred to the Olson store but still called Union, and there it remained until the store was closed. Since the closing of the store the mail has been taken to Lindsay and sent out on route.

A strong community spirit prevailed among them, and they had many good times at their picnics, dances, and visits together. Mrs. Pierce (Margaret Bidwell) observed that she hesitated to even mention the dances because the social function that goes by that name now is such a far cry from the family affair that a dance was then. At those dances the whole neighborhood got together and visited, music was provided by local musicians (probably the organ and a violin), and they danced until daylight because they couldn't see the trails to go home earlier. They emphasized that there was no drinking or carousing at these get-togethers. Again it was pointed out that no respectable girl would dance with a man if she suspected that he had been drinking. Girls were very much in the minority in those early days – perhaps three girls and fifteen or twenty fellows – so no girl ever had to worry about sitting out a dance!

There were no deer in the area then, but neighbors sometimes got together for a rabbit or coyote hunt. No closed season for them! One of the neighbors had hounds so they did quite a little hunting with the hounds. Once when they were down at the old Thurston Ranch after a light skiff of snow, they found where gray wolves had pulled down a three-year-old steer. They started tracking them and followed them for over ten miles, but then had to give up.

When anyone got a new book, it was shared by the whole community, passed from family to family to family, read aloud in the evening by the light of kerosene lamps. Just plain visiting provided much good fellowship and recreation with the neighbors. Telephones were introduced with fences serving for lines. At least it provided contact with one another. The organization of a Sunday School provided opportunity for both worship and getting together. At first they met in Hill's granary, then in the school house after it was built.

There was no bridge across the Yellowstone at Terry when the Bidwells first came, but after it was built they did most of their business at Terry. A trip to town was a trip in the lumber wagon. In later years when there was grain to freight, they'd make the trip to Terry with the grain one day, then bring back a load of coal the next day.

Bidwell specialized in livestock rather than farming and shipped in many fine stallions. Almost every year for a number of years after they came to Montana he'd ship in a carload of breeding stock and did much to stock the range with fine horses. Jim recalled a deal with F.W. Kinney, another local horse breeder, in which Mr. Bidwell traded a stallion to Mr. Kinney for some brood mares. He shipped out many horses and cattle as well as importing the good breeding stock. He was a director of the Federal Land Bank. Even after he was in Montana he did quite a little auctioneering, especially during the depression when many farmers were leaving.

In the summer of 1916 they had a carload of hogs to sell so they decided the most expeditious means of getting them to the railroad would be to drive them to Terry afoot. Accordingly, Ray and Jim with Harris Olson and Ralph Pierce started out, chasing those hogs – or trying to keep up with them. Some of the hogs the Bidwells had raised, and some they had bought from near Circle. The Circle hogs had been trailed to the Bidwells so they were more or less 'trail broke', but not so the homegrown. The boys drove the hogs about twenty miles the first day, then decided to camp for the night by a little water hole, but the hogs had other ideas. They would not bed down so there was no choice but to follow them another four or five miles to Cherry Creek where they did succeed in getting them stopped.

Ray and Jim spent the night sleeping on the ground, and when they woke up in the morning, they found one of those big hogs bedded down between them. Ralph and Harris slept on the hay in the grub wagon so they didn't have any trouble with the hogs, but they awoke in the morning to find themselves almost standing up because the team, tied to the back of the wagon for the night, had eaten the hay from under their legs! By the time they reached Terry with that drove of hogs all the hogs had names, some of them not suitable for printing in this story, and the fellows were all of the opinion that they'd take cattle for theirs.

But cattle could present problems too, they found. They had trailed a herd of about 100-150 to Terry for shipping and had them just at the edge of town along the railroad track, ready to drive them up the lane to the stockyards, when a train came along and blew its whistle. At the sound of that shrill blast the herd exploded. Cattle ran in every direction, through or over the fences, across the gullies, over the hills, and amongst the trees along the river. It took them half a day to get them rounded up and back to the stockyards again, and then the depot agent told them there was no reason for the engineer to blow his whistle. Evidently he just wanted to see what the cattle would do. He saw and so, through much sweat and hard riding, did the boys.

Horseback riding was almost as much a part of their daily schedule as eating. One day as Jim was jogging along at a leisurely pace across country from Circle, leading a team behind his horse, his saddle mount suddenly jumped to one side. Jim had been sitting loosely in his saddle and was almost deposited on the rattlesnake, coiled in the grass, that had caused his horse to perform such gymnastics. He managed to stay in the saddle, however, and dismount at his prerogative to kill the snake responsible for the incident.

Of the four children born to Mr. and Mrs. Oscar Bidwell, three are still living. Jim, the oldest found his bride-to-be in a schoolhouse. Frances Haggerty, daughter of Glendive's E.P. Haggerty, was teaching the district school when Jim met her. During the first years of their marriage they lived on a farm in the Union area, but in 1937 they moved to West Glendive, and Mr. Bidwell took up carpentering. Now he says he is retired, but he's still building cupboards.

Ray, the second son, married one of the neighbor girls, Mildred Pierce, and they now live in Terry. Mildred's brother George won the Bidwells' first daughter, Margaret, and they lived together in West Glendive until Mr. Pierce's death in 1960. Mrs. Pierce continues to reside in West Glendive and teaches one of the special education classes at the Washington School.

The youngest of the family, Alice, also married a neighbor, Oakley Tinkey. She passed away in 1935, the first to break the family circle. Their parents continued to live on the homestead until 1944 when they, too, moved to Glendive. Mr. Bidwell departed this life in 1953, and his wife followed him in 1960, both having lived a long, full life and making a notable contribution to their community.

154

Jim Haggerty

December 1969 – January 1970

Now that Jim Haggerty has retired from driving the Northern Pacific Transport and has returned from a California trip where he helped his mother celebrate her 100th birthday, he finally has the time to sit down and do a little reminiscing.

Jim is a native Montanan but he didn't come to Glendive until he was eight months old. Those first eight months were spent in Butte where he was born in 1907 – or so he's been told. In 1941, when he decided that he wanted his birth certificate, he had quite a time proving he was born. There was no record of that momentous occasion so he had to get affidavits to that effect.

It was June 1908, when his parents brought him home to Glendive and he has lived here ever since. His father, John Haggerty (everybody called him Jack), was around these parts much earlier than that, however.

Exactly when he first set foot into Montana would be rather hard to determine but in 1889 he was stationed at Fort Buford*. When a tribe of Indians broke out of the reservation in Oklahoma and started for Canada, Jack Haggerty was with a patrol between Fort Buford and Fort Keogh in Miles City so if he wasn't in Montana before that, he was then.

Jack Haggerty, although an Irishman, was born in Scotland. His dad had got mixed up in the revolutionary movement in Ireland and soon found he was persona non grata. When he got word that the authorities were coming after him, he left Ireland and slipped across the Irish Sea to Scotland. So that's how it happened that Jack Haggerty was born in Scotland. Jack didn't have much schooling; he went through the "Third Reader" – just what the equivalent to that would be in our school system he found hard to explain but his formal education was very limited.

When Jack was still just a small chap, small enough, he used to explain to his son, that he had to carry his lunch basket in the crook of his elbow rather than in his hand so it wouldn't drag on the ground – he went to work in the collieries (coal mines). In the mines they had boys sitting by the conveyor belts where the coal passes through, and they would pick the rocks and slate out of the coal. This was the job that Jack filled.

He was only fourteen years old when one day, as he and two other boys were going home from work, the British Navy Patrol picked them up. Just like that they were in the British Navy. After almost two years in the navy his ship went to Amsterdam, and he saw a chance to get away. He deserted and worked his way on a freighter to Philadelphia where an uncle was living. But he couldn't find the uncle. He also had a half-brother in New York so he went there next, but he couldn't find him either.

He got a job digging ditches in New York until the Panic of 1887 hit and he was out of a job. He went to a recruiting station and tried to join the army but he wasn't quite eighteen so they wouldn't take him. He asked where the next recruiting station was and at that one he was 'eighteen'. It worked fine then but years later when he applied for his pension he had a hard time getting it because of lying about his age when he enlisted. He got his pension though. His widow, incidentally, is one of about ten in the United States still receiving the Indian Wars Veterans Widow's pension.

After his enlistment he was sent to Jefferson Barracks in Missouri for just less than four months, then was sent up the Missouri River to Fort Buford. For a glimpse of life at Fort Buford, we have his own description, even though it is eighty years old.

In another attempt to contact his uncle in Philadelphia, he wrote a letter from his army post. He still didn't contact his uncle and the letter was returned to him unclaimed. His son still has that letter and permits us to quote it. The letter contains few periods but for someone whose formal education stopped with the "Third Reader" the letter is rather remarkable – particularly the penmanship and spelling. (Son Jim confesses he's never found a pencil yet that will spell right, and his schooling extended well beyond the "Third Reader."

The letter:

Fort Buford, Dec. 15/89

Dear Uncle.

After a long delay which I cannot attempt to excuse I will now try and write you a few lines hoping to find you all well as this leaves me at this time. I was in Jefferson Barracks three months & twenty-six days. After that I was transferred to the 8th Cavalry up here in Northern Dakota it was very warm in the Barracks but it is cold enough up here to make up for that I can tell you. It is from 15 to 38 degrees below zero right along. It is a very lonesome country here no sport at all no town or village near Williston is the nearest and that is thirty miles distant but there is plenty game such as prairie chicken sage hens & rabbits & deer there is any quantity of them my troop has got sixty this winter already but it is getting most to cold for hunting season & the hunting season closes on the 15th but it is to cold anyway we cannot go out without buffalo coats fur caps & fur gloves walking post is all done in the stables no out door work at all so you can see we are laid on the shelf for winter nothing to do at all only take care of our horses but we will have to pay for this in the summer time their will be no rest at all then. but if worst comes to the worst Canada is near by. we are only about 60 miles from the borders. no more news at this time.

Tell Dunn & wife I was asking for them and likewise John McHennie.

Love & best wishes,
write soon
Troop E. 8th Cavalry
Fr. Buford, North Dakota

While Jack Haggerty was stationed in Fort Buford, a tribe of Indians broke out of their reservation in Oklahoma and started for Canada. Mr. Haggerty was a member of the unit patrolling between Fort Buford and Fort Keogh at Miles City but the only Indians they ever located was a group of women and children. However, while they were at Fort Keogh, quite a group of Indians came in and surrendered. Haggerty became quite friendly with some of them and one of the chiefs gave him a tomahawk and a ceremonial pipe. Son Jim, in later years, loaned the items out to different organizations for display and someone got away with the tomahawk. Now, all he has is the pipe and he doesn't loan that out anymore.

When Jack finished his stint in the army at Ft. Buford, he took on the job of driving stage from Ft. Buford to Glendive. That was quite a job in those days. There were no roads at all, only trails across the prairie over which the stage jolted. When the ruts in the trail he was using got too deep, he just made another trail. There were no bridges either so streams had to be forded. In the spring of the year, or after a heavy rain, crossing the streams could be a real problem. Much of the year a stream might be almost or completely dry, yet be turned into a torrent by the spring thaw or a cloudburst. He always went prepared for the worst by carrying bridge planks tied to the side of the stage. In an emergency he could make a makeshift bridge. Probably the worst trip he ever made was the time when, because of bad weather and road conditions, it took him three weeks to make the trip from Fort Buford to Glendive and back again.

After son Jim had started driving the Northern Pacific Transport on its Sidney run, his dad went along with him and pointed out the old stage stops to him. The first stop from the Glendive end was at Neil Stuarts where the Tagues live now, near Intake – no Intake then. The next was at Tokna west of Savage – no Savage then, either. There was another stop at Newland in the vicinity of Sidney – but no Sidney. Jim doesn't remember the name of the one between the present towns of Sidney and Fairview but the next stop was at Mondak and there was a Mondak then.

After two years of driving stage, Mr. Haggerty (Jack) decided to go into the sheep business with Billy Easton. They bought 500 sheep which they ran 'in the shadow of the Divide' (the Yellowstone-Redwater Divide). Come spring, a big storm hit in lambing season and they lost the whole band – every one of them. And he was out of the sheep business faster than he went into it.

Next, he went to work for the railroad in the car shops. He was on the wrecker for a while. When he was laid off there, he went to Butte and found work in the mines. While in Butte he met Margaret. They were married in 1903.

Margaret Tinsley was born in England in 1869. When she was fourteen, she came with her married sister to the United States. They first located in Plymouth, Pennsylvania, then ventured into the 'Wild West', spending a couple of years at Rock Springs, Wyoming. In the 1880's, Wyoming hadn't had much taming. From Rock Springs they moved to Butte, which wasn't especially tame either.

In Butte she met and married the miner, Jack Haggerty. It was during this period when Haggerty was working in the mines that the miners were trying to organize and were meeting with resistance from mine management. He took on a job on the side as organizer and was fired. Not only was he fired but he was blackballed as well so he couldn't get a job in Butte at all. When he couldn't get work, the Haggertys left Butte and Jack worked in the mines at Boulder for a year or two, then they went back to Butte where son Jimmy was born.

When Jimmy was eight months old, they moved back to eastern Montana and more mines. This time it was a coalmine on Burns Creek. There they lived in a one-room tarpaper shack with a dirt floor and carried their water about a half-mile. The hardships apparently didn't hurt his mother – she's the one who lived to celebrate her 100th birthday.

They lived on Burns Creek about a year, then moved into Glendive – and son Jim has lived here ever since. They lived in a four-room house, the last house on the east end of Valentine Street, right under Hungry Joe*. Actually, there weren't very many houses on all of Valentine then.

Jim recalls his mother telling about once while they were living there some Indians came to the door selling beadwork. Scared at the sight of the Indians, Mrs. Haggerty grabbed Jim and his sister Anna and dashed up to the bedroom where they hid under the bed until the 'visitors' went on their way.

In 1916, they built two more rooms onto the house on Valentine only to have the entire structure burn down in 1917. They lost everything. Insurance? That was still a 'rich man's plaything' at that time. But they built another house on the same spot.

When Jack Haggerty brought his family to Glendive in 1907, he went to work for the railroad. After about four or five years he quit the railroad and joined Glendive's 'police force'. At that time the 'police force' boasted two men – Mr. Haggerty and the chief. Mr. Haggerty worked nights, twelve hours a night, seven nights a week, 365 days a year.

Although there were only two men on the police force, Haggerty's police dog, a collie named Robin, probably supplied more than the equivalent of another man (and the city didn't even have to pay him). On his night patrols, Jack would go down the alleys, and his dog, accompanying him, would run in and out, searching all the nooks and crannies.

Saloons were rough in those days and the drunks were just thrown out. In the dimly lighted or unlighted alleys, Robin would find the men, then Mr. Haggerty would take them to City Hall and let them 'sleep it off'. City Hall then was painted white with two plate glass windows in the front. It was located in the same place as the present city hall.

Another important service Robin rendered was escorting lone women home. Sometimes women would come downtown alone in the evening to a lodge meeting or a card party and often the policeman on duty would be asked to escort someone home. Instead of going himself, Mr. Haggerty would send his collie who would walk the woman home, then trot back to his master.

One night a fellow broke out of jail during Haggerty's shift so Jack pursued him. As he chased him down an unpaved alley, he shouted to the fugitive, "Stop, or I'll shoot!" But the fugitive ran on unheeding, so the officer fired at the ground. The bullet hit a rock and ricocheted, killing the man. The next morning Haggerty turned in his badge and gun.

After his resignation from the police force, Haggerty tended bar for a while until passage of the Volstead Act which ushered in Prohibition. Then he served for a time in the sheriff's office under Art Helland. About 1920 or 1921, he went back to the railroad and worked there until his retirement in 1938.

Jack Haggerty was a charter member of the Volunteer Fire Department and was the first to retire from that organization. He also served two terms on the city council. Since he had served in the army in this area during the last of the Indian troubles, he participated in the dedication of Custer's Battlefield*.

When Jack Haggerty died in 1940 of illness brought on by a heat wave in Los Angeles, he left a widow, a son, and a daughter. Although his widow has now outlived him by eighteen years and has passed her hundredth birthday, her long life cannot be attributed to ease.

During the devastating 'flu epidemic of 1918 Mrs. Haggerty, Jim Haggerty's mother, was attacked by the dread disease, but she successfully fought it off. She was up and about her work only a short time after her bout with the flu, when she was stricken with inflammatory rheumatism. Rheumatism kept her in bed for nine months but this woman with the iron constitution regained her health and was able to take care of her family again. When a neighbor woman, mother of five, died in 1920, Mrs. Haggerty took the two youngest children into her home and cared for them too.

The baby was nine months old, the other child was two. However, the extra work proved too much so another neighbor took the older child. But then Jim's aunt died and his mother took her four or five-year-old girl to raise.

In the fall of 1926 the inflammatory rheumatism struck again, this time incapacitating her for five or six months. Again she recovered and although she has lived more than forty years since then, the rheumatism has not recurred. Mrs. Haggerty lived in Glendive until after the death of her husband in 1940, then went to California to live with her daughter Anna in 1941.

When the family was still together, Anna used to play the piano while the others gathered around to sing. They weren't professional singers, Jim points out, but they'd have a wonderful time. This past November when the family gathered to celebrate their mother's hundredth birthday, Mrs. Haggerty told Anna to get to the piano so all could sing together again. Although her voice was weaker now, Mrs. Haggerty joined in with them and sang too.

Until this past year, Mrs. Haggerty was able to be fairly active. In the years after she moved to California she was accustomed to staying home alone all day until two years ago when her daughter retired. However, last year she had the Hong Kong 'flu, and since then she hasn't been able to regain her strength. She explains that she's 'just tired'.

In spite of that, she had a wonderful time at her birthday celebration. There must have been, Jim estimates, more than a hundred guests for that illustrious occasion. And although she may be 'tired', she is still mentally alert with a keen memory. Even so, she doesn't 'live in the past' as many older folks are inclined to do but she does enjoy reminiscing.

Son Jim may be kind of a 'spring chicken' compared to his mother but he reached retirement age this fall, and he can remember some things that mark him as an old timer. For example, he remembers when their house on the corner of Rosser and Valentine was the only house on the block with city water. No, they didn't have running water in the house but they did have a water hydrant in the yard. Since that hydrant was the only one in the block all the neighbors carried their water from it.

Every three months Jim and Anna would go around and collect thirty cents from each neighbor. Then their dad would go down to city hall and pay the water bill. That outside hydrant worked fine in the summer but what 'fun' they'd have in the wintertime, Jim recalls, trying to thaw it out! (Does our present blanket of snow give anyone a yearning to find an outdoor hydrant from which to draw your daily supply?)

While winter didn't add any pleasure to the water carrying, it did bring other pleasures. With few houses to interfere, you could slide from 'Laritys Hill' at the foot of Hungry Joe to where the railroad track cut off Mann Street. The sport was not exclusive to children. On a moonlit night men, women, and children could be found sliding down the hill.

The water tank atop Hungry Joe used to overflow every day and it would flow down into the gully where Dove Addition is now. There it would spread across the flat and provide a made-to-order skating rink.

While Jim's dad was on the sheriff's force, one of his duties was to guard the bridge to make sure no horse galloped while on the bridge and that only a limited number of cattle, sheep, or horses crossed the bridge at one time. One fellow made the mistake of galloping across the bridge on a stolen horse. He made a second mistake when he stopped at the ranch of the rightful owner. After a discussion which became rather heated, the horse was left in the barn. So was the saddle because it was too heavy for a pedestrian to carry. The hired man started for town to get the sheriff but didn't have to go far. The sheriff was already on the trail of the man who had galloped the horse across the bridge. (Kinney, "As I Remember, Volume I")

During the summer if the boys could sneak away they'd go swimming in the river, but if they were caught it would go hard with them. To make Jimmy less conspicuous the boys would go to the river in two bunches. The first bunch would stop and talk with Mr. Haggerty while the second bunch, with Jimmy in the middle, would detour and slide down the tree at the bank to the river's edge. "Dad acted dumb," Jim explains, "but he knew what was going on, all right." Of course, it isn't hard to understand why Mr. Haggerty preferred to let the boys 'sneak' to the river when he was close by rather than to have them there with no one to come to the rescue in case of a mishap.

Jimmy attended Lincoln School for the first four years of his formal education. Although he actually started in a little frame building beside the old brick building, he only went there about a week with Maggie Brown for his

160

teacher. Then, because the little frame building was too crowded, he was moved over into the brick building, the 'old' part of the present Lincoln School, and Miss Charlotte Koch was his teacher.

Miss Lucille Hennigar was principal of Lincoln School at that time. Interestingly enough, Miss Koch and Miss Hennigar still held the same positions when Jim's two daughters started school, and both of them started with Miss Koch.

When Jim was in school they had just one band – the city school band which included the grade school (fifth grade up) and the high school. But that was pretty good; most schools then didn't have any band at all. But Glendive had Miss Hennigar, and Glendive was the first town in Montana, Jim pointed out, to have a school band.

Miss Hennigar started the band on her own time, just because she felt that music was so important for school children. When she retired, all her former band pupils were invited to play in a few pieces which she directed during the program in her honor.

Jim Haggerty has spent more than half his life driving for the Northern Pacific Transport Company, twenty-eight of those years 'down the valley' – between Glendive and Sidney. In earlier years he drove a bus with capacity for twenty-nine passengers, and then sometimes cars had to take care of the overflow. But more recently he drove a combination passenger and freight van. With that he had room for eight passengers.

Now that he's retired he's taken on some of the projects that always had to wait for lack of time. There's some traveling he and Mrs. Haggerty want to do, too. If Jim feels nostalgic about retiring he doesn't show it. "It feels wonderful," he declares. "Now if there is a blizzard I can just sit here and look at it!"

161

Mrs. H. B. (Evangeline Siggelkow) Boehmer

October 1965

Mary B. Harvey, later to be Mrs. O.H. Siggelkow and mother of Evangeline Siggelkow Boehmer, didn't enjoy very good health in her native Wisconsin so she decided to try the climate in Montana where her three brothers had taken up ranching. She found that the Montana climate could go to extremes of heat in summer and cold in winter, but it must have agreed with her because she lived with it about sixty years.

Her three brothers, Jim, John, and George Harvey, had come to Montana in 1893 and started ranching about thirty-five miles northwest of Glendive. She was twenty-two years old when, as a young schoolteacher, she followed their trail to the Treasure State. Schoolteachers in bachelor-dominated Montana didn't have much chance of staying single for long, and after a couple years of teaching on Belle Prairie, Miss Harvey became the bride of O.H. Siggelkow.

Siggelkow, who had known the Harveys in Wisconsin, worked for them on the ranch for a time after he came west. In the years that followed he worked at a variety of jobs including brakeman on the railroad; painter and paperhanger, machinist's helper (again on the railroad), homesteader, and storekeeper.

When the Siggelkows were first married, they rented a house on Barry Street, the house recently torn down to make way for a filling station. A few years later, since they each owned two lots on Mann Street, they built a home of their own. It was to this house that Mrs. Siggelkow later built an addition and operated one of Glendive's first maternity homes.

Mrs. Boehmer recalls that when she was a little girl, the sidewalks (where there were sidewalks) were either cinder paths or boards. She found it a 'scary' experience to walk the planks that provided a crossing for the drainage ditch along the railroad tracks. The city hall was a little frame building and had, among other things, two jail cells. Once when her dad was working on a float for a parade, she went along over with him, and he put her into one of the cells as a joke. That was a scary experience too, and no joke to her.

They lived across the street from the Old Methodist Church, and Sunday for the Siggelkow children included Sunday School and church in the forenoon, Junior League in the afternoon, and Epworth League in the evening, usually followed by preaching. Since they were just across the street from the parsonage they were frequently called upon for witnesses at marriages. The witnesses were supposed to be adults, but on one occasion the adult didn't want to sign the certificate so Evangeline, though she was a minor, signed her name as witness.

Although they were living on Mann Street they had a barn in the back of their lots and kept a cow and horse. Old Marble, the horse, was so gentle that even the small children could ride her, and many were the happy times they had riding horseback. They had chickens, too, and Siggelkow specialized in fancy Rhode Island Reds. He always entered some of his Rhode Island Reds in the fair and brought home blue ribbons. The fair was one of the highlights of the

162

year. A feature she particularly remembers was the men's relay race in which they had to dismount from their horses, put on some item of feminine apparel (the more difficult to don, the better), remount, and continue their race. There were races, too, for Roman riding, chariot races, motorcycle races, and car races.

She also recalled the tragic ending of the first parachute jumper to perform at the fair. The day turned out to be a windy one, and the parachuter decided it would not be wise to try to jump, but some of the crowd persisted in heckling until he finally decided to go ahead. The fairgrounds then were located along the Marsh Road, and the young performer landed atop Eagle Butte where his chute pulled him onto some rocks, and he was killed.

Indians coming through town often camped where the stockyards are now or perhaps up where the Northern Pacific Hospital is located, and her parents would sometimes take the children over to visit them. Mrs. Boehmer still has the little pair of beaded moccasins bought from the Indians for her when she was just a little girl. The girls enjoyed taking bright colored hair ribbons along to trade to the Indians for beads.

The homestead on which Siggelkow filed was located near Forsyth, but he was working on the railroad at the time, and the residence requirements, even a few months a year, were difficult to meet. Because of those circumstances they finally relinquished the claim. Not, however, before the homestead had contributed considerable color to Mrs. Boehmer's childhood memories.

While they had the homestead Evangeline's two older sisters would usually stay in Glendive with their father when Mrs. Siggelkow and the two younger children went to the homestead. Neighbors were few and far between, and the Siggelkows had no means of transportation – not even a horse. Not surprising then, that at times it was a bit lonesome. Perhaps that was why Mrs. Siggelkow one afternoon yielded to her son's coaxing and agreed to walk with the two children to the neighbors – "Just a little way," he said.

But the neighbors weren't 'Over this little hill', nor over the next one. After they had walked considerable distance and still hadn't come to any neighbors Mrs. Siggelkow insisted they turn back toward the homestead. Even so, darkness overtook them on the way, and to make matters worse they found when they came to an ordinarily dry creek (it was dry when they crossed it that afternoon), a cloudburst farther upstream had filled the creek to its banks.

The old log they found for a 'bridge' made crossing precarious so his mother removed Harvey's suspenders and tied them to his arm so she'd have a better chance of pulling him out if he slipped, then let him cross and go for a plank. Their old dog, Caesar, went along with him and well he did, for on the way back with the plank Harvey went too far upstream.

Caesar kept pulling at him to go downstream so finally the boy called, and his mother answered from the direction the dog was pulling him. They managed to get the plank into place across the turbulent stream, and Mrs. Siggelkow and Evangeline joined Harvey on the homeward side of the creek.

There were other inhabitants in the area even though they didn't find anyone that afternoon. One of the neighbor ladies was afraid to stay alone, especially during a storm. One night when Evangeline was staying with her, a very severe hailstorm struck. The hail pounded so hard that it knocked the knots out of the knotholes in the siding, and the lightning was so intense that the house almost appeared to be on fire. The next morning the hail had quit but the rain hadn't. The woman decided she'd rather try to get to a neighbor than to stay in that shack so they started out, she carrying her baby, and Evangeline carrying baby clothes. Evangeline also carried an umbrella, trying in the wind and rain to hold it over the mother and baby, and at the same time clutching the baby clothes in her arms, trying to keep them from getting soaked. They made it to the nearest neighbors, some bachelors, who quickly took them in and kindly urged them to lie down and rest.

They were almost exhausted by their tramp through the mud and rain, but Mrs. Boehmer recalls that, tired though she was, she refused to take off her shoes and lie down to rest because there were so many mice in the place! During that same storm her mother and brother, over in the Siggelkow homestead shack, stood on chairs and held an umbrella over their heads in an attempt to stay dry. Later neighbors helped them put a new roof on the shack.

Going to town for groceries meant borrowing a team and buggy from neighbors. One day, returning with their groceries, the wagon broke down as they were crossing a soggy alkali creek bed. They had no choice but to leave the wagon and, carrying the groceries they had to have, walk on home – several miles. Little wonder they decided the homestead wasn't worth the sacrifice and work required to 'prove-up' so they relinquished their claim.

Another of Siggelkow's ventures was a store at 'Four Corners' between Lindsay and Bloomfield. He had a rather large two-story building with the store and living quarters on the ground floor while the second story was used more or less for social gatherings by the neighborhood. When the depression of the thirties hit, too many people who had bought groceries on credit failed to pay their bills and Siggelkow was forced to close the store.

Angeline attended the local schools, starting at Lincoln with Miss Charlotte Koch as her first grade teacher. After graduating from the local high school she taught at Allard until her marriage to H.B. Boehmer.

The Boehmers have two children; Bob, who works out of Chicago with the A.B. Chance Electrical Tool Company as a demonstrator, and Gloria Jean, who operates a beauty shop in Glendive. The same Miss Koch who taught Mrs. Boehmer in the first grade also taught her son and daughter in the first grade.

Mrs. Boehmer has a number of antiques, relics of another day, another era. The old Kimball piano, over sixty years old, has never been refinished and is still in good condition. She also has an antique secretary – combination desk and bookcase – and some dishes from each of her grandmothers. The pitcher is still intact from the washstand bedroom set which her mother bought with the first money she earned and gave to Mrs. Boehmer's grandmother. These and other antiques are in her home, two-and-one-half blocks from where her parents set up housekeeping as newlyweds sixty-eight years ago.

Jens Scarpholt

June 1966

Jens Scarpholt first saw Glendive on July 6, 1907 early in the morning. He came with a group looking for homesteads, but when he saw the black hills of Hungry Joe*, just like the badlands they had come through east of town, it didn't look like the wonderful farming country he'd been told it was. He decided right then that he didn't want any homestead here.

Jens had been working on a big wheat ranch in North Dakota. These were pre-tractor days so all the work was done with horses, and the ranch had about seventy-five head of work horses. Mr. Leach, the ranch owner, had his own threshing machine with a big steam engine to power it. It took them twenty-six days just to thresh his own grain. They set the outfit up in the field amongst the shocks*, and ten teams hauled in bundles all day long, while four men pitched into the machine.

'All day long' was just that – a long day. They ate breakfast by kerosene light to start the day, and they ate supper by kerosene light at the close of the day.

The men working on the ranch didn't really know how much land belonged to Mr. Leach except that it was sections* and sections. There were no fences in Dakota at that time to mark property boundaries, but there was usually a wagon trail on the section line which marked off the sections.

Mr. Leach had ten outfits plowing his land. (One outfit consisted of a teamster and five horses hooked to a two bottom plow.) One day when they had finished plowing the section on which they were working, they pulled across the road to the next section and made a few rounds around it.

They were just getting a good start when the foreman came chasing out to where they were working and told them they were plowing on another man's land! So the neighbor got about twenty-five acres plowed free of charge.

The plowmen weren't the only ones who overestimated their employer's holdings. One man was kept busy with just the chores – taking care of the stables, hauling in hay for the horses, and other chores. One day when Mr. Leach was in town he happened to meet one of his neighbors, who complained that someone had been stealing his hay. Later that day as they were going home the neighbor, driving ahead, stopped and waited for Mr. Leach to catch up with him. "Look!" he told Mr. Leach, "There's that man stealing hay right now! Come along over with me and we'll catch him at it."

Mr. Leach was quite ready to help him catch the thief and went with him. What a shock, then, to find that it was his own chore man who was helping himself to the hay! "Ole," exclaimed the astonished Mr. Leach, "this is not our hay!" Bewildered, Ole protested, "But I thought everything around here belonged to you!" Mr. Leach paid for the hay so that ended the matter as far as the two neighbors were concerned, but the other men had a lot of fun kidding Ole about stealing hay.

165

In the town nearest the ranch, McHenry, a group of business men and others who had money to invest, formed a land company and bought all the railroad land in two townships (19-54 and 19-55) in eastern Montana. They engaged an agent who was supposed to get homesteaders to locate on homesteads in the townships, then try to sell them adjoining Company land. The agent succeeded in interesting a group of home seekers, Jens Scarpholt among them, and brought them to Glendive by train. As they traveled toward Glendive the agent described in glowing terms the wonderful farm land awaiting their inspection.

At this time Glendive was not much more than a frontier town, with hitching posts in front of business places, extending from about Borden Street on one end to Power Street on the other. There was little beyond those limits except a few log cabins scattered among the sagebrush. Across the railroad tracks there were a few houses and shacks near the roundhouse, a few others here and there between Sargent Avenue and Hungry Joe but more sagebrush than anything else.

As for what is now West Glendive there was one residence on that side of the river, with log cabin, log barn, and corrals. It had originally been built for a combined ferry house and road house, but after the bridge was built the ferry was no longer needed so now the people living in it were running cattle on the river bottom.

When the train pulled into Glendive many of the passengers rushed for the Jordan Hotel bar. Prohibition was in effect in North Dakota at that time so those with a taste for alcoholic beverages lost no time taking advantage of their opportunity.

Jens had made up his mind about a homestead in the badlands, but others in the party wanted to go see the Company land, and the agent was taking them out free of charge so Jens figured he might as well go along. The agent headed northwest from Glendive with his home seekers. When they reached the Morgan Table, Jens began to take notice. This looked different! Tall, thick grass covered the Table and hay could have been cut any place. Jens reasoned, "Where you can grow grass you can grow grain." Maybe a homestead wouldn't be a bad idea after all.

Coming from Glendive they had passed two residences: Bamber's Ranch just out of Glendive a few miles, and now, on Morgan Table, N.B. Sackett's homestead shack (where Rudolph Nissley now lives). As they started down the gravel hill at the north edge of the Table, they saw a fence – the first fence they had seen all the way out from Glendive. It was Joe Mullet's homestead.

They had to follow a lane from there down to the Red Top School corner. There were two homesteads in the half section south of the school. Jacob Chupp had built a house, part of which still stands, just across the road from the present Elmer Borntrager dwelling, and Miss Emma Miller had a shack near the Thirteen Mile bridge, except there was no bridge there then.

West of the schoolhouse corner a short distance, where the Scarpholts now live, was the Dan Miller residence. Just across the road from them was Joseph

Borntrager's home. After the thirty miles from Glendive through almost totally uninhabited country, the concentrated little Amish settlement nestled on the wide prairies was something of a surprise to the stranger approaching for the first time.

The party from North Dakota ate dinner at Joe Borntragers. They also spent the night there after looking at homestead sites. Borntragers had a nice little two-story house, a good barn, and the place in general fixed up very well. The visitors were impressed with its attractive appearance. The Amish did not use curtains or table cloths, but everything was clean and spotless, polished until it shone. Here was an example of the real 'Dutch'* cleanliness.

After dinner they continued their trip, going northwest from Borntragers toward the hills where Jens picked out his homestead. As they traveled they saw three more homestead shacks; Miles Borntrager's, where Gregg Jones lives; Ezra Borntrager's, where Nick Ziegler lives; and Mose Mullet's, where Walter Senner lives. About two-and-one-half miles southeast of where Bloomfield now stands, Jacob Mullet, Sr., had the post office in his farm home, the first post office in that area. At that time it was called Adams.

On that trip Scarpholt selected a quarter section northeast of the site that was to become Bloomfield, and in November of that same year he came back to Dawson County to establish residence on his claim. Dawson County has been his home ever since.

When Jens returned in November, he found that a goodly number of houses had been built in the area since his initial visit in July. Most of these settlers had come in from Bloomfield, Nebraska. The next year, 1908, a man by the name of Ed Albright built a store in what is now Bloomfield. This general store was in the block where the Farmers Union Oil Station now stands. After the store was built the post office was moved into the store, and the name was changed from Adams to Bloomfield because of the large number of settlers from Bloomfield, Nebraska.

Mr. Scarpholt observes that very few of the homesteaders in the Bloomfield community lost their homes in the years that followed. On the contrary, a number were quite well-to-do by the end of the five years required for proving up* on their claims.

This sudden influx of homesteaders with their families into virgin territory gave rise to the need for schools where there had been no schools and no need before. Accordingly, a schoolhouse was built in Bloomfield in 1908.

A few years later, in 1912, Bert Crockett built another store in Bloomfield. This one was on the corner across the road to the west of the present post office. The building was a large one with a store in one side of it and a community hall in the other side.

At the time this store and hall were built there were many more people in the area than now. There were four families in most of the homestead sections because at first they could file on only 160 acres. With lots of people, they had many good times in the little town.

They provided their own recreation with rodeos (strictly home talent), ball games, and celebrations of one kind or another. Frequently people from Glendive would come out to share in the good times. Nearly every Saturday night there would be a dance in the community hall.

Mr. Scarpholt commented that in those days people weren't afraid to walk a distance. He recalled one time when Joe Walbrink, working on the ditch* below Intake, walked with another young fellow to Bloomfield on a Saturday night, danced all night, then in the morning walked to his homestead southwest of Bloomfield, about seven miles (the Chris Kampschror place). Intake is twenty-six miles from Bloomfield, and Joe started from below Intake so he had some exercise before he reached his homestead.

Jens himself walked to Glendive a number of times. He didn't farm those first few years on the homestead because of difficulty selling grain when there were no elevators so, with little to do, he'd sometimes just strike out and walk to Glendive.

Bloomfield in those days had a good ball team, and everyone turned out to watch the games. Some of those early players were Lud Ludstrom; Al, Rick, and Arthur Johnson; Dave, Mose, and Menno Mullet; Frank and Bill Bush; and Bob Trulock. Bob was a good catcher. He could hit the ball, too. Those who knew Trulock might wonder how he could run bases, but sometimes he hit the ball so far out on the prairie they couldn't find it, and then he could make a home run. Charley Bush used to be the umpire.

Vida also had a good ball team. Some of their players had been professionals, playing on city teams for salaries, but most of them were getting along in years. On a hot day they could play hot ball, but on a cold day they were not so good. If Bloomfield happened to be playing them on a hot day, their team manager would warn them they'd have to tighten up to beat them, but if it was a chilly day, they didn't have to work so hard.

Sometimes they put on home talent plays in the community hall. Mr. Scarpholt particularly remembers one in which the main character claimed he could change old maids into young girls. He was supposed to have come into the community with some sort of machinery that would do the trick.

They had a tent in one corner of the community hall, and in the tent was some kind of machinery that could make noise whether it could accomplish anything else or not. A woman would go in one side of the tent dressed as an old maid, the machinery would grind away, and she would come out the other side dressed as a girl.

Presently a crabby-looking old maid came and wanted to be changed, but not into a girl; she wanted to be made into a man. After she went into the tent the machinery began to make a frightful noise, then the audience heard an explosion. That machine couldn't change her into a man, and it broke to pieces.

In the early days it was customary for a man to carry a bedroll with him because it usually took a long time to get to where he was going, and even when he got there, he might not find any sleeping accommodations. A bedroll consisted of, first, a four by fourteen foot piece of tarpaulin or canvas. When a man was ready to 'hit the sack', he spread this canvas on the ground, then the blankets and quilts were laid on it, a little way in from one end to about the middle. After the 'bed' was made, the other half of the canvas was folded over the top. The canvas had snaps and rings to fasten the cover to the bottom layer of canvas to hold it in place. In this bed roll a man could lie on the ground in rain or snow and stay dry.

As an example of the protection it gave, Mr. Scarpholt told about an experience he had when he was working on a sheep ranch. Several inches of snow had fallen during the night, and the next morning as he rode from the ranch house to the sheep wagon, he saw a hump on the ground. He thought nothing of it, and didn't even turn aside, but his horse shied away. Just as the horse shied, the 'hump' came to life and snow flew in every direction while a startled sheepherder sputtered, "You ---! Don't ride over me!"

Mr. Scarpholt laughed to recall the Easterner who came to work for rancher Harvey. He was unfamiliar with the customs of the land, particularly in regard to sleeping accommodations. When night came, he asked Mr. Harvey where he was supposed to sleep.

"Well," Mr. Harvey drawled, "We have territory called our range about twenty miles in diameter, and these buildings are about in the center. You ought to be able to find a place to spread your bed without getting on the neighbors."

One night during threshing season, late in the fall with the weather exceedingly cold, Jens and some of the others of the threshing crew bedded down in a straw pile. It was so cold that even with what he thought was an ample bed roll, he rolled and tossed and couldn't get to sleep. At last he did get to sleep in spite of the cold, and when he awoke, he was so warm and snug he was reluctant to get out of bed. When he did get out, he found out what was making him warm; a big 400-pound hog of Isaac Stanley's had rooted into the straw beside him!

He remembers another time when he wished he had had two of Stanley's hogs. He was on his way to Glendive with his oxen and a load of grain. He had stopped at Geiger's on Seven Mile the first night and expected to get to Glendive before the second night. By the time he reached Deer Creek, however, his oxen were completely tired out and could go no farther so he had to camp for the night. He had nothing to eat, but he had his bed roll so he unhitched his oxen and tried to get some sleep himself. He was hauling in the winter, and the temperature was down to twenty degrees below zero so that was when he wished he had two of Stanley's hogs!

Grain hauling had to be done in the winter because in the summer they were too busy farming. That winter hauling had its disadvantages. A trip to Glendive required two days at best so while you could pick a nice day to go in, you might have a blizzard when you came back the next day. No radio to warn that a cold front or a storm might be moving in. It surely was a blessing when Ford made his Ford truck.

Scarpholt was not slow to buy one when he found out how serviceable those trucks were. He bought one of the first to come into that part of the country. Now the trip that had taken two days could be made in half-a-day so people could get to town more often.

Folks made fun of those little Fords in the early days, but they were serviceable, and anyone with common judgment could repair them. Now days you just about have to be a specialist for each make to repair a car.

As an example of the early motorist's resourcefulness, Scarpholt told about a breakdown Frank Kampschror had. Kampschror hauled mail with a Ford car between Bloomfield and Glendive quite a number of years ago. One day as he was carrying the mail a connecting rod gave out, but he didn't go to the nearest phone and call a wrecker because at that time they had neither.

He did have an extra rod along, however, and also a pail so he drained the oil into a pail, took out the old rod, put in the new, poured the oil back in and was on his way again.

Once when Jens himself was going to Stipek with his Model T, he was just starting down the hill toward Seven Mile Creek when he saw something pass him and roll down into the ditch. He found that one of his own rear tires had come off the wheel and traveled faster than he was traveling.

He retrieved the tire and put it back on the wheel, then inflated it, and he was ready to go again. A tire pump was one piece of equipment he always carried with him.

When the Thirteen Mile settlers started coming, the horse-drawn stage was still in use between Glendive and Snowden. The stage carried mail and passengers. The stage looked somewhat like a giant baby buggy, and was pulled by four horses. Scarpholt observed that, once on the road, the horses never walked and never galloped; they maintained a swift, steady trot all the way. They didn't even slow down for the streams and water holes, so as they crossed, water splashed both sides. So far as he can recall, there were no bridges in the county except one across the Yellowstone River at Glendive.

When the Bloomfield homesteaders first tried farming they had very little market for their grain, because there was no one in Glendive who would buy their produce and ship it out for them. All the market they had was the little the Glendive residents themselves used. Almost everyone had a driving horse (or horses), and many had a cow (or more) also so they bought hay and a little grain. Glendive was a ranch town, and they were hostile toward the homesteaders for taking the range. That was why no one would buy and ship grain for them.

The old Merchant's National Bank wouldn't even handle their money because they had so little. They didn't want to bother with that chicken feed. Instead they told the homesteaders, "Go over to that newcomer" (Tom Hagan; the First National Bank had opened for business in 1904). "He might handle it for you."

So they went to the First National and Tom told them, "Sure we'll handle your little chicken feed for you." Now, Scarpholt points out, Tom Hagan's bank has resources of $10 million and is one of the finest business houses in

Montana. The other bank closed its doors (sold out to the First National, in fact) a long time ago.

When Scarpholt came, the Dion Brothers were running a big general store, selling everything from buttons to binders, in the location still called the Dion Building. According to Scarpholt, the Dions evidently realized that the farmers were here to stay and seemed glad to trade with them. "And," he added, "the Dions are still here too."

In 1910 the railroad (Northern Pacific) laid tracks along the river to Sidney, and some outsiders came in and built elevators, so at last there was a market for the farmers' grain.

In the fall of 1908, Scarpholt and Louis Swanson had made a trip to North Dakota, and while they were there, they each had a chance to buy four head of oxen, they bought some second hand machinery at a farm sale, and also bought some seed grain for the next year. In the spring of 1909 they both started farming. Jens wanted to get a certain amount of seed into the ground that spring, but by the time he got it in, his food supply – and his money, too – was running quite low. About all he had left in the grocery department was a little flour, lard, baking powder, and beans.

Then he engaged some breaking for another homesteader, fifty acres at $2 per acre. That brought him a hundred dollars, and a hundred dollars at that time was quite a sum, so when he got that breaking done he was sitting fine.

Since the railroad didn't reach Stipek until the following year, he was glad for the chance to contract all the oats he grew in 1909 to the Hollecker Ranch. He had a good crop of oats that year so with the oats sold, he felt he was well situated.

He farmed with those oxen for five years, then sold them for thirty percent more than he had paid for them. Now if one buys a tractor and farms with it for five years, it won't be worth thirty percent of what he paid for it.

When he sold the oxen, he bought horses and farmed with horses the next five years. He did about as well with the horses, as he did with the oxen. Some of his original purchases were mares, so he raised his own horses. In a few years he had eight young horses besides the old ones he had bought.

By 1916 he had a family-size farm and was all out of debt after just seven years of farming. And he even owned a Ford car! In contrast, Scarpholt observed that now if a young fellow buys a farm, the price of land and machinery is so high, it just about takes a lifetime to pay for it.

"I've heard people say Uncle Sam didn't give much when he gave the homesteader 160 acres of land, but I say he gave me a lot," Scarpholt declared. "He gave me a start in business and gave me a home, something I had not had since I was thirteen years old."

Jens Scarpholt was born in Denmark, where his parents owned and operated a farm. When he was three years old, his father died, and soon after that his mother moved her family from the farm. Three months before he was fourteen years old, his mother also died, leaving him to make his own way in the world. Jens grew up in a little Danish fishing village and learned early about ships and the sea. Little wonder, then, that when he was out of school, he hired out on a ship.

His first trip 'out' they didn't get back to shore for about three weeks. If they had come in sooner, he speculates, his seamanship would have been ended. His mother was very particular about discipline in the home and especially about table manners. Good manners become second nature for children thus trained, and on the ship the other fellows weren't slow to notice that Jens was careful about such particulars.

This seemed to the others a good chance for some fun so they practiced the very worst manners possible, trying to drive him away from the table or make him sick. He caught on to what they were trying, though, and made up his mind, "You're not going to succeed." And they didn't succeed, even though many of the things they did were not fit to print. Spitting on the food in their plates and continuing to eat was one of the minor offences. When they saw they were not accomplishing their purpose, they finally gave it up, but then they started something else. They started giving him 'baymans'. That was rough. To give him a 'bayman' they held him behind the head with one hand while with the other hand they tried to press his nose back into his face.

He didn't dare protest such treatment because he thought they were all against him. After a few days of this his nose was bleeding all the time and was sore as a boil. Then he decided it was time for revolt. He figured they might as well kill him or throw him overboard (which he surely thought they would if he resisted) so when one of the sailors approached to give him another 'bayman', Jens clenched his fist and hit him on the nose as hard as he could.

Though only fourteen years old Jens was a big, strong boy. The fellow was so surprised that for a moment he could only stare with the ugliest expression, Mr. Scarpholt says, he ever saw in his life. As the sailor recovered from his surprise, the ugly expression faded and his face broadened into a grin, as he told the lad, "This is O.K., Tenderfoot; maybe you will become a man after all." The others laughed and patted him on the shoulder, and he realized that was what they had been waiting for. After that he was one of them.

Once while he was on a fishing boat, a sail boat with no propeller, they got caught in a storm out on the Dogger Banks in the North Sea. The storm was so severe they couldn't fish so they dropped anchor and hoped the weather would improve. For three days the storm raged with no sign of abating so they decided to head for the nearest port toward which they had good wind. During all this time the sea was so rough they couldn't cook so they had to live on cold lunch and coffee.

After they got on a sail with the wind the sea was fairly smooth so Jens was ordered to cook some pea soup. Dried peas, big and yellow (used like beans), were cooked with salt pork until mushy to make the soup. This was a favorite dish on the sea because they needed lots of fat to endure the climate. In the little 6'x6' kitchen on the deck, right back of the main mast, Jens set to work to make the soup. On each side of the kitchen was a sliding door, and above one of those doors was a little shelf. A big hunk of tallow was kept on that little

172

shelf and was used to grease the fork of the mainsail boom to keep it from making a noise where it rubbed on the mast.

The pea soup was coming along fine, but just as he lifted the lid to stir, the ship gave a lurch, and that hunk of tallow splashed into the kettle! As he was considering what he should do about the embarrassing situation, one of the older sailors made the situation even more embarrassing by sticking his head in the door. While he 'bawled out' the cook, the cook was desperately trying to figure a way out of his dilemma.

He had to get the sailor out before he could do anything so he told him to go get his dish (they ate cafeteria style when the sea was rough); the soup was ready. As soon as the man's head was out the door, Jens grabbed the ladle and tongs to fish out the tallow, only to discover the tallow had all melted. He decided there was no choice; he would just have to dish up the soup, tallow and all. By the time he had dished up the last man's portion, the first man was back, wanting another helping of that good soup. He patted Jens on the shoulder and told him, "This is the best pea soup you ever cooked! Now remember how you made it and always fix it just like this."

The next time Jens was supposed to make the soup, he debated a while whether he should put the hunk of tallow in, but then he decided the reason the other soup tasted so good was just that they hadn't had any hot food to eat for so long. So he left the tallow on the shelf.

The sailors on those old sail ships were always reported to be rough and hardy, and surely it was no place for a tenderfoot. They had no doctor on board so they had to take care of their own needs. Mr. Scarpholt recalled the time, sailing along the coast of Africa headed for Johannesburg, a young fellow crushed his finger when he caught it in the gear of the windlass*. Taking him ashore was out of the question because the shore was a week's sailing away, and even when they reached land, there still would be no doctor.

The captain was a man of action (he had to be) so he tied a string around the finger as tightly as he could, poured a glass of rum down the patient's throat for a sedative, and called for the cook's cleaver and meat cutting board. With the finger laid on the board, the captain placed the cleaver blade on the spot chosen for the amputation, then hit the cleaver with the hammer. One blow severed the injured member. Then he soaked the stump in carbolic acid and ordered the cook to make a small cloth bag and fill it with flour to stick against the wound to stop the bleeding. Those 'first aid' measures took care of him until they reached Johannesburg.

When a sailor had a wart or a boil or some other growth he wanted removed, he simply burned it off. They would place an iron pipe, with a hole just the size of the growth, over the spot to be removed, then insert a red hot iron and burn the growth off. The treated area never festered.

After almost sixty years on a dry land farm Mr. Scarpholt is still 'old sailor' enough to use that method when he feels the occasion warrants. When a blood blister hardened for him instead of going away, his wife insisted he should go to the doctor, but he couldn't see that it was necessary and burned it off instead. He got along fine.

When Scarpholt was twenty-one years old, a young man who had gone to school with him came back to Denmark after working in Wisconsin. He reported wages there were twice as high as in the 'old country'. Jens knew Wisconsin was near the Great Lakes, and he figured he could get a job sailing so he accompanied his friend returning to the States.

Instead of sailing, he got a job on a dairy farm and worked there for a year. That's where he learned to milk cows. Soon word reached him of homestead land in North Dakota and Montana. He went to North Dakota but found the desirable land there pretty well taken so that's how it happened Jens Scarpholt found himself with a party looking for homesteads in Montana.

For thirty-six years he lived on his homestead as a bachelor. He ran everything, both inside and outside, and he enjoyed doing it. It was his. By that time he had accumulated some property, and he got to thinking he might as well have someone of his own to give it to so, in his words, "I asked Clara Miller, whom I had known all her life, if she wanted to come share the stuff with me, and she finally consented."

"I have to laugh when I think of it," he went on. "I had known her when she was a little girl running around home with two little brown pig tails sticking out from the back of her head. If someone had told me then she was going to be my wife, I would have said, 'You're cuckoo!' But things turned out all right. We have six strong, healthy children, and I have yet a good lot of hair, and she has never given me any black eyes."

Mr. Scarpholt passed his driver's test without glasses just before his eighty-first birthday. Now he is eighty-two and still actively engaged in farming. So actively, in fact, that to be contacted for an unscheduled appointment he had to be followed to the field where he was summer fallowing* because he wasn't expected home until nine o'clock that evening.

After his unscheduled stop, he philosophically observed that a little delay didn't matter. Some people seem to think you have to get everything done today, but he figures what doesn't get done today will be waiting tomorrow. And if tomorrow doesn't come, it won't make any difference that it didn't get done. Perhaps that explains why he's still going strong at eighty-two.

After the Scarpholt column appeared in the newspaper, Jens sent a letter detailing a couple more experiences. The letter follows:

I was on a hot spot another time when I was trustee in the Bloomfield school district. The group that backed me for trustee said, "Now we look for you to get us some good teachers, and don't be stingy with the salary," so we offered an enormous sum of $90 per month to a teacher. With a Montana Certificate, other schools were paying from $20 to $75 per month, there were only a few teachers educated in Montana in those days, they practically all came from other states. A young woman *from one of the middle eastern states with a life certificate within her own state, applied for the job, and we hired her.*

When she had been teaching about two months, she was called in to take the Montana Teachers Exam, and she failed. Then the Superintendent gave us notice that we couldn't keep her, and had to hire another teacher. The country was full of marrying-sick men at that time, and she was already married. Her husband came to me and, oh, was he mad! He said I caused her to be fired because I was jealous. I told him I had nothing to do with it in that line and I'm not thinking of getting married at all.

It is customary that a new sailor be baptized, the first time he crosses the equator. Therefore they baptized me the first time I crossed. They wanted to put a rope on me and throw me overboard, but the captain said no, there's too many sharks. Then they took a barrel with one end out and filled it with water. Then they tied a rope around my legs then up through a pulley up in the rigging of the ship, and ducked me headfirst a couple times into the barrel. I came near choked. I made such a fuss about it that I tipped over the barrel. Then they called it good.

I have been telling you so much now so I think we better call it good. I have experienced so much in my life that it could fill a big book. I dictated and Clara wrote.

Jens L. Scarpholt

Jens Scarpholt breaking sod with team of oxen

Mrs. Walter (Anna Manning) Schultz

November 1965

Anna Manning was born and reared in New York. Because her father's health there left much to be desired (he suffered from asthma) his doctor advised him to seek a drier climate. Since Mrs. Manning had a brother living in North Dakota their thoughts turned in that direction, but Mr. Manning would not consider moving to such a remote region unless their children – four daughters (three of whom were teachers and one married) and a son – were interested in settling in the same area. This was agreeable to the children so in March of 1909 Mr. Manning headed west.

Homestead land in Montana invited him to settle in the Treasure State, and he filed a claim on eastern Belle Prairie. The family had agreed that it would be wise for Mrs. Manning to stay on the New York farm until Mr. Manning could determine whether the move would improve his health. However, two of the girls were attending the New York State Normal College and expecting to graduate in June. They planned to join their father on the homestead as soon as their school term ended and they had their coveted sheepskins.

They traveled westward on the Northern Pacific train #3, then the fast train. They had already passed through Fargo when the conductor informed them that the fast train did not stop at Hodges, but since their tickets designated Hodges they insisted upon their rights.

After several trips to the engineer, he agreed that he would stop the train at Hodges providing they would have their luggage right at the door so they could get off quickly and not delay the train. "You know," he explained, "that it costs the railroad company five dollars every time we stop the train." So it was that two prospective teachers and their precious diplomas – one had a school contract as well – arrived at Hodges, July 9, 1909, ready for whatever the West might offer. And it offered plenty.

Mr. Manning had only a saddle horse and a shack on his Montana claim. He couldn't very well meet his daughters at the train with either of those so he had arranged with the late C.A. Anderson to pick up the new arrivals and bring them to the homestead. As the shack came in sight and they saw their father watching for them, Anna jumped to her feet and began waving her open umbrella. In her eagerness to see her father she didn't stop to consider the possible reaction of the team of horses to a waving umbrella. The horses promptly bolted and the rancher, throwing his weight on the reins, implored, "Sit down, sit down!" When the waving stopped, he was able to bring the horses under control, and they arrived safely at the new little shack on the great Montana prairie.

They found life on a homestead rugged compared to life in the modern New York home they had left. Instead of turning a faucet to get their water, they walked a quarter-mile through the tall grass to their well and carried the water home by the bucket full. The grass was so full of sharp hay needles that they soon sent off an order to Sears-Roebuck for some high top shoes to protect their ankles from the spears. And the mosquitoes! They were so thick that as one girl carried the water pail her sister walked behind her and with a small branch or reed swished the insects off the burden-bearer's back.

The normal college* from which Anna had graduated offered a four-year course (one of the first in the nation) so Anna was qualified to teach in both elementary and high schools. She came equipped with a contract to teach in the Wibaux junior high and high schools, but before the term began she had to register her credentials in the office of the county superintendent.

To get to Glendive (then the county seat for Wibaux) she could come by train from Hodges, but she had to figure out a way to get from the homestead to Hodges, seven miles. She solved that transportation problem by borrowing a saddle horse from a neighbor. After tying her roll of credentials to the saddle horn she mounted and started jogging toward Hodges.

All went well until that roll jabbed the horse's neck and he started bucking. Her credentials had nothing to do with qualifying her for bronc riding, and she didn't stay in the saddle long when her horse started such unexpected contortions. Too surprised at first to know what had happened, she just sat on the ground for a few minutes. Presently her horse came back and sniffed at her, almost as though he, too, was wondering what had happened. This show of interest didn't accomplish much else, but it did make her feel a little more kindly toward him.

Sitting there didn't get her to Glendive, though, so she started winding up her hair again – that rough ride had shaken all her hairpins loose – and remounted. In spite of the unscheduled interlude she reached Hodges in time to catch the train for Glendive.

In Glendive she registered her certifications, then spent most of the day visiting with the county superintendent. As the day progressed she kept getting stiffer until by the time she was ready to board the four o'clock train to take her back to Hodges she was so lame the conductor had to help her up the steps.

She wasn't very enthusiastic about riding the horse from Hodges back to the homestead but felt she must so she started out, slowly. It was dark before she reached home so her father was waiting for her on the highest point above the shack, holding a lantern to guide her.

Anna taught for three years in the Wibaux schools. The Mannings had been warned that winters could be severe in this part of the country, and they weren't disappointed. They thought it best to be prepared so another Sears-Roebuck order brought shaggy fur coats. One winter while she was teaching in Wibaux the school had to be closed because of an epidemic of scarlet fever so Anna, when she had the opportunity, rode out to her parents' home with one of the neighbors who was in town with team and bobsled. The day was dazzlingly bright with the sun glistening on the snow, and Anna, bundled in her fur coat and blankets had no thought of getting cold. Later she was informed that the temperature was fifty degrees below zero.

Following her three years of teaching in Wibaux she taught for two years in Glendive. In the meantime she filed on a homestead out on Lufboro. Even while she was teaching in Glendive she made regular trips to her claim, renting a saddle horse from Helland's livery stable to ride the twenty-five miles to the homestead after school Friday, then riding back to Glendive Sunday afternoon.

One weekend instead of renting a saddle horse she rented a driving horse and buggy and drove out. The horse was very gentle and well broken, but on the way out to the claim the breast strap rubbed and made his chest muscles sore so when she prepared to come back to town Sunday afternoon the horse wouldn't pull. A neighbor lady who had been visiting with her was accustomed to handling horses so she led the horse until he was 'travel-minded'. Anna was then able to proceed as far as the Enoch Harpster home but then the horse balked again so she stayed there for the night. The next morning Mr. Harpster brought her on into town. He notified the Hellands that the horse was at his place so a livery boy went out to get it.

In spite of these efforts a claim-jumper threatened to get her homestead away from her so she moved out onto her claim and taught at the Lufboro School until she had proved up. She married Walter Schultz in 1916 and they settled down on his farm. Five years later he was accidentally killed while they visited in Minnesota. They were spending Christmas with his brother who owned a road outfit. As the two brothers walked along the edge of a gravel hill a sudden dirt slide caught Mr. Schultz and snuffed out his life.

Left alone with their small daughter, Maria, Mrs. Schultz continued to operate the farm for a few years. She wrote to the county agent, then Mr. Mendenhall, and asked him if he could send a reliable man who could carry on the farming. Mr. Mendenhall sent Jake Bashore, who proved most efficient.

She stayed on the farm until the third year when a hailstorm harvested a beautiful crop for her. Friends urged her to dig out her diploma from the bottom of her trunk and go back to teaching. That did seem the wisest so she rented the farm out on shares and started teaching the home school. After six-and-one-half years of teaching she was elected to the office of county superintendent and moved into Glendive.

When Mrs. Schultz took the office of county superintendent, she was well acquainted with the needs and problems of the rural schools. Accreditation of these schools was one of the goals especially dear to her heart. Rural seventh and eighths graders were required to take examinations in January and May in an accredited school. That meant they had to come to Glendive. Since two days were required to write the examinations, arranging for the pupils to take them was, in some cases, a real hardship.

Mrs. Schultz felt strongly that it was important for more of the schools throughout the county to be accredited. The tests then could be given in the pupils' own community. Transportation would present less difficulty for the parents, and the students, she believed, generally would do better in familiar surroundings.

To meet state requirements for accreditation schools had to maintain certain educational and physical standards. Teachers had to hold required certification, and the school had to have an approved library, unabridged dictionary, encyclopedia, and standard maps to qualify educationally. Physically, the old pot-bellied stove that roasted you on one side while you froze on the other had to be replaced by a furnace or a stove with a jacket*. Ceilings had to be a certain height; sixteen square feet of floor space per pupil was required, and cross lighting had to be eliminated. In schools where running water was not available (and in how many rural schools of, say 1930, was running water available?) the water bucket and dipper had to give way to a water cooler with a spigot on the bottom and individual drinking cups.

In order to work for and maintain these standards Parent Teacher Associations were organized throughout the county. (PTA was also a requirement for accreditation.) During her term in office eighteen or nineteen such groups were functioning. As Mrs. Schultz went throughout the county organizing these groups she got enthusiastic and efficient help from some of Glendive's civic-minded citizens. Dr. Everett's wife believed strongly in the PTA and was well informed on its possibilities and responsibilities so she frequently accompanied Mrs. Schultz. Marie Hildebrand, too, and her sister, Mrs. Davidson, often joined them.

At each PTA meeting the program had to include a business meeting, an educational feature, and a social period. After the business meeting Mrs. Everett would give a talk supplying the educational feature, then Mrs. Hildebrand presented musical selections as part of the social hour. Usually the county nurse or physical education teacher would also go along and lead the group in games during the social hour. This 'Sample Program' would serve as a guide for the parents and teachers who were organizing.

As soon as a school met the standards prescribed by the state it would receive accreditation. Then, instead of pupils coming to Glendive to take their seventh and eighth grade examinations, Mrs. Schultz could go to these schools and administer the tests.

Mrs. Schultz also instituted the practice of holding graduation exercises for the rural school 8th grade graduates. These exercises were held in the Dawson County High School to give the students an opportunity to become a bit acquainted with the high school and perhaps encourage them a little to go on to high school.

Often at these exercises it was the late Judge Leiper who would address the graduating class. Judge Leiper had a deep appreciation for, and understanding of, the rural environment. The very difficulties and hardships – the chores required on the farm, the school transportation problems, for example - oftentimes regarded as disadvantages, he considered to be great character-building agencies. He sought to impress upon them that, while the city student did have many advantages, the rural student had advantages, too.

When Mrs. Schultz was elected as superintendent of schools, various individuals – self-appointed prophets – would tell her, "You'll like all but ..."

this or that, depending upon the individual. But after she had spent fourteen years in the office she could declare that she had enjoyed every part of it. Even the office problems such as figuring and balancing the new district budgets (after the new budget law was passed) or working out transportation problems in districts where schools had been closed, she found to be interesting and challenging.

One phase of her work which she particularly enjoyed was consulting with the teachers, the school board members, and patrons as they came to her office with their problems and their successes. She especially looked forward to Saturdays when teachers – or others – were free so they could visit in the office. One Saturday her clerk counted the visitors who came and at the close of the day found that sixty people had called.

Some of the pre-term prophets had predicted that she would like 'everything but those long trips' to visit the outlying schools (she was to visit each school at least once a year). But the prophet was wrong there, too. She looked forward to each of those visits, regardless of the school's location.

She always tried to relate to what the pupils were studying when she visited. Perhaps it might just be presenting arithmetic examples on the blackboard, but then again, perhaps they might be studying the production of maple sugar. She, coming from an area where maple sugar is produced, would give them a first hand account of the process. Fort Duquesne was located in the town where she had attended normal school* so another time that might work into the history lesson.

Later, because of this participation, some parent would meet her with the remark, "I understand arithmetic is your favorite subject." Or another, "I hear that history is your favorite subject." The truth was that she enjoyed any of the subjects.

Her last afternoon in the office the teachers of the county planned a little surprise party for her. Because of a heavy snowstorm many of the teachers couldn't attend, but those who could come spent an enjoyable time together over coffee and cookies.

Mrs. Schultz expressed appreciation for the wonderful cooperation and interest on the part of the pupils, teachers, school board members, and patrons, as well as from the state department of education, during her entire fourteen years in office. Summing up those years she commented, "I had many inspiring experiences that leave me with happy memories."

Noel Carrico

May – June 1970

If boss Henry hadn't been down in the meter pit cleaning the fish out of the meter (that was a messy, smelly job) when customer Henry came looking for light fixtures, maybe Noel Carrico wouldn't have wound up in Montana.

Noel Carrico was reared on a Missouri farm, but it seems that he must always have been interested in electricity and related fields. He took an apprenticeship in utilities in his hometown, working twelve hours today – eighteen hours tomorrow. An apprentice (everyone else, too) went to work at six a.m. and worked until six p.m. Next day you worked from six a.m. until probably midnight. For all this he received the handsome remuneration of fifteen cents an hour. But he learned the utility business, and it paid off. At a time when $40 a month was considered top wages, he was making around $100 a month. That may not sound like much in today's inflated economy, but in the early 1900's $100 was a lot of money.

The utility field at that time was 'wide open' for expansion and development, and he had a good connection with a local business. He was in line for all the electrical wiring in that area, and he had a 1906 International truck with which he hauled ice – had a profitable business going.

In addition to these fields he was public relations man for the owner of the utility business. A German, the man was an excellent electrical engineer for those times, but his public relations score was at the bottom. He just couldn't get along with people, so he left all 'uptown' dealings to Noel.

Noel was doing right well; business was good and growing regularly. Another young fellow in town was also in a good financial position so the two of them, since they were the only ones that had money, every so often would put on a dance for the young folks of the town. A further indication of the disparity in the economy then and now: they could rent a hall and get an orchestra to come from St. Louis, all for $6.

The money scale was just different. Boys, far from receiving an 'allowance', were lucky to have fifteen cents to go to the Old Settlers' Reunion once a year. Didn't have much source of income – might get two cents a piece for rabbits. Mr. Carrico reflected that he must have been born with a gun in his hand. He loved to go hunting with that old muzzleloader, and hunting is still one of his favorite diversions.

But scarce though money was when he was a boy, things were coming his way now. If anyone's future appeared secure, it would seem that Noel's did. What, then, caused him to leave it all and strike out into the unknown? It may seem like a small spark, yet....

Carrico's neighbor was building a new house – a $5,000 house. Doesn't sound like much of a house? There again – times have changed. There were hardly ten houses in the whole town at that time that were that expensive, and this was a beautiful home in the making. But the owner didn't plan to wire it for electricity.

Noel thought that it couldn't be. A beautiful home like that and not even wired? He reasoned and explained, finally pointing out, "You're going to sell this house sometime, and it will cost you a lot of money when you do if it isn't wired." That got through to Henry – customer Henry – and he agreed to have it done.

The utility company for which Noel was working was the only place in town carrying electric light fixtures, and they offered a choice of two fixtures: both were the 'inverted bowl' type on a drop cord, but one was opaque, the other green on the outside and white on the inside.

Noel advised Henry to go pick out his fixtures so he betook himself to the plant. He arrived at an inauspicious time. Along with their other enterprises, the company pumped the water for the city, and sometimes at the power plant, fish would get into the meter pit and be ground up in the meter. Taking the meter apart to clean it was a 'smelly deal' and not likely to put a fellow in the best of humor. So when Henry came, wanting to look at light fixtures, he found 'boss Henry' down in the meter pit cleaning out the fish and in no mood to do business with anyone.

The language he used was no sales pitch, and customer Henry returned to his house in high dudgeon to tell Noel, "Don't put that meter in!" It was the last nudge Noel needed. He quit his job. Boss Henry tried to get him to stay, but in less than a week he was on his way to Montana.

Noel Carrico had a half-brother living at Ollie, Montana, so that's probably why, when he left his job and Missouri, he headed this direction. At that time there were no less than nine passenger trains a day through Glendive! (He came on number seven.) He didn't come to Glendive just then, however; since his brother was at Ollie, Noel got off at Beach.

But this time he was running a little short of money so he immediately started looking for a job. He soon found one, hauling wheat from Ollie to Beach by wagon train. He was familiar with cars and tractors – not too many men were, in those days – so this proved an advantage as the wagon train was pulled by a big Rumley*. The train itself consisted of five wagons – four loaded with wheat, one with water for the engine.

Hauling from Ollie to Beach, he could make the trip with his load in eighteen hours, the trip 'empty' from Beach to Ollie in sixteen hours. Fences posed no problem because they were almost non-existent. (You can still make the trip from Beach to Ollie without concern for fences.) But at that time there was no 'right of way' for the road; the trail just struck off across the prairie, following the most convenient route. But there was one stretch where a fence paralleled the trail.

Generally there were two men on a wagon train, and while one drove, the other would get off and walk – get off and rest – should we say? Anyway, one trip Noel was following behind the train when he saw the other driver start off the road. He couldn't shout loud enough to be heard above the roar of the

182

engine and the rumble of the wagons. He couldn't run fast enough to take over the driver before – before the fence posts started to crack. That big Rumley straddled the fence, mowing it right down. Noel couldn't do a thing except watch, but he philosophically figured the driver would wake up when he hit that pile of rocks ahead. He did.

Another time as he walked beside the engine (rather than behind the train), he almost met with disaster. He had arrived in Montana in November and those chilly nights it was comfortable to walk on the 'warm' side of the engine.

The drive wheels on the Rumley – huge things, high as the ceiling of a room – were equipped with steel lugs which protruded about four inches from the rim of the wheel. One night as Noel plodded along on the 'warm' side of the engine, he literally "went to sleep on his feet." The first thing he knew, one of those lugs nicked – just nicked – him in the back.

"I jumped almost out of Golden Valley County!" Mr. Carrico declares. And after that he always walked behind the wagon train, insisting that his helper do likewise. Needless to say, if that lug had caught his clothing and thrown him to the ground, the wheel, with its four-inch lugs, would have passed over him and that would have been the end.

One night they got into Beach with their wagon train and found they had lost the engine flywheel. Since they couldn't reverse the Rumley without the flywheel, they had to locate it before they could even back up.

The wheat owner also owned an automobile so Noel retraced his trail, searching for the missing part. He didn't have to worry about its being in a ditch because there were no ditches, just the flat prairie so it should have been easy to find, but it wasn't. He finally found it – of all places – in a straw stack. The flywheel, spinning as it left the engine, had rolled some distance from the trail, coming to rest at the stack.

Their finding the wheel was something of a coincidence. On the trip into Beach the night before they had slept awhile in that very straw stack. With their trips taking sixteen or eighteen hours, they got very little sleep and would just have to catch 'a few winks' when they could. Now, as they hunted the missing flywheel, they strolled over to look at their 'hotel room' of the previous night – and there was the missing piece.

They kept hauling until they had all the wheat from that ranch transported to the elevator in Beach. Sometimes wagon trains would be lined up for a mile at the elevator. The year of 1912 produced one of the biggest wheat crops in this area, and Beach, either that year or the next, was 'wheat capital of the world'.

Coming from the South, Noel Carrico figured Montana would be just about the equivalent of the North Pole, weather wise, so he was amazed to find balmy weather in November. All that month while he was hauling grain the ground barely froze at night.

Much in demand as a chauffeur because there were few who could drive automobiles, he drove an automobile to Ollie for a lawyer just a few days before Christmas. In sharp contrast to the frigid weather he had expected, the thermometer that day registered seventy-two degrees, and they breezed along in an open car, coatless, necktie streaming over the shoulder of his white shirt.

The mild weather continued until January 4; then winter came with a vengeance. Temperatures dropped and so did the snow – about two feet of it, before the month was over.

In such weather there was one thing he could still do; he could hunt jackrabbits. Rabbits were 'thicker than fleas' so he went back out to the ranch from which he had hauled the wheat, borrowed a saddle pony, and, with his trusty 12-gauge shotgun, started hunting. The horse they gave him, Mr. Carrico declares, learned 'jackrabbit hunting' faster than you could imagine. This pony after being reined on a couple rabbits, knew just what to do. As a rabbit jumped up, the horse immediately swerved toward it and took off in hot pursuit.

The hunt was progressing fine when a rabbit jumped up, and his horse made an abrupt right-angle turn to go after it. Noel didn't make a right-angle turn with him but went straight ahead. When landing he encountered his first experience with Montana cactus.

Carrico had a job lined up with the Jennison Light and Power Company in Fairview, but he could not start until March 1, 1914. While he waited he took a job hashing* on a night shift in a Beach restaurant open twenty-four hours a day.

The job gave him a good opportunity to get acquainted with the town populace. At Christmas some high school boys – about five of them – brought him a tree, completely trimmed, and set it up in the restaurant for him. He was curious – perhaps a bit suspicious – as to where they got the tree, but they insisted they came by it honestly, even when questioned some thirty years later.

In the case of some other young fellows, he was considerably more dubious about their acquisitions. North Dakota was a 'dry' state at that time so bootlegging was not uncommon. Young fellows – and not so young – found it easy to slip over to Yates or Wibaux on a Saturday night. One night some boys with a suitcase came in to the restaurant where he was working and asked him, "Do you want this suitcase full of whiskey?" When asked what they were doing with that 'stuff', being of high school age, they explained they had found 150 pints under the manure pile back of the livery barn. When informed he was not interested in taking the suitcase and contents, they wanted to leave it anyway. The 'Old Man', as the night cook was fondly called, was a heavy drinker – even to vanilla extract – so perhaps that's what gave them the idea they might be able to cache the loot with Noel. Whatever their reasons and reasonings, he wanted nothing to do with their escapade and told them so in no uncertain terms.

Carrico's first visit to Glendive was in November, not too long after his arrival in the Treasure State. To this day he remembers the striking impression made upon him by the fine red brick buildings distributed along Merrill Avenue. He was also impressed by the high school. It looked like a little oasis, surrounded as it was by trees when there were very few trees in Glendive. The building itself, constructed only a few years before, was attractive, too, its bricks still new looking.

Another recollection tucked away in his memory from the first trip to Glendive was the bricks and other materials piled, alone in the middle of nothing, on Prospect Heights. The new hospital was just coming to completion. As soon as Noel arrived in Eastern Montana he had made a point of finding out what was going on in utilities. He found the Glendive Heat, Light & Power Company located close by where the Midland Lumber Company* is now, with a new power station being planned for 1914 construction down by the river where it now stands. Upon completion of the new Glendive plant, the old plant would be moved to Sidney. Prospects looked good for a young man experienced in the utility field, since not many were in those days.

Since Carrico was to go to work for the Jennison Light Company in Fairview March 1, he boarded the train in Glendive the last of February and headed north. Tracks went only as far as Sidney so that's as far as he went on the train.

When he got off the train in Sidney, a town of 798 people, he walked uptown. He remembers that as he walked across the street toward the Yellowstone Mercantile he found a dime in the middle of the street. From Sidney to Fairview he had to travel by stage (a Model T Ford) so he waited around until time for the stage to depart.

Aboard the stage, waiting for the driver to get ready, Carrico found himself sharing the Ford with two other passengers, one man on the back seat with him and another, a distinguished looking fellow, on the front seat. Introductions designated the man in front as Dr. Reisland, eye doctor.

Dr. Reisland, in spite of the cold temperature that morning, was bareheaded so as they waited to leave town, Noel ventured to suggest, "Dr., I'd think you'd want to wear something on your head." The incident took place some fifty-six years ago, but Mr. Carrico clearly remembers the reply that Dr. Reisland gave him. "Young man," he said, "if you keep your head cold, your feet warm, your bowels open and your mouth shut, you'll get along all right in this world!"

Just a couple of weeks before Dr. Reisland's death, Mr. Carrico happened to meet him and his wife on the street in Glendive and reminded him of that first meeting.

Carrico worked in Fairview until the first of June, then moved to Sidney, June 7, 1914. A franchise had been granted by the city of Sidney to the Water Users Electric Co. Later Frank Hughes, owner and manager of the Glendive Heat, Light & Power Co., acquired the franchise, assuring the advent of electricity, and this was when Carrico became interested in Sidney.

There was no light plant in Sidney yet – the old plant from Glendive would be moved there as soon as the Gate City's new plant was completed about November 1 – but there was work to be done. Electricity couldn't do much unless buildings were wired, and at that time only one house in Sidney was wired.

In October of that year, while he was working in Sidney, his brother became ill so they sent him back to Missouri. About the last of the month he passed away, and Noel went back for the funeral. He decided to go by way of the Great Northern, leaving from Mondak. But to get to Mondak he had to cross the river, and there were no bridges. He had a friend take him as far as the river, then he found a farmer who rowed him across in a boat for fifty cents.

To get from the river to Mondak he had to walk through the woods where the 'rough element' hung out. (And the rough element in Mondak was indeed rough!) He had heard of the killings that had gone on there so it was with some trepidation he started across that stretch. He carried a 32 Colt in one hand and his suitcase in the other as he braved the forbidding territory but freely admits that, had he been 'jumped', he probably would have dropped both and run!

However, he reached Mondak without incident and put up at the hotel. That hotel, he mentioned incidentally, is the only hotel he's ever stayed in where the manager locked the door into the hotel. But this manager did. He had reason to do so. If Noel hadn't been sure what his reasons were when he registered he knew before he left town that night.

About 2:00 a.m. he decided to find out if the train was on time so he walked down to the depot. Here he found this rough element had invaded the premises and had gotten into a fight. During the fracas they tipped over the stove onto the floor. After the depot agent kicked them out, Carrico helped him set the stove upright again. The train came in on time, and Carrico departed with no regrets.

He returned to the Treasure State just as the old electric plant from Glendive was being moved to Sidney. He hadn't made complete arrangements with Mr. Hughes for working the Sidney area plant so upon his return from Missouri he went to see him. He presented his qualifications – apprenticed utility man, had fired boiler, worked in engine room, experienced in wiring – and he'd like to have a job with Sidney Heat, Light & Power.

Mr. Hughes referred him to the Sidney manager so Carrico again took the train north. It was eleven o'clock when he got into Sidney that morning, November 3, 1914. He went immediately to see Hughes' man who asked him, "When do you want to go to work?" Carrico replied, "Now." And he did, at one o'clock that afternoon.

According to Noel Carrico, he never really had a job; his work was always fun. The hours he worked, it's a good thing it was fun instead of a job. When Sidney Heat, Light & Power began supplying electric current, they operated only from dusk to eleven p.m. (How would you like to be on that power line now?) Soon, however, enough interest in electricity had been drummed up so they began operation from six a.m. until midnight. (For that matter, how would you like eighteen-hour service?)

The plant was powered by a big Corliss engine – the same engine that had been on exhibit at the 1893 World's Fair in Chicago. If the current was to be turned on at six a.m. the boilers had to be fired at five a.m. to get the steam up, so every morning at five a.m. Noel was on hand to get it going.

Getting the big Corliss (its flywheel was twelve feet in diameter) started was some job! There were only two men working at the plant so after Noel had started the engine, he ran it until eight a.m. then the other fellow took over and ran it until midnight while Noel 'went to work'. Going to work meant selling, wiring, and promoting building lines.

Utility companies must of necessity be promoters because they have to build load if they are to stay in business. When Sidney HL&P began operations January 1, 1915, they had 115 customers signed up for service. (Mr. Carrico has the list yet of those original customers.) That, of course, was not enough for the company to operate profitably, but a start had to be made some place. And now it was Carrico's business to 'build the load' so they could operate at a profit.

When Frank Hughes earlier had asked him to take over the promotion and selling, he had offered along with the request to turn over his $2,280 inventory. Carrico accepted and continued as promoter and also as manager even after MDU* bought the utility in 1924.

Frank Hughes had come to Glendive in 1904, and he had built the first light plant in Glendive – next to where Midland Lumber is now located. Frank's brother, George, invented the electric range, and who would be more interested in promoting electric cooking than a utility owner – especially if the inventor happened to be your brother? When gas was brought into Sidney in 1931, they had 240 electric ranges on the line.

Probably few men in the utility business have fired with as many different fuels as Noel Carrico has. During his apprenticeship in Missouri, he fired with 'cord wood' (hickory) to begin with. Then they modernized to soft coal. At Sidney they used lignite coal, and in Glendive, it was lignite, oil and natural gas.

In 1916 gas was discovered eight or nine miles south of Glendive along the river at what became known as Gas City. Eastern Montana Oil and Gas Company built a four-inch line into town, and some residents put in gas for cooking, while a few people heated with gas. However, the supply was limited, and about 1918 it petered out. That was the end of the first gas experiment in Glendive, and it was followed quickly with an experiment with oil.

With the advent of natural gas into Glendive, Mr. Hughes became very concerned about the cost of fuel for the boilers in the Glendive Heat, Light & Power Company plant. He felt that if natural gas was in the ground there could be oil underneath. He engaged the services of I.C. White, state geologist of West Virginia.

After investigation, Mr. White reported in part: "So far as geology can give any indications, no more favorable point structurally for the occurrence of either oil or gas in very large volume could be found anywhere in the United States than on the Cedar Creek anticline dome...."

This report, dated August 1, 1916, caused Frank Hughes to decide to try for oil. A well was drilled to a depth of 4,103 feet, but it was a dry hole. This was drilled under the name of 'The Montana Yellowstone Oil Company'. August 10, 1918, a letter went to the stockholders that the well was not a success. At that time, they simply did not have the equipment to go deep enough.

In 1917 Hughes sold his interests in the utility companies at Glendive and Sidney, and Eastern Montana Light & Power was formed. During World War I times were tough and prices high. The power company had these electric ranges on the line, and the elements kept burning out. Replacing them was too expensive for the customer so Mr. Carrico invented a compound, called Carricite after the inventor, with which to bond the break and keep the ranges cooking. If the elements had had to be replaced each time it's doubtful that they would have kept many ranges on the line during those hard times.

Mr. Carrico's inventiveness had manifested itself long before World War I. When he started his apprenticeship in Missouri, he found he had a lot of company in the plant – rats. That wasn't the kind of company he could appreciate so he devised a rat trap. There was an underground water disposal pipe coming to the plant and when there was no water in it, the rats would use it as an entrance hallway. Rigging up a metal grid he placed it over this pipe so that when a rat came in, his back would touch this grid and ground it, thereby turning on the current.

General voltage at that time was 1100 (compared to 2300 volts now) but that was more than enough to kill a rat. He found that his trap worked all right; it killed the first rat that came through, melted the grid and cut out power for the whole town! Mr. Carrico concedes that that wasn't the smartest invention of his career – nor the most practical.

In 1924 R.M. Heskitt of Minnesota sold his utility interests there and invested in Glendive. At the same time he bought the utilities in Sidney and Wibaux, Montana; and Beach and Sentinel Butte, in North Dakota, forming Montana Dakota Utility Company.

In the succeeding months Noel Carrico bought for the company many small utilities in western North Dakota in addition to the plant already acquired in Montana. Before long he found himself in the position of working for three utilities at the same time.

Actually, they all belonged to MDU and were in the process of consolidation, but until that was accomplished Mr. Carrico worked for all three – besides running his own business in Sidney. Those were busy days of line building. In the first seventy-seven days of 1927 he was home only seven days.

In 1926 MDU built a gas line from Cabin Creek (where gas had been struck at about 2,000 feet) into Glendive. The first gas in the Baker area had been discovered quite by accident when a well for water was being dug. At about 400 feet they found gas instead of water. Mr. Carrico still has a big flier advertising the celebration of 'Gas Day' in Glendive on July 30, 1926.

He continued his business in Sidney until 1928, but when he transferred to Glendive that year he sold his merchandising to MDU. Gas was not introduced in Sidney until 1931 so a new experience awaited him at Glendive; Here he worked with gas for the first time. So he didn't meet all his 'firsts' during his apprenticeship days.

One of the firsts he did learn during his apprenticeship stands out particularly in his memory. Switchboards were made of marble when Noel made his acquaintance with them. His first morning at work the boss, giving him a brace and a bit, told him to drill a hole in that marble. Noel went to work with a will – he intended to learn this business. But diligently though he drilled, he just didn't seem to make much progress. During the course of the morning 'old hands' would come around to see how he was doing, but never a hint there might be some easier way.

By noon he had drilled maybe half an inch, but he had been told to drill a hole in that switchboard, and he intended to do it. Finally, after dinner, the boss came around, surveyed accomplishments and then told him to pour on a little turpentine. He did, and his eyes almost bugged to see the drill go through that hitherto almost impenetrable marble! Just as though it were dough.

In the years that followed his move to Glendive he had a great deal of experience with gas, building lines to carry it all over eastern Montana and western North Dakota. As an indication of the growth of utilities in Richland County alone (where Mr. Carrico was 'in on it' from the start) taxes for that first year, 1915, were $345; when he retired from MDU in 1955 the taxes amounted to $46,433.74; and last year, 1969, records indicate that taxes were paid in the amount of $205,993.81.

In the fifteen years since his retirement as manager of MDU, Mr. Carrico has not lacked activities. In fact, it would almost seem that he'd have had to retire to take care of his many hobbies and interests!

His earliest hobby, which he started before 1909, is coin collecting. It all began when he was reading electric meters back in Missouri for that original utility where he had been employed. Warrenton, his hometown, was a college town, home of Central Wesleyan. One day – he was just a youngster (in those days you were still a 'youngster' at twenty) – when he came to read professor Saur's meter, the professor greeted him with "I wish you would come into my library."

Mr. Carrico recalls **wondering**, somewhat apprehensively, what the professor could want with him, even though a clear conscience assured him he hadn't thrown any rocks or broken any windows. He followed the eminent gentleman into the library, a beautiful room with bookcases of hand-carved wood. He had never been in a place like that before! Beautiful though it was, he sat on the edge of his chair trying to figure out what the professor wanted with him.

As the professor talked on – and on – he became uneasy too, because he had more meters to read. Finally Noel ventured, "Professor, I've got to go." The professor came to the point quickly then. "I want to give you something." He pulled out a little sack and explained, as he handed it to the young meter reader, "When you are as old as I am, these will be very valuable." (He was at that time eighty years old, just the age Noel Carrico is now.) The little bag contained all but six of the copper pennies dated 1793 through 1857. Little wonder Noel was all but overwhelmed! That incident of course, started him collecting.

During those years while he was working for the utility company in his hometown, he also had an ice business, delivering in small towns in the area as well as in his hometown. One day when he supplied a little ice cream parlor, the proprietor told him, "Look here – what those kids gave me."

Noel looked and could hardly believe his eyes; they had given him some half-dimes. He willingly paid the man what he had allowed the children and told him that any time he took in such coins he'd do the same. He even acquired two counterfeit gold coins that way. His collection, started more than sixty years ago, is now on display to the public at the First Security Bank.

Another of his collections features auto license plates from the state of Montana, complete from the first plates issued in 1915. Licenses issued prior to 1915 were not metal plates as now; the car owner was simply issued a piece of paper. He then would have a harness maker stamp his number on a piece of leather which he would attach to his car. The earliest 'plate' in his collection was issued in 1910 to Dr. Schrumpf (Art Schrumpf's father) of Miles City for his Buick.

Mr. Carrico also has a model of every radio made by RCA (He sold RCA radios for many years, prompting that collection). His radio collection is now on display and can be seen at Frontier Gateway Museum.

He bought his first radio in 1919, putting his antenna up the last day of the year. His radio was the first in the community, and it wasn't unusual for him to come home late at night and find someone (other than his family) listening to his radio. One night two of his neighbors were there when he came home after midnight and before they left he had sold each of them a radio.

These are only samples of the collections and files he has on a variety of subjects, many of them in some way connected with the utility business.

In 1916, Noel Carrico married Christine Finkelson in Sidney. They have four children: D'Arline, Elaine, William and Frank, all living. Mr. Carrico has led an exceptionally full and active life. Furthermore, at eighty years, he continues to lead an exceptionally full and active life.

Great Northern's 'Gallopin' Goose' at Fairview

Mrs. Albert (Grace Aldrich) Skillestad

March – April 1970

Recently Albert Skillestad, going through some papers that had belonged to his wife, came across an account she had written of their early days in Montana. Although she does not so specify, it was probably written in conjunction with an effort of the Home Demonstration clubs to gather historical information. Earlier in this column we carried Mr. Skillestad's remembrances of the homesteading period. Now we have the woman's version. Mrs. Skillestad died in 1961.

Looking backward to our days of pioneering, I want to say, my husband and I recall them as among the happiest days of our lives. Even though we went through many difficult experiences, the satisfaction of earnest endeavor to do our best outweighs extreme losses.

I'm forgetting to introduce our readers to some of our old timers, whose names will be mentioned here. I am Mrs. Grace Aldrich Skillestad, wife of Albert Skillestad, pioneer homesteader on Upper Clear Creek, and founder of the Union Post Office.

We came to Montana in March 1908, from Sisseton, South Dakota, and my husband filed on our 1/4 section claim shortly afterward. Our plans were to make it our permanent home so, shortly afterwards, we bought the necessary lumber for our shack, and the adventure of getting located began.

Many little incidents on our first trip came to my mind. I still treasure the memories, though they're not important enough to mention here. I recall the few ranches we passed, with their low-roofed, widespread buildings, many of logs. The high corrals were new and interesting to us. The Almy Ranch was nearest Glendive, but as we had no need to stop there, we proceeded on to the next one, owned and operated by Gene Williams and his brother-in-law, Frank Bryan.

Mrs. Bryan prepared dinner for us. She was a cordial, attractive woman, and our initiation to Ranch Hospitality began happily. The W.W. Woods Ranch came next, and near there quite a number of homesteads had been filed on. So we saw some tents pitched near Keg Springs. While the party we were with stopped to unhitch the horses and water them, we met several of the newcomers and talked with them.

Herchel Purdum's claim was nearby, and he was one of the tent dwellers. Another man we saw there was Roy Kimball, who dropped by on his saddle horse. I had fun picking the lovely native wildflowers along the creek bank and even succeeded in catching a baby turtle that seemed to invite capture.

The 35 mile ride out from Glendive on a load of lumber to the O.W. Cress homestead was tiring, but after meeting Mary Cress and enjoying her good supper, I knew for a certainty we were going to feel at home in Montana. We boarded and roomed at the Cress home while our shack was being built. Work on our 14'x16' house began immediately. My Aunt Bernice Stafford and husband, Charles, arrived from Fargo, North Dakota, May 15th, 1908, and with their assistance we moved into our shack three days later. We then invited them to share it with us until their own shack could be built.

The day following, Skilly and Charlie Stafford hired a team from Mr. Cress and hauled a load of cedar wood from the Divide*. On May 20th a furious blizzard struck, and we learned what warm comfort a cedar fire can give but how quickly it burns out.

Next morning Levi Hendrixson came by to inquire how we had fared through the storm, and the horse he was riding bucked him off into a snowdrift just outside our door. Levi got up laughing, unhurt, due to the soft landing place.

Busy days followed. The men exchanged work, digging wells, building shacks, putting up wire fences, mining coal, getting fence posts out of the Divide, and hauling wood for cooking.

It was several months before we had a well, and the nearest spring was nearly 3/4 of a mile from our house. This spring was cleaned out and made deeper so as to hold about a 10 or 12-quart pail full of water. A box and some boards were used to improvise a cover to keep livestock from finding our precious reservoir. Thus it necessitated a mile walk for a pail of water.

Aunt Bernice and I often visited Mary Cress when our husbands were working there. We assisted with preparing meals, and we never tired of helping her in caring for their two small children, Edna, about four years old, and Joe, going on two years.

Sabina Miller, wife of Andy Miller, and Mary Cress were sisters. Both families came here from Storm Lake, Iowa. Their homes were only one mile apart. There were many advantages having near neighbors. For instance, take the problem of sending and receiving mail. Whenever one made a trip to Glendive, he called for and brought mail for all in the neighborhood. It helped a lot, but as more and more people settled nearby, the need for a post office on Clear Creek became more apparent.

Petitions were circulated, signed, and sent to the Post Office Department in Washington, D.C. Information received in response revealed it would be necessary for a three-month trial be given to determine if it would be profitable to establish an office in our sparsely populated area. This required keeping a record of all incoming mail and stamp cancellations of all outgoing mail, etc.

Our first address was Glendive, miles from our homestead. There was a post office at Circle, and Lindsay supplied enroute. During this trial period we would be responsible for bringing in mail for our patrons from the Circle Star Route to our house and also taking the mail out. The records would determine whether we could make a showing enough to get on the map and warrant Uncle Sam's mailman supplying our needs.

Several names for the proposed new post office were submitted for the Postmaster General's approval. First choice was 'Clear Creek' since the community was already known by that name throughout Eastern Montana. Second choice was 'Union', and *this was the name approved by the post office department because there was already one post office in Montana named Clear Creek.*

Union was an appropriate name. Many times during the trials of the trial period I thought that if our community had not stood so closely united we probably would not have succeeded in establishing our post office. O.W. Cress volunteered a gentle horse broken both to saddle and single driving, for use by the mailman. Right at first the amount of mail was light enough to be carried easily on a saddle horse, but it increased rapidly. Each delivery brought new and more addresses and names of new settlers to our list, and it became necessary to charter a buggy from E.E. Gregory. The driver was from one home, the horse from another, and the buggy from still another. We persuaded Nelson Martin to act as temporary carrier.

By the time all these were assembled and speeding on their way to a knoll three-and-one-half miles away to meet a mailman whose passing that way could vary an hour or more either way in coming or going, you can understand why our trial period became just that. The difficulties were soon forgotten, though, when papers came making my husband postmaster of the Union Post Office.

During April Skilly had a severe spell of rheumatic fever, and he was just recovering sufficiently enough to be out of bed when he received his appointment as postmaster. Thus May 4, 1909, became a red-letter day as his commission became official. There was once a week mail service but later changed to twice a week.

Later orders were given for the Circle mail carrier to include our office in their regular mail delivery service. The first man to do so was none other than Peter Rorvik, well-known old timer of Circle. Earl Reno, brother-in-law of Rorviks, was one of our best carriers, and he continued driving during the peak of the land seekers rush in the Circle area and beyond. Passengers were allowed to ride with the mailman, and at times he had as many as eight or nine on one trip, seeking available homesteads.

Mr. Skillestad acted as postmaster for several years until Olson Brothers set up a general store and began making plans to start another post office in connection with their store. We preferred having our office moved to their location and keeping the original name of Union so moving arrangements were carried out, and the community is still known as the Union Community.

Exchanging help was always the rule in the early days. All the wells were dug by hand, requiring two men at all times. One worked at the bottom of the well, digging and filling pails with dirt with the other pulling it up, hand over hand with rope and tackle. It was a slow, tedious task and dangerous as well, demanding caution in the operation and care of the ropes. Tottering rocks, which might fall on the man below, also constituted a threat.

That first year we built our house, started fences, planted a small garden and a potato patch. We had no horses yet so we hired horses for plowing the garden and patch for the potatoes. We also hired horses for getting wood from the Divide – also fence posts and lignite coal. The expense was a day's work for our neighbor in return for the use of the team. Wood, posts, and coal were free for the getting.

Also that first year we bought a wild range cow, calf by side, from the Garfield Ranch. The second year we finished fencing 160 acres and bought one unbroken horse. We dug a second well, as the first one had to be abandoned because of large rocks.

We hired horses from ranchers to do some plowing, agreeing to break broncs to work for the use of them through the summer. Later we traded our western horse for a gentle eastern one.

The third or fourth year we hired Claude Gunnett to plow 20 acres to sow flax. It was a very dry year, and the seed did not start until the fall rains came. The following spring this field was seeded early to Durum wheat. Sufficient rains fell and the field gave promise for a bumper crop. In August, when the wheat was nearly ripe enough to harvest, a terrific hailstorm laid it flat.

Our first cash crop was a flax field, threshed November 20, 1912 after a number of unsuccessful attempts to harvest one. This, too, came near being destroyed. Sparks from the old time engine set fire to some flax straw nearby the machine. But for the speedy action of my husband and the threshing crew in quenching it, the fire would have claimed not only our flax crop, but also our neighbor's threshing outfit, hayrack and all.

There were no churches established near enough to attend regularly so a group of our Upper Clear Creek neighbors organized a Sunday School. They met every Sunday in homes and many took turns acting as superintendent and did their part as teachers.

Early Christian leaders were Mrs. Betsy Martin, Rev. Herman Seil (a congregational missionary), his wife, Florence Brown Seil, Mr. and Mrs. Edward Gregory, Lyle Pullen, Josephine Gathright, Mr. and Mrs. Charles Stafford, Mr. and Mrs. L.D. Hendrixson and the Skillestads. Later on, other communities organized Sunday Schools and missionary ministers were provided by various church denominations.

Some of our favorite Sunday School songs were: 'There Shall be Showers of Blessings', 'Throw Out the Lifeline', 'When the Roll is Called Up Yonder, I'll be There', 'Sweet Hour of Prayer', and 'God Be With You'. Several old timers had violins, a few had accordions. There were a few old fashioned school-type organs, all of which were brought into play.

Our first school was taught by Effie Bryan in a homestead shack that was vacant for a few months. It was carried out on a trial plan recommended by the county school superintendent, in the fall of 1912 or '13 to get a school district established.

I believe nine pupils were enrolled. We boarded and roomed one girl, Lorraine Schuld, whose home was too far distant for her to attend otherwise. Jeannie West stayed with my aunt, Mrs. Charles Stafford, during the trial term of school. The usual teacher's salary was about $35 to $45 per month. Some teachers were homesteaders or one of a homesteader's family.

Numerous nationalities were represented in our Union Community. Some were foreign born, but I'm sure the majority were American born. There were a few who had come from Scotland, some were of Irish descent, and many were of Scandinavian parentage, coming from Iowa, North and South Dakota, Minnesota, Nebraska, Michigan and Wisconsin. Other states farther distant were represented also.

Cedar and other kinds of trees were used for fuel, and lignite coal from the Divide and from local mines. Coal and wood ranges were used mostly.

Considerable mail ordering was carried on. Sears-Roebuck and Montgomery Ward were leading catalog houses.

Rattlesnakes were not troublesome in our area. We did have a few lambs killed by coyotes and we evened the score by trapping quite a number. Weasels were sometimes a pest, and killed quite a number of our chickens.

Yes, we do recall several severe storms, cloud bursts, wind storms, blizzards and dry spells. We learned about all phases, from 119 degrees above zero to 48 degrees below zero.

We could not patronize bakeries often during pioneer days. All breads and pastries were home baked so flour and yeast cakes were among the important items to keep on hand. We raised our own chickens and potatoes, after the second year. We kept a cow or two and raised a few pigs, so with a garden we had considerable homegrown food.

I did make sunbonnets and sun hats for garden use. Having no daughters, much of my sewing was making boys' blouses for our four sons. I used a divided skirt for horseback riding. We did some catalog ordering, and Mr. Skillestad became much used to buying yard goods, etc. Calico at that time sold for from .03 to .05 cents per yard, and good grade gingham was 10 cents per yard.

I used girls' type shoes for every day wear. They wore well and were foot formed for comfort.

It wasn't strange to see a woman don coveralls or overalls. I've done it myself when necessity arose. I recall being in favor of Women's Suffrage, but we were far from speaking or campaigners at the time.

We were not well enough posted to speak wisely upon the War question." (1918) "My husband sold war bonds during the years they were needed. Quite a number of German descent living in our community reportedly had said they wouldn't buy bonds, but when he contacted them, they all bought. No complaints, which proved they were more loyal citizens than they let on to their own fellow countrymen.

I recall several young women who homesteaded near our claim. Miss Josephine Gathright was our neighbor, and she paid for her improvements by dressmaking. Miss Olive Pullen proved up on her claim, kept house for her brother Lyle, and later she returned to Allegan, Michigan. Stella Utterback came to Union from Blair, Nebraska, with her family. After proving up on her homestead, she became the wife of Herchel Purdum. They were long time residents on Clear Creek. Besides serving *several years as Dawson County commissioner, Mr. Purdum took time to act as a 4-H leader for boys and assisted with other community projects.*

(Problems) Our long distance to a trading center and no railroad for so many years. Also low prices for everything we had to sell.

One rewarding phase was the opportunity of raising our boys on a farm where they could enjoy their own saddle ponies and pets of all kinds.

Our fears and anxieties were numerous at times, but put to rest, usually by an enduring faith that 'whatever is, is for the best'.

The generosity of our new friends and neighbors" (when the Skillestads moved into the Clear Creek community) "was thrilling, and their cordial acceptance of us into their circle was very heart-warming. One Fourth of July celebration in particular we recall with much pleasure. It was our first year here, 1908.

The Grant Gibson's Ranch was the place; folks came early and stayed late. A long picnic table was laid in the center of an ideal clump of shade trees, where both dinner and supper was served.

We had no horses at the time, but a promise to provide transportation came with the invitation. Sure enough, in the forenoon of Picnic Day, the Gibsons sent their two-seated surrey, with Dick Long as driver, to bring Bernice and Charles Stafford, Albert and I to their celebration. It was an unforgettable experience for us.

Before the day was over we had met most of the family folk, and toward evening more young people came to enjoy dancing. The trails over the hill and dale were not considered safe for night driving, which meant the dance must go on until daylight. Not that the crowd minded that; all were having such a good time they welcomed an excuse to prolong the fun.

Music was furnished by volunteers, chiefly, and it was surprising how many good fiddlers were usually found in attendance. Picnics, dances and celebrations were often held by the early settlers with many in attendance. People drove or rode horseback long distances to join in the merrymaking.

Home remedies were in demand on the frontier. Dr. Blackstone was the first medical doctor, answering calls near Union and Lindsay. Dr. A.F. Robson and Dr. Bidwell were our first dentists. Mrs. Betsy Martin, Mrs. Jane Kilbourne, Mrs. Hulda Burgeson and Gertie Hendrixson were our early day nurses. They attended most of the home confinement cases.

In the latter part of her memoirs Mrs. Skillestad evidently was answering a questionnaire. The questions are not listed, but her answers in most cases make the questions obvious.

Both my husband and I were members of farm families, having normal knowledge of livestock and farm activities.

Most of the tillable land open for filing before the change was made was taken by 1912. But we did take an additional 80 acres of hilly pasture land which we later sold to a neighbor, A.M. Heron, who owned the land adjoining.

196

Fannen Reece

November 1967

He has smashed his ribs four times, but he's still managed to live eighty-nine years – plus about five months. Fannen Reece (his first name is Robert, but he says no one would recognize that name) was born in North Carolina, but Montana has been his home for 'nigh onto' seventy years.

When he was just a young fellow, he joined a kid who wanted to go to Oklahoma, and the two headed west. His companion had an uncle in Montana and soon moved on, but Fannen stayed in Oklahoma about a year. His friend kept writing letters back to Oklahoma, telling about the big wages in Montana, so the next summer Fannen yielded to the lure of more money and moved on to the Treasure State, too. He went to Park City first – that was in 1899 – and landed a job in a sawmill, just across the road from the town.

His friend was right about the wages: right away he got on for a dollar a day. Down in Oklahoma he had been working for fifty cents a day. He stayed with the sawmill that summer, then went up to Columbus where he started herding sheep.

In 1902 grasshoppers took over the range in that part of the country and didn't leave enough grass for the sheep so Hemalux (his boss) moved his sheep to Dawson County, moving Reece with them. Nobody has explained why the grasshoppers confined themselves to the southern part of the state that year. Whatever the explanation, the sheep and Fannen Reece were now located between Redwater and the Divide*, where he spent several years. After herding for Hemalux a while he decided to start a band of his own so he bought a bunch of lambs from Hedley Robinson. He bought them in the fall and wintered them along with Robinson's own bunch on the latter's home ranch, close to where Richey is now but wasn't then.

He spent several years in the Divide country, then and later, a sheep wagon his home. If he wasn't good company himself he was out of luck because most of the time he was alone, and if the cooking wasn't to his liking he had no one to blame but himself because he was the chief cook.

In the sheep wagon he did his cooking and baking with a camp-size cook stove with oven. Baking powder biscuits were his specialty. He baked sourdough bread for a while, but finally he quit that because it was too hard to control in the summer. He'd mix the bread in the morning before he left camp, then bake it in the evening when he came home. During hot weather the dough would rise too fast, and when he'd get back in the evening, he'd find the dough all over the place so he switched to baking powder biscuits almost altogether. He earned a reputation for making good biscuits.

His menu generally called for pancakes for breakfast, biscuits for supper, and soda crackers at noon. Mr. Reece explained that in bygone days you could buy big soda crackers (about the size of four present-day crackers) in a big box. He usually carried a lunch along to eat at noon. His lunch typically consisted of big soda crackers spread with peanut butter (he'd like to be able to have some right now) and "those little weenies you get in a can."

In the winter he had fresh meat, in the summer he had bacon – and maybe ham. He'd buy a couple of hogs in the fall, cure the hams and bacons. Long as the weather was cold he could have fresh (frozen, but no deep freeze) meat, but with the warm weather he had to rely on the cured pieces.

As was customary then, he always bought enough groceries in the fall to last all winter. Didn't run to town to buy a loaf of bread. If you ran out of some item, you just went without. High on his grocery list would be a big sack of dried beans. Flour, potatoes, dried fruit (cases of peaches, apricots, apples, prunes), peanut butter and coffee were some of his staples. Sugar was included, too, but they didn't use much sugar then. He used his oven for baking biscuits, not for cakes or cookies.

Although Reece began his Dawson County sojourn between Redwater and the Divide, he has spent most of his Montana years (most of his life!) east of the Divide, chiefly between Glendive and Savage on the east side of the river in the northwestern corner of Wibaux County.

Before he settled down there he ranched awhile on Big Seven Mile Creek, about eleven miles from Glendive, then moved across the state line to Skaar, North Dakota. When he located there, he had all the space he could want, but before long the homesteaders started flocking in, and in a couple years there were "settlers all over the place" so he began looking for another range.

He found what he wanted in a remote corner of Wibaux County where it runs into the Yellowstone with Dawson County on one side and Richland County on the other. By this time he had switched to cattle, and in time he took on some farming, too.

One day when he was disking, he finished one field and moved his outfit to an adjoining field. It was such a short distance that he didn't bother to lift the discs out of the ground (maybe if he had had hydraulic controls....) and as he crossed the strip one of the discs caught on a rock.

It pulled back so far that when it finally let go, the jolt threw him from the spring seat to the ground right behind the horses. The horses took off and the disc ran over him, leaving him with a set of broken ribs. But he survived.

His ribs took another beating when the horse he was riding on a dead run fell with him. He was trying to head off a cow, racing across a meadow through thick, tall grass. A ditch lay ahead of them and he knew it, but his horse didn't. When they hit the ditch, the horse somersaulted, pitching Reece onto a pile of cactus and breaking his ribs. The horse wound up with his head in a bunch of cactus, too. His head was so sore it was months before he could wear a bridle again. His head was sore about as long as Fannen's ribs were.

With rib-breaking his specialty, he managed it again when he sailed out of a topless Model T Ford onto a railroad track. This happened soon after Fords began appearing in this part of the country. A bunch of fellows had gone fishing, and the Model T was loaded (as were some of the passengers). In one place the road turned before it reached the railroad track and when the returning fishermen reached the corner where the road turned – they didn't. They ran right onto the track and Reece, leaning over to shut the door, was thrown out of the car (no seat belt to fasten) onto the tracks. More broken ribs.

But the only time he took his ribs to the doctor was the time the mower ran over him. Got smashed up a little too thoroughly that time – although, he hastens to explain, it was the neighbors' doings, taking him to the doctor.

He had hitched a bronc to the mower along with a gentle horse and started for the field, but half-a-mile from the barn the clip came off the single tree. He stepped across behind the gentle horse to fasten the tug*, but for some reason Gentle started kicking, knocking him down. Away went the horses, bouncing him along in front of the mower for what seemed an endless stretch before the mower went over him and left him lying with his smashed ribs while his team promptly left the scene of the accident.

Crippled up as he was, trying to do anything about the team was out of the question, but he did manage to drag himself to the house. The nearest neighbor was five miles away so there was no going for help. He made the mistake of going to bed that night. Next morning he started trying to get up fairly early, but it was ten o'clock before he made it so from then on he just sat on a chair.

The accident happened on Tuesday, and it was Sunday before anyone came around. Some neighbors had planned to come help him brand, but when they found him he was in no shape to wrestle calves. Instead some of the fellows rounded up his team (the horses didn't get off without consequences; the reins were wrapped around the hames so tightly that they couldn't get their heads down to eat or drink) and cared for them, then carted Reece off to the doctor.

He managed to get along without a hospital until he was seventy-eight years old. That was when he retired, but he figures that if he'd stayed on the ranch and kept working he'd still be going strong. If it just hadn't been for that arthritis! It was because of the arthritis he had to retire, and after that all kinds of things went wrong with him.

But now that he's living in the Palace Hotel he doesn't have to do much worrying about cold and snow and ice and blizzards. He can just stay inside where it's warm and remember the times he stood guard in a blizzard all night to keep his sheep from scattering. Or the time seventeen of his calves drowned in the Yellowstone. The river had frozen over but left an air hole, and the calves fell in.

The winter of 1908 was one of the worst he went through, hard on man and beast. Fortunately it broke early – in February. If it had lasted until spring, Mr. Reece declares, even the magpies wouldn't have survived! It wasn't just that they had a lot of snow that winter (and they had plenty); they also had thaws and rain so the snow was crusted with layers of ice. Horses' legs had to be wrapped with gunnysacks to keep the ice from cutting them to pieces.

Fighting the elements is all right for a young fellow, but when a man gets to be eighty-nine-and-a-half – well, living in a Palace is a little easier on him than living in a sheep wagon. And as for the blizzards – it's nicer to have them on the other side of the plate glass window!

199

Mrs. Albert (Ivy Fluss) Brubaker

August 1966

Mrs. Albert (Ivy Fluss) Brubaker of Terry doesn't remember a thing about her arrival in Montana, so all she knows is what people have told her. But from what people have told her, the year she came was an eventful year. While one member was added to the family, another member came close to being subtracted. Lon Fluss and Irva Booth had been married five years when they moved to the Bar G Ranch near Mildred in September of 1908. That same fall Mrs. Fluss went back to Illinois to await the arrival of their first child while Mr. Fluss kept things going on the ranch.

They had 'gone modern' on the ranch with a gasoline engine to pump the water when the wind failed to turn the windmill, but one afternoon the engine would not start. It was dark in the dugout where the engine was located so after expending considerable time and effort trying to get it started, Fluss struck a match (what a boon, flashlights!) to see what was wrong. He started something, but it wasn't the engine. Somehow gasoline had leaked out on top of the water, and when he struck the match, the ensuing explosion threw him up behind a 2x4 on the door. On the heels of that explosion (if explosions have heels) the gas tank blew up and catapulted him out the door. In those split seconds while he was being tossed about, he was subjected to searing flames, which burned off all his clothes except his belt and singed every hair from his head.

Fortunately he was not alone at the time of the catastrophe. George Johnson, standing in the door while Fluss tried to start the engine, was also burned, but Gilbert Booth, Fluss' brother-in-law, was at the corrals and unaffected so he was able to take charge. Booth hurried to where the saddle horse had been picketed so he could use it to round up the team, but he was distressed to find that the horse had broken loose at the noise of the explosion.

Ordinarily the team declined to be rounded up without the persuasion of a mounted man, but this time – wonder of wonders – Booth was able to catch them even though he was afoot. While he was getting the team and hitching them to the spring wagon, Fluss made his way to the house. The storm door stuck, and as he tried to pull it open he peeled the skin off his fingers. In the house he smeared himself with lard and flour, the only first aid at hand, then staggered to the buggy. They made the trip to Terry in record time, the horses on the run the whole twenty-five miles. Even when they reached Terry there was no medical aid available so they waited at the depot for the train to come through to take him to Miles City. Badly burned though he was, he survived, and scars were not too evident. By the time Mrs. Fluss came back to the ranch in March, bringing their tiny daughter, Ivy, he was home from the hospital with a five-pound jar of Unguentine to aid his recovery.

Lon Fluss first came to Montana to work for his brother-in-law, George W. Burt, in 1898. Burt had extensive sheep holdings around Ismay, Mildred, and on the Powder River. The two formed a partnership, which lasted until 1911.

Mr. Fluss used to tell his children about his first encounter with Calamity Jane. Soon after he came to Montana he happened to be in the Drummond Hotel in Terry when she came in. He got up to give her his chair, but she checked him with, "Young man, just keep your chair. I'll brush off my pants and sit on the floor." And she sat on the floor.

One summer soon after he came west, the hay crop was scant, and they weren't very busy in August so Fluss, with the Burts, decided to take a trip to Yellowstone Park by team and sheep wagon! That trip wasn't of the few-hours going, few-hours coming, with a whirlwind-spin-through-the-park-sandwiched-between variety. They took a leisurely six weeks and thoroughly enjoyed the sights in the Park, including Old Faithful. The Gardiner entrance was the only one in use at that time so they had no problem deciding where to go in.

In 1903 Lon Fluss married his childhood sweetheart, Irva Booth. They were married in the house where Hubings now live, a house built, and at that time occupied, by George Burt, and lived in Terry at first. Lon tended sheep camps and Mrs. Fluss helped Mrs. Burt with the housework and cooking. During shearing season there was plenty of cooking to be done. A shearing crew consisted of about seventeen men while the 'cooking crew' was generally made up of three women who moved from one shearing camp to the next as the shearing crew moved.

Later while Mr. Fluss was taking care of the sheep down on the Powder River he and his young wife lived in a small log cabin on the ranch. They were very isolated with no contact with other human beings for days and weeks on end. With so little outside contact Lon would often tease his wife by pretending company had arrived, knocking on the door when he came back from the sheep sheds. She was wise to him, though, and he didn't fool her.

One day when he had been at the sheds she heard the knock so she just laughed and called, "Come in and quit fooling." He didn't come in so she, a little confused, called again, "Lon, come on in; I know it's you." Still he didn't respond so she walked to the door and gave an ear-piercing scream that brought her husband running from the sheds. As she approached the low door she had seen two long, black braids of hair, obviously not her husband's! Her scream scared the Indian almost as badly as he scared her, and it scared Lon, too. As it turned out, the Indian was entirely innocent and had no intention of frightening anyone. He had become separated from other members of his tribe and had merely stopped to inquire, little expecting a white woman to answer the door.

Mrs. Fluss wasn't in Montana in time to be included in the sheep wagon expedition to Yellowstone Park, but she did get in on a boat trip down the Mississippi. George Burt had a boat built in St. Louis, which he named the Lucille Burt for his daughter, then arranged an excursion for his family and Mr. and Mrs. Fluss. The group went by train to St. Louis, then sailed down the Mississippi to New Orleans. When they reached New Orleans, they were having such a good time the Burt family decided to cruise the Gulf of Mexico, too, but Mr. and Mrs. Fluss took the train at New Orleans and came back to Montana.

George Burt was a native of Illinois, and his decision to ranch in Montana had far-reaching influence. He was married to a Fluss girl, so after he brought her to Montana, two of her sisters came to visit her. In a country where women were outnumbered by men as they were in eastern Montana at the turn of the century there wasn't much chance of any escaping single, and the Fluss girls didn't. One of them married David Bickle, the other married William Fulton. Both stayed to rear families in eastern Montana. With Mrs. Burt's brother Lon added to the list (Lon brought his bride from Illinois so he didn't rob any of the natives of a prospective wife), three of the area's earliest families, in addition to his own, can be traced to Burt's decision.

Gilbert Booth, Mrs. Fluss' brother, also moved to Montana, but he didn't bring a wife with him, and he never married. He lived with Mr. and Mrs. Fluss until the time of his death. Lon Fluss' older brother, Les, was included in the party that sailed the Mississippi, and on that trip he worked as fireman's helper. As he and the fireman became better acquainted, the fireman showed a picture of his sister to Les. Les was apparently a man of action. He became interested in the sister and wrote to her, and she answered, a correspondence which culminated in marriage. They however, settled in Texas instead of Montana, and spent their later years in California.

In addition to Ismay, Mildred, and Powder River ranches Burt and Fluss also had a ranch on Coal Creek. While all the ranches were not always humanly inhabited, they were always kept well stocked with provision. In the summer of 1909 W.A. Brubaker's sister came from Ohio to visit him. (Mr. Brubaker was one of Terry's first settlers and founder of Terry State Bank). She was interested in seeing the country so Mr. Brubaker took her for a drive.

One of the places he showed her happened to be the Coal Creek Ranch. To the sister from the east, the unlocked doors were a source of amazement, but when she saw the food supplies inside she was almost overwhelmed. How could it be that people would store that much food in a cabin, then go off and leave the door unlocked. Mr. Brubaker explained to her the unwritten law of the range land that a man was permitted any time to stop in and fix himself a meal whether anyone was home or not. The understanding was, "Eat all you want, but be sure you wash the dishes!" As for vandalism, such as is commonly reported in current news accounts – it was unheard of.

Mr. and Mrs. Fluss spent fifty-two years together before Mr. Fluss passed away September 3, 1955. Mrs. Fluss followed him almost two years later, departing this life August 3, 1957. Lon and Irva Fluss had three children; Ivy, now Mrs. Albert Brubaker; Jay, and Leo. Mrs. Fluss went back to 'civilized' Illinois to have their first child, but the second one was born in Ismay and the third one on the Bar G Ranch.

Their only daughter, Ivy, attended Eastern Montana College, then taught school several years before marrying banker Albert Brubaker. They now live in Terry. Jay lives on the Powder River Ranch, and Leo lives in Clarkston, Washington. Leo left the range, but he hasn't deserted his heritage; he works in the livestock yards.

History of Red Top Mennonite Church

July 1967

The Red Top Mennonite Church, located five miles east of Bloomfield, this weekend is having a celebration to commemorate the fiftieth anniversary of its organization. The congregation had its formal beginning on April 1, 1917.

For some time a small group had been meeting in the Red Top Schoolhouse. (This school had originally been named Adams because of its proximity to the Adams – now Bloomfield – post office, but after the schoolhouse roof was painted red the name was changed to Red Top).

This group of Christians had no formal organization or affiliation with any church body, but they were desirous of affiliating with the Mennonite Church so they contacted the nearest bishop of that church, I.S. Mast of Minot, North Dakota, and made arrangements for him to come to the community.

He came and held a series of evangelistic meetings, at the close of which three persons were received into the church by water baptism and seven others upon confession of their faith.

While formal organization of the congregation is dated 1917, its roots go back to almost the beginning of the present century when several Old Order Amish families settled in the Thirteen Mile Valley.

Jacob B. Mullet, a pioneer at heart, kept moving ahead of the settled community until he found himself on a farm in Dawson County. Born in Ohio, he had moved to Indiana, then with his family to Bisbee, North Dakota, where he was living at the turn of the century.

Winters in northeastern North Dakota were cold with a lot of snow and many blizzards which made stock feeding difficult. C.A. Buller quotes him as saying he "felt there must be a better place to live" (and besides that, the surrounding area was getting pretty well settled) so early in the summer of 1903 he started west.

He was looking for a place where there would be homestead land available for the young people to locate (he had five sons) in the home community and be able to attend church more regularly.

He was considering Bozeman but stopped in Glendive where he was contacted by E.C. Leonard, a real estate agent who offered to show him a large plot of good land where they could either homestead or buy railroad land for a nominal sum.

With team and buggy they drove about 30 miles into the country, north to Thirteen Mile Valley. There indeed appeared to be good farm land and good grazing for cattle, with abundant grass and water. (That some of the water was alkaline, Mullet didn't realize until later). Fuel was easy to obtain as coal could be seen sticking out of the hills in places.

He bought half-a-section of railroad land at $2.50 per acre, and instead of going to Bozeman, he went back to North Dakota to report his findings.

Others, too, of the North Dakota community were eager to find land for new homes, and some individuals came on over that fall to file on homesteads.

The first homesteaders that moved to the valley were J.B. Mullet's oldest son, Joe Mullet, with his wife Ann; the Amos Millers; the Dave Chupp, Sr.'s; and bachelor John Kauffman. They shipped a carload of machinery and their household goods.

They found a wide, lonely prairie with the nearest neighbor, a rancher, five miles away. They lived in tents until they had their houses built, hauling all their lumber and supplies by wagon from Glendive.

Homesteaders at that time were allowed only a quarter of a section*. Amos Miller and Joe Mullet both located in the east half of the section now owned by Clifford Kauffman, a mile south of where the church house was later built. Only alternate sections were available for homesteads, and John Kauffman chose the northwest quarter of the next homestead section to the east of the other two new settlers. Dave Chupp settled across the road from the present Elmer Borntrager home.

In the spring of 1904, Jacob B. Mullet and his family joined the settlement, and that fall three more families – Eli Chupp, Dan Miller, and Johnny Miller – came. Dan Miller was an Amish preacher.

In the spring of 1905 the Jake Hostetler family swelled by five the population of the Valley. Jake's wife, Lydia was a daughter of Johnny Millers.

Up until this time all the settlers had come from northeastern North Dakota, but also in the spring of 1905 another Amish preacher, Joe Borntrager from Fayette County, Illinois, visited the little group and conducted worship services for the settlers.

Since his family included five sons as well as a daughter, he became interested in the homestead land and filed a claim before he returned to his home.

That fall, after his crop was harvested, he moved his family to the Thirteen Mile Valley. Thirty years later his grandson, Elmer Borntrager, was ordained as minister of Red Top Mennonite Church.

The Amish held their worship services in the homes of the members so no church building was erected. It was largely from the first generation descendants of these Amish pioneers that the later Mennonite congregation was formed.

Among the ten charter members of the latter were two of Jacob B. Mullet's sons with their wives and one daughter with her husband, and one granddaughter with her husband. Another charter member was the daughter of pioneer Jake Hostetler.

For two years the little group was without a resident pastor, then in May, 1919, R.W. Benner came with his wife and family from Pennsylvania to accept charge of the congregation. The Benners, however, stayed only a little more than a year. Because of health problems, Mr. Benner found a change of location necessary so they returned to the east.

Again the Red Top Congregation was without a resident pastor. Bishop Mast attempted to arrange for a visiting minister at least once a month, but because of distances and weather this was not always possible.

Thirteen years passed before their desire for a resident pastor was realized. On September 10, 1933, George Kauffman from Kenmare, North Dakota was ordained to the ministry to serve at Red Top. He continued in service there until 1938 when he moved to Oregon.

Elmer Borntrager of the local community was ordained in August, 1935, to assist in the pastorate, and he assumed full responsibility after the departure of Kauffman. With the exception of a period of two years when he attended Goshen College in Indiana, he has served in this capacity to the present time. During the two years he was absent L.A. Kauffman, formerly of Minot, North Dakota, took over his responsibilities.

The congregation organized in 1917 continued to worship in the school house until 1936 when their newly constructed church house, just across the road from the school house, was completed. An extensive remodeling program for the church building was effected in 1965, enlarging it considerably.

Although there was a time when in the mid-twenties, membership in the congregation dropped to seven because of a drought-caused exodus from the Valley, in the late twenties a healthy growth was experienced, and the number on the roll has continued to grow.

In 1949 a number of families from the Red Top community moved to Glendive and soon started a new congregation, Little White Chapel, in West Glendive. This second exodus caused another drop in enrollment (though far less drastic than that of the mid-twenties), but in spite of this the membership at present is sixty-three.

The fiftieth anniversary celebration, July 8 and 9, has brought together many former members and friends who, in these past fifty years, have scattered from coast to coast, border to border, and even beyond United States borders.

Amos Shrader

February – March 1971

When Amos Shrader came to Montana in the spring of 1912, there wasn't much unclaimed homestead land left in that part of Dawson County which still is in Dawson. However, there was plenty of land south of the Missouri River. When he decided to claim some, he was still ahead of the government survey.

Shrader originally hailed from Illinois. Starting west, he worked awhile for a farmer in South Dakota, and then drifted on into the Treasure State. The fact that he had an uncle in Glendive (Alfred Wilson, father of Grant Wilson who still lives in the Gate City) no doubt influenced the direction of his 'drift'.

Amos found there was considerably more room in Montana than in Illinois and he liked that. He decided he liked the climate better too – year round. Montana's temperatures drop lower – he's seen sixty degrees below zero in Wolf Point where he lives now – but Illinois is a wet state and all winter the temperature kept hovering between freezing and not freezing. In Montana you at least could freeze outright!

His first job in Montana was with N.B. Sackett who had a homestead on Morgan Table. Next he worked for Majors and Larson, also on Morgan Table. Albert Larson had the north half of the section, Majors the southwest quarter and Henry Dyer had the southeast quarter (where Florence Mullet now lives). No buildings remain on either Majors' or Larsons' claims to mark the home sites of these settlers but Dyer's little 'shack' still stands, serving as a tool shed.

Amos stayed with Majors through the summer, then Larson leased his farm to him and moved to Fairview. The Albert Motel in Fairview is named for Albert Larson. Amos then lived on the Larson place. He got through the winter on his own cooking but in the spring, his mother came from Illinois and started keeping house for him until she decided she might as well have land of her own and homesteaded on Prairie Elk, about twenty-eight miles south of Oswego.

Now everything is done by truck but when Amos Shrader was farming on Morgan Table they did everything with horses – all his farming, hauling, everything. He'd load up a load of grain and take it to Stipek, a four-horse team pulling his load. He could make the trip to Stipek and back in one day.

Haulers from Morgan Table were lucky because they had no real hills to pull 'toward town' except Coalmine Hill coming up out of Morgan Creek valley into the badlands. Once that climb was behind them they had mostly down hill, even through the badlands.

One of their chief diversions during the summer months was baseball and Bloomfield had a real team. Although it was known as the Bloomfield team, the players were from the country a long way around Bloomfield. Mr. Shrader especially remembers the Kolberg boys (they usually supplied the pitcher and the catcher); Frank and Charlie Babcock from down on Morgan Creek; Bud Brown; the Boje boys; the Mullets and the Johnsons. They had great times at those ball games. They used to have some exciting rodeos at Bloomfield too.

206

In 1914 after Amos's mother filed on her claim he helped her build a shack on it. Now that his cook had moved to Prairie Elk, he was reduced to bachelor existence again. Much of the time Cousin Grant was with him and occasionally Grant's mother would come over and do some baking. In 1916 Amos decided to file on a claim of his own so he joined his mother in Prairie Elk country.

When Amos filed on his homestead south of Oswego, it had all been surveyed but only about half of it had been accepted as homestead land. His claim was right on the township line – on the east side of the line the survey had been accepted but on the west side it had not. He had eighty acres east of the line, the remainder on the west. Even though the survey had not all been accepted, squatter's rights* protected settlers – you could keep where you had your buildings and lines established.

Before the land was surveyed, a man from the Circle country – he was an under-sheriff of Dawson County at that time – had chosen this site for a homestead. He had plowed around a strip of land to mark his claim but later he had given it up. This then, was the piece on which Amos filed.

When you filed on a homestead, you had to establish some kind of boundaries so if somebody else came in they would know where your claim was. In Shrader's case, his boundaries were already marked. Claude Elder and Bert Powell were about the only settlers in that part of the country when Amos moved there. It was quite a contrast to the Bloomfield country which he had just left. There the homestead land was all taken (all of it that was worth anything) with many more people living in the area than now.

Roads weren't quite the same then as now. When he traveled from Bloomfield to Glasgow (where he filed) he just struck out across country to Paxton on the Redwater and stayed there overnight, then went on to Vida. He found the Vida area all taken so he went on to Prairie Elk.

It was quite an experience to go out on a piece of land in the middle of nowhere – not a stick of timber on it – put up a shack, break up a little land, start putting in a crop. About that first shack on his homestead: Mrs. Shrader observed that if it hadn't been for the newspapers between the 2x4's, you could have thrown a cat through. Perhaps "We don't have winters like we used to have" is less weather than housing!

The closest town to the homestead was Oswego. It was closest but you had to cross the river to get to it - in the summer on the ferry, in the winter on the ice. In between, you didn't cross. He watched pretty closely so he wouldn't get caught and never had any trouble to speak of. About the worst he encountered was having to stay overnight one time in 1919 waiting for the ice to freeze solid.

The river froze early that year – in October. The county seat election for McCone County had been held October 19. That day it started to rain and the rain turned to snow. October 24 he and Rossie Goode were going to leave for the winter and started out from their homesteads, but they found the river full of slush ice and they couldn't cross.

They stayed that night in the John Munz home on the south side of the river. The next morning they decided to check again and met two men –

Clarence Chamberlain and Cleve Ranking – who had been caught on the north side of the river the day before. They had walked across on the ice from Oswego so Goode and Shrader figured they could cross too, and did. October 25, they crossed the Missouri River on the ice and went back east for the winter.

Oswego at that time was more of a town than it is now. It had two grain elevators, a depot, two grocery stores, two or three rooming houses, livery barns, a blacksmith shop, and a clothing store that carried much besides clothing. It was really a general store rather than a clothing store.

When Shrader homesteaded in 1916, he had taken a claim joining the land on which his mother had homesteaded in 1914. Now he built his shack just across the line from hers. Thus each met residence requirements, yet their dwellings were close enough together so she could cook and keep house for him and he could do her 'outside work'. The Prairie Elk country is now classified as a grazing district, but Amos found enough good acreage to break up to meet homestead requirements. He spent most of that first summer on his homestead, building fence and making general improvements. This was no 'remodel' job; this was starting 'from scratch', and there was much to be done.

Even though he was only twenty-eight miles from Oswego, Glendive was the county seat those first years on Prairie Elk. About all that meant to him, he explains, was that he had to pay his taxes in Glendive. They mailed out the assessment sheets and if you 'paid up', Glendive didn't bother you.

Before he had left the Bloomfield area in the spring, Shrader had made arrangements to work during the threshing season for Menno Mullet. Mullet had a threshing outfit and did custom threshing and Amos was to come with a bundle rack and team. Later in the summer Menno wrote him a letter and told him he could come right away and help with haying. However, with all his other work that summer, he hadn't built a hay rack yet for his wagon so by the time he had that ready and got down there, the threshing rig was just starting out.

In former years, Mullet had run a full crew, including a cook car with the cook. When he had talked with Amos in the spring, he had expected to do the same that fall. But now, Amos learned, catastrophe had struck the wheat crop. Oh, the crop looked good enough; drought hadn't stunted it; hail had not beaten it; grasshoppers had not eaten it. Perhaps more heartbreaking to the farmer than any of these obvious destroyers, rust had shriveled the kernels so that a fine-looking stand of wheat yielded only a small fraction of the promise it appeared to hold. So severe was the blight that the various farmers simply couldn't afford to hire a crew. Instead, they arranged among themselves to exchange work and thus cut the cost of getting their grain threshed.

That could have left Amos out in the cold because he had no crop there for him to be a part of the 'exchanging'. He had come down to work for wages. As it turned out, even though Menno couldn't hire him to go with the rig, every farmer on the circuit, hard hit though they were, gave him a job so he worked through the entire season after all. Almost fifty-five years have passed but Mr. Shrader still spoke appreciatively of the community as he remembered that harvest.

208

Robert J. Frederickson & Mrs. Virgo (Marjorie) Anderson

February – June 1965

If Rev. E.J. Lindsey had not chosen to come to Poplar as a missionary to the Indians, R.J. Frederickson probably would not be making his monthly rounds, reading Glendive's water meters. His mother, a sister to Mrs. Lindsey, came to Poplar about 1892 to visit the Lindseys who came in 1887.

While she was in Montana she met August Frederickson, Tokna rancher (near the present Savage). After a time the two were married, and she settled down as a rancher's wife. Bob Frederickson is the youngest of their five children, four of whom survive.

Traveling in the 1890's was a far cry from today's jet travel. An imaginary trip with Rev. Lindsey (imaginary for us, that is; there was nothing imaginary about it for him) vividly illustrates the contrasts. Following is a copy of a letter he wrote to a niece of his in Carlisle, Pennsylvania, describing the trip from his Poplar mission station to a mission meeting at Fort Yates, North Dakota, sixty miles south of Bismarck.

A Trip from Poplar, Montana, To Standing Rock, North Dakota

August 29, 1892, we left our home for Standing Rock, North Dakota. The Mission meeting which we attended was at Fort Yates, a place which you can easily find on the map. Our party consisted of ten wagons and (including children) forty-five souls. All were Indians excepting your Aunt Nancy, Winona, and I. A few of the Indians understood English, but most of them knew only their native language.

The first camping place was at Culbertson, Montana, near the line of the reservation. The second day we reached Fort Buford* and camped just outside of the Fort. Three things the Indians desire for a good camping place: grass, water, and wood. I name them in the order of their importance. We had a little muslin tent over which we threw a good heavy wagon cover which made it perfectly dry when it rained. The Indians made fires in their tents, but we had a little kerosene stove. We usually camped in a little circle. When we stopped, while the men turned the horses loose, the women quickly put up the tents. One night we traveled until nine o'clock before we found a camping place for the night, but fifteen minutes after arriving, every tent was up. I said the women put the tents up. There were two exceptions. My native helper and I were supposed to be the most civilized and then the men put up the tents. The women sometimes condescended to help. So much for civilization. However, your Aunt Nancy had all she could do taking care of Winona, cooking, etc. When the tents were up, some went for wood, others went for water, and soon the fires were burning, and the supper cooking.

On the fifth day, it began to rain at noon. We camped early that evening near a beautiful stream but, oh, how wet everything was! But what could we do but tramp the tall grass down though dripping with water, and while the rain came down on our backs, stake our tent! But this is not as bad as it might be and soon we were inside listening to the pattering of the rain on the canvases or sitting near an Indian fire warming our toes. Supper over and we were soon abed asleep. And how sweet! While many in beautiful palace and soft beds were inviting slumber to soothe their tired nerves, or troubled by frightful dreams, (perhaps some college student dreaming over Greek verbs or Algebraic Equations) and then wake feeling unrested, we slept, as they say Down East, 'like a log', and woke refreshed.

At daybreak all began to stir, and soon the breakfast over, the dishes washed, we assembled for morning prayers. We were usually on our way by 7:30 am.

On the sixth day we came to where we must cross the river; did you ever cross the Missouri River or anything like it? Well, such a crossing as we had I shall never forget! It was three o'clock Saturday afternoon when we arrived at the place of crossing. This was the Berthold Indian Reservation and the only means of crossing, flat boat rowed by hand. The Indians who had charge of the boat were away and we undertook to cross ourselves. First we took the ponies (30 in number) and then the wagons. But oh, how slow!

How well I remembered walking over those grand bridges between Pittsburgh and Allegheny in a minute or two, or the great Brooklyn Bridge with pleasure. Now it took an hour to make a trip, sometimes an hour and a half and it took seven trips in all. Sometimes we had to wade in the water and all had plenty to do. One would think we earned our ride, but now, about dark, an Indian police from Fort Berthold stopped us. We must pay or stop using the boat. We had our ponies on one side and the wagons on the other side. Your Aunt and Winona were on one side and I on the other, so we told the police we must have the boat, gave him $5.00 and continued our 'pleasure' trip. The last boatload arrived just before midnight. We camped for the night on the east bank of the Missouri. It was on a hillside, cold and stormy, but that is where we spent the Sabbath. About sundown while the men were working, some women, led by your Aunt, built a large fire on the riverbank and boiled us some coffee. At midnight we got a good meal and were soon asleep. After such a crossing with its labor and vexations I realized what a grand thing a river bridge is.

We spent the Sabbath on the riverbank. During the night it grew colder. Sometime before morning Lizzie Parson came to our tent saying that her sister Mary was very sick. We had no medicine but your Aunt had taken her 'hot water bag' along. Having heated some water and put it in the bag for her she rested easier. Mary had just come in from Carlisle a few weeks before. She seemed to be in good health but yet she was not used to camping out. As young people too often do, she and Lizzie had taken only a blanket and comfortable along for bedding, unknown to us. We gave them another comfortable but this was not enough. The poor girl got worse and worse and not many days after died in the hospital at Standing Rock. This cast a shadow over our little band, but all the others returned improved in health except Lizzie who suffered from rheumatism on her way home.

210

Our Sabbath was a dreary one. Our little kerosene stove could not keep the tent warm and the wind almost blew it down. I remember, however, that after breakfast and I had cared for the ponies, it did not seem possible to have a meeting under these circumstances, so crawling among the blankets, I fell into a sound sleep. But alas, I was soon awakened by your Aunt calling and pulling and saying that the Indians (I mean the Fort Berthold Indians) were on the other side of the river calling for their boat. Upon going out I found that nearly all the men of our party were missing. We finally gathered up a few and began pulling the big boat up the river before we could row it across as it floated down the stream. I felt that it was down right work, not at all a pleasure trip, and it was the Sabbath. Of course, I remembered the Fourth Commandment, but then in cases of mercy and necessity work was justifiable on the Sabbath. I concluded that this was necessity, surely not mercy, and so my conscience was eased. We got over at last, shook hands with our friends and saw how another kind of Indian people did. Sabbath evening we had a short service and then soon all was quiet for the night. Monday morning bright and early we were on the road again. Part of our way was among the Bad Lands. The roads now were rough and hilly and we were traveling 40 to 50 miles a day. How I pitied some of the poor ponies. Our way now lay across an uninhabited country. We saw not a few deer and one of our number shot two at one shot. By the way, we passed two 'sheep ranches' during the first two days and a little event occurred at one of them about which I must tell you.

At Fort Berthold, the party (an old man and woman) who went along of their own accord got a fine dog, a present. As these people here eat a great many dogs and consider this a very dainty dish, I suppose they expected to have a feast with their friends when they reached Standing Rock. But alas for the poor dog and his friends: Sometime during Monday I think it was, we spied the 'Ranch'. Finally we spied the nice large herd of sheep feeding. When within a mile of them I should judge the big dog started for them. The Shepherd was prepared for him — but not soon enough. The dog crippled a fine large ewe and then frightened by the shot of the gun ran back to us. Two white men met us and oh! How angry they were! As we were along they held us responsible. I said, "Shoot the dog." Also Moses Morrow, my native helper, said, "Shoot the dog." And so they did and the old man and woman loaded him on their wagon sad hearted, no doubt, but when at the next camping place they had some for dinner, I suppose their hearts were good again. But mind you no one else got any. But I want to say again that they did not belong to our party. So we had no dog meat; but we had mutton such as it was. To make peace we bought the sheep and took it with us. It cost us three dollars and was old and tough. But when our friend came in with two nice young deer and they gave us a hindquarter of one, we in our turn had a royal feast. Our hearts were good even if we had to look over across the circle at our friends feasting on 'that dog'. I think that there is nothing nicer than venison broiled on the coals or a stick over the fire and as we had plenty of it we almost lived on it for a few meals. Our bread had also run out. On Tuesday it began to rain. The roads were muddy and the grass wet. We did not go into camp until near dark. The night before it was after nine o'clock. During the two days we had traveled between 80 and 90 miles. There were some tired people and ponies. The grass was very long and wet and it was raining quite fast. Having staked our tent I gathered up some brush and built a fire before the tent door. Moses and one or two others did the same. Things were getting quite cheerful when some one stopped and hailed us. "Hello there" he said. "I want you people to be careful about your fires. Don't you know that the whole country is like a tinderbox and if the prairie-fire starts it will burn up everything? A man was nearly burnt out last night. I am a commissioner of this county and I feel somewhat responsible." Well we thought the tinderbox is getting pretty well soaked tonight; but "we'll be careful of the fires. We came from Montana and we know what prairie fires are," we said. "Well," he said, "I guess if you come from Montana you know" and drove on. But the rain had not yet damped his recollection of the fire of the night before. I do not wonder. We drove over many miles where the fires had swept everything before it and met the fires on our way home and after we came home lived among the fires for weeks. The only way of protection was for all hands to turn out and put them out. They burnt to within a mile of the Agency. The cattlemen have a novel plan to put out fire. They kill a steer and then two men on horseback drag the hide of the steer over the flames and others follow and 'whip' it out. In this way they put out twenty-five or thirty miles of fire in one night. But I have digressed. Next morning we found all the fires well put out and journeyed on. At nine o'clock we came to Mandan, a beautiful little town which lies just across the river from Bismarck, North Dakota. Here we got some provisions and passed through. Two miles below we passed through Fort Lincoln. It is now abandoned but here it was that General Custer lived and had his headquarters. And it was from here or Fort Rice nearby that he started on his last and fatal expedition. We were now 60 miles from Fort Yates, the end of our journey. The Indians were tired. Some of their ponies were almost gone. So they camped early in the day. But we made a forced drive to the Cannon Ball River. Then at 8:30 p.m. we found a comfortable lodging place. It seemed good to sleep in a house once again and get a good square breakfast. Next morning it was raining very hard. But after dinner we drove the remaining 24 miles and arrived safely at the place of meeting and found a warm welcome with the missionary there, the Rev. George Reed.

Our Annual Mission Meeting is a very interesting and profitable one. It consists of delegates and visitors from the different agencies of the Sioux Nation. Although there are many Indians in this country and many thousands of them are not Sioux, yet the Sioux Nation is by far the largest nation. I think it now numbers about 40,000 souls. These people live along the Missouri River from Nebraska to Montana. The Agency, Poplar Creek, is the most to the Northwest. The Sioux people call themselves Dakotas or Friends. So please remember that the Sioux and Dakotas are the same people. Among these people are now many Christian Churches or Mission Stations. From these, delegates or visitors attend our annual Mission Meeting which is at some one of the stations. The white Missionaries were entertained in the house of Rev. Mr. Reed, the Missionary at Fort Yates, and by two ladies who have charge of the hospital there. The Indians camped in a large circle around the Mission Building.

As the church was too small, a large booth was made of tree branches. The weather was rainy and interfered with the meetings. However, from Thursday afternoon until Sabbath evening, sometimes three separate meetings were in progress, viz: the 'General Meeting', 'Woman's Meeting', and 'Young Men's Meeting' with one exception, Sabbath afternoon. These meetings were in the Dakota (native) language. In the general meetings, subjects were discussed as 'Whom did Christ come to save?' 'Is it beneficial for Indians and white people to live together?' etc. etc. Most of these discussions and this business was done by Indians, though the white Missionaries did much of the counciling. At the Young Men's meeting and the Women's Meetings the discussions and business were such as these Societies have the country over.

Our collections during the past year were over $1,500.00 for our Native Missionary. This society supports 5 Indian Ministers who are sent out to needy fields among their own people. So you see that the Missionary spirit is cultivated. We have less than 1,500 members. So you see we give more than $1.00 per member. Do our white people do so well? A very friendly sympathetic spirit prevailed and though the pale-face and the child of the forest sat side by side and spoke from the same platform it was not as distinct races, but as brothers and sisters in Christ. It is nothing but religion that can break down race barriers and class distinctions and make all akin.

On Monday all seemed to be anxious to start for home. But as most of the people had to cross the river the ferryboat was very slow and some could not cross until Tuesday. Your Aunt and I accepted the kind invitation of Brother Reed and wife and did not start until Tuesday evening. Thence we crossed the Missouri, followed along the river up beyond Bismarck and Fort Stevenson to Fort Berthold where we accepted the kind invitation of Brother Hall to spend Sabbath at his mission school. Here we found 45 bright-eyed boys and girls under a full corp of teachers. But my letter is growing too long. Monday morning we started for home and after a safe journey we arrived at home the following Saturday noon. We were glad to get home though we enjoyed the trip. I have given you a very meager idea of this trip. Hope you will enjoy it and find profit in its perusal.
E.J. Lindsey

Robert J. Frederickson, Glendive's water meter man, was at first a bit dubious about trying to share with us concerning the contribution his parents had made to the history of Eastern Montana. There was history aplenty, that he knew, but he was only six months old when his father died, and he didn't think he knew enough about those early days to share much. He surprised himself with how much he did know when once he started thinking back to childhood days. His memory was further jarred and vague recollections substantiated by some old documents and books and relics in his possession.

There was, for instance, the personal property tax notice dated 1890 and addressed to his father at Newlon, Montana. (Newlon was a post office located about six miles southwest of Sidney.) The tax list wasn't very lengthy, but it did include, among other things, three mills for the school fund and another two mills for a special tax for School District Number 1.

An invitation to commencement exercises at the fledgling Montana Agricultural College (now Montana State University) in Bozeman revealed that this was the first graduating class. August Frederickson, Robert's father, and his brother, John, had come together from Sweden and had located for a time in Minnesota before venturing on to the wide-open spaces of Montana. August then busied himself in eastern Montana, but John entered Montana Agricultural College, and he was one of the three graduates in that first class.

The little pocket notebook (a notebook that came from Douglas-Mead* of Glendive with a calendar for 1899, 1900) containing the names of the ranches in the area and their brands, listed in Frederickson's handwriting the roundups in which he had participated. And the order books, dated 1909, with their records of merchandise charged, give an indication of the bargains available at Frederickson's Tokna Store. Some samples: 13 lb ham, $2.40; 1 c. ginger, 10 cents; 1 c. cinnamon, 10 cents; 1 gal. molasses, 75 cents; sugar, $1; 10 lb. lard $1.50; 1 pair overalls, 85 cents; 19 1/2 lb. bacon, $3.50; shoes $1.50.

The lustrous, flawless finish on the little corner table in the living room was a reminder that the table had every reason to be scarred and weather-beaten. It had come to Poplar in 1887 with his aunt, Mrs. E.J. Lindsay, and had been left with the Fredericksons when the Lindsay family moved from the region.

The Frederickson's log house had a dirt roof and a canvas ceiling so when rain saturated the dirt roof, water drained into the canvas, causing definite 'sag' along the middle. Presently the 'sag', too, would reach the saturation point, and then the water would begin to drip through. Any furniture in line with the drip had to be moved, and Mrs. Frederickson would hurriedly bring out the pans and pails to intercept the precipitation.

Fortunately the family's story, as well as much community history, wasn't left just to memory for preservation. Many an old timer's descendants have lamented, "If only we had written some of these things down while our parents were still with us!" But Robert's sister, Marjory (Mrs. Virgo Anderson of Sidney), had the presence of mind, while her mother was still living, to record incidents and facts pertaining to the early days as Mrs. Frederickson recalled them from time to time, and so preserved much lore that otherwise might have been lost. Mrs. Anderson also gleaned information from the early files of Sidney and Glendive newspapers which she has shared with us.

A glimpse of the valley's earliest inhabitants (white) is given to us in a feature, "Our Ranchmen" by Editor W.W. Mabee, taken from the GLENDIVE TIMES of 1884.

A short ride from McCone's ranch brings the wanderer to the Newlon and Porter's ranch, on North Fork of Burns Creek. This herd is managed by W.W. Newlon who has been a prominent man among the lower Yellowstone settlements for years. We also saw his recent shipment of seventeen Hereford bulls, which make a grand improvement to his herd. C.H. Mayo, in company with Douglas & Mead (of Glendive) is located further up South Fork than we could make this trip.

Leaving McCone's ranch we headed for the Yellowstone Valley and a ride of twelve miles over a magnificent country on which cattle, antelope, and deer were peaceably grazing in bunches, brought us to E. Dunlap's place, which is in the valley at the foot of the highland. We found Mr. Dunlap planting trees and vines. He and his neighbor Grant have made an irrigation ditch in which they bring the entire water of the creek (if desired) around the hillside and all over their farms. Mr. Dunlap has an excellent place and his buildings and other accommodations are of the best. The creek flows past the house and everything has a thrifty and homelike appearance. Mr. Dunlap also has a nice band of cattle. He has taken a half section under the desert land act and though the filing was rejected at the Miles City land office he proposes to carry it up.

A few hundred yards more and we reach Geo. F. Grant's ranch, which is just now enlivened by those famous twin girl babies. Besides these Grant expects to raise a good crop of potatoes and onions this year. He has also eight acres to garden stuff and a young orchard planted.

A ride of two miles finds the traveler at Scott's well-known Half Way house. He has a very large and comfortable building and the largest stable on the road. In addition to his hotel accommodations, he has cattle and numerous horses about him.

Six miles further on we reach Uncle Billy Shadwell's ranch. He has a small patch in cultivation and is comfortably situated. He is road supervisor for his district.

Two miles more brings us to the Crane ranch, which is being farmed this year by Chas. Tilyou and his father. Uncle Jimmy (Crane) himself has been sick most of the winter. For years this claim has been considered one of the best.

The next claim belongs to Howard Bickford, more familiarly known as Tex. He has crops in. The next place is also his, managed by the irresistible Otis.

Mr. Stewart is found a few hundred yards to the right of the road. We remember the disappointment of Mr. Stewart when he first came to this country with his family and effects. He is (now) manifestly pleased with this land of promise, and early and late can be seen in his field at the plow. Leaving Mr. Stewart's we at once are in the midst of the Newlon settlement.

From the TIMES, June 20, 1886.

John L. Burns is in Glendive building a stable to accommodate his stage stock. He takes the line from here to Buford, July 1.

From the INDEPENDENT October 13, 1888.

Obituary: Mrs. Jennie Dunlap, wife of County Commissioner Emmet Dunlap, died at Tokna, October 7, aged 45. She was born in Canada of Scotch parentage, her maiden name being McPherson. With her parents she moved to Minnesota in 1858, was married in 1875, and with her husband came to Montana in 1882, when they settled in the lower Yellowstone valley. The funeral was held in the Methodist Church in Glendive. She is survived by her husband and three daughters.

Again from the INDEPENDENT, August 10, 17, 1889.

Our Missionary Tour Down the Yellowstone.

....County Commissioner Dunlap's ranch, where we camp for the night, is another illustration of what can be attained by irrigation. The ditch, which begins 50 rods from the house, has a fall of a half-inch a rod, is 3 feet deep and clear as crystal. The ditch water covers 160 acres, which is mostly used for haying purposes. Potatoes and other vegetables are looking fine. The entire ranch is a patch of green. The dwelling house is surrounded by cottonwood and willow trees. He has 50 tons of hay stacked and 75 tons cut; intends to stack 200 tons. Miss Tokua Dunlap has no less than 25 pets, including 12 lambs, one antelope, one deer, two colts, four dogs, and five cats.

G.F. Grant, another county dad, whose ranch adjoins Dunlap's, uses water out of the same ditch. He has corn, potatoes and other vegetables. He also seeded timothy and alfalfa which is growing nicely. He has 25 horses and 25 cattle on the range on Tokna Creek. A.H. Thomas, at the mouth of Tokna Creek, has some hay meadows and ranges 40 cattle.

INDEPENDENT, January 9, 1897

August Frederickson has resigned as mail driver to become postmaster at Tokna. George Grant and family took their final departure January 1 after spending the last night of '96 and of their stay in Dawson County at J. O'Brien's.

In the years that elapsed between his arrival in Montana and his purchase of the Grant Ranch at Tokna, Mr. A.A. Frederickson had become well known throughout Eastern Montana and had earned a good reputation. In addition to ranch work, mail carrying, etc. his diversified activities included photography as is indicated by another news note date lined Newlon, Montana, July 6, 1896: *Messers. Ormsby and Frederickson, photographers from Poplar, are taking photos and views in the valley. Unlike that prince of frauds, Ward, who robbed everyone he touched, they are doing good work, delivering it promptly and giving perfect satisfaction.*

A few years after his purchase of the ranch he married Miss Margaret Hunter and brought his bride to Tokna, December 30, 1899. Miss Hunter had come from her home in South Dakota in 1892 to visit her sister, the wife of missionary to the Indians, E.J. Lindsay, at Poplar. She accepted employment while in Poplar and the visit turned into a permanent stay; Montana was her home until her death in 1958.

When Frederickson bought the George Grant Ranch, he bought the post office, too. A post office had been located in that vicinity since before 1889 but under various names, one of which was Dundee. It was usually named according to the postmaster and the home in which it was located. While the Dunlaps had the office it had acquired the name Tokna.

They had decided to name it after their daughter whose name was Tokua, but the application blank must not have carried the familiar admonition, "Please Print." The application was made out for a post office to be named 'Tokua', but down at Washington, D.C., someone evidently read it 'Tokna', and that was the name that was accepted. No one bothered to have it corrected so 'Tokua' remained 'Tokna' until it was replaced by the Savage post office two miles south east, even though others ran the post office during the interim.

After Mr. Dunlap had had the office for a time it was moved to the George Grant Ranch and Mr. Grant was the postmaster. Thus it was that when Frederickson bought the ranch, the post office came with it. For about ten years one of the rooms in his home was used in this capacity. Then in the spring of 1907, he started building the Tokna store and post office.

That same year he bought out the Northy and Cheney Mercantile line from Ridgelawn, Montana. Besides the store, he bought the fixtures, showcases and all merchandise. They had dry goods, shoes, and hardware besides groceries. They sold kerosene, too, but never carried gasoline.

Mrs. Frederickson noted as she reminisced to her daughter, Marjory, that when she took up residence at Tokna (December 30, 1889), School District Number Seven extended from the Missouri to the Yellowstone, and the Tokna School was the only one in session. Even that one had closed after a three month fall term (with Miss Corkrin as teacher) before she arrived. No school at all was held during the year 1900 so in the spring of 1901 they had to have a term of school or lose the district.

Mrs. Frederickson's sister, Ruth, had gone through the grades and high school at Watertown, South Dakota, and had graduated from Normal School* so her services were procured for a three-month term at Tokna. She agreed to come for $35 per month and thought she was getting big wages.

Before she came out, Mrs. Frederickson had written suggesting things they would do after school was out, but Ruth immediately wrote back advising not to plan anything because she was just going to teach three months and come right back home. She didn't quite follow through with her plans. She taught the three months at Tokna as she had planned, but while she was there school officials in Glendive contacted her and she agreed to teach there for the winter.

Consequently, she spent the summer months with the Fredericksons – and perhaps Mrs. Frederickson's plans for their mutual activities materialized after all. The following year she did go back to her Watertown home for the summer but then returned to teach two more years in Glendive.

By that time, Glendive lawyer Theodore Lentz (partner at law with Leiper) had succeeded in making some permanent plans with her, plans that did not include South Dakota. After their marriage they lived in Glendive for several years before moving to Missoula in the spring of 1909.

By that spring of 1909, the Fredericksons had five children: Alfred, (now of Sidney), Anna Marie (Mrs. A.O. Johnson, Fairview), the twins, Marjory (Mrs. Virgo Anderson, Sidney) and Marguerite, who died in her senior year of high school, and Robert of Glendive. A 1904 clipping from the Glendive paper announced: "Born – to the wife of the Postmaster at Tokna, a brand new span of girls. Reports are that the trio are doing nicely, and August, well, that is all there is about it, he feels. Now if this is the result from irrigation on a small scale, what will be in store for the rest of the postmasters down the line when the big ditch* comes: Newlon, Sidney, Ridgelawn and Dore yet to hear from."

Aunt Ruth and Uncle Theodore were still living in Glendive when Anna Marie got the button in her nose and occasioned a trip to the doctor. Doctor Hathaway removed the button and also made the acquaintance of the newest Frederickson, exclaiming when he saw Robert, "Well, this is a baby I never heard about!" Enter Glendive's future water meter man.

The stay in Glendive must perforce include a visit at Aunt Ruth's house. Aunt Ruth enjoyed the luxury of having running water in the house and had a sink. Anna Marie delighted in climbing up to the sink and dabbling in the water. The next morning after they were back home at the ranch, Mrs. Frederickson told Anna Marie to wash her hands, but that worthy demurred, explaining, "I did a little while ago up town."

The trip to Glendive had to be made with a team and buggy, but the return trip was made in style. While in the city, Frederickson had found that some parties in Glendive were getting new cars so he arranged a ride out to the Tokna Ranch for the family. One man from Sidney, who had a car and had driven it awhile, had motored to Glendive. There were three new cars participating in the excursion with the Fredericksons in the lead car. This was Mrs. Frederickson's first automobile ride and was an event to be long remembered.

Only a few months later tragedy struck the Tokna Ranch when death claimed Postmaster August Frederickson, leaving his widow and five children. Mrs. Frederickson felt that the post office was more than she could manage under the circumstances, but she was told from Washington that if she could get a new postmaster the office could continue.

She wrote to Lawrence Johnson, a nephew by marriage of Mr. Frederickson, and he agreed to come take the position, but when she made the application she unthinkingly gave Johnson's address as Minneapolis so Washington would not accept her nomination.

Even though, after less than ten years of marriage, she was obliged to carry on alone in providing for and rearing her family, Mrs. Frederickson was not too busy for the Lord's work. The 50th Anniversary booklet compiled for the First Congregational Church of Savage gives us a glimpse of the beginning of Savage as well as the beginning of the congregation and includes insights into the community and the lives of some of its members.

Quoting from the history: *The foundation for the organization of a church was laid before 1910, thru the efforts of the Dunlaps, Fredericksons, (who came as bride and groom in 1900), the Larsons, and others. The Dunlaps lived where the Seeve home is located. The Fredericksons operated a store and post office farther down the creek. The post office was named Tokna . . . Church services were held in the homes and schoolhouses in those early days. Ministers and missionaries came from Glendive and Sidney to visit and hold services, among them L.S. Schermerhorn, Wm. Dawe, brother of Bennie Dawe, Sr. and Lossie Dawe, father of Mrs. Wm. Lowery of Sidney. Rev. E.J. Lindsay, brother-in-law of Mrs. Frederickson, homesteaded north of*

Tokna, and with his family spent the summer months there and held regular worship services in the schoolhouse. Mr. Lindsay was a missionary among the Indians at Poplar.

After lots were sold for the town of Savage, people moved in rapidly and a Presbyterian Church was organized August 21, 1910. Services were held in the Brooks and Patterson Store annex until the church house was built by the interested men of the community. Rev. Lindsay was assisted by Earl Benbow, a student minister, during the summers of '10 and '11. Rev. Schermerhorn became resident pastor in 1912 and the present chancel was built on to the church for living quarters. The late Rev. F.C. Phelps served from '12 into '17. By 1922, this was a more or less isolated Presbyterian Church and there were comparatively isolated Congregational Churches at Mildred and Brockton, Montana. As a matter of convenience and in order to better serve the people, the state boards advised an exchange of these parishes. The congregations accepted this suggestion and ours became a Congregational Church March 24, 1923, being served mostly by ministers from Sidney's People's Congregational Church since that time.

Earl Benbow's letter clearly shows us that we live in a different era when he describes his journey from Glendive to Tokna: *It is good to recall early days when I was connected with the organization of the Savage Church. It was in the summer of 1910 that the Board of Home Missions of the Presbyterian Church asked me to spend the summer at the preaching point then known as Tokna, Montana. I was as green a theolog as any turned loose, after one year in seminary. But the West appealed to me, having been born in Iowa. I landed in Glendive early one May morning, to find that the land boom, promoted by the railroads, had filled the stagecoach with prospective buyers. I had to wait a day to get a seat on the bronco drawn bus that left the following morning. Never will I forget the thrill riding that stagecoach — a three seated spring wagon, with the horses on the gallop down the main street of Glendive, for several blocks, until they swung into a trot that they kept up until miles away.*

The Fredericksons, Mrs. F. and five children, lived in the ranch house at Tokna and had a store and post office. I stayed with them that first summer. I will always remember the big storm that swept thru the valley on July 22nd which demolished the little cabin in the garden, in which I was staying....

Elsie Dahl contributes a bit of humor as she describes her efforts on a committee for raising funds; "I recall an amusing incident when Mrs. (S.L.) Hood and I 'managed' a fundraising 'ice cream social'. We bought large containers of ice cream which was intended to be served with measured dippers. But we, instead, gave very generous helpings with the result that when we counted the proceeds we were 'in the hole'. That probably was the first time we served on such a committee!"

Mrs. Frederickson moved from the ranch about 1930, but the influence of her and her husband continues.

Mrs. George (Viola Barber) Coryell

March 1965

Memories of the days spent in the Bloomfield Valley and near linger on in Viola (Barber) Coryell's mind – a lot of happy ones and a few sad ones, as is the case in most everyone's life. Here in her own words is her account of that eventful period, as well as a summary of the years that followed:

We were one of the families to leave Bloomfield, Nebraska, to seek a new home in Dawson County. My mother, Mrs. Romaine (Antha) Barber, my sister, Mary, and I arrived in Glendive by train the thirtieth of June, 1909. My brother Charlie met us, as he had taken a homestead west of Bloomfield a year or so before, and brother Levi joined him a little later.

We ate our supper at a little Japanese cafe. I loved cake, and in the center of the table was an old-fashioned cake plate, on a stand, with a fancy napkin on it, then a lot of slices of cake. Since I was just twelve years old and sort of tired of basket lunches on the train, I'll always remember how good that cake tasted.

We were very tired from our three-day train trip, but Charlie said we should get started on our way home. He had borrowed a double-seated buggy, and he was driving a little gray team of broncs named Spider and Cricket. As I always loved horses, I was really happy when I climbed into the buggy beside him. I was wearing a light blue, lightweight linen suit, but I was lucky to have on long stockings (girls didn't wear anklets then, or go bare-legged) because as darkness settled around us the air seemed cooler and damp. The road was rough and winding. We noticed a light near a creek – I think it was Hollecker or Kinney ranch. Anyway, we had to cross the creek, no bridge. Just as we reached the creek, a couple barking dogs raced out from the ranch. The broncs didn't seem to care for dogs so just as the team hit the creek they lit out running. They raced up the bank, with Charlie trying his best to hold those horses in the road. Mother, Mary, and I were hanging on the sides of that buggy, rocking as if we were on the ocean. The creek water splashed us good, and gravel flew. By this time we were miserably cold; not even a light blanket to put over our laps. Spider and Cricket were real anxious to get home so they could be turned out on grass. They loped down hill and trotted up.

I kept watching as the sky began to turn rosy in the east – not a cloud in the sky. As we were crossing a tableland, high and flat, Charlie said, "We'll soon be home." As we neared the edge of the high land there before me was a beautiful sight I'm sure I'll never forget. A deep, winding trail led down the long side hill, and a thick green carpet of grass covered the valley. A little twelve by fourteen foot gray rubberoid-covered shack stood on the flat close to some cut banks, which were full of buffalo berry bushes. Our pet Jersey cow, that had come ahead of us from Nebraska in the immigrant car with other things from our old home, was eating young oats in a little field. The sun

220

was just coming over the hill, and it seemed so warm that first day of July. I've often wondered what my mother, a fifty-eight year old widow, (my father had died three years before) thought when she walked into that little shack, two windows, a home-made bunk bed fastened to the wall, a little home-made table, a few shelves built on the wall for dishes, two or three stools to sit on. No doubt she was very tired, but there were four of us to get breakfast for. She just smiled and soon breakfast was ready.

She was a wonderful person, I thought. She had a real sense of humor and enough grit for two or three people. She was a true, old-time pioneer, I'd say. She, as well as my dad, was born in New York State. Their home was in the Catskill Mountains. She often told me of their happy days there. Their house stood by a mountain stream. My two oldest sisters and brother were born there.

The Civil War changed their lives. My dad went to war, as did three or four of my uncles, for several years. When the war ended, he decided taxes and expenses that piled up during his absence were more than he could overcome, so he called a sale and sold everything. They boarded a slow train for Yankton, as far as the train went towards Nebraska, the land of promises, as well as lots of Indians. Mother said it was spring, but a terrible blizzard hit, late though it was, and she thought she would freeze trying to keep the three youngsters warm in the stagecoach on their way to wherever they landed in northeastern Nebraska. It was about eighteen miles north of Bloomfield, Nebraska, in what is the 'The Devil's Nest'. That's where I was born years later and lived until I was five years old, when we moved to Bloomfield, Montana.

Now to get back to Montana. My mother and brother Levi took homesteads about six miles northwest of Charlie's, up near the divide country. Nothing but thick, tall grass up there. My brothers tied a white rag around the wagon wheel to measure out the section of land. There were rolling hills, many buffalo skulls, rattlesnakes galore, and it seemed to me, hundreds of meadow larks singing – I love their songs.

Soon, my brothers had a tent staked down on a big hill. I'd say the tent was about twelve by sixteen feet, with sides about three feet high before they started to slope. The thick grass was our carpet, but soon it turned to plain dirt. A folding cot next to the side wall was my bed for all summer until frost came. Mother and Mary slept in an old iron bed. This was my mother's homestead.

It must have been about one-fourth mile down the side hill where Levi dug a little dugout in the bank. He put a small window in the door, poles over the roof, then some canvas, then dirt. It had sort of a sandy clay floor, which would get places worn here and there; then our five-legged table would teeter so badly sometimes our coffee or soup would spill. A single bed in one corner for Levi, in another corner a cupboard made of boxes, which we got from the store with groceries.

Really did get nice wooden boxes those days. We would use them as extra chairs, etc. I think that was, in fact, I'm sure, the happiest year of my life so far. I would go over in the 'badlands' with Levi when he went to cut nice cedar posts, beautiful trees there, then. He would get a large load – how I enjoyed climbing way up on that load.

When we got to the top of the divide, the horses would jog along over the old HS trail to a hill beyond our tent and dugout where Levi planned to build a shack and barn for winter. He worked so hard; cut a lot of ash poles, also, and made large frame for a barn and small hen house. Then it was haying time. First Levi was going to help Charlie put up his hay before he started up at our home. The two of them 'batched' at Charlie's, while Mother, Mary and I stayed alone. How brave my mother was!

The only way we could fasten our tent at night was to tie the flap strings. Some nights when we were sleeping the wind would start blowing a gale; the tent top would flop, and the ridgepole would squeak. It would jerk so hard at the side ropes we would think surely they would break and the tent would leave us. Then that terrible lightning would come, and the thunder. My head was only a foot or two, I'd say, from the side roof, and those big drops sounded real loud.

I'm sure Mother worried about rattlesnakes, that they might crawl under the beds or among the boxes of clothing, etc., for she told of a terrible experience she had on the homestead in Nebraska. She and my Dad both hated liquor and would never allow it in the home, but they did get a pint to keep in case someone got bit by a rattler.

One day when she was alone, soon after they moved to Nebraska, she was pulling weeds from a little garden. When she'd get about all she could pack, she would carry them away. She picked up a pile, and she heard the rattler rattle. She threw those weeds down, I imagine, ran to the little one-room log house, and grabbed the whiskey as she noticed some little red scratches on her arm. She drank most of it, I suppose. She said she just sat there with cold sweat on her, wondering what to do. Nothing unusual happened so she at last decided those scratches must be from the weeds, not the big snake, so she started back to finish her job of cleaning the garden. I can almost hear her hearty laugh now as she told that to us. She said her feet didn't track right. She would step so high, then blunder or sway all over the path. Mother was next thing to being drunk. That finished her drinking whiskey for the rest of her life, but she never did get over her horror of rattlesnakes.

My brothers killed rattlers out in the hay field or prairie, and would bring the rattles home. We kept them in a cup, and of course I'd get them out once in awhile and rattle them. Mother would shudder and tell me, "Put those pesky things away!"

That fall I met my future husband when he brought my sister Mary home from a dance at Bloomfield. Out in the west folks danced until sunup, then they had twelve miles to ride horseback. I was always an early riser. I still love to get up in time to see the first rays of sun, listen to the birds sing so happy, and it's usually so peaceful and quiet otherwise. I was really shy then, and when they came to the dugout door, I couldn't get out of sight. Mary found out George had a homestead just two miles east. He was an accountant in the office of the Burlington Railroad when his father, Frank Coryell, his mother Ida, and five brothers, Charlie, Earl and Verl (the twins) Cody, and Floyde, and sister Vera moved to the Thirteen Mile Valley two years before.

He soon decided he wanted to come west. Also, that office work wasn't a healthy life. Soon he landed in Glendive with a new, heavy saddle and fifty cents in his pocket. He worked as horse wrangler for Jim Cavanaugh until he got enough money and was old enough to file on his homestead.

I didn't go to school the first winter. I figured that was my last year. I read lots of books, but since it was twelve miles to the post office, no radio, no newspaper, no stupid TV to keep me sitting too much, I rode every horse I could borrow. How well I remember one fast ride I had on a beautiful, high-lifed, shiny, slender, black horse. It was late summer and I was at Charlie's shack. Frank Bush, a neighbor boy who lived about one mile north of Charlie's often rode over to visit Charlie and Levi. I had been admiring this horse; he held his head so high and just pranced around, champing at the bit, and at last I weakened. After Frank tied — I guess his name was Midnight — to the fence post, I waited until I thought they were real busy talking, then ambled up and untied the horse.

I just had a full-skirted dress on — girls didn't wear overalls or slacks then. I petted the strange black a little, then managed to climb up in the saddle and head him south up the deep trail to the top of the hill. My dream at last had come true. He danced, went sideways, etc., but I wasn't a bit afraid. After I turned him back towards the shack things were different. He really did run, but I got a firm grip on those reins and managed to slow him up near the gate. I tied him good. Frank said afterwards, "Violet" (he always called me that) "It's a wonder that horse didn't run away with you." Believe he said I was the first girl to ride him. Soon I rode both Spider and Cricket.

I think it was that first fall that Spencer Rust came to our dugout. He was from Minneapolis and decided to seek his fortune in Montana, even though he had been brought up in the 'big city'. He took a homestead cornering Levi's; built a very small shack. He helped Levi a lot, putting up hay. They filled the frame of the barn and hen house making thick walls and roof with prairie hay. How proud we were of our first chickens. I'm sure we bought them from Mrs. Wienke. But a sad thing happened. We had a bad winter, and there were many range cattle about us. No doubt they were very hungry. One real cold night — about fifty degrees below zero — those cattle wandered in in the night. They ate hay all night, I guess; anyway, they chewed holes clear through the hen house. When Mother went out to feed her treasured hens, they were all frozen.

I think Spencer Rust got very lonely over on his homestead. His shack was down in a coulee, and after real winter set in, about every evening he would walk over, and we would play cards. He would tell us stories of his life in Minnesota, and we would have lunch. It seems Mother always would manage to have something baked, like gingerbread or sugar cookies — nothing fancy. I played so many cards those first winters, I've never played cards since.

The next fall Charlie went to get the mail one day at Nettie Gibb's homestead, just a mile west of Bloomfield. She asked, I guess, if I was ever going to continue my schooling. She said I could come stay at her house, room with her daughter Grace, and go to Bloomfield School. Didn't take me long to pack my clothes. I think I had about two dresses and a blouse and skirt. I was so happy going back where I would see some youngsters my age again.

A one-room schoolhouse – a coal and wood heater, water in a jar in the hall. But we had a very good teacher, William McQueen. I'm sure there were over forty kids, some large teenagers. We would all run out of that school door at noon or recess and play games. I could run like a deer then. I spent the next two winters there. The second year Grace left for Nebraska to go to school, as she was two years older than I. Nettie then moved into Bloomfield, into the new store Charles Crocket, George's grandfather, built. I was then assistant postmistress, and also helped clerk in Grandpa's store a lot.

The next fall I was again home. No chance of ever going on to high school. Sometimes I could coax brother Levi into going to the dance at Bloomfield. It seemed that the dance, and once in awhile Sunday School in the schoolhouse, was all there was to go to. One thing I'll never forget was the nice lunches Mrs. Ed Albright used to serve in the store, even though she had, I think, eight or ten children, and she also clerked in the store. They would fix a long table in the center of the store, put on white tablecloths, and set the table so nice. She made delicious big layer cakes, frosted so pretty. How she accomplished all she did I'll never be able to figure out.

I still think of the – guess it was a Carnival or maybe just a get-together – at Bloomfield our first fall in Montana. Strange how some things always stand out in one's memory. About all I can remember about this celebration was a rig of some kind, trimmed up. Mrs. Lud Lundstrom was sitting at the piano playing such pretty music, and their big team of buckskin horses pulling the wagon so proudly. Then sister Mary, George's sister, Vera Coryell, and Nora Wienke were dressed as three old maids, hobbling along the street. I believe they carried a sign, "Wanted, a Man" or some such. I remember no more of the day.

While I was boarding with Nettie Gibbs, Mrs. M.O. Lanam used to walk several times a week the four miles from her homestead shack to Bloomfield for mail and groceries. Mr. Lanam worked at Glendive and for weeks at a time he didn't get home. One day she invited me to hike home with her and spend the night, and then next afternoon we would hike back. I was thrilled. Mrs. Lanam had a very good education. I'm sure she read the best of books. She was so interesting to talk with. It was a beautiful Indian summer fall day, so warm and bright. She carried herself so straight and sort of proud-like, always taking a fast gait.

I'd say I really hiked, but I didn't intend to let on I was tired. When we reached the top of the high hill known as the Lundstrom Hill, she pointed far out on the flat to a little black, tar-papered shack. Not another thing around the yard; not even a wire fence, nor a chicken nor a dog, nor a cat; just plain prairie each direction. She said, "There's our home." Well! I thought, "They say, it takes a heap of living to make a house a home. I wonder...." When we finished hiking down that long trail, leading downward all the way, she opened the door, and folks, it truly was a home. She rested a few minutes, then started a late dinner. She seemed to skip from stove to table to cupboard so fast. She put a dainty lunch cloth on and brought out such pretty hand-painted china and real silverware. She prepared a delightful and an unusual meal, the while talking so pleasantly that, to me, just a fourteen-year-old girl then, it seemed almost like being in fairyland.

She had rows and rows of wonderful history and other books. She also had lots of nice fancy linens, all handmade, that made the little one-room shack peaceful and attractive. I understood then for the first time how she could stay out there on the big lone prairie for weeks alone. She kept her mind interested, always learning. She had several beautiful hand-painted scenery pictures on the bare two-by-four walls.

When I was nearly fifteen years old, George Coryell asked me to go to his sister Vera's home over the divide for New Year's dinner. We went in a buggy, and the snow banks were terrible. A year later we were married at Grandpa and Grandma Crockett's home one mile from Bloomfield. The next day was a bitter cold day; I think really it was about fifty degrees below zero that ninth of January. My mother rode with me to my old home in a little buggy. I drove a small fast team, 'Kit' and 'Lady'. They knew they were going home, and all I could do was sit up there and hang tight to the lines. A hard crust had formed on the snow, which was several feet deep. One minute one wheel would cut into the snow, then both would be on top.

Those two little saddle broncs trotted up hill and loped down. When I let my sixty-two-year-old mother out at the old homestead door, she said, "Won't you come in and get a little warm?" But I said, "Oh, no, I must get on over home. George will be coming with the four-horse load of oats" (a grain tank). "He has the cow tied on that Dad Coryell gave us for a wedding present." I waved goodbye to my girlhood days and Mother as the horses took off on a gallop. When I went around the creek bend, Mother stood watching. Much later she told me, "I stood watching and said, 'I hope she makes it safely home.'"

We spent about seventeen years trying to win on that homestead. Four children were born to us, two on the farm, and the twins at Richey. Our first born, a sweet little blue-eyed girl, whom I named Eva, only lived one week. That was two years after our marriage. Patricia was born two years later, and Dolores and Dale five-and-one-half years later. I taught Patty until she was eight years old at home. After that, some of the time she hiked five miles alone to school. Later, when we got a big old Reo* car, I took her to school. Then a school was built on Steffen's corner, two-and-one-half miles from us. Patty drove a pet horse, 'Frosty', on a single buggy. The twins went to school also for several years there.

George had worked mining coal winters on our land. That's mostly what we lived on because the rains didn't come. We would plant a lot of acres, then watch it burn up from the hot, dry spell. Our cattle grew thin, and it seemed our horses thinner. Our taxes were past due. So many families had left it was rather lonely in our part of the *country. Patty finished the eighth grade in 1930 so I decided to move to Richey, figuring that if I could earn enough to pay the rent on a little two-room shack, maybe buy some of our groceries, Patty could go to high school.*

Uncle Sam was badly in need of money. World War I had been expensive so even though I had worked right along in the fields with George, often driving four, sometimes six, horses, plowing, harrowing, even breaking prairie sod; shocking* wheat, cooking for bachelor neighbors' threshers, helping haul grain to Intake, thinking we could keep down expenses, we were saved the trouble of trying any harder to save our home. It was sold for taxes that year.

We both worked at anything we could find to do for two more years in Richey. The Fort Peck Dam started so we moved there. We worked and saved and bought a little home, but trouble followed us. George fell while working and broke his leg. It didn't heal right so he was in hospitals for months and lost much work. I worked cooking in cafes for years. In fact, we all worked any time we could get work. Just when the twins finished high school, World War II was on, Dale, our son, spent three years in the Navy, the last two over on those terrible islands in the midst of the fighting. Dolores and Pat, our daughters were both married.

George and I were about broke again so we closed up our home, and left for Renton, Washington, where we worked at war work for several years, then returned to Fort Peck for a few years. Dale married after the war and moved to Cut Bank. George's health started failing when we were running a filling station at Fort Peck. Again I worked along beside him, getting along without hiring help. But after going to Rochester Clinic, we found out George had emphysema. We sold our home and moved to Cut Bank where we bought a nice little home.

I've tried through the years to put the memories of our first home that we were forced off of out of my mind, but that's easier said than done. I've never seen that little home on the hill in Dawson County since I rode out of the gate in 1930, intending to return in the spring in time to put in the garden and raise some chickens.

Our youngsters loved it there. I remember every clump of wild roses in the pastures; pretty odd rocks; large cedar fence posts, some with odd twisted knots; the old trailer sitting east of our large granary, where the girls had a playhouse; the round flower bed in front of our shack where I had spaded the sod and planted nasturtiums — even packed water from the windmill in the pasture to them, and how cheerful they looked, blooming with prairie grass around them; the row of pansies, out near the east fence, I planted on a dry, hard fire guard. They refused to die — bloomed so pretty.

Yes, often I think I can almost hear again the old time music that was played on our piano and violins at our home dances at our house. I always looked forward to those dances. So many friends would come, even from the Bloomfield country, each couple bringing along something to help out for lunch. I always loved to dance, and it was the only entertainment we had through those dry years after the war. I loved also to ride horseback, same as when I was a little girl. I had two nice bay saddle horses, but they were both killed.

The little house has stood there deserted, alone for many long years. No happy youngsters' voices, no light in the window, even though the rains came again, and the prairies bloomed again, I am told. Tall grass grew where there was only parched grass when we departed. Suitcase farmers drove large tractors and seeders over the acres where George had broken the sod with a walking plow and three horses when he was about twenty-one years old. All that the second crop of land-grabbers, money-loving persons, had was wheat; never really repairing the buildings, no memories of how that home was worked for. Yes, they made easy money from us homesteaders' efforts, but I doubt if they enjoy it very much. Surely their consciences must sometimes bother them.

I will always think how much wiser it would have been during the depression, drought years and wartimes, if our government had said, "We want you small farmers to stay on the land. The country needs farmers close to keep homes built up, etc. We'll just skip the taxes until normal times return." But no, that couldn't be — but they sure can send millions to folks overseas.

Our much loved home is deserted now, but will never be forgotten. George is an invalid, too weak to even walk outdoors, and so these four walls and our fifty by one hundred feet yard is sort of our world. We have lots to be thankful for, though. Three good, healthy, hard-working, married children; eleven grandchildren; our mail delivered to the door; lots of kind friends, both old and new, from coast to coast; our old player piano, a TV, lots of books. I raise beautiful flowers. And last, but not least — so many memories of the homestead days in old Dawson County.

Earl Coryell demonstrating his roping skills

"The Tender Foot's Turn" – sketch by Earl Coryell

Bill Steffen, Outfielder for the
Bloomfield Baseball Team

Dorothy Pickering on the 'porch'
at house on Blue Star Honey farm
built for her great-grandparents
Byron & Hannah Pickering

Irwin's bucking mule

1914 Runabout Model T
Bill Warmke, Fred Steffen, George Stephan, Cliff Sansborn, Mary Krause

Nick Degel

December 1971

The grocery business isn't what it used to be. Just ask Nick Degel. He's been in the business almost fifty years now, so he ought to know.

Late in the winter of 1930, Mr. Degel came to Glendive where the Steve Meissners lived. Mrs. Meissner is his sister. Steve owned a half interest in a meat market located in the 200 block on North Sargent. Meissner and his partner, a man by the name of Seifert, had been operating the meat market for two years. Now Seifert wanted to sell his share so the Meissners had written to Nick about buying Seifert's interest. This brought him to Glendive and in the spring he decided to invest.

This was not Degel's first acquaintance with Glendive. His home was in Gladstone, North Dakota, and he had visited here before the war – before World War I, that is. By the time he moved here in 1920, he found that the town had undergone some changes and had grown considerably.

Nick was thirteen years old when he came with his family from Hungary to Gladstone in 1905. None of his family could speak English when they came to America but they had lots of German-speaking relatives in the Gladstone community east of Dickinson so language was no barrier.

After about a year of operating the Sargent meat market with his brother-in-law, Degel and Ralph Messmer saw an opportunity in a meat market that had been closed on Merrill Avenue. This market was located in the one-story part of the building now occupied by the Coast to Coast store*.

They bought the market and ran it for one year. Then Steve Meissner decided he wanted to go to California so he offered the Sargent Avenue market for sale. Degel and Messmer bought it.

When Mr. Degel first joined his brother-in-law, their enterprise was exclusively a meat market. However, when he came back to the Sargent Avenue market after a year in the store on Merrill Avenue with Messmer, he found that Meissner had put in some shelves and had begun to stock a few groceries. This was Mr. Degel's beginning in the grocery business and he's been selling groceries ever since.

Meissner changed his mind about going to California and decided to stay in Glendive so he bought the fixtures in the shop Degel and Messmer had just vacated and reopened business there. This shop was known as The Glendive Meat Market. Years before, Harpsters had had a butcher shop in this building.

At this time the meat market building was separate from the building next door to which it is now joined. Franklin Miskimen's father had built the two-story part of the building now used by Coast to Coast. The second floor, known as Miskimen Hall, was used for dances and lodge meetings. W.F. Stuart had a bakery and variety store on the ground floor. Years later Franklin Miskimen used this floor for the Rite-Price Grocery and the second floor was divided into apartments.

230

After Steve Meissner's death his son, Nick, continued operation of the meat market. When Nick too, passed away, Miskimen bought the one-story building from the widow and joined the two structures to make one, then cut an archway between to allow access from one part of the store to the other.

In 1929, Mrs. Degel passed away leaving Nick with four small boys. He kept his family together and ran his business too. During these years, they bought most of their meat locally and would do the butchering right on the farm or ranch where it was purchased.

They also had a little corral back of the Sargent store toward the railroad track where they sometimes kept cows to butcher later. During the early years of their business Glendive was in a state of transition. Prior to this time many residents kept a cow or two or several. Now as the town became more 'modern', people were selling their cows and buying milk so some of these cows would spend some time in the corral on their way to the meat block.

After his boys were gone, Mr. Degel quit butchering but for a number of years continued to buy carcasses from the packinghouse and cut it up in his store. He still buys some fresh meat from Pierce Packing Company (the only one who still sells the way he wants to buy) but he freezes it because it doesn't move fast enough to sell fresh.

With the price of meat what it is these days, Mr. Degel reckons, people are scared to buy it! He recalls those early years – and this was for a long time – when roasts sold for eighteen cents a pound, steak for twenty-five cents a pound, T-bones for thirty cents. What a rush there would be to his store if he could still sell at those prices! As it is, he sells mostly wieners and bologna in the meat department.

He used to buy his groceries from the Bismarck Grocery* (remember when they were in the old school house where the First National Bank* is now?) but they moved to Sidney, then quit altogether. There are no more wholesalers in Glendive from whom he can buy so now he gets his stock from Gamble-Robinson in Miles City.

It used to be Gamble-Robinson carried only produce, but now they sell some groceries too, so he buys from them. The coming of the big chain stores changed things for the little grocery. They can sell for less than he can buy from the wholesaler. His biggest turnover is in bread, milk, and candy. Neighborhood children slip in to buy candy so the candy business is always good.

Mr. Degel continues to keep his store open about ten hours a day. Sometimes you can even find him there on holidays. No, the grocery business isn't what it used to be, but his health is good, he says, and running the store keeps him busy. Maybe keeping busy is what keeps him young.

Richey's History Traced

June – July 1966

The arrival of the Great Northern Railroad in Richey in 1916 called for a big celebration. Richey wasn't much of a town yet, but anticipation of the railroad's arrival had stimulated the interest of businessmen from widely scattered areas to investigate prospects for business there.

In 1916 there was no railroad to Circle, no bridge at Wolf Point or Poplar, and Glendive, the trading center for the area, was many miles away. Hence, trade from the vast territory in the western and northern parts of the county would be channeled into Richey once a railroad arrived.

Business prospects looked good so several businessmen squatted* on railroad land about a half-a-mile from where the town was later located. One of those early 'squatters' was Karl Henk. Henk had come from Bismarck early in 1916 to look over the situation, and on this trip he met E.G. Ufer, a Lambert businessman. They got together and started a hardware store.

Later, when the railroad offered lots for sale at the site chosen for the new town, Henk and the other 'early birds' bought lots at auction and moved their business to the present town site.

The little town grew rapidly. Soon there were seven lumberyards (yes, seven), two banks, several grocery stores, two implement dealers, two pool halls, and three big livery barns. John Kelly, a homesteader from the area, built a garage and started selling cars – Ford's Model T. Best car in the world, one of the 'old timers' declared.

Herman Tinsley started a drug store, and various doctors spent a period of time in the bustling trade center. Ralph Price ran a restaurant, Hogan and Brynildson a general store. S.M. Disher operated one of those first lumberyards, as did the Midland. Along with legitimate businesses, the town also had its share of gamblers and bootleggers.

The First State Bank was one of the banks, with Joe Normand and John Kelly the first two depositors. Another 'first' for Normand was that of assessor for the town. Later he also assessed the county, traveling about with horse and buggy. Normand homesteaded in 1910 not far from where Richey later 'sprouted'.

The town was made up largely of young people. Many would come in from their homesteads to work in the town. People from all walks of life found their way to the prairie town. It seemed they were all looking for a good time, and as soon as someone started something, the others all joined in.

All the little towns around, and there many more then, had a ball team, made up of farmers from the surrounding area as well as fellows from town. One of Richey's 'charter members' remarked that after the ball game they'd often have a rodeo, and usually there'd be a few fights, too, to liven things up.

Virgil Weidner had built a big bowery where the first businessmen had squatted, then later Luchsinger built a hall at the town's present site. About every Saturday night there would be a dance with Louie Patinoid playing the fiddle and Mrs. Vera Hise playing the piano. The dance would last from dark to daylight because there were no roads, and no way to see to get home.

Hedley Robinson, who had been a cowboy for the HS Ranch of Redwater, had started a ranch of his own at a time when buying or leasing land wasn't necessary because all the range around was free. With the coming of the homesteaders and the railroad, however, that changed and where his hay meadow had been, Richey grew up. Mr. Robinson passed away in 1956, but Mrs. Robinson still owns the farm just south of Richey, and recently sold twenty-eight acres to the state to make an airport where only a little more than half-a-century ago the cattle roamed at will, with no fences to interfere, and the team and wagon provided the standard transportation.

Among the early settlers there was a strong bond of neighborliness, which Mrs. Joe Normand illustrated by relating one of her own experiences. While her first husband, Ernest Glyshaw, was living they had homesteaded in what is now the northwest corner of Dawson County. On one side was a neighbor named Lord, on the other a man named Goodman.

While they were building their own log house, cutting and hauling the logs from the Missouri River bottoms, they lived in a neighbor's board shack, no finish boards at all on the inside. The weather turned bitterly cold, a storm raged, Mr. Glyshaw was gone, and the coal supply was exhausted. Mrs. Glyshaw (then) and little daughter (now Mrs. Bert Hilger) went to bed and covered themselves with all their quilts in an attempt to keep warm.

Prospects for keeping warm were becoming dimmer and dimmer when a knock came at the door. "There," Mrs. Normand describes the incident, "stood the good Lord, come to take us to a Goodman's house."

This spirit of helpfulness and concern for each other helped to build the country and the town, creating a prosperous, bustling community where only a few years before the grassy prairies were undisturbed except for the occasional passage of Indians or animals.

While Jack Milne was a bit young at the time of Richey's inception to take much interest in its business concerns, he remembers that a few years later (in 1920) his father, who had been farming, bought and began operating the Grady Hotel in Richey. He also owned a Model T, and traveling men would rent the car to drive to the surrounding towns. Mr. Milne recalls that his father used to remark that he made about as much renting the car as he did renting rooms.

Jack soon 'drummed up' a business of his own by meeting the train and carrying bags to the hotel for the businessmen who came in. Later he went to work for the McConnen Implement, the John Deere dealer. At that time they sold mostly horse-drawn machinery. In the fall of 1927 the farmers harvested a bumper crop and McConnens sold thirty-eight horse-drawn binders. Mr. Milne remembers that because he had to set most of them up.

They were selling tractors, too, tractors on steel wheels. These would have to be driven to the farm because they didn't have trucks that could haul the tractors.

In 1931 Milne went to work for Standard Oil as their bulk agent out of Richey. His first truck was a Model T with a 300-gallon tank on it for delivering gasoline. In 1941 Mr. Milne came to Glendive where he operates Milne Implement Co.

As roads and motor vehicles improved, as bridges were built and railroads reached other towns, the need for a trading center at Richey declined. Other Richey businessmen (Karl Henk and E.G. Ufer among them) besides Milne moved their businesses to Glendive or elsewhere until only a remnant of Richey's former commercial force remains.

Richey's Golden Jubilee celebration was a heyday for anyone interested in talking with old timers! They were there by the score and in a mood for reminiscing.

Honors for being the earliest homesteader present went to Floyd Davis from up near Vida. Davis came in 1894, well before the homesteading started, but after homesteads were available he filed.

Davis who had been 'on his own' since he was twelve, came to Dawson County from Wyoming. Ranches offered about the only 'job opportunities' in those days (certain it is there was no 'youth corp' waiting to look after young job hunters) so Davis went to punching cows and breaking broncs.

According to the testimony of those who knew Davis when he was a cowboy, he was tops among riders, and if anyone could stay with a horse whose chief aim was to unseat him, Davis could.

Mr. Davis didn't mention that distinction, but in relating one of his roundup experiences he did mention that he rode the rough string. One year when he was repping* for an outfit from over on Charlie Creek, the roundup had moved to southwest of Glendive, and they were camped on Clear Creek near Billy Wood's ranch.

The roundup cook complained that his butcher knives were dull so the boss told Davis to take the knives over to the neighbors (Billy Woods) and get them sharpened. He got the knives sharpened all right and, carefully carrying the knives in a paper sack, started out of the yard, but as he did so a barking dog rushed out.

The horse he was riding was a long way from broke and promptly 'blew up'. Mr. Davis laughed as he recalled how Billy, watching from the porch, stood and yelled, "Drop those butcher knives! Drop those butcher knives!" while that horse went through contortions designed for anything but the convenience of his rider. In spite of Bill's admonition Floyd determinedly clung to his sack. When he reached camp, the sack was full of holes, but he still had his butcher knives.

The oldest homesteader present for the celebration was Mrs. Louise Adkins. Mrs. Adkins, who came in 1912 to homestead, is ninety years old. She and her husband located twelve miles northwest of Bloomfield, right on the Divide*, yet they were a part of the Richey trading area.

The first year they were in Montana they lived on Bert Crockett's place while they got their homestead ready. Mr. Adkins carried the mail between

Glendive and Bloomfield that summer. Life wasn't always easy on the homestead – in the thirties they sold wheat for twenty-six cents a bushel and seventy head of cattle for $70 – but the homesteaders for the most part were a hardy lot and took the bad with the good.

Even though they were far from town, not all the excitement passed them by. One evening a stranger stopped at the homestead and asked to sleep in their barn that night. Mr. Adkins offered him lodging in the house but refused to let him stay in the barn because of the danger of fire.

As it turned out, the man wasn't so much interested in sleeping in the barn as he was in changing horses. He had robbed the bank at Lambert and wanted a fresh horse to speed him on his way. No radio then broadcast the latest news and alerted area residents to be on the lookout for suspicious characters.

Thanks to Mr. Adkin's precautions his horses were safe, and the fellow hired someone to take him to Terry where he boarded a train and skipped the country. After his departure one of her daughters asked Mrs. Adkins, "Mother, didn't you notice the top of that man's ear was shot off and bleeding?" The 'parting shots' at Lambert had come close.

Mr. and Mrs. Adkins left the homestead in 1941 and moved to Glendive. Four years later Mr. Adkins passed away. In spite of her age Mrs. Adkins still takes care of herself. She admitted she did get a bit tired at the Golden Jubilee, but she had a wonderful time visiting with other old timers and reliving the old times.

Hank Yeo, Richey businessman for fifty years, was home from the hospital and able to watch the festivities. Hank will be eighty-five in August.

Veteran of the Spanish-American War, he came to Montana and homesteaded near Plentywood. The winter was a hard one, and he was unable to get to town for supplies until finally he was down to a little piece of bacon and just a little flour. He could still make biscuits, but he wasn't going to be able to make many more of those so when a nice day came along, he decided he'd better start hiking for town and get supplies while the getting was good.

The snow was deep and walking tough, even in decent weather, but before he had covered many of the twenty miles between his homestead and Plentywood a storm came up. He struggled on, floundering through the deep drifts. Nearing exhaustion, he knew he dared not stop or that would be the end of him. When he thought he could not take another step, he found himself at the edge of town and managed to stagger into the first saloon. He drank a beer, but that's the last he remembers for that day. He passed out, and even when he woke up he was still so stiff and sore and tired he could hardly move.

After that ordeal he never went back to his homestead. As far as he was concerned, the Indians could have it. He engaged in business in the town of Plentywood for a time, then moved to the brand new town of Richey.

His first enterprise in Richey was a cafe. He had to borrow money to get enough meat from the butcher shop to serve his first meals but soon it was a going concern. Through the years he has been involved in a variety of businesses, including a bowling alley, an elevator, a hotel, a farm, and a men's clothing store. He still owns considerable business property in Richey and is one of the town's best-known citizens.

RICHEY

They lived here on the prairies, many years, and not much enjoyment had.
Amongst coyotes, antelope, rabbits and deer here was nothing to make them glad.
Their granaries they were full to the top. Their market many miles away.
Their pastures they were crowded with stock, awaiting that shipping day.
That eventful June day, they will never forget and the sight of that first train.
They had elevators, stores, schools and smith and now could ship out their grain.
But oh say, they were glad, very glad. Oh say how they were glad.
When they built the railroad in from the east. Oh say, how they were glad.
It is fifty years ago this June day since a train came this far west.
Most homesteaders now have passed away, to their eternal rest.
Where the old folks fell short, the young did come and improved on it with thrills,
Their ranches, farms, stores and home. In the town between the hills.
    By Jens L. Scarpholt

Roy Richey sketched a bit of personal history when he responded to the Mayor's welcome at Richey's fiftieth anniversary celebration.

Richey came to Dawson County in 1909 to homestead, the second to file in his township. That fall a Great Northern survey crew came, and by spring everything in the area but the badlands had been taken for homesteads.

In 1911 Roy Richey's brother Clyde joined the trek to Montana, and before long he decided that with all the people in that vicinity there ought to be a post office. Up until that time they had been going to Bloomfield to get their mail. Once he had the idea, he began to do something about it, and soon he had enough names to entitle them to a post office out there in the country. Washington granted his application for a post office in his home, then requested suggestions for a name for the office.

At this point Roy observed that he had often wondered if his brother had put his own name at the top of the list. Be that as it may, when the answer came back from Washington, Richey was the name selected for the new post office.

His brother ran the post office for four years before the town of Richey was started. He was paid according to the number of stamps cancelled so it's hardly surprising that he continued with his farming, and his wife took care of the office.

With such a large territory to draw from, businessmen in surrounding towns had their eyes on the prospective town and began opening branch offices there even before the town site was sold. They squatted where the ball diamond is now, then bought lots and moved to new locations when the site opened for purchase.

With the new town officially started, a town name had to be selected. Since it was Clyde Richey who had started the post office, people felt that that should

236

be the name for the town, so Richey it became and Richey it has been ever since. Mr. Richey (Roy) commented that every time someone said Richey the next year or two he thought they were talking to him!

As Mr. Richey continued with his review of the town's progress he explained that at first they didn't have very good fire-fighting equipment and they had many fires. After awhile, though, they got a well so they could put out fires, but the water was so hard they couldn't use it to sprinkle gardens; the plants wouldn't come up. In time, three more wells solved their water problem.

It took cooperation to build the town and, summing up, Mr. Richey concluded that Richey residents still cooperate. To illustrate his point he explained that the town has two general stores. Last winter the proprietor of one of the stores had a heart attack so the other proprietor cooperated and had a heart attack, too.

Another Richey old timer is Bill Blue. Blue homesteaded in 1909 just east of what is now Richey, but he wasn't satisfied to stop with that: he influenced about a dozen of his relatives to homestead in Dawson County too. His father, four or five brothers, and some cousins helped to turn the Montana prairies into farming country.

Blue had what was probably the first locally owned tractor in that locality. His big kerosene-burning Rumley* (he had to haul the kerosene for it from Glendive) could pull a big load.

He used the Rumley to haul his big wheat crop of 1912 to market at Savage. A thousand bushels a trip he could haul with that Rumley. It could pull seven grain tanks, each holding 150 bushels, so even though it rushed along at one-and-a-half miles an hour he still moved his grain in much less time than he could have with horses.

After unloading the wheat at Savage he reloaded the wagons, this time with lumber, for the return trip. At the same time he hired twenty-five men to help thresh so on that return trip, men and lumber stuck out all over those wagons.

He laughed to recall the amazement of the farmers as he moved his caravan up through the Burns Creek Country. At the strange roar they would stop their teams and crane their necks to see what could be coming, then they would continue to stare as long as the strange procession was in sight.

One of the highlights of the afternoon was the brief congratulatory message by Governor Tim Babcock. The Emcee in introducing him, explained that attendance at such functions was one of the obligations that goes with high office, but when Governor Tim took the microphone he gallantly corrected him with the assurance that, "It is not an obligation but a privilege." The governor also reminded the gathering that his parents, too, were Dawson County homesteaders.

Richey can well be proud of their performance at their Golden Jubilee celebration. Applause – a good round of applause – was surely due all those who worked so hard to make the Jubilee a success.

Mrs. Joe (Mary Giarrantana) Crisafulli, Sr.

January – February 1971

Mrs. Joe Crisafulli, Sr. came to Glendive in 1912 as a bride of two weeks. Glendive isn't a very big town yet, but it was a lot smaller when she first viewed it. The house which became her home had no gas, electricity, water, or sewer, but then – very few houses in Glendive did. The Crisafulli home did, however, have a septic tank so they had sewage disposal even though they did have to carry the water in.

No hot water tank kept a supply of hot water ready; she heated all her water on the kitchen range and chopped a lot of wood to do it. There were very few houses in her neighborhood when she came, and she recalls that she kept the door locked all the time. A stranger to the West, she hardly knew what to expect.

Born in Italy, Mary Giarrantana had spent several years in the United States before coming to Montana. She and her three brothers, with whom she had come, lived in New Jersey where she worked for $5 a week – a six-day week. It cost her ten cents a day for streetcar fare so her net pay for the week was $4.40. Hard to believe now, she admits, when many people are not satisfied with that per hour.

Although Joe Crisafulli had been born in Italy, too, they had never met on that side of the ocean. However, Mary was a good friend of his sister, and his family knew her well. Then one summer in New Jersey she helped in presenting the Passion Play. Her part was rather late in the play so she was selling tickets when Joe's uncle, Joseph Anton Glorioso, just returning from a visit to their homeland, bought a ticket to the performance. Uncle Joe, too, had known her in Italy so when he got back to Glendive, he told Joe about her, including the information that she was still single.

Joe was interested in what he heard and wrote, but not to the girl; he wrote to her brother. Her mother had died when she was three, her father when she was nine. "They didn't do things then like they do now," Mrs. Crisafulli pointed out. He also wrote to his parents in Italy, and in due time arrangements were made for the marriage. Joe went back to New Jersey, and two weeks after the wedding she came to Montana with him. The way they did things 'then' must have merit; the marriage lasted forty-six years, until Mr. Crisafulli's death in 1958.

Mr. Crisafulli had a three-room house, kitchen, living room, and bedroom, when he brought his bride home. His uncle and his uncle's brother-in-law had a little house in the back yard where they lived, and she cooked for them, too. She also cleaned their house for them and did their washing (no, not in an automatic; she scrubbed the clothes by hand on the washboard).

Mr. Crisafulli was working for the Northern Pacific Railroad, in the baggage room at the time of their marriage and continued with this job for about a year; then he started a store in the living room of their home.

When they sold the store some forty-five or fifty years later, the Great Falls Tribune carried a story relating some of the history of the store and the family. Quoting part of the article from the Tribune: *Crisafulli, as a young immigrant from Italy, landed in the United States in 1901 without much except the clothes he was wearing. He first worked on a plantation in Louisiana but quickly realized the limitations the South had in the way of progress and decided to 'go West'.*

Arriving in Glendive in 1907, he worked as a laborer, saved enough to buy some lots and then built a three-room home. That year his girlfriend from Italy arrived in the United States, and in Hackensack, New Jersey, August 11, 1912, Crisafulli and Mary Giarrantana were married. The next year they opened a little grocery store in their front room on North Sargent Avenue in Glendive.

As their business and family increased, their home and store were enlarged. During this time, too, Crisafulli was raising vegetables and supplying work trains on the Northern Pacific besides the limited market in Glendive.

When the Buffalo Rapids Irrigation Project was completed, his entire farm was put under the system, increasing the output of potatoes, corn, and all vegetables on a large scale so that the firm was trucking vegetables, not only all over Montana, but in other states. In 1945, they built a freezing plant on their farm and in 1946, shipped five carloads of frozen corn on the cob which was one-fifth of the entire output of the United States. During this time, they went into a stock business raising both hogs and cattle.

The Great Falls Tribune doesn't mention it, but they had bought acreage west of the river, where they greatly enlarged their truck farming operations. In order to have water for irrigating, they dug three wells and used motors from old autos – a Chevrolet, a Vim, and a Moore 30 – for power to drive the pumps. When the Buffalo Rapids irrigation ditch went through, they began using water from the ditch and could forget about keeping the motors and pumps working. (They didn't have the Crisafulli Irrigation Pump in those days!)

Mary Giarrantana had nine brothers (no sisters), and although her parents had died when she was very young, the family stayed together. Neighbors, Mrs. Crisafulli explained, were good about helping them.

One of her brothers, Joe, had come to the United States in 1900. A couple years later, Dominic came, and then in 1907 Frank, Joe's wife and little boy, and Mary joined them in New Jersey. They were on the ship eighteen days, coming from Italy to New York. Joe met their ship, but immigration officials told them they couldn't leave the ship until the next day so he went home. But then they were released almost immediately and officials put them on the very next train. They couldn't speak a word of English, but when they got off the train, they saw a policeman on the corner, so they showed him the address and he took them to Joe's house, about three blocks away.

When Joe and Mary married and moved to Montana, the three brothers stayed in New Jersey, but two years later they made the move to Montana as well.

For many years, Joe Giarrantana repaired shoes in Glendive. When he passed away in 1950, Dominic, who had been working on his brother Frank's homestead, took over the shoe repair business. Frank had homesteaded at Gas City, eight miles south of Glendive but when he came back to Glendive following World War I, he plastered houses. The Giarrantana's mother was a DeMaggio, and the famed Joe is a third cousin to Mrs. Crisafulli.

As the Crisafullis enlarged their scope of business and their back-yard garden graduated to the farm across the river, Mr. Crisafulli would be out there all day, 'during season', and Mrs. Crisafulli tended store. One evening she noticed a stranger walking back and forth, back and forth, in front of the store. When he'd get to the corner of the building, he'd stop and peer in, then walk back to the other corner, stop, and peer in again.

As he continued this disconcerting practice she began to feel alarmed and called the police but the police didn't come. Clearly, if anything should have to be done it was going to be up to her to do it so she slipped a baseball bat under the counter.

Mrs. Crisafulli is a tiny woman but it was probably a good thing for 'that man' that he didn't try to come into the store that night! But he didn't come in and at nine o'clock she locked the door and pulled down the blind. Then her husband came back from the farm and everything was fine.

Tending the store meant a lot of extra work for the woman with five children, but Mrs. Crisafulli says she enjoyed it. Many of the workers on the Northern Pacific's extra gangs were Italian or Greek so it was only natural that they should patronize Crisafulli's 'Italian and American Store'. Crisafulli's, of course, made it their specialty to supply Italian foods such as Romano cheese, olive oil, codfish, and tomato paste.

Joe Crisafulli, Sr. came from a long line of fruit growers and vineyard operators so it was natural that a 'green thumb' would find expression in gardening. Whether or not the boys' thumbs were green, as soon as they were old enough to know a vegetable from a weed they were working in the gardens. But along with their work, their father always stressed the importance of education. "Save your money," he would tell them, "and get an education." And they did. All five of the children graduated from Dawson County High School and three have university degrees. Joe and Rose are graduates of the University of Montana at Missoula and Leonard graduated from the University of Washington.

The children worked, but the parents worked harder. Mrs. Crisafulli recalls that often she and her husband worked eighteen or nineteen hours a day. That didn't leave much time for rest, "But," she says, "we made it. Thanks to God, everything came out all right. Hard work keeps a person healthy." She will be eighty in April so how many of us are in a position to argue the point?

During the flu epidemic of 1918, she and her husband were both very ill with the dread virus. Dr. Schillington came to their house to see Mr. Crisafulli and promptly took him to the hospital – the Northern Pacific Hospital. Next morning he came back to report to her on her husband's condition and found her even sicker so he told her she had to go to the hospital too.

She protested that she couldn't go because of the children, especially the three-month-old baby. Her brother, she knew, would stay with the older children, but he couldn't be expected to manage a small baby. Dr. Schillington assured her he would find someone to take care of the baby so off she went to the hospital – to the General because the Northern Pacific was filled to capacity. Each morning the doctor would go the N.P. and tell her husband how she was and then go to the General and tell her how he was. They went through some anxious days, but both came through all right.

Mrs. Crisafulli has had three major operations in her lifetime, all three at Rochester, but she still does all her own work. "My boys," she explained, "want me to get somebody to do my housecleaning, but I do it myself. You feel better," she explained, "if you have something to do. Sit, sit, sit, is no good for a person!" So she keeps active, even continuing to garden in the summer.

Every morning she goes to church, driving her own car. She chooses to go early when there isn't much traffic so she is in the church by six o'clock and is home again by seven. She used to drive any time of day (used to, that is, since she got her first driver's license at sixty-nine years of age) but one time a little girl gave her a bad scare.

Just as she reached Degel's butcher shop the child darted out from between two parked cars, right into the path of her car. She was able to stop but just knew the car following would hit her. He was also able to stop, though, and the little girl was uninjured, but since that time she has confined her driving to early morning when there is little traffic.

Mr. Crisafulli passed away July 12, 1958. They lived in the store building for forty-three years. Mrs. Crisafulli has been in her present home for fifteen years, since they sold the store in 1955. Mrs. Crisafulli finds that her big German Shepherd is good company – and more. "Lady is particular about who comes into the house. They finally put the meters outside because she wouldn't let the meter readers come into the basement."

Three of her sons – Joe, Jr., Frank, and Angelo – live in Glendive. They take care of all the business interests. Since their father's death, a new enterprise has been added to the list of those he started. They now manufacture the Crisafulli Irrigation Pump and have sales representatives all over the United States. They have had inquiries from many other countries as well, and former President Lyndon B. Johnson was one of their customers.

The Crisafullis' only daughter, Rose, now lives in Missoula, and their son, Leonard, a chemist, lives in Wisconsin. Leonard was a naval officer in World War II and is a commander in the Naval Reserve. The influence of the Italian immigrant who came to Glendive in 1907 reaches far.

Mrs. John (Grace Redfield) Buttelman

March 1967

Many a farmer in eastern Montana early in the century started his farming with Diamond G horsepower. Even before the turn of the century many ranchers, too, bought Diamond G's. The Diamond G Ranch was located in the Gallatin Valley, but a number of the horses had been 'transplanted' to Dawson County and formed the nucleus for the '52' Ranch on Bad Route.

Two brothers, John and Nick Buttelman, came from Germany in the early 1880's and joined their uncles, George and Henry Gerdes, on their Willow Creek ranch near Bozeman. In 1889 Nick and John trailed a bunch of the Diamond G horses to eastern Montana because of the good grazing lands in this locality and started a ranch between Union and Fallon. At first they used the Diamond G brand on some of their cattle, too but they soon started using the '52' brand exclusively. The brothers built a log house on the creek bank and a log barn, too. After almost eighty years, the log house is still standing, but a frame structure replaced it many years ago as a dwelling.

In 1897 Nick, the older brother, married Mary Conrad, a North Dakota girl. Now the ranch had a woman's touch, but sometimes just two hands couldn't touch enough. Extra help was needed for the cooking and baking and washing and cleaning that goes with a bunch of men. In time, Miss Grace Redfield happened to be one of those who provided "extra hands."

Miss Redfield was a Minnesota girl who came to Montana in 1902. Her cousin and husband were coming this way, and Grace decided she wanted to see the west too, so she came with them. They stopped in Glendive for a time, and he worked on the railroad, but when they went on farther west, she chose to remain in Glendive. There was something about these 'wide, open spaces' that appealed to her, coming as she did from the Minnesota woods. In 1902 there wasn't much besides wide, open spaces to appeal to her!

Domestic help was much in demand in the little town on the river, and also in the surrounding area. There weren't many inhabitants on the prairies, but single girls available to 'work out' were even scarcer so she had no trouble finding a job. She began working for Mrs. LaBelle soon after she arrived in Glendive. Then, about the time she was through there, Mrs. Nick Buttelman came to town looking for a girl to help on the ranch so Grace went with her.

She soon found out how much outdoor men eat! She learned, too, that when she prepared a meal for about six 'regulars' she could expect extras almost every day. Men coming through would stop in and eat with them. It wasn't the 'drop-outs' but the 'drop-ins' that concerned her then.

As with most ranchers of that day, they bought groceries twice a year, and they bought in great quantities because it took a lot of food to feed that many men. They depended much upon dried fruits, beans, potatoes, and canned meat. During the winter, of course, they could enjoy fresh meat. As for bread – she baked nine or ten loaves twice a week and didn't have any dry bread problem.

Before she had spent many months on the ranch Nick's younger brother John persuaded her to take on a permanent job. They were married in 1903. For about a year they continued to live at 'the big ranch' but then built a four room framed house about three miles down the creek. They were quite modern with a well under the kitchen and a pump just outside the kitchen door, but before long the pump quit working and they had to draw the water out of the well with a bucket on a rope, then carry it up the basement stairs.

That same well served as refrigerator. Jars of milk and cream, as well as other perishables, would be suspended from a rope into the water so they would 'keep'. For many years her washing machine was of the wooden tub variety. It had a hand lever, which was pushed back and forth to turn the agitator. They always kept water in the tub so it wouldn't dry out. Even that was a great improvement over the scrub board.

They had three children, two girls and a boy. The girls were ready for school before school was ready for them! When the oldest girl was eight and the second was six, Buttelmans offered their bunkhouse for use as a schoolhouse, just so they could get a school started. The first teacher was Miss Anita Groves who had a homestead about five miles up the creek. During the week she boarded at Buttelmans, then returned to her homestead over the weekend.

That first year they charged her nothing for room and board, so determined were they to get a school started. The next year she paid just ten dollars a month. After all, Mrs. Buttelman pointed out, the teacher only made $35 a month so they didn't feel it would be right to ask her to pay more.

In the first school little emphasis was placed on the equipment – it was all they could do to manage a school! Planks and boxes provided benches for the twenty-one pupils in the bunkhouse that first year, while the teacher's desk was a little kitchen table. Some of the pupils came from as far as three miles away – and they didn't come by bus, either! Two terms of school were held in the bunkhouse before a proper schoolhouse was built.

Almost every Sunday when the weather was nice neighbors visited each other. It seemed easier to visit when they had to go with team and buggy than after they had cars. They didn't have regular church services, but Miss Groves' brother, whose homestead adjoined hers, had studied for the ministry so while he was in the community he conducted services, in homes or in the school.

When their girls were ready for high school the Buttelmans bought a house in Glendive, and Mrs. Buttelman moved to town with the girls so they could continue their education. At first they spent summers on the ranch, but later they lived in town year round. Mrs. Buttelman noted that when she first came to Glendive in 1902 a man ran sheep where her home now is on North Kendrick.

In 1936 Mr. Buttelman passed away as the result of a heart attack. Now their oldest daughter with her husband and oldest son are on the old ranch. The old roundup wagon is still on the ranch, still stocked with some of the supplies so necessary when it rumbled across the prairies almost a century ago. Although it has not been used for more than a half-a-century, it symbolizes an era long gone, the era when the stockman ruled the range.

Jens Jensen Family

May 1974

Our parents, Mr. and Mrs. Jens Jensen, arrived at Kenmare, North Dakota, from Denmark in 1906. Mother, whose maiden name was Anna Sophie Kristine Kristensen, was accompanied by her sisters, Laura (later Mrs. Anton Anderson of the Crane Community) and Hertha (later Mrs. Julius Nelson of Bentley, Alberta, Canada). Mother and Dad were married at Kenmare, March 20, 1907. Dad worked on farms and in a coal mine which was owned by Henry Misfeldt, (who some years later lived with his family in Sidney), and Mother worked in private homes. They told of eating oatmeal with water because milk was in short supply.

In 1907 (April) they migrated by stagecoach to Mondak, and from Mondak to Sidney in a lumber wagon. I don't know where they stayed when they arrived in Sidney, but I remember hearing many accounts of help and kindness from Mr. and Mrs. Peter Anderson, Sr.

They immediately filed a homestead claim on a one-quarter section of land, located about five miles northwest of Sidney, in Mother's name. They selected this particular piece of land because of the presence of spring water and grass. This homestead became the farm closest to Sidney of the Brorson Community. They built a two-room frame house and a dugout barn. They acquired a few broncos and some farm equipment and started farming. Dad worked on a banker's farm in 1907 and also hauled freight by team and lumber wagon or sled between Mondak and Sidney to help them get their start. On one of these trips, coming home late at night, Dad spotted a strange light where none was supposed to be. He veered from his course, driving around the prairies looking for familiar landmarks. At last he decided to investigate. It was home. Mother had hung a lantern on the outside of the house to guide him. There was no window on that side, so there should have been no light.

In 1908 Dad worked on the construction of the irrigation canal.

I was born September 23, 1908. A midwife supervised my birth since no doctors were available. I was the first boy of Danish immigrants born in the Brorson Community. I was also the first boy of the same community to graduate from Sidney High School (1925).

Mother was alone with me much of the time while Dad was freighting. On one occasion the stove failed, so to keep warm she loaded me into a little 'Express Wagon' and pulled me, through the snow, across the prairie and hills to Aunt Laura's (Mrs. Anton Anderson), who at that time lived about four miles east in the 'Valley'. On another occasion one of the broncos broke loose, but he still stayed close to the haystack. Mother laid a snare for him and hid, waiting for him to step into it. He did, and she pulled the rope tight, secured it, and the horse was still there when Dad came home. There were no fences at that time except those Dad had built around the place and the land he had managed to break and seed. A trail crossed the homestead and Indians traveling it often camped near the open water close to our home.

It took three years to prove up* Mother's homestead. About that time Dad contested the claim on the quarter section bordering Mother's land on the west. The party who had 'filed' had failed to complete his claim and, hence, lost his right to the land. Mother and Dad then moved our house from her claim to his. I was only two years old, but I still retain a recollection of the house being tilted while being moved. The same house is still located on the land to which it was moved. Additional rooms were added as the family grew. It is, however, no longer occupied. The land is now owned by my youngest sister, Inger, and her husband, Aril Sunwall.

Shortly after the house was moved and a new barn dug into the hill west of the house, a prairie fire burned the barn. Dad was able to save the house by plowing around it, but some of his farm animals perished.

Dad was an exceptional horseman. He was able to get unbelievable accomplishments from them. Once, on a trip to an island in the Yellowstone River for a load of wood, some farmers were 'stuck' on the bare riverbank with two sled loads of wheat. They had hitched four horses to one sled, but were unable to move it. They asked Dad to hitch his two to the load along with their four. This he refused to do, but told them to unhitch all four of theirs and he would then pull the load up the bank. "Impossible," they said, and told him they would give him the load of wheat if he could. He hitched his team to the sled and pulled the load of wheat up the bank. They said he 'prayed' with the team. The last he saw of 'his' wheat, they were trying to salvage it after the team had become frightened at the elevator and overturned the sled on the grade.

The church and its work was the focal point of my parents' lives. They, together with other homesteaders, held the organizational meeting of the Pella Danish Evangelical Lutheran Church on February 26, 1908. On January 9, 1912, it was decided that a congregation should also be organized in the Brorson Community. Thus, our parents were charter members, first of the Pella Congregation, and later, of the Brorson Congregation. When our parents moved to Sidney upon their retirement, they again affiliated with the Pella Church.

Because our home was almost a 'midway' point between the two congregations (they were served by the same pastor), it became a stopping point for the pastor at which to rest or get a fresh team of horses, and to have a lunch or meal, or to stop overnight if the weather was bad. Also, when there was to be a burial in Brorson, it became a convenient stopping place for all involved when the sometime fierce winter weather made it almost impossible to proceed.

My sister Nora was born in 1910 and Ethel in 1912. In 1913 the farm was 'sold' and we traveled to Denmark where we stayed eight months. The party who had 'bought' our farm experienced a tragedy in the family, and he was unable to complete the sale. We then returned to Montana, living for a few months on Dr. Beagle's farm *northeast of Sidney. From there I started school in the spring of 1914, in the People's Congregational Church. Mrs. Jack Harnish was my teacher. She must have had her hands full and I must have been a problem to her, as I could speak no English. That summer we moved back to the homestead and I started school in what was known as the Carl Sorensen School. This was a three-mile walk for me. One morning I stopped to investigate some calves on the range and was chased by the cows. I managed to reach the safety of the fence around the Hendersons' quarter section and went back home. Mother immediately sent me back on my way with instructions to follow the fence lines. I was quite late for school. My teacher that year was Emma Hendricksen (later Mrs. Chris Rasmussen).*

When my sister Nora was old enough to start school Dad bought a black pony and saddle from Ed Henderson. This was to be our means of transportation. Our school then was the Seliger School, located about four miles northeast of home. Dad would direct our pony in the right direction and start him out with a buggy whip. We would go as far as Simard's where Avis climbed into the saddle with Nora, and I rode behind the saddle. Avis's dad, Arcade, would then start our pony with a blacksnake. I don't blame the pony for being so hesitant about going to school. The treatment he received left much to be desired.

By the time Ethel was old enough to go to school Hardy School had been built and we were able to walk the distance of only one mile each way.

My youngest sister, Inger, was born in 1917, but by the time she started school the pioneer days were history. Dad bought our first car, a 1925 Ford, and in the fall of 1925 I left home for college and I have lived most of my life in the state of Minnesota. Nora became Mrs. Fred Iversen, Ethel, Mrs. Jacob F. Miller, and Inger, Mrs. Aril Sunwall. Mother passed away in 1963 and father in 1970. Ethel's husband also passed away in 1970. Sunwalls bought the old homestead in 1945, and have farmed it ever since.

Henry A. Jensen
Minneapolis, Minnesota

Mrs. Forrest (Kathryn Farnum) Currens

February 1965

Lovers of antiques would have a heyday visiting Mrs. Forrest Currens. Most of the items in her collection, with which she can just about 'out-museum the museum', came to Glendive before the turn of the century, well in advance of her own arrival. Not that she's particularly interested in antiques; she has them because of their sentimental value.

Her father, Lovell G. Farnum, came to Montana in 1894 to join his brother-in-law, Hope Davis, in the druggist business. (An advertisement in a 1922 Yellowstone Monitor, congratulating the Northern Pacific Railroad on the completion of its new depot, informs that the business was established in 1881). Together they operated the firm as Davis & Farnum.

The firm's name was changed to the present Farnum and Gabert when Farnum associated with Leslie Gabert in 1929. When Farnum died in 1954, he was the oldest registered pharmacist in Montana, the eighty-second to be registered.

In the fall of 1897 Mr. Farnum went back to his former home community of Clarkston, Michigan, and married Miss Clara Taylor on October 6, then returned to Glendive with his bride. Here they made their home. When the new Mrs. Farnum came to this raw frontier town, she brought with her much of her furniture. Many of these same pieces are still being used by Mrs. Currens.

One of her most prized possessions is the melodeon on which her mother played as a girl and on which she later gave lessons. The melodeon wasn't working when Mrs. Farnum brought it from her eastern home, but Mrs. Currens had it repaired two years ago so that it once more yields its charming harmonies. When a friend told Mrs. Farnum, even when the melodeon was not working, that in Chicago she could get her a thousand dollars for it without batting an eye, Mrs. Farnum retorted, "If it's worth a thousand to somebody else it's worth two thousand to me!" So it's still in the family. An Edison phonograph, with several boxes of its cylindrical records, is also still in the family, stored away in the attic. Mrs. Currens recalls that her mother many times mentioned giving a phonograph concert (phonographs were quite a novelty then yet), charging a ten-cent admission fee and collecting enough money to buy a stained glass window for the church.

In addition to a complete set of bedroom furniture which belonged to her grandmother Farnum, Mrs. Currens also has her grandmother's silver tea set and many exquisite dishes dating back considerably before her own time. Her grandfather's pocket watch (which has to be wound with a key) and his pipe – with a stem well over a foot long – also adorn her china cupboard shelves. Gracing her living room is a little table which once belonged to her grandmother Taylor.

Shortly before his death the late George Copping found out about a chair in her back yard that was about to be consigned to the dump grounds. When he learned that the chair had come to Glendive by way of a steamboat on the Yellowstone River, he lost no time making arrangements to obtain the chair for the Gateway Museum.

During the Farnums' earliest years in Glendive they lived in a little house on the corner of Anderson and Mann streets. It was quite a trip from the little house on the south side to the Bill Jordan home on Meade Avenue. It was so far, in fact, that when Mrs. Farnum pushed her small daughter in the baby buggy across town to the Jordans' for an evening, they'd stay all night and walk back in the morning because it was too far to walk back after dark. No paved streets or sidewalks, then, you know; just some board walks, and only a few blocks of those. But there were enough boardwalks. Mrs. Currens recalls, that when, as a little girl she'd drop her pennies, they'd roll into the cracks between the boards so she couldn't get them out.

Mrs. Farnum was entirely satisfied with their little house on the south side, but her father, a lumber yard owner back in Michigan, thought she should have a more pretentious dwelling so he insisted upon building a house for them on Meade Avenue. Her mother didn't at all want to move, with the result that Mrs. Currens remembers the sinking feeling that she, too small to understand what it was all about except that it was something her mother didn't want to do, had when they moved to the big house.

Each fall her grandfather Farnum came to Montana to hunt. He'd load up a buckboard* and head for the Jordan country where he'd spend six weeks leisurely pursuing his game. No license was required then, and no game limit halted his hunting before he was ready to quit. The black iron pot in which he did his cooking on these hunting expeditions now serves as a receptacle for a large plant in the Currens' front room.

When in 1909, a mild earthquake shook the area and the dishes fell off her plate rails, the frightened Mrs. Farnum called her husband at the store for some reassurance. His reassurance was, "If you saw all the bottles falling off the shelves, you'd know something was happening!"

The advent of the first automobiles caused quite a stir, and for the Farnums it caused more than a stir. When one of the first proud owners among their friends invited Mr. Farnum for a ride, he accepted, and they started out in the open car for the pleasure jaunt. They headed in the direction of the present airport, but there was a huge ant pile in the middle of the road. The driver either didn't realize how big the ant pile was or didn't realize how fast he was going because he hit it too hard, and Mr. Farnum flew out of the car, breaking his arm. Trying days followed for Mrs. Farnum: baby Jo had colic, daughter Kay had an ear abscess, and Mr. Farnum had a broken arm!

While Glendive was still a frontier town there were those who recognized the contribution music can make to a community, and credit must be given to those who struggled to build up the music department in the local school system. This department was still struggling with its growing pains when Mrs. Farnum, during the teacher shortage of World War I, was asked by Professor R.L. Hunt to take charge of it. The war soon ended, but Mrs. Farnum was

248

retained; and her success in molding both vocal and instrumental sections into commendable performers was evidenced by their showing at the first State Interscholastic Music Meet held in Big Timber. According to the story in the Dawson County Review, "Our boys and girls of the Dawson County High School did not win the cup, but came dangerously near. Had entries been made in all of the musical numbers, Glendive without doubt would have carried off the honors. They did, however, bring home pennants and medals in eight of the nine events contested by Glendive.... Glendive's orchestra was so far ahead of the Bozeman contingent that the latter voluntarily de-rated their organization to Class B orchestra. When one considers that Bozeman is twice as large as Glendive and should have greater musical talent than the smaller city" (Bozeman won the meet) "the showing made by the young ladies and young men of the Dawson County High School is the more remarkable.

"It reflects splendidly on the skill, patience and instructive powers of Mrs. Lovell Farnum, who trained and coached them. Hers is largely the credit for the victories secured at Big Timber. She was ably assisted at the meet by Mrs. P.J. Moe and Thomas Hunt, who acted as chaperones and guardians of Glendive's interest. There are few men so enthusiastic and so active in the musical development of the Gate City as Thomas Hunt." Such was Glendive's beginning in state musical competition.

Mr. and Mrs. Farnum were charter members of the local Congregational Church* and active in helping promote the building of the structure which was torn down this past summer to make way for the newer and larger building. Mrs. Currens reflects that she had a part in that one, too. The Women's Society ran a concession booth on the corner of Town and Merrill to help finance the building, and since the back of the drug store was conveniently located near the booth, the items and necessities that had been overlooked would be supplied from there. So she wore a path and wore out shoes, running the errands.

The Farnums had two daughters, Kathryn (Mrs. Forrest Currens) and Jo. Miss Jo Farnum resides in Minneapolis, while Mr. and Mrs. Currens live in the house on Meade that her grandfather built for her mother.

Clifford Pierce

October 1970

Clifford Pierce came to Montana in the spring of 1909. His father, Thomas S. Pierce, and his older brother, Ralph, had come out in the spring of 1908, in time for Ralph to get caught and almost perish in a late snowstorm.

Two of Cliff's uncles, Frank and Charlie Ferguson (his mother's brothers), had preceded his father and brother to Montana. Coming out in the spring of 1907 they had been so enthusiastic about the homestead opportunities they had persuaded Mr. Pierce to look, too. They had returned to Iowa for the winter of 1907-08, then when they came back to the Treasure State, Mr. Pierce and Ralph came too.

Ralph and his cousin Harvey had gone to visit Charley Anderson, about a mile from Fergusons. When they started out that afternoon of May 20, they had no reason to guess that the day might close in any but the usual way (the weather bureau wasn't issuing traveler's warnings in those days, and there was no radio to convey the message if they had). Before they got back home that afternoon the snowstorm hit, hit with such intensity that they lost all sense of direction. They wandered all night in the whirling snow. Next morning, their strength almost spent, they sighted Herschel Purdum's tent and staggered to it. They were five-and-a-half miles southeast of their intended destination!

Three feet of snow had fallen that night. Since the storm came so late in the year, baby birds were already hatched out, and many were fluttering about over the snow. How many perished no one knows. Birds were not the only casualties in that storm; even cattle and horses, not to mention sheep, drifted with the wind, huddled against a bank, and suffocated when snow drifted over them.

Tom Pierce filed on a homestead about seven miles southeast of Union that spring of 1908, and he and Ralph spent the summer in Montana. During the summer, they built a house – just a 'homestead shack', that first one was, and a barn. That fall they returned to Sac City and spent the winter, then in the spring of 1909, they made the permanent move to Montana. The men came with their immigrant car which brought furniture, farm machinery (a far cry from the array of machinery which would be required now to start farming), five horses, one cow, one bull, some baled hay, a wagon, and a buggy.

Before coming to Montana Mr. Pierce (Cliff's father) had been a house mover – he moved other buildings too. He also did carpenter work which stood him in good stead when the time came to build on the homestead. But now farming became his full-time occupation – and farming was full-time when it was done with horses, even if you had four boys, as Tom Pierce did.

When they moved to Montana, Mr. and Mrs. Pierce had four boys: Ralph, George, Lloyd, and Cliff; and two girls; Mildred and Dorothy. Caroline was the only one of the Tom Pierce family born in Montana.

While the men came with the immigrant car, the 'women folk' came by passenger train, arriving in Glendive March 3, 1909. It had been a long train

250

trip, and now there was a long buggy trip ahead of them. Crossing the Yellowstone Bridge that first time was a memorable experience. They didn't have a choice of three bridges then and the one bridge they had was a shaky, wooden structure that left them a bit shaky, too, that first time they crossed it.

They were glad for the pleasant weather that greeted them and prevailed for their fresh-air ride. Those of us who came along in later years naturally tend to think of an oiled highway to Lindsay, Circle, and on. But the early settlers didn't even find roads, much less pavement. There were just wagon trails across the prairie – and not even a wagon trail to the newly selected homestead site. Those same trails were followed until the ruts became too deep to follow, then another trail was started beside the first until there might be two or three sets of parallel ruts. Quite a jolt for anyone who might try to cross at right angles.

The trail to the Union community led through tall, thick grass waving in the wind, and seldom did they see a fence. There were no trees except ash and chokecherry in the brush coulees. There were cedar trees in the badlands, but that was on beyond Union. Buffalo berries were abundant in the fall, and as for the hunting enthusiasts (or the bread winner) there were plenty of grouse and sagehens, and lots of antelope.

When the Tom Pierce family settled on their homestead in the spring of 1909, their nearest neighbor was Billy Wood, six miles away. More neighbors were coming though. Dr. Blackstone, a medical doctor, came with his immigrant car on the same train that brought the Pierces. Although he settled closer to the Divide than Pierces did, other neighbors were settling in their community. Three dentists homesteaded in the Union-Lindsay area: Dr. Bidwell (he was there when Pierces arrived), Dr. Moe, and Dr. Robson. Anyone know of any other rural community that could boast that many dentists? Probably few towns in eastern Montana at that time could equal that number!

Posts for fencing and much of the material for the barn and other outbuildings came from the cedars in the badlands. Pierces built on the west prong of Clear Creek, and for the first two years they used a spring in the creek for their water supply. They couldn't seem to find time to dig a well so they sank a barrel around the spring and found it a source of good, clear, cold water. Later they dug a well closer to the house.

The winter of 1909-1910, their first winter in Montana, was a winter of heavy snow. They had surrounded the haystack near the barn with a fence, but as the snow drifted deeper and deeper, the fence was completely covered, so the cattle could (and did) walk right over the top of it. They built another fence on top of the first, sinking the new posts into the snow beside the original posts, wiring them fast. By the time the snow melted in the spring they had a fence ten feet high. With the snow gone they could reduce the fence to normal height.

There were no schools in that part of the country so Tom Pierce worked for the organization of a new district, then he and his sons hauled lumber out from Glendive and in 1910 built the schoolhouse that became known as the Pierce School. Later other schools were built as more settlers came.

The school was used as a community center as well as a schoolhouse in those early days. Many dances were held in it, and when a Sunday School was organized in the community, this also was held in the schoolhouse. Church services were held whenever a minister was available. Years later (1923) Harry Green donated land, and a hall was built at Union with the neighbors donating the labor. This hall was then used for a community center.

Lignite coal was plentiful in their area, and during their first years in Montana, they mined their own coal. Later they began buying at the Peuse mine, about twelve miles west of Glendive. They'd haul a load of grain to Glendive, then take a load of coal home.

One of the outstanding events during their early years in Montana was the last big cattle roundup. The days of open range vanished with the coming of the homesteaders, and the range cattle had to be cleared out. Farmers were fencing their fields, leaving no free range for the vast herds of the big cattle companies.

The XIT was one of the biggest holders in Dawson County – A Dawson County that extended to the Missouri River and well beyond its present western and eastern borders. In the fall of 1910, the XIT rounded up the last of their cattle and shipped them off to market. While they gathered cattle in the Clear Creek country one of their roundup wagons camped on the flat by Pat McGovern's place. They butchered a beef and invited homesteaders from miles around for a barbecue. Several cowpunchers sang for the group, and it was a great event for the homesteaders. The cattle were held overnight on the flat, then next morning they were started down the long trail to market.

One time when the Pierce boys were still living at home, a strange bull paid a call. Visits from strays were not encouraged so the boys tied an empty five-gallon gasoline can to the bull's tail. He took off across the hills on a run, stopping every now and then to chase the can. He'd go round and round in a circle trying to get rid of his pursuer, then give up and run again. He didn't come back a second time.

Mr. Pierce recalls that they used to have quite a problem with wagon wheels in a hot dry summer. The wooden wheels would shrink, and the spokes came loose from the hub. Sometimes, as a temporary measure, they would drive shingles between the iron tire and the fellow*, but to 'cure' the situation they'd drive the wagon into the creek and let it stand a couple of weeks in the water (they were fortunate to live near a creek that had that much water in it!) to make the wheels swell to normal size again.

Today's woman, with all her modern conveniences, fast and efficient transportation, ease of communications, must have difficulty feeling empathy with the pioneer women of sixty years ago. Even those pioneer women who remain may find it hard to think of their present selves in those circumstances, vivid though the memory of 'those days' may be.

In view of the role these women played in the development of the frontier – and the frontier is not very long gone in eastern Montana – they deserve a salute for their fortitude, courage, and resourcefulness. Perhaps, if she was one of the fortunate, it was the job of the men and boys to pump and carry the water and pack the coal, but even so the males weren't always around. And how many of the women regularly worked in the fields – not on a tractor with an air-conditioned cab (not that all tractors today have cabs) but driving horses.

The only air-conditioner in the home then was the coal range in the kitchen, and by the time it had conditioned the kitchen, with the temperature outside already close to 100 degrees, it was about enough to encourage fasting! Mrs. Pierce, Cliff's mother, cooked on a Monarch coal range many years.

In the absence of refrigeration other means had to be utilized for preserving meat. Canning, of course, was common, and the Pierces often corned* part of the beef to keep it. Pork they 'fried down' – fried the meat, packed it in a crock, and poured hot lard over it to seal it. Chicken was an important item on the menu, and wild game was used considerably.

When Cliff was a boy growing up on the farm, his great ambition was to be a cowboy. Imagination could transform a calf into a bronc, and he practiced diligently. He got so he was handy riding steers by starting with those calves, but that's about as far as he got with that particular ambition. By the time he was grown the day of the cowboy had passed so he settled down to the more prosaic farming. His dad bought their first car in 1907. That Model T Ford was high class then! The rough roads were enough to shake a car to pieces, but at that, those little old Fords lasted ten to twenty years.

Women in the Clear Creek community wanted fellowship with one another so they started a women's club. Prior to that they got together occasionally for quilting or such, but they wanted to meet regularly so about 1915 they decided to organize the Clear Creek Women's Club and meet monthly. It was a women's club, but it really involved the whole family. Most of them still depended on horse and buggy for transportation so the husbands took their wives, and the children, of course, went along too. Each woman would bring something for the dinner, and they would spend the entire day together. At first they met in the homes, but after Union Hall was built they met in the hall.

These monthly get-togethers meant much to the women, isolated as they were. Trips to town were infrequent and there was little contact with the outside world, so visiting their neighbors was a welcome break in the routine of the work. The Clear Creek Women's Club, organized well in advance of the Home Demonstration Clubs later sponsored by the Extension Department of Montana State University, celebrated their fiftieth anniversary a few years ago.

Cliff Pierce came to Montana in time to see the last freight boat on the Yellowstone. It was probably the first year he was in Montana, 1909, but he isn't positive about the year. It was loaded with cement for the Intake Dam and rails for the new railroad being built between Glendive and Sidney.

In 1924 Cliff married Ivy Black, in St. Paul. They have one daughter, Betty Henke of Glendive, and one son, a high school teacher in Bellingham, Washington. The Pierces spent part of their married life in Minnesota, but since 1934 they've been back in Montana. He worked on the Fort Peck Dam for three years and on the Buffalo Rapids project, surveying for a couple years. In 1940 they moved into Glendive and have lived here since.

Jean Sellers

January 1968

Wooden sidewalks in the business district – no sidewalks at all north of the Jordan Hotel – the Jordan Annex where Brenner Drug now stands – a gully angling from Hungry Joe* to the river past the depot – two or three feet of water on Main Street – if you remember these you've been around Glendive awhile. Jean Sellers has. She came to Glendive in 1910 to work for the Northern Pacific Railroad after teaching school in Beach and Gladstone, North Dakota.

At that time both the Beach and Gladstone schools were one-room schools where one teacher taught all eight grades. In fact, Gladstone then didn't have even a one-room school. The Northern Pacific section foreman's wife had died so they held school in his former home.

The winter she taught at Gladstone the school ran out of coal during a cold spell and in the middle of a snowstorm in the bargain. During the same storm a Northern Pacific engine had stalled at Gladstone so, since they had to have coal if they were going to have school, they asked permission from the railroad superintendent to get some coal from the idle engine. Permission granted, they formed a bucket brigade and hauled enough coal from the engine to the school to feed the pot-bellied stove until the storm subsided and a new supply could be brought to the school.

Jean was born in Wisconsin, but her family moved to the Black Hills when she was three years old. The last lap of the journey, from Pierre to Sturgis, had to be made by stage. Sturgis was a rough town in those days. They became accustomed to the cry, "Man for breakfast this morning," meaning that a man had been killed the night before. The town was on the freight line from Bismarck. All freighting was done by bull team, and many of the 'bull whackers', though of course not all, were a rather rough lot, contributing considerable color and sometimes violence to their surroundings.

Handling the bull teams was a man-sized job; some of those bulls were mean. One especially memorable critter was an old blue bull with a bad temper and long Texas horns. When he got into a bad mood, he'd go out and lie down in the meadow north of town (now there are houses instead of meadow) and sulk. No one, not even his driver, dared go near him when he was in that mood, but after two or three days he would get up and it was safe to catch him and put him to work again.

The Sellers family located on a homestead soon after moving to Sturgis. At first Mrs. Sellers and the children kept things going on the claim while Mr. Sellers stayed in town, taking care of his truck garden. Once a week he would come to the homestead to bring supplies and see how they were getting along, but he came late and left early so the children didn't often get to see him.

One night when they were alone, the mother was terrified to see Indian signal fires burning close by. There was no place to hide from them, and the only possible course of action she could think of in case of attack was to run – a mother with a pair of twins four years old and another pair of infant twins. But she determined to try if need should arise.

She had a large homespun shawl so she planned that, at any sign of danger; she would put the two babies in the shawl and tie it over her shoulder, take the two older children by the hands, and run. All through the long night she watched (to the older children the night was memorable because they were allowed to play on the bed!), but the Indians made no attempt to molest them.

Jean became a school teacher and taught first in South Dakota then moved north and taught one year at Gladstone and two at Beach before coming to Glendive in 1910 where she worked for the Northern Pacific until her retirement in 1946.

When she first came to Glendive she boarded at the Jordan Hotel but roomed at the Jordan Annex because at the annex rooms could be rented by the month. There were no sidewalks north of the Jordan (and those in front of the Jordan were wooden) so often it was necessary to wade through mud to get from the annex to the hotel.

During one of her early years here the Yellowstone River flooded and backed two or three feet of water up the main street of Glendive. The train master came to work wearing hip boots so he carried the women employees to the depot (not the present structure, incidentally) so they could go to work.

The Gate City has grown a bit these last fifty-eight years. Now there are miles of cement sidewalks – the streets are paved – not quite so many saloons in proportion to the other businesses – some of the original buildings have been torn down or moved or remodeled, and many have been added. Yes, Glendive has done some changing since Jean Sellers first saw it.

Fred Rong

December 1968

Fred Rong doesn't remember when his parents came to Montana for the simple reason it was before he was born, but as he remembers his father telling it, it was 1904.

The family moved to Montana from Nebraska, making the move with a team and wagon. Fred recalls his older sister describing the trip, the family crossing rivers by walking on the railroad bridges while Mr. Rong swam horses and wagons across.

Rancher Adams on Morgan Creek showed the newcomers around and helped them locate a suitable tract of land for a homestead. Mr. Rong didn't want to get too far from town and found what he was looking for about twelve miles north of Glendive.

Not many homesteaders were that close to a town, but Rongs didn't even have to go twelve miles to shop; they were only about two miles from Stipek, and Stipek, particularly a little later on, was quite a shopping center. Even so, they went to Glendive perhaps once or twice a month, a team and wagon their means of transportation.

The family came to Dawson County in the fall of the year, and of course houses didn't come with homesteads, so while they were getting their first dwelling built, Mr. Rong worked for Hi Griffith, and they lived up Morgan Creek.

Their first house was a three-room log building, and it was in this house that Fred was born. His father had hewed logs in Nebraska part of the time for a living so he was experienced when he went after logs for his homestead shelter. They used split logs for the roof, sealed the cracks with mud, and covered it with scorio*. It was a warm house, despite its rustic appearance.

Fred's mother died when he was less than a year old. She cut her hand with a kitchen knife and lost her life when blood poisoning set in. One of his older sisters, Carrie, practically raised Fred and his next older brother, Jim.

They lived close to the main road, the road that is now Highway 16, but it was not a paved highway then. It was just a country road, the ditches very shallow. About 1910 cars began coming into use so roads had to be improved.

As improving cars demanded improving roads, Mr. Rong got a job doing roadwork, building, grading, and maintenance. Fred remembers 'the big book' in which his father kept records of the men working for him, wages paid, roadwork scheduled, and all the other information necessary for efficient operation.

Fred described his father's section of road as "past our place, past the Adams Ranch, through Devil's Gulch, up Coalbank Hill." Coalbank Hill, he explained, was rather steep, with a sharp turn toward the top. Two or three fellows, he heard, ran off that turn after cars came into use.

Although deer were scarce in Dawson County during a period between the main influx of homesteaders and more recent years, they were still in plentiful supply when the Rong family came to Montana in the early 1900's. Fred recalls hearing his father talk about how the deer would graze right with the cattle at first. They changed their habits, however, as the country became more thickly settled and they became the target of more hunters.

The ten years following the Rongs' arrival in the Treasure State brought many changes to an almost primitive land. Homesteaders flocked in by the hundreds, and soon many homestead sections were being called upon to support as many as four families to a section. They hadn't learned yet that four sections to a family was a more likely balance.

Mr. Rong engaged in farming, but he also ran cattle and horses so had a couple sections for pasture up Morgan Creek, west of the now-Highway 16. The horses were very important to his farming operations for about the first twenty years in this area, prior to the purchase of his first tractor.

While they used horsepower in the flesh they farmed about 100 acres. They'd use three horses on the plow; four on the drag*; three on the drill; four on the binder; two on the mower. (Not all at the same time, of course!) They started out with just a few horses but kept raising colts – always breaking a horse or two or more – until they had thirty head in the early thirties. In 1934 they sold all but five head.

After they bought their tractor in 1924, they increased their tillage to 300 acres. "It was kind of comical," Fred reflected, "to run that little Fordson around the field." Comical or not, the tractor increased their efficiency considerably.

About 1916 Mr. Rong built a new house and married a new wife. Daughter Carrie had been the principal housekeeper after her mother's passing until her father's second marriage. In contrast to the little three-room log house, which they had first built on the homestead, the new house was a frame building with eight rooms. Fred's uncle was a carpenter, and it was he who built the big house. The new house was about a ten-minute walk from the log dwelling, and it was about a year before they had outbuildings ready for use at the new site so they got plenty of exercise going back and forth for the milking and other chores. They tore down the log house and used the materials to make a barn closer to the new house. The new calf barn was solid, built out of railroad ties. They dug a trench and stood the ties upright, side by side. With the building of the new house, everything else had to be built new, too.

The winter of '16 was a hard one, and Rongs had to buy hay to feed their 150 head of cattle. Montana hay simply wasn't available so they had to buy North Dakota hay. The hay was made from slough grass, and its thick stems made it hard for the cattle to eat. And that was no North Dakota joke!

One spring as the ice broke up they beheld a most unusual sight. They lived about half-a-mile from the river and had spent the forenoon working in the timber at the river's edge. When they went home for dinner, they saw nothing unusual about the river, but about one o'clock they noticed that it looked 'funny'.

They walked down to 'Camp 6' (the Indians name for the place; the flat above the house was 'Camp 5') so they could see better and saw the ice rolling toward them. As they watched they saw a sheepwagon coming down the river with the rolling ice! There was no one with it – just the wagon. They heard later that the herder had drowned, but of him they saw nothing. Another time they saw the horse that rode a cake of ice down the river during a spring breakup. The horse was rescued farther down the river.

In 1936 Fred's father died. At the time four of them were still living at 'home' – Fred, Jim, Carrie, and their oldest brother, Amedoce. In 1938 F.L. Gabert bought the place, and the Rongs moved closer to town, out by the old fairgrounds. The four, although they moved about in the years that followed, stayed together until one by one, they passed on. Now Fred is the only one remaining, and lives in the General Nursing Home.

Fred philosophically observed, "When I was a kid, I thought everything was just fun, but when I got older I found out if you want something you have to work for it." – a lesson worthy of passing on to each succeeding generation!

'Ford' of the early settlers, 1917

Mrs. G.P. (Aurilla Drummond) Drowley

April 1966

It was in the little cow town of Terry that Mrs. Aurilla Drummond Drowley, one of the present directors of the First National Bank, first saw the light of day. Her father, J.W. Drummond, was one of Terry's early pioneers

Drummond was a native of Iowa, but, of an adventuresome nature, he headed west when he was only seventeen. In 1877 he, accompanied by two brothers named Carter, set out from Iowa with an ox team and buckboard*. At Cheyenne they decided they'd gone far enough so they stopped there and found jobs. Young Drummond spent the next two or three years in the vicinity of Cheyenne and Laramie, working with cattle. From there he went to Buffalo and joined the 71 outfit. About the time he was old enough to vote the Flying E, under Fred Hess, took him on as foreman.

The Murphy Brothers, along in 1890 or '91, bought the Flying E, 76, and the LX Bar outfits and consolidated them under the LX Bar brand. They moved a large part of their stock to Montana, and Mr. Drummond was made general manager with headquarters at Terry, Montana in 1891.

In Terry he became acquainted with another pioneer family, the C.E. Jouberts – and their daughter, Pauline. The Jouberts, along with two other French families from Wisconsin, Mr. And Mrs. George Landre and Mr. and Mrs. Lanscigne, Sr., had come as far west as the Northern Pacific Railroad could bring them and a little farther besides. They didn't stop at Fallon where the N.P. rails ended but went on to Terry.

Besides operating a farm a mile east of Terry, the Jouberts ran a hotel, offering room and board in Terry. With the paucity of feminine citizens on the frontier and the corresponding lack of housekeepers and cooks, boarding houses offered the predominately male population about the only alternative to trying to survive on their own cooking and to keep their quarters 'hoed out'.

In 1893 Drummond abandoned the bachelor ranks and married the Jouberts' daughter, Pauline. He continued as foreman of the Murphy Cattle Company, now called the LX Bar. Their range was along the Yellowstone Valley and benches from Powder River to Sandstone and Fallon Creeks, until they sold out their entire holdings about 1897.

After the Murphy Brothers sold out, Drummond thought it was a good time to see how things were going back in his native state so he and Pauline spent the year of 1898 in Sioux City, Iowa, where he worked as stock inspector. Returning to Terry he was soon in the cattle business again but not to the exclusion of other interests. He engaged in the hotel business and also operated a stage line between Terry and Sandstone.

With all of his business interests he still found time for community service. He served one term as deputy sheriff of Custer County just prior to the creation of Prairie County. Mr. Drummond also served several terms as a school board member, starting when Terry School District No. 5 was a part of Custer County.

During the time he was serving as a trustee the 'new' Terry schoolhouse (while Terry was still a part of Custer County) was completed. On that occasion the Terry Tribune carried an article on Drummond, commenting, "Naturally public-spirited, as a member of the board of school trustees Mr. Drummond was one of the first to take up the matter of better school facilities and has been untiring in his efforts to push the project since it was first taken in hand. He is as proud of the new schoolhouse as if he were personally proprietor of it, and while one of the most genial and good-natured citizens of the village, some of his friends are jokingly inclined to remark that the only possible instance in twenty years of 'Jim's' Terry residence that they have been able to notice his needing a larger hat was when the new school house was completed. By some he is considered the best looking member of the board – and he has certainly deserved credit as one of the most faithful and efficient."

The Drummonds were the parents of five children, among them Aurilla Drummond Drowley. At the time Aurilla was born the Drummonds were living on the Kempton Ranch, and it was there on the ranch that she made her entrance into this world.

Aurilla wanted to take a commercial course when she finished elementary school but no such course was available in Terry so she came to Glendive and stayed with her aunt, Mrs. Warren Voorhies, and attended Dawson County High School where Mr. G.G. Hoole taught a business course. After her graduation she was employed in Glendive and on June 23, 1918, she married Gilbert P. Drowley. Mr. Drowley was associated with Glendive's First National Bank.

Mrs. Drowley observed that three generations of her family are buried in the Glendive cemetery – her grandparents, Mr. and Mrs. Joubert (the Jouberts moved to Glendive in their later years, purchasing and operating the rooming house that was later bought by the Fowlers); her parents, Mr. and Mrs. Drummond; and her husband, the late G.P. Drowley. Four generations of her family are in her house almost every day – Mrs. Drowley, her daughter, granddaughter, and a great granddaughter.

Some pieces of her furniture go back several generations, too. She has some tables and chairs that were sent up the Yellowstone by steamboat before the railroad came through.

Mrs. Drowley is perhaps the only woman living – certainly one of the very few! – to have been 'baby-sat' by the famed Calamity Jane. One day while their mother was gone, Aurilla and her brother were playing around the windmill. He told her to stick her finger through one of the holes in the pump rod so, since he was a year older, she innocently did what he told her. The windmill chose that particular instant to turn, starting the pump and breaking her finger.

When Mrs. Drummond came home, no less a personage than Calamity Jane was trying to comfort Aurilla, walking the floor with her and singing "There'll be a Hot Time in the Old Town Tonight!" – probably the nearest thing to a lullaby she knew.

Although G.P. Drowley was not one of the founders of the bank, he was associated with the bank from the time he came to Glendive in 1916, twelve years after it opened for business, until his death in 1955. Mr. Drowley was born in Caledonia, Minnesota in 1894 but later moved with his parents to North Dakota. After his graduation from high school he attended Grand Forks Business College, then started his banking career at Sarles in Northeastern North Dakota. He made rapid progress after joining the Glendive bank where he was elected assistant cashier in January 1920, a director in 1932, cashier in 1942, and president in 1946. He was the third man to serve as president in the entire history of the First National Bank.

In addition to his many years of service in civic affairs, he was active for a number of years in the Montana Banking Association. He was president of that organization in 1952 and in 1953-54, he served as vice president for Montana of American Bankers Association.

At Mr. Drowley's instigation, the bank in its fifty-year celebration held an open house, presenting to every woman visitor a rose, to every man a cigar, and souvenirs to all. It also exhibited a current collection of the Federal Reserve Bank of Minneapolis. This consisted of samples of all paper money in use in the United States since the earliest days. In speaking of the bank's growth Mr. Drowley said, "This growth would not have been possible without the faith and friendship of people in this area. Our open house was planned as a means of expressing at least partial appreciation for this."

In addition to his major business connection, Mr. Drowley was a director of the Glendive Building and Loan Association. He was a member of the Glendive City Council for twenty years and served for many years on the library board. Very active in the Glendive Chamber of Commerce, he served as director and treasurer for many years.

A member and past commander of the American Legion post, he long held the office of department finance officer. He was a member of Glendive Lodge No. 1324, Benevolent and Protective Order of the Elks, and had served that lodge as exalted ruler and secretary. He was also a member of the lodge of the Free and Accepted Masons, the higher bodies of Masonry, and Al Bedoo Temple, Ancient Arabic Order of Nobles of the Mystic Shrine at Billings. A communicant of Glendive Congregational Church, he served on its board of trustees.

Soon after his marriage to Aurilla Drummond in 1918, Mr. Drowley entered the Service and was sent to Fort Lewis where he was stationed until cessation of hostilities. He returned to the bank as soon as he was discharged and continued with it until his sudden death on November 24, 1955.

Mr. and Mrs. Drowley had one child, a daughter June, who also is one of the present bank directors.

Pete Boje

August – November 1972

Pete Boje is one of those old timers who knew my parents well, but I had never met him until last week when he was in my cousin's home. When I entered the room and she asked him if he knew me, he looked searchingly a moment, then ventured, "You must be Menno Mullet's daughter; you look just like your mother." Others may not see the resemblance, but he guessed correctly.

Mr. Boje, a 'young' eighty, is a little hard of hearing and evidently didn't catch my married name nor just why I wanted to interview him for after we talked a bit, he inquired, "Are you going to put this in the Glendive paper?" "Yes," I explained again, "in the 'As I Remember' column." "Do you write that now?" he asked. "I have written it ever since it was started," I replied. He looked a bit puzzled as he pursued, "I thought a – a – Kauffman wrote that." We assured him he was correct, and as the light dawned he laughed, "I guess I was still thinking Mullet."

Pete Boje first came to Montana early in the winter of 1909. Two of his brothers, Louis and Adolph, already had homesteads in Dawson County, but Pete was the 'kid' brother and wasn't old enough yet to homestead.

Louis had come to the Treasure State from Nebraska in 1906, and Adolph had come a year or so later. Adolph expected to join Louis here when he came, but when he arrived, he couldn't find Louis.

He sent a post card home – a post card with a picture of Glendive's Grace Hospital – reporting that he couldn't find Louie. By the time his card arrived, home folks back in Nebraska had had word that Louis was in the Grace Hospital with typhoid fever.

Christmas of 1908 Adolph and Louis went back to Nebraska for the holidays, and Pete, who had been shucking corn in Illinois, was also home for Christmas. Even though he wasn't old enough to homestead, he wanted to come to Montana too, so when his older brothers returned to their homesteads after New Year's Day, Pete was with them.

Sixteen-year-old Pete's ambition was to be a cowboy, but his brothers had other ideas. "They were afraid I would break my neck," Pete explained, "so they wouldn't let me go out on a ranch." Instead he wound up cooking for the boys that spring and summer.

Both Louis and Adolph had claims in the Bloomfield area. Louie's claim was two miles east, one-and-one-half miles south of Bloomfield (Charles Senner now farms that land; no one lives on the place). Adolph was located one mile east and two miles south of Bloomfield. Where Adolph's little 12'x14' shack stood, there are now two houses: his widow lives in one, his son Floyd lives with his wife and family in the other.

Pete came by train with his brothers to Glendive, but that was the end of mechanical transportation. From there on to the homesteads they were on their own – their own feet, that is. Some of the homesteaders were freighting to Glendive, but they'd have a load going out, too, so the three Bojes walked behind the wagons the thirty miles to the homesteads. Sometimes going downhill they would jump on the wagon and ride awhile. They left Glendive well before sunup, but it was long after dark when they reached Adolph's shack.

Because of homestead regulations Adolph and Louis Boje each had to have a dwelling on his claim, but those dwellings didn't have to be very elaborate to qualify. Theirs weren't. Not all, but many of the homesteaders just put up tar paper shacks – 2x4's with ship lap nailed on the outside and tar paper over that. On the inside of the 2x4's – nothing. Such was Adolph's shack where Pete would spend the next eight or nine months.

How would you like to spend a Montana winter in that kind of house? You might even decide we still have winters "like we used to have!" If you heated your house the way they heated theirs, you might be more persuaded. Adolph's little cook stove served to heat the shack as well as to cook their meals.

Forerunner of the later wood-coal ranges, the stove had a fire box with a top for surface cooking, and it even had an oven – for baking biscuits. The fire box was really too small to adequately heat the 12'x14' shack during the cold of winter, especially a shack with no inside walls, but Pete assures us they didn't pay much attention to that. On the contrary, he says, they enjoyed it. Surely that kind of environment would be easier on three bachelors than on a family with small children.

For a roof, many of these homestead shacks had just a 2x8 in the middle for a ridge pole and the boards bent over it, but Adolph's shack had a peaked roof. Although Louie had a shack of his own and slept there enough to meet homestead requirements, he generally ate his meals at Adolph's, and it was at Adolph's Pete spent most of his time during his first year in Montana.

Furnishings in the little shack were as simple as the shack itself. Much of it was improvised from wooden boxes and packing cases. Wooden boxes were used much more then than they are now, Pete pointed out, and were easily obtained. They used boxes for chairs. They used boxes for cupboards. The table was a simple affair they had tacked together – probably from a packing case – and nailed to the wall. They could fold it up against the wall when it was not in use and make a little more floor space available, and they could let it down when they needed it. The bed was on a frame nailed to the wall. That, with the cook stove mentioned before, just about made up the furniture in the little homestead shack. But it was enough.

When 'spring's work' started on the homestead, Pete found himself chief cook. Meal planning wasn't too much of a problem for him, he explains, because they either had (dried) beans and baking powder biscuits or baking powder biscuits and beans.

Sometimes when Adolph and Louie were gone Pete would wander over to Jake Mullet's homestead on the quarter section* just east of Adolph's and follow Jake around. One spring morning he was alone so he went over to Jake's, but no one was home there, either. Jake had planted potatoes and Pete found, tossed out on the ground, the little potatoes that Jake had thrown away. Pete carefully gathered up the scrubby little marbles, took them home, and scrubbed them up for dinner. When his brothers came, they were surprised to find potatoes for a meal and curious as to where he had got his treasure. Potatoes during the winter and spring months were too expensive to buy so these were a welcome change from the beans and biscuit fare.

When Pete Boje came to Montana in 1909 to spend some time with his brothers, Louis and Adolph had each broken ten acres on their homesteads as regulations required. In addition to their own, they were also farming Frank Coryell's land.

Coryell had come to the Bloomfield (Montana) area with some of the earliest immigrants from Bloomfield, Nebraska. He was already set up for farming with perhaps 80-100 acres broken and the equipment to work it. At this time, however, he was driving stage between Bloomfield and Glendive. He'd make the trip into Glendive one day, then back to Bloomfield the next, providing mail and passenger service every other day. Mr. Boje suggests that maybe that's where Amtrak got the idea!

Be that as it may, his stage job didn't leave much time for working his land so he made the deal with Louie and Adolph to do his farming. Pete isn't sure whether they bought his equipment or whether he furnished it as part of the deal, but they used it on his land and theirs. They did buy four horses from Coryell.

When the Boje boys filed their claims, they could only get one quarter section of land, but while Pete was with them, a new law was passed allowing half a section. Those who had already homesteaded could file on an adjoining quarter if one was still unclaimed. Adolph's section was all settled, but one quarter in Louie's was 'up for grabs' when the law was passed.

There was no radio or TV to flash the news as soon as the law was passed, not even a telephone, so out in the Bloomfield country they hadn't received word of any such privilege. Louie however, just happened to be in town when the new regulation went into effect. He noticed people sitting by the courthouse, waiting for it to open, so when he found out why they were waiting, he joined the crowd and waited, too. As a result he was able to get the quarter just north of his original homestead.

Much of that winter Louie and Adolph, Pete with them, were hauling lumber for the Crockett house that was being built east of Bloomfield. In contrast to many of the homestead shacks, the Crockett house was a real house for that time. (This house has been moved to a location west of Glendive where it still serves as a family dwelling.)

Each trip to Glendive with the team and wagon for lumber called for two days. They'd go into town and load up the first day, then haul the load out the second day. They'd carry drinking water along in a canvas bag, and their lunch usually consisted of hard-tack and the old faithful beans. For the return trip their menu was likely to be sardines and crackers – sometimes a bottle of beer.

They didn't frequent hotels when they made those trips; instead they took along a tarp and a roll of bedding and slept outside.

The provisions on their cupboard shelves back at the homestead weren't much more elaborate than the lunches they carried on their freighting trips: flour, baking powder, soda, salt, Pennick syrup, (no butter) and, of course, dried beans.

Pete Boje well remembers when Jens Scarpholt and Louie Swanson arrived in the Bloomfield country with their oxen. He thought they were Indians. The boys were always kidding him about Indians coming, and he had never seen oxen around there before, so what else could it be? One of the men had two oxen, the other four. Pete was home alone when he happened to look toward the south and see the strange cavalcade slowly winding its way down off the 'Table'. "I figured they would sure get my scalp!" Pete laughs now, but it was no laughing matter then.

When they pulled up – the main road then was a mile east of where it is now, and went right past Adolph's – he was relieved to see that they were white men, and they only asked for water for their oxen. At this time Adolph did have a well on his place – Pete had helped with the digging of it earlier that spring – and it was enough to supply them for household purposes but not enough for watering livestock. However, he told them they were not far from Thirteen Mile Creek, and there was plenty of water there for their teams so they went on. No Indians ever did come around while Pete was there.

One of the events of the winter of 1909 which stands out in Pete's memory was Grandma Chaney's funeral. There were no church houses built yet in that frontier community so the funeral was held in the Red Top schoolhouse. Already, although the community was scarcely five years old, a cemetery had been started on the hill north of the schoolhouse.

The schoolhouse had no piano or organ so Pete helped Art Kitchen haul the piano with team and wagon from the Bloomfield school the five miles to Red Top. There was no minister in the community yet, either, so N.B. Sackett, one of the homesteaders, conducted the service.

Red Top was about the center of the Amish community, and they all came to share this time of sorrow with the Missourians who had come to Montana less than two years before. Pete notes that this was his first contact with the Amish and admits that he 'looked and looked' at their unique appearance – hooks and eyes instead of buttons on their clothing, their beards, the type of hair cuts. But he soon became acquainted with them and accustomed to their appearance. Later he became good friends with the boys and often accompanied them to church. They held their worship services in their homes, then all joined together for a meal following the service.

There were a lot of young fellows in the Bloomfield area during the early homestead days, and one of their favorite forms of recreation – during the summer months, that is, was playing ball. When Pete Boje joined his brothers in 1909, he joined in playing ball, too, any time he had a chance.

Some of the grandsons of some of the players on that original Bloomfield team still get together to play in the summer. Some of the sons and daughters can be found in the crowd, watching, but those first players are about gone. Pete is one of the few – perhaps the only one – left. Pete used to be either pitcher or shortstop. Even now, he confesses, when he gets a ball in his hand, he can feel how it should go, but at eighty his arm just doesn't work the way it did at seventeen.

One Sunday afternoon he and the other fellows had walked into Bloomfield to play ball. They played until it was too dark to see the ball, then started discussing the circus somebody had heard would be in Glendive the next day. The upshot of their discussion was that they decided they would all go to town and see it.

They were afoot at the ball game, so they walked down to Mose Mullet's place first, ate up all the beans and biscuits he had, then walked on over to Adolph's and ate the beans and biscuits he fixed up. Then they were ready to start for town so they hitched up the team, piled into the lumber wagon, and headed for Glendive. They drove all night and got there in time for the circus the next morning. After spending the day and the evening, too, at the circus, they decided to sleep in town instead of driving another night.

Frank Coryell, the Bloomfield stage driver, had a stall at the Goodrich-Call Lumber Yard where he kept his horses on his nights in town. When the homesteaders came to town, they'd often sleep at the lumber yard – in the office if it was cold, outside when it was warm. That way they wouldn't have to get a hotel room.

The Goodrich-Call Lumber Yard had been the Douglas-Meade Lumber Yard. It was located about where Kampschrors* and the city parking lot are now, across the street from the Douglas-Meade Department Store. The Douglas-Meade yard, in addition to selling lumber and related merchandise, sold Studebaker wagons and later had the agency for E.M.F. cars when they came out.

After the circus, the night was hot so the boys rolled out their bed rolls beside the barn. They were young and sleeping hard after two full days with no sleep the night between and were totally unaware of the storm rolling up. Coryell woke up, though, and tried to rouse them, shouting, "Boys, get up! There's a storm coming." There was more to it than that, Mr. Boje recalls, that he felt need not be quoted verbatim. Mr. Coryell finally succeeded in getting them awake so they all grabbed their covers and ran for the shelter of the barn where they spent the remainder of the night. Next morning they got up early and headed back for the homesteads.

Pete Boje stayed with his brothers until after grain shocking that fall of 1909, but he didn't wait for the threshing. His brother Bill and Mel Roberts had come out on the train about that time to look over the homestead situation so when they went back to Nebraska, he went along with them. He was still four years short of homestead age so there wasn't much chance he could get started farming for himself for awhile.

266

Bill had tried for a homestead in South Dakota but wasn't very happy with what he found there. They drew numbers for the claims available, and when his number failed to win him a claim, he bought a relinquishment from a fellow who did get one. He moved his family – in a covered wagon – to South Dakota, only to find when he got there that his land was all rocks. He suspected then that he knew why the first fellow relinquished! He, too, decided to let it go and went back to Nebraska.

Back in Nebraska Bill got a job as road boss, building roads for the county. Pete had worked for him two weeks before they went back to Nebraska in the fall of 1909, and explains, "He was boss over me, anyway."

Building road grades then was quite different from the present operation. They did all their dirt moving with horse-drawn slips. They had two slips so they used four horses. Pete worked for Bill until time for corn shucking, then he went to Illinois and Bill moved to Montana.

Bill hadn't been able to locate a homestead in Montana on his first try so he bought a quarter* of railroad land. Then in 1910, after he moved here, he did find a homestead about ten miles south of Richey. Adolph and Louie bought his railroad land, and Bill moved onto his homestead to begin proving up.

When Bill first moved to Dawson County he lived with Adolph, but then he made a dugout in a coulee, put a roof over it, and that was home until he got a house built. Now days a complete set of farm buildings may go begging for occupancy because the man farming the land has his own home on another farm – or even in town. In 1910 the story was different and chances were slim that you would find any land with vacant buildings on it.

It wasn't until the fall of 1916 that Pete was able to put roots down in Montana. In the intervening years he had been 'working out' in the Midwest and saving his money to buy land. He came to Montana from Eagle Grove, Iowa, in June and worked for his brother Bill for a couple of months, then bought 160 acres of land four miles south of Richey. In the fall he went back to Iowa to pick corn, then the last day of February 1917, he and a pal of his, Arthur Carpenter (Carpy for short) loaded an immigrant car and began their journey to Montana.

Of the preparations for their trip to Montana, Pete in his own words, relates, "I had $1,400 saved up to start on, and I bought the land on a ten-year contract from the Northern Pacific Land Company: a tenth down, and one-tenth payment every year for ten years. It looked easy, but it wasn't easy – not for me at least.

"I made a deal with Carpy to come with me so he bought three horses, and I bought a team of white mules and a horse, making six head all together. I also bought a wagon, three sets of harness and horse collars, and an old sulky breaking plow* in Iowa.

"I also bought enough barb wire to fence in my 160 acres of land, open prairie in those days. I bought a sixty-bushel load of ear corn in Iowa to feed our horses on the way out in the immigrant car and here. We bought oats and hay after we got out here to feed.

"Well, we loaded our immigrant car with what we had and our six head of horses and mules. We had plenty of room for our horses and feed and water barrels. We really felt proud and had lots of hopes for going west and getting a home of our own. We just knew we could make it here in Montana. Someone wrote in big letters on our immigrant car, "MONTANA OR BUST."

"The hardest thing was to leave our friends and girlfriends back in the East and come out here to start 'batching' in the open prairie when neither of us had even learned to boil water – ha.

"Well, we were in St. Paul March the first and were delayed there for fifty-two hours in the Railway Transfer Yard, waiting to have our livestock or horses inspected. We just could not get transferred to the Great Northern Railway until they got us switched up to the Transfer Office, they told us.

"It seemed like the whole yard was nothing but immigrant cars, just lots of trainloads of immigrants and seemed like most were going to Montana, a few to Canada and a few to North Dakota.

"It was a real mess there. We tried to tell them that we had plenty of room in our car and plenty of feed and water for our horses, but to no avail. We decided to walk out of there and try to find a liquor joint and restaurant to get us a warm meal to eat. We found one not too far away; had a hot meal, and then we bought two quarts of whiskey to take along."

When Pete and Carpy got back to the transfer yard, they rounded up the yardmaster and promised that if he would come with them to their car they would give him a drink, and he would see that they had plenty of room and water and feed so that it wasn't necessary for them to unload to feed.

When he looked in their car, he agreed, and, after a big drink, filled out some papers for them to take to the transfer office. It didn't take long to get out of there after that, so that was once, Pete opined, that a little whiskey went a long way.

They had plenty to eat in their car so they did not starve and had a good bed with plenty of bedding and horse blankets to keep them warm, even if it was cold and their food froze a bit. They had a little kerosene heater with them, but it had to be watched, as it would turn itself up. At nights they turned it out and let things freeze. "We didn't mind it," Pete assures us; "we were both pretty rugged in those days and could take it."

It was a slow, long trip; nine days and nights to get to Richey – but they rode in their immigrant car all the way. They were delayed twenty-four hours in Snoden because of a train wreck on the Richey branch, but luckily there was a restaurant not too far away so they were able to get some hot meals.

They arrived in Richey about 10:30 p.m. First thing they did was look up a livery stable for their horses. The train had left them close to the depot rather than at the stockyards, but the snow was so deep that the horses could jump right out of the car into a snow bank. The horses were glad to get out of the car but surprised to hit a snow bank.

Temperatures were cold when Pete Boje and 'Carpy' reached Richey, but Pete assures us it was mighty nice to know they were in Richey. Next morning, as soon as they had fed their horses and eaten their own breakfast, they started to unload their ear corn onto their wagon.

Soon a man came along and asked where they were going. They told him they were going to Bill Boje's, but he protested, "Boys, you can't get out there with a wagon. It just can't be done." He told them where his ranch was (it was Kelley, a garage man in Richey besides a rancher) and offered to let them go get one of his sleds to use. Pete figured that with six horses, they should be able to pull a wagon through the snow, but Kelley pointed out to them, "No, you will just spoil the sled tracks. You will meet lots of loads of wheat coming in, and the ones going out of town have to give them the road so they don't upset."

Instead of borrowing Kelley's sled they thought they would just take their horses out to Bill's, but then they found Bill in town – he was kind of looking for them but didn't know just when they would get in. They loaded the corn on his sled, and Bill rode his jack mule, tailing the other five behind him.

They did meet a lot of loads on the way out that day, and one of them was Mr. Milt Hill from the Bloomfield country. He was so interested to see a load of good old Iowa ear corn – nice, big ears – that they let him have a few ears to take home with him.

They got to Bill's all right, without upsetting the load of corn. Bill had a good, steady team of horses, and they were adjusted to all the snow so next day they borrowed his sled, took Pete's team of mules, and went back to Richey. They made two trips, a load of wheat to town each time, a load from their immigrant car on the return trip.

They continued hauling the next few days. As soon as their car was unloaded they started hauling lumber for the 12'x14' shack they would build on Pete's place and the 16'x28' barn. 'Carpy' was a carpenter in more than name so, with Bill and Pete, they 'slapped' things together in a hurry. As Pete remembers, they stayed at Bill's about a week until they could move into their own shack and start 'batching'.

Before they left Iowa, Pete's brother-in-law had given them two 250-pound hogs to butcher and had cured the meat for them so, while it lasted, they had pork to eat with their pancakes and beans and biscuits.

To build their house they had cleared a place of snow, and when the snow was gone, they found they had built right in the middle of the road or trail going to Richey. At first people simply turned out for their house, right in front of it, but when they had their flax crops in and the 160 acres fenced, travelers had to make a different trail to Richey.

As soon as the ground thawed in the spring, they started breaking sod. They had a fourteen-inch breaking plow they could ride, and brother Bill let them use his walking sod breaking plow, also fourteen-inch. That meant one of them could ride, but one of them had to walk.

Pete was, to use his expression, "brought up behind a walking plow," so he was the one who did most of the walking. Carpy was a town boy and had had only one year of experience on a farm so Pete let him use the riding plow.

269

After Pete Boje and Carpy had their 1917 crop planted they turned their attention to building a fence around Pete's new farm. It had to be a good fence as they were in the middle of the prairie in free-range country. There were many range horses and range cattle running around and rubbing on the fence posts, especially in the spring of the year when some were lousy and itchy.

The fence built, Pete and Carpy went to Glendive to try for summer jobs with the Northern Pacific Railroad. There were openings just then for firemen. Carpy failed to pass his physical examination required for firemen so he got a job in the roundhouse, but Pete passed and was sent on a trial run to Forsyth.

He soon found there was more involved in being a fireman than he realized. He says that he thought he could scoop as much coal as any man, but they didn't tell him before hand that he'd have to scoop left-handed.

When the engineer relayed that bit of information to him, he exclaimed, "You might as well let me out of here as I just can't scoop left-handed and gauge the scoop to hit that little hole." The engineer assured him he would learn, but Pete was not optimistic. Besides gauging the scoop to hit that little hole, he had to place each scoop full in a different place: four scoops full on each side of the firebox and two on each end, as he remembers. Just learning to stand up in that moving, pulling locomotive was a job, he declares. They had a very heavy load so it, to quote him, "Wiggled around quite a bit."

Although he 'worked like a horse', he simply could not keep the steam up so the regular fireman had to take over – shake the grates, dump the ashes, look after the water. It looked easy for him, but it all had to be learned.

A new fireman had to make three student trips and be O.K.'d by three engineers before he drew any pay. The engineer couldn't O.K. him on the trip to Forsyth but did on the return trip. He urged Pete to stay with the job when Pete declared his intention of quitting, assuring him he had done better than any student he had had on the first trip.

Back at the roundhouse, black with coal dust, galled from sweat, Pete took a bath and changed into clean clothes, then went uptown to eat. Who should he run into but Brother Louis. Louis took a dim view of Pete's railroading ambitions, insisting he belonged on the farm. Nevertheless, Pete let the call boy know where they were staying that night.

Lo and behold, at three that very morning, the call boy came knocking for him to come to work. He tried to get up, but he was so stiff and sore he could hardly move so he told the call boy he was giving up trying to be a fireman. There were no other job openings at the roundhouse so Pete went home with Louis and helped him and Adolph on their homesteads.

Carpy worked for the N. P. until harvest, then came out to help get their crop harvested. It had been a woefully dry summer, and there wasn't much crop to get. Brother Bill had a grain binder so they worked with him. Pete and Bill took turns running the binder, changing horses so they could keep the binder going long hours.

Pete took the early morning shift, then Bill would run it from about ten in the morning until four in the afternoon, when Pete would take over again and run until dark. Carpy did the shocking, with Bill and Pete helping him when they weren't on the binder. When they had their crop all harvested, they found they had 115 bushels of flax from their 117 acres.

Back in 1916 and '17 Pete, in Iowa, "had received lots of literature from the N.P., advertising their land for sale with lots of nice pictures of farms in Montana, all built up, with groves around the farmsteads and nice big grain fields that really showed off nice."

With a couple brothers out here who had had some very good crops and a good start right off the bat, coupled with what Pete himself had seen when he was here in 1909 – weed-free prairies, nice, clean stubble in the fall – little wonder the literature did its work. The only trouble was, his fields in the fall of 1917 didn't look much like those in the pictures.

After their meager harvest Brother Bill suggested that renting a coal mine two miles southeast of his place might yield them some cash so they tried it, but business was slow in a dry year, even though they sold their coal for a dollar a ton. There were a lot of places where people could just pull in and mine their own coal to heat their homes, and they couldn't afford to buy much. Coal was one advantage this country offered the early settlers!

Also that fall they made a deal to rent Hannah Jurgensen Lockhart's homestead, and they moved into the house there, only about 100 rods from Bill's. It had forty acres broken on it. Her brother had broken it with a team of bulls. Bill had loaned him one bull, and he had bought another from Mr. Cole at Bloomfield to use on the walking sod breaking plow.

Hannah, one of three sisters who homesteaded and taught school in this new country, was a sister to Bill's wife so the Bill Boje homestead was a gathering place for schoolteachers. Each teacher had a saddle horse to provide her with transportation. On Friday after school they would ride to Bill and Anna's, stay until Sunday afternoon, then ride back to their schools. Bill had a big Buick car and often he'd take them all to town on Saturday.

One Friday two of the teachers started for Bill's after school, but darkness overtook them, and they got lost on the open prairie. Not many fences (or roads) to guide them in those days. They pulled the saddles off their horses, used their saddle blankets for beds, tied their horses to their own feet, and slept on the ground until daylight. Then they could see Bill and Anna's house only a mile west of where they had spent the night.

The year 1918 the Lockhart place would provide Carpy's share, and Bill would get the harvest from his land. That fall their wheat made eight bushels to the acre, and Carpy's flax made four bushels to the acre. Not so bad that year. Then after harvest they went back to Iowa and got a job picking corn so made a little money on that.

"They were really going good in Iowa those World War I years," Pete explained. "They got good prices for their grain and hogs and had big crops so the farmers were really going high, wide, and handsome – and a little bit too wild, I thought," he added.

271

"Everybody seemed to have plenty of money – all but me, who came back from Montana broke. All my old buddies were wearing silk shirts and some even had Model T Fords, and I had to keep my nose to the grindstone to make my payments on the Montana land I had bought and pay my taxes on it. Our taxes here in the Richey School District were plenty high, I thought – almost $100 a year on my 160 acres, as Richey had built a new, big brick schoolhouse."

Pete admits he was tempted to throw it all up, but his brothers coaxed him to hang onto his land. It wasn't easy for a young man to quit his buddies and girl friends and keep saving to make his land payments, but he did.

He sometimes wonders if he did the right thing by not getting married and having a family, but in his early teens he had worked for a family who had six children and some sickness and were very hard up. When the work was all done in the fall, there wasn't enough money left to pay the hired man. "And who," Pete asks, "would take the food out of a hungry child's mouth? Not me. So I didn't get all my pay I had coming."

"I figured I would not get married 'til I had a home of my own so I could feed my wife and kids and give them a good home. Well, that time was slow in coming as age doesn't wait for anyone." (Pete was sixty when he married a widow, Tillie Graber Wienke.)

Carpy and Pete spent the winter of 1918-19 in Iowa. In the spring Pete came back to Montana alone and put in the crop on both places. The last part of May Brother Adolph persuaded him to go along back to Iowa for a visit. Pete protested that he had no money, but Adolph was planning to drive his little Baby Buick and insisted Pete go along.

Together they dug out a spring on the Lockhart place so the horses would have water, and Adolph put his horses in there, too. Bill's wife and two daughters decided to go along to visit relatives, but Bill stayed to "keep the home fires burning." When they left June 4, some of the early seeding looked very good, even though there had been no rain.

They didn't have highways then like we have now. They took the old Yellowstone Trail to Aberdeen, and the only road markers were rocks painted yellow. When you found a yellow rock, you knew you were on the right trail.

In the Dakotas they ran into lots of rain and found swamps full of water and mud holes where the road was supposed to be. That meant detouring and staying overnight here and there.

"There have been lots of changes in highways and cars since that time," Pete reminds us. "It's almost unbelievable, how far we have come in our short life time, when we stop to think back."

In one place the trail was up hill and washed out so they had to straddle the wash. They were all having a good time, and Pete guesses that Adolph was doing too much talking and joking and not watching the road because all at once they slipped off the trail and got high centered with all four wheels a foot off the ground.

They had brought along a new shovel so now the shovel was put to work (so were Pete and Adolph). They had to dig the car down for maybe 200 feet back down the hill and then start over. But they finally got to Bazille Mills, Nebraska, where their mother lived. They spent a whole week going to Nebraska, and now they make the trip (about 800 miles) in one good, long day.

They had a good time visiting, but it was quite a blow to Pete, who used to have plenty of money, to come back from Montana broke, especially when his buddies still had plenty.

About the first of July they got a letter from Bill in Montana telling them to come back because everything was dried up, including their spring. Bill had to pump water by hand for their twelve horses out of a ninety-foot well – hard pumping. This was in addition to pumping water for his own horses and cattle.

They stayed and celebrated the Fourth of July, then headed back toward Montana. About twenty miles west of Huron Pete was driving – it was dark – and he missed a detour. He suddenly was confronted with a big lake over the road. He and Adolph were both dog-tired so they just settled down, right there by the lake, and went to sleep in the car.

The mosquitoes, Pete declares, were as big as wasps, and stung like wasps. They (Pete and Adolph, not the mosquitoes) had a big fur robe in the car, so they crawled under that and slept. It was a hot, sultry night, but they slept soundly until daybreak when they backtracked and found the detour.

Conditions in Montana were just as Bill had described them – "hot and drier than a bone." Another blow for Pete. Finally he decided he'd better move back to Iowa and work on a farm for $100 a month, then pick corn in the fall for twelve cents a bushel.

He was responsible to Lockharts for harvesting their place so he sold the crop to Frank Benes for $45 and Frank would give Mrs. Lockhart her share. Brother Louis loaned him a hundred dollars to rent an immigrant car to take his stock and equipment to Iowa to sell where he could get a good price, rather than taking a loss on it here. The wagon for which he had paid $90 before he came out, sold for $150 when he took it back to Iowa. The harnesses brought $50 more than he had paid for them new. He was able to get a job right away so it only took him a month to repay Louis.

Pete stayed in Iowa and worked out until 1924 before he tried in Montana again. By that time he was able to make a go of his farm. When he started he had hit three of the driest years Montana ever had – and that's dry!

"It was," Pete admits, "kind of a headache, all right, for a young man to run into that when he wanted to get a home of his own in the Wild, Wild West. But God was with me and gave me courage to carry on and to hang on to my land through thick and thin."

"Like the old saying goes, 'Stick through thick and thin, and you will come out slick as a pin!' So I am thankful to God for everything. In all things He has been good to us, letting us have the land to work and a good home to live in while here on earth."

Mrs. Ludvig (Annie Wold) Field

March 1965

Back in Black River Falls, Wisconsin and the surrounding countryside, a land agent was making his rounds, offering for sale Northern Pacific Railroad lands in Dawson County of Montana. It was the fall of 1908, and as an added inducement the agent was careful to point out that homestead land was also available so that the wise buyer who chose his location carefully could get a bonus of a quarter section free. As he extolled the latent possibilities in the virgin lands, just waiting to be developed by enterprising pioneers, he was able to interest a number of families, and about a dozen men went to Montana with him to inspect, buy, and file.

Among those who came was Richard A. Wold, father of Mrs. Ludvig Field. The tract of land which the agent was selling lay northeast of the present town of Lindsay. On December 3, 1908, Mr. Wold filed on a homestead in section four, township nineteen, range fifty-two, in addition to buying one quarter of land adjacent to the homestead and another quarter half-a-mile away. Mrs. Field's older brother, Johnny, is still living on his father's homestead.

Returning to Wisconsin, Mr. Wold made preparations to bring his family to Montana. The Wolds were not alone in their plans; a number of their neighbors were planning, too. In the spring nine immigrant cars were loaded, and the Wisconsin exodus began.

The Wolds had a silver collie named Trouble, and when the cattle and horses were taken from the farm, Trouble left, too. The family didn't have time to locate him before they left so Uncle Ole took the job upon himself. Word got around, and soon it was a big joke with the whole town that Uncle Ole was going up and down every street in Black River Falls looking for Trouble.

Mr. Wold accompanied the immigrant car (as did the other men) while Mrs. Wold and their seven children followed on the passenger train. Mrs. Field reflected that the Theodore Johnsons would have been the first of the Wisconsin contingent to reach their homestead, but there was no highway leading to Lindsay in those days so the Johnsons lost their way and had to camp overnight. That evening after dark the Wolds, bouncing along in their three-seated buggy, passed the Johnson camp about two miles from the homestead so Wolds arrived first.

By the time the family arrived, Mr. Wold had the barn framed up so they moved into it for temporary quarters. He hadn't had time to get the shingles on so for a substitute they stretched a tent over the top. That kept the rain out, but it didn't do a very good job keeping the cold out. Mrs. Field recalls that trying to bake bread while there was 'trying'. The bread baking was her job, and she just couldn't get the bread to rise in that cold 'bakery'. In a few weeks they had the house on the hill ready for occupancy, and it was with no regrets that they made the move.

The day after they reached the homestead sheep started moving off the range. They watched a band of Lindsay's sheep, about 5,000, come over the hill, moving slowly toward the south. They had a bench with a wash bowl on it outside the door, and as the band moved past a pet sheep deviated from the route to drink the water from the bowl. Before the day was over an even larger bunch, belonging to a rancher over in the Bad Route country, also trailed past, mute (or, knowing sheep, perhaps not so mute!) testimony to the arrival of the homesteader and the end of the open range.

As more settlers moved into the locality the need for a post office became apparent so an application was made and authorization granted. Mr. Wold was appointed postmaster, and Mrs. Wold was assistant, but it was seventeen-year-old Annie who was practicing postmistress. Her father was busy with the fields, her mother was busy with the children, so she was busy with the Wold Post Office. Henry Roher carried the mail. Later the post office was moved to Theodore Johnson's, then replaced by route service from Bloomfield.

Johnny filed on a homestead of his own as soon as he was eligible, and Annie, second oldest of the children, also filed when she reached age twenty-one. They owned the first tractor in the community – a big Hart-Parr – with which they did considerable breaking for others as well as for themselves. They owned a threshing rig, too, and the third fall they were in Montana near-tragedy struck the family.

They moved the rig from one farm to another, threshing for the entire neighborhood, but one day they failed to meet their schedule. One of the neighbor women was expecting the crew for dinner, but they got stuck and didn't make it until evening so she just covered and put away the beef roast she had prepared for dinner and served it to them for supper.

Of course, there was no refrigerator in which to store the meat that hot day, and as a result, the whole crew came down with food poisoning. Most of them escaped with fairly mild cases, but not so with Johnny. He became desperately ill, and doctors despaired for his life. They successfully battled the poisoning, but it was followed by typhoid fever, then pneumonia, and finally two lung abscesses. He was in bed seven months less one day. He recovered, though, and apparently the siege didn't shorten his life because he's now almost seventy-five, living alone on his farm doing his own work, both household and outside.

The winter that Johnny was sick the snow was so deep the drifts piled to the barn roof. Their chicken house was located between the barn and the big granary, and it was completely snowed under so they had to dig a tunnel to the door. When the weather break finally came, the chinook took the snow so fast that, according to Mrs. Field, the hill by their house looked like Niagara Falls.

The same year that the Wolds came from Black River Falls, Wisconsin, Ludvig Field came from Westby, Wisconsin, to homestead. Annie Wold met him a week after she arrived here, but it was nine years before she married him. A short time before they were married Louie sold his homestead and bought a farm a few miles from Lambert. There they spent their first five years together.

The fellow who bought Louie's homestead soon found that the life of a pioneer Montana farmer was neither a life of ease nor 'get rich quick'. He found it easier to mortgage his property than to pay off the mortgage so he gave it up. The Fields bought it back and moved to the homestead. Mrs. Field traded her homestead (she had proved up about a year before she was married) to her mother for cattle and horses.

The Fields lived for more than thirty years on the farm, rearing their five children there. (One son died in infancy.) As the children reached high school age, Mrs. Field moved to Glendive with them during the school term so they could get their high school education. The children now are scattered from Yankton, South Dakota, to Eureka, Montana (one daughter, Mrs. Eldridge Zolman, lives in Glendive), and her grandchildren are scattered even farther.

In 1953 they sold their farm and bought a home in Red Lodge near one of their daughters. They returned to Glendive in 1957, and it was here that Mr. Field passed away two years later. Mrs. Field, who is a week-and-a-half younger than seventy-three years, lives alone. Besides her housekeeping and walking, she keeps herself busy making quilts and rugs, along with other sewing.

Mrs. James (Marie) Pechar

August – September 1968

Mrs. Marie Pechar gave birth to the first baby born in Glendive's 'new' Northern Pacific Hospital. In the fifty-five years since then, both hospital and baby have changed names – and ownership, but both are still with us: the Glendive Community Hospital and Mrs. Adrian Skillestad.

Mrs. Pechar was reared on the plains of Kansas, but after her marriage to James Pechar in 1909 she came with him to Mandan, North Dakota. Mrs. Pechar chuckled as she recalled how Kansas friends had planned a charivari* for them, but her husband foiled their plans by hustling his bride to the train and departing for points north.

Mr. Pechar worked for the Northern Pacific Railroad, and in 1912 he was transferred to Glendive. Soon after coming to Glendive their first child was born – on January 23, 1913, a week before the hospital was dedicated. Though not yet dedicated, the hospital was open, and five patients were registered. At the dedication ceremonies a week later nurses carried baby Marie back and forth, showing that they already had a baby in the hospital.

1912 had been a year of bumper crops for the farmers who were getting a start in eastern Montana, and Pechar was soon receiving reports on every hand of the bonanza awaiting the homesteader. The government gave you free land, and all you had to do was go out and make your fortune!

It sounded good (if it sounded too good to be true, it's because it was) and he decided to try it. However, even though his railroad wage was small, it was steady so it seemed best to hold onto his job until the homestead could be developed. That meant that Mrs. Pechar, with little three-month Marie, would have to establish residence on the homestead. As it turned out, she had to do far more than establish residence.

Although they homesteaded just twelve years after the turn of the century, the best farm lands had already been taken. They did, however, find a desirable half-section on Morgan Creek so they filed, only to discover after it was done that the land agent advising them had made a mistake. Instead of a location along the creek, the claim they filed on was in the middle of the badlands. Although they were not among the earliest homesteaders, surely Mrs. Pechar 'out-pioneered' many of the first pioneers.

They homesteaded on the five year plan which required residence only a few months of the year. They planned that Mrs. Pechar and baby Marie would live on the homestead from April to August, then move back to Glendive for the winter months.

When they moved out to the claim, there was nothing except the hills of the badlands so they set up housekeeping in a tent. Mrs. Pechar had been told that snakes wouldn't cross a rope on the ground so she hopefully strung a rope around the tent.

Whether or not it was the rope, the snakes didn't come in, but snow did. Even though it was April they found that the winter wasn't all past. They had some late snow storms that year, and more than one morning she found snow drifts on the floor inside the tent. Fortunately the baby was still small enough that keeping her off the floor was no problem.

One of the first tasks was to build a more permanent dwelling. Since Mr. Pechar was working a split shift on the railroad, he couldn't get out to help. If he had had a '68 model car he could have 'buzzed' out in half-an-hour, helped a couple hours, and buzzed back for the remainder of his shift. As it was, he didn't even have a Model T so there was no way he could manage.

Mrs. Pechar was happy that her father, a Kansas farmer, was able to come help her long enough to get a shack built to meet requirements of the homestead law. As soon as the shack was up he had to return to Kansas for harvest so once more Mrs. Pechar and the baby were left alone on the homestead.

Mrs. Pechar's only means of transportation on the homestead was horse and buggy. They had bought their first horse from E.J. Barry in Glendive. Mr. Barry raised racing horses but this horse, though registered, was no longer a racer. He was still a good buggy horse, though.

On the homestead such a short time, she and baby Marie were fortunate to have a roof over their own heads, and there had been no time to build a shelter for any animals so the horse had to be staked out. Since they were in the middle of the open range, range horses would often come around and fight with her horse. One night the horse got loose and vanished, leaving her stranded in the badlands. Little chance she had of finding him when the only way she had to hunt for him was on foot so she advertised and offered a reward for his return.

After two months – two months afoot, miles from town, for her – the horse was finally returned and the reward collected. Significantly, the horse bore collar marks indicating that he had not been on vacation those two months, but nothing was said about that.

Not only did the range horses give Mrs. Pechar a bad time that first summer on the homestead, but so did the range cattle. That spring Mr. Pechar had hired someone to break ground for a few acres of flax and also a patch for a garden. Mrs. Pechar wasn't raising a garden for cattle feed, but she found herself constantly contending with the cattle on that point. Many times she had to get up in the night and chase them away as well as chasing them many times in the day. She could relate with amusement now how she'd run after those cattle with the baby astride her hip, but there was nothing amusing about it fifty-five years ago.

Understandably, she was more than a little concerned about getting fences built – especially around the yard and garden. Around the hen house, too, was fence priority. Coyotes were frequent visitors around the little home in the badlands, and they had special interest in the chickens.

First thing she would see in the morning would be a coyote on the horizon, waiting for a chance at a chicken when she let them out of the hen house. One morning a luckless chicken was grabbed, but Mrs. Pechar saw it in time to fire at the marauder with the 22. She didn't get the coyote, but she made him drop the chicken. The chicken was injured, but she got it in time to butcher it so it wasn't entirely wasted.

One or two coyotes yapping could sound like a whole pack (and sometimes there would be a whole pack) and to hear them start howling was enough to make chills run up and down her spine. In later years she became accustomed to their serenade, but that first year they were most unwelcome callers.

With so many things to do that first summer, only the most urgently needed fences were built, but in succeeding years about eight miles of fencing was constructed on the homestead. No power-take off tools lightened the work in those days, and every post hole had to be dug with a hand digger. Many times rocks had to be dug out before the hole could be completed. Since Mr. Pechar's time on the farm was so rigidly limited, much of the fencing fell to Mrs. Pechar's lot.

Another problem facing Mrs. Pechar that first summer was water. Those individuals who have never had to put forth more effort to get water than turning a faucet and whose greatest inconvenience in that line has been occasional rationing by the city water department may have difficulty appreciating the problem facing the lone woman on the homestead.

Since there was no spring nearby, she had to haul water from the nearest neighbor, rancher Ivan Kalberg, one-and-a-half miles away. During the time that her horse was missing she had to use a little express wagon (commonly considered a child's play wagon, but it was a work wagon on the homestead) for the hauling. Loading the baby and the largest container she had into the wagon, she'd walk, pulling the wagon, to Kalberg's, get her water, and walk back again. She'd also set out every container she could get her hands on whenever it rained so she could catch rain water for washing, thereby minimizing the amount that had to be hauled.

Although she wasn't able to find time to dig a well during her first summer on the badlands homestead, Mrs. Pechar gave that project high priority the second summer. She had to dig a well as she did most other things by hand.

Since she was digging with a shovel she had to make the hole wide enough to give her 'elbow room'. At first she threw the dirt out over the top, but when she got down too deep for that, she rigged up a windlass*. That meant getting down into the well to fill the bucket, climbing out to empty it, then back down to fill it again.

When she was down about sixteen feet Mr. Griffith, a neighboring rancher, came by. Finding her in the well, he asked her, "What are you doing down there? That is no place for a woman!" She agreed, but what could she do but keep on digging? She kept on digging until she had water. Then she took the stone boat and scoured the nearby badlands for flat rocks to build up the curbing. At least she had no trouble finding rocks! After the well was completed they drew water from it by lowering a bucket on a rope into it, then pulling it up hand-over-hand.

Fuel for heating and cooking came from the surrounding badlands. The first summer on the homestead, of course, she didn't need much coal. Any 'hauling' that year she did with the little red wagon – the same little red wagon she used for hauling water. Child's play wagon? What would she have done without it!

She could get both coal and wood close by so while the baby was asleep, Mrs. Pechar would take the little wagon with a nail keg on it and "run to beat the dickens," to quote her, to get some coal and get back before Marie woke up. She hauled wood with the wagon, too.

Taking the baby and a jug of water in the wagon, she'd gather the wood from one or another of the deep coulees on the homestead, tie it into bundles, and haul it back to the little shack. Wood, of course (especially cedar), was her chief fuel during the summer months.

When Marie was a little older, she added to her mother's worries by her fascination with the stove. During the winter months fire had to be kept burning all the time. When the weather was too cold to take Marie along out with her to do chores, Mrs. Pechar would carefully admonish her to stay away from the stove; yet many times when she came in she would find little hands trying to poke a stick through the holes of the ornament on the front of the stove door! Fortunately no serious harm ever came from it.

When they started staying on the homestead the year-round Mrs. Pechar hauled the coal – lignite was plentiful in the hills of the badlands – with the big wagon and a team of horses. They needed about ten ton for a winter.

One time as she was hauling a load of coal through the snow one of the horses stumbled in a drift and fell. That had happened many times, but this time he was so entangled she thought she was going to have to cut the traces to get him up. Reluctant to commit herself to harness-mending, she struggled in the snow and cold until she was able to get him unhitched.

The first year she didn't have to worry about laying in a big supply of coal because they moved back to Glendive the latter part of August and stayed in town until the following April, but spring found them back on the homestead again.

Mr. Pechar, meanwhile, continued his job with the railroad. Working conditions were considerably different then from now, and his job included the work done by three different men in later years. He worked in the old depot which was heated by a wood-coal furnace, and one of his responsibilities was firing the furnace. He also took care of the mail, hauling it to and from the post office on a cart pushed by hand. His third 'job' was that of express and baggage man.

Many more salesmen then traveled by train, and many of them traveled 'heavy' – suitcases and trunks loaded with their wares. Mr. Pechar was rather small of stature, yet his job required him to do much heavy lifting. Little wonder that a few years later his health broke under the strain.

After he was changed to a straight shift he was able to get out to help with the work on the homestead sometimes. On those occasions Mrs. Pechar would get up very early in the morning and go to Stipek to meet his train. After the work was done she'd take him back to Stipek, he'd catch the train, and she'd go home alone – with the baby, that is.

Working the homestead was hard for Mrs. Pechar, but it was hard for Mr. Pechar, too. The heavy work on the railroad was breaking his health, yet whenever he could he would join his family on the farm to help with the many projects that must be carried out.

He'd work as fast as he could while he was there, but the time was short. If the work was urgent and he wanted to stay longer than the train schedule would allow, he'd finish his task, then his wife would take him all the way to Glendive with the horse and buggy.

Mrs. Pechar remembers many times falling asleep on the homeward trip, holding little Marie on her lap as the horse plodded along. Sometimes in early spring or late fall the weather was cold enough to make those trips a real trial. She could wrap Marie in a big bundle and keep her warm enough, but sometimes her own feet froze. At one time she thought she was going to lose her toes from freezing them. Then the chill blains….

The first couple years after they homesteaded Mrs. Pechar and Marie spent the winter in town with Mr. Pechar in the five-room house they had rented, but after the farm was built up a little they let the house go and moved everything to the country – everything from a five-room house into the one-room shack.

By the time they had everything moved into the shack, there wasn't room for Mrs. Pechar and Marie to sleep there so, until they could get organized, they slept in the bunkhouse. The bunkhouse was built into the bank and intended for quarters for hired help as needed. It was also used as a granary or for whatever purpose it might come in handy.

One night Mrs. Pechar was awakened by a glow from the direction of the shack and hurried to the window to see the house in flames. The shack burned to the ground, and with it burned all their household furnishings as well as their wedding presents, their marriage license, their good dishes, two cases of silver, her collection of books – everything.

When the fire cooled down, they found some melted silver, some dishes broken and charred, but nothing they could save. They also found where the fire had been set outside the house, on the side from which the wind was blowing. Homesteaders were not always welcome in range country!

They moved into the dugout 'temporarily' but they stayed there until they moved from the farm in 1934. They did, however, build on another room. Since the railroad still claimed much of Mr. Pechar's time, Mrs. Pechar had to do much of the cement mixing and building of the addition.

Their first cow was escorted to the homestead by a man whom Mr. Pechar hired for that purpose. They had no way to haul her so Mr. Pechar gave the fellow directions for finding the little farm in the heart of the badlands, and he walked, leading the cow, all the way from Glendive. Then he walked back to town again.

There were no public roads to the Pechar property so Mr. Pechar applied for and was granted a one-and-one-half mile right-of-way in to their property. So far as rights were concerned they had assurance of getting in and out, but sometimes in the snow and mud they weren't altogether sure the 'right' would do them much good, especially when they were using the car.

They were on the homestead a number of years before they had that particular problem – the problem of getting in and out with a car. They bought their first car from Gust Kolberg when he went off to World War I. According to Mrs. Pechar her first and only driving lesson went something like this: "This lever is for this; this lever is for that, and there you are."

She can see herself yet, she tells us, sitting on the fender of their newly-acquired automobile, studying the folder that came with it to get acquainted with its structure and operation. It was necessary that she get acquainted with its structure as well as operation because if something went wrong it was up to her to fix it.

Thinking of their early motor transportation must inevitably bring memories of cold weather starts: setting a pan of ashes under the oil pan; pouring water over the manifold; jacking up the hind wheel. And when everything else failed (as it usually did) pulling it with the old faithful horses until it started.

Behind the 'dugout' into which the Pechars moved when their house on the homestead burned was a big hill. Sometimes snow drifted out from the hill and almost covered the house.

The deep coulees of the surrounding badlands were natural receptacles for snow. After one particularly heavy spring blizzard the coulee where the horses had drifted was so full of snow that the horses were walking among the tree tops. They couldn't get feed, of course, so Mrs. Pechar carried feed to them. She had to cover her face to brave the fury of the storm as she dragged the corn shocks* to the hungry animals. Each excursion left her soaked and cold, but she saved the horses.

The badlands weren't very productive crop-wise (or otherwise). Some years they didn't even get their seed back, but some years were better. She recalled one year they had a fair crop, but after she cut the wheat with the binder and stacked it herself, she had to pay the threshers and hire someone to haul it to Stipek. When she figured up all her expenses she found they had made seven cents a bushel. (Maybe some of today's farmers think she was lucky at that!)

If drought didn't curb their wheat yield it might be hail or grasshoppers. One year there were so many grasshoppers that after they had been poisoned a hard rain washed them into drifts six inches deep – in the coulees, not on the level, Mrs. Pechar hastened to explain. Then she added dryly, "They couldn't have been six inches deep on the level because we had no level fields!" The hills in the fields were so steep, she declared, that when she was cutting grain she had to hang onto the binder so she wouldn't fall off!

To fight grasshoppers they didn't have the sophisticated sprayers that farmers use now. Instead they mixed the poison by hand, then scattered it by

282

hand. One year they mixed so much that Mrs. Pechar became ill from absorbing too much of the poison. She spent six weeks in the hospital before she fully recovered.

Several years later she was hospitalized again when she underwent an operation. They had no insurance to cover hospital bills and surely no money to spare from their meager income, but just when she was due to be released, Mrs. Pechar learned that the hospital cook had resigned.

She promptly applied for the job, but the doctor shook his head. She persisted, however, until he agreed to let her try it. She took the job of cooking the meals for the staff and patients – about seventy-five people – and stayed with it until spring's work opened up on the homestead. The operation had been performed in January so she was able to pay her bill.

All of their field work in the early years on the farm was done with horses. Although they hired the first breaking done, later they bought their own implements, and Mrs. Pechar plowed with four horses on the sulky plow*.

She walked miles behind the harrow and filled the drill box from hundred-pound wheat sacks. When the bull wheel broke on the binder, she changed it by herself. When the canvas laths broke she repaired them.

She hauled used railroad ties and heavy planks with team and wagon for building projects that succeeded their first shack. One of the horses, when she was hauling lumber, was wild and continually watching for a chance to bolt so she had to be continually watching that he didn't get it. Especially at the gate she had to be careful. The gate through the fence around the homestead was on a hill where it was bad enough to have to stop under the best conditions. That bronc in her team didn't make for the best conditions.

When she stopped for the gate, she'd carefully climb down from her perch on the wagon, open the gate, and lead the horses through. Then she'd edge quietly past the horses back to the wagon and quickly climb back on. As soon as she put her foot on the hub of the wheel, the team was in motion.

Once when she was husking corn in the field (picking the ripe ears from the stalks and throwing them onto the hayrack) something spooked the horses, and they took off on a run. They tore through a fence, breaking a couple posts, and kept running until they reached the barn yard. There, because the barn was too solid to go through and too high for them to go over, they stood and waited for her to come up to them.

When little Marie was big enough to toddle around, Mrs. Pechar used to tie a red kerchief on her head to make it easier to keep track of her in the tall grass. Almost before the red kerchief days were over, Marie started to school.

Schooling on the frontier generally presented a problem, but in Marie's case it was rather premature. A neighboring rancher, Ivan Kalberg, had two children ready for school, but there was no school for them to attend, and the law required that a district have a minimum of three pupils before a teacher could be hired.

It was time for Lars and Dorothy to be in school so to get a school started Marie, four-and-one-half years old, was enrolled. Once a school was opened it could continue for two pupils so Marie was more or less expected to drop out, but Marie had different ideas.

It was lonesome for one small child on the homestead, and she thoroughly enjoyed the new experiences coming her way. Once she had started she sailed right on through school until she graduated from the eighth grade. Even then she took a post graduate course.

Her mother had to go with her that first year the mile-and-a-half to school in Kalberg's yard. That winter she even had to carry her through the deeper drifts. Later on a schoolhouse was built, and then Marie had three miles to go. By that time, however, she was big enough to ride horseback and could go by herself.

Marie was eight years old before she had a playmate at home. She had long prayed for a baby sister, had written to Santa Claus, had done everything she could think of to get a sister so when the baby arrived, she was overjoyed.

While the mother and baby were still in the hospital Marie was allowed to go in with the neighbors to visit. On the return trip as her comprehension absorbed the full import of the visit her jubilation increased until it could no longer be contained. Jumping up and down in the back of the car she began shouting, "I've got a sister! I've got a sister!"

Although Alice was born the twenty-eighth of August, she came home in a snowstorm. Mothers then were kept in the hospital for two weeks, and by the time Mrs. Pechar was released an early September snow was falling and blanketed the occupants of the open buggy as they jogged along.

Marie had been in school that day as usual but was home and eagerly watching for the first sight of the buggy with its precious cargo. The sight of the snow-crusted bundle in Mother's arms made a deep impression upon her, an impression which remains with her to this day. The bundle was large for so small a baby, but the many blankets separating her from the cold did their job well.

By the time Alice was ready for school they had more problems. The district had become so depopulated that they didn't even operate a school, so for even her first eight grades Alice had to go to Glendive. Driving back and forth daily was impossible so they had to find a place for her to board in town.

Mr. Pechar had quit the railroad two years before Alice was born so for five days of the week she was alone as far as her family was concerned. Weekends she usually had no problem getting home as other farmers farther on took their high schoolers to town on Monday morning, left them there for the school days, then picked them up again after school Friday. Alice would meet them at 'Coal Mine Hill' to ride in with them Monday and reverse the procedure Friday afternoon.

About 1934, however, Mrs. Pechar and Marie both found employment in Glendive during the winter months so then they all lived together in a small apartment. In 1936 they moved to Glendive the year around.

Mr. Pechar had kept his railroad job until 1919. His tenure with the railroad preceded employee-employer bargaining days, and the heavy work took its toll on his health – all for $69 a month. By the time he quit his health was broken. In spite of his physical condition he struggled with the farm when he wasn't in the hospital, but his last fourteen years before his death in 1947 were spent in the hospital.

Opportunities for attending formal church services were few and far between while the Pechars were on the homestead. Marie was introduced to Sunday School when Martin Peterson, a Baptist preacher, homesteaded several miles up Morgan Creek. Peterson did not forget his calling while he farmed but ministered to the spiritual needs of an isolated community, holding services in his own and other homes in the neighborhood.

Marie recalls that Peterson's son, James, assured them that when he grew up he was going to be president of the United States. Although he hasn't demonstrated great political aspirations since growing up, his name has become familiar to many TV watchers – Dr. James Peterson, marriage counselor on the Art Linkletter show.

When Petersons moved from Morgan Creek, the community was again without organized worship services. Pechars could seldom get to Glendive for church, but Mrs. Pechar assures us, "We stayed Christians anyway. We prayed at home."

Women of the community –'community' including women living fifteen to twenty miles apart – met together for Ladies Aid regardless of their denominational affiliation. Reflecting on their gatherings, she surmised half-a-dozen or more denominations must have been represented among the hardly more than a dozen women. In spite of this difference they got along harmoniously and had good times together.

When Mrs. Pechar first moved to the homestead the only women close enough for her to get to know were Mrs. Andy Anderson and Mrs. Ivan Kalberg. Mrs. A.A. Kent wasn't much farther away, but the road then didn't go past Kents, and it was some time before they became acquainted.

Neighbors 'neighbored', and company was a real treat – not a social custom to be endured. The bachelors were likely to 'happen' to drop by at mealtime, but that was fine, too. Daughter Marie recalled the feeling of importance she had when she was drafted to make a fourth with her parents when one visitor would stop in for a game of '500'.

Another real treat was their first radio. Uncle Tony thought they needed a radio in their isolated farm home so he sent them one. Perhaps it's hard for anyone caught up in the rush and bustle of today to realize what a radio would mean in such circumstances. Even though they could get out but little, now they could bring the world to their living room.

Marie recalled, too, her first and last attempt at flying – on her own power. She rigged up a cape and had it all figured that if she'd flap her arms as wings when she jumped from the top of the shed by the barn, she'd just naturally fly. As she leaped from the shed she found that it wasn't so natural after all so her attempt at flight ended ingloriously in the manure pile.

It was probably a good thing, she conceded ruefully, that she landed where she did or she'd likely have broken both ankles. Seeing a circus had put the idea (and quite a few other ideas) into her head, but for some reason most of the ideas didn't seem to work for her.

Stipek was kind of 'home town' for Pechars, less than half as far away as Glendive. Marie recalled J.J. Stipek's campaign to attract business to the then 'booming' village. The campaign included some posters lauding Stipek's possibilities for development, but some skeptics with less vision than Mr. Stipek had scrawled some indelicate initials across the posters.

The insult, however, did not faze Mr. Stipek in the least. When he saw the scribbling he nodded his head vigorously and exclaimed, "That's right! That's right! Boost Stipek! Boost Stipek!"

Mrs. Pechar still owns the homestead, but she rents it out now, living elsewhere since 1936 – Glendive, Missoula, Butte, Deer Lodge, and in Arizona. Marie is now Mrs. Adrian Skillestad and lives in the Union country, while Alice, also married, lives in Moses Lake, Washington.

After her husband died in 1947 Mrs. Pechar continued to work at Deer Lodge until 1954 when she suffered her first major heart attack. She lived with her daughters between 1954 and 1956, but arthritis made life difficult for her.

When an arthritic friend wrote from Mesa, Arizona, urging her to try the climate there, she decided she would and moved to Mesa in 1956. She finds that she does indeed feel better there so she spends her winters in the south, but she comes back to Montana for the summer.

As Mrs. Pechar reviewed for us the hard years on the homestead she recalled, "I used to get so tired I'd pray the time would come when I could be just a housekeeper instead of doing a man's work." The time came, but not with any rush.

In spite of her eighty years, arthritis, and heart trouble, Mrs. Pechar is still alert and still has a sense of humor. Perhaps her philosophy could be summed up in the verse on a birthday card which she recently sent to an eighty-nine-year old friend:

Don't worry about that birthday;
It doesn't mean a thing.
We're both the same spring chickens
With just a little less spring.

Nils J. Trangmoe

Note: The following article on Nils Trangmoe, a pioneer Dawson County homesteader, was compiled from notes and written comments by his son, Henry. The report was nearly complete at the time of the unexpected death of Henry in October 1969. John Trangmoe, a grandson of the subject of the report, made final preparation of the material.

Nils J. Trangmoe was born Nils Johnson. When he homesteaded on Whoopup Creek Flat, his nearest neighbor was also named Johnson. Two neighbors with the same name can have problems, especially with mail. Tiring of the 'mix-ups' that kept occurring, Nils inquired, when he happened to be in the courthouse whether a man could change his name. Assured that he could, he chose the name Trangmoe, meaning 'Long Meadow' in Norwegian. That settled the mail problem!

Nils J. Trangmoe was born in Norway in the state of Norland, which is north of the Artic Circle. The home place in the native land was a small farm with one horse, a cow, pigs, and a few sheep. The main crops were hay, oats, and potatoes. Since potatoes are a basic ingredient of lefsa and many other Norwegian foods, they were a mainstay for family food. Also, livestock were fed potatoes during the winter.

Nils spent his boyhood summer days herding community livestock in the mountains. Winter was the time to hunt, ski, and skate. As a young man his trade was boat building and fishing. Being north of the Artic Circle there was a problem of telling when was yesterday or tomorrow as the sun never rose over the horizon for several weeks in winter.

Nils came to the United States with his wife, Christine and daughter, Hannah, in 1905. It took over three weeks to come from Norway to Grafton, North Dakota. Here a year was spent working on a farm to get acquainted with the new country.

All the farm buildings at that time were built in the shelter of trees along the Red River. It was the general opinion that homesteaders could not survive the winter on the treeless plains of eastern North Dakota. After seeing the Red River flood the farmland, they decided to go to Montana to try for a homestead in the semi-desert. Nils, after spending the day viewing homestead land prospects, was invited to stay with Martin Evans on his sheep ranch. They slept in a dugout in a cut bank. During the night the thunder of hoofs right over the roof announced a stampeding sheep flock.

Nils, not being brave enough to settle on the better land thirty or forty miles out in the roadless hills, decided on a homestead site ten miles from Glendive on Whoopup Creek flat. The view of the badlands and the trees along the Yellowstone River may have influenced him in choosing the site. Trees for logs were available along the river so it was natural that the homestead shack be built of logs. It was constructed without nails as the logs were notched together at the corners and at the doors and windows. The floors were made of boards, as was the roof with the log rafters showing. For insulation, and to keep the rain out, the roof was covered with gumbo.*

For income, it was necessary to work for the railroad section crew, living in the bunk car and eating at the cook car while the family held down the claim. As money became available, a couple of horses and a walking plow were purchased. This made it possible to grow a garden and grain crops and to put up hay. Also, now they could have a milk cow, a few chickens, and pigs.

As the years went by, additional sod was broken and crops grown so the railroad job was abandoned. In winter, for additional income, the badland cedar was harvested and sold to homesteaders for fence posts. This also made it possible to do contract fencing for the city farmers that were speculating or farming on state and railroad land.

In those early years of Trangmoe's sojourn on Whoopup Creek Flat there were only crude trails and no bridges so sometimes we had to wait until a flash flood passed before being able to cross. Once a month to town was average. Surplus cream was made into butter with a barrel churn turned by hand. We really enjoyed the wild fruit that was made into sauce, pudding, pie, jelly, jam, and wine. The wild currents, chokecherries, plums, and buffalo berries grew in coulees with underground water.

A few sheep were kept for wool and mutton. The wool was made into woolen bats that were the fillers for quilts. We also had wool made into yarn, which was knit into stockings, mittens, caps and sweaters. We also had a feather tick, which was a quilt sized bag filled loosely with feathers. This was really nice to cuddle in and was warm to sleep in on those cold windy nights when the coal stoves would burn out.

Dad dug a well by hand that turned out to be the best, clearest, coolest water in the valley. People would always stop as they passed through for a drink so this gave Dad the opportunity to visit. This visiting, I think, was his greatest enjoyment. One such visit was with a government geologist who told him that the Cedar Creek anticline crossed the homestead and so the dream was that someday there would be oil.

I must tell about the steam engine that came to help break the sod. It pulled ten plow bottoms and disc, packer, or anything you wanted to hook up behind. It burned wood and coal and used lots of water for steam. The whistle was used to signal that coal hauler or water wagon to hurry. Also, this engine was used for power for the threshing machine to harvest the grain bundle in the fall.

Now came graded roads passing by the homestead. At first it was called the Red Trail but later was named the National Park Highway. There were only a few cars but the roads were not graveled so when it rained for three days in June, many tourists would wait at the homestead until the rain stopped and the sun dried the gumbo.

The Gypsies still used horses to pull their covered wagons. They traveled in caravans, sometimes two miles in length. The lead wagon usually dropped off a lady dressed in long robes with a half dozen kids. They would beg for milk, eggs, chickens or anything in sight. They always said that they had a sick grandmother in the wagon. They would tell your fortune if you gave them what they requested; they would bless you. If you did not honor their wishes, they supposedly had the power to put a curse on anything on the farm. They also needed horse feed, so as they drove by a field of oat bundles, someone from each of the wagon would run out and grab bundles.

Another incident that came with the National Park Highway was feeding two heavily armed men one day when the folks were in town. Only the three youngest boys, ages four, seven, and ten, were home as these men walked in and ordered coffee, bread, meat, and the like. One of the men turned out to be the third most wanted criminal. The FBI shot and killed the one and arrested the other before they reached Fallon.

So, with the spirit of togetherness, the community telephone was born. At first, the old barbed wire fence was used but the wire was so rusty the phones only worked when the weather was dry. So, gradually new, galvanized wire was used. Eventually, an old abandoned telephone line, poles, and insulators were purchased and served until the present dial service came. The six original charter members of the Prospect Valley Telephone Company were Joseph Rock, August Schaal, Nils Trangmoe, Swen Oftendal, Edwin Cook, and Charlie Meseberg.

With World War I came heartaches, disappointments, sacrifices, the flu epidemic, the 1919 drought, the record breaking severe winter following the drought and the $60 slough hay from North Dakota — subjects of which several chapters could be written, but for now would rather be passed and partially forgotten.

Then in the twenties, the slogan for the farmers — diversify or go broke — got the Trangmoe farm on sound economic foundations with hogs, laying hens, milk cows, and a variety of crops. This opened up to a better living with an ice house to store winter ice for use in the kitchen ice box, for homemade ice cream, and for ice cold drinks.

As the Trangmoe children, Hannah, Lawrence, Henry, Andrew, and Morten were now growing up, I might mention the recreation of the day was horseback riding, swimming, games, ice skating, skiing, sliding, etc. Entertainment was the playing of musical instruments such as the accordion, mouth organ, jew's harp, as well as the home organ and singing mostly those Methodist hymns. By this time 4-H was active. Church was held occasionally at the Kinsey School, mostly sponsored by Mr. and Mrs. August Schaal. These good neighbors also provided the means for the early Sunday School classes for the community, mostly held at the schoolhouse during the summer.

The United States Government did reserve the right of way for irrigation canals on the homestead land in the valley; so to promote and get irrigation water from the Yellowstone River, a group of valley farmers were organized by County Agent Mendenhall to go in person and view the Huntley Irrigation Project near Billings. Those making the trip were Joe Rock, August Schaal, Ed Starr, Swen Oftedal, Ed Cook, Nils Trangmoe, and Fred Yale. They traveled by Model T Fords taking a long day to drive this distance with the usual boiling radiators and blown tires. After spending the second day viewing this irrigation project, these farmers were convinced that irrigation was a must for the valley.

Then came the stock market crash with economic disaster for the people of the East, soon spreading west with people coming from the East looking for work on farms. To make economic times worse, the dirty thirties came to the West with wind, heat, drought, insects, and poor farm prices. But by now a new generation of native sons began to devise new ways to survive on farms and ranches. To survive the grasshopper plague, a turkey flock was used in the fields to reduce the insect population. It was also necessary to have a watchman with the flock to keep the coyotes away. Even though several sections of land were farmed, it was necessary to harvest weeds, 'roots and all' on the summer fallow* in order to have something to feed the livestock during the winter of 1930-31.

To make use of the wind, a wind electric plant was built to charge batteries for lights for the farm buildings and to charge batteries for the radio.

The depression brought about the New Deal in government, which was responsible for W.P.A. workers constructing the Buffalo Rapids Irrigation Project. Prior to this there were only seven ranchers in the valley making a living from the land between Glendive and Fallon. So Dad Trangmoe lived to see irrigation water with green crops growing. Suddenly the farm shelterbelt grew tall. Now came new young neighbors and about two hundred farms in this area, along with the long-awaited electric power to make possible a modern way of life with the conveniences of the city.

So after a half century of interesting life, Dad Trangmoe passed away leaving a homestead for his sons to carry on. I now realize it would take a book to hold all the experiences of this homestead.

Christine Trangmoe with the chickens in front of the old homestead shack

Mrs. Frank (Entonie) Benes

June – July 1968

Entonie Benes had never in her life seen such hills as she saw from the window of the train approaching Glendive – and she had seen a lot of country on both sides of the Atlantic. Then she saw Indians on their ponies and became really alarmed. She had started out for a homestead some place in eastern Montana, but from the looks of the country and the Indians, she wondered if she was being taken to some Indian reservation instead.

Only a year before Entonie had come to the United States from her native Czechoslovakia. Many immigrants from Europe came to America in the hope of bettering their economic position, but that had little to do with Entonie's decision to come. Her family, while not wealthy, was comfortably situated, but, as Mrs. Benes explained, "Young people get big ideas. You hear what others do and think you can do the same things." Then she added, "You forget you don't talk the language." That language business proved to be a formidable obstacle.

When Entonie first arrived in New York, she almost wondered if the people in America belonged to a different species. Did they – fantastic thought, but – did they have two stomachs? What else could explain why so many people, on the train, the street, everywhere, were working their mouths when they obviously were not eating? She finally expressed her bewilderment to the guide responsible for taking them from their ship to the train that would get them to the proper address. The guide was amused and explained that the people were chewing gum; that you chew the same stick all day. She gave Entonie a sample so Entonie chewed it until the sweetness was gone, then disposed of it. When her guide asked her what she had done with it, she frankly told her she threw it away. Maybe other people could chew a stick all day, but after the flavor was gone she was ready to get rid of it.

Entonie had come to the New World with a girl friend. Rosy had a cousin in Pennsylvania so they were depending on him to help them get acquainted and get jobs. However, when they reached Pennsylvania, they found him ready to return to Czechoslovakia. Cousin had a farm back in the old country. He hadn't been able to get work in Pennsylvania so he had decided to go back to his farm. He met the girls, but the day after they arrived, he and his family left to go back whence they had come.

The language barrier had never loomed so large. How many jobs are open when you can't understand or make yourself understood? Job opportunities for women were much more limited early in our century than now, even if you spoke the same language, so for the girls the prospects seemed rather dismal. In spite of this problem Rosy found a job in a home where there was a pair of new twins, but Entonie had to look longer. When she found work, she found more of it.

The home in which she worked had eight children, the latest a new baby. Entonie never saw so much washing and ironing in her life – washing on the scrub board, ironing with flat irons heated on the kitchen range. There was lots of work but little to eat for Entonie. The children went to their grandmother, who lived nearby, to eat; the mother ate a little milk and Entonie, well, there just didn't seem to be much of anything for her except a little bread and coffee. She had some money, so in desperation she finally went to the store to buy some food, but the grocer didn't know anything about Czech money so the bread and oranges went back on the shelf, and Tony went hungry.

Another Czechoslovakian girl who had been in the community for some time came that very evening to see how Tony was getting along. When she found that the new immigrant wasn't getting enough to eat, she hurried home and told her grandmother. Grandmother ordered, "Bring her here right away," so Tony stayed there until she found another job. She was supposed to be paid $12 per month, but she hasn't got her money yet.

At the next place she worked her wages were only $10 per month (and there she was paid), but there were just two people and her work was much easier. The woman had broken her leg and needed help until she could be on her feet again. Mrs. Entonie Benes remembers her with gratitude, but her memories of the woman's husband are less pleasant.

He was a heavy drinker and, though life would go along smoothly for five days, weekends were harrowing. After one particularly hair-raising weekend, Tony decided she would have to leave. 'Mr.' planned to go fishing, but when it was time to collect his equipment to go, he couldn't find the new fishing line he had just bought. He hunted and Tony hunted (his wife couldn't because her broken leg immobilized her), but the line was not found. Suddenly from the bedroom 'Mrs.' called, "Tony, Tony, come!" so she hurried to the room and found him with his revolver pointed at the helpless woman and threatening, "If she doesn't tell where the line is, I will shoot her." (He, of course, was the only one who had had his hands on the line.)

'Mrs.' jerked Tony in front of her, but he warned, "I'll shoot her, too!" And Tony, terrified, thought, "I came to America just to get shot!" She didn't, though. He consented to another search and Tony, with sudden inspiration, thought of his smoking table. She found it there, and saved more than just 'the day', evidently, as he growled, "You are lucky. You can still walk."

He was gone five days on his fishing trip and returned with three small fish, already stinking. He ordered her to prepare it for his supper, but 'Mrs.' circumvented him that time. She sent Tony out to buy a fresh fish to prepare. Said he when the fish was served, "If I had known the fish would be that good I would have brought more."

Tony was sorry to leave the woman who had been so kind to her, helping her learn English and showing her every consideration, but her nerves were so jumpy she couldn't stay there any longer.

Just at that time Rosy lost her job, too. One of the twins for whom she had been caring died, and the mother could take care of one alone, so both girls were looking for work when a letter came from a girl they had met on the ship crossing the Atlantic. This girl had gone to St. Paul and wrote that there she was getting $16 a month, and the other girls might as well get that, too. Tony was inclined to be cautious, but Rosy wanted to go so she agreed. They reached St. Paul to find that the girl's employers had gone to Florida and had taken her with them!

Mrs. Benes's comment, "It was not a very happy thing," is perhaps a classic understatement. They didn't know a soul in St. Paul, and the only address they had was that of a girl who wasn't there. They found a man at the address, another Czech, and he informed them that the folks had moved, and he and his wife now lived at this address. He took them and their problem to his wife, and though they were not a wealthy couple, they told the girls they were welcome to stay with them until they found work. They also assured them they would help them find work.

It was Thanksgiving Day when they landed in St. Paul, but when they reached the address of their acquaintance to find her gone, it seemed a day for despair instead of thanksgiving. Before the day was over they could hardly believe things could have changed so dramatically.

As they went to the depot to pick up their trunk after the supper their benefactors had shared with them, they passed an open church. They didn't know what kind of church it was, but their hearts were so full of gratitude they felt they must go in and thank God. The caretaker was just ready to close the church, but he waited until the two immigrant girls had given their thanks for the way God had provided.

Both girls found work quickly in private homes, even though they couldn't speak the same language. A little later Tony had an opportunity for employment in a hospital fixing trays. And she was paid $16 a month, too! Soon Rosy, also, was able to get on at the hospital.

While she was working in the hospital she received a letter from Frank Benes in Montana. Frank was also from Czechoslovakia. Her family was acquainted with his, but he had left his native land a number of years before so she didn't know him.

Back in Czechoslovakia, Entonie's family lived about as far from the Benes family as it is from Bloomfield to Richey, about twenty miles. Since Frank and Tony were both in America, her mother gave her address to his sister, who in turn had sent it to him. Mrs. Benes explained, "They thought America was so small that everyone knew everyone else!"

In the first letter Frank wrote to her he told her that he lived on a homestead in Montana. She had no idea what a homestead was so she took the letter to the woman who had befriended the girls when they first reached St. Paul (they had become good friends) and asked her about it. Her friend didn't know either, but she had a kind of vague idea that it was some sort of rough place.

He wrote several letters and one of his neighbors started writing to Rosy, but the girls were in no hurry. They liked their jobs at the hospital and were getting along well. Then one day at work Tony caught her hand in the dummy that lifted the trays to another floor at the hospital. She thought she was dead, she recalls, but she wasn't. It made her think, though. St. Luke's Hospital, where she worked, was a 'high-priced' hospital so if she had required hospitalization, she'd have had to go to the city hospital, whose reputation was not the best. That thought scared her and perhaps caused her to give a little more consideration to Frank's next letter.

He sent her money for train fare, assuring her, "You don't have to stay. Just come and look it over." She and Rosy still stuck together, and together they decided to come to Montana to 'look it over'. A year after their introduction to Minnesota they had their first glimpse of the badlands (and Indians) of North Dakota and Montana.

Frank Benes, accompanied by a neighbor, met them at the train. When Frank and Entonie did decide to get married, Rosy and the neighbor (Charley Cezeh) were their witnesses. Charley wasn't the homesteader who had written to Rosy in St. Paul, but perhaps meeting her at the train put him in on the ground floor. However it came about, it was Charley who married Rosy a few months later.

He fully intended to come before Christmas to claim her as his bride, but there was so much snow they had to change their plans. Rosy was spending the intervening time with the newlyweds on their homestead south of Richey. The two newcomers had never seen such weather in their lives! There were no roads then, and the trails were buried deep under the snow. When Charley came calling, he had to walk from his homestead to theirs – about six or seven miles 'across country'. All through December and January the snow kept them imprisoned, making a trip to the county seat for a marriage license impossible. In February the weather moderated so they started for Glendive.

The plan had been that Frank and Tony would take Rosy to Cezeh's place so she could look things over and see what she might want to buy while in Glendive, then they would all go on to town. The plan was more reasonable than the weather. Temperatures rose so rapidly there was soon water every place. They left the Benes homestead with team and sled, but they were able to get only as far as George Coryells. There was water, water everywhere, creeks and coulees turned into rivers.

Coryell's horses were sick, and they didn't think it wise to put healthy horses in with them so, though the people found refuge there, the horses had to be taken on over to Hank Zimdars. Riding one and leading the other, Frank took them over. Next day he rode over to Cezehs to let him know they were at Coryells. Charley started to come with a team and wagon (no sled!) to pick up the wedding party and go on to Glendive, but water in the creek was so high he almost drowned his horses. There was nothing to do but stay at Coryells until the water went down.

The wedding party waited at the George Coryell home until water in the creeks and coulees had subsided and mud had dried enough to allow wagon travel. As soon as conditions permitted they started for Glendive, but when they reached the Yellowstone at Glendive, they found that the river had 'gone out'. There was so much ice and high water they couldn't get across the bridge.

294

But the pioneers were resourceful people – they had to be. They turned back to Stipek where they left the team and wagon and boarded the train. At long last they reached the county seat where Charley and Rosy were married. Another wait of almost a week followed before the ice cleared away enough for them to make the return trip. They could have taken the train back to Stipek, but they wanted to load the wagon with supplies before they went back to the homesteads. Little wonder they didn't want to make another trip right away.

As soon as the way was clear Cezeh took the train to Stipek to get his team and wagon, and they loaded, then started for home. They hadn't left Glendive very far behind when snow started falling, and before long they found themselves enveloped in a blizzard. As they struggled on they could hardly stay on the trail, but they knew they had to make it to the Hamilton ranch if they were to survive. Hamiltons had a roadhouse between Bloomfield and Glendive, and that night their house was filled up. The Benes party slept upstairs, but there were people everywhere, even sleeping on the floor around the stove. The stove was a big one and they kept shoveling in coal all through that bitterly cold night. By morning the storm had subsided so the travelers reloaded their wagon and started on. As he loaded, Cezeh found a horseshoe so he threw it into the wagon box because, he explained, a horseshoe is for good luck.

Maybe a horseshoe is for good luck sometimes, but in this case, as the wagon jolted along over the rough, frozen ground, the five-gallon can of kerosene which they were bringing from town jolted onto the horseshoe. Instead of jolting off again it stayed right there and bounced on that horseshoe until a hole was worn through the can. By the time they discovered it, all but about one gallon of the kerosene had leaked out of the can.

Charley delivered Frank and Tony at Coryells where they got their sled and team and went on home. The high wind had swept the ground bare in places, but even where it was bare it was now frozen so they could use the sled. It was good to be home again!

Tony had no idea what a Montana winter could be like, but that first year she learned. The cold and snow had started early, and the one small stove in their little house had to be kept filled all the time. In February she thought spring was coming, but in March the snow came again.

Frank Benes homesteaded about six miles south of Richey in 1912. In Czechoslovakia he had been a tailor, but he couldn't stand the steam. His brother Jim had earlier emigrated to Nebraska so Frank decided to join him. Frank worked for a relative in Nebraska for a time, but then Jim moved to New York to farm, and Frank came to Montana with Tom Jones. He filed on a homestead in Dawson County and started farming for himself.

Although Entonie had had no idea what a homestead was when she first heard the word, she soon began to understand. She enjoyed being outside and always liked to help her husband with his work. One of her first experiences helping him was in breaking some new ground. (Most of the country in that vicinity was still 'new' ground). She was to drive the team for him while he held the plow. He hung his bright colored cap on a fence post across the field from where they were to start and told her to go straight toward that cap. She fixed her eyes on the cap and started toward it, but when she came to a little coulee, she went around it. When she came to some brush, she went around it. When they reached the end of the field, they looked back and the furrow was so crooked he couldn't use it.

One of Mrs. Entonie Benes's most unforgettable experiences on the homestead came when they were ready to start harvesting grain the first harvest season she was in Montana. Her husband hitched four broncs to the binder, then handed her the lines with, "You hold the lines, and I will hurry and get on the seat." He hurried, but the horses reared and plunged. Before she could give the lines to him all four horses were piled on the binder platform! He had to use a knife and cut them loose to get them off the platform, then he riveted and patched the harness and tried again.

When Frank Benes built his first shack on the homestead, he built on the south side of the creek. The first shacks Entonie saw dotting the prairie gave her the impression you could put a couple ropes on them and tie them to your back. In the country from which she had come the houses were built of rock.

The second year Frank and Entonie were married they decided to move to the north side of the creek. (They didn't put a couple ropes on the shack and tie to anybody's back.) Often the creek was hard to cross, and people couldn't get in to visit them. They had such good times when the neighbors came to spend the day, visiting, singing, and playing records on the gramophone, visitors were always welcome.

In the days when they traveled with a team and wagon, going places took much longer, and it wasn't unusual for visitors to stay overnight before starting the long trip back home. After they relocated across the creek on their present home site, getting in and out was much easier for themselves and others.

Many of the early settlers struggled long before finding a satisfactory solution to the water problem. For Frank Benes it meant digging two wells on the south side of the creek and three more on the north side. They had very good water from a spring creek to start with, but they had to carry it too far so they started digging wells. In the sandy soil the wells would cave in so the last one Mr. Benes dug by hand. He rocked up the curb as he dug and the sand didn't cave into that one. For many years they carried the water from the well to the house, but about 1950 they piped it in. Because they are so far from the Rural Electrification Association power lines, they still have their own windcharger to supply their electricity. Bottled gas furnishes the fuel for heating, cooking, and refrigeration.

In May, 1932, Mr. and Mrs. Benes lost everything in a hailstorm, even their house. They were away from home when the storm struck, and the hail knocked the chimney down. That caused a fire to start in the attic so the house and everything in it burned to the ground. Their chickens and geese were killed by the hail. One cow, driven by the storm, fell into an old well; and even some of the horses were cut by the hailstones. The catastrophe was of major proportions, surely enough to cause all but the stoutest hearts to give up, but

Mr. and Mrs. Benes started over and built up their place again. Two years later a granary full of oats burned to the ground when it was struck by lightning, but they just kept on 'keeping on'.

Three children, two boys and a girl, were born to the Beneses. The parents talked Czech in their home so the children did not learn to speak English until they started school. Some of the neighbors thought this an injustice to the children. One Czech friend told Mrs. Benes, "I would be ashamed to send them to school when they couldn't talk American", but Mrs. Benes had her reasons. She was well aware that her own English was very broken, and she reasoned that if they spoke English in the home, the children would talk just the way the parents did. If they waited and learned in school, then they would learn to speak correctly. When so many well-meaning friends insisted she should teach them English at home, she consulted the schoolteacher about her problem. The teacher agreed that they should wait and learn at school. Mrs. Benes noted, "They learned good American in one year at school. Otherwise they would talk just like me."

Mr. Benes passed away in 1948, but Mrs. Benes still lives on the homestead. Their oldest son, who has never married, lives with his mother, while the other son is on a farm about three miles northwest of the home place. Their one daughter lives in Richland County.

It took a long time, Mrs. Benes reflected, to build up the farm. They started slow and built piece by piece. Sometimes they had a crop, sometimes not. "You forget a lot of little things, and some other things you would like to forget," she observed. While life on a Montana homestead involved many heartaches and hardships, she has been satisfied.

John Quick

Submitted by Georgia Ross, daughter

June 1965

My father, John Quick, came to Montana in the year 1907 from a little town called McHenry, North Dakota. Everywhere was advertising of the free land in Montana to homestead and also there was a real estate man, Owen T. Hart, who lived in McHenry who was bringing men out to Montana to locate them on homesteads.

My father had rented farmland and had always had high hopes of owning his own farm and home. So this Owen T. Hart, real estate man, brought my father to Montana and out twelve miles northeast of Bloomfield and thirty miles north of Glendive, he found our home and to my fancy, the nicest land in Dawson County — Section 20, Township 20, Range 5.

My father filed on the land and hired Glen Borntrager to build a little shack (car roof) tar papered, 12'x12', out in the middle of a big prairie.

My dad was a fairly good cook, which was fortunate because he had to do his own cooking before the family came out. He was especially good at making baking powder biscuits, but one day he ran out of lard and had to make them without shortening. When Glen (he was building the shack then) sampled the biscuits, he observed, "John, I don't believe the biscuits are quite as good today." Dad replied, "Oh, yes, Glen." So Glen conceded, "Well, maybe so."

He then came back to North Dakota and there was lots of discussion as to whether we should come to Montana or stay there. The next year he came back to Montana and stayed awhile to hold his rights on the land.

I heard him tell the story of how one night he had gone to bed and he heard strange noises and looking out of the window he could see long horned Texas cattle rubbing on the shack and it was shaking and squeaking. He said there must have been a hundred of them. He was afraid they would stampede and trample his shack if he frightened them so he gently tapped on the window and the cattle close in kept moving around and around and pushing the others out and finally when they were far enough away he opened the door and yelled at them. You can imagine how fast they got out of there! That was a night to remember a long time.

We decided to come to Montana to live and the fall of 1908 my father shipped all our stock and household goods by railway freight and came to Montana.

My mother, brother Harold, and I spent the winter in Illinois with our grandparents so we could go to school. It was four years before we got to go to school out here in the West. We came in March, 1909, and were met in Glendive by my father and neighbor, Leon Kinch, who had come to meet his sister, Cora Johnson, with a team and wagon. It took us all day to drive thirty miles.

We stopped at a half-way ranch on Morgan Creek. The peoples' name was Griffith. We had dinner there. When we got home it was real nice to walk into the house with all our furniture there and pictures on the wall (enlarged pictures of all of us). It really looked like home. Father had built another room of the same size but oh, such a big vast country. This was the beginning of our homestead days.

My first week in Montana was spent in bed with the measles. I was exposed to them on the train, we thought. Our closest neighbors were one and a half miles, also homesteaders, the Ernest Johnsons. When she or my mother wanted help they would hang a white dish towel on the clothes line — we could see each other's house real plain.

We had a team of ponies we drove and our first trip to Bloomfield to buy groceries, we took shavings along (from the new posts we were cutting to fence our land) to mark our way so we could find our way home again in this big sky country. Glendive was the nearest big city, but we drove to Bloomfield for our mail until a few years later when it was delivered by a rural carrier from a post office called Marco (down on the river between Intake and Savage, and now gone a long time ago). Later we got our mail at Intake.

Intake and Stipek had elevators and stores, so we hauled our grain there. Both little towns were really booming then. They had a livery barn, store, saloons, dance halls and hotels. We drove to Glendive about twice a year and stayed over night, but we didn't get to Glendive until we had been here about three years.

All of our plowing was done the first year with a walking breaking plow and I believe thirty acres was probably our first year's crop. The next year a steam engine plowed some for us.

We would get about $60 in groceries every fall from Sears-Roebuck which would be navy beans, pail of fish in brine, and canned goods. Some years we didn't have the $60 so lived on what little we could raise the dry years, and navy beans, which were always cheap and went a long way. I still think they are good food. One year it was so dry there was no grass or hay or straw so we fed our stock Russian thistles. They survived.

Our first water was hauled with a stone boat (a flat bed on homemade sled runners), drawn with one horse about one-half mile. Later we could afford to have a well drilled which was thirty feet deep and wonderful cold water.

We had many experiences with rattlesnakes. Probably our worst was one of our cows that came home one night to be milked and we noticed she was breathing real hard. We thought she had eaten too much and was too full. After a few moments we saw her jaw was swollen and knew she had been bitten by a rattlesnake. My mother tied a white cloth around her head and poured kerosene on the cloth. The oil would drip off and was green. The cow lived. Maybe the coal oil saved her, we never knew for sure.

Our little dog was also bitten by a rattler over his eye and my mother poured whiskey on a rag and tied it around his head and the 'snake medicine' ran down his face into his mouth. I believe he was slightly intoxicated. He would lap it up. He also got well. We killed many rattlers through the years. There were also lots of coyotes, and they would get our chickens.

We were in Montana four years before we had school. By then there were enough children to build one, with a little maneuvering. Mrs. Bob (Kate) Kennedy was under eighteen so they listed her as a pupil to make up the quota, as I remember my dad talking about it. Then they needed more voters for the election so they listed her as a voter, too. And they think they have school problems now!

I do not remember how many there had to be, or how far a distance, but I do know the schoolhouse was built three and a half miles from our place. I rode to school and back, although the first year I stayed with the teacher. She had a homestead in the same section next to the schoolhouse. I went over to her on Sunday and came home Friday. Her name was Mabel Reed and she was a cousin of Clara Cavanaugh (this Clara is a cousin of Mrs. Desmond O'Neil). The schoolhouse has since been moved on a section adjoining the George Zody farm.

We gave basket, pie, and cake socials to buy an organ for the school, and it was bought from the Sears-Roebuck catalog. I believe it cost about $40 at that time. I now have that organ in my home. I had it refinished and fixed so it is like new and very dear to me as I corded while Bob Prigan (killed overseas in World War I) played the violin for dances. Lyle Lundstrom also played sometimes. We had dances at the schoolhouse. I also played for the other pupils to sing. Guess it was rather crude music, but they liked it.

Besides Mabel Reed homesteading in our neighborhood, there was one other lady named Minnie Cole. She had a homestead on the south fork of Burns Creek. She later married Dr. Danskin and now lives in Billings.

When we first came here, all the neighbors took turns meeting at each other's home and everyone brought something to eat. There were the Ernest Johnsons, Ed Kinch, Leon Kinch, Oscar Kinch, John Sullivan, Wood Quick, Ray Kneble, Harry Thompson, Noah Long, Albert Gerlingers, Thad Jones, Charles Williams, August Elpel and John Quicks. Needless to say, we had some good times. We had picnics at the Windmill Ranch on South Fork of Burns Creek and barn dances in the old Sutton Barn over by Virgil Gregg's. We had a phonograph with a horn we used to play at home and we would dance in our kitchen and call square dances. We probably never had a full set in the square but we had lots of fun.

It seemed like all the young folks came to our house and we had such good times. 'Redwing', 'Rainbow', 'Silver Bell', 'When the Sunset Turns the Ocean Blue to Gold' were some of the hot tunes of that day. Violins were played at country dances and maybe a banjo helped out.

A midwife – I believe her name was Mrs. Shay – lived over on Burns Creek. I remember the day John Twedt came driving into our yard, his team all played out. It was forty below zero and lots of snow, and he wanted to get Mrs. Shay to deliver their baby. My dad used his team to take Mr. Twedt on over to the Shays and back to our place, then Mr. Twedt's team was refreshed enough to get back to his homestead where Mrs. Shay was in time to deliver a sound, healthy baby girl whom they named Margaret – now Mrs. Gregg Jones.

Doctors were far away so good old home remedies were used unless something was real serious and then they had to be taken to Glendive or Lambert. My mother was called out many times in sickness and childbirth although she wasn't a midwife. She was just a practical nurse – and she also helped to lay out a few people in case of death to be taken to Glendive.

When Mrs. John Sullivan's mother died, it was in the dead of winter and bitterly cold. They couldn't get to town to buy a casket so my uncle, Elwood (Wood) Quick, built the casket and lined it with some black material from a skirt. She was buried in the Red Top Church cemetery, then later moved to the cemetery at the Bethlehem Mennonite Church.

We dug lignite coal for fuel and had a coal range and a heating stove and burned kerosene lights. If we ran out of kerosene my mother would put a rag in a saucer and cover it with lard. It was sort of a poor light but better than nothing.

Wood was plentiful in Montana on Burns Creek, anyway. My father lost his eye in an accident while chopping wood.

Chokecherries and wild plums were our fruit. Sugar wasn't always available but we would can the juice and make jelly when we could.

I rode horseback to a school in South Valley to church. I do not remember the minister's name or where he came from.

Watkin's medicine man made a trip through the country once in a while.

My father and mother have both passed away and our dear old homestead is gone long ago, but I always make one or two trips out there every summer and drive by and think of all the good times and some of the heartaches of long ago. I live in Glendive and have worked as a PBX Operator for the Northern Pacific Railway Company for many years but recently retired. I hope I have brought back the days of homesteading and related some of the experiences. I am thankful I was brought up 'out there' and can say we were one of the first homesteaders in Dawson County, Montana.

LuLu (Knapp) Quick

February 1974

It was the last part of October 1911 when my father, Mason Knapp, was ending up his business at Cooperstown, North Dakota, and prepared to move to Circle, where he and our housekeeper, Amanda, had filed on claims five and a half miles northwest of Circle. My mother, paralyzed for seven years, had passed away on July 1.

Papa loaded a boxcar with three horses, two cows, and a heifer calf, also machinery, household goods, furniture, trunks of clothing and bedding. About October 25, the freight train pulled out for Glendive, Montana with Papa and Gail, my brother, four years older than me, in it. I had just turned nine. Papa stowed Gail away in the boxcar. About the 27th, Amanda and I took the passenger train for Glendive, the closest railroad station to Circle, about seventy miles. We arrived early the next morning and got a room in a rooming house next to the Reynolds store. We rested awhile, then went down town for breakfast. On the way, Amanda asked me what I thought that big bank was over on the horizon. I said, "A cloud." No, she said it was a huge hill called 'Hungry Joe'. We had not walked very far before we met Papa and Gail. They had arrived the night before.

After breakfast Papa and Gail started unloading the boxcar, putting the hay rack and buggy together. The next morning we left Glendive, papa driving the two mares 'Bessie Tannow' and 'Oakwood-Princess' on the hay rack, loaded very heavy with furniture, trunks, etc. the heifer calf with the two cows were tied behind. Amanda drove 'Little Dick Lochhart' hitched to the buggy with suitcases and as much as we could pile in there, including me, also and my cat.

At first Gail and I walked gathering pretty stones, but I soon got tired and crawled under the blankets in the buggy. The cows got tired and began pulling back, making it harder for the horses with their heavy load. So Papa turned the cows loose and Gail had to drive them behind the load. There was only a wagon trail to follow and darkness set in early and we got off the trail and got lost.

Papa kept going and finally saw a light. We went to it and they were such kind people, father and mother, two little girls and a boy. They gave us supper and put us to bed and fed our livestock. The next morning they gave us breakfast and sent us on our way. They would not take anything, but Papa gave the children a dollar.

By noon Papa decided we had to lighten the load so we pulled into a place by the name of Baggs. There we left some furniture and the heifer calf, until he could come back after it. That helped. That night we stayed at the Garfield Ranch. They had a big sod house plastered inside with clay. The next morning Mr. Garfield made us pancakes and sausages and we were on our way again.

We had not gone very far when it started to snow, making it very hard pulling for the horses on the wagon, as the snow balled up under their feet and they just rocked on them. And poor Gail, tired, sore and wet feet trying his best to keep the cows up with the wagon. Going up the divide, 'Antelope Mountains' they were called, was difficult, but once we reached the top it was easier, as it was downhill all the way to Circle. We reached Circle just as it was getting dark. We pulled up to the hotel, run by Njaas then, got rooms and Papa and Gail put the horses and cows in some kind of a barn.

After a good breakfast we started out on the last lap of our journey. When we had gone about three miles we saw a meteor fall from the sky. It seemed right in front of us, but I suppose it was many miles away. Anyway we never heard anything about it, but all four of us had seen it.

When we reached the homestead, someone was living in Papa's shack, so we drove to Amanda's. Papa and Gail walked up the hill to see if they could see where anyone lived. They saw a house about three-quarters of a mile away, so they walked up there and were able to get the horses and cows in their dugout barn. Mr. and Mrs. Ed Coburn lived there. When Papa and Gail got back we moved into Amanda's shack, a 12'x16' foot shack with only boards over the 2x4's and a curved roof.

The people living in Papa's shack were Mr. and Mrs. Henry Hinds, who were building a house one and a half miles west of us. Papa and Gail helped them, then they helped us build a dugout barn as soon as Papa could freight out lumber from Glendive. They made a four double stall dugout barn.

On one trip to Glendive, Papa stopped at the Baggs homestead to get the rest of the furniture and the heifer calf, but Mr. Baggs would not let Papa have the calf. He kept it for storage of the furniture. This made Papa very unhappy, as in two years she would have been a cow.

We had a small laundry stove but nothing to burn, no coal or wood, so Gail and I would pull the buggy up one hill and down, gathering cow or buffalo chips. The snow had gone by now. When the buggy was full we'd go home and the chips would burn like wood, if good and dry. We had no well yet but down the coulee a ways was a spring. After the barn was finished and Papa was freighting, Gail and I would lead the cows and Little Dick down to the spring, and water them out of a wash tub.

Before the barn was built, Gail walked up to Colburn's every morning and night to feed the cows and Dick. Once he rode Dick home in the evening and tied him to the corner of the shack. Papa was freighting, of course, and Little Dick was lonely out there and kept whinnying and now and then would kick the side of the shack. We could not sleep with that going on, so Amanda told Gail to go out and get Dick and bring him in. Gail did, and tied him to the foot of the bed. Dick became so contented and quiet, never making a sound. He was such a pet and just one of the family.

When Papa was away we would sit around the little laundry stove to eat and to keep warm. Amanda could make only one pancake at a time, and she would give the first one to Gail and the next to me. I don't know when she would get one.

The neighbors would go together seven or eight miles to Redwater River to mine coal, lignite. They would go early and come back late. One night someone knocked at the door. It was a sheepherder who was lost. Gail and I had seen the sheep wagon just before dark, so we could tell Papa just where to go as soon as he came home. Amanda gave Papa and the sheepherder supper, then with a lantern they struck out to find the sheep wagon. They found it and it was OK. The sheepherder had left a fire in the stove so was very nervous for fear of everything burning up. He kept asking what time it was, but just as they were going out the door he said, "Why, I have a watch." The next day he came back with a dressed sheep to show his appreciation for what we had done for him. He was so thankful, and how good that mutton did taste.

Amanda had canned twenty-five or thirty quarts of June berries in Cooperstown and lots of other fruit to bring along, but we were hungry for potatoes and meat and vegetables. One day Mrs. Coburn brought half a gunny sack of potatoes, onions, carrots, rutabagas and turnips. I have never tasted such good turnips since. Amanda gave her canned June berries for it.

Another time Amanda went through some pockets of old suits that Papa had worn in Cooperstown while he was sheriff. She had packed the suits thinking he could use them on the homestead. In one pocket she found a $20 bill. Papa immediately hitched Bess and Oakwood to the stone boat. He put foot-wide boards on the sides and ends and a spring seat across it.

With blankets we rode very comfortably. We went to Circle, 'Old Circle'. It was later moved about half-a-mile, but I am not sure in which direction. Anyway, we bought half a pig, fifty pounds of flour and other groceries from Pete Rorvick, who had a grocery store in his sod house. The post office was there also.

We got our mail only once a week, on Saturdays. The St. Paul Dispatch made lots of reading for the following week. Papa had subscribed to it before leaving Cooperstown. I remember seeing La-Follette's picture with his high bushy hair combed in a pompadour. He was then running for president. Also I remember the people talking about the sinking of the 'Titanic', how John Jacob Astor helped his wife, of a few months pregnant, get into a life boat, and he went down with the ship as they played 'Nearer My God to Thee'.

We had three carpenters for awhile, tarpapering the shack, and putting rubberoid on the roof. Before the roof was covered, we could look up and see the stars. When it snowed our beds would be covered with snow. Water in the water pail would be frozen and water in the wash basin bulged. Also the carpenters helped put up the barn. That made seven of us to sleep, eat, and live in the 12'x16' foot shack. Gail slept with Amanda and me, two men with Papa and one on the floor. The poor man must have gotten awfully cold but he never complained. No one ever did. Everyone was always so contented and happy.

Our first Christmas, we were invited to Henry Hinds. Oh, what a good dinner she had and plates of candy sitting around. We got started for home late and as usual darkness set in all at once. We got lost. Amanda lost her glasses. Papa stuck the 'Go Devil' stone boat tongue up the snow so in the spring we would know where to look for them. And we did find them in the spring. Well, we saw Hinds' light, so we went back there and stayed all night. In the morning we went home, a bright sunny crisp morning. As the road rounded the hill we could see Little Dick peeking around the corner of the shack. He had been out all night. As soon as he was sure it was us, he came running, whinnying, kicking up his heels, so glad to see us.

No school the first year for Gail and me but the reader, arithmetic, and spelling books Amanda had brought along. But the beginning of the second year, the Lost Creek School was built and Gail and I walked four and a half miles to it. George Tribe was our teacher, a bachelor, and a very educated and kind hearted man. He had done lots of traveling, so for opening exercises he would tell us of his travels. While walking, Gail and I would see something shiny. He would tell me maybe it was a diamond and the first one to reach it could have it. Of course he could outrun me, and when we got there it was only a tin can left by some sheepherder. After it got cold, Papa rigged up a cart and we drove Little Dick. We would leave him in Bill Knight's barn and walk half a mile to the schoolhouse. Some afternoons would be stormy and we would stay all night at the Knight home.

Ethel and Gladys, their two girls, went to school, too. One afternoon, Gail thought the bit was too cold to put in Little Dick's mouth so he told me to try it out first. It was cold, it stuck to my tongue and of course I pulled, taking the skin off my tongue, which was sore for a very long time.

In freighting, the men camped out in nice weather. They hobbled* the horses and cooked something to eat. They would jab their knives, forks, and spoons into the ground and they would come out so shiny and clean.

Papa broke up land with the three horses and planted it to oats. It was a beautiful crop but he could not get a threshing machine, so with the neighbors' help, he stacked it. I believe there were five big round stacks. He fenced it but the CK cattle, hundreds and hundreds of them broke down the fence, ate and trampled it all down. We never had another good crop like that. We had good gardens but not enough rain for the crops. Papa would sit out in the yard at night watching clouds come up but they would either go to the north and follow Lost Creek or to the south and follow Horse Creek. Papa would come in not saying a word and go to bed.

Reverend Beam came about in 1913 and took up a homestead one and a half miles north of us. He had been a missionary in China and held services in the schoolhouse. Rev. Beam married Papa and Amanda in 1914. They lost both claims and left the homesteads. Later Papa became sheriff of McCone County for twelve years.

Francis Miller

February – April 1973

Back in 1907 cars weren't the common mode of transportation they are now so when Francis Miller decided to investigate homestead opportunities in Dawson County, he rode his bicycle.

Francis was working for Pete Yoder in Mylo, North Dakota, when he heard about the Montana homestead land. He pedaled his bicycle to York where he could catch a train for Culbertson, Montana. At Culbertson he was interested to find that one of the men he met already had a homestead in Dawson County.

The Missouri River was very high due to heavy rains, but there was a ferry so he and his bicycle crossed on it. They couldn't make the first landing so went ashore at the second landing.

He – and his bicycle – then took a stagecoach. The bicycle was tied on behind. "Six horses of good sturdy build," Francis reports, "drew the stage coach. Every twenty miles the team was relieved by a fresh team and the coach rolled briskly on."

His journey began at nine o'clock in the morning and he arrived in Glendive at ten o'clock that evening. He had originally planned to get off the stage at Headgate (now Intake) and ride across country the thirty miles to the Jake Chupp home. However, by the time they reached Headgate, it was already dark so he went on to Glendive. Riding across that country on a bicycle even in daylight would be no mean feat so a stranger was wise to go on to Glendive. He stayed at the Jordan Hotel that night and, after a restaurant breakfast, started his bicycle trip northwest. He wasn't traveling on an oiled highway, either.

It was about nine o'clock when he started. He had pedaled only a few miles when Jerry Steffus came along with an empty hayrack. Steffus picked him up and in good time delivered him at the Jake Chupp home. (Mrs. Chupp was his first cousin.) If you should have a condescending view of the speed and comfort of a team and hay rack transportation, try riding a bicycle twenty-five or thirty miles on an unpaved surface. Francis was glad for the lift.

Jake Chupps lived almost a mile south of the Red Top schoolhouse, on the east side of the road. The house which Jake built is still standing even though it is in rather dilapidated condition and it's been twelve or fourteen years since anyone has lived in it.

At church the next Sunday Francis met Enos Yoder who lived one-and-a-half miles north of the Red Top School. Enos had a team and buggy and offered to take Francis homestead hunting the next week. They spent the first half-day looking in the vicinity of Enos's place but everything in that area seemed to be claimed so the next day they ranged farther abroad. About seven miles to the northwest they found a quarter section that was nice land and still to be had for the filing so Francis went back to Glendive and filed on it. This was in July of 1907. Several years later they bought more land adjoining this original piece until they had a whole section.

306

The homestead law gave them six months time to build a shack so after he filed, Francis went back to North Dakota to work in the harvest. His wife, Lena, worked in the cook car – a kitchen (and dining room, if you please) on wheels that moved about with the harvest crew. In November that same year, Francis and Lena moved to Montana. They lived with Jake Mullet while they built their shack. They also built a small barn at this time.

Francis Miller was born February 4, 1884, at Mt. Ayr, Indiana. His mother died when he was less than four years old. A year later his father remarried. When Francis was eighteen, his stepmother too, passed away. The following year his father again remarried, this time a widow. When he brought his new wife home, he also brought along her daughter, Magdalena (Lena). "He did not realize," Francis observes, "that he was bringing home a bride for me also but that is just what happened. Three-and-a-half years later, I married my step-sister."

Since his father was an Amish farmer and owned several farms, Francis learned a lot about farming – from experience, starting at an early age. He attended school for eight years and continued working on the farm after he was out of school. He also had experience working in a coal mine.

Shortly before he and Lena were married, Francis met Jake Mullet who was visiting in Indiana. It was very easy to get acquainted with Jake and Francis speculates that Jake must have talked about his home in Montana although he doesn't remember specifically. He probably talked about North Dakota too since he had just been working there so it was he who first stirred Francis' interest in 'the frontier'.

It was about this time that several of Lena's cousins from North Dakota visited in Indiana and they definitely stirred up an interest in the West, telling about the nice farm land and job opportunities in North Dakota.

After Francis and Lena were married they had to decide where they were going to live. They thought they'd try North Dakota. Five days after their wedding they boarded a train heading for the Flickertail State. This was in March of 1907.

Almost as soon as they reached North Dakota, Francis went to work on Pete Yoder's farm. Then in July he made the trip – by bicycle, train, stage coach, and hay rack – which landed him on a Montana homestead.

When Francis and Lena moved to Montana after the North Dakota harvest, they found a number of young people living in the 'young settlement'. (With the exception of a few ranchers, the earliest settlers along Thirteen Mile Creek had only been there about four years.) While the home site Francis had located was several miles north of this community, Jake Mullet, with whom they lived the first few months, lived in the Thirteen Mile Valley.

Just one mile away from Jake was the Chaney home with four young people, Clyde, Ora, Cordia, and Sylvus. "We had a real good time together playing games," both Francis and Lena aver, adding, "Ora, who married Menno Mullet (brother to Jake), still visits us here in Virginia in late years." They seem to enjoy each other's company just as much now as they did sixty-five years ago.

During their first January in Montana, Lena and Francis went with Jake and Joe Mullet to Red Water Divide to get cedars. They camped along the divide during this time, near Clay Butte – the highest point in Dawson County. This was eight miles from Miller's homestead.

While they were camped in the divide getting the cedars out they lived in a twelve by fourteen tent pitched in a little canyon. There was a coal vein nearby where they dug coal to supply fuel for the stove they kept going in the tent. Lena cooked for the men. New Year's day the temperatures were so warm they walked around in their shirtsleeves.

When Francis and the Mullet boys went to the Divide to cut cedar posts, Jake took two teams of horses – his own and a team belonging to his brother Mose. Mose had a pair of big, beautiful horses that pulled without a driver, simply following the team ahead.

Jake hauled hay to Glendive occasionally and brought back supplies to the Divide camp. Francis cut the cedars using one horse to snake out the posts. Joe drove a team back and forth picking up posts already cut. Jake and Francis each cut 1,500 posts during the month of January. They used these to fence their homesteads.

Inside the tent they slept on bedsprings. They carried water for drinking and washing from a spring down the canyon. One night during a strong wind their tent blew down. Before it collapsed they were able to carry the stove with the fire in it outside and set it down. Then the tent fell.

One day during this post-cutting period, Francis was sick and had to stay in bed. As he lay there he heard loud and repeated calls from Jake, high up on a hill. Thinking Jake was being attacked or threatened by grave danger of some sort, sick Francis jumped from his bed, snatched up his rifle and tore up the hill to rescue him. When the rescuer arrived, a sheepish Jake explained that he was merely shouting to test the echoes. What a letdown for the sick hero! He never did find out how many echoes Jake heard in answer to his yells.

The last few days in January turned snowy and cold so they closed the post-cutting operations, took down the tent and went home. They were well pleased with the supply of posts they had gathered. 'Home' now was the little shack they had built the preceding November. For five years they lived in the little ten by sixteen foot house. That first year in Montana they planted about two acres of wheat and twelve acres of oats. They also had a garden.

On May 18, 19, and 20, they had a blizzard, which deposited more snow than they had had all winter. (Does this hold any portent of what we might expect after our mild winter months this year?) The first two days Francis was able to get to the barn to do the chores but the last day it wasn't safe to venture outside. On the fourth morning when he was able to make his way to the barn, his horses were really happy to see him.

After he had fed them, he went to check on the two pigs which were in a pigpen beside the barn. When he got to where the pen was supposed to be, he could see nothing but a big snowdrift. He figured the pigs would be dead by this time but he got a shovel and started digging. Soon he could hear the pigs grunting so he knew they were still alive after all.

At the other end of the barn was a drift just about as high as the barn itself. Everywhere you looked there were big snowdrifts. Many ranchers and homesteaders throughout the country suffered considerable loss of livestock in that May storm.

In the fall of 1908, the Millers returned to North Dakota for a few months during harvest and threshing season. Before leaving their Montana homestead Francis cut and stacked his grain. While he was threshing in Dakota, Lena again worked in the cook car. Back in Montana a threshing crew came to their homestead and threshed their first year's crop which yielded about fifty-six bushels of wheat (from two acres) and 250 bushels of oats (from twelve acres). Since he had not yet built a granary, they stored the grain in the house – the little ten by sixteen foot shack in which the Millers lived during their first five years in Montana.

When Francis and Lena came back to the homestead early in the winter, he had to fix up a bin in the barn for the grain first thing so they could get into their house again. It took him most of the first day to fix the bin so he didn't get much grain transferred from house to barn.

Earlier in the day their neighbor had come up and told them they should sleep at his place that night. However, a Chinook wind started blowing and the snow started melting. A creek separated them from their neighbor's place and that evening when they attempted to go, they found the creek so swollen they couldn't cross it. There was nothing to do but go back to their own shack so they fixed a bed on top of the oats and slept there.

Francis recalls many interesting experiences connected with his grain hauling. The first years he had only one team of horses, as did some of the other homesteaders, so it was a good idea to travel with another grain hauler. Then if they came to a hill that was too steep for one team, they could help each other by hitching both teams to one wagon, pulling it up the hill, then taking both teams back for the second wagon. This of course consumed quite a bit of time but at least they were able to get over the hills.

One time Francis, Fred Erbaugh and Lloyd Hatch all started off together with their wagon loads of wheat. (They bagged the wheat for hauling although sometimes they would have loose grain in the bottom of the box, the sacks of wheat on top.) It took them five hours to go the five miles to the blacksmith shop. At that point they decided it would be best to leave the loaded wagons there, take their horses home and spend the night, then get a good start the next morning. Francis and Fred left at five the next morning. It took them almost two hours to get to their loads and get started on to Glendive and the rest of the day to get on into town.

On such trips they usually planned to spend one day in town before starting home again. While in town their loads were standing at the blacksmith shop, and the birds found their grain and had quite a feast. Francis and Fred figured they probably lost several bushels. Lloyd Hatch, who had left his load there for several days before he could get back to take it on to Glendive, had quite a substantial loss. They started back the next day and it took them about ten hours to get home with their empty wagons.

Back in the days when grain was cut with a binder and threshed later with a separator, farmers of necessity did much of their grain hauling in the winter – and income tax had nothing to do with their decision.

One winter morning Francis Miller and Ike Stanley, traveling together, started for Intake with a load of grain. It was a pleasant day with a nice breeze from the west on their backs.

They made it to Intake without incident, unloaded, and spent the night at the hotel, prepared for an early start next morning. They planned to leave by six o'clock, but at six the temperature was forty-five degrees below zero.

They waited around until ten o'clock. By then it felt warmer so they started for home. It wasn't too bad until they reached the Table, but then a cold wind hit them directly in the face. Francis was wearing two coats – a sheep skin and a fur coat – but even that wasn't enough. The wind came up under those coats and chilled him through and through.

He tried walking beside the wagon and then behind, but neither way made the situation any better so he got back up on the wagon and tried to keep warm by clapping his hands and stomping his feet. That effort also was far from successful. The lead team had icicles over a foot long hanging from their noses before they reached shelter that night. Mr. Miller still seems to feel a bit of that frigid weather as he remembers how long it took him to thaw out after arriving home. But such experiences were all a part of the 'the good old days'.

During the time the Millers lived in the little ten by sixteen house two daughters, Vera and Margaret were born. In 1912 they hired a carpenter neighbor, George Greb, to help them build a new four-room house in which they then lived six years. Shortly after they were settled in this new house, daughter Agnes was born. Roy, Abner and Clara were also born while they lived there.

The first years they were on the homestead their nearest neighbor lived three miles away. He was a rancher who was not in sympathy with the homesteaders. Although they lived only nineteen miles from Richey, Mrs. Miller never visited the little town. She couldn't have at first because the town didn't get its start until several years after the Millers homesteaded, but even after the railroad came in and made it a business center she never made a trip there. Francis, of course, found this closer terminal advantageous for hauling grain. With a team and wagon, every mile counted.

Rattlesnakes were common in the area, and Francis killed quite a number while he farmed in Dawson County. One day a hawk alighted on a little rise near the house so he took his shotgun, hoping to get close enough to shoot. Creeping along on his hands and knees through an oat field to keep out of sight of the hawk, he suddenly found himself only about six feet from a good sized rattler. He couldn't find a rock to throw so he threw a chunk of sod. How that snake rattled and hissed and struck! With nothing satisfactory to throw, Francis decided to shoot him even if he scared the hawk by the blast.

He had a double barreled shot gun, one barrel with large shot and one with finer shot. He figured it best to use the small shot for the snake and save the big shot for the hawk, but in his excitement he pulled back the wrong hammer. Bang! At such close range he couldn't miss! He never did find the snake's head and found only part of the rattles. Nine were left. By that time he forgot all about the hawk. Mr. Miller, in his Virginia home, still shows eleven sets of rattles taken from rattlesnakes he killed while in Montana.

When Francis and Lena Miller moved to Montana, a small group of Amish lived in Thirteen Mile Valley. They met for worship in each other's homes, but since the Millers lived eight miles from the other members, they didn't attend every Sunday. They traveled to church services in a hay rack so, although the actual number of miles may be the same, certainly the distance seemed much greater than it would now in a car which would cover that same distance in a few minutes.

A year or so after they moved to Montana, a Mennonite Church was formed in the community where they lived, and in 1909 they became members of this church. They had no resident minister at first so C.J. Schmidt asked H.A. Baughman, a minister and head of the Freeman Bible College, Freeman, South Dakota, to come to Bloomfield and baptize his children. The minister did come, the children were baptized, and the following day some of the girls visiting in the Miller home, told of their experience. Mr. and Mrs. Miller wanted to be baptized, too, so Lena suggested that Francis go talk to the minister who was still at the Schmidts.

He went over the same day and talked to Schmidt, but the minister was in the house and Francis was too shy to ask to talk to him. So he rode his horse the three miles back to his own home, rather discouraged over prospects for baptism. However, the following day Mr. and Mrs. Andrew (Grandpa) Buller learned of the problem so they told the minister and he called at the Miller home. After counseling with them he agreed to baptize them.

The next day a special meeting was called. Mr. and Mrs. Enos Yoder, Mr. and Mrs. Joe Borntrager, Mr. and Mrs. Andrew Buller, and the Schmidt family were there in addition to the Millers and the minister. Mr. Miller recalls of that day more than sixty years ago, "Brother Baughman read from John 15, 'I am the vine, ye are the branches.' At the close of the service, the rite of baptism was administered to us. Then we had communion together. When the offering was lifted at this meeting, I gave all I had – a total of sixty-four cents."

About this time sentiment became strong for more regular services. John Schwartz, Joe Graber, and Peter Senner all with big families had moved in from South Dakota, and they wanted Sunday School. Gerald Boese, father of Alfred Boese, was also an attendant at these early meetings.

Their first meeting was held in the barn belonging to Fred Buller. Because of this they decided to name their group Bethlehem. To this day the church is called Bethlehem Mennonite Church. P.P. Tschetter was the first resident minister, and has been a lifelong friend of the family. He was single so he took turns staying in the different homes.

During World War I the Bethlehem Mennonite pastor (John Franz at that time) was seized by a mob. Their church was non-resistant and Pastor Franz helped some of the young men fill out their questionnaires as conscientious objectors. Also, the Franzes received a newspaper, printed in German, from their home town of Mountain Lake, Minnesota. Church services were held in German so Pastor Franz was accused of being pro-German. Feelings were running high against Germans, culminating in mob action on a Saturday when twelve masked men kidnapped him.

Pastor John Franz and his wife had gone to a school meeting at the Independent School northeast of Bloomfield. Soon after the meeting convened, a stranger came in and asked Pastor Franz to come outside. The minister complied and was immediately seized and dragged to a waiting car. Mrs. Franz, realizing something was amiss, hurried out to the car but she was knocked down and left unconscious as the car drove away. As they headed toward Glendive, a rope and shovels on the floor of the car mutely announced their intentions.

Any doubt as to their intentions vanished when they stopped beside a large tree and looped one end of the rope over a branch. While this was being done the men argued among themselves, and Pastor Franz prayed. As they led him to the tree where the noose hung ready, he noticed the county attorney and the sheriff in the group. He pointed out to them that he was an American citizen, as was his father, and his grandfather was a naturalized citizen. "If you kill me," he told them, "you will be murderers. Think of that!"

Some of the men had been drinking and were in no mood to listen to reason but the sheriff, realizing they could run into serious consequences, managed to persuade them to take Franz to the jail in Glendive. In the meantime, the church members gathered to pray while some of the leaders of the congregation took Mrs. Franz to Glendive where she was allowed to see her husband.

Nothing was done about the matter Sunday but Monday a trial – at least a period of interrogation – was held. Franz was then returned to jail and bond was set at $3,000. Officials were sure the money could not be raised but within three hours of the time they received the information, his church had the $3,000 ready. This show of confidence in, and concern for, their pastor amazed county officials.

John was allowed to return to his home on the condition that he report to Glendive each month to answer any questions that might come up. However, before the end of the first month the bond money was returned and a letter informed him that he would not have to come in for questioning. Later friends around the Mennonite community learned that the county officials had heard false stories about the Mennonites. Lawyers urged Pastor Franz to sue the officers and business men responsible for his abduction but he just quoted the

Bible verse, "Vengeance is mine; I will repay, saith the Lord." And he let the Lord take care of the matter.

After Francis became a Christian his Bible was in daily use and he frequently alluded to it in conversation. One of his neighbors, named Fred, used to laugh, "Ho, ho, I don't believe it." Then in 1910 came terrible forest fires. Although the fires raged far to the west, the sky in eastern Montana was filled with smoke and ashes. One morning the smoke was so dense that the Millers, not realizing what time it was, stayed in bed until ten o'clock. Only when the chickens made their way to the house demanding breakfast did Francis get a light (you didn't just flick a switch then) and check the time. He could hardly believe it was daytime when it was still so dark.

Later in the day an uneasy Fred came calling. He was afraid the world was coming to an end. Once after this, during threshing, the men were discussing something from the Bible. Again, Fred laughed saying there was nothing to it. Francis then reminded him of the day he thought the world was coming to an end. Fred said no more about not believing the Bible.

Francis Miller not only believed the Bible; he believed in its practicality for every day living. Harold Stanley of Billings tells of an experience he had with his Uncle Francis. They had overhauled a Nicholson-Shepherd gasoline tractor, but when the time came to start it, all efforts were in vain.

"Wait a minute," said Francis to Harold. He pulled out his Bible which he kept on the tractor. Quietly he read a portion of Scripture, then prayed and asked God to help him. Again he tried to start the tractor and it responded immediately. This experience made an unforgettable impression on the younger man.

In 1910 Harold's parents, the Isaac Stanleys, had moved to Montana. Harold's mother, Amanda, was a sister to Francis, and it was his influence, of course, that brought them to the Treasure State.

Stanleys worked on the Cavanaugh Ranch at first, then bought a quarter section of land just south of Millers and lived in Millers' granary until they were able to get their shack built. Then in turn, when Millers in 1912 replaced their homestead shack with a four-room house, they lived with Stanleys until their new house was ready for occupancy.

In 1917 Francis' sister Mattie with her husband and family (the Levi Millers) moved to Montana. They also lived in Francis' granary for a while. Levi worked for Francis when they first came to Dawson County.

Descendants of Francis and of Mandy have all moved from this area, but some of Mattie's grandchildren and great-grandchildren still live in Dawson County. Mandy passed away in Oregon, Mattie in Glendive. Francis lives in Virginia.

Montana may have seemed like the land of promise from a distance, but they soon found it didn't always keep its promises. In 1910 they had only four inches of rain from the time they planted their seed until they harvested. They didn't have much to harvest.

There were other hindrances to a good crop, too. One year they had a bad hail storm with stones the size of peaches. Even chickens weren't a sure 'crop' because sometimes the coyotes ate those. It wasn't all smooth sailing 'in the good old days'.

There may not have been much actual difference in the winters then and now, but there certainly was a difference in housing and transportation. By the time they drove thirty-five miles in a bobsled to Glendive, even with heated sad irons or stones to warm the feet, below-zero temperatures were bound to make more of an impression than when that same trip is made in a late model, heated auto.

In 1918 and 1919 Francis had the flu so often that for almost a year he was unable to work. Several times he thought that the end of his life had come. He promised the Lord that if He spared his life, he would live for Him the rest of his days. Well into old age Francis talked to prisoners in jail services and assisted in a little city mission within driving distance of his home.

Even now, although he recently celebrated his eighty-ninth birthday, he goes to the jail every Sunday to speak to 'his boys'. They have not been going to the Mission Church for about seven years, but they did help there for fourteen years.

Because of his continual bouts with the flu, Mr. Miller's doctor recommended that they move to the west coast. He liked Montana so well that he would have remained here the rest of his life if he had been physically well enough to do so. As it was, they left Montana in 1919.

When they moved, they took their trunks on a sled over the snow to Glendive, leaving most of their household goods behind. They moved to the state of Washington, and after taking twelve treatments he was able to go to work.

Ben Holzworth farmed his land for awhile, then in 1944 the late William Senner (sister Mattie's son-in-law) bought the place.

The Millers lived in Washington for three-and-one-half years, then moved to Nappanee, Indiana, so they could be with and help care for his aging parents. In 1940 they moved to southeastern Virginia where their home has been since.

Francis still has three diamond willow canes that he made while in Montana. One cane he gave as a gift to his father, and a fifth he sold in Washington while they lived there. He has a couple hundred pounds of agates as reminders of his homestead days, and also some petrified wood which is a source of interest to visitors. These souvenirs help to keep fresh their memories of the years spent in the Treasure State.

Mrs. Earl (Elsie Cravath) Grow

July - August 1970

Mrs. Earl Grow of Enid is a history writer's 'dream come true'; she kept a diary! In 1907 her father, F.J. Cravath seeking range for his Percheron horses, moved his family and livestock from Anamoose, North Dakota to eastern Montana.

Railroad transportation was available, but Mr. Cravath chose, instead, to come by covered wagon and drive the horses and cattle overland. In the party were Mr. and Mrs. Cravath, their six daughters: Winifred, Elsie, Florence, Marjorie, Alice, and Marion (four years old); Winifred's husband, Walter Revo; and a cousin, E.R. (Bob) Haven.

Mrs. Grow (Elsie) has written an introduction to her day-by-day chronicle and has added some comments. She writes:

On Saturday, August 17th, 1907, at about 10 a.m. we left our summer camp which was on a very high hill a few miles north of Seabolt's Lake and started on our trip overland to Montana. Papa drove Dapple and Dick on the covered wagon; Walter drove Billie and Romeo on the open wagon; Mama, Winifred, and Marion rode in the spring wagon, driving Hattie and Robert's Babe.

Robert rode Pinto; Florence, Little Bill; and I rode Gentle. We three usually drove the bunch of horses, numbering 110, and Marjorie and Alice, riding Prince and Kitty drove the cattle — about 22 head. Sometimes we changed off for every one wanted to drive the horses and no one the cattle. Sometimes we tried to drive the cattle just behind the horses, but that did not work very well because they were so much slower.

(Eighty-year-old Mrs. Grow looks back to that trip 63 years ago and notes that she rode horseback every step of the way, mainly so she could, in coming years, look back and say that she did).

Our first drive was through a Russian settlement, and besides the adobe houses, the most noticeable things were the immense stone piles at the corner of each field. One particularly large one, which looked like a stack of hay, was, we judged, about 10 or 12 feet wide, 25 feet long and 8 feet high. Beside one of these stone piles we stopped for our first meal on the road. We ate from the cupboard in the back of the wagon, the front of which let down, making a small table.

After driving about ten miles that afternoon we reached Crooked Lake where we made camp for the night. Making camp was usually done about this way — Papa and Robert, assisted by some of the girls, would take care of the work horses, picketing some, hobbling others, and leaving a few of the quietest loose; milk the cows and help unload the wagons the things needed for the night.

Walter and Mama pitched the tents — the round cooking tent in which were put the sheet-iron cook-stove and the cupboard and the two sleeping tents — one a wall tent and the other a Miner's A. In these Mama and the girls spread out the rolls of bedding.

Usually dry wood for the cook-stove could be found near the camping place or else had been picked up along the way. After supper one of the men would go out to herd the bunch, which I had been watching until then at a short distance where the grazing was good. Usually Walter or Robert night-herded, Papa occasionally taking his turn.

Sunday, August 18th: During the night a little colt was born so we had to lay up for a day. Papa, Mama, Florence, Marion, and I drove over to visit Jim Hotchskins who lived a few miles up from the lake. The year before they had lived on our old place at Anamoose. Florence and I went because we wished to see Charlie Burroughs, an old school friend. Mrs. Hotchskins gave us garden vegetables and flowers.

That evening at camp a man whom Robert had met (on his trip to look up the route) brought us some ducks. We also rowed on the lake and went in bathing.

Monday, August 19th: We let the little colt have another day to rest. Marjorie, Alice and Marion visited at Harmon's and played with their three children. After dinner Mrs. Harmon and the children came to camp. The children were so pleased with everything. The little boy wanted to take one of the dolls home, so Alice gave him a clothespin doll. He was greatly pleased.

August 20th: Tuesday morning after rolling up bedding, loading tents, stove, cupboard, etc., we resumed our journey. Went by Frye's at the end of Strawberry Lake, through Horseshoe Valley, and to Miss Boe's claim where we stopped for dinner. Miss Boe and her sister Lilah went with us until night when we camped near a ranch and a small alkali lake. They greatly enjoyed the riding and camping.

The boys had said that Gentle's little colt Polly should be the mascot on the trip. She was always a great pet and soon got to be rather a nuisance around camp. Whenever anything was going on she would be right there to see all about it and would bound like a rubber ball.

There was a bunch of four thin orphan colts, The Royal Four. The smallest and poorest Marjorie fed oats and named Princess. The boys called her The Mule.

August 21st, Wed.: In the morning Papa took Miss Boe and Lilah home and then overtook us. We drove through a hard country. There were many grain fields, all unfenced, along the road, and it was difficult to keep the horses out. They ran through one wheat field and the owner wanted $125 damages. Papa was willing to pay within reason, but as the man would listen to nothing less we just drove on and left him alone with his wrath. We camped at night about two miles east of Garrison where we remained for the next day, Papa going to Garrison to arrange for the inspection of the horses. Marjorie, Alice, and Marion played by the shore of the lake most of the day.

August 23rd: We drove to Garrison and pitched camp just south of town. Florence and Marjorie held the horses about a mile from town, waiting for someone to come and help them corral. While they were waiting the McLean County constable paid them a visit and ordered them off. He said, "Why, your father has no more right to put his horses here than he has to turn them into a man's wheat field." They told him all he had to do was to notify them and they would take them off. The next thing he said was that it was a nice bunch of horses. Then the folks came to help get the horses into the stockyards in town. But we could not get the inspection so the boys took the horses out east of town and herded them until late. They corralled in town without water as there was no place they could get it. While we were eating supper at camp Walter came home with some ice cream, which was quite a treat for us.

Saturday, August 24th: In the morning we found that the cattle had got out of the stockyards. Florence and I went after them and found them taken up a quarter of a mile from town with $2.00 damages against them. Florence stayed and herded them. Dr. Robinson inspected the horses and found them to be all right. After looking them over he said to Papa, "Would you take $100 around" (considered at that time a very good price) "for the bunch?" "Oh, no, of course not." "But would you take $110?"

At about 2:30 we left town and drove to some very deep little lakes before we had dinner. As the horses had had no water for a day and a half they were dreadfully thirsty. Did not drive far that afternoon and camped by a creek.

Sunday, August 25th: As we drove along we took several pictures, one of an old cabin with the logs running up and down and others of the badlands near Old Garrison and Fort Stevenson. We passed right by the large vacant buildings of the fort. That night after crossing a big bridge at Douglas Creek we camped in a loop of the creek. We placed the wagons and tents across the opening of the loop and stretched a lariat between one of the wagons and a tree to keep the horses on that side. Then Walter and Rob slept near the bridge to keep any of them from going back. The banks along the creek were so steep and high they would not cross so they were in a corral and did not need night herding.

We made camp quite early, and as it was very pretty along the creek, Marjorie and Marion went for a walk. They came back with their hands full of the most beautifully colored poison ivy! Mama had them wash their hands in strong soda water and Marion was not poisoned. But Marjorie was not so fortunate. They also picked chokecherries for supper.

Monday, August 26th: The girls spent the forenoon playing on the bridge with their feet hanging over, a load of smarties went by and hollered, "Hello, boys!" And they were quite insulted. They also played with a very nice girl and her brother from a farm about a mile away.

In the afternoon Papa, Robert, Winifred, Florence, Marjorie, and Alice drove to Expansion to see about ferrying the horses across the Missouri. They had to drive about half a mile on a sandbar to reach the ferry landing. On his trip looking up the trail Rob had made arrangements to have them ferried.

The next day we drove across the old Military Reservation. By this time the horses had become so used to traveling that in the morning as soon as they saw the tents being taken down they would begin to work toward the wagons, and by the time we were ready to start, Lady's three-year-old, Leo, would fall in behind the last wagon. Lady and her younger colts would follow, and then the whole bunch with Spera and Guybert always in the rear, walking along side by side. We took a picture of the bunch on the trail in the badlands and of Robert, Florence, Marjorie, and me up on one of the buttes. We camped at night just east of the Fort Berthhold Indian Reservation. Some of the horses got tangled in wire near the reservation, but there were no bad cuts.

August 28th: It rained nearly all day so we did not break camp. Two Indians visited in the afternoon. One was a young man and the other quite old and badly crippled with rheumatism. He was dressed partly in Indian garb with his black hair in two braids tied with strips of colored cloth. They sat in the tent all the afternoon, saying little and when spoken to, answering in monosyllables, grunts or motions, but seeming very friendly and accepting our invitation to stay for supper. We had soup and, in accordance with Indian customs, Mama gave them large bowls full and very thick slices of bread to signify generosity.

August 29th: We started across the Fort Berthhold Indian Reservation. When watering the horses at the first creek a very old Indian riding an Indian pony came to help us. All he wore was a pair of buckskin leggings and a cotton shirt. His head was bare and bright strips of cloth were braided in his hair. As long as we followed the Missouri Valley where there were plenty of trees and water there were many Indian dwellings with some gardens and very small fields of oats. Then we went up on the hill back from the river valley and stopped on the open prairie for dinner.

An old Indian riding a white horse with a feather and very bright green ribbon in its tail, stopped to ask for something to eat. We took a picture of Mama giving him dinner but, like many of the others, it was not good.

We girls climbed a very high hill to see a small volcanic crater at the top. There beside a boulder of lava I found a large Indian pipe bowl made from red pipe stone. Then we drove on across the prairie. We met a load of Indians driving in a democrat wagon*. In the back, sitting on the bottom of the wagon, was a very large, fat Indian woman in a very bright red dress who waved and pointed and motioned about the roads until they were some distance past.

Walter, Winifred, Robert, and I climbed another very high hill to get a view of the Missouri River and valley. It was beautiful. We took two pictures but as the sun was low, they were not very good. At the very top of the hill an iron pipe was driven as a geological mark. Near it sat a very old Indian watching the sunset. He could talk a little and said for us not to cross the reservation.

As we drove on across the prairie we saw fewer and fewer Indian farms until we came to an entirely open country. That night we drove until late trying to find water. We crossed a strip of fresh burning, which was miles wide. It was dusty and choking and we all got so tired. Mama and Winifred drove ahead to look for water, but as they did not find it we stopped as soon as we were across the burning. It was about ten o'clock and all were so tired that we stopped right in the road; did not wait to put up the tents but slept in the covered wagon and on the ground. But the horses smelled water and ran ahead to Lucky Mountain Creek. Walter was night herding and being afraid it might be muddy or too steep, went back for Papa and Robert to help hunt for a crossing. They got to the creek in time to see the last one plunge over the bank. None of the horses were injured.

To drive across an Indian reservation one is supposed to write to the Department of the Interior at Washington, D.C. and get a permit. But that often takes so long as to make quite a delay. So instead of doing that we had made one day's drive onto the reservation and then in the morning Rob rode back to Fort Berthold to report to the Indian Agent. As Papa expected, he said it would be easy to put us off one side as the other, and sent an Indian police back with Bob to overtake us and accompany us off the west side.

In the meantime we had been driving on. We went through a long coulee and by a little ranch. An Indian boy riding bareback and managing his pony with a lariat rope around its neck, helped us drive the bunch for some distance. We drove down between high bluffs on one side and the river on the other, across a very rough road.

We twisted around the curves of the river until when we stopped for dinner, we all thought we were headed a different way. As we could come to no agreement we decided we were facing straight up. Walter caught a fish in the river.

Sometime during the day we met an Indian who talked with Papa in sign language, explaining that the river road was longer but the other road had many hills.

As we were leaving the river we crossed a little gumbo flat where we had a very severe electric storm. The lightning and thunder were terrible, and the rain about the hardest I have ever seen. The horses were quite frightened, so we had to stay with them and of course were soaked through. Mama was in one of the wagons holding the team when the storm broke. Bell being very frightened started to run under the wagon, but ran through behind Romeo who kicked at her. So Mama started him up, which ran the wheel onto Bell.

Mama stopped when she yelped and the wheel was directly on top of Bell for a few moments until Mama could start on. Then they put Bell in the wagon but her hind legs seemed to be paralyzed and Papa thought he would have to kill her. But we begged him to wait and see if she wouldn't get over it.

After the rain was over, it was terribly muddy, but we went on away from the river, through a few oat fields, onto the prairie. Bob and the Indian policeman overtook us just when we were uncertain where to go. The hill ahead was so steep and muddy they did not think the teams could pull the wagons up. The Indian guided them around. We made a very wet camp at Shell Creek. It was not necessary to night herd as we were in range country. That evening after supper we were all sitting around the tent when the Indian suddenly pointed without saying a word at Alice's skirt. She had fallen asleep on the ground and a lizard was crawling over her skirt.

Papa got it on a stick and took it away. Bob said it was poisonous, but when Papa asked the Indian he said, "No." He was a well-educated man, but never spoke unless he was spoken to and then answered in as few words as possible.

The next day we drove northwest and went out the north side of the reservation. The Indian guided us, leaving us suddenly to be gone an hour or more, then as suddenly returning. We camped just off the reservation. An Indian came to look for horses and stayed to dinner. In his hair, also, were braided bright strips of cloth.

We stayed in the same camp over Sunday. We herded the horses along the reservation fence. Went to Black's ranch on Knife River, and I took a picture of the house. It looked so pretty – a house of gray stone set together with green cement with trees all around it.

Monday morning, September 1st: We started on, taking the river road for a long distance. In places it was real dangerous. The rains had washed deep ruts in the road, and the river was washing under the banks and great pieces of the land kept sliding down into the river. As we drove the horses along it was impossible to keep some of them from crowding out toward the bank.

Once one of the old gray mares and about ten others went out where the ground had washed away under the bank. Papa would not let any of us go out to drive them back and said he guessed we would lose that bunch. But they came back safely. At night we camped in the timber and watered the horses at the river by driving them for a long way along a path through the thick brush.

Sept. 2nd: Walter, herding in the morning in a heavy mist, found some very strange, huge formations of sandstone on a high hill. There were also trees, larger than any standing there, that were fallen and turned into rough stone. These trees were not like agatized wood, but plain stone and broken into lengths, evidently from their fall. There were some formations that looked like huge butter bowls. That afternoon we passed Chilcot P.O and had dinner at White Earth Bridge. Then we went wading in the creek. Kitty's colt, Ginger, got a bad cut on his neck and shoulder in the wire at the bridge. We were delayed doctoring him. When we started on we turned back from the river again with Mama, Winifred, and Marion driving ahead to inquire the way. We camped on a very high table above White Earth Creek. It was so high that the valley below us looked far, far away, and the houses and stock very small. We stayed there the next day to rest Ginger.

Sept. 4th: Art McGlynn helped us start in the morning. We drove through a farming district to Harkness' place where we camped at noon. Mama, Winifred, and Marion were invited to the house for dinner. We got a supply of eggs from them.

Sept. 5th: Robert, Florence, Marjorie, and I cut across the hills with the horses and cattle. The camp outfit followed the road, got ahead, and waited for us at Hofflund. Alice came out on old Billie, bareback to help us drive the bunch. There was a ditch to cross and instead of stepping over, Billie stood still and gave an awful jump. Alice stayed on but was rather frightened.

When watering the horses at a rather deep hole in Nessin Creek a thin young mare got stuck in the mud and the men had to work quite awhile getting her out. We camped at night just beyond Hofflund near a place where a French lady lived with her two sons and a daughter-in-law. She took a great liking to Marion and said her mouth was 'a perfect cupid's bow'. She gave me three French books which had belonged to her daughter who had died a few years before.

Sept. 6th: We went back to the creek to water, then drove to Nessin P.O. and Jack McKay's ranch. We camped up on a hill a mile beyond the ranch. Mr. McKay was an old friend of Papa, Walter, and Winifred. The next day it rained so we did not move on. The boys brought home some lovely chokecherries.

Sept. 8th: We were all invited to Mr. McKay's for Sunday dinner.

Sept. 9th: We stayed another day and did a big washing. Took some pictures of washing in camp. When going out to look for the horses, Pinto ran away with Papa circling around on a side hill.

Sept. 10th: The next morning we resumed our trip but as the cattle were so sore-footed that they could travel only a few miles a day we left them with Mr. McKay's bunch, to go back after them later. We went on across a rolling prairie, stopped at Turax, a little country store, and got a lot of supplies. Papa wanted to give them some trade as they were so far inland.

Later when we were following the old Fort Buford and Fort Berthhold Government Trail we passed a timbered coulee and just beyond a lot of mounds beside the trail. It looked to us as if Indians had been in ambush in the coulee and attacked a government party. Then we passed over the height of land and were in sight of the Williston country. We camped in open country and turned the horses loose over night.

The next day we drove within three miles of Williston where we made camp. We watered at a dairy ranch. There was a large dammed waterhole which got terribly muddy when they drank. The next day was rainy and we remained in camp. A family named Ellis lived near. They were very poor but seemed to have such good times together. They offered us all the peas we could gather from the garden.

The following day the men took a little lame colt to Williston to get him shod. They put on the cutest little shoes, hardly larger than a dollar. We were all crazy to have one when they were taken off, for a souvenir of the trip. But the colt wore them all fall until they were worn through and lost.

Sept. 14th: We drove to Williston and held the horses for a short time on a vacant lot, where they were looked over and admired by a good many people. Then as we drove through the main streets of the town we were stared at by everyone. Mama and Winifred stopped in town to do a little trading. They got Marion a white sweater which buttoned on the shoulder and a toque, both trimmed with pink. There was a red sweater they wanted to get her, but she would not have it. Since, she has admitted that the reason was that it buttoned down the front and she thought it looked like a boy's. We camped three miles beyond Williston.

September 15th: We drove through Trenton about sundown and camped a few miles this side.

September 16: One of the colts was very sick and as far as we could tell had been snake-bitten. We hauled it that day in the back of the wagon. We went through Buford to Mondak and drove a mile-and-a-half to the hills north of town where we could get range for the horses. Papa brought some whiskey from town with which to doctor the sick colt. But it died anyway.

September 17th: We drove to the Mondak ferry in the forenoon and began the difficult task of crossing. There was a long corduroy road made across deep mud, too soft for the horses to walk in and too thick for them to swim.

The channel on the west side was narrow, deep and swift. We had been told that if any of the horses went off the road into the mud we would surely lose them. They were so used to stringing out and following Lady and Leo that when we got them started on the corduroy road we attempted to drive the whole bunch over together.

It was difficult to get them started for the road gave some and they were afraid. I was riding Gentle, and Polly ran ahead and went on with the horses. We had most of them on when the head ones came to a place where the road sagged with their weight, making the branches and leaves shake.

They snorted, wheeled, and ran back, frightening those behind so all rushed back off the road. We were unable to stop them. Three grown horses and Polly were crowded off into the mud. They went in almost to their backs. Immediately Marion began to call for "Someone to help Polly out quick." But she was the first one out. She was so quick, active and light that she climbed out in no time.

Two others regained the road with much difficulty, but the fourth, the runaway mare, was unable to make any progress. She was soon in up to her head. The men threw a rope around her neck, and after working a long time succeeded in pulling her with the saddle horses to the road.

The minute the rope was around her neck, she forgot that she was drowning in the mud and did her best to fight the rope. The mud was very light-colored and it was more than a week before it was all off from them.

Next we tried driving a small bunch onto the road and finally got them across to the ferry. I went across with the first load to hold them on the other side. It took all day to cross them all. And it was a very hard day indeed!

It was extremely hard to get them onto the corduroy road and then after driving them across the sand bar it was hard to get them onto the ferry. Once when they got a few leaders on the road, Mama went behind them on foot to keep them going while the riders drove on more behind her.

Suddenly the leaders turned and ran back, and as the road was narrow, one of them knocked Mama down, one of his feet going on each side of her head. Another time the ferryman did not tie the ferry, and when all but a few of the load were on, the boat began to push off. Guybert, who had just gone on, turned around deliberately, and by the time the boat was a few yards from shore, stepped carefully off and immediately went in all over. Of course, he had no trouble in swimming and wading to shore.

As more of the horses were brought across Marjorie came over to help me hold them. Some of them fed quietly but others, separated from their bunches, ran up and down along the bank, whinnying and trying to find a place where they could get down to the river. As it was a high cut bank, there was no place they could get down, except at the ferry landing, and that we had to watch carefully.

Late in the afternoon the last bunch crossed, and we riders went ahead with the horses while the teams were crossing. The fences on this side were in poor shape, and some of the horses ran into a tangle of wire. A yearling colt got a wire twisted entirely around his neck and drawn tight. In some way he got out without a scratch before we could do a thing to help him. I never saw anything done which looked more impossible.

When we got back from the river bottom, we let the horses stop to feed. Johnnie Reed (on whose ranch we later lived) came to see us and spent the evening at our camp. At midnight men taking Mr. Durand, who had been nearly killed in a fight, to Mondak, stopped to borrow a lantern by which to follow the road.

September 19th: We drove on to Sidney. The fine white dust lay inches deep in the road. It rose in clouds that nearly choked us and we could hardly see the horses. Tired and dreadfully dirty, we reached Sidney at noon and ate our dinner back of old Mr. Kemmis' place.

We had our mail forwarded from Anamoose to Sidney and got an awful lot. Mama and I drove to the schoolhouse to see the teacher, Miss Jackson, about our attending school there and my taking high school work. As we drove up a little girl with white curls sat on the gatepost. It was Frances Gardner. She told us later that they thought we were gypsies. "And to think my teacher was there," she said.

Then Papa and Mama drove out to the ditch camp at Obergfells where Uncle Marshall had a ditch contract. The rest of us drove on to Newlon and waited for them there. We drove up Fox Creek, past the forks, and went a short distance up the North Fork where we made camp — our last camp on the trip. The following week we did little but rest and hunt for agates and lucky stones along the creek.

On the night of September 28th Cravath Edgar Revo was born in the Sibley tent. We all thought him wonderfully cute — Mama and Papa's first grandchild and the first great-grandchild of Grandpa and Grandma Cravath. Later Walter, Winifred and Cravath moved into their own little house at the Obergfell ditch camp where Walter worked on the ditch." (Mrs. Grow explained that Walter had expected to have a little home built for them before the baby came, but the trip had taken longer than expected). "Florence boarded at the camp and attended school in Sidney. The rest of us stayed at the camp on Fox Creek until about the first of December when we moved onto the Reed Ranch east of Sidney on Bennie Peer Creek, just across the line in North Dakota.

There we spent a very enjoyable winter, one which we all look back to with pleasure. We called it our 'happy home'. The ranch house was built of logs and stone, and the living room especially was cozy. In February Aunt Mabel and Uncle Harley *came there. Floy was then only a few weeks old. Winifred and Walter were there of course. Also George Plymat. Robert, Earl, and some of the other boys were there part of the time. They were baling hay and cutting cedar posts up in the cedar hills.*

In the meantime, I had taken the teachers' examinations and after the holidays began teaching the primary room in the Methodist Church at Sidney. In the spring Marion visited my school quite often. She was then five years old and had curls. The children all thought her so cute. She would go to the blackboard so quietly and write the numbers so neatly somewhere up into the thirties. They thought it quite wonderful.

In April the folks moved into the little black shack in Sidney. The following October, Marion began school, I being her teacher.

In another account Mrs. Grow told of traveling to Glendive and some of her experiences:

At that time Richland County was still part of Dawson, and the county seat was at Glendive. I was preparing to teach school and so had to make several trips to Glendive by stagecoach to take teachers' examinations and to attend teachers' institute.

Each morning a four-horse stagecoach started from Mondak and drove to Glendive, and another one started from Glendive and drove to Mondak, carrying mail and passengers. With roads as they were then this was not an easy day's drive. The horses were always driven at a very fast trot or gallop. There was a stage stop every 15 to 18 miles. The man at the stage barn had four horses already harnessed and waiting. The change of teams was made as quickly as possible, and the stage was on its way again without much delay.

In fair weather the most desirable seat in the stagecoach was the one beside the driver, but if it was cold it was much better to ride in the coach. Even there one could get very cold on those long rides.

I remember once when we came over a high hill and there below us were the lights of Glendive — what a welcome sight! But there were still many miles to go, and I was really cold when we reached our destination. There was one very long, very steep hill, known as Devil's Gulch. At the foot of the hill the road made a sharp curve to the bridge over the gulch. It was a strict rule of the stage company that their drivers must always stop at the top of the hill and 'rough lock' the wheels (chain the two wheels on one side of the wagon). But once in a while when a stage was late, a driver would be reckless and take the hill on the run. That was really a wild ride!

School had started that fall in the one-room schoolhouse at the south end of Sidney with Miss Myra Jackson from Michigan as the teacher. But the room was overcrowded and the school board decided to hire me to teach a primary room after the Christmas vacation. This was held in the old stone Methodist Church, now a warehouse for the Gurney Electric Company. I was not yet 18 years old.

With my first month's wages, which was $50.00, I bought a Miles City saddle. I taught for three years for $50.00, the fourth year for $60.00. As many weekends as I could I went to see my folks, but there was the problem of getting across the river.

There was a cable ferry, but at times it could not run because of ice. When the river was freezing up there might be strong ice along each shore. The passengers would walk across the ice, a rowboat would take them across the open water to the ice on the other side. Then they would walk across that ice to the farther shore where they would be met with a team and sleigh. When the river went out, it would be full of floating ice; the ferry could not run, but passengers were taken across in a rowboat, weaving its way among cakes of ice. When the pontoon bridge was built, that seemed wonderful, but the ice took that out too.

Mrs. Grow's father, F.G. Cravath, had a horse camp on Fox Creek where the family stayed in the summer months, moving to Sidney during the school term so the children could attend. Elsie (Mrs. Grow) became so involved with teaching that she never did get around to attending high school.

Later Mr. Cravath built up a ranch east of Lambert which was headquarters for his ranching business, always his main interest. He built up a very fine bunch of Percheron horses, always using purebred sires, many of them imported from France. He had come to Montana because here there was open range for his horses, while in North Dakota there was a herd law.

Elsie and her sister Florence did a lot of riding for their father on account of his horses. Mrs. Grow recalls once when they stopped at a shack where two girls were homesteading. One of the girls, Christine Finkelson, later became Mrs. Noel Carrico; the other Mrs. Fred Mielke. Elsie and her sister never carried guns, but it happened that before they started out on this particular ride that a young fellow, just for fun, had buckled a holster around Florence and shoved a revolver into it. As they got ready for bed, Florence took off the holster and gun and laid them on the bureau beside the bed. (The gun was unloaded, but that doesn't show when you just look at the outside of a gun.) Since this was their first meeting, their hostesses were a bit apprehensive, not sure just what kind of transients they were sheltering! But they found their guests to be quite harmless and as they became better acquainted, turned out to be good friends.

After four years of teaching school, Elsie married Earl Grow. Many of Sidney's leading citizens began their formal education under her instruction. We'd like to name some of them, but we'd be sure to omit some that should be included so perhaps it's better not to start. Even though more than 60 years have passed since she stood before her first group of primaries, Mrs. Grow is still active and alert and much interested in what goes on about her.

Earl Grow also came to Montana in 1907 and filed on the first homestead on McCone Heights south of Lambert. He drove a mule team on a scraper* to help built the 'Big Ditch' on the lower Yellowstone irrigation project. Most of his life he engaged in ranching in eastern Montana. In later years his hobby was trapshooting. He participated in trapshooting meets at such places as Phoenix, Las Vegas, and Reno, winning several first-place trophies.

The Grows had five children, three boys and two girls. Mr. Grow passed away in 1966. Mrs. Grow, with two of their sons, lives at Enid, still in the area that's been 'home' for these 63 years.

Percy Sawyer

January 1965

Anyone who made the trip to Glendive by stagecoach in 1897 surely qualifies as an old timer. Percy Sawyer probably wasn't doing much of the directing of that expedition since he was only three years old, but he was no doubt contributing plenty for diversion of others in the party.

He came with his mother and sister from Seattle, destination: the William Lowe home. His mother had kept house for the Lowes when she came to Glendive in the 1880's until she married and they moved to the Seattle area. Upon her return to Glendive she resumed this position and continued there until her death in 1938. Thus the Lowe home was also the home of the two young Sawyer children. Mr. Lowe died in 1912, but Mrs. Sawyer continued to keep house for Guy and her own son. After her death Guy and Percy 'bachelored' together in the Lowe home on Anderson Avenue until Percy's marriage to Ethel McGaughey in 1943.

Lowe had come to Glendive in the early 1880's and established a hardware store. This first store located where the Stockman Bar is now had a dirt floor, but later Lowe moved his business to more pretentious headquarters in the present Hagenston Hardware* location. Lowe was then well up in years and retired in the early 1900's, allocating most of the responsibility for the store to his two sons, Ray and Guy.

Mr. Sawyer describes the elder Lowe as a devout Methodist. The entire household attended church and Sunday school regularly, and grace was always said before meals. Every evening before retiring they all gathered in the parlor and knelt together while Mr. Lowe led in evening prayers. The town had its rough faction, but it also had its meritorious element.

Sawyer commented that as a youngster he spent most of his free time at Glendive's roller skating rink in the building now occupied by the Glendive Machine Works*. The rink was built by his uncle, carpenter Jim Sawyer. Later the rink was converted into a theater, accounting for the fact that the building is higher in the back – to accommodate the drops. In addition to building many of Glendive's early homes, Jim Sawyer has the distinction of being the first person to drive a wagon across Glendive's first Yellowstone bridge.

Sawyer states that one of the things that stands out most distinctly in his memory of childhood days is the celebrations they used to have at fair time and Fourth of July. Indians always came for the fair, then put on their shows and dances. He recalls seeing them camped on Muxlow hill, drying meat in the sun. They cut the meat into thin strips, then hung it on a rope stretched between two poles in the sun so it would cure. The meat hanging there in the hot sun didn't exactly tempt the appetite, but the meat dried! He remembers, too, seeing cowboys ride into town. They always wore their holsters but didn't carry their guns in town.

The river was the boys' main source of recreation. The slough near the bridge used to be running, and that was their 'swimmin' hole'. Once when he, with some other boys, had swum across to the pool and then had tried to swim back, he collapsed about two-thirds of the way across and one of the Twible boys pulled him ashore.

Percy Sawyer took an early interest in the garage business. The first garage in Glendive, run by Leo Magne and Frank L. Soare, did business where the Subway Husky Service* is located. Soare, father of Franklyn and the late Art Soare, was an engineer on the railroad but also had an interest in the garage. Percy didn't work there, but he did do a good deal of 'hanging around', observing what went on. A bit later when W.H. Frank built a garage at the present Hilger Garage* site, Percy was old enough to work for him, cleaning up, helping the mechanic, and so forth.

His next job, about 1910, was that of delivery boy for the Kellogg Meat Market, located in the Beasly block*. His deliveries were made, not with a pickup or van, but with a horse-drawn cart. While he was working there the butcher came to work one Monday morning still chuckling over one of his pranks the preceding Saturday night – and still wondering a little if he was going to get by with it. He always carried a sharp little penknife, and he told Percy how he had managed, in the roughest saloon in town, to cut off a fellow's bright red necktie just below the knot, then dashed out before the fellow could gather his wits enough to retaliate. He never did say who his victim was, but about twenty years later Percy at Christmas time gathered up all his neckties that he didn't like, draped them over a coat hanger, and started downtown, generously making a gift of a necktie to anyone he met who liked one of them. Presently he met Jack Plahn, who, seeing a bright red one, seized it with the exclamation, "That's the first I've had a tie like this since some #%&$! cut mine off twenty years ago!"

Percy took one year of high school when Professor Hunt was principal, then went to work in Whistler's Garage. In 1912 he went to Flint, Michigan. During his two years there he worked at everything from building motors for Little Car (the name was changed to Chevrolet in 1913) to nailing bottoms in buggies for the Flint Buggy Works.

When he came back to Glendive in 1914, he took a job running the grader for the county. That was the first year the county used mechanized road equipment – in fact, the first year the county graded roads! They pulled two graders, a big one with a smaller one fastened behind it, with a '48 Caterpillar. He went to a Caterpillar school in Great Falls, and the next year he drove the Caterpillar. He stayed with this job until he was drafted for World War I, then spent twenty-three months in the Army, fourteen of those months overseas in France and Germany.

After his return to civilian life he worked at a variety of jobs, including more road grading. That summer he was grading down by Marsh, he says, was the hottest summer he can remember. It was so hot that all that could grow were grasshoppers so the chickens lived on grasshoppers, and the eggs had such a strong taste they could hardly eat them – and in the home where he stayed, they lived on eggs!

One other job 'way back when' that Sawyer mentioned was that of delivery boy for the Hollecker Store. That's where he learned to eat olives. The olives were kept in a big keg in the basement so whenever any of the employees went to the basement for something, they'd sample them. It took a long time, but he finally learned to like olives.

He managed to get in some flying, too, about 1927, but after he soloed, he didn't do much more with it. In 1929 he and Byard Patterson went into partnership, bought out Haskell's Body Shop and moved it to the corner of Kendrick and Clement. Later he bought out Patterson and he continued to run the shop until 1962 when he retired and leased it to Al Koschel.

Mrs. Lee (Leone Burton) Hubing

August 1966

Only one thing keeps Mrs. Leone Hubing from being a real 'old timer' – she wasn't born soon enough. Her parents were in Montana by the turn of the century, as were the aunt and uncle who reared her after her mother died. Her father, Harry Burton, settled near Savage when he came to the Treasure State. When the 'Big Ditch'* was constructed for the Lower Yellowstone Irrigation Project, he found employment there.

Mr. and Mrs. Burton had several children before the arrival of their twin daughters, Leone and Ione. When the twins were just small, their mother died, so their father accepted the offer of his sister and her husband, Mr. and Mrs. Alfred Wright, to care for the little girls.

The Wrights had no children of their own and were as mother and father to their nieces, Mrs. Hubing explained. Mr. and Mrs. Wright lived in Terry so Terry became the 'home town' for the little Burton girls, and it was with the history of the Wrights that Mrs. Hubing became familiar rather than with that of her own parents.

Mr. and Mrs. Wright were both natives of England, but they had to come to the United States to meet, even though they had grown up within ten miles of each other.

Fannie Burton's parents brought their family to Wayne County, New York, and her father found employment on the 'Shaker Tract'. He was working there when Alfred Wright came to the U.S. Alfred was only twenty-one when he came to Wayne County and also found work on the Shaker Tract. So it was the young couple met and later married.

Alfred worked there for about two-and-one-half years, then evidently heard the call of that era, "Go West, young man, go West!" because in March of 1891 he landed in Terry. How a remote, sparsely populated area such as Terry could have called loudly enough to be heard almost across the continent might be a bit of a mystery. Wright didn't know a soul in the entire region, and had the handsome sum of five dollars in his pocket when he arrived. Perhaps that's why he didn't go any farther.

Whatever his reason for stopping there, he went to work at the first job offered him, which happened to be digging post-holes and building fences. After a month of that he went to work as a ranch hand for his employers, the 'T.D.' outfit. By the end of that summer he had enough money to send for his wife who had remained in New York when he came West.

Although they had never met in England, living just ten miles apart, they had not been in Montana long before they knew everyone within considerably more than a ten-mile radius – and still didn't have a very large circle of acquaintances. To be more exact, the circle was large, but the number of acquaintances wasn't.

They spent their first winter in Terry where Fannie had a little restaurant, and Alfred ran a livery stable. In the spring (1892) they went back to the 'T.D.' where he again worked as a ranch hand, and she did the cooking.

In the fall of 1893 Mr. Wright took a bunch of sheep on shares, anticipating a quick profit. The profit didn't materialize. Under the Cleveland administration wool dropped from eighteen to eight and three-fourths cents a pound. Mr. and Mrs. Wright had planned to take a trip around the world 'next year' with their wool profits, but when the price of wool dropped, they found themselves broke instead.

Wright would have been glad to sell his lambs, but there was no demand for them so he had to keep them, and he was in the sheep business permanently. He built up a place for his sheep on Fallon Creek near Ismay and continued with sheep until 1906 when he sold his spread and moved to Terry. By the time he was ready to sell he had bought eighteen sections of railroad land for less than a dollar an acre so when he sold his land and his sheep, he found that it had been a profitable venture despite the plummeting wool price in his early years of sheep raising.

During his ranching years Fannie's brother, Frank Burton, had joined them in Montana for a partnership for raising horses. When they were ready to sell, the brother accompanied a train carload of horses to New York. Mrs. Hubing still has the letter which he wrote back to his brother-in-law Alfred, informing him of his safe arrival and his disposition of the first of the horses.

The letter read in part: "Dear brother, Got here all right. Eleven days on the road. Had an auction and sold eight for good money. The others I bid on and shall have another sale at Palmyra, Saturday 15 and I shall let the most of them go. When I get rid of my horses, I shall visit around a little. Did you ship my stuff yet?"

Exit one carload of Montana horses. Burton planned to stay in New York State, rather than return to Montana, but he contracted typhoid fever shortly after the foregoing letter was written and died.

While they were on the Fallon Creek ranch the Wrights bought the piano which stands in the Hubing's living room. Mrs. Hubing still has the receipt, dated 1903 showing payment for the piano. Mr. Wright had hauled their year's wool to Miles City, and on the return trip freighted out the piano in the wagon for his wife.

In a letter to her mother in England in the summer of 1906 Mrs. Wright outlined their plans for leaving the ranch and moving to Terry. Mrs. Hubing has that original, too. In the letter Mrs. Wright explained, "We haven't moved to Terry but expect to do so in a short time." She went on to explain that they had "had so much rain. 500 sheep were killed by the rain." They had just been sheared so when the cold rain came, they "chilled and chilled."

She also mentioned that "The store is going up." The store was the Roylee Mercantile Company which Wright built in partnership with J.W. Stith. Later the name was changed to Wright-Nelson-Stith Company. After the death of Mr. Wright the store was sold to the F.T. Reynolds Company.

330

The letter continued, "We have another railroad going into Terry." (The Milwaukee) "We have already an order for goods for the railroad men so that means a lot. I think it will do well.

"We bought our house just right as property has gone up terrible. We would have had to pay a $1,000 more for it. We gave $2,500 for it and there are twelve lots of ground belonging to it." The house which they bought was the house built by George Burt, one of Terry's earliest settlers. That was the house in which Mr. and Mrs. Lon Fluss, parents of Mrs. Albert Brubaker, were married in 1903.

The house was originally built of logs, but the Wrights sided it over. A windmill had been used to pump water, but they discovered an artesian well so they built an elevated tank into which the well overflowed, and from the tank water was piped into the house – probably the first house in Terry with 'running water'.

In Terry Mr. Wright engaged in other businesses besides the Roylee Mercantile Company. He was also a member of the Terry Drug Company and one of the organizers of the Terry State Bank. Wright was evidently a man of diversified interests with vision to see the needs of a burgeoning community. Another of his enterprises was the building of the original telephone plant at Terry. Mrs. Fanny Reynolds Fisher of Ismay, who died this year, was the first telephone operator.

Mrs. Fisher had come from England when she was still Miss Reynolds to visit her cousin, Mrs. Fannie Wright. While here she met Billy Fisher, and as was the case with many a single girl who ventured into the masculine-dominated West, she married, and her visit became permanent.

Wright also assisted in starting the electric light plant and a brick manufacturing plant and built a restaurant and recreation hall in Terry. He was mayor of Terry for ten years, during which time the Yellowstone Bridge was built and a water works plant was installed.

Even after he moved into Terry Wright did not forget his livestock interests. He continued to raise fine horses, importing purebred Shires from England. Mrs. Hubing has several of the transfer certificates from the Shire Horse Society of London, which certified some of the imported animals. The earliest one in her possession is dated 1906, but others, dated as late as 1916, indicate he continued his imports over a period of years.

One of Terry's most influential and active citizens, Wright passed away January 19, 1937, and Mrs. Wright September 9, 1941. Their niece, Leone, and her husband bought the Wright house from Mrs. Wright in 1940. There they reared their family, four daughters.

Their girls are all married now and have homes and families of their own. Three of them live in Montana and one is in Minnesota. Mr. and Mrs. Hubing continue to live in the old home, now completely modern, in Terry.

DCHS Reunion 1965

July 1965

An air of anticipation and conviviality prevailed Thursday afternoon as Dawson County High School alumni began assembling for the reunion of students who had attended between 1900 and 1930. From Arizona, Michigan, Oregon, Minnesota they came to visit with friends, some of whom had not seen each other for forty or fifty years. Some of Eastern Montana's earliest settlers were represented by a son or daughter, themselves now grandparents.

Grace Bean Reeves

Grace Bean Reeves isn't sure when her folks did come to the Treasure State, but she knows she was born here in 1898 and that her sister, fourteen years older, was also born here. How long before 1884 her parents may have come she isn't sure. As far as she knows, they lived down along the Yellowstone River when they first came, at a place known as 'Tobacco Corner'. That's where they were living when her sister was born, anyway. When Grace was four years old, her father bought a ranch on the Redwater River. During the summer the family lived on the ranch, but during the winter they lived in Glendive so the children could attend school.

Their family was well acquainted with Senator McCone and his family. His daughter Alice (Farris) and Grace were school chums and both graduated from DCHS in 1916. Mrs. Reeves describes the Senator as a great story teller and recalled for us one of the tales he told them of his pony express days. Another pony express rider, near Hardin, had been killed by the Indians. They took the mail he was carrying, but then didn't know what to do with it. Included in the mail pouch was a corset someone had ordered from Sears, Roebuck, and Company so they took the staves out of the corset, stuck them into the ground, upright, in the form of a circle, and tossed the mail sack into the circle. The mail was found but not the rider. McCone (pre-senatorial days) was sent to locate the rider and found his body buried in a wheat field.

Grace's mother had journeyed from Kansas City to Pike's Peak in a covered wagon, then later had pressed farther north into Wyoming. That's where they were living when Fred Bean, from far off Maine, found his way to Wyoming and in time, found a bride, too. From Wyoming the young Beans moved to Dawson County and made it their permanent home. Mr. Bean was an active citizen and served, along with other responsibilities, as county assessor for (to quote his daughter), "years and years and years."

Mrs. Reeves with her husband moved from Montana in 1922 to Wyoming, then to Idaho, back to Wyoming, to Montana again, and finally to Michigan. Her husband passed away ten years ago, but Mrs. Reeves still resides in Lansing. She spent twenty-six years working for the Michigan State Police with the identification bureau in the fingerprinting department, retiring four years ago.

She was surprised to be greeted with such a green Montana and so much rain in July when she arrived for the reunion. Her relatives are gone from the area, except for a nephew, Ward Bean, who ranches near Burns Creek, but she was having a wonderful time at the reunion and commented that she certainly enjoyed meeting all these people again.

Cristine Kolling Smith

The family of Cristine Kolling Smith arrived in Montana about 1908. There had been much upheaval in Europe, including their native Hungary, so the Kollings immigrated to the New World in search of a more stable environment. Her father established a grocery business in Glendive and built the building now used for the Southside Tavern. Even while selling groceries her father dreamed of having a chicken farm in California and that dream finally became a reality when they moved to California. He also operated a feed store in conjunction with his poultry producing. Her father has passed away, as well as four of her brothers, but her mother still lives in Glendora, California. Mrs. Smith herself lives in Monrovia, California. Two of her brothers and five sisters are still living.

It's been fourteen years since she visited in Glendive, but coming to Glendive was just coming HOME. She expressed herself as being real happy that she could attend the reunion and said she was having a lot of fun.

Ward Hill

A brief chat with Ward Hill, class of 1925, revealed that his parents had come to Glendive in 1912. His father became the manager of Dion's Mercantile, the largest department store east of Billings in those days. Mr. Hill remarked that since his arrival for the reunion he had made a point of noticing and had counted four stores now in the space occupied by Dion's at the time his father became a partner with Cummins to establish the Cummins-Hill Store.

Mr. Hill recalls how, as a youngster, he used to go down along the river and pick up moss agates. Two of his Oregon friends are enthusiastic rock hounds so one of his aims in coming to the reunion was to pick up some agates for them. He finds, however, that the agates in the area near town don't seem to be as plentiful as when he was a boy. Mr. Hill now lives in Portland, Oregon.

Roy Kinney

The family of Roy Kinney, class of 1909, came to Glendive in 1904 from Amboy, Minnesota. His father, Carl Kinney, was Chief of Police in the Gate City for fifteen years. He also held the positions of Street Commissioner and Fire Marshal. In these various capacities he had his fingers in a good many projects for the improvement of Glendive. He promoted installation of the first water filtering plant and establishment of the sewer system, and pressed for fire escapes on hotels and schools.

His father was a carpenter by trade and built many of the early houses in Glendive, among them their own house (then) at 404 North Merrill, the Baldwin house, Herrick's house, and the Jordan house on Meade Avenue. He also supervised the construction of the building across the street from the City Hall for its owner, his brother Frank Kinney.

The 'gandy-dancers', men laying track for the railroad, had a miserable place to sleep so another of his projects was to arrange with the Northern Pacific to have box cars converted into comfortable living quarters for them. This brought him into great favor with the men. Most of them were Italians and couldn't speak his language and he couldn't speak theirs, but they managed to communicate and they esteemed him highly.

Roy left Montana in 1917 to enter the armed forces but returned after the war. Later he re-enlisted. In 1924 his parents moved to Eureka, California. Back in Montana again Roy spent many years teaching in rural schools throughout Dawson County, retiring in 1945. Since his retirement he has lived in Minneapolis, a bachelor, doing his own cooking. He is a director of the Senior Citizen Council House and holds offices in four different Senior Citizen Clubs. He is also active in the Latter Day Saints Church and, at seventy-seven years of age, is still finding plenty to do.

Myrtle Foss Aasness

Myrtle Foss Aasness from Bremerton, Washington, graduated with the class of 1924. Her family came to Glendive a few years before this country entered World War I, and lived at first in the Fowler Rooming House. A little later they ranched west of Glendive near the Kinney Ranch. Mr. Foss also worked for the Northern Pacific Railroad while they lived in this area. He passed away in 1929. Montana Dakota Utilities Company probably wasn't especially interested in matchmaking, but they were responsible for bringing her husband-to-be to Glendive where he and Myrtle could meet. His father was the first manager of MDU when they brought natural gas service to the city in 1925. Mr. and Mrs. Aasness have spent most of their married life in Washington but enjoyed getting back to Glendive to visit with old friends at the reunion.

Mildred Herrick Palmatier

Mildred Herrick Palmatier has to look way back to find her family's earliest connections with Glendive. Her father came in 1882 from Jamestown, New York, to help with some mules. He didn't care for that so he took a job hauling water for the construction crews building the Great Northern Railroad, and that's how he got his start. His start may have been modest, but he went on to become one of the big stock shippers on the Northern Pacific. In addition to big herds of cattle, Mr. Herrick ran many sheep, the first rancher in this part of the country to have both cattle and sheep at the same time. He was here a good while before the Exchange State Bank, but later he became its president.

The folks who bought the ranch from him found some dynamite so they put some in the stove to see if it was still good. It was. It blew up the house!

Mildred, a 1923 graduate, now lives in Grand Rapids, Michigan. She and her husband, Jackman Palmatier, were both present to add their contribution to a successful reunion.

George David Hollecker

The Hollecker family was another that was prominent in Glendive's early days. George Donat Hollecker, father of George David Hollecker who came to the reunion, moved to Glendive in 1893 and associated with A.M. Coleman, owner of one of the very first general stores in the city.

Hollecker had been a sales clerk for the John V. Farwell Co. back in Iowa. The department manager some how knew Coleman in Glendive and knew that Coleman, getting up in years, was looking for a reliable young man to work for him who might be interested in buying into the business and taking some of the load from his shoulders. The Farwell manager thought Hollecker might well "fill the bill" so he recommended Hollecker to Coleman and Coleman to Hollecker. Hollecker did come and did invest in the business. Before much time had gone by Coleman became ill and wanted Hollecker to buy him out. So it was that Hollecker found himself possessor of the Hollecker Department Store.

For many years Walter King was in charge of Men's Furnishing in the store, while Archie Mack was in charge of the Grocery Dept. The store also had a dry goods section. After Mr. Hollecker's death in 1931, his heirs sold the store to Andersons and it became Anderson's Department Store*.

In addition to his department store Mr. Hollecker had extensive land holdings and also owned a farm implement store where the Farm and Home Furniture is now located. In the implement store they featured John Deere plows, roller-bearing wagons, and Light Kentucky drills. They sold bobsleds, too, and anything else needed (when available) on the farms. John Deere specialized in the manufacture of plows at first, but later as they expanded to manufacture other implements – drills, for example – Hollecker would switch to theirs until finally John Deere was manufacturing a full line of farm machinery and Hollecker was selling the full line.

Mr. Hollecker was a member of the school board and also of the Cemetery Association until his death. He was influential in many areas of Glendive's development, and the family is still remembered as we enjoy Hollecker's Lake, the community recreation facility a short distance from town on Highway 16.

Mrs. Hollecker took great interest in collecting Indian relics. Crow Indians traveling through frequently camped on the river bottomlands just below the Hollecker home on the corner of Towne and River so Mrs. Hollecker would take advantage of the opportunity to go down to their camp and bargain with them for various articles. As a result she was able to gather an interesting and unusually complete Indian collection. Several years ago the Hollecker children presented the collection to the State Historical Museum in Helena where it is now on display. A plaque bearing the names of Mr. and Mrs. Hollecker identifies the collection with the names of the children as the donors.

Mr. Hollecker raised Shetland ponies so ponies, to young George, were an integral part of growing up. Riding and races occupied a prominent place in their recreation. 'Things to do' weren't handed to them on a platter in those days. Certain it was they didn't sit and watch TV! But they managed to find plenty to do, perhaps too much sometimes. One of their winter diversions was hunting cottontails on Sawyer's Island after the river had frozen over so they could cross. George recalls that when Glendive's first swimming pool was built, the digging was done with tractors and fresnoes*. His sister Marie helped with the tractor driving. Marie is married to Herman Diekman, former agriculture instructor at DCHS. He is now retired, and they live on a fourteen-acre grape farm in California. Jessie (Mrs. Schommer) lives in Chicago.

George and his wife, the former Louise Greenwood, live in Great Falls where George has run the John Deere branch house for the past sixteen years. He noted that even now they get an occasional order for a bobsled.

A native of eastern Montana, Louise lived in Forsyth until 1917 when the Northern Pacific transferred her father to Glendive. They moved here just before World War I. Perhaps her most vivid memory of those first years in the Gate City is that of the flu epidemic, and for good reason. Louise, along with the other three children in the family, were all hospitalized at the same time with the dreaded virus. That trip to the hospital, with blankets thrown over their heads to contain the germs, was a trip not soon to be forgotten. Their mother was already ill and confined in the hospital on Merrill Avenue across from the high school. But the ordeal ended on a happy note when all recovered.

Both Mr. and Mrs. Hollecker reported of the reunion, just the best time renewing acquaintances. They visited with people they hadn't seen since graduation, and felt strongly that those who took time to organize the event were deserving of much credit.

Hjelmer Foss

Hjelmer Foss, a student of Glendive High School (it didn't become Dawson County High School until the term of 1906-1907) didn't attend the reunion, but he has some very early documents relating to the schools. "The Constitution and By-Laws of the Glendive High School Alumni Association" were adopted August 9, 1904. Iit lists all graduates up to that time, beginning with the first class of 1895. That year – 1895 – there were three graduates: Charles Day, Bell Brown, and Mabel Schryver. Harry Dion, well known Glendive resident, was one of the six graduates listed for 1898.

All teachers who had taught up to that time were listed as honorary members. These included E.O. Busenburg, Theodore Lentz, R.W. Pattengill, Edward Keeler, Lydia Berry Brooks, and F.D. Smith. Mr. Foss explained that the first year (1894-1895) Mr. Busenburg was the only high school teacher, but later, as the number of students increased, so did the number of teachers.

When Hjelmer's sister, Hilda Foss, graduated in 1902, Theodore Lentz was the principal and Lydia Berry was high school teacher. So the 1902 commencement announcement, of which Mr. Foss has a copy, informs us. The announcement further indicates that the commencement exercises were held in the Opera House. The Opera House was on the second floor of a two-story building which stood where Kampschrors* Store is now. And why not in the high school auditorium? At that time there was no school of any kind on the

900 block on North Merrill. Glendive's first school, 'The Brick School', was built in 1893 and later used as a warehouse for the Bismark Grocery* before it was torn down to make way for the new First National Bank*, now under construction. The second school was the present K.C. Hall, completed about 1899. At first the high school occupied the second floor of the Brick School, but during the time that Hjelmer was in high school the classes were held in the 1899 building. The original North Merrill high school was built about 1909, Mr. Foss estimates. He was old enough to vote in 1907, but 1908 was the first voting year after his twenty-first birthday, and one of the issues that year was a levy for building the new high school. The 'new school' included an auditorium that could accommodate such occasions as commencement.

Names listed on the Board of Education in 1902 are still familiar in Glendive: F.J. Kilpatrick was president, and other members included J.C. Sorenson, Henry Dion, E.P. Baldwin, and James Marshall. By 1902 (Mr. Foss has a copy of that commencement announcement too) the list had changed to Henry Dion, president; and other members, J.C. Sorenson, James Marshall, J.C. Taylor, and Frank W. Kinney. Fred Dion was one of the graduates of 1903 according to the announcement.

So the reunion has recalled for us the days when the 1909 building was the 'New High School', and brings us up to the time when the 1930 addition was just becoming a reality, with the 1963 facilities still far off. The general impression received from chats with alumni is that it is not so much the building, but what goes on within its walls that determines the quality of education and the effect upon the lives of the students.

Malena Vashus Bervenjust

The opportunity to visit with old friends and acquaintances was something Malena Vashus Bervenjust never expected. She graduated with the class of 1920 and had a wonderful time renewing acquaintances.

Malena's family came to Glendive in 1903. Her father, Olaus Vashus, had come from Norway five years earlier but had gone first to Kansas. Upon his arrival there he might well have decided to turn around and go back when he saw how raw and ruthless this new world could be. His uncle had been scalped by Indians just a short time before. Friends had found him, still alive, buried with only his head above ground. But Olaus stayed. After a few years in Kansas he brought his family to Montana. When he came to Glendive he worked for the Northern Pacific Railroad for a time and later for Harpster's Meat Market. In 1914 the family went back to Norway for a visit, and the visit turned out to be longer than anticipated. While there World War I broke out so they couldn't leave. Mr. Vashus had to wire President Wilson to get money out of the bank before they could return. Political wheels oft times grind slowly so it was six weeks before they could start home.

Malena was married the same year she graduated from high school. She and her husband continued to live in Glendive until 1926 but then moved to Seattle. There they stayed until 1961 when they moved to Yakima.

Stefie Gondek Evans

When Stefie Gondek Evans first got word of plans for a reunion, she made up her mind, she says, that she was coming, no matter what. By Saturday afternoon she was ready to declare, "I wouldn't have missed it for the world!"

The Gondeks came to Dawson County from near Kansas City, Kansas, in 1908 and settled on Crackerbox. Stefie's grandfather had come about three years earlier and filed on a homestead so at first they helped him, then expanded operations to include a farm of their own. Their first home was a log house but later they built a frame dwelling. The country was all open at that time, and horseback riding was one of their chief diversions. Their elementary education was obtained in a little country school. Came a series of hard years with hail about five years in a row, and the Gondeks decided it would be better to move to town. They left the farm about 1920, and Mr. Gondek began working for the Northern Pacific Railroad.

Stefie graduated with the class of 1927. She, along with a sister and a brother, decided to try Chicago, and it seemed a little easier to find employment there. Later the entire family moved there. It was in Chicago that she met her husband, John Evans, presently foreman at the International Harvester Company with whom he has been associated twenty-nine years.

Mrs. Evans noted that Glendive had done considerable growing since they moved from here. Her sister, Caroline Gondek Banaszak, class of 1925, also from Chicago, came to the reunion too. Both of the sisters exclaimed at the moderate registration fee and marveled at so much for so little!

Elsie Holton Sater

Elsie Holton Sater was another Washington representative at the reunion. Her family came from Wisconsin, and in Glendive her father continued to work as a butcher. She married a railroad man, and in 1933 he was transferred to Seattle where they still reside. A 1924 graduate, she found many old friends with whom to visit and thought the reunion marvelous as it made this possible.

Olive Lokken Blaszek

Olive Lokken Blaszek, a 1930 graduate, came to DCHS from a ranch near Circle. She explained that in order to go to high school she worked for her room and board at Hildebrands. She hadn't been back here for a long time, and as she glanced quickly around, just at the close of registration at the high school Thursday afternoon, she concluded that it was certainly different from when she was in high school.

Ferol Halvorsen Nelson

Ferol Halvorsen Nelson, class of 1923, graduated in a class of thirty-five students. Allard was quite a little community when her parents homesteaded there in 1910, but now everyone has moved away. The family still owns the old homestead, but there are no buildings on it now because of an odd transaction some years ago. The Halvorsen family moved from the homestead to Billings in

338

1926, but Ferol's cousin, Hjelmer Foss, continued to live in the Allard community. One day he called the Halvorsens and excitedly reported that someone had stolen their house! The bewildered Halvorsens figured a house might be a bit cumbersome to steal, but it had vanished, that much was certain. They started an investigation, and soon learned that a man from Glendive had bought a house near theirs for taxes, but when he had it moved, he innocently got the wrong house. The Halvorsens were reimbursed for their house, but it 'stayed gone'. As Mrs. Nelson exclaimed, "It could only happen at Allard!"

The Halvorsens came to Montana from North Dakota. Mr. Halvorsen had been working in a store there, but it burned down so he began looking around. Everyone was homesteading, and the Foss family (relatives) were at Allard so when he found a very good piece of land there, he filed on it, loaded his machinery and household goods into an immigrant car, and moved to Montana.

When a day in August failed to produce any light, they began to wonder just what sort of country they had moved into. There was no radio or TV to explain the phenomenon, making the darkness more eerie. Some thought Haley's Comet had returned, others were sure it meant the end of the world. Whatever it was, Mrs. Halvorsen wouldn't let the children outside to play the whole day. Newspaper and other mail were their only communication with the outside world so it was not until the train came through the next day and left the paper that they found out forest fires were so rampant in the western part of the state that even in this area the smoke completely obscured the light from the sun.

The first school they attended was a log cabin with a dirt floor and a sod room. The 'blackboard' was a buggy top. A packing case provided a desk for the teacher, and she sat on an ordinary kitchen chair. The children brought their own 'desks' and chairs from home. Ferol's desk was a keg, cut to accommodate, and she sat on her little rocking chair because that was the only chair her size they had at home. But they got good instruction in that school! Mrs. Steele Nelson was the teacher, a very good one, and they learned. They had school in that building two years before their new school was built – a very modern school: it had floors, roof, and windows.

After graduation from high school Ferol attended a summer session of normal school*, then came back and taught two years at the home school – one of its first pupils, and now the teacher. She taught a term at the Three Mile School also before she married and moved to Glendive, where they lived until her husband, an N.P. telegrapher, was transferred to Deer Lodge.

Mrs. Nelson is another of the alumni who wouldn't have missed it (the reunion) for anything. She declares she never enjoyed anything so much and feels that a vote of thanks is certainly due the committee for a wonderful job.

Ruth Lunsford Christie

Ruth Lunsford Christie's mother homesteaded twenty-four miles northwest of Glendive soon after the turn of the century. In order to go to high school Ruth and a friend, Cordia Chaney (Cordia lived in Thirteen Mile Valley, a few miles farther north), roomed together in the Kelly Apartments in Glendive.

Transportation then wasn't what it is now so they didn't get home very often, or even get to see the 'home folks' because they seldom came to town. The girls stood it as long as they could, but finally about the middle of March, they got so homesick that, in desperation, they started walking toward home. They had walked about thirteen miles when someone came along and gave them a ride, taking them within half-a-mile of Ruth's home. By this time they had had ample time to consider their rashness, and the closer they got to the home, the more qualms they had anticipating Mrs. Lunsford's reaction to such an escapade.

When their wagon ride came to an end, they decided to walk another four miles on down into the valley and visit Cordia's sister instead. They spent the night with Mr. and Mrs. Menno Mullet, and by morning their homesickness was sufficiently assuaged so they felt they could face the city for another indefinite stay and the Mullets took them back to town again.

After her graduation in 1914, Ruth taught school in Dawson County for several years before her marriage. She now lives in Bozeman.

Cordia Chaney Plummer

Cordia Chaney Plummer, whose parents homesteaded in Thirteen Mile Valley in 1907, arrived in Glendive just two weeks before the reunion – in her casket. Cordia had married a Methodist minister, A.E. Plummer. She had shared a number of parishes with him in Montana before they moved to Colorado in the late 1930's, where they continued to serve. Cordia, who graduated in 1914, was one of twelve eligible for the reunion known to have passed away between the time reunion plans were instigated and their culmination.

Margaret Nye Tebbe

The Northern Pacific Railroad was responsible for bringing many families to Glendive, and Margaret Nye Tebbe is one of them. Her father, Walter F. Nye, was sent here from Carbondale, Pennsylvania about 1902 to work for the railroad. He stayed with the railroad about a decade but then decided to try homesteading and chose a site about six miles east of Lindsay. In 1917 they returned to Glendive and Mr. Nye held the position of county clerk and recorder from then until 1925 when he ventured to Florida, Mrs. Nye following later. Margaret had graduated in 1923 and the year he went to Florida, she went to Seattle to enter the University of Washington. She graduated from Library School in 1929 and accepted a position as county librarian in Klamath Falls, Oregon. There she met her husband-to-be and was married in 1935. Since that time they have lived from coast to coast and at present are living in Missoula.

Margaret's grandmother, Mrs. Chase, lived to be 104 years old and was well-known in the Glendive area. She passed away at the County Rest Home where she had spent her last years.

Mrs. Tebbe surmised that a great deal of work must have been done to organize the reunion and considered the organizing superbly done. She, along with many others, reported a wonderful time.

DCHS Reunion 1975

July 1975

The reunion of the 1900-1935 Dawson County High School classes proved to be, in some cases, not only a reunion of school mates, but also a reunion of families. The four remaining members of the Greenwood family were having a good time visiting with one another. At the class reunion five years ago they were all together for the first time in thirty-five years. Their father was still living then to share in their reunion. This time it was just the four 'children' to visit because their father passed away two years ago. Owen 'Bud' Greenwood lives here in Glendive; Sam lives in The Dalles, Oregon; Louise in Great Falls; and Alice in La Crescent, Minnesota.

Three daughters of Frank Brown – Weltha Terry, Pearl Coombs, and Eunice Longelf – also were enjoying their opportunity to visit with each other. Their father had brought his family to Glendive in 1913. He had been a blacksmith in the east before coming to the Gate City and continued in that occupation here. For many years he ran a blacksmith shop on the corner of the alley across Kendrick from the courthouse. Newcomers to Glendive wouldn't be familiar with the big pile of horseshoes (by 'big pile' we mean stacked many feet high as well as wide), but you don't have to be a very old timer to remember it. Or do you? How old do you have to be to be an old timer? Was the pile there until World War II?

In addition to his blacksmithing Mr. Brown became interested in politics and served as county commissioner for about sixteen years. He always had a supply of ice water at his shop so men would congregate there to 'jaw' and have a drink of cold water. Dawson County readers will remember Mrs. Coombs for the years she spent in the public library. She could always be counted on for her interest and help.

The Halvorsen family likely had the highest representation, both numerically and percentage wise. Six brothers and sisters, 100% of the living members of the family, were present. One brother lost his life with the marines on Guam in World War II, and both parents have passed away. The three brothers, John, Bud, and Joe, all live in Sidney, as does their sister, Betty Halvorsen Eyer. Esther Eyer lives in Bellevue, Washington, while Eleanor Thomson's home is in Klamath Falls, Oregon.

For many other graduates there was no family reunion, yet coming back to Glendive was 'coming home'. Bernice Brown Shuman first came to Glendive with her parents in 1912. Her father, R.H. Brown, was superintendent of the city schools here until 1926 when he moved on to St. Cloud, Minnesota. Bernice graduated from high school with the class of 1921 so she was here for her junior and senior high years. Glendive, she says, is still more like home to her than any of the other places she lived.

The family came to the Gate City in the spring, and Mr. Brown filed on a homestead about five miles east of town. It is now a part of the Eaton ranch, but it is still known as the Brown place. While they were on the homestead they one day heard such a rush and roar they thought a tornado was coming so they ran to the root cellar. They were correct in anticipating a storm but it was rain and hail. Then they had a problem getting back to the house.

During his tenure in the Glendive schools Mr. Brown was granted a two year leave of absence to get his doctorate at Columbia University. When they returned from New York they found that some tramps had broken into the little house on the homestead and burned part of it (all the vandalism wasn't reserved for our day) so they didn't stay out there any more, even during the summer. Their town home was on Meade Avenue and Bernice recalls that several times high water from the river came uncomfortably close to their back yard. Bernice and her husband, 'Tag' Shuman, are living in retirement in Arizona, but she thinks it would be nice to be able to come back to Glendive to live.

Pearl Longbothum Mack didn't graduate from – or even attend – the local high school, but she felt that she just had to come to the reunion of the classes of 1900-1935; she wanted to see some of her first and second graders.

Mrs. Mack came from Cuba City, Wisconsin, to Glendive in 1914 to teach in the Lincoln School. After two years of teaching she married Don Mack, a conductor for the Northern Pacific Railroad, but she continued to substitute as a teacher until 1948. She has lived in the same house since 1923. Among her 'first graders' that she visited at the reunion was Chuck Goodspeed.

Chuck's father first came to the Gate City when Montana as a state was only about six years old. He had been a typesetter in a printing office in Minnesota, but when the typesetting began to affect his eyes, he decided to heed the adage of the day, "Go West, young man, go West." He had a sister living in Glendive, Mrs. Herrick, so that helped point his direction.

He stopped off at Mingusville (Wibaux's former name) to look for work. There was no state employment service available then to get employers and employees together. The local saloon was the closest approximation of that office so he stopped in at one and did some inquiring about job possibilities.

About that same time a cow puncher came to town looking for a hand for the winter so Mr. Goodspeed spent that first winter in Montana working on a ranch. The next spring he got on with the Northern Pacific Railroad as a freight brakeman and stayed with them for forty-seven years.

The Goodspeeds' first house was located where the present Catholic Church stands. Chuck, his brother, and his sister were all born in the same bed. His sister has now passed away, but his brother lives in Washington DC.

When Chuck and others of his school mates who had gone away to college graduated from the university, the nation was in the grip of the great depression. There were no jobs to be had in Glendive – or in eastern Montana, for that matter – so they had to look elsewhere for a livelihood. Chuck looked and found employment with the Federal Reserve Bank. Now he is retired and lives in Seattle.

As Mrs. Mack moved about through the reunion crowd gathered at the Moose Hall she located others of her 'first graders'. Among them were George Krug, George Hollecker, Eleanor Haggerty, Jimmy Dvorak, and Don Larimer. Some of her former pupils were a little hard to recognize, especially those who have been gone from Glendive fifty years or so, but the weekend was really a highlight for Mrs. Mack as it was for many others.

Mel Plagmann, for example, missed the last reunion but determined he was going to get to this one. Mel lives in Vancouver now. He wasn't sure of the reunion dates so he finally called Ann Meissner, a former Glendivian living in Seattle. He called on Friday and she told him the reunion started the next Thursday. Mel wasted no time and flew in to visit with his classmates and other friends.

For many years Mel's father, Lou Plagmann, ran a cigar store on Main Street, a few doors from the Rose Theater. Mel recalls that one of his greatest delights as a youngster was to hang around his dad's store and listen to the conversations of those who stopped in to visit.

Glendive, when the Plagmanns came in 1917, had dirt streets, wooden sidewalks, and every second business was a saloon. The rains we've been having this summer reminded Mel of the big flood in Wibaux in the late twenties. He helped clean up after that flood so he remembers it well.

Even though he lives in Washington, Mel keeps in touch with his hometown through the Ranger-Review. Several years ago he came back to Glendive for a visit and while here, stopped in to renew his subscription. He pointed out to editor Burke that he was such a loyal subscriber he had driven 1,200 miles to renew his subscription. Unimpressed, Burke retorted (with embellishments you can supply if you read "Frank 'n Sense"), "You're just too tight to spend eight cents for a letter!"

Abram Greenwood

July 1975

The four children of Abram Greenwood were among the DCHS alumni attending the June reunion of the 1900-1935 classes. While the Greenwoods did not come to Glendive until 1918, Mr. Greenwood made his Montana debut about 1902, Mrs. Greenwood about 1904. He was 'Mr.' then but she wasn't 'Mrs.'

Before Abram Greenwood landed in Montana he had been in every state west of the Mississippi. He was about sixteen and had completed two years of high school when he started his roaming. His father had died a couple years before and his mother was also dead. He received an allowance from the estate, but he decided he'd rather go it on his own and struck out.

In Idaho he worked on a cattle ranch where the cattle would come out of the brush covered with ticks. For awhile he tried hoboing. One time he sold his horse and saddle because he wanted to go by passenger train. That was fine, but when he got to where he was going he was afoot. That wasn't quite so fine, but he made out.

In Wyoming he bought his first overcoat in J.C. Penney's first store – from none other than J.C. Penney himself. At the time, buying an overcoat from J.C. Penney was hardly momentous.

Arriving in Butte he soon found work in the mines. Most of the other miners were Welsh, and Greenwood became known as "the guy with the paper 'poip.'" Mining was dirty work, a feature he did not like, so the young, independent Greenwood drifted east into Forsyth-Miles City country.

His first job opportunity was as a cowboy so he spent some time at that, then took on a job driving stagecoach. There was nothing fancy about the stagecoach he drove. It was just a plain wagon, drawn by a team of horses. Although the wagon was not enclosed, he hauled passengers, mail, freight – whatever needed hauling. His route followed Rosebud Creek and Arnold Creek with stops at Ashland, Lamedeer, Colstrip, and all points along the way where someone might want him to stop. He drove over prairie trails, and there were no fences to hinder his course.

Driving stage provided him with a variety of experiences and plenty of adventure, in case he happened to be looking for experience or adventure. Just after Christmas he headed for Ashland with a school teacher, returning to her school after vacation, as a passenger. The day was beautiful when they started out, but before they reached their destination they found themselves enveloped in a blizzard, and their visibility was close to zero.

After a time he realized they were going in circles so he unhitched the horses, put the teacher on one of the horses and mounted the other himself, then let the horses have their heads. Thanks to some good horse sense, they arrived safely at the next stop.

Another time while he was driving stage he and his passengers were caught in a summer storm. When hail started pelting them, they got out of the open wagon and crouched beside it, trying to find a little protection from the vicious balls. The horses, however, found no protection whatever. They endured what they perhaps considered a reasonable beating, then took off, despite his efforts to hold them. They scattered mail all over Forsyth Flat, but at least they didn't scatter passengers. He and his passengers took advantage of what little shelter a ledge offered and picked up mail as soon as the storm subsided.

It was common in those days for sheepherders to come to town and drink up all their wages. The bartender would save enough money to send them back on the stage to their post. When one drunk insisted upon getting fresh with a school marm, Greenwood put him off the stage, even though they were out in the 'middle of nowhere'.

Driving stagecoach gave Mr. Greenwood ample opportunity to size up the country. When he saw an opportunity to get a good piece of land by homesteading on it, he took up a claim. However, before he proved up on it a young woman established a claim on him. Living out in that tarpaper shack, miles from everything and everybody, didn't appeal to her so he sold the land. His claim was a part of what later became the Colstrip mining territory, but he and his bride didn't know then that it might some day be worth more than surface value.

Bertha Linnabary arrived in Forsyth from Missouri in 1904. Her father, a railroad engineer, had been killed in a wreck. Later her mother had remarried, and the family had moved to Forsyth. There Bertha met and married Abram Greenwood.

Since Bertha was less than enamored with homestead life, Abram took a job with the Northern Pacific in 1908, firing the boiler on the old steam engines – engines that burned fifty tons of coal a day. After two years on the road, he was transferred to the roundhouse and fired a stationary boiler another two years. In 1912 he got on as a brakeman, and he liked that better than firing. Firing was dirty work, and he had a hang-up about dirty work.

Some of his brakeman experiences with hoboes were a bit reminiscent of his stagecoach days and drunken passengers. On one occasion he and another brakeman, Steve Boor, were on a run from Glendive to Forsyth and were making their customary check along the train for hoboes. They found a hobo, a hobo brandishing a 'Hogleg' – a 44 pistol. Even though there were two brakemen, the gun seemed to give the hobo a majority, but they watched their chance to jump him. When they took the pistol away from him they found that it wasn't even loaded! They took no chances on returning it to him though. Instead they sold it at Forsyth.

One experience which Mr. Greenwood never was allowed to forget was humorous to his companions if not to him. On their layovers between runs they just lived in the caboose rather than rent a room. One time when he removed his partial dental plate so he could rinse his mouth, he carefully laid the plate on some papers. When he finished rinsing his mouth, he absently rolled up the papers and dropped them into the potbellied stove they used to heat the caboose. No sooner had he let go the papers than he realized his teeth had gone, too, but it was too late. While he lived, he never did hear the last of that episode.

In 1918 the Greenwood family moved from Forsyth to Glendive, and in 1924 Mr. Greenwood was promoted to conductor. He worked out from Glendive until his retirement November 1, 1943. When his son, Bud (Owen), began his career as a brakeman with the Northern Pacific, father and son worked together.

Mr. Greenwood was all set to retire from the railroad at the customary age of sixty-five. He had his papers made out, ready to sign, but because World War II was in progress and he was badly needed, he agreed to stay on for awhile.

Then came a rough winter. One cold night they had problems all the way into Dickinson, problems that only a railroad brakeman could appreciate. By the time they reached that terminal he decided he'd had enough. He walked into the office and announced that he was retiring.

Mr. Greenwood had been accustomed to activity all his life and continued active after his retirement. When he was close to seventy-nine years of age, he was visiting his daughter Alice on the farm and decided he wanted a horseback ride. His son-in-law saddled up a buckskin, and the old cowboy swung into the saddle.

He let the buckskin go and Alice, watching the horse run, was too petrified to do anything but scream, "Get him off! He'll kill himself!" He didn't kill himself and was soon back at the barnyard, none the worse for wear.

Mrs. Greenwood had passed away in 1928, and Mr. Greenwood had never remarried. After Alice's first husband died and she moved into Glendive, her father lived with her for a time.

He was an avid reader, interested in history but interested in progress, too. He thrived on the news and took in all the sporting events in town. People used to tell Alice they could set their clocks by the time he went to the post office each day.

While not an extremist, he was something of a food faddist and once went to see Bernard MacFaddon. When Alice and her sewing club friends would meet and invite him to have a cup of coffee with them, he would tell them, "Nope. You girls are just heading yourselves to an early grave." In view of the fact that he lived to within a few weeks of his ninety-sixth birthday, who wants to argue?

Mr. Greenwood lived with Bud and his wife for awhile, too, but then he succumbed to an urge to go to California to live. After about five years of sunshine unlimited he went through a period of poor health. About that time he heard of the opening in Billings of St. John's Lutheran Home and decided that was where he wanted to 'settle down'.

He was one of the fourteen charter members of the home, and he loved it there. "The only trouble with St. John's," he once confided to Bud, "is that there are so d--- many old people."

His family celebrated his ninety-fifth birthday with a reunion, the first time they had all been together for thirty-five years. Since Bud was a conductor on the railroad with his run between Billings and Glendive, he continued to see his father regularly, but other family members had to content themselves with less frequent visits.

On one of Bud's visits Mr. Greenwood suddenly announced that he wanted Bud to go to the bank with him so he could turn everything over to him. Bud pointed out that his sister in Great Falls was the administrator, but his father insisted that the matter be taken care of at once so the transaction was completed. Two weeks later, while in the hospital awaiting surgery, Mr. Greenwood died very suddenly of a heart attack, January 18, 1973. He would have been ninety-six on February 4.

Thanks to his foresight, many legal entanglements had been avoided, quite different from the circumstances surrounding his own father's estate. Although Abram Greenwood lived to be almost ninety-six, he did not live long enough to see his father's will probated, even though his father had died when Abram was fourteen!

Less than a year ago all four of Abram's children received a letter that their grandfather's will was in probate. Although he died eighty-four years ago, his estate is being settled in 1975! The matter came to light when some homeowners on a particular tract of land in Utah attempted to get clear title to their homes. The delving into past transactions revealed that the estate of William Greenwood had never been properly settled.

During his long life Abram Greenwood had spent very little time in the hospital and continued to be alert until death overtook him in the hospital corridor while he waited to be admitted for surgery. They brought him back to Glendive for burial, and Bud, his conductor son, brought in the train that carried his body.

Randal Stewart

November 1965

An old proverb tells us, "It's better to light a candle than to curse the darkness." Randal Stewart and his father didn't just light a candle, they turned on the electric lights for an entire town!

Randal's father had come to Fairview in the spring of 1913 to set up an electric light plant – the first light plant to supply electricity to the lower Yellowstone on a commercial basis. Randal and his younger brother joined him that fall and the former immediately went to work helping on the light plant.

The two young Stewarts came to Fairview by way of the Great Northern Railroad as far as Mondak, then a thriving Missouri River town on the Montana-North Dakota state line. From Mondak a 'taxi' – a Model T Ford – transported them to Fairview.

When they reached that bustling little town, unemployment was no problem – no problem, that is, unless you wanted to stay unemployed. According to Mr. Stewart, "You no more than set your foot down and looked around a little, and there would be a dozen bosses or straw bosses asking if you were looking for a job."

In addition to the light plant that was in the process of construction and the coalmine that was being developed, Fairview boasted a flourmill and a brick yard among its industries. So there was plenty to do, but Randal's work was already cut out for him.

The Stewarts had come from Sioux City, Iowa. The elder Stewart, an engineer, had gone first to Williston where he was chief engineer in C.W. Jennison's flourmill. Fairview then, to quote Mr. Stewart, "was in her swaddling clothes and just beginning to grow." Mr. Jennison decided Fairview would be a good site for another flourmill, but he didn't stop with a mill. He saw a need for a light plant, too, and possibilities for developing a coal mine.

While Stewart was building the light plant – setting up the boilers, engines, and generators – Jennison was sinking a mineshaft ready to start operation. By the time the light plant was ready to start operation, the mine was ready to supply the fuel.

Mr. Jennison had worked out a handy setup for loading coal and fueling the boilers. The coal was in a big bin, and when a customer wanted coal, they just let down the chute and in about five minutes the coal was loaded and ready to go with no shoveling. All the screenings fell into the light plant's boiler room and supplied the fuel for firing the boilers, and all of it was done with a minimum of effort.

By November the light plant was ready to go. Randal Stewart was the engineer who opened the throttle to start the engines, and his father threw the switches to put Fairview on the electric line, fifty-two years ago this month.

Mr. Stewart has added reason for remembering that anniversary; the same day they turned on the electricity for Fairview, he lost part of his finger. As he

348

succinctly explained, "I put my finger in a place where it shouldn't have been and got it cut off!"

With Fairview 'all lit up' Sidney had to have electricity, too, so when Glendive built a new light plant, Sidney bought their old one (in 1914), and the Stewarts set up a light plant for Sidney also. This plant was used about six years, but it wasn't very satisfactory. An investigation convinced them they could buy electricity from Fairview more cheaply than they could make their own so a highline was built from Fairview to Sidney – the first highline in the valley.

A very busy time for the Stewarts, father and son, followed the introduction of electricity as they wired houses so the new power could be used. People were glad to say goodbye to the dim kerosene lamp to the chore of cleaning lamp chimneys each morning.

Jennison owned the Fairview electric plant for some years, but later the Glendive company bought it and modernized it. This was the beginning of the Montana-Dakota Utilities Company. Mr. Stewart points out that the big M.D.U. plant southeast of Sidney is a good example of what can come from a small beginning.

Meanwhile, after they had Fairview's and Sidney's light plants sending out the current, Randal's father accepted the position of engineer in the new mill that the Russell-Miller Milling Company built in Sidney. In the fall of 1915 Randal, too, went to work for the flourmill and worked there, with the exception of one year, until the mill closed in 1952.

Although his father has long since passed on, Randal Stewart still lives in the valley where he helped make history with the introduction of electricity. During his fifty-two years in the valley he has seen many changes and much progress. As far as he is concerned, he declares, there is no better place than Montana.

Maude (Smith) Ritchey

April 1969

Maude (Smith) Ritchey came to Montana almost sixty years ago so she could breathe. She's still breathing that Montana air and wouldn't want to live any place else.

Maude was born and lived her first years in Goshen, Indiana. When she was in her second year of high school she was forced in February to join the dropouts because of her health. She had great difficulty breathing, and the doctor told her parents they'd have to get her to a dryer, higher climate.

Her uncle previously had bought two sections of land near Beach, North Dakota, so when he returned to Indiana on a visit and learned of Maude's physical condition, he urged her father to go west, too. There were still a few homesteads available, he said, and the climate was higher and dryer. So in March of 1910 Billy Smith (her father) and Harry (her brother) made a trip to Montana.

In the immediate vicinity of Glendive the homesteads seemed to be pretty well taken so they kept on going – clear out around Paxton and Jordan. There was plenty of free land there yet, but there were plenty of Indians in that part of the country, too. Smith was sure his wife would never be happy there, so they returned to Glendive.

They were feeling rather glum over their land-hunting venture as they stood in front of the Chinese restaurant talking with a couple farmers. As they visited, Smith mentioned their failure to find homesteads, whereat the men informed them that two claims were available out in the Pleasantview area. One had never been filed on and another the homesteader would relinquish. That sounded fine so they investigated – and filed.

Smith built a little 12'x16' shack on his half section that summer, and it was to this that he brought Maude and her mother that fall. He went back to Indiana in October to complete moving arrangements. They loaded an immigrant car with furniture and equipment and also brought along 500 quarts of fruit that Mrs. Smith had canned. Once they were settled on the homestead, Mrs. Smith delighted in making fruit pies for neighboring homesteaders to whom the fruit was a real treat. Commercially canned fruit wasn't available then as now, and they had to depend mostly on dried fruit.

Smith had told his 'women folk' much about Glendive and the surrounding area, and brother Harry had sent some picture post cards (including one of the old Jordan Hotel with the portico) so Maude and her mother felt somewhat acquainted when they arrived.

The town, Mrs. Ritchey recalls, looked good to her after their long train ride. She remembers that at that time there were two big cottonwood trees – just two – along Merrill Avenue between Towne Street and the high school. There were a lot of big cottonwoods along the river, and residents had taken an interest in beautifying the town so a lot of small trees had been set out, but there were only two big ones along Main Street.

In 1910, the only sidewalks were wooden and there weren't too many of those. There was only a vacant lot where the H&M stands and also where the Cedar Grill is. E.C. Leonard's land office occupied the building now housing Berg's Shoe Shop, and on the other side of the vacant lots was a Chinese restaurant where the Oasis now stands.

Instead of the Glendive Community Hospital (or even the Northern Pacific Hospital) up on the hill there was a pasture where the town residents kept their cows and horses during the day. In the evening they'd drive them home, in the morning chase them back again.

Maude spent her first night in Glendive with her father and mother in a room above what is now the Stockman's Bar. For years after that her handprint was in the plaster on one wall of that room. As she slept she had flung her hand against the wall, and the plaster was so fresh and soft that the print stayed.

Next day, November 5, she just about froze riding in a wagon to the homestead. Although there was snow on the ground, it really wasn't so cold, but with her patent leather shoes and no overshoes she just wasn't dressed for November in Montana. Later they moved up in style and purchased a top buggy for such trips, leaving the wagon for heavy hauling.

The little 12'x16' shack to which Mr. Smith took his wife and Maude on the homestead may not have been impressive by today's standards. Not only was it small; it had no plumbing, no electricity; for the first month or so they had to haul or carry water from a spring two-and-one-half miles away. And all the water they carried in had to be carried back out again.

Where were the poverty programs to deliver people from sub-standard housing? Who was there to improve environmental conditions and help people develop economically and culturally? Since the pioneers had never heard of such programs they just went ahead and did their own developing. They had chosen their environment — Maude soon "felt like a million dollars" instead of struggling just to breathe — and had many wonderful times. Before Mrs. Ritchey left the homestead permanently forty-six years later she had built it up to a 4,000-acre ranch with a lovely modern home on it.

In December her dad, her brother Harry, and a neighbor started digging a well close to the house. They dug by hand, filling a bucket with the dirt and passing it up to someone on the surface as the well went deeper. Mrs. Ritchey vividly remembers yet the thrill of "Water in!"

Since Mr. Smith was slimmer than Harry and could work more easily in the cramped quarters as the well got deeper, he was down in it doing the digging and passed up a bucket of dry dirt just as they were called for dinner that twenty-sixth of December.

At dinner he jubilantly confided to his 'women folk' that he had reached water. He had had a hard time trying to find enough dry dirt to fill that last bucket he had passed up to Harry, but he wanted it to be a surprise when they went back to work after dinner. When they returned to the well Harry was duly

351

surprised to find the water flowing in. They had struck very good water in ample supply, and the well has continued in use to this day.

A little more than a year after they came to Montana they started building a new house and moved into it in March 1912. This was a good-sized house with four nice rooms on the main floor and an upstairs besides. They thought they had a mansion, Mrs. Ritchey asserts. And well they might, after living seventeen months in the little shack.

The little shack was not to be abandoned, however. Farmers, ranchers who lived much greater distances from Glendive – from Circle, Jordan, Paxton, as well as points around and between and beyond – had begged them to start a road house to accommodate freighters. The nearest roadhouse was four miles on west, upgrade. That extra eight miles, on into Glendive and back in one day, made just a little too much of a trip so that was why the haulers wanted the Smiths to arrange to put them up there.

They weren't asking for fancy accommodations – just a place to spread their blankets and to be able to get meals. So the original 12'x16' shack with a sixteen-foot square room built on to it was converted into sleeping quarters for the travelers. Mr. Smith built wooden frames for beds, covered them with ticks filled with straw.

It was the extra cooking required to feed the men that put the real burden on Maude and her mother. They'd serve breakfast so the men could start on for Glendive at six o'clock in the morning where they'd unload their wool or grain or whatever they happened to be freighting. Then they'd reload with lumber (materials for Jordan and other towns west, as well as for the new farm buildings, came largely from Glendive) or whatever they might be needing and return to Smiths for another night. It might be ten or eleven o'clock at night when they arrived, but the women would get supper for them. In the morning another breakfast and the men would be on their way with their six or eight horse teams.

The first school in their community was a three-month term the first spring the Smiths were there. The second year of school the county superintendent of schools wanted Maude to teach. She passed the required tests, all right, but she didn't want to try the home school. The boys attending were too big – fifteen and sixteen years old. She was only seventeen herself, and she just didn't feel that she could handle them.

She would have liked to teach the Hasty School rather than the school in her home district. Hastys lived eleven miles straight north of the Smith homestead. Maude greatly admired Mrs. Hasty and could have boarded there during the week, returning home for weekends. Her father, however, objected to that plan. He wanted her to teach the home school so she could be home nights, but since she didn't think she could handle discipline in that school, she settled it by not teaching school at all. Instead of becoming a teacher she became a bookkeeper. But that was a couple years later, in 1914.

One of her reasons for wanting to work in town was to get her mother out of the cooking business. By this time the cooking for the roadhouse had become quite a burden to her, but there seemed to be no way out of it. With Maude in town it would be altogether too much for her so Smith would find it easier to firmly refuse trade. It worked that way, but even then when an old faithful customer would stop they'd take him in. To the general public, though, the roadhouse was discontinued when Maude moved to Glendive to work.

Her first job was as bookkeeper for the Hughes Oil Company. The company was located where the Standard Oil Bulk Station stands now. She rented a room over the post office (in the building now occupied by MDU) and stayed in town because commuting with horse and buggy wasn't quite what it is now with cars. For that matter, the roads weren't quite the same, either. (Is someone saying that many of the roads throughout our county leave much to be desired yet?) Even though she was working in town, all she made went into fences and stock and other things for the farm.

She worked for Hughes until 1919 when she went back east for a time. While there she received a telegram from the Dion Mercantile Company asking her to come work for them. She came back and took over the position vacated by Louie Elliot (stepson of Henry Dion, Sr.) when he went to work in the courthouse. She worked for Dions until she married in 1921.

After her marriage she and her husband lived in Minnesota for two years, but they didn't like it there and returned to the Treasure State and the farm. Her father had died in 1918, so when she came back to Montana she took her mother to live with her on the farm and kept her with her until she passed away in 1941.

Although much work went into building up a farm starting from nothing – not even a furrow turned – Mrs. Ritchey looks back upon her years in Montana as wonderful years. She'd be glad to live them over if she could. While some people may dwell upon the hardships and inconveniences of pioneer life, Mrs. Ritchey remembers the wonderful people and the good times.

Neighbors in those early years the Smiths were in Montana would get together at one of the homes and dance from dark until dawn. Often there wouldn't be room in the house for the people and the furniture, too, so they'd move the furniture into the yard.

Mr. and Mrs. Hardy, who lived in the same section as the Smiths, usually played for the dances – all night for five dollars. He played the violin, she played the organ or piano. They had a happy community, Mrs. Ritchey reflects.

Along with her bookkeeping and farming-ranching experience, Mrs. Ritchey also had the experience of running a furniture store in Glendive a number of years. Her brother Harry had started the store, and in 1928 she bought him out. In April of 1943 she sold the store. At present she and her son, Harry, operate the Cedar Grill and the H&M Bar.

In 1958 Mrs. Ritchey went to New York on a carpet-buying trip and stopped two hours in Goshen, Indiana (her birthplace), long enough to get her birth certificate. The brief stop was long enough to remind her that she wouldn't want to go back there to live. Her roots are in Montana, and here is where she wants to stay.

Bernie Storm

March 1966

When Bernie Storm was ready to move to his Dawson County homestead in the fall of 1910, he thought it would be easier on his wife if she stayed with her parents in Nebraska that winter while he prepared a home on the claim. She agreed and they made the trip to southern Nebraska, but when he got back to the home they were leaving, there was a telegram waiting for him. It said, "Send for me. I want to go with you." So Mr. and Mrs. Storm came together and spent over fifty-two years together in the sod house they built on the claim.

Mr. Storm had come in the spring of that year to file on his claim. Old Jack Wyman, a former Nebraska neighbor, had written glowingly of the big crop harvested in 1909 and urged his friends to come and get in on the free land. Dr. Cross, a veterinarian, had already responded to the challenge and was shipping his machinery, livestock, and household goods by immigrant car so he arranged with Bernie Storm to come in the car to look after his belongings. After reaching Glendive Mr. Storm found a site to his liking in section 10, township 20, range 55, filed and returned to Nebraska to prepare to move that fall.

If Mrs. Storm had stayed behind when her husband moved, she'd have missed out on plenty of excitement. Probably the most memorable experience of those first weeks was her flight from some long horned range cattle that roamed the area. The Storms stayed at the Cross home while their own house was being built, three miles to the east. Each day Mrs. Storm would walk over with dinner for her husband and the lad that was helping them build. Often she walked back again after dinner, rather than waiting for the working men, and one afternoon as she was returning alone to the Cross home, some of the long horns saw her and gave chase. They weren't accustomed to seeing two-legged creatures on the prairie, and they lost no time investigating the phenomenon.

As the wild cattle bore down upon her, Mrs. Storm cast about desperately for some kind of shelter but found none. A sudden inspiration prompted her to throw her coat toward them, and that inspiration saved her. While the cattle paused to maul her coat, she fled over the hill and found hiding in the brush of the coulee. She left her coat in the custody of the cattle for the afternoon, and that evening her husband went back to get it for her.

That was by no means their last experience with the long horns. One evening, about two weeks after they had moved into their new home, they heard some of the cattle start bawling just over the hill, and in an incredibly short time, three hundred head had gathered to join the serenade. What a commotion they made! The new homesteaders had no fence around their yard, and two big steers who hung out along the creek appointed themselves for guard duty. Mrs. Storm's sister stayed with them at this particular time, and every time one of the women would step out of the house and start for the chicken house or the well or wherever, those two steers would bellow, their heads would go down and their tails would go up, and they would give chase.

354

The women were getting desperate, but Mr. Storm was inclined to treat the whole matter as a joke. It was a joke, that is, until one day the steers took after him when he started for the well. He beat a hasty retreat into the house, but only to arm himself. Filling a shotgun shell with salt, he loaded his gun, then stepped out again. When the steers charged, he let go with a blast of salt. Those steers changed their course in a hurry, and the women had no more trouble.

Other trouble with the long horns wasn't entirely due to the perverse nature of the wild cattle; some of the perversity was from ranchers. Ranchers could hardly be blamed for resenting the encroachment of homesteaders upon 'their' land – even though it was theirs only because they had squatted* on a desirable location and turned their livestock loose to roam the ranges for miles around. Now, with the homesteaders and their fences, the free range was fast disappearing, and many of the ranchers were trying to 'fight back'.

Part of the Storms' homestead included that part of the 'table' land where the ranchers held the cattle for branding after they had been rounded up and they didn't take kindly to the prospect of having that area fenced. Mr. Storm didn't at first fence there, but he did put up a fence around the forty acres he had put into flax. More than once (and disconcerting it was) he found that fence cut and range cattle in his flax field. One of the other homesteaders found the answer for keeping the cattle out of his potato patch, however. Cattle can't read, but for some reason, after he put up a sign 'Paris Green', the cattle didn't get in.

Building their house had taken only about a week. A young fellow who was working for Cross helped him, and in return Mr. Storm gave him a six-shooter that he had brought along from Nebraska. The walls of the 14'x24' house, two-and-one-half feet thick were made of sod, while the floor, roof, and window frames were made of lumber. He hauled the lumber from Savage with a team that Dr. Cross let him use. Once that house was finished they had a solid house and well insulated, too. Heating was never any problem in the winter, yet in the summer the house was always cool. They lived in that same sod house until they moved into Glendive in the fall of 1964.

A good water supply was always a primary concern for the homesteaders. Some, for want of good water on their claim, were compelled to haul it, but the Storms built along a creek and found they had a good supply just twelve feet down. Mr. Storm dug their well with a shovel. When he got down into the well too far to throw the dirt out over the top, he'd fill a bucket with dirt, then Mrs. Storm would pull it up with a rope, dump it, and lower the bucket for another load. The bottom was full of gravel so he had to curb it up as he dug down.

The spring after they came to Montana Mr. Storm went to work for the Brown and Dahl plowing outfit. Their gasoline-powered engine pulled eight plows, and they could get a lot of breaking done, but so many wanted breaking done that by the time they got to Storm's homestead the season was well advanced. Neighbors proved friends indeed and, because it was so late, helped him put his forty acres into flax. If the plowing rig was busy in the spring, the threshing outfit was even busier that fall. It was February before he was able to get his crop threshed. Then Switzer from Savage knocked it out for him.

In the early days of settlement very little land was plowed so fires were a great threat. Once started in the luxuriant grass, there was nothing to stop them so rancher and homesteader alike dreaded the alarm, "Prairie Fire!" The Storms were not long in Montana before they were initiated into the Order of Fire Fighters. It was on Easter Sunday, and they were eating dinner with the Cass families, former Nebraska neighbors. Suddenly their neighborly visiting was interrupted by the cry, "Fire!" Rushing outside, they saw the fire bearing down upon them. Sunday clothes were forgotten (and 'Sunday duds' were scarce) as the men quickly formed a fireline and started beating at the flames while the women drew water from the well (there was no pump, the water was pulled to the surface in a bucket on a rope) and carried it to the fighters.

In spite of their strenuous efforts the flames would not be stopped, and all the men, women, and children were forced to flee into the dugout for shelter while the fire roared over them. What a blessing that this homestead dwelling was not a frame structure! When they could venture out again, it was back to beating out the tongues of flames that continued to lick at anything the big blaze had missed.

Mrs. Storm's sister was married to a druggist in Nebraska, and he decided a homestead would be a good investment. He didn't figure it was such a good investment that it was worth giving up his business, however, so he came and filed, then went back to 'business as usual' except for a few visits, while his wife stayed in Montana to prove up* on the homestead. She stayed with Storms as much as possible, spending just enough time on the claim to meet requirements.

On one of his visits, Charley borrowed a team and a sulky plow* from Mr. Storm so he could do some work on his homestead. He was doing all right with his plowing, but then he saw a gopher and jumped off the plow to give chase. Even then he might have got by, but he cracked his whip at it, and at the crack of the whip the horses took off, the plow with them. They plunged across the field, the plow jolting behind, until it tipped over and broke loose, leaving the horses to run unhampered. It was a sadder and wiser druggist who concluded that gopher-chasing and plowing –with horses, anyway – shouldn't be mixed.

Range horses as well as range cattle frequented the area, and they could make trouble, too. One stallion in particular was liable to chase anything in sight, even a cowboy on horseback. One day as the children were playing outside, Mrs. Storm was appalled to see that stallion approaching. She had heard that if you looked an animal straight in the eye he would back down so, grabbing the broom in one hand and a lard pail in the other, she dashed out to confront the beast. As she marched toward him, looking him in the eye while she pounded the lard pail with the broom, she felt far less courageous than she tried to appear. Whether it was the looking him in the eye or the din from the pail and the broom, she was never quite sure, but whichever it was, she was vastly relieved when the horse finally wheeled and left. The ordeal left her weak, but not too weak to gather up the children and take them into the house, just in case he might decide upon a return engagement.

356

In years long past by the time the Storms moved to Montana the route for the McCone Pony Express Trail to a point on the Missouri River crossed what later became their homestead. Even after their arrival the trail was still plainly visible. By the time they took an interest in eastern Montana mails, however, mail was delivered on a route from the Marco post office. (Marco preceded Intake as the post office for that region.)

At first mail was just delivered once a week. The mail for all the neighbors was left at the Storm home, so they were assured of a house full of company at least once a week. Everybody was on hand when the mail came! Later mail delivery was increased to three times a week, but during severe winter weather this was sometimes cut to twice a week because of the difficulty in getting through the snow, even with a team and sleigh. At such times the mail carrier would make the trip to Storms one day, spend the night, and return next day.

Davies, the mail carrier, drove a pair of little buckskin Indian ponies. He had to cross Burns Creek no less than seventeen times between Marco and the Storm homestead. When the weather was cooperating, he could manage, but when the creek was full of snow or water, he had a problem.

Mr. Storm recalled that one afternoon in early spring when the creek was flooding, Davies reached his place with the buckskins wet up to their ears. Quickly stabling the horses, they gave them a good rub-down to get them warm, then kept them covered with blankets all night to ward off any ill effects. One fall Storm had a tremendous crop of potatoes, and so did everybody else. There just wasn't any market for the tubers, and spring found his cellar still full. He didn't know what he could do with 290 bushels of potatoes, but when he mentioned it to the mailman, Davies agreed to take them to feed to his pigs. He hauled away three double wagon box loads, and the next time he came with the mail, he brought along a little pig for Mr. Storm.

They couldn't keep that rascal in its pen, but it marked the beginning of a new venture on the farm. Mr. Storm went in for hog-raising. Some of his neighbors were also raising hogs on a rather large scale, so when the hogs were ready for market, the farmers decided to ship together and ordered two boxcars at Intake to load them out. Even though they ordered the cars in the winter, they could hardly be expected to know that it was going to be fifty-five degrees below zero the day they were to haul the pigs. Cold or no, Mr. Storm went ahead and hauled his to Intake, but they had to hold up the car one day because one of the other consigners waited until the next morning to bring his in. It was just forty degrees below zero that morning. Mr. Storm was well pleased when he learned that his consignment topped the St. Paul market at 190 pounds.

Back home, while he was delivering those hogs, things weren't going too smoothly. The first day, though it was bitterly cold, there was no wind, but the second day it started to storm. Instead of a brick chimney the little sod house just had two stove pipes, one for the kitchen range and one for the heater, sticking up through the roof. The wind reached such velocity that it blew down the cook stove pipe. Although the heater did a good job of heating, it wasn't designed for cooking, but now it was going to have to substitute. An elaborate ornament decorated the top of the stove, but it was on a hinge and could be swung to the side, uncovering a small flat area. Swung to the side it was, and, though they couldn't very well cook a full course meal there, there was room to boil a kettle of potatoes so Mrs. Storm made potato soup and let the stove pipe wait until Mr. Storm got home to fix it.

Before he left for Intake Mr. Storm had arranged with a neighbor to come over and do the chores during his absence, but when the weather turned so cold, the neighbor didn't show up. That meant Mrs. Storm had to brave the wind and snow and cold to do the feeding and milking besides coping with fallen stove pipes and other problems under such adverse conditions.

A little side light to the hog-raising project debunks the theory that a pig will eat anything. Mrs. Storm, her family testifies, could make wonderful baking powder biscuits and cakes and pies, but when it came to bread – well, sometimes the bread wasn't quite all that might be desired. One day when Mr. Storm had gone to Savage, the bread turned out much worse than usual – hard, gray, heavy. Eating it was out of the question, but it was a shame to waste all that flour. The only answer seemed to be to soak up the bread and feed it to the pigs. The real shock came when the pigs refused to eat it! When Mr. Storm came back, the evidence of the bread failure was all over the hog pen.

Horses were raised in great numbers and had considerable value. With horses running loose over a wide range, perhaps it is not surprising that some men whose principles were not too strong in the first place might yield to the temptation to try to get away with some that didn't belong to them.

One day while Mr. Storm was helping a threshing crew on Pleasant Plains he saw a bunch of horses running and recognized one of his in the bunch. He quickly jumped on his saddle horse and galloped to meet them. When he confronted the riders (he knew them all), one of them unhesitatingly assured him, "I'll turn her loose and head her back toward your place." But Mr. Storm never saw his black mare again.

In time the rustlers were apprehended, and after one of the gang had 'taken the rap' for the rest of them, another member came out to Storms' looking for his brother who had been working there. Brother happened to be gone, on a visit to his folks, but Joe stayed around anyway. He was carefully avoiding Glendive because he figured the climate there might not be too healthy just then so he stayed around Storms. He worked, of course, while he was there, so Mr. Storm had a hired man and all it cost him was the fellow's 'grub'.

Horses weren't the only things stolen. Another time a fellow, using two five gallon cans, carried off a barrel of kerosene. This, too, was during threshing season, and when he showed up the next day, Mr. Storm accosted him, but he, while his clothes reeked with kerosene, protested, "You can't prove it."

For many years church services for the area were held in the South Valley School. From 1912 to 1914, Rev. A.E. Plummer had held services in the Independent School a couple miles to the west, but it was not until 1928 when Rev. Birch moved into the community that permanent services were begun.

358

The summer of 1929 meetings were held in a tent erected on the southeast corner of the Thede Jones homestead. The next year a tabernacle was erected there, and from then on the pattern was to meet in the tabernacle during the warm months and in the schoolhouse during the winter months.

During the summer of 1944 they were meeting, as usual, in the tabernacle and were expecting a series of nightly meetings to start the next week when the worst flood inhabitants had witnessed in that area swept down Burns Creek. It wasn't unusual, during times of high water, for water to get into the tabernacle, but this time it didn't merely get into it; it took a good part of the tabernacle and its furnishings right on down the creek with it.

The only wall of the tabernacle left standing was the platform end. They chased planks from the benches clear down to Storms, four miles down the creek. The organ that had been standing on the platform was washed out of the building and smashed to pieces. The steel cabinet in which supplies and records were kept had likewise been washed out and all its contents soaked.

Markings showed that a wall of water at least eight feet high had roared through the tabernacle grounds in spite of the distance from the main creek bed. Seven inches of rain had fallen in one-and-one-half hours to turn loose the torrent of water. Damage to the tabernacle was only a small part of the destruction. Most tragic was the loss of two little children, swept away from their trailer home as their parents attempted to take them to safer quarters.

As Mr. Storm began to assess his losses, he found that his barn had washed away (the water had come to within one foot of the house), and the grain bins that had been built around it were gone too. With the bins went 500 bushels of wheat, 200 bushels of flax, and an undetermined amount of oats.

Three cows and three calves were among the flood casualties. Mrs. Storm, awakened by the storm, had seen, by flashes of lightning, the water coming down the creek and had wakened her husband to get the stock out of the barnyard, but by the time he had dressed he couldn't get to the barnyard.

They found two cows six miles down the creek, but the third cow had simply disappeared. Finally Mr. Storm noticed the dog sniffing up a tree so he looked, and there was the third cow! The wind and water had bent the trees almost to the ground (many had been uprooted) so getting the cow into the tree wasn't quite the feat that it might at first appear. Much damage was done to fences, fields, and machinery by the floods, not only on the Storm farm, but over a wide area, one of the most destructive floods the county has ever seen.

Floods – fires – drought – hail – blizzards – grasshoppers – the Storms encountered them all through their years on the homestead. In spite of the adversities, the years were rewarding.

Mr. and Mrs. Storm had two daughters: Hazel is married and lives in the Black Hills while Mayme keeps house for her father. After Mrs. Storm's passing in January 1963, Mr. Storm and Mayme continued to live on the farm for more than a year and a half, but in the fall of 1964 they moved to Glendive and rented out their land. Now the sod house stands alone on the homestead.

Helen Trocinsky

April – May 1972

Most of us would probably consider living more than eighty years something of an accomplishment, but to live eighty years at the same location – that is something! Helen Trocinsky wasn't around when her parents came to Glendive in 1889, but she arrived the next year. They had, by the time she came along, bought a house on the south side, and with the exception of two years when the family was in Anaconda, she has lived at that same location all her life.

Mr. and Mrs. John Trocinsky came to Montana from Wausau, Wisconsin. Mrs. Trocinsky's sister, Mrs. Joe Meyers, had moved to Glendive earlier, and it was through her influence that the Trocinskys immigrated to the Treasure State.

Mrs. Trocinsky wasn't at all impressed with Glendive's grandeur when she arrived. No sidewalks, hardly anything you could call a street – certainly no pavement! In 1889 the town was very new – new and raw – and very limited in population. Chief asset of the town itself was the railroad. Since this was fifteen years before homesteaders started flocking into the surrounding country, the area boasted only a few ranches, and they were far apart. At least it didn't take long to get acquainted with everyone!

The Trocinskys bought two lots with – they thought – a house on them. However that section of the 'town' had not yet been surveyed, and there were just a few houses on that side of the tracks. When it was surveyed, they found that the house was in the street so they had to move it onto their front lot. This they did and, except for the Anaconda sojourn, lived in it until 1928. Then they built a new house at the same location. John Sterhan, an up and coming young building contractor, built their new house for them. This is the house in which Helen Trocinsky still lives. They bought their lots from Thomas Kean who owned a large part of the south side.

Mr. Trocinsky worked on the railroad for a time, then decided he wanted to move farther west. He started for Missoula but stopped in Anaconda and liked it so well he decided to stay. He went to work for a construction company and sent for his family. Mrs. Trocinsky liked Anaconda. For one thing, it had better school facilities, and her children were reaching school age.

But when Helen was seven, her father was killed instantly in an accident on the job, leaving her mother with four children, ranging in age from five-month-old Tom to seven-year-old Helen. Mrs. Trocinsky would have liked to stay in Anaconda, but her relatives urged her to move back to Glendive so she wouldn't be alone. Since she still owned their Glendive home, she finally agreed.

Perhaps most people associate speeding with automobiles, but the problem goes back farther than that. The Glendive Independent, Saturday, October 9, 1897, quoted an item from the Butte Miner, October 5, 1897, in connection with the accident which took the life of John Trocinsky.

The call for Dr. Murray was an immediate one and instead of waiting for his own carriage he jumped into a hack and told the driver to get him to the depot as fast as he *could without endangering their lives. The driver, Fred Smith, carried out his instructions so well that when he came back up to town the police arrested him for fast and reckless driving. He was released on a $25 bond and when the facts become known he will probably be dismissed.*

Again, it was Mrs. Joe Meyers who influenced the widow with her four small children to return to Glendive, just as it had been Mrs. Meyers who influenced the Trocinskys to come to Montana in the first place. Mr. Meyers ran the ferry across the Yellowstone. Their son Joseph was the sole survivor of the Snyder party along the Marsh Road that drowned in the Yellowstone River flood of 1899. (Dion story, Volume I, page 219.) The Meyers family is closely connected with the railroad history of Glendive. The railroad was booming then, and all seven Meyers children made their livelihood through the railroad. The boys worked on the railroad and the girls married railroad men.

One of the girls married a conductor, T.P. Cullen, who later became a state senator; another married Jim Clayton, an engineer; yet another married J.N. Rapelje who, starting as a brakeman, worked his way up until he became superintendent. The fourth girl didn't marry until after the family moved to California. The Rapeljes stayed in Glendive when the rest of the Meyers family moved to California and Helen cherishes warm memories of the trips she took with them in their private railroad car.

Back when Mrs. Trocinsky was left a widow, there was no social security – no aid to dependent children, and getting help from the county was the worst disgrace. Mrs. Trocinsky was determined not to turn to the county for help.

She received $2,000 insurance which helped tide her over that early adjustment period ($2,000 in 1897 of course, went a lot further than $200 would in 1972). She still had their Glendive home so she was assured a place to live without paying rent. She bought a cow and sold milk; soon built up a flock of chickens again and sold eggs (yes, they were living on Nowlan Avenue). She'd work for various neighbors as they needed help and was able to supplement her income in that way. "Ma had a pretty good head on her," Helen avers. The children helped, too, as soon as they were able, and her relatives, who were in comfortable circumstances, also assisted them.

Frank, Helen recalls, was not yet fifteen when he went to work for the railroad. Mrs. Trocinsky didn't like the idea of his taking on such a job so young, but many young fellows did. A lot of the railroad employees at that time were from foreign lands and they would tell her, "He's big enough; my kids started to work by the time they were his age." There was no doubt in Frank's mind that he was 'big enough', and he was bound to go so, reluctantly, she let him start. There was no denying that his wages were a big help.

Helen Trocinsky remembers when the stores provided more than just delivery service. They'd come around in the morning and take the orders as well as delivering the orders later in the day. They had a spring wagon* and team to provide this door-to-door service.

The children used to play 'Pom Pom Pull Away' in the street – Nowlan Avenue – with never a worry about cars. The grocery wagon would come down the street each day, but that was about the only 'traffic' to interrupt them. The water wagon came around too, but not every day. When town folk wanted water, they'd put up a red flag, and when the wagon came by, the driver would fill the barrel. One time a traveling salesman came to town, saw all those red flags and wanted to know, "What have they got here? Smallpox?"

The water in the barrels was so 'riley' or muddy that Mrs. Trocinsky (and others) would put bread in it to settle it. They thought they were really fortunate to be able to get steam water from the roundhouse. They'd put a boiler on a little wagon and go to the roundhouse to get it. It was nice soft water, wonderful for laundering and other household chores, but of course they couldn't drink it. (Could it have been worse than the water in the barrels?)

When the town first graduated to a pumping plant and water mains, there would be a water hydrant out on the street every block or so, to service homes in the area. Everyone would go to the hydrant to get their water. Sometimes in the winter the hydrants would freeze up, and what a time they'd have!

Mrs. Trocinsky sold their original house to Mr. Cargill to move from their lots. He was having so much trouble with it that Mrs. Trocinsky was sorry she sold it to him and wanted to take it back. He insisted he wanted it and kept working at it, but then the ceiling fell on him, and he died from the injuries. Mrs. Trocinsky was much distressed and lamented that she had ever sold the house to him, but there was nothing she could do about it.

Mrs. Trocinsky also owned a house on River Avenue and she wanted to move over there, but the children were much opposed to that idea. They wanted to stay on the south side where their friends were so she sold the River Avenue house and stayed on Nowlan.

Even though they lived on the south side, Helen and her brothers went to school on the north side, in the red brick school building that used to stand where the First National Bank* is now located. The reason was simple: There was no other school at that time. They had to cross the tracks to get to school because there were no subways in Glendive when Helen Trocinsky was getting her formal education. With no sidewalks – much less, shoveled sidewalks – they often had to wade deep snow in the winter.

School received much less emphasis in 1900 than it does today. The main thing then was to learn reading, writing, and arithmetic and a trade. Even graduating from the eighth grade didn't seem too important. Helen remembers one year when just one girl – Bertha Todd – graduated from Glendive's elementary school. Bertha later married Bert Butler. No doubt many Glendivians remember receiving care from her after she became a nurse. For a number of years she was director of the General Hospital.

As a girl Bertha lived close to Trocinskys, and they played together constantly. Helen remembers how, before they moved to Anaconda, they'd run to meet their father as he came home from work, carrying his lunch box. Bertha would be playing with them, and she'd run to meet him, too. One of his fellow workers had no children and would often send something – a piece of cake or such – along home with Mr. Trocinsky for his children.

Even when Mrs. Trocinsky and her little brood came back from Anaconda, no one had a car yet. Everyone walked unless they were lucky enough to have a horse and buggy. The walkers included even the doctors. It was customary then for a doctor to go to his patients, rather than the patients go to the doctor. Perhaps lack of transportation was part of the reason. It was easier for a healthy doctor to walk to the sick than for the sick to get to the doctor.

When Helen's brother Tom was five years old, he broke his leg so Dr. Ireland came to the house to set it. He ran out of chloroform and had to walk over to the drug store and get some more before he could finish setting the leg. But he finished it and did a good job because Tom has never had any trouble with it. Helen laughed as she compared their transportation then to the present. Then they walked and walked. Now they go to the moon!

Even though they walked wherever they went, people did go, and they visited. The stores remained open until nine o'clock Saturday evening so everybody went downtown, mostly just to walk around and visit. In the winter when darkness came so early, they had to carry a kerosene lantern with them in the evening. The Trocinskys had a big old phonograph, and they'd take their last forty cents, Helen averred, to buy the new record that came – Redwing – whatever it might be. These records, of course, were the cylindrical type. Friends often gathered to listen to the phonograph, too. Saturday nights they'd pull up the rug, and Jimmy Osborne would bring his concertina to play for their quadrilles. "People don't visit any more like they used to," she concluded.

Mrs. Trocinsky was determined that all her boys should learn a trade, "Even," she declared, "if it's peddling!" None of them was a peddler, however. Tom and Frank learned the machinist trade and worked in the local Northern Pacific Railroad shops, Leo joined the navy when the United States entered World War I, then went to Chicago where he attended the Coyne Electrical School, and trained to be an electrician – a relatively new field at that time. He worked for the Bureau of Reclamation, in Glendive and elsewhere, including Fort Peck while the dam was under construction. In Glendive the MDU workers called him 'Uncle Sam' because of his affiliation with the Bureau.

As for Helen, she worked for a time for Mr. Widmeyer in the printing office ("How the printing business has changed!" she exclaimed!), and also did a good bit of baby sitting, helping with housework or whatever was needed.

In 1969 she broke her hip. A pin was put in, but the pin came out and her problems really started. She was sent to Billings where four more pins were put in, then she spent four months in a convalescent home there so the doctor could keep her under surveillance.

Now she is able to manage in her own home again, thanks to a combination of Mrs. O'Connell, her basement renter, and brother Tom and his wife next door. Because of arthritis, her arms aren't strong enough to support her on crutches so she is confined to a wheelchair. Even though her body, admittedly, is handicapped, her mind is still active and alert in spite of her almost eighty-two years. And she still likes to visit.

Mrs. Eugene (Eva Martin) Wester

August 1965

As Mrs. Eva Wester watched her eight children grow up in Glendive, so she watched Glendive itself 'grow up'. She came to the Gate City June 10, 1905 as a bride of five days and has lived in the same location ever since, albeit in a different house. Her husband had been working on the Northern Pacific Railroad's section gang and had built a little tarpaper shack over on Sargent Avenue to have a place to stay on the weekends while the rest of the gang was hanging around the beer joints. The little shack was fine for a single man, but Jack wanted a better house for his family so as soon as he brought his new wife he started building a new house in which Mrs. Wester lives to this day.

There weren't many houses on Sargent Avenue when they started to build: a few little tarpaper shacks and one or two 'real' houses. The sagebrush was so tall that when Mr. & Mrs. Keene, who owned most of the land on the South Side, walked over town, the sagebrush completely hid Mrs. Keene.

Mrs. Wester was born September 5, 1886, in Russia and came to the United States when she was thirteen. Her aunt was living in Mandan, North Dakota and wanted her father to join them. She and her husband sent a pass for him and also for each of Eva's two oldest sisters. Mr. Martin (Eva's father) just didn't feel that he wanted his two girls to come that far without their parents so he sold everything he had in Russia and brought the entire family to the New World. The 'entire family' then consisted of the parents and nine children. Two children had died in Russia and three more were born in North Dakota.

Crossing the ocean took seven days and Mrs. Wester observed that she was sick all seven. None of the family could speak English so the children were careful to stick close to their mother. When the ship docked in New York, Grandfather and the two oldest sisters were held back. A strange land – a strange language – three of their party taken from them (would they ever see them again?) – little wonder that panic began to overtake them. But then they found someone who could speak German and explain for them. Since those three had come on passes the authorities had considered it necessary to wire to Mandan before allowing them entrance to the country to make sure they would not be dependent upon the county. When that assurance was received, the 'prisoners' were released and the family reunited, to their great relief.

Once they reached Mandan, Mr. Martin filed on a homestead (this was in 1899). Thirteen-year-old Eva and her eighteen-year-old sister went to work washing dishes in a restaurant, Eva for $6 a month and her older sister for $8 a month. Their dishwashing sinks were two washtubs placed side by side. A man would fill the water heater for them and they would draw their dishwater from a spigot at the bottom of the tank. To empty the water her sister took one handle of the tub, Eva the other, and they carried it to the back yard and poured it out.

Later she began working in private homes in Bismarck, her highest wage $15 per month. While she was working in Bismarck she met a young man

364

named Jacob Schloss. She became acquainted with a cousin of his while both were visiting there. Three years later they were married, a few months before her nineteenth birthday.

Jacob (or Jack, as everyone called him in this country) was also born in Russia. He had been left an orphan so when his oldest sister and her husband immigrated to the United States in 1897, they brought Jack with them. He was able to get a job on the Northern Pacific Railroad and though he was transferred to Glendive, he continued to visit his sister and so met Eva Martin.

The day after he brought his bride to her new home, Jack took her to the Douglas-Meade* Store and they bought their housekeeping equipment. Brides weren't 'showered' then, and they didn't have even a spoon or a dish. They selected those items and also bought a wood and coal range for $35, which she used until the gas line was laid to their house after Mr. Schloss's death. They hauled their purchases home with a horse and wagon but then realized they had neglected to get a clothesline so they had to go back for that.

Kerosene lamps, of course, supplied their lights. Most Glendivians who did not have their own well bought their water by the barrel from a deliveryman (water so dirty it had to settle before they could use it) but Mr. Schloss carried theirs from the roundhouse, good water and clean. Usually he just took a couple of buckets, but on wash day he took a little two-wheeled cart which he pulled by hand and hauled a barrel for her. She heated the water in a boiler on the stove, then emptied it into the washtub to suds and scrub the clothes.

After their marriage, Mr. Schloss worked in the N.P. carpenter shops for a few years, then began working as a contractor in partnership with William Ullman. In a few years a young fellow by the name of John Sterhan began working for them, and later Mr. Schloss and Mr. Sterhan formed a partnership, working together as long as Mr. Schloss lived.

Mr. and Mrs. Schloss had seven children. When their youngest son was born, the flu epidemic was raging across the country and six were in bed with the flu in their house. That spring they had taken a homestead north of the present Helland Ranch so Mrs. Schloss and the children stayed on the homestead with Mr. Schloss coming out on weekends. However, when the flu presented such a threat they moved back to town and gave up the homestead.

A concrete wall fell on Mr. Schloss in 1924. He survived, but ten months later he dropped dead as he walked to work. The doctor explained that his heart had been enlarging ever since the accident and that had caused his death.

In 1927 Eva married Eugene Wester who died in 1933. They had one son. Now Mrs. Wester has six children living, thirty grandchildren, and twenty great grandchildren. Seven of her sisters are still living, Mrs. Wester the oldest.

When she came to Glendive sixty years ago as the bride of Jacob Schloss, she didn't know anyone in Glendive except her husband, but she liked it here then and likes it here now. This is where she chooses to live.

Earl Baggs

March 1967

Probably most of us have not had the experience, as did Earl Baggs, of a bunch of Indians sitting in our front yard eating their supper, but then – most of us didn't have a front yard on Hay Creek the early part of the 20th century.

Hay Creek happened to be on the route the Indians from Wolf Point customarily used each spring when they went to visit their South Dakota relatives for the summer, then again in the fall when they returned.

Mr. Baggs had built close to some springs on the creek, and these springs were often used by campers, including the Indians. One year, after the advent of automobiles, a big car loaded with Indians drove up, and they asked permission to camp a little to the east of his buildings. He didn't mind their camping, but everything was so dry he didn't think it wise to make an open fire so he suggested they come in and cook their meal on his wood stove.

When they had their ham cooked they all filed out into the yard, then sat down in a circle and ate their meal. By the time they were ready to eat, the second carload of Indians had arrived so they sat in the circle and ate, too. Although this time the Indians were in automobiles, in the early days they had come with their ponies and dogs. They were always orderly and made no trouble for the settlers in the area.

In the fall of 1908 Mr. Baggs had come from Iowa to file on a homestead in Dawson County. In Jefferson, Iowa, the banker had heard about the homestead lands opening up in eastern Montana and began promoting Treasure State opportunities. He had contact with Charles Miller, Glendive real estate agent, and would send prospective settlers to Miller who would then locate them.

After Mr. Baggs had picked out his future home site on Hay Creek, three miles west of Lindsay, he went back to Iowa, and that next February he married one of his former schoolmates, Della Richards. Her brother had come out and filed on a homestead the same time Earl had filed, and the first of March the two men headed out again so they could put up some buildings before the women folk arrived the first of May.

That first year on the homestead, what with building and making the improvements necessary for habitation where there had never been human habitation before, they didn't get much farming done. The next year, 1910, they did some farming, but they didn't get any harvest from it. That was one of the driest years in Mr. Baggs' farming experience. Besides being uniquely dry, even in a dry country, that summer furnished them another unique experience – the day without daylight.

Mr. Baggs' father was visiting them, and one night seemed to have no end. Finally, even though it was still dark, they decided to get up and found that it was already eight o'clock. Even the chickens were fooled that morning so Mr. Baggs lit the gas lantern and hung it in the henhouse to wake them up.

Earl had been cutting oats the day before so about ten o'clock he went out to the field. He couldn't see more than forty rods but he cut until mid afternoon. By four o'clock it was dark again. Many people thought this must be the end of the world, but they later learned that forest fires in Minnesota had combined with forest fires in Montana's western mountains to blanket the area with smoke cover so dense the sun's rays couldn't penetrate.

Baggs had not yet engaged in cattle raising so that next winter – since he didn't have livestock to feed and demand daily attention – he took on the job of freighting for Pete Rorvik, Circle merchant. Earl's brother-in-law was likewise employed. They used sleds and four-horse teams to haul from Glendive to Circle. Most of the way there was plenty of snow and in places more than plenty, but the Yellowstone Bridge was always bare, as were the high ridges through the Redwater-Yellowstone Divide*. Ordinarily they would have avoided the highest ridges, but there was so much snow on the regular trail that they were compelled to seek out the high spots. Those bare gravel ridges made tough pulling for the horses, but they kept going.

The Baggs homestead was about midway between Glendive and Circle which was handy when he freighted between the two towns. He could make it to Glendive from his place in one day (in one day, that is, if his day started at three o'clock in the morning) to get his supplies.

The second day he could get back to his home where he'd spend the night, then the third day it was on to Circle. Since his brother-in-law was freighting, too, the nights that the men had to be in Circle or Glendive their wives would stay together. Redwater, of course, had to be crossed before they could get to Circle and the bank was steep. One trip they pulled up to Redwater late at night so they decided to just leave the loaded sled on the east side rather than attempt that crossing in the dark.

Unhitching the horses, they each mounted one and took their teams on into Circle, stabling them in Rorvik's barn. It was easier to find a place for the horses that night than for themselves. There was a ball in progress, and the town was crowded so Mr. Baggs and his brother-in-law slept on the floor of the post office. At daybreak they went back to Redwater to get their sleds and complete their mission.

For making those long trips in the cold and snow (it was fifty degrees below zero one morning when he started for Circle) with team and sled his remuneration was a dollar per hundredweight. But it gave them some income during a winter when otherwise they'd have had no income, following a summer with almost no income.

1912 was the year of the big crop, including a big flax crop. At that time Glendive had the only elevator for miles around, and it had only one – the one on Merrill Avenue in the vicinity of the high school. The bumper crop had to be hauled to this one elevator, and Mr. Baggs recalled with amusement the races that sometimes took place on Main Street as teamsters vied to 'get there first'.

The big, slow-moving tractors of that day were used by some to haul grain. These machines could pull six or seven wagons behind them so when they reached the elevator, it took a long time to unload. Little wonder the teamsters weren't eager to pull in behind one of those outfits. Waiting in line that long meant you would be late getting your horses to the livery stable.

Mr. Baggs usually patronized the Helland Livery Barn, at that time run by Ole Mosshes, located on Kendrick. There was another stable on Bell Street near the bridge, and Ed O'Neil had an establishment on the corner of Kendrick and Towne. Instead of a gas station on every corner, it was a livery stable – or a saloon. There weren't enough corners for the latter, however.

When making the thirty-mile trip with a load of grain, Mr. Baggs would leave home about three in the morning, aiming to reach Eleven Mile Spring by noon to water the horses. He'd eat his lunch there, then come on into town. He'd stay in Glendive overnight, then return home the next day, usually arriving there about eight o'clock in the evening.

Watching the big cattle shipments come in was a sight Mr. Baggs well remembers. The old bridge (the wooden structure pre-dating the 1922 Bell Street bridge) had a chute so that train doors could be opened and cattle unloaded directly onto the bridge. Every year the CK, as well as other ranches, shipped in thousands of cattle. These cattle then were trailed to the ranch, northwest of Circle in the case of the CK. The cattle were so thin from their long trip up from Texas that many would die on the trail to the ranch.

As late as 1916 thousands of horses were shipped in, too. One rancher brought in 15,000 that year with 3,000 a little later. The government had bought great numbers after the outbreak of World War I, but later the demand for horses abruptly declined, and ranchers were left with no market except the cannery at Miles City.

Prairie fires were an ever-present hazard which the pioneers faced, and whenever a fire started, farmers and ranchers for miles around turned out to fight the blaze. One fire Mr. Baggs mentioned burned from Lindsay almost to Glendive. Mrs. Christmas had emptied her ashes at her home just east of Lindsay, and the wind caught some sparks. The grass in 1909 was tall and thick so there was plenty of fuel to feed the blaze. What a time they had getting that fire out! When the ranchers fought fire, they split a beef carcass in half, then tied it to their saddle horns and pulled it along the front of the fire. Mr. Baggs knows from experience what it is to wake up at night and see a fire that looked as though it was just over the Divide, then ride for three hours (horseback) before reaching it.

In 1912 the folks around Lindsay built the community hall. That summer they met there for their Fourth of July celebration. Not only the Lindsay people but also many from neighboring communities and Glendive attended as well. Mr. Baggs guessed there were probably a thousand people in the little town for their celebration. The hall was used extensively for community gatherings a number of years, but after automobiles became common the hall was used less and less. After the 'old Lindsay' store burned, the hall was moved down to the present Lindsay site.

Mr. and Mrs. Baggs made their first trip back to Iowa to visit in 1913. The next year he started raising Angus cattle, one of the earliest herds in the state.

In 1950 Mr. and Mrs. Baggs moved to Glendive, but he continued farming until 1962 when he was compelled to quit because of his health. Mrs. Baggs passed away in 1954. Three of their five children are still living. One daughter with her husband is on the home place, another daughter lives in Circle, and the one son is in Wyoming.

As Mr. Baggs thought back over the last fifty-eight years he observed that he wouldn't take a million dollars for his pioneering experiences, but on the other hand, he didn't think he'd want to go through it again, even for a million. Of course, at eighty-one years one doesn't have to make that choice – even if the frontier were still to be conquered.

Yellowstone River and badlands at the mouth of Thirteen Mile Creek

Bill, Francis 'Peg', and Rob Kelly
Ray LaBelle and Ole Knutson

Blue Star Honey
from the Pickering Farm

Well driller pulled by team of horses

Studebaker 'Straight 8'
Fred & Margaret Steffen, Kathleen, John, Clarence, Frederick

'Democrat Wagon'

J.K. Ralston

1974 Unpublished

When J.K. (Ken) Ralston, famed Montana artist, depicts ranch scenes, he knows whereof he paints – or draws. As he was growing up he was exposed to cowboys daily and joined their ranks at an early age. Ralston was born in Western Montana and came with his parents to Dawson County in 1906. Northeastern Montana was the last stronghold in the state for cattlemen, and it was in this refuge that his father ranched.

His grandfather had come to Montana in 1864, lured by gold in Alder Gulch. He had left Independence, Missouri in 1859 for Pike's Peak – and gold – and prospected there until 1863 when he headed for Idaho. He didn't intend to spend the winter in Idaho, but when he tried to get over to Alder Gulch, he found more snow than he could navigate so he stayed in Idaho after all.

Next spring he put in his delayed appearance at Alder Gulch, then followed gold from one place to another in Montana. In 1876 he built the first house in Marysville and the town was named for Ken's grandmother. His grandfather had a livery stable and butcher shop in Helena, a ranch in Prickly Pear Valley (Helena Valley now). In the late '60's (1860's!) Ken's father was peddling beef to miners in the gulches. They'd leave a note giving him their 'order'.

In 1878, when Ken's father Will Ralston was in charge, they moved the cattle to Teton. He started a ranch of his own near Choteau in what became known as Ralston's Gap. In 1885 he married Ellen Matthewson, and they lived on the ranch which they called Cold Spring. That's where the children were all born: Bess, Allen, Frank, Billy, and last, Kenneth. But then Ken's dad was struck with gold fever and sold out to follow the strikes in Idaho and British Columbia. They lived for awhile in Spokane and in Rossland, BC.

In 1903 they came back to Montana and he made a deal with a rancher by the name of Tatum to set up a ranch for Tatum's boy when he was out of college. Will Ralston took over as manager of the Flying U Ranch, again in Choteau country.

Cowboys could be identified by their range 'lingo'. One thing, you'd always find at least one Englishman. Research on the Battle of the Alamo reveals that the state with the most men was Tennessee. The second largest group was from England. Two Englishmen worked for Old Man Day, and one married J.K.'s aunt.

From Choteau Will Ralston moved his family to northeastern Montana and became manager of the Capital P Ranch, just south of the Missouri River on Charlie Creek. Culbertson, north of the river, was the nearest shipping point and was a wild cow town. The country at that time was all open range with no fences except where someone may have fenced a piece of public domain for a pasture. But those were few.

The Capital P had a big log house on it with an 18'x24' living room. People kept asking when they were going to have a dance so before fall roundup started in 1906 they accommodated. They whittled candles to wax the floor of that big living room.

That was the wettest year since white man's history! The day of the dance rain started falling again. This would have been late August or early September. Every steep place was a potential mud slide. But people came from miles around.

The Hilger girls were visiting the Fred Sullivans and came with them in a spring wagon*. Butler, a friend of Will Ralston from Prickly Pear Valley, and his wife from the '14' came with a top buggy. Some came on the 'flag' train from Culbertson. A flag train would stop and let you off wherever you designated. Henry Miller rowed them across the river to the dance.

Miller brought the music from Culbertson. The piano didn't get there, but they had music. Floyd Davis met his future wife Clara Hilger there. Davis (Volume I, pages 22-33), riding a bronc (what else?) was breaking horses for Henry Miller at the time and came with probably eight or ten other horseback riders. He was off to one side a little when they came to a cut bank about four miles from the ranch. They tried to go around it, but he went over the bank. Fortunately, he wasn't hurt and neither was the horse so they went on to the dance.

Sullivans, with the two Hilger girls, were close to West Charlie Creek, coming up through the hills, when they attempted to negotiate a sidling hill. The buggy tipped over, scrambling cakes and other food (and people), but they, too, continued on. There were about six cowpunchers to every girl at the dance so some fellows tied a handkerchief around a girl's arm to establish his claims, especially for the square dances.

Families brought their children along as was customary in those days. Supper was served at midnight: big pots of coffee, sandwiches, coleslaw, and cakes. People sat around the edge of the hall to eat.

There was lots of room at the Capital P. Besides the 18'x24' living room there was an 18'x18' kitchen and four bedrooms. There were plenty of corrals, but they owned not one foot of land. The land was claimed by the federal government.

Mrs. Ralston, Ken's mother, filed the first homestead claim in that township and submitted a petition to have it surveyed. No surveying had been done south of the river, but a surveyor was working north of Culbertson where he had perhaps a dozen townships to survey. He had to come across the river and survey this one township before he could be released from his contract with the government. Ken's father had used his homestead rights at Teton so couldn't file. Ken and his siblings did file, but now Billy is the only one still in the area. He has the home ranch plus his own. Capital P was out of business by this time; this had been their outfit.

Mr. Ralston didn't dwell much on his fame as an artist, but his paintings, too numerous to name, are known internationally and have been seen in Canada, Europe, Australia, and other countries. Prelude to a Tragedy shows Custer coming on to the field just before the battle. It was used in a series by the British Broadcasting Company. <u>After the Battle</u>, depicting the aftermath of Custer's defeat by the Indians, was leased by the United States Department of Commerce in Washington as part of the collection <u>Treasures of the West</u>. The collection has been shown in Europe and is slated to go to Australia. <u>The Winter Ranch</u> is popular on greeting cards.

Mr. Ralston explained the various components of the roundup crew. Obvious, of course, were the cowboys. Since the roundup covered hundreds of miles and cowboys might not get back to the home ranch all summer they had to have a support crew. Any roundup had to have a cook and a mess wagon. The cook drove the mess wagon, which carried the food, the cooking utensils, and the mess tent. In the back of the mess wagon was the grub box. It would stick up above a double wagon box. This was covered with a wagon sheet over two wagon bows, high enough to clear the mess box. The seat was on stilts well above the horses. Mr. Ralston mentioned that he has eaten at the mess wagon which is now in the Mile City Museum. The wagon boss's bed was also in the cook tent.

The bed wagon carried the water barrel and a little extra wood, anything they didn't want to put in the mess wagon. There was a bed rack on each side of the wagon, then piled up from there. From the rack in the back they could hang chaps and ropes. It looked like a hay load coming down the road – if there was a road! On roundup each puncher would have six to eight horses in his string. They made temporary corrals for the remuda* with ropes staked to the bed wagon wheels.

Ken has his sister Bess to thank for introducing him to his future wife. Bess was attending summer school (for teachers) in Miles City. When Ken and some of his friends went to Miles City for the Fourth of July rodeo, Bess introduced him to her new friend Willo Athaud. Bess encouraged Willo to apply for a country school near the Ralston ranch and Willo was accepted. The cowboy did his part to welcome the new teacher into the neighborhood, and the next summer they were married.

The Ralstons have two children, Margie and Kenny. Margie is married to Harold Scott, a CPA in Bozeman. They have two daughters and a son. Kenny works for Boeing in Seattle. He and his wife Eleanor have two sons and a daughter.

Floyd Davis, a neighbor of the Ralstons, was Ken's boyhood friend and hero. When Davis requested Ralston's photo of the Pot Hound Pool remuda be borrowed to accompany his story in the Ranger-Review column (January, 1969) the Ralstons graciously loaned their highly prized photo, only because of their esteem for Davis. Mr. Ralston added a note that, "the Gobbler (Davis) was a top cowboy.... met his wife at a dance at our place, the old Capital P, in 1906." After the article ran, Mrs. Ralston sent the following note:

Dear Mrs. Kauffman:

We received the copies of the Ranger-Review with the story of Floyd Davis, and enjoyed them very much. His life and Clara's make a very entertaining tale.

Our photograph of the Pot Hound Pool remuda which we loaned you was also returned promptly and safely by the Review. The picture came out very well in the paper. Glad you could use it.

Thanks for having the papers sent to us. We will be writing to the Davis's about the story, now that we have read it.

Sincerely, Mrs. J.K. (Willo) Ralston"

The first letter from J.K. Ralston accompanying the loaned photo is printed below. These communications with the Ralstons regarding the Floyd Davis story led to this interview with the Ralstons themselves in 1974.

JK RALSTON
2103 ALDERSON AVE
BILLINGS, MONTANA 59102

December 31, 1968

Mrs Morris Kauffman:
417 Grant
Glendive, Montana

Dear Mrs Kauffman:

　　We have your letter of December 17, and am sorry we have not answered sooner but were out of town over Christmas.

　　At your request I am mailing you the photograph of the Pot Hound Pool remuda - the spring roundup of 1906. I prize this photo very highly and would not lend it except that you wish to use it with the story of my old friend Floyd Davis. I am backing it with plywood to put in the mail so it will not get broken.

　　The "Gobbler" was a top cowboy. He repped for the Pot Hounds and various other wagons. Had a cabin on the river below our ranch, and as he has probably told you, met his wife at a dance at our place, the old Capitol P, in 1906.

　　I would like very much to see your story when it comes out in the paper and will appreciate your sending us a copy.

　　Please do not loan this photograph to anyone and do not have copies made other than for use in your story in the paper. Credit line: "loaned by J.K.Ralston" .

Sincerely,

J.K.Ralston

John Diercks

1975 Unpublished

When John Diercks's father joined a roundup crew in Montana, he realized he was facing life in the raw. He rode over a hill and found, not the stray cattle he sought, but a man hanging by the neck from a tree. This was during the cattle, sheep, and squatters war and no one could be neutral so he moved to quieter territory.

August John Diercks, John's father, was born in Germany and brought to the United States when he was very young. The family did not get beyond New Jersey, but John kept drifting west until finally, about 1890, he wound up in Montana. While he was still with his mother in New Jersey, she had remarried. He and his stepfather were not too compatible so he farmed out as an apprentice to a sheet metal worker. That didn't work out, either, so he went to live with his uncle in Iowa.

A lot of range stock was brought into Iowa from states farther west, and through this contact young Diercks met a South Dakota cattle rancher. The rancher took a shine to the youngster – he was only fourteen or fifteen – and took him along back to South Dakota. Ranch life was completely new to John, and when the rancher assigned him a horse and a job, he rode all day and wound up back where he started without ever getting to where he was supposed to go. He quickly learned, though, and by the time he reached Montana he was well on the way to becoming a cowboy.

He soon found that the life of a cowboy was not all glamour and romance. They traveled light, and they traveled long, especially when on roundup: bedroll and the inevitable sack or plug of tobacco. Rarely did they carry a lunch with them, even though they might be away from the ranch or wagons most of the day. When John – Buck, as he was known in Montana – became roundup cook for the XIT he found himself serving breakfast between three and four in the morning; dinner at two, when riders began bringing in the cattle they had rounded up that morning; and supper around five. Irregular as eating hours sometimes were, a cowboy generally ate heartily when he had opportunity.

As cook on the roundup Buck moved the chuck wagon from one location to the next, where he'd set up camp in time to have the noon meal ready for the hungry riders returning from the morning circle. He had no road, usually not even a trail to follow over the prairie or through the badlands so he made his own trail. One morning as he was heading for the new camp he started down a steep grade, and the wagon went over a bank. Riders within sight saw equipment flying in all directions, but he managed to keep the wagon right side up and collected his scattered pots and pans so he came out all right in the end.

On roundup they simply used ropes for corrals, but when they needed something more permanent, they went out and cut timber for it. Buck decided on a shortcut for loading a rather large tree. Instead of cutting it down, then loading it onto the wagon, he backed the wagon up to the tree and felled it into the wagon. Only one problem – it went right on through the wagon.

The law of the open range allowed you to eat when you came to a ranch or a line* cabin, occupied or unoccupied. Cabin or ranch – the door was never locked. If you needed food you helped yourself and cleaned up after yourself and nothing was said about it. One night he came up to a line shack dug into the side of a hill so he bedded down for the night. He woke up to a pounding overhead. He tried to figure out what was going on but couldn't imagine. Finally he got up courage to go investigate and found a horse on top of the cabin!

Another time when he was looking for cattle, he came to the end of the day with no habitation in sight. He just threw his bedroll down so he could sleep. He heard a snake rattle, but it was dark and he didn't dare move around hunting for it so finally sleep got the best of him. Next morning he found the snake was under his bed. He'd been sleeping on it all night!

One time he was heading for a different set of ranch buildings and decided to have a little fun. Although it was out of the way for him, he swung around to where he knew he'd find a sheepherder who stuttered. Finding the herder, he asked the way to the ranch. The stutterer started, "It's b-b-b-b-b-b-b – It's b-b-b-b-b – It's b-b-b-b – Oh, you know where it is, you &%#! Go get it!"

Ranchers in eastern Montana didn't have specified sections where their cattle ranged. Rather, their range extended from the Missouri River to the Wyoming line, from the Musselshell to the Dakota line. Diercks's main headquarters were at Miles City or thereabouts. Some winters when work was slack he set up a trapping line in the Wolf Mountains south of Miles City, trapping wolves and coyotes. John still has a robe made of eight coyote pelts with tails attached. His stepfather had the pelts made into a robe, and John has a picture of the stepfather holding the robe.

Some winters he spent at ranch headquarters. One particularly bad blizzard they played cards to see who would have to feed and water the saddle stock in the barn, with loser out – literally! Dad lost so he put on his big coonskin coat with just a little peek hole to look out, but even then he had to turn around now and then to catch his breath. After the storm they found their yard full of deer. One of the fellows went for his gun, but before he could use it the other fellows knocked him down for even thinking of shooting deer after such a storm.

Once when the ranch had sold a bunch of horses to the army, Diercks delivered them to Fort Keogh and wound up in the guardhouse for failing to salute an officer – a young lieutenant who had just come into the area. Diercks spent most of the day in the guardhouse before he could get a hearing, but then he was promptly released because as a civilian he was under no obligation to salute.

It's hard to grasp the immensity of the operation of some of the ranches, but one fall one of the big ranches started loading cattle at Fallon for eastern markets on September 1. They loaded seven days a week, from sunup until after dark and kept it up until Thanksgiving. Then from Thanksgiving until the first of the year they loaded three days a week.

Fallon at the time was the largest stock shipping point in the world! Once when they were herding a bunch of cattle across the river at Fallon, his horse lost its footing and threw him into the river. George Twible (later sheriff in Dawson County) was on hand and pulled him out.

Dad used to go to Cheyenne and pick up the trail herd from Texas and bring them up into Montana. Montana Bill was one fellow who came from Texas on the trail that Dad picked up in Cheyenne. Bill later managed the Range-Riders Museum in Miles City and they were friends to the last. For a time Dad considered staying in Wyoming, but that was during the era when you had three choices: you could be a rancher, a sheepman, or a farmer. Whichever you chose you were target bait so he came back to Montana.

On one of the big ranches the cowboys told the rancher they would like to have different fare and talked the rancher into buying cereal so they could have cereal and fresh milk for breakfast. The only problem was that no one could ever find time to milk the wild cows so the cereal idea was abandoned.

A couple fellows came through this country and raided a couple bunkhouses, taking what little some of the cowboys had. They were found out and chased to the Musselshell River where they were 'disposed of'. Justice was dealt summarily in those days. No years of appeals.

On another occasion a couple cowboys were having bad words with each other and decided to settle it with a duel. However, Diercks saw what was happening and stepped between them. He ordered them not to turn around. They complied and the matter was settled.

When one of his childhood friends from New York planned a trip west, he contacted Diercks to find out where he was located so they could visit. Diercks told him where he'd be 'ranging' so the friend came, and whenever he'd meet a cowboy he'd ask for A.J. Diercks. Invariably the answer was the same: didn't know him. Finally in one camp the cook was inquisitive enough to do some further inquiring. Happened to tell John a stranger was there looking for a fellow from New York named A.J. Diercks. John informed him promptly, "That's me." Not too long after Diercks hit Montana some Indians had given him the name Pawny Buck, and that was the name he went by. Nobody knew Diercks, but they knew Buck.

One time after a hard ride on the range he came upon an Indian encampment. He was tired and hungry so when they invited him to eat, he accepted. They had a beautiful stew, and it wasn't until after he had eaten that he found out it was dog stew.

After the turn of the century the homesteaders began coming in, and the range was being fenced so it was time to look for some other means of livelihood. About 1904 or '05 he started working for the Northern Pacific Railroad in Glendive. Years later he took the first N.P. train to Brockway as locomotive engineer. When he was first up in that country if he would have said something about bringing a train to Brockway they would have shot him for being crazy. Now he rode the iron horse instead of a flesh and blood horse.

February 10, 1908, he married Jessie (Gillies) Sanders in Passaic, New Jersey, and brought his bride to Glendive. They had gone to school together in New Jersey. Her friends and folks were reluctant about her coming out here among the Indians and bad men of the west but she was willing.

From their home in the 100 block of South Nowlan Avenue she could look over the town – what there was of it. She had a brother who was a traveling agent for the N.P. out here. One night Dad was out on the road. When darkness came Mother pulled the shades, lighted the kerosene lamp, and sat at the table reading. They had a board sidewalk and presently she heard someone clumping up the walk onto the porch, followed by a rap on the door. Instead of answering she turned the lamp down. Three times the rap came. Finally a voice bellowed, "For heaven's sake, Jess, aren't you going to let your brother in?" She did. In those days nobody locked doors – except people who came from New Jersey. She brought her habits with her – didn't trust anyone who came to the door.

In those early days of marriage Dad was always talking about ranch butter – better than dairy butter. Mother shopped at Douglas Meade*, and one shopping trip the clerk told her, "Mrs. Diercks, I have some fresh ranch butter just brought in this morning." The young bride, wanting to please her husband, bought it, brought it home, happily put it on the table. Hubby looked at it. "Ranch butter?" "Yes." "Where did you get it?" "Douglas Meade." "Who made it?" "Blackwell said it was fresh – just brought in this morning." John persisted, "But who made it?" She couldn't answer that so he wouldn't eat it. When he was out on the range he had stopped in at a ranch house where the woman was churning butter and a mouse had dropped into the cream. She had pulled the mouse out and continued making butter. In another instance a woman was kneading bread when the baby, nearby, had an accident. She changed him and continued kneading bread. Those experiences made him wary about what he was eating. That's why he wanted to know where and whom it was from and who made it. She used the fresh ranch butter in cooking.

About 1924 they bought a car so he thought he'd like to go visit some of his old ranch friends. He knew where they were and how to get there, but he didn't know the roads. Finally in frustration he exclaimed, "If I had a pair of fence clippers I could take you there with no problem at all!"

He was involved in one small skirmish with a renegade band of Indians on Powder River. Nothing serious came of it. A few shots were exchanged but that was all. He knew a lot of the early ranchers and he was friends with everybody. He never questioned a man. A lot of these fellows were renegades at home, got into trouble of some kind and were seeking a new frontier. If a fellow wanted to tell you, okay, but if he didn't, that was okay, too.

In September 1920 Buck and Jessie bought a home in the 400 block of North Kendrick Avenue where they continued to live until Dad died in 1950 and Mother in 1962. When he left the range he left it. Life as cowboy was harsh and hard – but it was freedom. That you don't have today.

Russell Evans

1975 Unpublished, Updated 2006

When the house in which Russell and Jessie Evans reared their family was built (long before either of them made their debut into this world) all the lumber was sawed in Minneapolis. It was shipped by rail to Glendive on the relatively new (1881) Northern Pacific tracks, then hauled some twenty miles to the ranch by team and wagon.

A man by the name of Lovejoy built the house in 1883. The site on which he built was not yet surveyed so he squatted* close to Lower Seven Mile Creek. The later survey showed the buildings were on the section line. Rural roads in general followed section lines where feasible, but by the time a road was built Isaac Evans had purchased the ranch. The county deferred to him by making a bow in the road to the east rather than splitting his homesite.

When Lovejoy started his operation, there were no fences so his cattle ranged from the Redwater River to Thirteen Mile Creek. Until the killing winter of 1886-87 most ranchers expected their cattle to graze all winter, and Lovejoy was one of those who had no hay. He lost most of his cattle, as did many another rancher, so in the spring he rounded up the remnant, swam them across the Yellowstone River, and sold them to Pierre Wibaux.

That fall he sold his buildings and squatter's rights to an English nobleman who was in trouble with his family and was paid to stay out of England. He brought with him some of his English life style, keeping polo ponies and trotting horses. He would hitch four horses on a buggy, two in the lead and two next to the buggy. He even had a racetrack east of the buildings.

After about ten years he sold his holdings to Bob McNeeley and Bill Jones, a couple of railroad engineers from Glendive. McNeeley seems to have been the manager of the ranch. During this time he filed for water rights which meant no one could build a dam on the creek above their property. When Isaac Evans purchased the spread in 1910, his water rights extended from section 22 through section 24.

Evans was born in Norway and came to St. Paul in 1890. While in St. Paul he stayed with a fellow Norwegian, David August Rivenes. In the spring of '92 Evans moved to the Sweetgrass Hills near the Canadian border in north central Montana (not to be confused with Sweetgrass County in southern Montana), but Rivenes had come only as far as Glendive where he joined Wester in the hardware business.

The men kept in touch through correspondence, and it was Rivenes who interested Evans in eastern Montana. Evans came to check prospects in the area, and Rivenes with team and buggy took him out to view the country. As they followed Lower Seven Mile Creek they came in sight of McNeeley's buildings. Evans commented on how nice they were, to which Rivenes responded, "That's the place I'm taking you to see." Evans was so impressed with it that he bought it May 2, 1910.

He went back to Sweetgrass Hills to take care of his business there, then brought his wife and family to Dawson County in June. At that time he and his wife Dorothy had four children: Walter, Helen, Russell and Margarite. A son Robert was born after they moved to the eastern part of the state. The original purchase consisted of only 840 acres, but as time went on he bought more land. Four thousand sheep also came with the place, as well as some cattle and horses.

Besides the house, the buildings included two barns and some sheep sheds across the creek. The horse barn had five box stalls on the north end for trotting horses. These box stalls were 10'x12', all closed in. The hay barn was built up on cedar poles with a calf shed underneath.

In 1918 Evans hired a man to build a larger barn. The man sawed piles of lumber. And more piles. Isaac told him he'd pull the men in from the field when he was ready, but the man kept sawing until Isaac was beginning to wonder. Finally the day came. They brought the men in, and in one day the barn was erected! Of course, there was finishing to do, but the basic structure was complete. No time wasted while the men waited for more lumber to be prepared.

Many a newcomer to the area had to haul water, but this place boasted two wells. One well was close to the barn, the other in the basement of the house with an ordinary pump on the kitchen floor. That well still supplies water for household use. Few houses in those days were blessed with indoor water. Most had only the water they carried in. Often even what they carried in was first hauled from a distant spring or other water source.

When McNeeley sold the ranch he kept back a forty-acre desert claim on the northeast corner of section 28. He left that to his nephew in Scotland. The nephew sent money over every year to pay the taxes until World War II when he was not allowed to send money to the States. Instead he asked a relative, Robert Ayre in Glendive, to pay the taxes for him. The Scotland nephew never resumed paying the taxes so Ayre continued to pay, and after he died his son Dave made the payments.

The nephew in Scotland died and his heirs contacted Dave Ayre about the land. The land was basically worthless to them so they gave it to Dave because he and his dad had paid the taxes all those years. That was when Dave went to check out the land and talked to Russell, who by this time owned the ranch. When Dave Ayre died, he left it to his son Bill who retains that forty acres carved out of the Evans ranch.

McNeeley had run sheep and hired herders to care for them. In 1914 Evans sold the sheep that had been included in the original purchase of the ranch, but ran a small bunch again in 1929-1931. At that time he fenced the pasture with woven wire to contain the sheep so they didn't have to have a herder with them all the time.

After he retired Mr. McNeeley wintered in California. He'd come to the ranch to visit each summer and would always bring a present for each of the four children. He'd ask the boys if they still had their jackknives, and when they would respond negatively, he'd reach down in his pocket and produce more. Mr. McNeeley died in 1917. He is buried in the Glendive cemetery on the hill in the same area as David Ayre.

One of Isaac's neighbors owned a team of mules and was notorious for his unwillingness to let anyone pass when he was driving. One time crossing Gumbo Flat (also known as Wilson Flat) Isaac came abreast of the wagon pulled by the mules before he realized it was the mule driver so, whipping up his horses, he went around and kept going. Years later the neighbor had not forgotten the incident. As they stood visiting on the street in Glendive he declared, "If I'da seen you coming, you never would'a got around me!"

After his father died in 1937 Russell rented the place for nine years before buying it in the spring of 1946. At that time he married a neighbor girl, Jessie Mullet. She had been working on the west coast and after a twelve-year absence, had come home the previous spring to help with the crop planting because of her father's illness. One of their daughters recalled hearing her mother tell about the inauspicious beginning of their romance.

Jessie and her parents had gone to neighbor Charlie Hillier's auction sale. Such sales were social events as well as commercial. Russell noticed Jessie holding a newspaper over her head to ward off the hot sun so, always the gentleman, he offered her his hat to protect her head. Next day he appeared at the Mullet farm, 'looking for horses'. (Looking for horses was always a valid reason to account for your whereabouts.) He didn't find any horses, but of course Mr. Mullet invited him to stay for dinner (noon, not evening) as was still a frontier hospitality custom. They visited until about three and before he left, Russell asked to take Jessie to a movie that evening. The beginning of the romance? Maybe, but....

Many years had intervened since Jessie's sister Lillian, the first child in the family, started to the rural school, driving a horse and buggy. She was so shy that Jessie was allowed to go with her to keep her company. Children of the pioneers routinely accepted responsibilities that today would probably be decried as child abuse, but Lillian didn't really have to drive the horse. A well-trained horse could be relied upon to deliver his charges safely. And Menno Mullet's horses were well trained. The girls were probably safer than children walking on our city streets today.

What the two little girls could not do was stable the horse and remove the harness when they reached the school. Eighth-grade Russell appointed himself caretaker for the little girls, daily assisting them with those tasks, morning and afternoon. Not all heroes are featured in headlines. Certainly no romance was involved at that time, but maybe the seeds....? Russell and Jessie were married the spring after that auction sale. In the succeeding years they bought more land until the ranch was more than ten times the size of Isaac Evans's original purchase.

In the late 1940's or early '50's an older fellow visited them on the ranch. He told them he had worked for Lovejoy in 1883 and helped build the house. If he needed to establish his credentials, he did so quite convincingly by telling

382

them there had been a log entrance on the back of the house. They were dubious about that until they went around to the back and looked. He was right. They could still see where the entrance had been.

Isaac had focused more on cattle and horses than on sheep. Horses, of course, were their only means of transportation – unless they walked. They bought their first car, a Model T Ford, in 1917. After driving it for twenty years, they sold it to a young fellow in Glendive for twenty-five dollars.

Isaac was good at handling horses, took good care of them, and could get a lot of work from them, but if a horse was a little rough, he wouldn't ride it. He left the rough ones for his boys. Russell started riding in rodeos in 1923 but had started breaking horses well before that. Generally horses then weren't broken until they were five to seven years old. The first one he broke was a six-year-old mare. She wasn't even halter-broken when he took her in, but his dad said he could have her if he broke her.

Russell was riding a 'green' horse one day when it started running and wouldn't stop. He managed to head the horse up a steep hill, thinking that would tire him and slow him down. It didn't work. As the hill grew steeper, the horse ran faster. At the top of the hill the horse paused just long enough to survey a route down, then whirled and ran down the hill as fast as he had come up. Russell didn't try that strategy again.

Russell's adventures and misadventures could fill a book by themselves. When he was still a boy, he was with his mother coming home from Glendive with team and wagon when one of the horses jerked a rein from his mother's hand. Russell climbed onto the wagon tongue in an attempt to reach the line, but the horse spooked and the team took off running, causing Russell to slip under the tongue where he clung desperately. He finally had to let go and fell to the ground as the wagon careened on behind the runaway horses. His mother, concerned for Russell, teetered to the back of the wagon and slid off, skidding along the ground and rubbing the hair off her fur coat. A wheel ran over Russell's finger, breaking it, but neither he nor his mother sustained serious injury.

He was only sixteen when he broke his leg and spent four months in the hospital. He was chasing horses out in the hills with Earl Fairchild and Bill Dobson when he roped a horse that ran in front of him. His rope was secured to the saddle horn, and when the other horse hit the end of the rope, it isn't clear whether the impact jerked Russell's horse off his feet or whether the saddle cinch broke. Whichever, he was forcefully deposited on the ground and his leg was badly broken. While he lay there, his companions desperately sought help. The nearest neighbors, Applebys and Browns, were not home. Russell's father had taken his two sisters to Glendive, and his mother was visiting at neighboring Ingrahams. Earl gave her a ride home on his saddle horse, but there was still no one to transport Russell.

Several families of Geigers lived farther up Seven Mile to the west. Even without telephones, word spread of the injured rider, and John, whose son Walter was out alone, thought that it was Walter who had broken his leg and began scouring the countryside with his car, driving through fences trying to find him, until he had wire wrapped around his front axle. Although the injured was Russell instead of Walter, to John it was just as bad. He had a heart attack and was never able to work after that.

Bill had gone to the road and stopped a car with six women in it to ask for help, but they were on their way to a ballgame in Bloomfield and refused to give assistance. Finally it was Louie Geiger with his Studebaker who took Russell to the doctor. A silver plate was put in his thigh, and he spent four months in the hospital with more time on his back after he returned home. What can you do when you are lying in bed? During his convalescence he learned to quilt, and his daughter Pat still has the quilt he made.

Another time when he was riding to school his horse slipped on the ice and fell with him, cracking his skull. But that and other mishaps didn't stop his riding. He became well known in rodeo circuits, both for riding and officiating. As the years went by, his family learned to assist in the running of the ranch, but he continued to rely on his saddle horse until the end of his life. In spite of all his mishaps he lived until July 3, 1995, just a few months short of his ninetieth birthday. He was buried on the ranch, and his saddle horse led the procession to the gravesite.

2006 update: His wife Jessie continues to live on the ranch, and all but two of their children remain in the area: Bernard, Don, Gene, Sheryl and Larry are in Dawson County; Patricia lives in the Gallatin Valley, and Richard is in Indiana. The house on Seven Mile Creek, built in 1893 (with subsequent additions) has been occupied by the Evans family since 1910, almost 100 years.

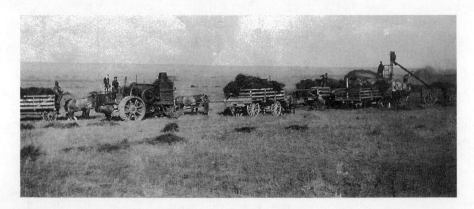

Threshing on the Evans Ranch

Joseph Pipal

1975 Unpublished, Updated 2006

In 1898 Joseph Pipal, a Czechoslovakian immigrant, brought his considerable skills as a blacksmith to the Indian Agency on the banks of the Missouri River. Before coming to Montana he had been a farmer in South Dakota. Now he was commissioned to create and maintain a water system for the little hamlet of Wolf Point.

Old Town Wolf Point had its beginning as a trading post. It was a refueling stop for the steamboats that plied the river, servicing the fur traders. Trappers would stack wolf hides at the Trading Post to be picked up in the spring. In 1842 a traveler on the river made notes in his journal that he had sighted many wolves at a point along the river. The obvious name for the later settlement was Wolf Point.

After the coming of the Great Northern Railroad in the 1880's the town was moved about a mile north along the train tracks as opposed to being on the river bank. Sherman Cogswell operated a trading post and store in this Indian country. Now Joseph Pipal constructed a water system, complete with windmill and holding tank, to supply water for the Indian Agency and for irrigation. He had been schooled in his trade while still in Czechoslovakia. A recent drought had caused the starvation of many Indians so the irrigation system was created with the hope of preventing such a tragedy in the future.

Joseph Pipal brought with him his family of eight children, including five boys. His boys, too, were gifted with engineering skills. His son John built the first power ferry across the Missouri River at Wolf Point. Prior to that a big rowboat had been used to cross the river. Wagons and other cargo would be loaded onto the boat and rowed across while the horses swam the channel.

Joseph's grandson Harry, who granted this interview, recalled seeing the Mandan Steamer, a snag puller, the last steamer to come up the river. Mother and a neighbor took the children to watch the exciting event. The Corps of Engineers was responsible for keeping the river open to traffic until Fort Peck Dam was built, ending the river commerce. The old bridge was built high enough to allow ships to pass.

When the first bridge, a pontoon, was built in 1915 John sold the ferry, then opened Pipal's Garage and Service Station the following year in Wolf Point.

All five of the boys homesteaded on Sand Creek, south of the Missouri River, as land became available and they reached legal age. Joe E. and John, Joseph's sons, settled near the mouth, the others further up the creek. Bill's place was about halfway between Circle and Wolf Point, and the road connecting the two towns went right past his homestead. Travelers, particularly grain haulers, would stop at his place overnight and go on the next day. Bill built a bridge over the creek to facilitate crossing.

A layout at the mouth of Sand Creek presented something of a mystery. The site in question had a rectangular outline with a gap where there had been a gate. It appeared to have been a stockade. They thought at first it might have been old Fort Charles but, with the help of Merrill Burlingame from Montana State College, the location of Fort Charles was determined to be southeast of Wolf Point rather than west. Harry noted that his dad (Joe E.) knew about it but never discussed it beyond warning, "Don't back into those holes," when they were fishing. Later it was learned that the property had belonged to a man named DeLong. He had a business there and had indeed built a stockade. He ran into trouble with the Crow Indians who killed him and burned his store and stockade.

Fort Charles had been established in 1861 but abandoned in 1862 after the river cut through the Oxbow, changing its course and causing the bank to cave off. A boat picked up the stranded people. This change in the river's course caused the holes near the fishing access.

Joseph Pipal had three daughters as well as the five sons. 'Baby Lillian' was much younger than her siblings. The others had gone to school in South Dakota. It wasn't mandatory then that children stay in school until a prescribed time so when Lillian enrolled in Wolf Point, she was the only white child in the school and she couldn't speak English. In the Joseph Pipal home they spoke Bohemian or Indian so that was all Lillian knew. She spoke of her playmates saying, "All my friends are little Indian kids." Later (much later) Lillian married Sig Cusker, well known cowboy and rancher.

Joe E. (so designated to distinguish from Joseph, who was known as Grandpa Joseph) sometimes worked in Cogswell's store. Harry spoke of sometimes going to the store with him and remembered seeing the Indians in their traditional dress; shawls, braids, feathers. Cogswell would give him candy – a real treat when Harry was a boy. Dad and Cogswell conversed in the Indian language.

2006 update: Over the years, most of the Pipal family have scattered to the four winds. Of the original five Pipal homesteads on Sand Creek, only one is still in the family. Fourth-generation Allan Pipal farms his grandfather's homestead and one daughter of Joe. E., Alma Hall, resides in Wolf Point.

Tim & Betty (Lee) Babcock

Compiled from submissions from Tim & Betty Babcock

The Boy from Crackerbox

Excuse me. Milford Babcock was a governor of Montana, you say? Are you confused about names or history?

Neither. According to his birth certificate, Milford Babcock was born October 27, 1919, in Littlefork, Minnesota, to Erwin and Olive Babcock. And according to history, he became governor of Montana in 1962.

When he was just a baby, one of his aunts started calling him Tiny Tim. Soon others followed suit. The name Tim clung to him all through his school years, clung so tenaciously that when he enlisted in the military his mother had to sign an affidavit affirming that Milford and Tim were one and the same person. (Tim and Betty still have a copy of that document.)

Tim's grandparents (yes, from here on he is Tim) Martin and Emma Rhinehart in Minnesota heard glowing reports of free land in Montana: 160 acres, yours for the taking if you settled on it and made minimum improvements. Martin Rhinehart made a trip to Montana in the fall of 1909 to see what was available. Then in October, 1910, Martin with his wife Emma, two sons Alfa and Ovid and their daughter Olive, loaded an immigrant car and set out for Montana.

Also in the party were Erwin Babcock and Virginia Gosselin. Virginia was no relation to the Rhineharts, but she did have relatives in Eastern Montana who urged her to come in hopes her asthma would improve. (It did.) Erwin wasn't related, either, but that soon changed. He and Olive were already engaged, and this seemed like a good opportunity to get a home of their own. Erwin Babcock and Olive Rhinehart were married November 25, 1910.

Upon their arrival in Montana, Erwin and the other men filed for homesteads on Crackerbox Creek southwest of Glendive. They put up a two-room shack, just a shell with no insulation so it went up quickly. Other buildings on the other homesteads came later. A dugout barn housed pigs, cows and horses. They dug a well, and by the next spring they were ready to plant a big garden so there would be fresh produce as well as plenty to can. Chokecherries and wild plum bushes provided some fruit. Meat was cured to preserve it. Fuel for heating and cooking came from a coal mine on their property. It seemed like a wonderful beginning.

Olive and Virginia had no problem finding housekeeping jobs in the Glendive area. Virginia (Volume 1, page 315) related that while she was working for an older man on a homestead, she and Olive had ridden horseback to a dance. They returned later than he thought they should so he had locked them out and they had to sleep in a haystack.

For nine years the Babcocks struggled to make a living on the homestead. Their first two children, Merle Irene in 1912 and Donald Erwin in 1915 were born during this period. Times were hard, prices for farm products were low. The 'glowing reports' that brought them to Montana hadn't mentioned anything about drought, hail, or grasshoppers, nor that 160 acres of dry land would not support a family in Eastern Montana. Relatives in Minnesota wanted them to return and wrote of farmers and loggers needing horses.

Since Erwin had been raising horses, they decided this would be a good time to visit relatives and see what it was like in the old hometown. Erwin and Olive with Merle and Donald left Montana in 1919. They looked forward to an easier lifestyle, but that was not what Littlefork offered. Winters were severe with temperatures as low as fifty degrees below zero. Hardships were many.

Erwin and his brother-in-law Bill Henry made several trips to Glendive and back, buying and hauling horses to sell. It was during this period that the third child was born into the family on October 27, 1919.

Although Tim was born in Minnesota, he grew up on the farm where his parents had homesteaded in 1910. His parents had moved back to Montana when Tim was six months old. His formal education began in the Crackerbox School. One of the neighbors made a leather harness for Tim's dog, Pup, and hitched it to his wagon for him. He drove it to school, but sometimes ran into difficulty for when the dog would see a rabbit, he would take off after it. When they came to a fence, Tim would have to roll off the wagon, then eventually catch the dog with the wagon or sled to continue on his way. Tim always had a wonderful way with animals and always tried to mechanize everything to make life easier.

About the time Tim graduated from the eighth grade, the family bought a house on the west end of Glendive. The farm was not a paying proposition so Erwin, Tim's dad, went to work for the County, and they started a second hand store, buying and selling things in a small building next to their house. It was too far from the high school for Tim to walk so that first year he stayed with Mrs. Mace.

After graduating from Dawson County High School in 1939 he went to California where he worked for Douglas Aircraft Company. With World War II in progress, Tim enlisted in the army. During his three years of service as a combat infantryman he was awarded three battle stars and the bronze star for valor in action at the Remagen Bridge. He was honorably discharged as a Staff Sergeant.

In 1941 Tim had married Betty Lee, and they lived in California until Tim left for the army. While he was serving in the army she with their daughter Lorna returned to Glendive where she first worked in the ration office, then later weighing sugar beets.

When Tim returned from the War, he joined her in Glendive. Her father was in the trucking business and asked Tim to be his partner. Together they formed the Babcock and Lee Petroleum Transportation Company with Tim as both driver and manager. As the company grew from two tankers to fifty they were forced to move headquarters to Miles City and later to Billings, Montana.

It grew to be one of the Rocky Mountain Region's most successful motor transport firms by the time they sold it.

Tim had developed an interest in politics and is one of the very few Montanans elected to the State Legislature by the people of two different districts. In 1952 he was elected from Custer County, then after moving to Billings he was elected to serve two terms from Yellowstone County. In 1960 he was elected lieutenant governor running with Don Nutter for governor. Almost exactly one year later he found himself catapulted into the chief executive's chair when Governor Nutter was killed in a plane crash. He was then elected to his first full term in 1964.

In 1966 the town of Richey in Dawson County celebrated its fiftieth anniversary and asked Governor Babcock to speak. He added a little levity to the occasion with a story about a survey, asking older people how they accounted for their longevity. They found a feeble fellow with a long, white beard sitting along a curb. In answer to their questions he replied, "Wine, women, and song!" Surprised at this unconventional reply they pursued, "And how old are you?" His answer, "Twenty-nine years!"

While he is no doubt best known for his role as governor, that was by no means the end of his political involvement. Space does not allow a complete listing of his accomplishments, but he remains active in both politics and business in his eighth decade. Tim enjoys golf, horsemanship, hunting, flying, antique cars and trucks, but with his busy schedule, does he have time to indulge? He currently serves on various boards and maintains membership in civic and service organizations. His wife Betty has been active along with him and remains so as well.

Betty Lee is also of pioneer stock. She was born in Aplington, Iowa, to Otis (more often called Bill) and his wife Ruth. Betty was only two years old when her mother suddenly became ill. In a few short hours she had died, and from then on everything went down hill for Bill Lee. His sister, with ten children of her own, offered to take care of Betty, but a series of tragedies/mishaps necessitated removal from that home. The next home was also unsatisfactory so then Ruth's sister Jess and her husband became involved. Unfortunately, that seemed to be 'out of the frying pan into the fire'. The husband was an alcoholic and the sister had a violent temper.

In desperation, Bill Lee wrote a letter to his brother, Richard Elwood Lee and his wife Katherine in Montana, and asked if they would be interested in caring for Betty. They had no children so when the letter arrived, 'Wood' handed it to his wife, observing that here was her chance to 'get a kid'.

They were living at that time with her parents, Isabella and Jack Martin, in Glendive. The Lees had come to help when Katherine's sister was ill with spinal meningitis. The sister had died, but they continued to help the Martins.

Katherine was excited and very willing to take the child, but Isabella 'threw a fit'. "You'll never raise her," she warned. "She'll be nothing but trouble!" (Isabella didn't know she was talking about Montana's future First Lady!) She was used to having things her way, but this time was an exception. Elwood told his wife that he wanted to help his brother and she should have this child if that was what she wanted. He made arrangements for Kitty, as he called his wife, to take the train to Iowa and pick up the child.

Betty had been told of the plan and was so excited when Katherine arrived that she threw her arms around her aunt's neck and wanted to leave for Montana immediately. When they went to the depot to leave, Betty's brother Sonny had a basket of fruit to give them, but he was so depressed at seeing his little sister leave he forgot to give it to them. On the train to Glendive Betty wasn't at all shy and didn't hesitate to talk to strangers. She asked some Nuns if they had feet because she couldn't see them under their long habits. It didn't bother the Nuns, but it did embarrass Katherine.

Katherine soon became Mom to Betty, and Elwood was Daddy Wood because she still had Daddy Bill back in Iowa. She readily claimed the Martins as her grandparents but called Isabella Mother Martin or just Mother because that was what Katherine called her.

Grandmother Martin was born in Scotland. She told Betty of working in the laundry of the queen's palace in Scotland when she was sixteen. She loved everything about the queen, Queen Elizabeth the First. Isabella had an uncle, Duncan McIntyre, and a sister Jessie Narrun who lived in Sidney, Montana, and they encouraged her to join them there. Soon after her arrival as a young woman she met John (Jack) Martin, originally from Prince Edward Island, Canada. They were married in Lewistown, Montana, December 5, 1890, and homesteaded on Burns Creek, between Intake and Savage.

Betty recalls Mother Martin telling about the time a bull snake dropped down through the rafters and landed at her feet as she was rocking one of their babies in their sod house with dirt floors.

Sometime later they built a log house caulked with adobe mud between the logs. The roof was covered with dirt and scorio* rocks. The ceiling was covered with flour sacks sewn together, then painted with white calcimine. They were fortunate to have water in the house, even though it came from a pump.

She cooked on a large wood stove with a reservoir that provided hot water. There was the typical bowl and pitcher on a stand by the back door where every one washed up before meals. Of course the outhouse served its purpose some distance from the house.

During a severe thunder and lightning storm Isabella was holding Baby Ethel in her arms as she stood by a window. Little Florie, about two-and-one-half years old, was standing at her side when lightning struck, knocking them to the floor. Isabella and the baby survived, but Florie was killed.

The Martins had to get their supplies from Glendive so Jack would make the trip with team and wagon about once a year. During the small pox epidemic he bought the necessary vaccine and vaccinated his own children at home. They acquired more land that eventually became a large ranch in partnership with John Diercks, where they ran about 1,500 sheep. Jack Martin is often mentioned in As I Remember, Volume 1, as an employer of newcomers.

The Martins had four girls. When it was time for them to go to high school, they built a beautiful home in Glendive at 222 West Town Street. Mother Martin maintained a rigid schedule: breakfast at 7 a.m., dinner at 12 noon, and supper at 5:30. Except in the summer, they lived there all the time Betty was growing up. Her best friend, Leta Thompson, lived only a block away. They shared joys and sorrows, victories and defeats. They walked to school together, even when the temperature dropped to forty below zero. Betty recalls that they wore long black stockings and had scarves tied over their noses so they wouldn't freeze. It was when Betty was a sophomore at Dawson County High School that she met Tim Babcock and married him in 1941.

Betty and Tim are the parents of two daughters, Lorna Lee (Mrs. William) Kuney and Marla Kay (Mrs. Michael) Fillinger. Marla was killed in a car accident September 24, 1985.

Betty has been no less active than her husband. She, too, served in the Montana State Legislature, 1975-77. During her tenure as First Lady she carried many responsibilities but found time to author and edit the First Ladies Cookbook. She updated it in 1973 and again in 1996. The third printing was for the benefit of the Shodair Children's Hospital in celebration of their hundredth anniversary and to help with the building of their new hospital. Pages would be required to list her civic, benevolent, social, and political contributions and achievements. She enjoys entertaining, genealogy, history, historic preservation (in 1996 she was appointed by Governor Marc Racicot to the Montana Capitol Restoration Foundation), and her family.

Instead of retiring, both Tim and Betty seem to have just retreaded.

Betty Lee (Mrs. Tim Babcock)

Former Montana Governor
Tim Babcock

Fred Steffen

Compiled from memoirs of Fred Steffen submitted by John Steffen

The Kaiser's conscription of fourteen-year-old boys into the Prussian army contributed to the Steffen family, three generations later, homesteading in Montana. August Steffen lived in the seaport town of Stettin, Prussia. He had been a flag bearer in the Prussian army, but as his oldest boy, Johnny Steffen's grandfather William, was nearing the age of fourteen, August made plans to leave.

A friend of his was a sea captain with a sailing vessel and arranged for August and his four children (no mention is made of a wife) to escape in 1869 on this friend's vessel. An earlier attempt to leave had been stymied by the Prussian government, but this time their escape was not noticed by Prussian officials until they were well away from the coast so no attempt was made to retrieve them.

Always adventuresome, during the ocean voyage almost-fourteen-years-old William climbed to the top of the mast. When the captain sent seamen up to bring him down, William took to a guy rope and slid to the deck. Frontier America was settled by risk takers.

August Steffen settled in Wisconsin, but William at age twenty (1875) moved to St. Paul where he learned brick laying. In 1878 he married sixteen-year-old Elizabeth Danner. Three years later he moved his family to a homestead near Cooperstown, North Dakota. There they broke sod with a team of oxen. John notes that when he was compiling these memoirs his dad, Fred, still had some of the ox yoke in his possession.

Ferdinand (Fred) was the oldest of twelve children born to William and Elizabeth. He and his brother Bill (second oldest) wanted to get away from farming so they decided to come to Montana and raise livestock. Fred came first in July 1907, to find a place. After getting off the Northern Pacific train in Glendive, he ran into an old friend from Cooperstown, Sam Helland. Helland helped him find a rig to rent so he could go look for a good place to ranch.

The first night they stayed at Joe Borntrager's on Thirteen Mile Creek near the Red Top School. Joe had been one of the earliest homesteaders, filing on his claim in 1905. The next day they went north over and across Retah Table, which was a sea of grass, reaching to the horses' bellies. Not one homesteader yet! But Steffen was looking for hillier country with more protection for livestock so they went closer to the Redwater/Yellowstone Divide. At the head of the middle fork of Thirteen Mile Creek he found the place he wanted, west of the present site of Bloomfield. Later Fred filed on the southeast quarter* of section 32-20-53. Bill filed on the southwest quarter of the same section. Charlie Fiske and Joe Sansborn each filed a claim nearby.

After filing they went back to Cooperstown, and that fall Bill and their father William returned to build claim shacks. The shacks were built side by side, straddling the boundary line so they could live in the same building, yet

392

prove up* on both homesteads. A dugout barn was built into a red hill nearby to shelter the team they shipped from Cooperstown. In 1910 their sister Christine came to Montana to homestead and later married Glenn K. Coutts. Bill Warnke married their sister Edna.

Fred arranged to ship forty-five mares and colts and one registered Percheron stallion. They also shipped in a carload of Galloway cattle: eighteen cows and one bull. These cows became the nucleus of the largest registered herd of Galloways in the United States. His brand was A-L.

Some of their neighbors (the term neighbors is used rather loosely as it might mean anywhere from five to ten miles) were the Harvey brothers – Jim, George, and John; Jim Cavanaugh; Charles Sterner; Roy Svenvold, John Stephan, Olaf Waag, and Sam Sansborn.

In 1914 Margaret Rusche came with her cousin Mary Stephan for a visit. Here she met Fred Steffen, and in 1915 they decided to get married. But first Fred wanted a new house. Claim shacks were all right for a couple bachelors but not for a bride. He hired the Larson Brothers, contractors, to build a bungalow-type house over a full basement with a Mueller central hot water system, plumbing for bath and running water for kitchen sink and laundry. H.M. Hanley of Glendive secured the heating and plumbing contract. He did the whole job for $650. This was the first home north of the Yellowstone River in Dawson County that had modern plumbing and heating. The same house still stands today with the same heating system, as good as the day it was put in. Sons John and Clarence make their home here on the old A-L homestead.

Four children were born to Fred and Margaret: Fred Junior, who is older than Clarence and John, and the youngest, Kathleen (Mrs. Wilbur Eggebrecht).

John reports that his dad (Fred) often told of an exciting adventure in 1912 when he made a deal with Frank J. Steihl of Buford, North Dakota, to exchange bulls. Steihl also had Galloway cattle with his headquarters at Mondak. They agreed to meet at Culbertson to make the exchange. Dad trailed his bull to Culbertson in two-and-one-half days, stopping at ranches along the way at night. He purchased a second bull from S.D. Sweetman at Snowden.

When he reached Culbertson he had to cross the Missouri River on a ferry built of logs and planks with one railing on each side. On the return ferry trip the two bulls, strangers to each other, started fighting and the big bull knocked the smaller bull into the river. Dad roped him and pulled him to shore, but before they reloaded him they tied the big bull to one corner of the ferry, then loaded the smaller one and yoked them together with a rope. It worked! No more fights.

In 1920 Fred and Bill dissolved partnership. Fred sold his interest in the cattle to Bill and moved twenty-five miles north of Glendive where he farmed on the Ditch. At that time Burns was his post office. After ten years they moved back to the homestead and continued ranching until 1956, then moved to Glendive. In 1957 the parents sold their share of the homestead to sons John and Clarence.

Bill also prospered and expanded his holdings along the Redwater Divide. When he died November 1, 1969, he left one of the oldest, hardiest, continuous herd of cattle under one brand in Dawson County range history. This estate herd of Galloway cattle was liquidated by sale November 13, 1970 at Glendive and ended sixty-one years of herd history in Montana.

The Steffen story would not be complete without mention of Croppy. (It is far from complete even with mention of Croppy!) The Steffens had owned hundreds of horses over the years but none compared to Croppy. Space does not permit the attention he deserves, but at times his discernment – 'horse sense' – rivaled that of a human being, considerably exceeding that of some! John can tell you many examples of Croppy's perception and exploits. One example of his superior intelligence was demonstrated if he happened to be driven in and corralled with a bunch of other horses. If he was needed, all Dad had to do was point his finger at him, and Croppy would walk right out of the bunch and come up to him.

He was capable of tricks, too. They had a big horse barn, and usually the doors were left open in summer so the horses could come in for shade. The oats bin had a flat door covering with a hasp. A piece of wood was pushed into the keeper to fasten it when closed. They had a pair of draft colts, and one of these colts had learned to pull out this piece of wood (Croppy wasn't the only one with smarts!) and open the door.

One day when Croppy and the colts were in the pasture, Dad and Uncle Bill saw Croppy suddenly turn back his ears and start hazing the colts toward the barn. They decided to watch this maneuver, carefully keeping themselves hidden. When the colts were in the barn, Croppy posted himself in the doorway, blocking the way out. He just stood there, watching the colts and switching his tail. After a bit of time, the 'gifted' colt started nosing the feed box and 'did his thing'. As soon as the box was open, Croppy sauntered over, cordial like, and joined them for a feed of illegal oats.

Dad (Fred Steffen) lived to the ripe old age of ninety-three years, passing away in 1973. Mother Margaret Steffen died in 1979 aged 91.

In conclusion John paid tribute to all the homesteaders of this era. "We, the sons and daughters of the homesteaders, owe you a debt of gratitude. You suffered and sacrificed much for us. You have given us a less rigorous, more enriching and rewarding life than you endured. You gave us a heritage surpassing monetary worth. You gave us a sense and appreciation of values, a love of country, family, and neighbor. In the western ranching and homestead areas of today, this heritage is reflected in our present day youth who show a greater sense of balance than their counterparts in other areas of America."

John A. Kelly

Compiled from submissions from Bernard & Bev Kelly

Bernard Kelly's grandfather, John A. Kelly was an inveterate adventurer, always looking for new worlds to conquer. He left his New Jersey home when he was a teen, heeding the call of the day, "Go West, young man, go West."

John spent some time in Minnesota and Colorado, then in the 1870's he and another fellow decided to build a raft and float the Mississippi River from Minneapolis to New Orleans. After that adventure he joined a traveling baseball organization and toured the Midwest, playing professionally. He was a good athlete, and a medal he won for hurdle racing is still in the family's possession. Among his other talents, this Irishman could tap dance. (Both his parents came from Ireland but had never met until after they were in the United States.)

A survey crew took him to Montana, and while in Deer Lodge he married Margaret Peoples. The Peoples family also came from Ireland, and Margaret had been born there. They lived for a time in nearby Granite, and their first son, Francis (Peg), was born there before they moved to Eastern Montana in the 1890's. William J. was their first child born after that move. Four more children were born to the family in eastern Montana: Robert E., Frances M., John R., and James J. When they first saw Glendive, 'old town', it was on the flat above the present site, about where the fairgrounds are now.

They settled on Bryan's Plains* and both started working for the Sheep Hook ranch on Cedar Creek, southeast of Glendive. After working for several other area outfits they started ranching on their own, under the brand 'WP Quarter Circle'. At that time ranchers didn't own land but just ran cattle and horses on public range.

The children attended the Bryan's Plains school, a one-room log cabin. One teacher taught all eight grades. About 1910 a new school was built of lumber, but it was still just one room. On account of schooling, the family also moved back and forth between the ranch and Glendive for a couple school terms.

In 1902 eleven-year-old Fran was thrown when his horse shied, and his foot caught in the stirrup. The horse panicked and bolted, dragging the boy and breaking his leg. His teacher at the rural school saw the accident and hurried to his rescue, then summoned his parents. The nearest medical help was Glendive so they loaded him into a horse-drawn wagon (what else?) and took him the twenty-five long miles. Even when they reached Glendive more time elapsed before they were able to locate a doctor. When the doctor finally saw the broken leg, he said the leg would have to be amputated. Mrs. Kelly refused that option and took him by train to Bismarck, but by then it was much too late. His leg had to be amputated halfway between the knee and the ankle.

In spite of the loss of his leg, Fran refused to be 'handicapped'. In order for him to get around after he returned home, a peg leg was fashioned of wood from local trees. A leather belt held it in place, hence the nickname Peg. These peg legs were outgrown or broken rather often and would have to be replaced.

He made most of these himself. After he was full-grown he started reinforcing the wooden peg legs with iron. They were more durable and withstood his rigorous life better for he determinedly pursued all the activities others did with two legs of flesh — and excelled, whether it was breaking broncs, calf-wrestling, foot or horse racing, jumping, or roping.

He routinely participated in rodeos, from Miles City to Pendleton, Oregon, and was billed as 'the only one-legged bronc rider in the world'. He was proficient at breaking and training horses, both for riding and for driving. The three oldest Kelly brothers — Peg, Bill, and Bob — were regulars on the roundup circuits as well as being widely known for their rodeo participation.

The coming of the homesteaders ended ranch life as it had been practiced since the late 1800's. No more could livestock freely roam over thousands of acres. Barbed wire fences blocked the range, grasslands were plowed under, and wild game disappeared. By 1910 the open range was basically a thing of the past in the Glendive area so the Kelly family gave up ranching and moved to town.

Mr. Kelly (John) found employment with the Northern Pacific Railroad. With the outbreak of World War I, Bill and Bob were called into military service. After the war they also went to work for the railroad. Others in the family secured jobs in various capacities, from the sugar beet factory in Sidney to Mountain States Telephone & Telegraph to bus driving, but none in ranching. They had been successful stockmen but chose not to continue due to the loss of the open range.

John and Margaret Kelly saw dramatic changes in the span of their lives, John from 1862-1933, Margaret from 1868-1943. Both are buried on the hill above Glendive.

Rob Kelly making candy

Myron Pickering

Compiled from memoirs of Myron Pickering and notes from Marian Robbins submitted by Dorothy Bullington

Myron Pickering states that his earliest memories are of a home in Wisconsin where their house was of unhewn pine logs roofed with rough split shakes in place of shingles. The cracks between the logs were chinked* with pieces of wood fitted in the cracks and then plastered over with mud. The roof did a fair job as a shelter, but as he lay in the upstairs bedroom he could see a star through the roof.

His father was a natural born pioneer, and after scouting around a couple years he settled on a claim near Fairview, Montana. In 1905 he brought his family to his homestead. (The town of Fairview celebrated its one hundredth anniversary in July 2006.) They dug a room in the east side of a hill, 12'x20', and covered it with a board and tarpaper roof with a door opening on the side.

In late November they loaded all their possessions on a hired dray* at Berthold and headed for their new home. They could save miles by cutting across the prairie instead of following the road, but the first try they missed the dugout. They lost a lot of time looking for it, and it was late in the evening by the time they were all unloaded. Furthermore, a blizzard was starting.

The drayman had planned to return the twelve miles to Berthold but now he realized he would not be able to make it so they had to figure out a way to get all inside, two horses as well as three grown people, two babies, and a load of household goods and food. They made it, and the next morning the drayman hitched his team and departed, leaving the newcomers to clean up and do the best they could to get it in living condition.

From their homestead Myron walked twelve miles to Berthold where he was able to get a job with the railroad, helping unload and pile rails and ties. Sleeping accommodations were in a boxcar with other men. He worked there until he came down with the grippe. Roasting and then freezing, he kept getting worse until finally he went home. He found his wife and two babies at the neighbor's place about half-a-mile from their home where his wife was working for them.

About this time a letter came from back home with $20 in it! With this they bought half a hog, and that, along with a barrel of apples they had brought with them, gave them a nicely balanced diet.

In order to prove on their claims, the family had to live there a certain amount of time so his wife and two daughters stayed on the claim that summer.

In March the brothers Earl, Allie, and Myron, struck out for work in the direction of Minot and were able to ride in the caboose of the snowplow that was clearing snow from the railroad tracks. They reached Minot before nightfall and found a reasonably priced hotel where they paid for one bed and had just enough money left to buy crackers and cheese for breakfast the next morning.

The three brothers walked twelve miles to a coalmine to try to get work and were hired. Myron made it a practice to see his family every second weekend. To get home he had to walk to DeLacs, ride a freight train to Tagus, and walk the six miles home with a reversal to get back to work.

Myron did not finish his memoirs so family added that he spent two or three years doing carpenter work in Sidney where he built many of the original houses and some of the business places. Allie had the first photo studio in Sidney. In 1911 Myron moved his family to what was to be the 'home place' near Crane. He ran a flour mill at Crane, and in 1914 bought his first swarm of bees, the beginning of the Blue Star Honey Farm. The name came from a wildflower on the land that looked like a blue star. They delivered honey to stores in Western North Dakota and Eastern Montana and Myron was a beekeeper the rest of his life.

Following are a few random notes from Marian Robbins, Allie Pickering's daughter. She states, "There is no continuity in these memories. They are like a kaleidoscope, flashing in and out."

Uncle Myron's 'honey-house', was not built for a honey house; it was their home to begin with. He knew about cyclones and built his home against a 'hillside'. Anything more than five feet tall was a 'hill'. The first floor was of concrete. No wind would blow it away! Downstairs was a kitchen and one bedroom. Upstairs was of lumber covered with tarpaper to keep the wind out and was sleeping quarters for the children. It also was a great place to play. Beth was very good at planning games.

There was also a cellar, dug into the hillside beside the house. It had a door on it and was the place to keep garden surplus through the winter — potatoes, squash, cabbage, etc. One time a porcupine got in and when we children found it, we thought it great fun to poke it so it would throw its quills! It wasn't nearly so much fun when Uncle Myron made us get in there and pull all the quills out of the potatoes!

Everyone had cows and chickens and gardens. There was milk and cream and butter and eggs enough for everyone, but flour, sugar, salt, spices, and many of our clothes, including shoes (but that is another story) came from Sears Roebuck or Monkey (Montgomery) Ward. When the new catalog came there was a great time looking at all the things now available. Among them, believe it or not, were houses! You could select the type of house you wanted and buy it from the catalog, boards, nails, shingles, everything! Uncle Myron and Aunt Mary decided they could afford a bungalow. And so it was built. It had everything, from a front porch with two steps up, and dormer windows upstairs, a fireplace, a dining room, or was it a kitchen so big that it served for all one's meals too? And when it was finished there was a celebration.

I learned about spontaneous combustion when Uncle Myron's barn burned because the alfalfa hay was a little too damp when he put it in the loft. And I learned about spontaneous explosion when the flour dust got a little too 'hot' and the mill blew up! Uncle Earl was an excellent shot. He practiced constantly so that he could hit the

398

spot he wanted to with great accuracy. There were wild horses running loose in the prairie and when he needed one he would go out and 'crease' it. Which meant shooting to hit it just at the top of the shoulder, barely breaking the skin, but stunning the animal. Then he would go up, put a rope around its nose, just as the Indians used to do, jump on the horse and ride it till it stopped in exhaustion. He never 'broke' his horses, they loved him and would let him do anything he wanted with them. No one else could handle them, though. They hauled coal for him all winter, and when the wagon was empty you could hear him a half-mile away, the horses running at full gallop with him laughing and urging them on!

The morning that the dynamite blew up in Dad's face they took him into Sidney in about twenty minutes. I will never forget when we kids got to school one of the older boys came up and said, "I hear your dad got his face blown off this morning!" He must have healed up good after the dynamite blew up in his face because I never noticed a scar on his face.

One sunny afternoon mother said that I might go stay with Ione all night. Ione had come by on her horse, so I saddled my horse and we rode to the farm. We had scarcely gotten there when Uncle Myron came running out grabbed the horses bridles and told us to get in the house NOW! We were so frightened we scarcely asked why, because the rule was, if we wanted to ride we had to take care of our horses. To have them snatched away from us was really scary. We hurried into the house and Aunt Mary rushed us down cellar just as the wind came on – a cyclone! That cellar had always seemed a nice big place, but with seven of us huddled together it was pretty crowded. After awhile the wind passed on and Uncle Myron went out to assess the damage. I wanted to go home – to see if I had a home to go to. But Uncle Myron wouldn't let me. I suppose I slept that night, but I didn't wait for breakfast next morning. I went home.

Before I even got there I could see that the straw stack was gone. The chicken house was gone. And when I got to the house it was empty except for a lot of litter of breakfast dishes and clothes flung about. Imagine yourself ten years old – and this! After I recovered from the first shock, I slowly began to put things right again, and eventually the family came home. I have forgotten where they went or why. I was still too upset and crying when they came. They said they had all huddled around the two stoves, which were in the center of the house, hoping their added weight would keep the house from blowing away. It must have worked! I never want to live through a cyclone again.

In Sidney I remember the grocery store where I waited for the man to cut a dime in two so I could have two nickels! I also remember the earthquake that actually moved the back steps away from the house.

Washday in 1914 at the Pickering home: Monday Morning

Utensils necessary for the wash:

1 boiler – a large oblong copper tub used on the stove
3 galvanized tubs, though usually we could only afford two
1 wringer to be moved from tub to tub as needed
1 washboard – a small board covered with a wrinkled brass mat
1 or more bars of very strong naphtha soap
1 bag of clothespins and 1 long clothesline

Right after breakfast all the dirty clothes in the home, usually everything that wasn't being worn at the moment, were gathered up and sorted. 'White clothes' were the things associated with food such as dishtowels, napkins, aprons, (cloths used for straining milk were always washed by hand every morning and carefully sterilized and placed where they could be kept sterile). Sheets, pillowcases, underwear were usually 'whites'. All the 'colored' clothes were in another pile, and the stockings, socks, and small things were by themselves. During the season of winter colds handkerchiefs were washed separately before being put in with the other white things.

Now we were ready to fill the various tubs with water. The boys and men were called on to do this, as it meant carrying water from the pump or the creek. The boiler was brought to a boil by building up the fire under it and keeping it burning for an hour or more. A bar of naphtha soap was sliced into the boiler and the first of the white clothes were added. It was necessary to stir them frequently with a stick while boiling. The stick was usually an old broom handle. When the washerwoman decided they had boiled long enough they were moved into a large pan and put through the wringer into the first tub. A second boiler of white clothes began boiling while the first batch was being scrubbed on the scrubbing board. It was handy to have a small daughter who would rinse the clothes as they came from the washing tub, and wring them into the second tub. Here another rinsing usually removed the suds that were left from the previous work. It was important to get all the naphtha soap out or the result was itchy clothes and red skin. Lastly the white clothes were put through a 'bluing' rinse which would help to restore that brand-new whiteness they had before they were used.

Clothes were hung to dry, then folded and sorted for ironing the next day. Washday was not over until clothes were dry and sorted, and the tubs were rinsed and hung to dry. By this time it was time for supper.

Tuesday was then ironing day and Wednesday was for mending. Thursday was for miscellaneous chores and cleaning, and Friday and Saturday were bake days. Sunday was a day of rest and after the morning chores were finished, we all put on our Sunday go-to-meeting clothes and walked up the hill to church. After Sunday dinner, which was always the best meal of the week, Dad and Mother would take a much-needed rest and we children sat on the porch and learned scripture verses. When our parents got up again, we had to report on what we had learned. There were still evening chores to do, and a bedtime story to be read. It had to be a day of rest!

400

C.H. 'Dick' Nefzger

Compiled from memoirs of Dick Nefzger submitted by Deanna Hostetler

Vida or Clarence, which should it be? August Nefzger submitted the names of his two youngest children when he applied to the Postmaster General in Washington, D.C., to start a post office. Vida was chosen so that became the name of the post office and the town between Wolf Point and Circle.

August, looking for good farm land, migrated to Montana from Lima, Iowa in 1910. Earlier he had moved his family in a covered wagon to Oklahoma but wasn't satisfied with what he found so he had moved back to Iowa. Now, however, railroad agents assured him that there was plenty of land and water, just for the settling in Montana so August and his neighbor Robert Durfey came to check out the reports. They each staked claim to half a section of land in northern Dawson County. Later as the county was divided he lived in Richland County, then in McCone without ever moving.

A short time after they had a sod house built an Indian rode up and told them three squaws were waiting for them at the Poplar depot. To their surprise they found Robert's wife Lizzy and August's wife Johanna with their daughter Vida. They were ready to start pioneer life on the prairie.

August's son Charles Henry, or Dick as he was known, also wanted to move to Montana, but he was renting a farm in Iowa when his father moved and felt obligated to seed the crop for the owner the next spring so he asked August to locate some good land with a spring on it for him. In March of 1911 Dick, with his wife Katie and their three children, arrived in Wolf Point by train. There were only two houses at that location then.

They expected Dick's brother Clyde to meet them, but he wasn't there so Dick arranged a ride for him and his family with young Joe Heser. Joe had brought his two brothers to the depot to catch the train for Glasgow where they had dental appointments.

The railroad was north of the Missouri River so they had to cross the river. They found water running three feet deep on top of the ice. To cross they sat on the backrest of the wagon seats with their feet on the seat itself and their suitcases on their laps. Such was Katie's initiation to homesteading in Montana.

As they continued on their way there was just a trail winding through the brush and trees and mud holes. One of Joe's broncs gave out about the time they reached the U P Ranch so Joe unhitched him, took him into the log barn, and came out with a fresh horse. He didn't see the man who lived there, but he knew it would be all right to change horses. Such was Katie's further introduction to Montana.

They stayed overnight with Joe's folks, who welcomed them like family, then started on the next morning with fresh horses for August's place. They had gone only a few miles when they were met by Dick's brother Clyde and Jake Kluth with team and wagon so Joe turned back for home. Dick tried to pay him but he wouldn't accept any thing. More introduction to Montana.

They spent the night with Dick's parents, then the next morning Dick with his brothers Clyde and Clarence started for Poplar where their immigrant car would be unloaded because there was a ferry at Poplar while there was none at Wolf Point. The water over the ice was even deeper than the day before so Clarence turned back for home with the team and wagon.

Jack Mail lived near the ferry boat and was getting ready to come get Dick and Clyde when an Indian came riding down on the ice with his saddle horse. The ice was bulged in the middle with deep water on either side. Dick mounted behind him and the rider took him to the ice in the middle, went back for Clyde and took him all the way across before he returned for Dick. Dick could see that the Indian was scared but as for himself, he wasn't afraid because he didn't know how dangerous it was. Afterward the Indian told him he had crossed the river many times, but he wouldn't cross it any more. Dick expected to have to pay as much as $10, but his conveyor only asked for two bits.

The immigrant car had to be unloaded, but the river was so dangerous no one dared cross it. Dick rented a house and barn in Poplar where he kept his cattle, hogs, chickens, horses, and machinery while he waited for the ice to go out so the ferry could cross. He waited thirty days.

After the ice went out it would be a few days before the ferry could be put into the water, but Dick was impatient to get out to see the land his dad had picked out for him so Jack Mail, a good river man, took Dick and Clyde across the river in a rowboat. He had Clyde stand in the front of the boat with a ten-foot pole to push the big ice cakes away. They made it all right, then Dick and Clyde walked the thirty-five miles to their folks' place that night. It was the first 320 acres Dick had ever owned, and he wanted to see it. He said it was a good feeling, and years later could say he was thankful he had settled in Montana.

August, with the help of his three sons, built a sod store in the summer of 1911, and that's when he applied for the post office. The application was granted in about three weeks, and August then built a new frame building on the northeast corner of his half section to provide better service. When the town was moved to its present location one mile west of 'Old' Vida, August's store was also moved and now is the first building on your left as you enter Vida from the south.

When the permission for the post office was granted, August appointed his son Dick as the Deputy Post Master, a position he held for many years. Besides doing the bookkeeping and working in the store, Dick hauled the store's freight and took the mail along on those trips. There wasn't a fence or a tree or a house between his house and the Heser Valley. It took three days to make one trip so he would stay overnight at Merl Purdy's or at the U P ranch, then the next day cross the river. If it wasn't safe to cross with the horses he would use Cogswell's horse and wagon (Cogswell had a store in Poplar) to take the freight and mail to the river, then haul it across on a hand sled to where his team waited on the other side. By the time he reached Vida and unloaded freight and mail, it would be dark, and he still had three miles to go to his homestead. There was no road and no landmark so his wife would hang a lantern on the end of the ridgepole of their old sod house to guide him.

Ed Schillinger built a wooden store and later a new brick building for the store and post office in 'New' Vida, and August's grandson Raymond was the postmaster there from 1963 to 1990. Today August's great grandson, Darrell Nefzger, occasionally fills in for the postmaster so there is still a Nefzger behind the window at the Vida Post Office, forty-six years later.

While permission for the post office was granted in about three weeks, it was a different story getting a route out from Wolf Point. Then homesteaders started coming in thick and fast, and in 1913 the government notified the Vida post office that they were putting out bids for a route from Wolf Point to Vida. Rob Durfey was the first mail hauler.

There were only a couple buildings in what later became Wolf Point when the Nefzgers first came, but as more settlers came in, other buildings started going up. Also, in 1912 John Pipal built and put in the river the first ferry boat at that locality. The first school was built where Masonic Lodge stands now. The Sherman Hotel was another structure that was put up about that time. Since Dick was in on 'the ground floor' of the area settlement, he could (and did, in his memoirs) list the original locations of various establishments.

Dick and Katie's first home had been a 10'x20' sod house built against a creek bank, but later they built a two-story, hip-roofed house for his growing family. Their house stood out on the prairie and was a landmark for miles around. There they reared their family, four boys and eight girls.

Donald spent most of his life in the Vida area with the exception of his years in the military. During those years he completely circled the world and later chronicled his travels in a book, Around the World the Hard Way.

He retired to Glendive in 2001. He was a great storyteller and would have said of his age, he was "Thirty-nine and some months." Those months added up to about 541! His widow Anna continues to live in Glendive as does his daughter, Deanna (Mrs. Craig) Hostetler. His son Dan maintains a Nefzger presence in Vida, and son Darrell lives in the Bloomfield area.

Dick Nefzger concluded his memoirs with an expression of gratitude that he settled in Montana and added, "I say thank God for good old Montana. I have so much to be thankful for. God has been good to me."

Glossary of Terms and Landmarks

Anderson's Department Store – 107 North Merrill

B. & B. Gang – Bridge and Building railroad gang (as opposed to track building)

Bachelor's biscuits – Baking powder biscuits, a main staple of early bachelors

Bamber Hill – About two miles north of Glendive on the old Sidney Highway

Bayou – A marshy inlet of the (Yellowstone) river

Beanery – Northern Pacific Lunchroom at the depot

Beasly block – 300 Block of North Merrill

Big bone – Large dinosaur bone discovered summer of 1967

Big Ditch – Lower Yellowstone River irrigation project, starting at the diversion dam at Intake, Montana

Big Dry country – The wide open area of East Central Montana named for Big Dry Creek

Bismarck Grocery – At Kendrick, Valentine & Douglas, later First National Bank, later Public Library

Break a horse – Tame or make obedient (a horse)

Break sod – Plowing sod to prepare as a field

Breaking Plow – Plow used to break (plow) sod

Broncpeeler – One who breaks horses for riding

Bryan's Plains – Ranching community south of Glendive near Cedar Creek

Buckboard – Four-wheeled open carriage; Seats rested on the floorboards

Bum lamb – An orphan lamb or a twin rejected by the mother

Buttrey – Now Albertsons in West Glendive

Callboy – Railroad employee who would go to the home of an employee to call him to work

Chaps – Leather trousers without a seat, worn over ordinary trousers by cowboys to protect the legs

Charivari – A mock serenade with kettles and drums to a couple on their honeymoon

Chinking – Plaster or similar used to fill chinks or cracks in walls

Citron Melon – Watermelon with hard, white flesh, used only candied or preserved

Coast to Coast store – 112 South Merrill

Comfortable – Comforter, quilted bed covering

Congregational Church – 120 West Power

Corned – To preserve or pickle with salt granules or in brine

Coulee – A gulch or ravine, usually dry in summer

Cradle – A frame attached to a scythe so the grain can be laid evenly as it is cut

Custer's Battlefield – Now known as the Battle of the Little Bighorn

C.Y.A. Hall – Catholic Youth Association Hall on Douglas, later Knights of Columbus Hall

Delco lights – Generator powered electric lights (32 volts DC) used by rural families 1900 to 1935

Democrat Wagon - A light wagon on which could be added two or three seats in order to take passengers

Dinky – Combination freight and passenger train between Glendive and Sidney

Dion Block – 100 Block of South Merrill featuring brick buildings from 1886

Divide – See Redwater-Yellowstone Divide

Douglas Meade – Large general store at 119 1/2 North Merrill

Drag – Six-section drag – farm implement used to uproot weeds in a field

Dray – Low, sturdily built, horse-drawn cart with detachable sides, for carrying heavy loads

Dutch – Pennsylvania Dutch, a German dialect of the Amish

Fallow – Plowed ground, typically seeded every other year and allowed to lie unplanted in alternate years to conserve moisture and help control weeds

Fellow – The rim of a spoked wheel

First National Bank – Kendrick & Valentine, later the Public Library

Fort Buford – U.S. army fort at the confluence of the Yellowstone and Missouri Rivers

Fresno – A type of horse-drawn road scraper

Gangplow – Plow with a number of shares side by side to make several furrows at the same time

Gate City – Glendive's nickname

Glendive Machine Works – 110 West Benham

Goose (the) – A short line train between Sidney and Richey

Greyhound Bus Depot – Across the street from the city hall

Gumbo – A fine, silty soil which becomes sticky and nonporous when wet – and very slippery!

Hagenston Hardware – 103 North Merrill

Hashing - Cooking

Hilger garage – 301 North Kendrick

Hobble – Hampering movement of a horse by tying hind feet together

Homestead – Land given to settlers by the government in exchange for living on it and making improvements

Honeyockers – The disparaging term ranchers applied to the homesteaders

Hungry Joe – The rugged hills towering above Glendive on the east

Immigrant car – Railroad boxcar used by immigrants to transport belongings to their new location

Jacket – Protective metal wall around a wood stove to prevent people (children) from being burned

Kampschrors – 606 North Merrill

Lambing – Tending a flock of sheep during the spring when the lambs are born

Lean-to – Makeshift shed or storage area adjacent to another building

Line Rider - Cowboy who rode the perimeter of the range checking on cattle

MDU – Montana Dakota Utilities, 113 West Towne

Midland Lumber Company – 100 North Merrill

Normal School – Teacher training college

Picket pin – Stake driven into the ground as a hitching post for animals

Prove up – Satisfy government requirements to own your homestead

Pumphouse – Building (sometimes a residence) along the railroad housing a pump, often for the purpose of filling a water tower etc.

Q.B.&R. – Quanrad, Brink and Riebold Auto Parts, 400 North Kendrick

Quarter – See section

Rawleigh Wagon – A peddler's wagon, selling spices and extracts – and candy for the kids

Redwater-Yellowstone Divide – The dividing line between the watersheds of the Redwater / Missouri Rivers and the Yellowstone River

Reo – Reo (Ransom Eli Olds) Motor Car Company, Lansing, Michigan, 1905 to 1936

Remuda – A group of extra saddle horses kept as a supply of remounts during roundup

Repping – Each ranch would send a representative to the roundups to claim their livestock

Riprap – Reinforce the river bank

Rodman – A person who carries the leveling rod in surveying

Roustabout – An unskilled or transient laborer

Rumley – Also Rumely; Large tractor produced by the Rumely Company, forerunner of Allis Chalmers

Sad iron – Used for ironing laundry and heated on the stove

Sandstone – No longer on the map, south of the current town of Plevna

Scorio Road – (or scoria) A road graveled with a red, cinderlike lava

Scraper – A wide scoop pulled by horses to move dirt

Section – One square mile, 640 acres (quarter section = 160 acres)

Shocks – Bundles or sheaves of grain

Slip – Same as a scraper

Sou – Former French coin similar in value to a penny

Speedcar – Small vehicle designed to run on rails and used to transport workers

Squatted – Established residence on land without legal formalities

Spring Wagon – Wagon with box mounted on springs instead of directly on the axle

Squaw Man – A White man married to an Indian, usually living with her tribe

Stoneboat – A flat bed on homemade sled runners

Subway Husky Service – 322 South Merrill

Sulky – Carriage with a seat for only one person

Sulky plow – Plow with seat for riding (instead of walking behind the plow)

Summer fallow – See fallow

Tender – Horse's feet sore from walking; also weakened from hard work without grain

Treasure State – Montana's nickname

Tug – Heavy strap connecting the harness to the crossbar of a wagon

Wagon reach – A pole joining the rear axle to the forward part of the wagon

Windlass – A simple winch used to lift a bucket out of a well

Zion Lutheran Church – Sargent & Riverview, originally at Sargent & Power

List of Interviews

Following is a complete list, in alphabetical order, of the interviews Mrs. Kauffman conducted between 1964 and 1975. Each entry is referenced with volume and page number. Interviews without page numbers do not appear in either volume.